Gateway to the West:
The History of Jefferson Barracks from 1895 – December 7, 1941
Volume II

Marc E. Kollbaum, Curator (Retired)
Jefferson Barracks Historic Park

Marc E. Kollbaum
e-mail: Mkollbaum@yahoo.com

Front cover: No. 1 Grant Road. This building, built ca. 1894, served as the Post Administration Building. The Commandant and his staff officers maintained officers in this building from the time it was completed until the pot closed.

Back cover: The 6th Infantry Regiment in formation on the Parade Ground. Col. Joseph A. Atkins stands in front of the formation, which is arranged by company. The 6th Infantry called Jefferson Barracks home.

Contents

List of Illustrations
Preface
Acknowledgments

Illustrations

4

Preface

During the years between the founding of Jefferson Barracks in 1826 and the closing of the Cavalry Recruit Depot in 1894, Jefferson Barracks served as the country's first Infantry School of Practice, as a ready reserve for the troops needed to settle the West, as a hospital during the Civil War, as an Engineer Depot, and as a Cavalry Recruit Depot. It had ranged in garrison strength from six to eight soldiers {who requested additional troops from the Headquarters in St. Louis so that the local farmers' livestock could be kept out of the barracks}, to being the largest military post in the country during several years in the 1880s.

Many historically significant military figures served at Jefferson Barracks during the 19th century. One such figure arrived at the post several months after his graduation from the U.S. Military Academy at West Point in 1828. Jefferson Davis had been assigned to the 6th Infantry Regiment after graduation, and after a furlough he joined his unit at Jefferson Barracks. While there, 2nd Lt. Davis accompanied the 6th Infantry north to take part in the Black Hawk War. He then served as adjutant of the Regiment of Dragoons, the first mounted regiment in the Regular U.S. Army, which organized at Jefferson Barracks in 1833.

Also in the 1830s, 1st Lt. Robert E. Lee joined the Barracks as an engineer sent to adjust the flow of the Mississippi River so that it once again flowed to the docks on the Missouri side of the river. Lee appeared at Jefferson Barracks again in 1855 as lieutenant colonel of the Second Cavalry which was being formed at the Post.

In 1844 2nd Lt. Ulysses S. Grant made his first appearance at the Barracks as a member of the 4th Infantry Regiment. In addition, other prominent Civil War figures such as William T. Sherman, Edwin V. Sumner, Ambrose Burnside, Joseph Hooker and Philip Sheridan (for the North) and Albert S. Johnston, Joseph Johnston, Richard Ewell, William Hardee, James Longstreet, and Edmond Kirby Smith (for the South) are just a few of the two hundred or so Civil War generals that served at Jefferson Barracks before they became generals during the Civil War.

General Order No. 45, Adjutant General's Office, ordered the Headquarters and six companies of the 3rd Cavalry to occupy Jefferson Barracks as the Cavalry Recruit Depot had been discontinued as of 1 October 1894. In compliance with this order, units of the 3rd Cavalry departed for the Oklahoma or Indian Territory during the first week of October 1894 en route to Jefferson Barracks. When Lt. Col. George A. Purington, 3rd Cavalry, arrived he assumed command of the Post.

Many changes were in the offing for Jefferson Barracks, already 58 years old. The Grand Old Post would be completely re-built and turned from an old 19th century military reservation into a modern training facility for the new Army Air Corps. However, there would be many twists and turns along the way.

At the end of the 19th Century the 3rd Cavalry and numerous other regular Army units departed from Jefferson Barracks to take part in the Spanish-American War and the Philippine Insurrection. In addition, Missouri volunteer units rendezvoused at the post, were inducted into the Army, and started on their way to participate in the conflict. U.S. volunteer units also organized at Jefferson Barracks before making their way to Cuba, Puerto Rico, and the Philippines.

During World War I Jefferson Barracks served as the largest induction station in the Midwest. Many of these men received their basic training at the post. After the war many units and men made their way back to the post to be released from service.

The years between the world wars Jefferson Barracks continued to train new recruits, but life at the post tended to be rather dull and routine causing many men to desert from sheer boredom. Finally, when war in Europe began the routine at Jefferson Barracks began to take on a new life. Facilities expanded and in 1940 the Army Air Corps took over control of Jefferson Barracks from the 6th Infantry. Jefferson Barracks became the first AAC basic training center. By 7 December 1941, Jefferson Barracks had developed a new role and life was no longer the same old routine it had been for the past forty years.

After the U.S. entry into World War II the process of readying recruits for combat duties became the primary focus of training. A new Reception Center and Induction Station operated 24 hours a day and could take in 1,000 men a day. Basic training took place on the main post, and schools such as a Camouflage School, Chemical Warfare School , and a Bakers and Cook School began operation. Life was hectic and the old lazy days long gone, replaced by continued frenetic activity.

Chapter 1 - October 1894 Through 1897

The 26 August 1894 edition of the *St. Louis Post-Dispatch* carried a major story on Jefferson Barracks. The story stated that four troops of cavalry would immediately be stationed at Jefferson Barracks with eight more troops to follow. Fifty thousand dollars had been set aside for new construction at the Post. The *Post-Dispatch* story went on to point out that "the War Department now fully determined to relinquish the small outposts in the Western country, where they are absolutely useless...."

A year or so before the *Post-Dispatch* story, the War Department had established a policy of concentrating troops at large posts and closing the abandoned reservations. Since 4 March 1893, the Army had turned over 741,000 acres of public land to the Department of the Interior. Only a few years earlier, in 1888, there had been 120 military posts throughout the country, but by the end of fiscal year 1895 (30 June 1895) there were only eighty-three.

At first, the Army determined to cease all recruiting and training of recruits at Jefferson Barracks as of 1 October 1894, but reconsidered and decided to continue as before until the completion of new cavalry stables and the size of the garrison required the cessation of these activities. Until that time the Army had operated thirty general recruiting stations; one of these being located in St. Louis. Recruits were quickly forwarded to one of four recruit rendezvous, David's Island, New York; Columbus Barracks, Ohio; Jefferson Barracks, Missouri; or Fort Sheridan, Illinois. A recruit then received three months of instruction at the rendezvous. However, by the Act of Congress dated 1 August 1894, recruits were to be forwarded to regiments from recruiting stations and rendezvous as soon as possible. The Act also provided for changes in who could be enlisted, which helped in the streamlining of the Recruiting Service.

In accordance with General Order No. 23, Jefferson Barracks was abolished as a Cavalry Recruit Depot on 1 October 1894. Then, in accordance with General Order No. 45, Adjutant General's Office; Troop D, 3rd Cavalry, commanded by Captain George F. Chase left Fort Supply, Indian Territory, on 1 October and proceeded by rail to Jefferson Barracks. The troop arrived at 7:00 p.m. on 2 October. Capt. Chase relieved Lt. Col. Samuel S. Sumner, who departed Jefferson Barracks on 5 October to return to duty with the 6th Cavalry. Troop K, 3rd Cavalry departed Fort Reno, Indian Territory, on 3 October, traveling the 664 miles to Jefferson Barracks by rail, and arriving on 4 October. Capt. George K. Hunter commanded Troop K. By 4 October 1894, regular army troops had re-established themselves at Jefferson Barracks.

Lt. Col. George A. Purington, commanding the Post and regiment, had been ordered to Fort Leavenworth, Kansas, from 6 to 16 October, and did not assume command of Jefferson Barracks until the 16th. Other 3rd Cavalry officers arriving in October included Capt. Samuel R. Jones, Quartermaster Department (QM), who arrived 10 October, to serve as Post Quartermaster; Major Alexander S.B. Keyes, 3rd Cavalry, who had been on Detached Service commanding Fort Ringgold, Texas, from 21 March 1893, until 22 October 1894; 1st Lt. Parker W. West, appointed Post Adjutant; 1st Lt. Franklin O. Johnson, Troop K, was put in charge of the Post Mess, Post Exchange and served as Acting Commissary of Subsistence; and 2nd Lt. Julius T. Conrad, Troop K, appointed Superintendent of the Post school. Major Robert H. White, Medical Department, also arrived to serve as Post Surgeon. The colonel of the 3rd Cavalry, Anson Mills, although assigned to Jefferson Barracks, had been serving on the Mexican Boundary Commission since 12 December 1893, and he continued in that capacity. In addition to Lt. Col. Sumner; Capt. John B. Kerr, 6th Cavalry; 1st Lt. Richard B. Paddock, 6th Cavalry; and Capt. Charles H. Ingalls, QM Department; were relieved of duty and departed Jefferson Barracks during October. Thus, by the end of October 1894, nine 3rd Cavalry officers and 140 enlisted men had taken station at Jefferson Barracks. In addition to the 3rd Cavalry personnel, the Jefferson Barracks garrison consisted of 45 enlisted men in the recruit detachments or casually at the post.

The aforementioned General Order meant that Jefferson Barracks was to become the headquarters for the 3rd Cavalry with the colonel commanding. His staff and the regimental band were all to be stationed at Jefferson Barracks. Troops C, E, F, and G received orders to take station at Fort Ethan Allen, Vermont.[1]

Little took place at the Post during the last two months of 1894. The officer contingent remained the same and the number of enlisted men changed only slightly, with a total of 161 enlisted men of all categories present.

The Saint Louis Powder Depot, occupying the northern section of the military reservation, remained under the command of Major (Brevet Lt. Col.) John A. Kress. Kress had 18 enlisted men in his charge during the last three months of 1894, then dropped one when First Class Private Patrick O'Brien received his discharge on 13 December.

The construction program that had begun in 1892 to replace the old limestone buildings with modern red brick buildings continued during 1894. With the cavalry returning to Jefferson Barracks, the War Department authorized fifty thousand dollars to be spent for the construction of four brick cavalry stables and a Quartermaster and Subsistence storehouse. The stables were to cost a total of $38,476.00 and the storehouse $7,364.00. The remainder of the appropriation was to be used for repairs to existing structures.

It should also be noted that a two-room brick addition to the lodge at the Jefferson Barracks National Cemetery was constructed in 1894. The War Department report for fiscal year 1895 describes the Jefferson Barracks National Cemetery as consisting of 50 acres, with 20.5 enclosed by a stone wall. Water was supplied by a cistern and the Post waterworks to a 5-room brick lodge, a 2-room brick office, and a brick outbuilding. Interments were 8,806 known and 2,906 unknown for a total of 11,712.[2]

In the War Department Report, the Surgeon General of the Army reported that Jefferson Barracks had the highest hospital admission rate in the Department of the Missouri with 1,330.27 admitted per 1,000 strength, compared to 1,127.76 for the entire Department. However, even with the highest admission rate, the Post's non-effective rate remained low, at 23.42 per 1,000, compared with 34.29 for the Department. The Surgeon General also reported that Jefferson Barracks had rates lower than average for venereal disease, alcoholism, and rheumatism, but higher than average rates for malarial fevers, tonsillitis, and diarrheal diseases. The Post also had 50% more injuries and accidents than was usual at a military post in time of peace.

One further event of interest took place during the latter part of 1894, when the *St. Louis Post-Dispatch* ran a story in its 29 October issue reporting the death on 26 October of Brevet Major General Amos Beckwith. General Beckwith was laid to rest in the Jefferson Barracks National Cemetery after a long, distinguished military career. Beckwith graduated from the U.S. Military Academy in June 1850 and had risen to the rank of Captain in the Commissary Department by the outbreak of the Civil War. He received a promotion to brevet lieutenant colonel and to colonel on 1 September 1864, for gallantry and meritorious service in the campaign against Atlanta; then to brevet brigadier general on 13 March 1865, for his service in the campaign terminating in the surrender of the insurgent army under General Joseph Johnston; and to major general on the same date, for faithful and meritorious service in the war.

The service at Jefferson Barracks contained all the pageantry of a military funeral for someone of General Beckwith's stature. Col. Purington received the funeral cortege at Jefferson Barracks. Captains Chase, Hunter, and Adjutant West rendered the traditional "Present Arms" and a detail of eight cavalry sergeants marched four on either side of the hearse from the Barracks to the burial plot, where they lowered the casket into the ground.

Before proceeding, it may be appropriate to quote a description of Jefferson Barracks contained in the 26 August 1894 issue of the *Post-Dispatch*: "Jefferson Barracks is situated on the high bluffs above the Mississippi River three miles south of Carondelet, or the extreme southern city limits. It is one of the most beautiful and picturesque spots about St. Louis, and is moreover a historic spot with tradition galore.

The bluff on which the reservation is located commands a view of the Mississippi for ten miles. To the north the city of St. Louis with a faint cloud of smoke hanging over it may be seen, to the east the American bottoms stretch away to the bluffs in the distance far over in Illinois, a low green plain with bits of bright water glittering here and there.

To the south there is a grand view of the Mississippi, with the bluffs its western shore and several green islands in the distance. At the foot of the bluff below the reservation on a ledge of stone left specially for the purpose are the tracks of the Iron Mountain Railroad..."

The year 1895 began much as 1894 had come to a close. Lt. Col. George A. Purington, 3rd Cavalry, remained in command of the Post. The garrison consisted of four officers and 13 enlisted men on the Post General Staff; the 22 enlisted men of the 3rd Cavalry Band; and Troops D, K, and M, 3rd Cavalry, with 12 officers and 186 enlisted men. In addition to the regular garrison, a Mounted Recruit Detachment consisted of one colored and 11 white recruits and a Foot Service Recruit Detachment contained 4 colored and 21 white recruits. There were also 11 enlisted men on casual status and 2 military convicts at the post.

Brigadier General Thomas H. Ruger, commanding the Department of the Missouri; his Aide de Camp 2nd Lt. Charles G. Lyman, 2nd Cavalry; and Capt. Jesse M. Lee, 9th Infantry, Assistant Inspector General of the Department of the Missouri inspected the post on 16 January. All must have been found to be in order as no major discrepancies were noted.

The only addition or subtraction in the Post officer corps occurred on 15 January when 1st Lt. Henry L. Ripley joined from Detached Service. 2nd Lt. Julius T. Conrad also joined from leave on 11 January, and was appointed Post Engineer and Signal Officer. 1st Lt. Gonzales S. Bigham, 9th Cavalry, and 1st Lt. Stephen H. Elliott, 5th Cavalry, remained attached officers on duty with the Recruit Detachments.

Major Kress remained in command of the St. Louis Powder Depot at Jefferson Barracks. Kress had 20 enlisted men in his command.

During February the Army in Washington, D.C., appointed boards of officers to meet on 28 February for the mental and physical examinations of appointees to the United States Military Academy. At Jefferson Barracks, Major Robert H. White, surgeon; Capt. Charles B. Ewing, assistant surgeon; Capt. George K. Hunter; 1st Lt. Franklin O. Johnson; and 1st Lt. Stephen L. Elliott, all of the 3rd Cavalry, were chosen to conduct these examinations.[3]

February, March, and April 1895 saw little change in the activities or personnel at the Post. Aside from the normal garrison duties, one day each month the garrison took part in fire drills. The importance of fire drills soon became apparent.

In May, the command got a break from the routine and boredom of regular garrison duty. On May 9, Major Keyes took the 3rd Cavalry Band, consisting of 23 men under the command of 1st Lt. Franklin O. Johnson; Troop D, 3rd Cavalry, 44 men commanded by 2nd Lt. Kirby Walker; and Troop K, 3rd Cavalry, 44 men commanded by Capt. George K. Hunter and left Jefferson Barracks, proceeding by rail to Camp Schofield near Memphis, Tennessee to attend the Interstate Drill and Encampment. While there the men took part in enlisted men's drill training.[4]

Their return trip certainly offered another break from the routine, when during the afternoon of 22 May troops discovered a fire in one of the cars used to transport the horses, presumably caused by a spark from the train's engine. Five of the 94 horses being transported were injured and had to be put down after reaching Jefferson Barracks.

Again, in June, the command attended an Interstate Drill and Encampment, but this time they only marched to St. Louis. Heavy rain fell during the night of 30 June and all day on 1 July, but arrangements for the drill to last a week proceeded as planned. Most of the troops had already arrived and had been given quarters in Camp Hancock, which was named in honor of General Winfield Scott Hancock. Major Keyes again commanded the men of the Band and Troops D and K, who marched the 15 miles to the encampment on 30 June. The 3rd Cavalry troopers took part in drill with state militia troops. In addition to the 3rd Cavalry troops from Jefferson Barracks, troops that had arrived included the Indianapolis Light Artillery; the Dallas, Texas, Artillery Company; the Rockville, Indiana Light Artillery; the Neely Zouaves from Memphis, Tennessee; the Mount Pleasant Drum and Bugle Corps from Washington, D.C.; the Walsh Guards, Company F; and the Branch Guards of the 1st Regiment, Missouri National Guard.

Scheduled to arrive the next day were the National Rifles of Washington, D.C.; the Bullene Guards and Hale Zouaves from Kansas City; the Chicago Zouaves from Aurora, Illinois; the Belknap Rifles from San Antonio, Texas; and the Fletcher Zouaves from Little Rock, Arkansas. Several other units not named were also scheduled to take part in the drill and exercises.[5]

Earlier in the month, Jefferson Barracks had received three distinguished visitors. The Honorable David S. Lemont, Secretary of War; Brig. General Richard N. Batchelar, Quartermaster General; and Major General George W. Davis, Military Secretary, arrived on 19 June on a tour of inspection. The visit resulted in a recommendation for an appropriation of $18,000 for the purchase of a target range. [Davis, after serving the duration of the Civil War, was appointed Lieutenant Colonel and Aide de Camp (A.D.C.) to Lt. Gen. Philip Sheridan from 15 April 1885, to 10 October 1885. He was promoted to Brig. General of Volunteers on 4 May 1898; to Brig. General U.S.A. on 2 February 1901; and to Major General on 21 July 1902. He retired on 26 July 1903. Batchelar began his military career as a 1st Lieutenant and Quartermaster of the New Hampshire Infantry on 2 May 1861. He rose through the volunteer ranks in the Quartermaster Department during the Civil War. He received brevets to major, lieutenant colonel, colonel and brigadier general of volunteers on 13 March 1865, and major, lieutenant colonel and colonel U.S.A. the same day for faithful and meritorious service during the Civil War. He was awarded the Medal of Honor on 20 May 1895, for most distinguished gallantry in action against Mosby's guerillas between Catlett and Fairfax Stations, Virginia, 13 October to 15 October 1863, while serving as Lieutenant Colonel and Quartermaster of Volunteers, Chief Quartermaster, Second Army Corps. Batchelar died 4 January 1901.

During the summer fire destroyed the old barracks that housed Troop D, 3rd Cavalry. A new building, No. 26, was erected in its place.

Lt. Col. George A. Purington, 3rd Cavalry, brought the regiment to Jefferson Barracks in October 1864 shortly after the Cavalry Depot closed. He assumed command of the post on 17 October 1864, and remained in command until he retired on 17 July 1865.

The old limestone barracks. These buildings were arranged in a rectangle open at the Mississippi River end. In the early 1890s the construction of red brick buildings to replace the old dilapidated limestone buildings began and continued through the early years of the 20th century.

Samuel M. Whitside served as a United States Cavalry officer from 1858 to 1902. He commanded at every level from company to department, including at Fort Huachuca, which he founded; Jefferson Barracks and Fort Sam Houston; the Department of Eastern Cuba and Santiago and Puerto Rico. He retired in 1902 as a Brigadier General.

After a long and distinguished military career that spanned 35 years, Lt. Col. George A. Purington retired 17 July 1895. Purington began his military career as 1st Sergeant of Co. G, 19th Ohio Infantry on 22 April 1861. He became Captain of the 2nd Ohio Cavalry on 27 August 1861; Major on 10 Sept. 1861; and Lieutenant Colonel on 10 July 1863. He honorably mustered out on 1 November 1864. He became a Captain in the 9th Cavalry, U.S.A., on 28 July 1866; then a Major in the 3rd Cavalry on 25 Oct. 1883; and a Lieutenant Colonel on 20 October 1892. He had received brevets to Major on 2 March 1867, for gallantry and meritorious service in the Battle of the Wilderness, Virginia; and to Lieutenant Colonel for gallantry and meritorious service in the Battle of Cedar Creek, Virginia. Purington died 31 May 1896.

Lt. Col. Samuel M. Whitside arrived at Jefferson Barracks and relieved Major Keyes on 20 August 1895. Whitside was relieved by Col. Guy V. Henry on 4 October 1895. Col. Henry remained in command of Jefferson Barracks for almost two years.[6]

In August 1895, the 3rd Cavalry Band accompanied Ascalonis Commandery No. 16, Knights Templar of St. Louis on their pilgrimage to Boston to take part in the 26th Tri-Annual Conclave. The band was marked for its excellence, as the *Boston Globe* wrote: "One of the principal features of the division was the 3rd United States Cavalry Band from Jefferson Barracks, Missouri. These regulars marched with an ease and precision that caught every eye along the route, while the sweetness and novelty of their quicksteps pleased the ear already tired with a surfeit of Sousa music." While in Boston, the 3rd Cavalry Band with its officers, the sponsors, maids of honor and chaperones was being entertained at one of the palatial homes of the city. While the band played, ex-Senator Jones of Iowa came up. The venerable statesman lifted his hat, and when the selection was completed, he requested that "Dixie" be played. The request was complied with, to the gratification of the assembled throng. The 3rd Cavalry contingent returned August 30 having traveled 2,388 miles.

Troops A & B, 3rd Cavalry, left Fort Reno, Indian Territory by rail on 7 October 1895, to take station at Jefferson Barracks. They arrived at 9:00 p.m. on 8 October. Then on 21 October, Troops H and I, 3rd Cavalry, departed Fort Sill, Indian Territory on orders to take station at Jefferson Barracks. The troops marched 29 miles to Rush Springs, Oklahoma, where they boarded rail cars with their property and proceeded to Jefferson Barracks, arriving the afternoon of 24 October. This brought the garrison strength in 3rd Cavalry personnel to 13 officers and 309 enlisted men.

Although Jefferson Barracks had been discontinued as a Cavalry Recruit Depot, other recruits continued to be transferred to their permanent units and stations. In September, 68 recruits transferred; and in October, 70; in November, 41; and in December, 55 recruits transferred.[7]

One aspect of training that had not heretofore been prevalent became a regular aspect of 3rd Cavalry training. Col. Henry believed in hard training and, as such, practice marches became a staple of the training regimen. In November, all 3rd Cavalry troops at Jefferson Barracks traveled 36 miles on practice marches and on 6 December, Troops A, B and I traveled 22 miles in 3 hours; then on 11 December, traveled 23 miles in 3 ½ hours.

Post construction continued during 1895, when a forage storehouse with a capacity of 300,000 pounds, a wagon shed large enough to accommodate 12 wagons, a barn for the Quartermaster to house 22 horses, a blacksmith shop, a bakery with a capacity of 700 loaves of bread a day, a 300-ton coal shed, bachelor quarters for eight officers, and a double barracks building large enough to accommodate 126 men were all completed. Work was also started on a large Quartermaster storehouse. A substantial fence about six feet high was erected around the Post in late 1895, and finished in early 1896. The fence consisted of two boards at the bottom and three strands of barbed wire at the top.

On 21 December 1895, the War Department granted a franchise to the Southern Electric Railway to build, maintain and operate an electric street railway into the Jefferson Barracks reservation. On 7 November 1895, the *St. Louis Republic* contained an article stating that the city of St. Louis owed Col. Henry its thanks for his efforts to improve the appearance of Jefferson Barracks and add to its attractiveness. If Col. Henry's plans were carried out, Jefferson Barracks would soon become a popular suburban resort for the people of St. Louis. The Post was connected to the city by water and rail, and the Southern Electric Railway would soon extend its line to the Barracks. Authority to cross the bridge over the River des Peres had been granted by St. Louis Mayor Walbridge. This removed the last obstacle to the proposed extension. The line was completed and operations began in 1896.

After brief tours as commanding officer at Jefferson Barracks by Samuel M. Whitside and Alexander S.B. Keyes, Col. Guy V. Henry assumed command of the post on 4 October 1895. Henry remained in command for nearly two years. Henry had graduated from the U.S. Military Academy in 1861 and been posted as a 2nd lieutenant in the 1st Artillery. He became colonel of the 40th Massachusetts Infantry on 9 November 1863, mustering out of volunteer service 30 June 1865. He then served as a captain in the 1st Artillery until he transferred to the 3rd Cavalry 15 December 1870. He became a major in the 9th Cavalry on 26 June 1881, lieutenant colonel of the 7th Cavalry on 30 January 1892, transferring to the 5th Cavalry on 22 September 1894. After a brief tour with the 5th Cavalry he returned to the 3rd Cavalry. He then served as colonel of the 10th Cavalry beginning on 1 June 1897, brigadier general of volunteers on 4 May 1898, and major general of volunteers on 7 December 1898. Henry was honorably discharged from the volunteers on 12 June 1899, and served as a brigadier general U.S.A. Henry died 27 October 1899. Henry was awarded the Medal of Honor on 5 December 1893, for having led the assault of his brigade upon the enemy's works at Cold Harbor, Virginia on 1 June 1864.

The "Dinky" connected St. Louis with Jefferson Barracks. It began carrying passengers in late 1896. This is one of the earliest known photographs of the electric streetcar.

Streetcar station ca. 1900 letting off and taking on passengers. Note: the guard mount in forefront. The station was located where the current Archery Shelter is now located.

In November, excitement of another kind surfaced at Jefferson Barracks when charges and counter charges were filed involving Col. Henry, Surgeon Major Robert H. White, and Surgeon Captain Charles Ewing. Major White accused Capt. Ewing of attempting to cast a stigma upon him, personally and professionally. He portrayed Ewing as a man who professionally could lay no claim to distinction as a physician, much less as a surgeon, and whose personal character was such that he had not hesitated to repeatedly falsify his public accounts. When Col. Henry received the charges from Major White, he forwarded them to higher headquarters in Chicago with the following endorsement: "I have investigated the charges and believe they can be sustained." Capt. Ewing then preferred charges against Major White. Ewing accused White of making a false statement, in saying that the officers and their families would not receive the treatment of Capt. Ewing. To back up his claim, he got written statements from nearly all the officers of the post saying how White had treated them and that in each instance White's treatment was all that could be expected. Also, that the Post Surgeon had falsified his public accounts by certifying that he owned a private horse and by this means he drew pay at the rate of $15 per month for forage, when the truth was that the horse in question belonged to August von Clossman, the Post Hospital Steward. It was also alleged that when Col. Henry received the charges he merely, without taking any action, forwarded them to General Merritt, Department Commander.

It was expected that shortly an inspector would be sent to investigate the charges or a court-martial would be ordered. The charges against Capt. Ewing were looked upon as very trivial, but the charges against Major White, if sustained, would go hard against him. All the officers involved in the charges kept very quiet, understandable given that Col. Henry, their commanding officer, was involved. It also came out that Capt. Ewing was the brother-in-law of U.S. Senator F.M. Cockrell.

There were, also, charges preferred against Col. Henry by Lt. Col. Samuel Whitside. Henry had relieved Whitside in command of Jefferson Barracks. Apparently, shortly after Henry succeeded Whitside, Henry had been quoted as saying that he had been sent to take charge of the barracks because he was more able and fit to manage it than anyone else. When this caught the eye of Whitside he took it that Henry was reflecting upon him and so he was said to prefer charges which were in the hands of General Merritt. There was also trouble between Capt. Hunter and Capt. Jones that resulted in charges filed against Hunter.

One jovial officer told a reporter that it was very probable that General Merritt was waiting until all the charges came in before ordering an investigation. The officer argued that as so many charges had been filed, General Merritt probably thought there was a lot more to come and therefore concluded to wait until they all arrived, and he could save the government considerable money by sending one court-martial brigade to try all the cases before they left. Taken altogether, the matters were very serious.

The Jefferson Barracks garrison had grown during 1895. By the end of December, the 3rd Cavalry counted 13 officers and 327 enlisted men; the 3rd Cavalry General Staff consisted of two officers and 13 enlisted men; the 3rd Cavalry Band and Field Staff, 5 officers and 23 enlisted men; the Recruit Detachments, Mounted Service, 10 enlisted men; and the Field Service, 21 enlisted men. Attached and casual personnel amounted to 1 officer and 9 enlisted men. One schoolteacher also served the post. Thus, the total garrison complement at the end of 1895 consisted of 21 officers and 403 enlisted men.[8]

The St. Louis Powder Depot at Jefferson Barracks continued to function as normal throughout 1895. Major (Brevet Lt. Col.) John A. Kress remained in command. His command consisted of between 18 to 20 enlisted men throughout the year.

News was received in February 1895 that the School Sisters of Notre Dame had elected Sister Casimira Schul of the motherhouse in Milwaukee, as mother superior for the new motherhouse for the Western province established near St. Louis. Sister Emerentia Eichhammer was selected as first assistant, and Sister Borgia Meek as second assistant. Mother Casimira was born in Lancaster, Pennsylvania, and had a large amount of experience. Sister Emerentia came to St. Louis from Chicago, where she was in charge of St. Michael's school. Sister Borgia was only 38 years of age and was located at Chippewa Falls, Wisconsin. She was the youngest official of the order. Work on the buildings was to begin during the summer of 1895, but completion was not scheduled until 1897. There was a building on the grounds that was to be taken charge of by Easter, 1895.

The site of the new motherhouse was to be called "Sancta Maria in Ripa," St. Mary's on the River. The School Sisters of Notre Dame still occupy the grounds and buildings adjacent to Jefferson Barracks to this day.[9]

1896

The year 1896 started much as 1895 had come to an end. On 7 January, the 2nd and 3rd Squadrons of the 3rd Cavalry traveled 25 miles in 4 ½ hours on another practice march. Even in the dead of winter Lt. Col. Henry felt training must continue.

The garrison strength remained fairly constant. For example, in January 1896, the garrison consisted of 21 officers and 390 enlisted men. [Not included in these numbers are the 25 enlisted men in confinement serving sentences imposed by General Courts Martial]. In June there were 18 officers and 362 enlisted men and in December, 25 officers and 368 enlisted men. With a few exceptions, the troops performed normal garrison duties throughout the year.

A general court martial convened at Jefferson Barracks on 7 January 1896. Major Robert H. White, Medical Department, served as president and Lt. Daniel H. Boughton as Judge Advocate. The following officers composed the detail for the court in addition to those named: Major Henry W. Wessells, Jr., and Major Alexander S.B. Keyes; Captains John B. Johnson and George F. Chase, 3rd Cavalry; and Samuel R. Jones, Assistant Quartermaster; Lieutenants George H. Morgan, Franklin O. Johnson, Parker W. West, Adjutant; Tyree R. Rivers, Quartermaster; and Arthur Thayer, 3rd Cavalry. As the detail indicated, it was thought that an officer was being tried, but no name was forthcoming.[10]

Just a week after the above court martial convened, Major Henry W. Wessells, Jr. preferred charges against Lt. Parker W. West for conduct unbecoming an officer and a gentleman. The specifications alleged vicious and insulting language by Lt. West.[11]

It appears that January 1896 was a time of courts martial for several Jefferson Barracks personnel. Capt. Charles B. Ewing, Medical Department and Post Surgeon at Jefferson Barracks, was found guilty by a court which tried him at Fort Leavenworth. There were three counts filed against Capt. Ewing. The first specification was "conduct to the prejudice of good order and military discipline." The first specification related to certain correspondence between the accused and the Post commanding officer. Capt. Ewing was found guilty of only certain charges preferred against him and sentenced to "suspension from rank for three months and to confinement within the limits of Jefferson Barracks reservation for the same period."[12]

Apparently, the charges against Capt. Ewing resulted from an ongoing quarrel between Capt. Ewing and Major Robert H. White, Medical Department. While on trial at Fort Leavenworth, Capt. Ewing preferred counter charges against Major White. It appears that the War Department wanted to end the feud as Major White was transferred to the Presidio of San Francisco on 14 February. In return Major Girard was transferred to Jefferson Barracks from the Presidio. After ordering the transfer of Major White, the War Department evidently intended to take no further notice of the counter charges filed against him by Capt. Ewing.[13]

On 3 March 1896, Secretary of War Daniel S. Lamont approved the recommendations of Capt. George F. Chase, 3rd Cavalry, stationed at Jefferson Barracks, for the purchase of 1,100 acres of land for use as a rifle range in the Arcadia Valley. The tract of land could be purchased for $17,300. Capt. Chase had been authorized by the War Department to examine land in several locations adjacent to St. Louis with a view to purchasing land to be used as a rifle range for the troops at Jefferson Barracks for target practice.

Capt. Chase spent several months riding over the country and finally secured options near Arcadia, Missouri to purchase 1,100 acres in the Arcadia Valley, three miles of lowland with a mountainous background. For a time, Secretary Lamont seemed somewhat indifferent to making the purchase or recommending it to Congress, as nearly every other post in the country desired their own rifle range. Many of the posts had put in requests for appropriations from $50,000 to $100,000 to buy the land necessary for a rifle range, but Capt. Chase made a better bargain and convinced Lamont to recommend the immediate purchase of the Arcadia Valley land to Congress. The land was purchased and troops from Jefferson Barracks made yearly trips to Arcadia for target practice.[14]

Troop A of the 3rd Cavalry and the Band served as escort and played taps at the funeral of Col. Frederick W. Lewis on 19 March. The cavalry troops along with members of the Washington Lodge of Masons; General Lyon Post, Grand Army of the Republic; and the Legion of Honor accompanied the remains from Lewis' house to the Methodist Episcopal Church in Carondelet, where services were held. A procession was then formed, and the march was taken to the Odd Fellows' Cemetery, where interment took place.[15]

Not normal was the death, due to diabetes, of Capt. John B. Johnson, Troop D, 3rd Cavalry, on 5 April 1896. He was laid to rest in the Jefferson Barracks National Cemetery. Johnson had been sick in quarters since February. He had been commissioned a 2nd Lt. in the 6th U.S. Colored Infantry on 8 September 1863, with a promotion to 1st Lt.

on 15 February 1865. After the Civil War, he became a 2nd Lt. in the 7th Infantry on 23 April 1866. He was promoted to 1st Lt. on 12 October 1867; and then assigned to the 3rd Cavalry on 31 December 1870, where he served as Regimental Adjutant from 15 May 1871 until 4 April 1878, when he was promoted to Captain. At the time of his death Johnson commanded Troop B.

April seemed to be a month of the non-routine, as fire destroyed Barracks Building No. 26 early in the morning of 22 April. In a letter to the Quartermaster General of the Army, Captain and Assistant Quartermaster Samuel R. Jones reported that a fire was discovered in the basement of B-26 at 1:30 a.m. The entire command turned out to fight the fire in minutes, but due to the density and pungency of the smoke, it was impossible for the men to get close enough with buckets. At risk to life a hose was taken into the basement, but due to insufficient water pressure no water could reach the basement ceiling, which was burning fiercely. The low water pressure was due to the fact that the auxiliary pump at the city limits did not work between 11:00 p.m. and 4:00 a.m. As the only communication between the Post and St. Louis was by mounted courier, valuable time was lost in getting water and assistance.

The building was a total loss, but nearly all the moveable property above the basement level was removed. Building No. 25 caught fire from the heat, but was saved by hard labor. Building No. 48 became badly scorched, but was also saved. Building No. 23 caught fire and would have been destroyed, but for the timely arrival of a steam fire engine from St. Louis.

Although the exact cause of the fire could not be determined, investigation determined that the fire broke out in some packing boxes in the basement. Therefore, spontaneous combustion among some old rags used for cleaning oil lamps and the packing boxes was probably the cause of the fire.[16] Building No. 26 housed Troops A and D, 3rd Cavalry. None of the men were injured in the fire.

By an Act of Congress approved 11 June 1896, $300,000 was appropriated for construction at military posts. This sum of money could be appropriated to individual posts as the Secretary of War deemed necessary. Jefferson Barracks received the fourth largest appropriation, $19,472.[17] This appropriation, together with money already allotted for the construction begun in 1892, resulted in the construction in 1896 of four additional barracks buildings, each with a capacity of 126 men, and facing the parade grounds from the south. A pavilion capable of accommodating 32 patients was added to the post hospital. A lodge for the gate keeper, four stable guard houses a fully equipped fire station, and a band barracks for 26 men were all completed in 1896. Also, the old brick water tower was demolished and a steel tower with a capacity of 50,000 gallons of filtered water was constructed near the west limits of the post. Jefferson Barracks was assuming its position as one of the best equipped and most important military posts in the country.

A cyclone partly destroyed a large portion of the city of St. Louis on 27 May 1896. Jefferson Barracks sustained little damage, but troops from the Barracks took an active role in patrolling the damaged areas, cleaning debris, and restoring order.

When darkness temporarily interrupted the search for storm victims during the night of 28/29 May, three hundred fifteen people were known to be dead on both sides of the river, and although the complete list of the dead was not yet known, it was estimated that approximately 400 were killed in the two areas. Of course, the number of injured was even larger, and many of the injured would not survive. The property loss would reach into the millions. Miles of wrecked buildings had not been explored as of 29 May, and the numerous collapsed factories could hide any number of people who perished during the storm. The crew and passengers of the ferryboat *Christie* had a remarkable experience. When the storm hit the boat was torn from its moorings at the foot of Spruce Street and blown downstream with fearful velocity. The passengers were crazed with fear and 16 two-horse teams stampeded on the lower deck. The water rushed over the boat, filling the hull, but by a miracle, it remained afloat and was driven before the storm down the river. The river was like a roaring sea and the crew were unable to launch any boats. The passengers crouched in the cabin, expecting any moment to go down. The boat drifted as far as Jefferson Barracks, where she sank in shallow water. The horses on the lower deck were drowned, but the 15 passengers were rescued.[18]

The *St. Louis Republic* reported on 1 June that Grand and Florissant avenues in St. Louis, the main thoroughfares of Bellefontaine and Calvary Cemeteries were covered with a continuous stream of carriages following the victims of the storm to their last resting places. The appearance of the hearses in the sad procession alone punctuated the points where one funeral ended and another began. There was a sunless sky and the somber clouds dripped a misty rain. Fifty-one of the victims were buried in St. Louis and thirty-nine in East St. Louis, Illinois.

Recruiting at Jefferson Barracks was resumed in 1896 with officers from the 1st, 2nd, 3rd, 4th, 5th, 7th, 8th and 10th Cavalry Regiments assigned to recruit duty at the Post.[19]

Once each year, all the troops stationed at the Barracks had to travel to the rifle range at Arcadia, Missouri, for target practice. One group, commanded by Major Keyes, that included Troops B, I, and K, 3rd Cavalry, left the post at 8:00 a.m., on 11 June. They marched 17 miles to Antonio, Missouri, on 11 June; 18 miles to DeSoto on 12 June; 22 miles to Potosi on 13 June, and the final 32 miles to Arcadia on 14 June. They remained at Arcadia for about a week, when they retraced the route back to Jefferson Barracks. In July the 3rd Cavalry Band journeyed to Arcadia and in August, Troops D and H participated in target practice.[20]

On 9 June, 1st Lt. Charles A. Hedekin and three privates left Jefferson Barracks en route to Springfield, Missouri, to examine the roads and countryside preparatory to a practice march. Then on 5 October, Lt. Col. Henry, accompanied by Major Henry W. Wessells, Jr.; 1st Lt. Parker W. West, Adjutant; Capt. Charles B. Ewing of the Medical Department; and Troops A, B, D, H, I, and K, 3rd Cavalry, left on a practice march to Springfield. They returned on October 25 having traveled almost 500 miles. Along the way, they made camp at St. Claire, Bourbon, St. James, Franks, Richland, Lebanon, Marshfield and finally, Springfield. They began their return trip on October 16, and made the same stops with an additional camp at Pacific, Missouri.

Also in July, in compliance with Special Order No. 115, Department of the Missouri, Troop A, 3rd Cavalry, commanded by Capt. James O. Mackey, left Jefferson Barracks by rail for Cleveland, Ohio, to encamp with the Ohio National Guard. While in camp at Cleveland, the Troop performed the usual garrison duties until 12 August, when they marched to the camp rifle range, where they remained until 31 August. Troop A re-joined the Post on 12 September.

The health of the soldiers at Jefferson Barracks continued to be a major concern during 1896. The hospital admission rate was 1,573.91 with a constant sick rate of 67.23 per thousand of strength. This was high when compared to an admission rate of 1,158.68 and a constant sick rate of 37.23 for the Department of the Missouri as a whole. The high admission rate at Jefferson Barracks was attributed to the high incidence of malarial and venereal diseases at the post and a slight increase in injuries. The malarial admission rate stood at 356.52 compared with the Army rate of 83.08 per thousand of strength and the venereal disease rate of 211.59 compared with 78.08. Jefferson Barracks also had ten cases, three fatal, of typhoid fever, during the fiscal year 1897. [1 July 1896 to 30 June 1897]. Disease resulted in six discharges and six deaths during the same time period.[21] As a result of the alarming sick and non-effective rates at Jefferson Barracks in November 1896, the Commanding General of the Army, Lt. General Nelson A. Miles, directed the Commanding General of the Department of the Missouri, Major General Wesley Merritt, to make a thorough examination of the Jefferson Barracks reservation. General Miles further directed General Merritt to detail the Department's Medical Director, Lt. Col. Albert Hautauff; Post Commander, Lt. Col. Guy V. Henry; Post Surgeon, Major Alfred C. Girard; and Post Quartermaster, 1st Lt. Tyree R. Rivers, to assist in the examination. This Board of Examiners was also to report on the sanitary condition of the rifle range at Arcadia, Missouri. Merritt visited Jefferson Barracks on 24 December 1896, with remarks that the post at Jefferson Barracks could be made as healthy as any other Post in the country with certain necessary improvements. The old buildings needed to be torn down and replaced on another site, the sewer system needed to be upgraded, and the water supply increased. As for the rifle range, Merritt said that a more suitable location than Arcadia could not be found in Missouri or Arkansas.

Merritt submitted a second report detailing the costs involved in order to bring Jefferson Barracks up to the standards required for a permanent military reservation. The estimated total cost of the improvements came to $206,979.33. This amount included not only the tearing down of old buildings and replacing them with new, an improved water and sewerage system, but also the draining and filling in of six sink holes with standing water.[22]

It appears that the Board of Inquiry held a series of meetings at Jefferson Barracks that took testimony from interested St. Louis citizens. This developed into a fight to stop the abandonment and closure of the Post. It appears that the committee from the Loyal Legion and the Merchants Exchange had sent a memorial to Washington supporting the improvement and continuance of Jefferson Barracks.

According to the *St. Louis Post Dispatch,* the afternoon session of the second day of hearings heard comments from four St. Louis committee members who had escorted General Merritt to the Barracks. Col. James O. Broadhead, General John W. Turner, ex-Congressman W.M. Kinsey and Hugh E. Weber addressed the committee on the necessity of making Jefferson Barracks a first-class military post. They were assured by both General Merritt and Lt. Col. Henry that the commission would do nothing to injure the Barracks.

The chief feature of the discussion brought out by the St. Louisans was that General Nelson Miles, General-in-Chief of the Army, was the prime mover in an attempt to remove troops from Jefferson Barracks. The aforementioned position taken by General Miles came to light in a letter, dated 14 December 1896, from Senator G.G.Vest to General John W. Noble. This letter was read to the Board of Inquiry by Col. Broadhead, who acted as chairman of the joint committee for the Loyal Legion, the Business Men's League, the Master Builders Association and the Merchant's Exchange. The letter was as follows: "My Dear General - Yours of the 7th Inst., transmitting a communication in regard to the Jefferson Barracks, has been received. I do not know that I can add anything to my published statement as to this matter. The Secretary of War, Mr. Lamont, informs me that Gen. Miles is urging the removal of the troops from the Barracks, and its discontinuance as a military post. I do not think there is the slightest danger of his success during this Administration, but when the new Secretary of War comes into office, it will devolve upon yourself and other influential Republicans in St. Louis, to counteract the influence which Gen. Miles will be able to exert. Of course, I have not the vanity to assume that I can make any valuable suggestions to gentlemen so experienced in public affairs as yourself and your associates upon the committee. My only object in writing is to assure you that everything I can do to maintain the Barracks as a military post and to make necessary improvements there will be done...."

Just why General Miles wanted Jefferson Barracks removed from St. Louis was a question that could not be decided offhand. It was the opinion of several gentlemen who were familiar with the situation that his hostility was due to the fact that two years before when he was the only candidate in sight for the position of Commander-in-Chief of the Loyal Legion, the St. Louis delegation to the National Convention arrived in Washington and defeated him by supporting General Gibbon and working for the latter's election.

The *Globe-Democrat* went on to state that General Merritt told a *Globe-Democrat* reporter that he believed that the Post could be put in first-class sanitary condition and that he was unalterably opposed to its removal. General Merritt was in favor of making Jefferson Barracks a first-class Post, in every sense of the word.

The *Globe-Democrat* also wrote that the Republican delegation from Missouri in Congress would hold a meeting that Friday evening in regard to the agitation over the condition of Jefferson Barracks and other matters of interest to Missouri. The delegation would make great efforts to secure an appropriation to make such improvements in the post as would do away with the sources of complaints. The general opinion among the Missourians over the condition of the post, far from doing it harm, would be to its advantage. The delegation wanted to impress on Congress the necessity of making a sufficient allowance to put this important station in first-class shape. Heretofore when suggestions of improvements in the Post had been made they had been rather regarded as the efforts of Missouri Congressmen to please their constituents and not as being urgent.

Many improvements to Jefferson Barracks' buildings had already been started. New barracks and other buildings had been built and others were in the process of building or plans had been approved. This would continue for the next ten years until Jefferson Barracks had been completely rebuilt. If indeed, General Miles wished the abandonment of Jefferson Barracks, he did not succeed.

Desertion continued to be a major problem for the Army. The Department of the Missouri, of which Jefferson Barracks was a part, consisted of nine posts in Missouri, Michigan, Kansas, Arkansas, Illinois and the Indian Territory. Jefferson Barracks had the most desertions of any post in the Department, forty-five, with an average enlisted strength of 404, this equals an 11.11% desertion rate. The next highest percentage occurred at Fort Logan H. Roots, Arkansas, which had a percentage of 7.63 with ten desertions from an average enlisted strength of 131. The overall percentage of desertions within the Department stood at 4.13%, a decrease from the 6.74% of the previous year. Jefferson Barracks' rate stood well above either percentage.[23]

In the fall of 1896, the electric railway from St. Louis completed its track to the post. This made the Barracks more accessible and drew visitors in large numbers. Formerly, visitors to the picturesque and historic post had to take the Iron Mountain Railroad or a river steamer, but with the completion of the Southern Electric Railroad from Carondelet to the Barracks with a connecting link to the city, the journey was an hour and six-minute ride.

A morning at Jefferson Barracks furnished a unique interest to those who could spare a few hours to observe the movement of that contingent of regular Army stationed there. Here is the daily program omitting the exceptions, those being Saturday and Sunday. Saturday was a day of inspection of quarters and Sunday a day of rest. Boots and Saddles was at 8:25 a.m., with assembly of troops at 8:30 a.m. First call for dismounted drill came at 9:00 a.m. and assembly took place at 9:10 a.m. A dress parade took place at 9:50 a.m., followed by first call for guard mount at 11:15 a.m. At 11:30 a.m. came the guard mount, which was an inspection of the arms of the guard enlivened by music provided by the 3rd Cavalry Band. While men who performed guard-duty filed out to the small parade ground in the center of the garrison, the band played the march "Greater New York," and as Lt. West inspected the guns the band gave that sweet serenade, "Under the Stars." The "King John March" was played while the 30 men, with arms shouldered, marched about the grounds, and as they passed in review under the eyes of Col. Henry, who stood with folded arms near a flagstaff whose colors added to the military character of the scene, the band glided off into Sousa's "Yorktown Centennial."

On Friday mornings the regimental drill, longer and more imposing than the others, took place under the direct command of the General, and at the end of the month was the special ceremony of receiving the standards, when all the colors of all troops passed in review before the commanding officers and the new regimental flag, a handsome silken standard sent out by the War Department that year, was brought into requisition. When there were enough visitors to justify this variation of the usual procedure of the day, the ceremony of receiving the standards was given for their entertainment.

Every evening at 8:00 the band gave a concert with the exception of Sundays, when the concert was at 3:00 p.m.[24]

Troops from Jefferson Barracks continued to take part in celebrations around the country. Lt. Col. Henry commanded the Field and Staff, the Band, and Troops A, D, H and K, who left Jefferson Barracks by rail on 29 May to take part in the Tennessee Centennial Exhibition. They arrived on 30 May and remained in Nashville until 4 June, when they departed for Jefferson Barracks, arriving the next day. The 3rd Cavalry troops were joined in Nashville by four companies of the 6th Infantry from Fort Thomas, Kentucky; and six companies of the 5th Infantry and the Band from Fort McPherson, Georgia, attending the inaugural ceremonies of the Tennessee Centennial Exhibition at Nashville on the 1st and 2nd of June.[25]

As the result of an epidemic of typhoid fever at Jefferson Barracks in September 1896, more than ten ill and convalescent soldiers were left behind when the troops started a practice march on 3 October. As of the morning of 19 September, there were 54 patients on the sick report. Many were thought to be so ill that recovery was almost impossible. The hospital wards were so crowded that tents had to be pitched on the ground in order to accommodate the overflow.[26]

Six troops of 3rd Cavalrymen, between 250 and 300 officers and men, left Jefferson Barracks on 3 October. They arrived in Lebanon, Missouri, on 12 October. They were on a practice march with Springfield, Missouri, as their final destination, a distance of 210 miles. They arrived in Springfield on 14 October, averaging 25 miles a day on their march. It gave them a taste of real army life, and the boys seemed to enjoy roughing it.[27]

In October 1896, Major General Wesley Merritt issued a circular to the Department of Missouri directing a thorough course of military gymnastics at the posts of his command, including Jefferson Barracks, during the next four months.

In addition to the regular drills, a course of light workout with dumbbells, barbells, jumping, vaulting and running were taught, with athletic competitions recommended. Abdominal breathing was to be taught, commencing with half-minute runs each day without accouterments and gradually adding the rifle and pack until the men passed obstacles such as ditches and fences, fully equipped for service over long distances.[28]

An item of note took place in St. Louis during November 1896, when the twenty-eighth reunion of the Society of the Army of the Tennessee took place. General Grenville Dodge, who had served at Jefferson Barracks in 1865, was re-elected President of the Society. The assembled group approved a report from a committee accepting the contract of Carl Rohl-Smith of Chicago to erect a statue of General William T. Sherman in Washington. Upon the arrival of Col. Guy V. Henry, commanding officer of Jefferson Barracks, the Society and its guests proceeded to Jefferson Barracks on 19 November, where General Wesley Merritt, commander of the department, inspected the 3rd Cavalry regiment. A soldier's welcome was next given the visitors at the Officer's Club, where a luncheon was served.[29]

While attending the reunion of the Society of the Army of the Tennessee, Col. Frederick D. Grant, son of General Grant, and Col. Guy V. Henry called on Mrs. Jefferson Davis and her daughter Winnie at the Planter's House Hotel. Henry had received his warrant of commission at West Point from Jefferson Davis. Mrs. Davis and her daughter were in St. Louis for a meeting of the Daughters of the Confederacy.[30]

A look at the new red brick barracks constructed in the late 1890s. The water tower is in the foreground. Note the wooden plank sidewalks

Troops at the Arcadia Rifle Range for their yearly target practice. Firing for record during the last days of their stay at the range could be extremely important as it could earn a soldier extra pay each month. The Arcadia Range was used until a new range at Moss Hollow opened during World War II.

Major John A. Kress remained in command of the St. Louis Powder Depot located on the northern section of the military reservation. Kress' command consisted of nineteen enlisted men in January of 1896 and seventeen men in December of the same year.[31]

It was not always serious military matters at Jefferson Barracks. The Social Dramatic Club of Jefferson Barracks presented a three-act comedy entitled "Snowed In" on the night of 21 December. A large audience composed of the Jefferson Barracks garrison watched as the leading lady Miss Kress, the beautiful daughter of Major John Kress, made her part, Kittie Rosemary, a brilliant success. It was hard to tell whether Capt. Boughton, Troop B, or Lt. McNames, Troop I, was the leading man, as both had about the same amount of hard work to do. Each made a success of his part. Miss White, Mrs. Captain Ewing, Lt. Bell and Robert Ashton Kissack of St. Louis all played parts in the comedy. Music was provided by the 3rd Cavalry Orchestra. The proceeds from the play were used for the benefit of the children's Christmas tree, which was given the next Thursday at the post mess hall and contained presents for every child at the post.[32]

1897

As the new year 1897 began, the post garrison remained unchanged for the most part. Lt. Col. Guy V. Henry remained in command of the post and the 3rd Cavalry Regiment. The garrison consisted of the Band and Troops A, B, D, H, I, and K, plus one officer of Troop L and eight enlisted men of Troop M. The 3rd Cavalry had an aggregate strength of fifteen officers and 354 enlisted men. There were also four staff officers, bringing to nineteen the number of officers present for duty. Twelve additional enlisted men were present for duty.[33]

These troops performed the routine and mostly monotonous garrison duties throughout the year. There occurred an exception to the routine when a fire was discovered around 11:20 a.m. on 19 February. The fire originated in the roof of the building occupied by the Post Office, Recruiting and Printing Office, the Post Adjutant, Sergeant Major, and quarters for married enlisted men. Due to the effectual work of the troops trained and under the supervision of the Post Fire Marshall, 1st Lt. Tyree R. Rivers (who also served as Commissary Quartermaster), the fire was brought under control by 12:30 p.m. The building, however, was completely destroyed. Lt. Rivers had a very narrow escape while on top of a building fighting the fire. He stepped on one of the skylights, which gave way. But for the quickness of Pvt. Black, Troop D, who caught the Lieutenant as he was going down, Rivers would have been killed.[34]

Another fire during the summer destroyed the Post Laundry. A new laundry became part of the year's reconstruction program. From 1 July 1891, to 1 November 1897, a total of $557,429.09 was spent on the reconstruction program [35]

The *St. Louis Republic* reported in its 10 January edition that a military commission was likely to report in favor of extensive improvements to Jefferson Barracks. These improvements would make the post a first-class military station. However, two days later the newspaper reported that General Nelson Miles, General-in-Chief of the Army, wished to know what these proposed improvements would cost before allowing them to begin, thus putting the entire improvement project on hold until another report could be put together.

Then, on 15 January, the *Republic* reported that the commission appointed to investigate the sanitary conditions at Jefferson Barracks had not received any word from the War Department relative to its report sent some time before. Col. Henry stated that he had not received any intimation of a desire on the part of Gen. Miles to have the report amended, but he went on to state that he was prepared to cheerfully supply any information that may be lacking. Henry then stated that the general opinion in military circles and shared by himself was that Jefferson Barracks was to not only be improved, but also be enlarged.[36]

By the end of January 1897, the *St. Louis Republic* reported that $270,000 was the estimated cost of the improvements to be made to Jefferson Barracks. This figure came from Capt. Summerhayes, Post Quartermaster, who was to supervise the proposed work. The plans called for a complete renovation with all the old limestone buildings to be torn down and replaced by new and modern structures.

Another of the improvements called for an immense new parade ground, fully 60 acres in size, taking up the entire central portion of the reservation. The quadrangular form of the Post was to be retained, with the parade ground in the center. The officers' quarters were to form the north side of the quadrangle, while the south side was to contain the new barracks for the soldiers, the riding hall, mess hall and other smaller buildings. The west side was to be made up of the Quartermaster's Office, the Guardhouse and buildings of that nature, while the entire east side was to be left open to the river.

Probably the most important improvements were to be in the water supply and sanitary arrangements. Instead of the 6-inch main which had furnished water to the post, Capt. Summerhayes recommended that a 12-inch main be laid from the city limits at the River des Peres to the government reservation and that a new pumping station be built with a capacity of 500,000 gallons every 24 hours.

A new system of sewers was to be laid that, when coupled with the natural drainage, would provide a complete and vastly improved sanitary condition for the post. Drainage would be so good that within an hour of a hard rain the Parade Ground would be ready for drill.

The scheme for new buildings called for the erection of five new residences to be used for officers' quarters along the north drive; a new riding hall, 400 feet square; six new double barracks, for use of the soldiers; a new Quartermaster Office and several minor buildings.

Summerhayes expected that at some time Jefferson Barracks would be made a regimental post. He also expected a battery of artillery would be stationed at Jefferson Barracks.[37]

By the end of April Capt. Summerhayes had completed a supplemental report requested by the War Department and forwarded it to Washington. Over the previous two months, Capt. Summerhayes and a surveyor had been making a plat of the reservation. The plat showed all the depressions and sink holes on the reservation and the report which it accompanied gave estimates of the cost of permanently putting the sinkholes in a sanitary condition. The survey effectually disposed of the theory that during high water the river reached these sink holes. The bottom of the deepest hole was 15 feet above the high-water mark and 35 feet above the normal river stage. It was hoped that an order to commence work on the proposed improvements would be forthcoming within ten days of the receipt of the Summerhayes report.[38]

In early June, Quartermaster General George H. Weeks inspected Jefferson Barracks and his report promised to bear fruit as the needed improvements to the post seemed about ready to commence. An order to tear down the old Quartermaster's Exchange Building had been issued. This building stood directly north of the Guardhouse and occupied 200 square feet of land. All the officers at Jefferson Barracks looked with satisfaction upon the destruction of this building as it had long been an eyesore. No repairs had been made to the building since it had been half destroyed by fire in 1894. Another important improvement to be made was the establishment of a pumping station near the entrance to the reservation, having engines with sufficient force to give Jefferson Barracks as good a water supply as any locality in the city.

On 4 June, the first of the improvements was turned over to the government by Construction Quartermaster Capt. J.W. Summerhayes. This was a set of barracks to replace the barracks that had been destroyed by fire. They were the finest set of buildings on the post and occupied the site of the old barracks that had been destroyed. The new barracks was a three-story structure with room enough to quarter two troops, A and D, and had all the modern improvements.

Capt. Summerhayes and his wife left for his new assignment in Washington, D.C. the next day. Summerhayes had done an outstanding job during his short stay at the Post and would be missed.[39]

In March, Memphis, Tennessee, was hit by a major flood and called on the government to provide all possible relief for flood sufferers. In response, the War Department ordered the Quartermaster at Jefferson Barracks to ship all the tents that could be spared to Memphis. The tents were packed and ready for shipment by March 25. Jefferson Barracks was the closest military station to Memphis.[40]

The annual drill of the troops at Jefferson Barracks began on 6 April. Six men out of each of the six troops were detailed for the drill, which lasted until the middle of May when the troops departed for the Arcadia Rifle Range.[41]

Ten bachelor officers at Jefferson Barracks gave a ball the night of 23 April. It was held in the large mess hall, which had a dancing capacity of 200 couples and it was crowded. The hall was gorgeously decorated with United States flags, signal flags, cavalry sabers, trumpets, flowers and tropical plants. The ladies' dressing-room, gentlemen's hat room and the café were Army tents. Everything had a military air. The first dance was announced at 10:00 p.m. by a trumpet call and supper was served at midnight.

Lt. West served as master of ceremonies, assisted by Lts. Bell, Conrad and Hawkins. The Legion of Honor was well represented. Among the prominent guests were: Mr. and Mrs. Niedringhaus, Mr. and Mrs. W.P. Turner, Major and Mrs. H.T. Sharpe, Mr. and Mrs. Tower, Mr. and Mrs. D.C. Taylor, Mr. and Mrs. Edwards Whitake,

General and Mrs. Wilson, Captain and Mrs. Waterman, Misses Whitaker, Walker, Warner, White, Wilson, Christine Tutle, Marie Turner and many additional lovely young ladies.[42]

A major re-organization took place in June. Lt. Col. Guy V. Henry, the other Headquarters Staff officers, and the 3rd Cavalry Band, consisting of thirty-one enlisted men, departed Jefferson Barracks 7 June 1897, for Fort Ethan Allen, Vermont. The move, in compliance with Special Order No. 111, Department of the Missouri, and Special Order No. 116, Adjutant General's Office, transferred the Headquarters of the 3rd Cavalry to Fort Ethan Allen. In addition to Col. Henry, Major Henry Jackson, 1st Lt. Tyree R. Rivers, the Veterinary Surgeon, Sergeant Major E.M. Thornton and Quartermaster Sergeant Joseph Badgery transferred to Fort Ethan Allen.[43] Major Henry W. Wessells, Jr. relieved Lt. Col. Henry in command of Jefferson Barracks and the 3rd Cavalry troops at the Post.

Born at Fort Smith, Indian Territory (now Arkansas), 9 March 1839, Guy V. Henry graduated from the U.S. Military Academy on 5 May 1861, and served throughout the Civil War and Indian Wars as Lieutenant, Captain, Major, Lieutenant Colonel, Colonel, and Brigadier General in the Regular Army. Henry received brevets for gallantry and distinguished service for action near Pocotaligo River, South Carolina on 20 February 1864, in the Battle of Olustee, Florida; and in front of Petersburg, Virginia, during the Civil War. He was awarded the Medal of Honor on 5 December 1893, for his Civil War service at the Battle of Cold Harbor on 1 June 1864, where he was serving as Colonel of the 40th Massachusetts Volunteer Infantry. However, Henry made his greatest reputation as a fighter during the Indian Wars after 1870. He chased the Apaches in Arizona and the Sioux in the Dakota hills. Henry received a wound that penetrated both cheeks, severing the optic nerve during the Battle of Rosebud Creek. He was breveted a Brigadier General for his bravery in this action. Soon after hostilities broke out with Spain in 1898, Col. Henry was appointed Brigadier General of Volunteers, then on 7 December 1898, he was made Major General of Volunteers. He commanded a brigade under General Nelson Miles in Puerto Rico. Later he became the first American Governor General of Puerto Rico. General Henry died at his home in New York City on 28 October 1899, from pneumonia. He is buried in Arlington National Cemetery.[44]

Much was made of the removal of most of the 3rd Cavalry and especially the Band to Fort Ethan Allen. It was suggested that Jefferson Barracks would be abandoned or significantly reduced in importance. However, in a letter written by Congressman Bartholdt and received 21 June by St. Louis Mayor Ziegenhein, Jefferson Barracks was not to suffer any loss of significance through the recent changes ordered by the War Department.

Bartholdt related the contents of a conversation he had with Secretary of War Russell Alger in the course of which Alger gave Bartholdt positive assurances that Jefferson Barracks would be garrisoned in the near future with a regiment of Infantry, four troops of Cavalry and a Battery of Artillery. General of the Army Nelson Miles had agreed in principal to this.[45]

On 25 June, Missouri Senator George Graham Vest had an interview with the Secretary of War in which the Secretary repeated much the same information regarding the future of Jefferson Barracks. The only difference was that the Secretary stated that only two troops of Cavalry would be coming to Jefferson Barracks. Secretary Alger went on to state that he intended to visit St. Louis during the summer to inspect Jefferson Barracks and the old arsenal grounds for the purpose of determining intelligently all the questions involved. The Secretary had considered selling the arsenal grounds with the proceeds going to improve Jefferson Barracks.[46]

Henry W. Wessells, Jr., was the son of Brevet Brigadier General Henry W. Wessells, who began his military career at West Point in 1829 and retired 1 January 1871. Wessells, Jr. began his military service at the Naval Academy in September 1862, but dropped out 12 November 1864. He then served as a private and sergeant in Companies D and K, 7th Infantry, from 1 March to 6 August 1865. He received a commission as a 2nd Lt. to date 21 July 1865. He transferred to the 3rd Cavalry on 31 December 1870; was promoted to captain on 20 December 1872; to major on 16 August 1892; to Lt. Col. on 8 May 1899; and to colonel on 19 February 1901.

Cavalry drills are performed in order that each cavalryman learns and maintains proficiency in Cavalry maneuvers. However, drills do not always go according to plan as witnessed by the 3rd Cavalry drill on 22 May. On that morning Troops A, C, E, I and K, comprising about 300 men, were out for drill. With red and white banners fluttering gayly in the breeze and the backs of their well-groomed horses glistening in the sun, they wheeled and galloped around. Just at the final roundup of the Cavalry as Troop A wheeled into line, Pvt. McDonald's sorrel horse slipped and fell in making a turn carrying his rider with him. A melee at once resulted, with the result that Pvt. Nicholson of Troop C was thrown from his horse, sustaining a bad injury to his right side and arm that laid him up for a few weeks. Pvt. McDonald's fall was the more serious. He was unconscious when he was picked up and he suffered from a slight concussion of the brain, which, while not fatal, may be alarming in its results.[47]

Decoration Day, 31 May 1897 brought forth a grand ceremony. The regular program did not commence until afternoon, but the monthly inspection and muster, all dismounted, took place at 9:00 a.m. and guard mount at 10 o'clock. Upon the arrival of the Grand Army of the Republic, a 21-gun salute was fired. At 2:00 p.m. the command, mounted, received the Grand Army veterans on the north parade grounds and after reception of the standard, it passed in review at a trot. The change of direction continued toward the band barracks, in a column of fours. When north of the quartermaster and commissary buildings the regiment dismounted, and in column of threes headed by the 3rd Cavalry Band and followed by the Grand Army veterans, they proceeded to the cemetery.

After the addresses and speeches had been made, the regiment fired three volleys over the graves, and the trumpeters sounded "Taps, The Soldiers' Last Tattoo." The decoration of the graves then commenced and continued until evening.[48]

The 3rd Cavalry gave an exhibition sham battle on the afternoon of 4 June, for the benefit of Inspector General Peter D. Vroom. The 2nd Squadron under the command of Maj. Henry.W. Wessells and composed of Troops K, L and B, appeared against the 3rd Squadron commanded by Capt. G.F. Chase and composed of Troops A, D and H. The object of the sham battle was to show the line of defense, attack, and the different maneuvers that would be resorted to in time of war. The drill lasted 40 minutes and a large crowd turned out to watch.[49]

Major General Jonathan R. Brooks inspected the Post on 10 June and on 27 November 1897. No major problems were noted. While at Jefferson Barracks, Brooks intimated to members of the Businessmen's League that his report would be in favor of the retention of the Barracks and most liberal appropriations for improvements.

A correspondent for the *St. Louis Republic* reported on 14 June that he had consulted with leading officers of the War Department, and they had all stated that the Barracks would, in time, with the improvements contemplated by the department, be made one of the best posts in the country. The correspondent's report went on to state that the War Department had proposed to spend $16,000 for a new guardhouse, constructed of brick and modeled after the best in the United States. Also, a new water pipe to St. Louis, upon which about $10,000 was to be spent, was to correct all that was needed to satisfy sanitary conditions at the Post.[50]

A most unusual event started on 15 June 1897, when 24 men of the 25th U.S. Infantry started on a ride of nearly 2,500 miles from Fort Missoula, Montana, to Jefferson Barracks. What made this unusual was the fact that the men rode bicycles. This was an experiment to determine if bicycles were to be used in the Army. Full Infantry equipment, including cooking utensils and shelter tents were carried on the bicycles.[51]

The Bicycle Corps reached Jefferson Barracks on 24 July, and on 17 August, Lt. James M. Moss and the other members of the Bicycle Corps of the 25th U.S. Infantry left Jefferson Barracks by rail for Fort Missoula. When Lt. Moss reached his destination, his first duty was to prepare a detailed report of the trip and forward it to the War Department. This report was to furnish information on the quantity of rations carried, the details of their consumption and distribution, the weight of accouterments and the detailed manner of their shifting the arrangement of the repair problem, so that the entire Command was never delayed, the physical capacity of the men to cover certain distances in certain times, the effects of hunger and thirst, and the ability of the wheel, topographical and meteorological conditions. The information contained in Lt. Moss' report was used to determine the feasibility of the use of bicycles by the Army.[52]

The 3rd Squadron, 3rd Cavalry, Troops A, B, and H, commanded by Capt. George F. Chase, left Jefferson Barracks on 8 July for its yearly target practice at Arcadia. They arrived at Arcadia on 12 July.

On 20 July, the 2nd Squadron, 3rd Cavalry left Jefferson Barracks and the 3rd Squadron left Arcadia for Chicago. They attended ceremonies for the unveiling of a statue of the late Major General John Logan. They returned on 24 July.[53]

After returning to Arcadia from Chicago, the 3rd Squadron completed target practice on 7 August. The Squadron marched to Farmington on 7 August, to Platton Gap on 8 August, to Kimmswick on 9 August and to Jefferson Barracks on 10 August.

The 2nd Squadron, 3rd Cavalry, Troops B, I, and K, left for target practice at Arcadia on 12 August. They finished target practice and broke camp on 15 September and arrived back at Jefferson Barracks on 18 September after marching the same route as the 3rd Squadron.[54]

General Wesley Merritt commanded U.S. troops in the Philippines. He had commanded Jefferson Barracks during its Cavalry Recruit Depot days and is credited with playing a major role in saving the post from the chopping block when General-of-the-Army Nelson Miles wanted to close it.

25th Regiment, Bicycle Corps

Gazebo next to the parade ground with a gentleman out for a stroll around the post.
To the left is one of the old limestone barracks and in the center is one of the new red brick barracks.

By the middle of August, the proposed improvements to Jefferson Barracks had taken on definite shape. Bids for construction of barracks, officers' quarters, and other buildings had been received and examined by the Quartermaster General and contracts were awarded to the following bidders:

For tearing down and removing the gymnasium building, C. Stafford, 513 Union Trust Building, St. Louis, with a bid of $475. The same bidder got the contract for removing the office of the Constructing Quartermaster with a bid of $765.

Samuel I. Pope Company of Chicago received the contract for construction of a pumphouse and boiler. The bid was $5,389.

J. Clark & Sons Century Building of St. Louis won the contract for a new guardhouse. The bid was $10,469. Guardhouse plumbing went to Ring & Reardon of St. Louis for $553.

Construction of three double barracks was awarded to William H. O'Brien, 8626 Cozens Avenue in St. Louis. The War Department was pleased with the amount of the bids.[55]

In compliance with Special Order No. 159, Department of the Missouri, Troops A, B, D, and H, 3rd Cavalry, proceeded by rail on 14 September to Nashville, Tennessee, to take part in the Tennessee Centennial Exhibition . Major John S. Loud, who had been promoted from Captain, 9th Cavalry, arrived from Fort Washakie, Wyoming, on 31 August, and was in command of the troops. The troops returned Jefferson Barracks on 31 October.

Troop K, 3rd Cavalry, three officers and forty-nine enlisted men, left Jefferson Barracks on 23 October, for duty at the annual St. Louis Horse Show. They rejoined on 31 October.[56]

George D. Meiklejohn, Assistant Secretary of War, arrived in St. Louis the morning of 16 October 1897, from Washington, D.C. The Secretary was accompanied by A.J. Schofield, Chief Clerk of the War Department. Meiklejohn was on a general inspection tour of western military installations. Capt. G.F. Chase met Meiklejohn at Union Station and drove him to the Southern Hotel, where quarters had been arranged. After breakfast, the Secretary was driven to Jefferson Barracks, where a dress parade and a general review of the troops was held. This was followed by an inspection of the Post.[57]

A regimental review and drill by the 3rd Cavalry was given in honor of the St. Louis Railway Club, the afternoon of 12 November. The public was urged to take the Southern Electric Railroad from 6th Street in St. Louis, for the one-hour ride to Jefferson Barracks.[58]

The post mortem on the body of one Jacob Weinand, who was found dead in his kitchen on the evening of 22 December, revealed a peculiarly fiendish method used by the murderers to get rid of the old man. When found, Weinand, besides being gagged and bound, had a towel tightly twisted about his neck. The post mortem showed that far down the old man's throat, tightly imbedded at the bronchial tubes, was a wad of thick cloth which had been wrapped with horse hair. Fingers could not have reached that far, therefore a stick of some kind was probably used to ram the wad down his throat. Then the old man was garroted with a towel.

What makes this murder most interesting is the fact that in 1893 a soldier at Jefferson Barracks, who had saved about $14,000 which he carried in his pocket, was found murdered in his room. He had been bound, a wad of cloth and horse hair had been pushed down his throat and he had been choked to death with a twisted towel. The similarity of the two murders caused excitement in police circles and an all-out effort was made to solve these crimes, but to no avail, as they were never solved.[59]

This ended the rather uneventful year of 1897. The year saw 427 recruits transferred to permanent duty stations. Major John A. Kress commanded the St. Louis Powder Depot for the entire year. At the end of the year he had twenty enlisted men in his command.

Chapter 2- Jefferson Barracks and the War with Spain

Although momentous changes were in the offing, the year 1898 began with the same routine that had exemplified the previous several years. Major Henry W. Wessells, Jr. commanded the Post and the six troops of the 3rd Cavalry Regiment that made up the majority of the garrison.[1] The entire garrison consisted of 24 officers, 355 enlisted men, and one schoolteacher. The February 1898 Post Return also listed property consisting of 312 horses, 20 mules, one Dougherty wagon and one sprinkler wagon. The primary enlisted personnel consisted of Zachariah T. Woodall, Ordnance Sergeant, who had been at Jefferson Barracks since 10 October 1893; Henry Donaldson, Post Quartermaster Sergeant, at Jefferson Barracks since 30 June 1896; 1st Class Private John Healy, Signal Corps, at Jefferson Barracks since 28 February 1896; James Hanaghan, Commissary Sergeant, at Jefferson Barracks since 3 February 1896; and August von Clossman, Hospital Steward, at Jefferson Barracks since 28 November 1892.

Capt. John T. Knight, Acting Quartermaster, officially turned over a new guardhouse for use on 1 February 1898. Major John P. Baker paid the garrison on 7 January and 7 February 1898.

However, during February events took place that led officers, soldiers, and civilians alike to the impression that war with Spain was inevitable. Preparations for just such an event began in earnest.

During the evening of 15 February 1898, the battleship U.S.S. *Maine* lay at anchor in the harbor of Havana, Cuba. Capt. Charles D. Sigsbee, a seasoned veteran who had served during the Civil War at Mobile under Admiral David Farragut, was certainly qualified to command a capital ship assigned hazardous duty and the *Maine* was undoubtedly performing hazardous duty, Sigsbee sat in his cabin writing about the experiences of his command in troubled Cuba.

On 25 February 1895, a group of dissidents in eastern Cuba had signaled the start of an armed uprising against Spanish authority. Fighting began and Spain had been unable to quell the rebellion. Even prior to this latest rebellion, Cuban dissidents had fought Spanish authority from 1868 to 1878, known as the Ten Years' War [1]

The United States had become deeply interested in the struggle between the Cuban insurgents and the Spanish garrison in Cuba. The *Maine* had been ordered to Havana in late January 1898, to protect American citizens in Havana after riots there threatened serious trouble. Adding to the seriousness of the situation for the *Maine* was the fact that two weeks after the arrival of the *Maine* at Havana, relations between the United States and Spain had deteriorated when an American newspaper published an indiscreet letter written by the Spanish minister to the U.S., Enrique Dupuy de Lome, who was highly critical of President William McKinley. Sensing heightened danger, Capt. Sigsbee had prohibited unescorted visits to his ship and posted sentries on deck. Ammunition had been placed next to the 1-pound and 6-pound guns.

Suddenly, at 9:40 p.m. a massive explosion tore through the *Maine*. The blast occurred in the forward section of the ship near the living quarters of the enlisted men. The *Maine* sank in minutes. Of the 354 officers and men aboard the *Maine*, 266 were killed and many more were seriously injured.[2]

Despite Capt. Sigsbee's initial report that advised against making a judgement as to the cause of the explosion, most Americans immediately jumped to the conclusion that the Spanish were responsible. Sigsbee soon put forth the theory that before the *Maine* had been moored in Havana harbor, a mine had been placed beneath the birth assigned to the ship. Secretary of the Navy John D. Long attributed the accident to an internal explosion. A more typical view came from Capt. Sherman Vanaman of the schooner *Philadelphia*, who had been in Havana harbor on the night of the explosion. Vanaman was convinced that a torpedo launched against the *Maine*, presumably by the Spanish, had caused the ship to sink. Despite the expression of shock and sympathy by the Spanish government, the public outcry in the United States demanded American intervention in Cuba.

President McKinley reacted in a calm and measured attitude, stating that "We must learn the truth and endeavor, if possible, to fix the responsibility. The country can afford to withhold its judgement and not strike an avenging blow until the truth is known."[3]

An American court, on 21 March 1898, held that a submarine mine, set off outside the *Maine* by persons unknown, had caused the forward magazines of the vessel to explode, the force of the explosion causing the *Maine* to sink. The next day, March 22, the Spanish inquiry came to a different conclusion: the *Maine's* forward magazines had indeed exploded, but from internal causes.[4]

On 11 April, President McKinley took the step he had long avoided: he sent a message to Congress asking for authority to intervene in Cuba. McKinley's message summarized the course of prior negotiations and stated the grounds for armed intervention. McKinley offered four reasons for armed intervention: it would end bloodshed in Cuba; it would afford protection to American citizens in Cuba; it would preclude further damage to trade and property; and it would remove the menace to peace that had proved so disruptive in recent times.

On 19 April 1898, the joint resolution providing for intervention in Cuba passed the Congress. McKinley signed it the next day at 11:54 a.m. It called for Cuban independence; immediate Spanish withdrawal from Cuba; and if necessary, intervention by the armed forces of the United States. It disclaimed any American intention to absorb Cuba.[5]

The American ultimatum to Spain required that Spain indicate its future course by noon, 23 April. Before American Minister to Spain Woodford could deliver this message, Don Pino Gullon Iglesias, Spain's Foreign Minister, on 21 April, ordered Spanish minister Polo de Bernaba to leave the United States, and informed Woodford that Spain had broken diplomatic relations with the U.S. Spain declared war on the United States on 23 April 1898. The president, on 25 April, asked Congress to make a formal declaration of war. The House and Senate responded immediately, specifying the beginning of the conflict as 21 April.[6]

Preparations had already begun at Jefferson Barracks. The Second and Third Squadrons of the 3rd Cavalry departed Jefferson Barracks by rail on 19 April, en route to Chickamauga Park, Georgia. They arrived on 20 April, and on 21 April marched to Camp George H. Thomas. This left only a small detachment of the 3rd Cavalry at Jefferson Barracks. With the departure of the officers of the 3rd Cavalry, only Assistant Quartermaster John T. Knight and Assistant Surgeon E.B. Ewing remained as regular Army officers. Knight assumed command of Jefferson Barracks upon the departure of Major Henry Wessells, Jr. Capt. Francis A. Winter, Assistant Surgeon, arrived in late April, and Major Joseph B. Girard remained assigned to Jefferson Barracks, but had left for three months leave on 2 April. Thus, the garrison totaled four officers; Zachariah Woodall, Ordnance Sergeant; Henry Donaldson, Quartermaster Sergeant; James Hanaghan, Commissary Sergeant; Alfred Silverstone, Hospital Steward; Gustave Cooney, Troop M, 3rd Cavalry, in charge of the General Prisoners; Sgt. William DuPerow, 3rd Cavalry, on duty with the Recruit Depot; and Sgt. Joseph L. McGee, Troop M, 3rd Cavalry, on duty with the Recruit Depot; and a total of six recruits and seven general prisoners. The entire garrison consisted of the grand total of twenty-four men.

Jefferson Barracks did not remain practically deserted for long. President McKinley put out a call to Missouri Governor Lon V. Stephens on April 29 asking for five regiments of Volunteer Infantry and a Battery of Light Artillery. Volunteers had been awaiting this call, but Governor Stephens had put a damper on their ardor by announcing that the state had no funds available to pay the expenses of transportation and mobilization. He also declined to call a special session of the State Legislature to authorize a special appropriation. This obstacle was eventually overcome by deficiency spending and by using Federal funds.

Light Battery A, Missouri National Guard, which had been training on the outskirts of St. Louis arrived first, reaching Jefferson Barracks on 4 May. This unit had been recruited and enrolled in the City of St. Louis. It was commanded by Capt. Frank M. Rambouillet. Other officers included 1st Lt. Edward B. End, 1st Lt. John E. Weber and 2nd Lt. William J. Murray. 1st Lt. Leacher Hardeman mustered Light Battery A into Federal service on 9 May, to serve for two years unless discharged sooner. Light Battery A, Missouri Volunteers, remained at Jefferson Barracks until 16 May, when it departed for Camp George H. Thomas at Chickamauga Park, Georgia, arriving on 17 May.

At Camp Thomas the unit became part of the Light Artillery Brigade. On 19 May the company received their guns and horses making it one of the best organizations at Chickamauga [7]

In response to the second call for volunteers, Capt. Rambouillet and Cpl. Allen C. Rick returned to St. Louis to enroll the required 53 men. They had the luxury of picking only the men they desired as the Artillery had greater appeal and appeared more romantic than the Infantry. By the end of June, the recruiters and their new recruits were back at Camp Thomas.

Orders arrived on 20 July to proceed at once to Newport News, Virginia, where the regiment was to embark for Puerto Rico, as part of the First Army Corps under Major J.B. Rodney [8] The regiment left Chickamauga Park on 24 July and arrived at Newport News at 11:00 p.m. on 27 July. Capt. Rambouillet learned that he had orders to sail at 4:00 p.m. the following afternoon. Capt. Rambouillet also learned that there would probably not be enough room on the transport for the entire 1st Corps. He rushed his men and equipment on board the *Roumania*, an old freighter pressed into service. There was no time for order and everything went into the hold in the order it could be dumped. After a wild, disorderly scramble the entire Battery managed to get on board, and the freighter set sail.[9] Conditions on the ship can be described best in Capt. Rambouillet's own words: "A tug boat with one gun could capture us, the *Roumania* is so poorly fitted up. There are 780 men in the steerage, 18 inches to a man. You can imagine how it smells. There are 700 head of horses and mules, and these are on either side of the officer's quarters. There is no way to dispose of the droppings, therefore, we could not sleep and had to eat on deck."[10] Rations taken consisted of canned beef, tomatoes, beans and coffee. No provisions for cooking existed.

The *Roumania* arrived at Guanaco on 3 August. However, the ship ran aground on a reef and it took 12 hours to extricate it. The transport then proceeded to Ponce and on to Arroyo. Arroyo had no facilities for unloading, so the men improvised a wharf by sinking two lighters and using planks from the horse stalls. It took 10 days to unload the tangled mess that had been thrown in, in one day. At Arroyo, the regiment reported to Major General John R. Brooke on 12 August. General Brooke decided to drive the Spanish from their position near Guayama. Battery A was assigned the second position in the column of attack. The attacking force advanced to within three miles of Guayama, took up a position in front of the Spanish blockhouse, set and sighted their guns, when a messenger arrived with news of the armistice.[11]

The next few weeks the men of Battery A endured many hardships. The rains came, making the roads a quagmire and making food scarce and of poor quality. Fortunately, their stay was short, as Battery A boarded the *Concho* on 7 September for their return trip to New York. Upon arrival in New York, the Battery proceeded directly to St. Louis, arriving on 17 September. A crowd of around 10,000 turned out to greet them. On 24 September, a celebration and banquet feted Battery A at the Exposition Building.

Battery A lost three men from typhoid fever. Cullum Whittlesy was the first Missouri volunteer to lose his life on Spanish soil. After a sixty-day furlough, the Battery mustered out on 30 November 1898.[12]

Arriving later in the day on 4 May was the 1st Regiment, National Guard of Missouri. The 1st Missouri Volunteer Infantry was recruited and enrolled in St. Louis. The 1st Missouri was the first to fill its ranks. It had been drilling in the armory on Pine Street for some time before war was declared. When orders arrived on May 4 to proceed to Jefferson Barracks, the regiment paraded through the streets of St. Louis, accompanied by Union and Confederate veterans of the Civil War.

The first days at Jefferson Barracks proved to be a trying experience for the men of the regiment. Upon arrival at Jefferson Barracks, the men found there was no available means of transferring their baggage to the camp grounds. The men finally carried their own tents and blankets to their camp area. When they eventually reached their assigned camp area, around 7:00 p.m., they discovered that no orders for provisions had been made.[13] They finally managed to obtain food and their camp life at Jefferson Barracks got underway.

The camp for the Missouri Volunteers was named "Camp Stephens" in honor of the Missouri Governor. The first days in camp proved every bit as trying as their arrival had been. It rained and was cold and gloomy. The tents leaked and there was not enough blankets or straw for mattresses. If that was not enough, the food was poorly prepared by amateur cooks.[14] The regiment's officers tried in vain to improve conditions as they feared the men would demand their discharge. To make matters worse (if that was even possible at the time) on 10 May the regimental band notified Col. Batsdorf that it would not accompany the regiment unless each musician was paid three dollars a day. Charles Seymour, the Band's Chief Musician, offered to raise a volunteer band, and the old band members received their discharges.[15]

On 11 May, they held an election in which Edwin Batsdorf was elected colonel and commanding officer; John H. Cavender was elected lieutenant colonel.; Alfred G. Kennett, major; Clarence A. Sinclair, major; and Alexander M. Fuller, major. Major and Surgeon John R. Hereford rounded out the senior staff officers. Lt. Leacher Hardeman mustered 47 officers and 981 men into United States service on 13 May 1898.[16]

The Rambouillet family moved to St. Louis in 1868, where Frank attended the public schools and later Washington University's School of Medicine. He received his M.D. in 1884, and that same year he established a medical practice in St. Louis.

The Spanish-American War in 1898 interrupted Dr. Rambouillet's medical practice. Rambouillet had a long involvement in the Missouri National Guard, first enlisting at 14 in 1876. This led to his commissioning as a captain in Light Battery A, Missouri Volunteers. Capt. Rambouillet saw action in Puerto Rico as part of the American contingent rushed to secure Puerto Rico before the expected Spanish surrender.

Rambouillet transferred to the 32nd Infantry and again saw action, this time in the Philippine Islands as a member of the American occupation troops attempting to crush the Filipino insurrection. Capt. Rambouillet received a commendation for meritorious service in the Philippines.

In 1909, Missouri Governor Herbert Hadley asked Rambouillet to become Adjutant General of Missouri. He accepted and served in this position until 1913.

Three years later Rambouillet became involved in the Mexican Border Crisis of 1916, as a colonel in the Missouri National Guard. President Woodrow Wilson ordered Guardsmen to the Mexican border after tensions created by Poncho Villa's raids into the United States led to talk of war. Luckily, it remained only a "talking war" and within a year the Missouri troops came home.

America's entry into World War I saw Rambouillet again answering the call to arms. After training at Camp Doniphan, Oklahoma, Col. Rambouillet, in command of the 128th Field Artillery attached to the 35th Division, journeyed to France as part of the American Expeditionary Force. Rambouillet saw action in the Argonne Forest fighting. He remained in France until 1919, when he returned to St. Louis.

After the World War, Rambouillet remained active in Missouri National Guard affairs. He was reappointed Adjutant General from 1925 to 1927. Frank Rambouillet died in 1937.

The 1st Missouri Volunteer Infantry remained at Jefferson Barracks until the evening of 19 May, when the regiment boarded a train bound for Camp Thomas, Chickamauga Park, Georgia. The train was divided into two sections, each consisting of a Pullman sleeper, eight passenger coaches, two baggage cars, a freight car, and a stock car. Although the Army provided rations, the trip took considerably longer than expected, requiring the men to depend on the generosity of the people in the towns through which they passed for provisions.

While en route, calamity struck on 21 May, when the first section of the train wrecked. Pvt. George Walker was killed and seven other men received slight injuries.[17]

The regiment reached Chickamauga Park during the night of 21 May. The men marched a short distance from the train station, rolled up their blankets, and went to sleep without supper. In the morning Battery A, which had preceded the 1st Missouri, served the men black coffee and dry bread before the First formed up and marched the three miles to the camp ground. The regiment received orders assigning it to the 1st Brigade, 3rd Division, 3rd Army Corps, commanded by General James F. Wade.[18]

While in camp, the regiment performed the usual garrison duties. Camp life consisted of problems, certainly not concerned with the war in Cuba. The most pressing problems dealt with food, water, and cleanliness. The men's diet consisted of Army rations, i.e., beans, rice, potatoes, bacon, and fresh and canned beef. Bread and fruit proved to be scarce commodities. The company cooks' baked biscuits were barely edible, but better bread became fairly plentiful after the regimental bakery was established. The problems with the meat supply could not be overcome as easily. The canned beef proved to be in poor condition and almost unpalatable. Fresh beef arrived by train, but when unloaded on the station platform it oftentimes laid in the hot sun covered with flies for hours. The result was a spoiled and putrid meat supply before it even reached the cooks.[19]

The water supply became a serious problem the longer the 1st Missouri and the thousands of volunteers from other states remained at Camp Thomas. Chickamauga Creek and a few wells provided the water for the 50,000 to 60,000 men camped in the park.[20] The creek served as a source of drinking water, as well as a place for washing clothes and bathing. The soldiers did not properly dispose of waste products, causing them to seep into the creek. Within a few weeks typhoid fever had appeared. The 1st Missouri was more fortunate than most units, as it had discovered an old well that provided a more healthful supply of water. Dr. Hereford also proved to be an extremely proficient physician. Of even more help was the almost fifteen hundred dollars in the regiment's treasury, which was used to purchase extra food and supplies.[21]

However, on the subject of uniforms and equipment, the 1st Missouri did not fare as well. The State of Missouri had issued the 1st uniforms, arms, and blankets, with the expectation of being reimbursed the price of new uniforms, which the Federal Government refused to do. Missouri Adjutant General Bell ordered the regiment to turn in all their uniforms. The problem once the uniforms had been returned was that there were no U.S. uniforms to be had. The men wrapped themselves in blankets and remained clothed in this manner for some time. Not until 10 June did the troops receive new uniforms. There was also what proved to be a major delay in issuing the 1st Missouri troops equipment. Not until 21 June did Col. Batsdorf report that his entire command was fully equipped.[22]

In a second call for volunteers issued on 25 May, company strength was increased from 81 enlisted men to 106. 1st Lt. and Adjutant George B. Webster; Capt. Charles W. Holtcamp, Co. D; and Major Kennett returned to Missouri to recruit the additional 355 men needed to fill out the regimental ranks. They opened a recruiting office in the armory in St. Louis on 16 June. Recruiting the additional men proved difficult and by 26 June only half of the needed recruits had been enrolled. News of the fighting in Cuba re-aroused interest and by the end of June the necessary men had been enrolled.[23]

In another rather unusual circumstance, the 1st Missouri witnessed first-hand the effects of the political spoils system. In late July, Governor Stephens appointed numerous inexperienced men directly from civilian life to be officers in the regiment. Col. Batsdorf and Lt. Col. Cavender stated that as the 1st Missouri was a part of the United States Army and no longer under the command of Governor Stephens, they did not have to accept these officers, which they refused to do. Of course, this action did not sit well with Governor Stephens, and in late July when the regiment's officers received their signed commissions, Batsdorf, Cavender and Webster did not receive their commissions.[24] However, in a 29 July statement the War Department upheld the actions of Batsdorf and Cavender.

Meanwhile, the status of the three officers remained in abeyance. Rumors circulated that the regiment would have been chosen for active combat service if not for the status of the three officers.[25] Finally, on 20 August, the War Department returned a decision that stated that men legally mustered into the United States service were not subject to recall by the Governor. Stephens could not remove the officers, but he still refused to issue the signed commissions. While all of this was transpiring news of the cessation of hostilities reached Chickamauga on 12 August, and the men realized that they would not get a chance to fight the Spanish.

The 1st Missouri received orders to break camp on 5 September. The regiment arrived at Jefferson Barracks on 6 September, where they received a joyous welcome by the mayor of St. Louis and a large crowd of citizens. On 29 September, the volunteers were entertained at the Exposition Building, and on 31 October, Lt. Ralph Harrison mustered the regiment out of U.S. service.[26]

Pursuant to orders the 2nd Regiment of Infantry, National Guard of Missouri proceeded to Jefferson Barracks on 4 May, arriving the next day. The 2nd Regiment had been recruited in the western and southwestern parts of the state. Once at Jefferson Barracks, the 2nd Missouri received physicals resulting in a three percent loss of personnel. The regiment, consisting of 45 officers and 943 men, mustered into United States service on 12 May 1898, as the 2nd Missouri Infantry, United States Volunteers, to serve two years, unless discharged earlier.

The regiment left Jefferson Barracks for Chickamauga Park, Georgia, where it arrived on 20 May 1898. The regiment's commanding officer, Col. William K. Chaffee, wrote a letter to the governor reporting the regiment's arrival at Camp George H. Thomas on 20 May. Chaffee went on to report that upon arrival, he reported to General John R. Brooke and the regiment was assigned to the 3rd Brigade, 3rd Division, 1st Army. It was at this point that Chaffee put forth his sternest complaint writing: "to be greatly regretted that some method was not devised to equip Missouri troops. Humiliating to bring to camp a regiment so inadequately provided with uniforms and equipment. It was also hard to explain that Missouri did not pay her troops. Missourians, from practically 1 April, served until 4 July 1898, without a dollar of pay; received on 4 July from U.S. pay from May 4. The lack of early preparation as to equipment, has, in my opinion, prevented Missouri's being represented in any of the expeditions which have so far left this country, and officers and men alike have been humiliated and disheartened." Chaffee went on to write that six deaths had taken place in the regiment; that the water supply was inadequate, having to be hauled four miles; that there were no bathing facilities; and that typhoid fever had become epidemic with sixty-nine cases in the regiment.

The ranking staff officers in addition to Chaffee, from Carthage, included Lt. Col. Harry C. De Muth, from Sedalia; Major Harrison Mitchell, from Nevada; Major Franklin E. Williams, from Joplin; and Major and Surgeon Samuel K. Crawford, from Sedalia. The companies comprising the 2nd Missouri were recruited and enrolled at the following points: Company A, at Carthage; Company B, at Butler; Company C, at Lamar; Company D, at Sedalia; Company E, at Pierce City; Company F, at Clinton; Company G, at Joplin; Company H, at Nevada; Company I, at Sedalia; Company K, at Springfield; Company L, at Jefferson City; and Company M, at Springfield.[27]

The history of the 2nd Missouri at Chickamauga Park proved to be a repetition of the experiences of the 1st Missouri, i.e., spoiled food, bad water, and lack of equipment. Col. Chaffee reported that 1,040 out of 10,000 at Chickamauga Park were sick, many with typhoid fever.[28]

The officers in command of the companies composing the 2nd Missouri experienced numerous problems. Several companies proved to be rowdy and unruly, and many soldiers deserted. Dissatisfaction with lack of pay resulted in the men accusing the officers of appropriating money sent by relief organizations at home.[29] Meanwhile, the men waited anxiously for orders to move to the front.

Finally, on 27 June instructions from Washington arrived ordering that all men be supplied with full field equipment and that the entire 1st Army Corps be held in readiness to move.[30] Despite the excitement that these orders generated among the men of the 2nd Missouri, when the next orders arrived, the 2nd Missouri was not included. The troops believed that a lack of equipment caused their exclusion. Resentment aimed at Governor Stephens increased, both among the troops and at home.

The 2nd Missouri remained in service even after the cessation of hostilities. On 27 August, the 2nd Missouri received orders to move to Camp Hamilton, Ky. Once there, they became part of the 2nd Brigade of the 2nd Army Corps.[31] The regiment finally mustered out of service on 3 March 1899. It had lost sixteen men from disease, two by accident, and forty-four by desertion.[32] During their trip home, the train wrecked and seventeen men were injured.[33]

The 3rd Regiment of the Missouri National Guard, under the command of Col. George P. Gross and stationed in Kansas City in April 1898, was in extremely poor condition. It had little equipment and its ranks were far from filled. As a matter of fact, the idea was prevalent that it would remain in Missouri to be used for home defense. Adjutant General Bell ordered recruiting offices opened in Kansas City, Independence, and Liberty and through the efforts of Col. Gross the 400 men required to fill its ranks were enrolled [34]

The twelve companies of three officers and eighty-one enlisted men with Field, Staff, and Band left Kansas City by train on 7 May 1898, and arrived at Jefferson Barracks the next day. While at Jefferson Barracks, the men complained about the quality and quantity of the rations being issued to them. It would seem that they certainly had a valid complaint regarding the quantity of rations as the regiment was being issued rations for 980 men when nearly 1,150 men were present for duty. The *Kansas City Times* reported that on Sunday, 9 May, the troops held a day of fasting and prayer - "Fasting because there was nothing to eat - prayer for the eatables to come."

The 3rd Missouri Infantry mustered into Federal service on 14 May with 50 officers and 974 enlisted men, 100 having been rejected during their physicals. Col. George P. Gross commanded the regiment with Lt. Col. Charles E. Wagar, Major Sidney E. Kelsey, Major Fred W. Fleming, Major Thomas H. Slavens, and Major Surgeon Charles E. Wilson comprising the ranking field and staff officers.[35]

The entire regiment came from Kansas City with the exception of Company F, which had been recruited in Independence.

The last regiment to depart, the 3rd Missouri boarded the train to take it to Camp Russell A. Alger, Virginia, on 26 May. At Camp Alger, the regiment became part of the 3rd Brigade, 2nd Division, of the 2nd Army Corps.[36]

The conditions at Camp Alger almost mirrored those at Camp Thomas. Bad food and water and overcrowding caused disease to become prevalent. On 31 May, Congressmen Dowherd, Dockery, and Cockran visited Camp Alger and were extremely disturbed by the lack of equipment issued to the Missouri troops. They complained to the U.S. Army Adjutant General, and by 9 June, the entire regiment received uniforms.[37]

Due to the poor conditions at Camp Alger, on 3 August the 3rd Missouri, together with other troops at the camp, traveled to Thoroughfare, Virginia, and from there to Camp Meade, Pennsylvania, on 22 August. Conditions at Camp Meade were much improved.[38]

News of the armistice arrived and on 6 September, the 3rd received orders to return home to Missouri. The regiment received an enthusiastic welcome when they arrived in St. Louis. The 3rd proceeded to Kansas City where a reception committee had prepared a banquet for them at Fairmount Park, where they were to camp. Ignorant of the welcome plans, the men decided to stage a parade through the streets of Kansas City. When their officers refused permission, the men threatened to mutiny and the officers finally consented. The men paraded through empty streets, while the reception committee waited until late afternoon.[39]

All the men who desired a 30-day furlough received one and the regiment remained at Fairmount Park until 18 October. The weather turned cold and the men moved to Graham Park in Kansas City, as there was no permanent shelter at Fairmount Park. The regiment mustered out on 7 November. It lost 13 men to disease and 7 men deserted.[40]

The 4th Regiment, Missouri Volunteer Infantry, was organized from a nucleus of eight companies of the 4th Regiment of the National Guard of Missouri. After an act of Congress dated 25 April 1898, four additional companies were raised. Its headquarters was at St. Joseph, where Col. Joseph A. Corby had been drilling men before war had been declared. At the outbreak only the 1st and 2nd regiments were thought to be needed, so Col. Corby gave permission for any man of the 4th who wanted to see action to join the 2nd , which needed recruits. When word came that the 4th Missouri would be called, recruiting began with renewed vigor. By 24 April, the four St. Joseph companies had been virtually filled and recruiting officers went to towns in northern and northwestern Missouri where four new companies were raised.[41]

The regiment rendezvoused at Camp Stephens at Jefferson Barracks on 9 May 1898 and mustered into Federal service on 16 May. A total of 48 officers and 959 enlisted men belonged to the 4th Missouri Volunteer Infantry at the time of muster.

Col. Joseph A. Corby, of St. Joseph, commanded the regiment. The other high ranking field and staff officers included Lt. Col. William B. Burnham, U.S. Army; Major William E. Stringfellow, St. Joseph; Major Wilson S. Hendrick, St. Joseph; Major Clay E. MacDonald, St. Joseph; and Major Surgeon Harry D. Kreidler, St. Louis.

The 4th Missouri Volunteer Infantry departed Jefferson Barracks on 25 May 1898. The regiment occupied more comfortable travel accommodations than the previous Missouri units. The train carrying the 4th Missouri consisted of sleeping cars and two parlor cars. They had rations for three days and the officers had been given cash to purchase coffee for the men. The regiment arrived at Camp Alger on 27 May and was assigned to the 2nd Brigade, 2nd Division, 2nd Army Corps. In addition to the 4th Missouri, the 6th Pennsylvania and the 7th Illinois Volunteer Infantry made up the 2nd Brigade. Col. John W. Scholl, 6th Pennsylvania, commanded the brigade, with General George W. Davis commanding the 2nd Division, and Major General William M. Graham in command of the 2nd Corps.

In spite of a lack of uniforms and equipment, the men remained enthusiastic and drilled faithfully. President McKinley visited Camp Alger and reviewed the troops on 28 May. Col. Corby created a sensation when he paraded his regiment in ragged civilian clothes and without arms.[42] His object was to impress the President with the regiment's lack of equipment and to show how quickly raw recruits could be whipped into shape. The exhibition achieved the desired results. By 1 June, the regiment received its uniforms.[43]

In response to the second call for volunteers, on 16 June officers were sent back to Missouri to recruit each company to 106 men. By 22 June, the additional recruits had been enrolled, most from farms around Bethany, Missouri.

As with the 3rd Missouri, the unsanitary conditions at Camp Alger necessitated a change and the 4th Missouri transferred to Camp Meade. Col. Corby made the 4th one of the best organizations at Camp Meade, and it was chosen to go to Puerto Rico with General Wade, but the armistice negated the move to combat. On September 12, Col. Corby was promoted to Brigadier General and became Brigade Commander, and Lt. Col. Burnham became Colonel of the regiment.

The regiment remained in service after the armistice, transferring to Camp Weatherall at Greenville, South Carolina, on 16 November 1898. At Camp Weatherall, the regiment mustered out on 10 February 1899. It lost one officer and 23 enlisted men from disease and 33 from desertion.[44] Several of the boys joined the regular U.S. troops and later saw action in the Philippines.

The 5th Missouri Volunteer Infantry organized under the provisions of Special Order No. 19, dated 17 April 1898, Adjutant General Office, Jefferson Barracks, Missouri. The 5th Missouri organized under completely different circumstances than the other Missouri Volunteer units previously mentioned. It had no nucleus of men or officers from which to build. It had to be hurriedly recruited from raw recruits and supplied with an Officer Corps. Political interference and jealousy occasioned by a mad scramble to obtain commissions caused dissension within the new regiment. Three methods of selecting officers were possible. They could be elected by the men and officers of the line, appointed by the Governor, or regular U.S. Army officers could be appointed. Election was the general rule in the selection of officers. Officers of the field and staff were usually both elected and appointed. Politicians saw an opportunity for the governor to enhance his political status in the possible appointment of 48 officers. After corresponding over the course of several weeks between Adjutant General Bell and the War Department, it was decided to let the men and officers of the line elect the officers, but the Governor had to give his approval to those elected.[45] For all practical purposes, this procedure gave the Governor control of appointments.

Adjutant General Bell gave official orders to Milton Moore to organize the 5th Missouri Regiment on 28 April 1898.[46] Since the new regiment was to be recruited primarily in the Kansas City area and Col. Craig of Kansas City had already organized a body of men which he called the 1st Missouri Volunteers, everyone expected this organization to form the nucleus of the new regiment.[47] Although Moore had been recommended to President McKinley for the position of Brigadier General of the State of Missouri, this never materialized.[48] Thus, Moore became Colonel of the 5th Regiment. Governor Stephens then decided that only five companies would come from Kansas City with the remainder to be raised in and around Harrisonville, Carthage, Higginsville, Excelsior Springs, Greenfield, and Mexico, all areas where the Governor hoped to curry political favor.[49] Then the appointment of Col. Charles H. Morgan to be Lt. Colonel of the regiment relegated Craig to the position of Senior Major. As a result, Craig and all the other officers of the 1st Missouri Volunteer Regiment resigned and the unit disbanded. Col. Moore announced enlistment for the 5th open, and five companies of the old regiment re-enlisted and mustered into state service on 3 May.[50]

Although pushed vigorously, recruitment proceeded slowly due to numerous difficulties, not least of which was a lack of tents, uniforms, and blankets. The students of the University of Missouri in Columbia responded immediately and formed a Cadet Corps.[51] This Cadet Corps became Company I of the 5th Regiment. Capt. J.H. English, from Kansas City, commanded Co. I, which became the most proficient company in the regiment. The cadet band became the 5th Regiment Band.[52] Companies A, B, C, D and F came from Kansas City. Company E came from Harrisonville, Company G from Carthage, Company H from St. Louis, Company I from Columbia, Company K from Higginsville, Company L from Mexico, and Company M from Excelsior Springs.[53]

Col. Moore commanded the regiment. His senior staff consisted of Lt. Col. Charles H. Morgan of Lamar; Major William T. Stark of Kansas City; Major William M. Abernathy from Kansas City, who resigned June 5; Major George D. Moore, U.S. Army; Major Henry S. Julian, from Kansas City; and Major Surgeon Nathan O. Harrelson, Kansas City.

Lt. Leacher Hardeman mustered the 5th Regiment into Federal service at Jefferson Barracks on 19 May 1898. At the time the regiment consisted of 40 officers and 976 enlisted men. The 5th Missouri left Jefferson Barracks by train on 25 May. It reached its destination, Chickamauga Park, Georgia, on 27 May, and was assigned to the 2nd Brigade, 2nd Division, 3rd Army Corps.[54]

Now at camp, the men of the 5th Missouri needed almost everything a soldier could possibly need. The regiment did not even have uniforms until late June.

The experiences of the 5th Missouri Volunteer Infantry at Camp Thomas were much the same as the 1st and 2nd Missouri Volunteer Infantry. But unlike the 1st and 2nd Missouri, Col. Moore enforced strict adherence to sanitation regulations, which kept the sick list of the 5th Missouri comparatively low.

After the armistice was signed, the 5th Missouri received orders to return home. On 27 August, the regiment went to Lexington, Kentucky, where it became part of the 1st Brigade, 3rd Division, 1st Army Corps. Then on 6 September the regiment received orders to return to Missouri. The regiment arrived in St. Louis on 8 September, where a reception committee of women furnished lunch for the men.[55] After lunch the regiment continued its homeward journey, but at Jefferson City Major Julian, without Col. Moore's permission, stopped his section of the train and paraded his command in the streets, to please Governor Stephens. Col. Moore, extremely angry over Julian's violation of orders, decided not to press charges against Julian since the regiment was to be mustered out.[56] Although the men wanted to parade when they reached Kansas City, Col. Moore refused and took them directly to Fairmount Park.[57]

The 3rd Missouri was also encamped at Fairmount Park and some unpleasantness arose between the two regiments. After a 30-day furlough the regiment mustered out of U.S. service on 9 November 1898, at Kansas City. The regiment lost 16 men from disease and 17 by desertion. The organization then disbanded. Its purpose had been fulfilled and it was not needed for state service.[58]

As previously mentioned while relating the experiences of the five volunteer regiments that Missouri furnished, President McKinley, through the War Department, put out a second call for volunteers on 25 May 1898. Adjutant General Bell received a telegram from the War Department asking him when Missouri would be ready to furnish the 1700 additional men the second call required.[59] Bell replied that Missouri had indeed filled her quota, then realized the next day that with the second call existing companies increased in size from 81 to 106 men, or 700 additional men and that a thousand more men were to be recruited for a new regiment. The existing regiments sent officers to the districts in which the regiments had originally been recruited to enlist the necessary men. Although these new recruiting officers encountered some problems in raising the additional men, within a few weeks the new requirements had been fulfilled.

On 18 June, Bell received definite orders to raise a sixth regiment of Missouri Volunteer Infantry.[60] Independent companies had continued to form even after the first five regiments had departed Jefferson Barracks. The Adjutant General's Office received enough men to organize three additional regiments. Since southeastern Missouri had not furnished any men during the first call, volunteers from that section of the state received preference. Lt. Leacher Hardeman, appointed Colonel of the new regiment, proposed a plan to organize a new National Guard of 36 companies. The twelve best would form the 6th Missouri Volunteer Infantry.[61]

Recruiting for the new organization moved rapidly forward in southeastern Missouri and in and around St. Louis. The "Busch Zouaves" volunteered on the second call. Washington University raised a company called the "University Rifles," which drilled at Grand and Hickory.[62] St. Charles raised a company as did Carondelet, St. Louis County, and four companies in St. Louis City. Col. Hardeman announced that he had selected the following companies: one each from Willow Springs, Brookfield, California, Doniphan, St. Charles, Bloomfield, Kennett, Lutesville, Carondelet, and Webster Groves and two from St. Louis to be chosen by lot from the four existing companies.[63]

The men elected John R. Dyer as Captain of the Webster Groves company, even though George A. Kauffman had been instrumental in forming the new company.[64] A quarrel ensued and Kauffman and his supporters withdrew and enlisted in Company C from St. Louis. Capt. Dyer and his company mustered into state service. But due to the notoriety of the quarrel, Adjutant General Bell and Col. Hardeman refused to accept the Webster Groves Company, and the unit had to serve three years in the state militia.[65] A company from De Soto took its place.[66]

The selected companies rendezvoused at Jefferson Barracks and mustered into Federal service between 20 and 23 July 1898. At the time of muster, the regiment consisted of 27 officers and 1,265 enlisted men. Col. Leacher Hardeman, 10th U.S. Cavalry, commanded the regiment, with Lt. Col. Harvey C. Clark, of Butler, Missouri; Major Orlando F. Guthrie, of St. Louis; Major Jacob J. Dickinson, of St. Louis; and Major Surgeon Keating Bauday, of St. Louis, making up the senior field and staff officers.

Orders arrived on 12 August to proceed to Jacksonville, Florida, where the regiment arrived on 15 August. It was assigned to the 2nd Brigade, 3rd Division, 7th Army Corps under General Fitzhugh Lee.[67] Camp "Cuba Libre" at Jacksonville proved to be a pleasant, healthful location where Col. Hardeman drilled the men and established a high degree of efficiency. On 16 October, the regiment transferred to the 2nd Brigade, 2nd Division, 7th Army Corps.[68] On 6 November, the 6th Missouri left Jacksonville for Savannah, Georgia, where they encamped at Camp Onward. On 21 December, the 1st Battalion boarded the Transport *Obdam* and the 2nd and 3rd Battalions boarded the Transport *Roumania,* for their trip to Havana, Cuba.

Upon arriving at Havana, where the 1st Battalion arrived on 21 December and the 2nd and 3rd Battalion on 24 December, the regiment marched to Camp Columbia-Quemados at Marianao, Cuba. While in Cuba, the regiment performed occupation duties. Possibly the most important of these duties was simply to show themselves around the Cuban countryside. As such, on 20 February 1899, the 2nd Brigade, 2nd Division, 7th Army Corps, of which the 6th Missouri Volunteer Infantry was a part, left camp early in the morning on a practice march. They continued to march about the countryside passing through villages such as Arvays, Arriba, Punta, Varones, and San Antonio de los Banos, where they remained from 23 to 25 February. On 26 February, they marched through four more villages ending at Calabazar. They set out again on the 27th and continued until they returned to Camp Columbia on 9 April. At one of the villages Company E of the 6th Missouri visited a village cemetery. The gate was locked, but shortly several Cubans appeared from some nearby woods carrying the skeleton of a dead man they had found. The cemetery keeper opened the gate and the Missourians entered. The graves were all in rows and numbered, but in the back left corner of the cemetery they discovered a boneyard, a place about ten feet by twenty feet and eight feet deep, half full of human bones. They discovered that the graves were rented and when the rent stopped the bones were removed from the grave and thrown in the boneyard. The grave was then ready for the next renter.[69]

On 9 April 1899, the regiment marched to Havana where it embarked on the Ward Line Steamer *Havana* for Savannah. They arrived on 11 April and went into quarantine for five days on Daufuskie Island. The regiment then went into camp at Savannah until it mustered out on 10 May 1899. At muster out, the regiment consisted of 53 officers and 1,357 enlisted men. During its period of service, the regiment lost one officer and 23 enlisted men who died of disease. The State of Missouri issued a medal to the volunteers who served in the 6th Missouri Volunteer Infantry. The 6th Missouri was the only Missouri unit to see active service.

The seven regiments of Missouri militia did not constitute the total Missouri representation in the Spanish-American War. Many other Missourians served during the conflict having already belonged to the Regular Army or Navy when the war began. Also, many men enlisted in the U.S. forces after the outbreak of hostilities.[70]

On 25 April, a Navy recruiting office opened in St. Louis with Lt. Commander John M. Hawley in charge. Within a few days around 500 men had applied, but as most wanted to enlist as skilled machinists, they failed to qualify. The Navy accepted 54 men, primarily as firemen and the office closed.

Some Missourians did serve with distinction during the war. At least eight took part in the Battle of Manila Bay. A.L. Smith of Sedalia served as one of Admiral Dewey's expert gunners.[71] Edward P. Stanton, of St. Louis, is officially credited with raising the first American flag over Manila. Serving in Cuban waters, Commander James M. Miller commanded the collier *Merrimac*. James P. Morton served as chief engineer on the cruiser *Vixen.*[72] Ensign Leigh C. Palmer served on the battleship *New York* and made a reconnaissance of the land batteries at Santiago, going within 100 yards of shore under intense fire.[73] Ensign Arthur L. Willard, of Kirksville, won a hundred dollar offer by the *New York Herald*, for planting the first American flag on Cuban soil, when he accomplished this feat at Diana City, Cuba.[74]

Missouri Volunteer camp at Jefferson Barracks ca. 1898

6th Missouri Volunteer Infantry, Company E, in Cuba
Capt. Giboney Houck, Cape Girardeau, Missouri, commanded Co. E with 1st Lt. . Martin, St. Louis, and 2nd Lt. James W. Pettyjohn, Brookfield, Missouri, the other company officers.

This half-dollar sized medal was awarded to volunteers who served
in the 6th Missouri Volunteer Infantry. The regiment served in the
occupation forces in Cuba. The obverse of the medal shows the crossed
rifles of the infantry and reads "U.S.V. 6th Missouri". The reverse reads
"Enlisted for Spanish American War at St. Louis July 1898. Mustered out
at Camp Onward 10 May 1899"

Company E, 6th Missouri Volunteer Infantry discovered this boneyard at a cemetery in one of the small villages it
visited in February 1899. The boneyard measured about ten feet by 20 feet and was eight feet deep. The men
discovered that the graves were rented and when the rent stopped the bones were removed from the grave and thrown
into the boneyard and the grave was ready for the next renter.

Almost all branches of the U.S. Regular Army opened recruiting offices in Missouri. Early in May, Lt. C.M. Fuller, 2nd Cavalry, opened a recruiting office in St. Louis, Sedalia, Jefferson City and Springfield. By June 3, he reported that the regiment had been raised to 1,300 men, 700 from Missouri.[75]

At different times, nine different recruiting offices opened in St. Louis for the recruitment of men to serve in the U.S. Infantry Regiments.[76] The 10th, 11th, 16th, and 19th Regular Infantry Regiments and the 5th U.S. Volunteer Infantry opened recruiting offices in St. Louis during May and June. The 10th, 11th, and 16th went to Cuba. The 10th and 16th took part in the Battle of El Caney and the Santiago Campaign. The 11th Infantry went to Puerto Rico and took part in the Battle of San German.

Several Missourians distinguished themselves during the war. Frank Fulton, of St. Louis, in the 16th Infantry, planted a flag on San Juan Hill.[77]

One other Missourian of note took part in the Spanish-American War. Lt. John J. Pershing, 10th Cavalry, whose gallant conduct at El Caney brought him to the attention of General Leonard Wood, who recommended him for promotion. Pershing was promoted to the rank of major in the U.S. Volunteers on 18 August 1898. He later served with distinction in the Philippines, and then in 1917 became commander of the American Expeditionary Force during World War I.

While Missouri filled its quota for troops for the Spanish-American War, we have seen that few actually saw combat duty. However, the Regular Army troops who left from Jefferson Barracks did distinguish themselves. The 3rd Cavalry fought at the battles of Santiago and El Caney, and the 11th Infantry won an important battle at San German in Puerto Rico.

The 3rd Cavalry had been stationed at Jefferson Barracks since the Cavalry Depot closed in October of 1894. It departed Jefferson Barracks for Cuba via Tampa, Florida, shortly after the opening of hostilities with Spain. On the morning of 1 July 1898, the 3rd was camped at El Poso, Cuba. About 7:45 a.m., it received orders to move out, which it did at 8:00 a.m., taking the main road to Santiago de Cuba, in the rear of the 6th Cavalry. While following the road much delay ensued from some reason unknown to Major Henry W. Wessells, Jr., commanding the unit. The regiment was under fire from 8:20 a.m. until nightfall. This first fire was from shell and shrapnel and caused some loss. About 10:00 a.m. the 3rd reached the San Juan River and formed on the left of the road in two lines and there deposited their packs. Soon after, Wessells received orders from the brigade commander, Col. Henry Carroll, that when the regiment moved it was to go forward in two lines and that it was eventually to be on the left of the brigade. Afterwards Wessells was told by Capt. Robert L. Howze to move to the right, and again by Col. Carroll to take position to the left of the 6th Cavalry commanded by Major Thomas C. Lebo. Wessells was prepared to do this when Lt. John D. Miley told him positively that the 3rd Cavalry was to be north of the road and on the right-hand side, and this was immediately confirmed by General Stephen Sumner.

The regiment waited in two lines, with its left immediately on the road, seeking cover, but still men were being shot. About 11:45 a.m., Capt. Howze ordered the 3rd to advance, which it immediately did in two lines, the 2nd Squadron, Troops B, H, I and K, with Capt. Charles Morton commanding, in the first line, and the 1st Squadron, Troops C, E and F with Major Henry Jackson commanding, in the second line. In moving forward, the first line became at once entangled with other regiments, but moved on, and finally Troops H and K reached the most northern house. Troop I went more to the left and to the crests of the hills in their front. Here Wessells was wounded and left the field for about four hours. On returning, he found the 2nd Squadron holding a ridge north of the most western house. Wessells passed the 1st Squadron where it had been stopped by Gen. Sumner. Later it joined the first line. The regiment did its whole duty. In this action during the Battle of Santiago de Cuba, the 3rd Cavalry had six officers wounded, three enlisted men killed and 48 wounded.[78]

At the Battle of El Caney Major General Joseph Wheeler reported that the 3rd Cavalry lost three men killed and six officers and 45 enlisted men wounded out of a total strength of 22 officers and 420 enlisted men. Wounded officers that had left Jefferson Barracks only a couple of months earlier included Major Henry Wessells, Capt. George K. Hunter, 1st Lt. Arthur Thayer, 1st Lt. O.B. Meyer, Capt. George A. Dodd and 1st Lt. Alfred C. Merillat.[79]

During May, shortly before the departure of the Missouri Volunteers, several incidents took place at Jefferson Barracks. Shortly before 7:00 p.m. on 8 May, while many of the soldiers were at mess, a fire broke out in the house of civilian clerk William Campbell, chief clerk to Capt. John Knight. A Private McGuinness discovered the fire and alerted the men at Camp Stephens by having Bugler Allen blow the fire call. The regulars on duty at the Barracks arrived first armed with a hose and buckets. Then about 200 Missouri Volunteers arrived. They climbed ladders and poured bucket after bucket of water on the shingle roof as the regulars aimed the hose at the roof, but with no effect. Only after the Jefferson Barracks Fire Corps arrived did anyone imagine that the clerk's house could be saved.[80]

Only two days after the fire, the citizens of St. Louis journeyed to Jefferson Barracks to show their support for the Missouri Volunteers going off to war. On 10 May, the Southern Electric Railroad carried a record 66,000 passengers, almost all to Jefferson Barracks. A spokesman stated that "everything that would roll without jumping the track was pressed into service...." It was the largest day's earning in the history of the company.[81]

As most of the Missouri Volunteer Regiments departed Jefferson Barracks in late May 1898, most of the activity at the post centered around recruits for the Regular Army. This was certainly not a new activity for Jefferson Barracks. In June, 617 recruits transferred from Jefferson Barracks to their permanent units. The 3rd Cavalry received 568 of these recruits.

Capt. Knight remained in command of Jefferson Barracks and Brevet Lt. Col. John A. Kress continued to command the St. Louis Powder Depot at the post. These officers represented the only two Regular Army officers present at Jefferson Barracks during the entire month of June. 1st Lt. Edwin M. Suplee, 3rd Cavalry, left Jefferson Barracks on 10 June conducting 3rd Cavalry recruits to Lexington, Kentucky. Major and Surgeon Joseph B. Girard left on detached service to Fort Leavenworth on 29 June and Capt. Charles B. Ewing, Medical Department, had been on detached service with the 5th Cavalry since 3 May. Capt. Francis A. Winter, Medical Department, had been with the 3rd Cavalry since 19 April. The enlisted population of Jefferson Barracks amounted to a mere 48 men at the end of June.

As the fighting in Cuba and Puerto Rico wound down, the recruit activity at Jefferson Barracks did likewise. Only 29 recruits transferred from the post in July and 20 of these were in the Hospital Corps and transferred to Tampa or Chickamauga Park.

Capt. Knight remained in command during July. Major Girard returned from detached service July 6. Brevet Lt. Col. Kress was relieved from command of the Powder Depot on 20 July and departed on 27 July. Lt. Col. John A. McGuinness replaced Kress, but did not arrive until 4 September. The manpower of Regular Army personnel stood at two officers and 25 enlisted men, plus 24 enlisted men assigned to the Powder Depot. However, Jefferson Barracks was not as deserted as these figures might indicate, as the 6th Missouri Volunteer Infantry organized at Jefferson Barracks in July.

August 1898 saw the return of more Regular Army troops to Jefferson Barracks, when 72 enlisted men of the 15th U.S. Infantry under 1st Lt. George McD Weeks joined the post on 2 August, from Fort Huachuca, Arizona Territory. Capt. Knight transferred to Montauk Point, New York, on 6 August, to be replaced by Capt. Thomas Downs, Quartermaster Department, the same day. Major Henry R. Brinkerhoff, 3rd Infantry, arrived August 9 and took command of the post. Lt. Weeks commanded Jefferson Barracks from 3 to 9 August and took charge of the General Mess, Commissary and Post Exchange.[82]

September 1898 proved to be an active month at Jefferson Barracks with the arrival of many new troops returning from Cuba. The 12th Infantry Regiment broke camp at Camp Wikoff, Long Island, at 9:00 a.m. on 16 September and boarded a train for their 1192- mile trip to Jefferson Barracks. They arrived and took station at Jefferson Barracks at 11:00 a.m. on 19 September. This contingent consisted of 12 officers and 575 enlisted men. Battery E, 1st Artillery, consisting of 105 enlisted men commanded by 2nd Lt. Alston Hamilton, left Montauk Point, Long Island, at 6:30 a.m. on 21 September and arrived at Jefferson Barracks at 9:00 a.m. on 24 September.

Major Henry H. Humphreys, commanding the 12th Infantry in the absence of Col. John N. Andrews, who was on detached service as a Brigadier General of U.S. Volunteers, relieved Major Brinkerhoff in command of Jefferson Barracks on 19 September. Major Henry W. Wessells, Jr., also joined in September, although he was still recovering from wounds suffered in Cuba.

This brought the strength of Jefferson Barracks up to 19 officers and 718 enlisted men. In addition, the Powder Depot consisted of Lt. Col. McGuinness and 24 enlisted men.[83]

A regiment of black soldiers, known as the 7th Regiment of Immunes, mustered in at Jefferson Barracks on 21 July. The demise of Missouri's black companies was not unique. By 1898, black militia units served in 15 states and the District of Columbia. Although Governor Stephens refused to acknowledge the martial spirit of black Missourians, they had served under arms before. During the Civil War, the state had furnished at least 8,344 African-Americans for the Union Army. The quick response of St. Louis' Attucks Guard during the Great Railroad Strike of 1877 had earned the unit respect in St. Louis.

It remained for the Federal Government to provide a new opportunity for African-Americans to serve in the war with Spain. Congress approved increasing the Regular Army's authorized strength, and its four black regiments, three of which had previously organized and spent time at Jefferson Barracks, added more than 800 men. Secretary of War Russell Alger also wanted to recruit at least six regiments of "yellow fever immunes for service in Cuba." In May 1898 Congress authorized President McKinley to authorize Alger "to organize an additional volunteer force of enlisted men possessing immunity from typhoid diseases, not to exceed 10,000 men."

Many erroneously believed that the African ancestry of black Americans, as well as the fact that most of them lived in the South, made them especially suited for service in hot climates and less susceptible to tropical diseases. Booker T. Washington wrote the Secretary of the Navy that Cuba's climate was "peculiar and dangerous to the unaclimated white man. The Negro race in the South is accustomed to this climate." President McKinley, after much deliberation, authorized the formation of the 7th through the 10th U.S. Volunteer Infantry regiments comprised of black enlisted men and lieutenants, with white company commanders and field and staff officers in the regimental headquarters. The 1st through the 6th U.S. Volunteer Infantry regiments were to be all white.

To organize the Immune regiments, the War Department divided the South into ten recruiting regions, General Order No. 60, dated 1 June 1898, assigned the states of Arkansas, Missouri and part of Tennessee to the 7th U.S.V.I., but eventually the regiment accepted a company from Des Moines, Iowa. Of the other 11 companies three came from St. Louis; three from Little Rock, Arkansas; three from Columbia, Kansas City, Memphis, Moberly and Springfield. Col. Edwin A. Godwin was to be its commander. Godwin, born in Preston County, West Virginia, in 1850, had fought in the Civil War as an underage cavalryman before graduating from West Point in 1870. He had been promoted to Captain in the 8th Cavalry, a rank he had held since 1886.

Originally, Memphis had been designated as headquarters for the 7th Immunes, but in June it was announced publicly that the 7th Immunes was to be a black regiment and its headquarters moved to Jefferson Barracks. The first companies were organized in St. Louis, which had a black population of about 35,000. Lt. Col. Charles D. Comfort, a St. Louis businessman with 23 years of service in the Missouri National Guard, had been appointed as the regiment's second-in-command. He established a recruiting office in the city's post office annex in late June, but the War Department's refusal to commission black officers above the rank of 1st Lieutenant initially caused many prospective recruits to turn a cold shoulder to the new regiment. According to the *St. Louis Post-Dispatch*, the 7th recruiting was "the flattest thing which has struck St. Louis recently," but during the first week of July, it improved considerably. Godwin attributed the wave of patriotism to "the noble conduct" of the black troopers of the 10th Cavalry in the fighting at Santiago, Cuba.

Col. Godwin established the 7th camp at Jefferson Barracks, a short distance from the end of the electric car line that ran between St. Louis and Jefferson Barracks. According to the *St. Louis Republic*, the Immunes' tents were set up at "the most desirable location on the government preserve." Another reporter who visited the site noted that the black soldiers looked "quite picturesque" in their new uniforms and side-brimmed hats and that they drilled in small groups, they never failed "to salute in true soldierly fashion anyone who approached them." He also quoted Godwin's assessment of his local recruits, "I have found the St. Louis men to be active and intelligent. They are learning to drill rapidly and will make fine soldiers."

On 25 August, after several weeks of diligent training, Col. Godwin sent a telegram to Adjutant General Henry C. Corbin proudly proclaiming, "This regiment is now ready for orders to move." Three weeks later, the 7th Immunes proceeded to Lexington, Kentucky. After arriving at Lexington, the 7th established its camp at Weil's Farm, a few miles west of the city. It was brigaded with the 10th Immunes, whose companies had been organized along the eastern seaboard from Washington, D.C., to Jacksonville, Florida.

Lt. Col. Marion P. Maus, of the Inspector General's Office, came to Weil's Farm to inspect both black regiments. Maus reported that the 7th enlisted men "appeared well and marched well, but for the fact that they were very poorly dressed, would have presented an excellent appearance." He also noted; "They were very respectful, stood at attention, saluted their officers properly, and impressed me as being well instructed for the short time they had been in the service." Major William H. Daly, a surgeon accompanying Maus, supported the Lt. Colonel's favorable opinion by reporting that the regiment presented "a strikingly fine appearance" on drill or parade and that their "Column for marching [was] rarely excelled by any nation's soldiers. I should expect this to be a rare good fighting regiment."

7ᵗʰ Immunes at Jefferson Barracks

Some of our brave colored boys who helped to free Cuba.

On 21 November, the regiment moved to Camp Haskell, about three miles from Macon, Georgia. After spending more than three unpleasant months in Georgia, the 7th United States Volunteer Infantry mustered out of service at Camp Haskell on 28 February 1899.[84]

An unusual event did take place at Jefferson Barracks when the body of an unknown man was discovered in bushes just north of the pumphouse. Michael Mike, who had associated with the man while alive, discovered the body. The body exhibited no marks to indicate a cause of death. From accounts, he had given of himself, he was a cross tie maker and had left Arkansas for fear of yellow fever. He had been in City Hospital, but had left to avoid an operation. He was about 65, above medium stature and had a beard. He had been loafing around the Barracks for several weeks, subsisting on the scant contributions of soldiers and townspeople.[85]

Since the arrival of the 12th Infantry in September, the regiment had been busy recruiting back to full strength. By the end of October, this had almost been completed as the twelve companies of the regiment consisted of twenty-one officers and 1,070 enlisted men, plus six officers and twenty-two enlisted men in the staff and band. The garrison also consisted of eight officers and 113 enlisted men of Battery E, 1st Artillery and five attached officers and sixty-five enlisted men. The total strength of the Jefferson Barracks garrison stood at forty-two officers and 1,270 enlisted men. In addition, Lt. Col. McGuinness remained in command of the Powder Depot which consisted of 23 enlisted men. It should also be remembered that the 1st, 2nd, 3rd and 6th Missouri Volunteer Infantry regiments had returned home and were at Jefferson Barracks. The post was a busy and congested place.

Some exciting news reached the area on 16 October, when the *Post-Dispatch* ran an article stating that: "President McKinley has ordered that Jefferson Barracks near this city, be made as large a military post as any in the country. The order was given to the Assistant Secretary of War in the presence of a number of St. Louisans at Omaha. This guarantees that Jefferson Barracks will be as soon as possible put in shape to receive a full brigade of troops."

November 1898 saw the bustle of activity and congestion at Jefferson Barracks decrease considerably as the Missouri Volunteer Infantry regiments were either on furlough or mustered out of service. Then on 12 November, a battalion of the 12th Infantry, consisting of Companies E, G, I and K, commanded by Capt. W.W. Witherspoon, departed the post for Fort Riley, Kansas, arriving on 13 November.[86]

Lt. Col. Smith remained in command of the post, which now consisted primarily of the remaining eight companies of the 12th Infantry and Battery E, 1st Artillery. The total strength of the Barracks stood at twenty-four officers and 975 enlisted men. Approximately 162 recruits transferred during November. Twenty-four enlisted men served under Lt. Col. McGuinness at the Powder Depot.[87]

One other development that took place toward the end of 1898 is of particular interest. This event, of which today we would not even take note, in 1898 made for a major newspaper article. On 9 November 1898, the *St. Louis Republic* ran an article entitled *Telephone to the Barracks: Long-Distance Service Will Soon Be Established*. Think of that, "long-distance" service between Jefferson Barracks and St. Louis. We certainly take this type of service as beyond routine. The article pointed out that arrangements had been made to establish long-distance telephone service between Jefferson Barracks and St. Louis, with work on the new line to begin at once. Lt. Col. Smith, Quartermaster Department in St. Louis and officials at the Barracks had been trying for some time to establish this service, but Bell Telephone Company had demanded an exorbitant rate that the government refused to pay.

Since hostilities began between Spain and the United States the amount of business between the Quartermaster Department in St. Louis and Jefferson Barracks made telephone service almost a necessity and negotiations began in earnest. The President of the Southern Electric Railway, C.H. Spencer, had been working on the matter and set-up a meeting between the Bell Telephone manager, Mr. Durant, and the Army. Durant proposed that his company would establish a telephone pay station at Jefferson Barracks, provided the government grant permission to set poles and string wire on the military reservation. The Army accepted Durant's proposal. To save time Spencer gave Bell Telephone permission to string wire on the Southern Electric Company's poles until the telephone company could set their own poles.[88]

December 1898 witnessed another decrease in personnel when 200 men of the 12th Infantry, in the charge of 1st Lt. Wilbur E. Dove, left the post at 8:30 p.m. on 3 December for Fort Logan A. Root, Arkansas. It is also interesting to note that two wagons and 56 mules were shipped from Jefferson Barracks to Macon, Georgia, on 14 December. This left 12 wagons and 65 mules at the post. At the end of December 1898, the post's strength stood at twenty-seven officers and 780 enlisted men, plus twenty-three enlisted men at the Powder Depot.[89] On the last day of the year Lt. Col. McGuinness was made chief ordnance officer of the 8th Corps and departed Jefferson Barracks bound for the Philippine Islands. Thus, ended one of the most eventful years in the 72 years of Jefferson Barracks' existence, but with hostilities continuing in the Philippines the frenetic pace of activity at Jefferson Barracks had just begun.[90]

A story of a different nature occurred at the Powder Depot on the night of 10 December when Chief Clerk Louis Jacobson of the Powder Depot found a woman and two small children lying on the banks of the Mississippi. The night was the coldest of the season and the suffering of the three was intense. Mr. Jacobson gave them shelter in his house until morning, when he accompanied them to St. Louis, where he turned them over to Mrs. Gilbert, police matron. The woman gave her name as Mrs. Lizzie King. The family was forwarded to the Provident Association.

While in the detention rooms at the Four Courts, Mrs. King told a pathetic tale of their wanderings. Several years ago, she said, they lived in Memphis, Tennessee. Misfortune drove them away from that city and they settled in Huntsville, Alabama, where her husband got employment on a plantation.

About six weeks previously, they started to walk to Bayard, Iowa, where Mr. King was said to have relatives. They came to St. Louis, arriving worn and ragged. They settled in an old log cabin near Jefferson Barracks and King got a job as bartender in William Horn's saloon in Harris' Grove. When King did not return last Friday, Mrs. King began looking for him and failing to find him started to St. Louis for help. Night overtook her near the Powder Depot and there she spent the night, until found by Jacobson.[91]

Chapter 3 - Philippine Insurrection - 1899

As 1898 came to a close and the year 1899 began, activity at Jefferson Barracks seemed to be returning to normal after the frenetic activity at the post resulting from the War with Spain. Regular Army troops returning from the war took station at Jefferson Barracks and the Missouri Volunteer units were mustered out. However, normalcy did not last very long.

In the Philippines, as also in Cuba, native revolutionaries had been fighting the Spanish occupation forces when the Americans arrived. The first American contingent arrived in Manila Bay shortly after the declaration of war with Spain on 21 April 1898. Commodore George Dewey, commander of the United States Navy's Asiatic Squadron, sank the antiquated Spanish fleet at Manila, on 1 May 1898.

One of the Union's Civil War brigadier generals, Major General Wesley Merritt, was placed in command of United States ground forces bound for the Philippines. Merritt assembled a capable and efficient staff, including his second in command, Major General Elwell S. Otis. To Merritt's displeasure, the majority of his forces consisted of volunteers from the western states. These volunteers were enthusiastic, but they lacked discipline and equipment needed for tropical service. Merritt had them camp near San Francisco, where he and his staff attempted to provide the necessary training and supplies. Although successful in many of his efforts, Merritt was hampered by a War Department ill-prepared for a major war. He could not obtain all the Regular Army units he wanted, and a shortage of transportation forced him to dispatch his army piecemeal. His men steamed off to the tropics in heavy wool clothing, armed with obsolete black powder Springfield rifles instead of the modern Krag-Jorgesons. Despite these problems, the first brigade of 2,500 men under Brigadier General Thomas M. Anderson left San Francisco on 25 May. A month later, Merritt sailed. This meant that 10,600 American soldiers were either en route or had arrived in the Philippines.[1]

The Philippine Islands that these Americans embarked for consisted of around 7,000 islands with a total area of 115,026 square miles. Half of the country's population of over seven million lived on Luzon, the largest island and the site of the capital city of Manila. Luzon's 40,420 square miles are divided by topography into several virtually separate regions. Within the island's population are five major linguistic groups including the Tagalogs, who provided the majority of the Philippine revolutionary leadership against both the Spanish and the Americans.

The most effective of the leaders was Emilio Aquinaldo, a 27-year old Tagalog "principal" from Kawit, Cavite. When the revolt began, Aquinaldo raised a guerrilla band, assumed the title of general and soon controlled much of eastern Cavite.

When Merritt landed on 26 July 1898, he chose to work independently of the Filipino nationalists. President McKinley's orders stated that the powers of the military commander were immediately in effect in the islands, and because of this, Merritt did not think it wise to establish direct relations with Aquinaldo. He intended for his attack on Manila to be conducted solely with his own troops and then to issue a proclamation stating American aims.[2]

The siege of Manila evolved into two separate campaigns, with both Americans and Filipinos conducting their own operations, while ostensibly cooperating. Aquinaldo's Army, a bush-whacking force of brave and adventurous men, but of very loose organization, was not able to storm the city by itself. The U.S. Army, able to capture Manila by itself, wanted to prevent Aquinaldo's forces from seizing much of the city under cover of the American attack. Faced with starvation and fearing a bloodbath if the revolutionaries broke into the city, the Spanish commander agreed to surrender after token resistance, if the Americans would keep the Filipinos out of the city. The resulting Battle of Manila on 13 August, contained enough gunfire and casualties to satisfy both Spanish and American honor. For the Filipinos, it provided the revelation of how little they were valued as allies. When the battle began, they joined in the attack and seized control of a few Manila suburbs, but the Americans turned them back from the city. Aquinaldo's forces retreated to their trenches and began a second siege of Manila.[3]

Merritt did establish contact with Aquinaldo and assured him that "if the Americans did not stay they would be sure to leave him in as good condition as he found by the Government." At the same time, Merritt appealed to the Filipino people. On 14 August, he issued a proclamation declaring that the Americans had not come to make war on the Filipinos and promising the preservation of personal and religious rights. To prove his point, Merritt restored the water supply in Manila and had the streets thoroughly cleaned.[4]

On 10 December 1898, the Treaty of Paris formally ended hostilities between the United States and Spain and transferred sovereignty of the Philippine Islands to the United States.[5]

The relations between the Army and Aquinaldo's forces had improved somewhat after Merritt's August 14 proclamation. However, Major General Elwell Otis relieved Merritt in late August 1898. Otis had been in the military since 13 September 1862, when he had been appointed a captain in the 140th New York Infantry. He had received brevet promotions to colonel and to brigadier general during the Civil War for meritorious service at Spotsylvania and Chapel Hill.[6]

Otis's record clearly shows him to be a most able and competent Army officer. The trouble between the United States and the Filipinos came about because Otis did not possess the diplomatic and administrative skills necessary to maintain a peaceful and working relationship with the Filipinos. Soon after taking command Otis decided that Aquinaldo and his revolutionary forces represented either Tagalog despotism or lower-class anarchy. He felt a firm policy toward them would secure support from "men of property." In a situation that required tact and flexibility, Otis proved to be pedantic and self-righteous.[7]

Otis insisted that Aquinaldo's forces totally withdraw from Manila's municipal limits. This meant that the Filipinos even had to abandon territory that they had captured. This infuriated the Filipinos, resulting in numerous armed confrontations. On 4 February 1899, while serving picket duty in a disputed area, Pvt. William Grayson of Nebraska fired on a Filipino patrol that refused to answer his challenge. In a matter of a few hours, gunfire spread up and down the lines. The Philippine War had begun.[8]

In the operations following the outbreak of hostilities, the United States Army quickly established its military superiority over the Filipino Nationalist forces. U.S. forces easily overcame Aquinaldo's men in battle, inflicting extremely heavy casualties. During April and May, U.S. forces drove the Filipinos in the provinces of central Luzon. These victories, while carried out with efficiency and exacting heavy casualties, proved ineffectual. Otis's forces numbered only 26,000 troops, with less than half available for active campaigning in Luzon. When the monsoon season arrived in late May, the Army was exhausted. Some units suffered from a sick rate of sixty percent. Otis was forced to wait for the arrival of a new army, before he could again take the offensive.[9]

Jefferson Barracks played an important role in the formation of this new army for the Philippines. If the United States intended to remain in the Philippines, it had to raise a new army. An Act of Congress, dated March 2, 1899, and passed due to the insurrection among the Tagalogs on the island of Luzon, gave authority to again increase the Regular Army to a strength not to exceed 65,000 enlisted men, and to raise a force of not more than 35,000 volunteers, to be recruited from the country at large, to serve until 1 July 1901. During the summer and fall of 1899, the Army organized twenty-five regiments of volunteers, including two black regiments. When organized, the Regular Army numbered 61,999 enlisted men and 2,248 officers, for a total of 64,247 and a new volunteer force numbering 33,050 men and 1,524 officers, an aggregate of 34,574.[10]

Jefferson Barracks began 1899 with a relatively small garrison that consisted of a contingent of the 16th Infantry, [one officer and thirty-five enlisted men] and Battery E, 1st Artillery [two officers and 152 enlisted men]. The Recruit Detachment contained a total of 149 recruits. On 14 January, eight companies of the 12th Infantry, commanded by Lt. Col. Jacob H. Smith, arrived from Fort Wayne. The 12th Infantry consisted of twenty-nine officers and 933 enlisted men. Company E, 7th Infantry [seventy-nine enlisted men and Capt. James M. Burns] also arrived from Fort Wayne on 14 January 1899.[11]

However, the major influx of personnel did not remain for long. In compliance with General Order No. 22, Headquarters, Department of the Missouri, dated 22 December 1898, all elements of the 12th Infantry left Jefferson Barracks on 11 February 1899, via train for Jersey City, New Jersey, where they boarded the U.S. Transport Sheridan, on 24 February. Battery E, 1st Artillery, left Jefferson Barracks the last day of February en route to the Philippines. It sailed on board the U.S. Transport Sheridan with the 12th Infantry troops that had departed Jefferson Barracks earlier in February.[12]

The garrison did receive three additional officers and 348 enlisted men of Companies F, G, I and M, 16th Infantry. Major Joel T. Kirkman, 16th Infantry, arrived on 13 February and relieved the departing Lt. Col. Smith in command of Jefferson Barracks the next day.

Jefferson Barracks seems to have become a popular destination. The St. Louis Republic published a story on 7 February regarding a proposed electric train line from Maplewood to Jefferson Barracks. It seems that Joseph T. Donovan, John F. McDermott, Michael Hammel, Joseph E. McGuinniss and H.J. Weber, under the corporate name "Maplewood and Jefferson Barracks Railroad Company," asked St. Louis County for a franchise to construct and operate a double-track electric street railway line from Maplewood to Jefferson Barracks. The proposed new line was to run from the intersection of Marshall Avenue with Manchester Road.

Captain Thomas C. Woodbury relieved Major Kirkman in command of Jefferson Barracks on 5 March. His command during March consisted of eleven officers and 766 enlisted men. This figure also included 150 men in the Recruit Detachment. Company L, 7th Infantry arrived from Fort Sheridan, Illinois, on 30 March.[13]

This figure did not include Major Frank Heath, who arrived and assumed command of the St. Louis Powder Depot on 14 March. Heath had twenty-four enlisted men in his command. Heath had relieved Capt. William S. Pierce.[14]

Capt. Woodbury remained in command during April 1899. The garrison still consisted of Companies F, G, I and M, 16th Infantry and Company L, 7th Infantry. The passage on 2 March 1899, of an act of Congress had begun to take effect as the number of enlisted men in the 16th Infantry had risen to 488. Company L, 7th Infantry had increased to 108 enlisted men. The number of recruits in the Recruit Detachment had also grown to 349. One hundred twenty recruits had been transferred to permanent units during March.[15]

Also, in compliance with General Order No. 61, Headquarters of the Army, dated 4 April 1899, Troops G and K, 3rd Cavalry, Capt. Francis H. Hardie, commanding, had departed Fort Ethan Allen, Vermont, on 19 April by rail and arrived at Jefferson Barracks on 22 April. This increased the garrison by three officers and 186 enlisted men.[16]

One other change occurred in April, when Major and Brevet Lt. Col. John A. Kress returned to Jefferson Barracks. He arrived and relieved Major Heath on 17 April.[17]

One major development affecting troops at Jefferson Barracks took place in April 1899. The purchase of 1,275 acres of land for use as a rifle range had been confirmed on 11 April. This land, in the vicinity of historic old Fort Davidson, was approximately ninety miles southwest of Jefferson Barracks. The Arcadia Rifle Range would be used by Jefferson Barracks soldiers until a new range opened at Moss Hollow, in 1943.[18] Troop K, 3rd Cavalry was the first to use the new range. Troop K, with two officers and eighty-four enlisted men, marched eighty-three miles and arrived at the Arcadia Rifle Range on 13 June 1899.[19]

Capt. Woodbury, who had commanded the post since March 5, transferred and Capt. Francis H. Hardie, Troop G, 3rd Cavalry took command on 23 May. At the time the garrison consisted primarily of Troops G and K, 3rd Cavalry [four officers and 145 enlisted men] and Company 1, 7th Infantry [three officers and 104 enlisted men]. The Recruit Detachment contained only twenty-nine recruits. The St. Louis Powder Depot, commanded by Major Kress, had twenty-three enlisted men in its garrison.[20]

In an interesting sidebar, the Post Returns for May 1899 reported that the Army employed one civilian clerk at the recruit rendezvous, four clerks in the Quartermaster Department, one messenger, and forty-nine civilians and trackers.

The Jefferson Barracks garrison got even smaller in June. Company 1, 7th Infantry [three officers and 111 enlisted men] left Jefferson Barracks on 1 June en route to Benicia Barracks, California. They arrived 6 June, then departed for San Francisco on 25 June, arriving the same day and left on the steamer *St. Paul* en route to Alaska.[21]

Capt. Hardie remained in command of the post. Troop K, 3rd Cavalry, traveled to the Arcadia Rifle Range in June for its annual target practice. This left Hardie in charge of only three other officers: 2nd Lt. Godwin Ordway, Acting Assistant Surgeon T. von Clossman, and Capt. W. Allen, U.S. Volunteers, who had joined June 7. The enlisted strength of the garrison came to 135 including twenty-two recruits.

Major Kress remained in command of the Powder Depot. His command consisted of twenty-four enlisted men.[22]

Troop K, 3rd Cavalry broke camp at the Arcadia Rifle Range at 6:00 a.m. on 18 June and spent the next four days marching back to Jefferson Barracks, where they arrived at 8:15 p.m. on 21 June. They had marched a total of eighty-three miles. Thus, at the end of June 1899, the Jefferson Barracks garrison numbered over 200 officers and men.[23]

As July began with Capt. Hardie in command, the garrison consisted of seven officers and 227 enlisted men. There was no change in the complement assigned to the Powder Depot. For the most part these troops performed the usual garrison duties during the month.

August 1899 saw the tempo of activity at the post increase markedly. Col. George S. Anderson, 38th U.S. Volunteer Infantry, arrived at Jefferson Barracks to organize a new volunteer regiment. Col. Anderson, who had transferred from the 7th Cavalry to the 6th Cavalry in January 1899, arrived and assumed command on 2 August.

Troop M, 6th Cavalry [one officer and eighty-three enlisted men] departed Fort Reno, Indian Territory, at noon on 5 August and arrived at Jefferson Barracks at 4:30 a.m. on 7 August. Troop K, 3rd Cavalry, left Jefferson

Barracks on 8 August en route to Manila, Philippine Islands, via Seattle per General Order No. 138. Troop G, 3rd Cavalry, left the post 18 August en route to Fort Myer, Virginia.

Recruitment and organization of the 38th U.S. Volunteer Infantry began at Jefferson Barracks in August. The 38th Volunteer Infantry had been authorized by the act of Congress passed on 2 March 1899. Major Willard A. Holbrook, formerly 1st Lt., 7th Cavalry, and Major and Surgeon James D. Glennan, assistant surgeon, U.S.A., also joined in August. By the end of the month, sixty-seven enlisted men of the 38th were at Jefferson Barracks.[24]

Recruitment and organization of the 38th U.S. Volunteer Infantry continued at a frenetic pace throughout August and September. By the end of September, thirty-eight officers and 1,386 enlisted men had been received and assigned to the 38th. Col. Anderson remained in command of the 38th Volunteer Infantry and the post. Major Holbrook was appointed commander of the Second Battalion of the 38th. In addition, Major Charles H. Muir, formerly a captain in the 2nd Infantry, joined on 22 September; Major Lewis E. Goodier, formerly a lieutenant colonel in the 203rd New York Volunteers, joined 20 September; 1st Lt. and Adjutant William A. Covington, formerly 1st Lt., 4th Tennessee Volunteers, joined 19 September; and 1st Lt. and Assistant Quartermaster Frank F. Krebs joined 6 September.[25]

One of the two black regiments authorized by the 2 March 1899 act of Congress, the 49th U.S. Volunteer Infantry, began recruitment and organization at Jefferson Barracks. The enlisted men and most of the line officers were to be taken from the most efficient non-commissioned officers then serving in the four black regiments of the Regular Army upon the recommendation of the colonels commanding those regiments.[26] By the end of September, nineteen officers and 273 enlisted men had joined Jefferson Barracks.[27]

Lt. Col. Arthur C. Ducat, formerly a captain in the 24th Infantry, joined 22 September. In addition, 1st Lt. and Regimental Adjutant Robert C. Greg and Major and Surgeon Thomas E. Evans joined during September.[28]

The organization of the African-American 49th U.S. Volunteer Infantry at Jefferson Barracks did not come off without some difficulty. A prime factor in causing problems came from the attitude of southern soldiers to serving with black soldiers or to having black officers at the post.

Henry Leigh, a private in the 38th U.S. Volunteer Infantry, refused to salute a black captain of the 49th. Leigh, a native of Lampasas, Texas, was walking along the sidewalk leading from the canteen when he encountered a black captain. At about twenty paces from the officer Leigh assumed a swaggering gate and commenced singing "All Coons Look Alike to Me." Upon coming up to the captain Leigh made no movement that could pass for a salute. The captain turned sharply and in a stern voice called Leigh to attention.

The command had no effect on Leigh except to start him singing another verse of the song. The offended captain then called for the corporal of the guard. When the corporal of the guard arrived, the captain ordered him to arrest Pvt. Leigh.

"But," said the corporal, "you are not the officer of the day, nor commanding officer of the post, which two officers, you know, alone command the guard."

"That is all right. You do as I tell you and I'll be responsible for the act." The corporal then arrested Pvt. Leigh and took him to the guardhouse, followed by the hisses of a crowd of soldiers, whom the incident had attracted. The incident created quite a lot of talk among the officers and men of both regiments.

Pvt. Leigh was released from the guardhouse after promising that he would not commit the offense again and would in the future salute all commissioned officers regardless of the wearer.[29]

On 21 and 22 October 1899, Col. George S. Anderson commanding the officers and men of the 38th U.S. Volunteer Infantry departed Jefferson Barracks for the Presidio of San Francisco, California, en route to the Philippine Islands. The 38th Volunteer Infantry followed the contingent of the 3rd Cavalry that had left Jefferson Barracks earlier en route to the Philippines. Lt. Col. Henry W. Wessells, Jr., with Troops A, C, E, F, K and L, 3rd Cavalry had sailed from Seattle aboard the transport *St. Paul* on 25 August and had arrived in the Philippines on 1 October 1899.[30]

Another regiment, the 6th U.S. Infantry had also sailed for the Philippines. The 6th Infantry, under the command of Brigadier General John C. Bates, had boarded the transport *Sherman* on 22 May 1899 and sailed for Manila. They arrived at Bacolod, Philippine Islands, on 2 July 1899. Eighteen days later, on 20 July a detachment of the 6th Infantry defeated a robber band near Tolon. This was the first action for the 6th Infantry in the Philippines. Eight days later, on 28 July, another detachment of the 6th Infantry encountered an insurgent force near Valdez, in the Visayan District of the Philippine Islands.[31]

The first 6th Infantry officer killed in action in the Philippines was 1st Lt. Hayden Y. Grubbs. Lt. Grubbs was killed in action with insurgents on 1 October 1899, at Tabuan Island, Negros, Philippine Islands.[32]

Col. William H. Beck, former captain in the 10th Cavalry, joined the Post on 145 October 1899. Col. Beck had been appointed colonel of the 49th U.S. Volunteer Infantry.[33] During September and October, the 49th had been recruited to its maximum strength of forty officers and 1,431 enlisted men.[34]

Capt. DeRosey C. Cabell, who had been on Detached Service at Dallas, Texas, joined the post on 30 October, and assumed command of Troop M, 6th Cavalry and the post. The garrison, in addition to the 49th Volunteer Infantry, included four officers: Cabell, Major Surgeon Joseph B. Girard, Capt. Walter Allen, 2nd Lt. Patrick W. Guiney, and 134 enlisted men. In addition, Lt. Col. John A. Kress commanded the St. Louis Powder Depot at Jefferson Barracks with its twenty-three enlisted men.[35]

Of the men enlisting in the new volunteer infantry regiments, 1,198 came from Missouri, forty-seven more than the Missouri quota, and 2,318 came from Illinois, 213 above that state's quota.[36]

In compliance with General Order No. 189, Adjutant General's Office and General Order No. 19, Department of Missouri, the 49th U.S. Volunteer Infantry broke camp at Jefferson Barracks on 15 November. Field, Staff, Non-commissioned staff and Band, and Companies A, B, C, D, E, F, G and H, constituting the 1st and 2nd Battalions, left the post. Companies I, K, L and M, third Battalion, broke camp on 16 November and departed under the command of Major George W. Kirkman.[37]

Shortly before leaving Jefferson Barracks, the 49th Volunteer Infantry suffered its first death when Capt. Louis McNabb, 35-year-old commanding officer of Company K, committed suicide by blowing off the top of his head with a pistol. He had recently been promoted from 1st Sergeant in the 24th Infantry. No reason for the suicide was reported [38]

Capt. McNabb was well known at Fort Harrison, Montana, where he had been stationed since returning from Cuba. He had been promoted for conspicuous service at San Juan Hill, when a Spanish general officer mounted on a white horse attempted to rally his troops. "Give me your gun, Sergeant," Capt. Ducat had said to McNabb, "I believe I can knock that devil off his horse." McNabb handed Capt. Ducat his Krag-Jorgeson and Capt. Ducat quickly raised it to aim but before he could fire, Capt. Ducat was himself hit by a bullet. Sgt. McNabb seized the prostrate officer and dragged him about fifty yards down the slope and out of the reach of bullets that were singing over the brow of the hill. For an hour Sgt. McNabb watched over his captain. When the ambulance corps arrived, McNabb returned to his company and took command. Every officer of the company, including the first sergeant, had been shot, and as McNabb was the senior sergeant, command fell to him. For six hours of severe fighting, he had command of the company.

When the regiment returned to the United States, McNabb was promoted to first sergeant. He had been a sergeant in the Regular Army for 13 years and a soldier with a good record all the way through. He had served in several Indian campaigns and in one of them was mentioned for bravery. Capt Ducat had recommended him for promotion and about two weeks prior to this he had received orders to join the 49th at Jefferson Barracks.[39]

While the activity involved in the recruitment and organization of the 38th and 49th U.S. Volunteer Infantry regiments at Jefferson Barracks was taking place, one of the most noticeable landmarks at Jefferson Barracks was in the process of coming to the post. On 9 August 1899, the commanding officer of the New York Arsenal received orders to turn over a Spanish cannon to the Mayor of St. Louis. Today this cannon sits on the top of the hill behind the Administration Building overlooking the Mississippi River.

The story of the cannon has been in question since it came to Jefferson Barracks. The original story has the cannon being taken at the capture of Santiago de Cuba by General William Shafter on 7 July 1898. It was supposedly recovered from the Spanish battleship *Oquendo* which was sunk in Santiago Bay on 3 July. A brass plate on the breech bears the following inscription: 14 CMTR Artilleros Del Nervion Bilbao 1894, No. 27. This plate is presumed to have replaced the original when the cannon was remodeled from a muzzle to a breech loader. A plate which formerly attached to the cannon read: "16 CM Muzzle Loading Bronze Gun. One of five captured at Santiago de Cuba when the city capitulated 16 July 1898, Spanish American War." Whatever the true story, the cannon remains a Jefferson Barracks landmark. Hundreds of soldiers and civilians have had their pictures taken sitting on the barrel of this gun or standing beside it.[40]

Capt. Cabell remained in command at Jefferson Barracks, during November 1899. With the departure of the 49th U.S. Volunteer Infantry, the garrison was reduced in size to six officers, 114 enlisted men and three general prisoners. Brevet Lt. Col. Kress remained in command of the St. Louis Powder Depot with twenty-five enlisted men assigned. The post also employed twenty-two civilians.[41]

Early in November 1899, it was reported that Jefferson Barracks had become the Training Center for Army mules. It was officially entitled the National Mule Headquarters for the Army. This included the National Training Center for Army Muleteers and the Training Center for White Bell Horses. This breed of horse was vital in leading the mule pack teams. From the beginning of the war with Spain, more than 2,500 mules, mostly native to Missouri, along with some Texas mules, were mobilized and trained for pack service at Jefferson Barracks.

All the pack mules in the Army underwent their preliminary training at the post. Their handlers also went through a thorough course of instruction at the Barracks before being accepted as muleteers.

It required more time and hard work to get a pack train ready for duty than it did to organize and drill a regiment for duty in the field. Mule recruits had to be drilled hard every day for three months before they were qualified to take their places in the single file caravan that carried the Army equipment and supplies through country not suited for wagon travel.

A pack train consisted of sixty-three mules, thirteen men and a bell horse. Fifty mules carried packs or cargo, and thirteen were saddle mules. The bell horse served as the drum major of the train, and if the mules could be induced to follow his lead the proper discipline could be maintained.

The head trainer was a Missourian named W.W. Witt. Mr. Witt had previously taken a mule train to Alaska in connection with a rescue expedition for miners in the Klondike. Since Jefferson Barracks had served as the Army's Cavalry Recruit Depot, it seemed the best place for the Mule Headquarters, since it contained many vacant stables.[42]

As the year 1899 came to a close, Capt. Cabell remained in command of Jefferson Barracks. The garrison remained relatively unchanged. Brevet Lt. Col. Kress commanded the St. Louis Powder Depot at Jefferson Barracks with twenty-five enlisted men assigned.[43]

Col William H. Beck, commanding the Headquarters and Companies A, B, C, D, E, F, G and H, 49th U.S. Volunteer Infantry, and a detachment of the Hospital Corps, totaling thirty-five officers and 863 enlisted men, sailed aboard the transport *Warren* on 2 December 1899. The contingent arrived in the Philippine Islands on 2 January, 1900. The remainder of the 49th Volunteer Infantry, under the command of Major George W. Kirkman, sailed on December 6 aboard the transport *Sherman*. This contingent consisting of twenty-six officers and 622 enlisted men arrived in the Philippine Islands on 2 January 1900.[44]

The two 3rd Cavalry troopers killed were Pvt. Harry Sweger and Pvt. Charles W. Frazee, Troop A. They were killed in action on 14 December 1899.[45]

6th Infantry men killed or wounded included Pvt. Daniel E. Adams, Co. A; and Pvt. Charles N. Cotay, Co. A, both killed in action on 15 September 1899; and Pvt. William F. Stoval, Co. A and Pvt. Horace B. Hutchinson, Co. C, wounded in the same action.[46]

1900

At Jefferson Barracks, the 20th century began much as the 19th century had ended. Capt. DeRosey Cabell, 6th Cavalry, remained in command of the post. 2nd Lt. Patrick W. Guiney, Troop M, 6th Cavalry, served as Post Adjutant, Signal Officer, Post Treasurer and was in charge of the Post Library, Recruits, and the General Prisoners.

Troop M, 6th Cavalry with two officers and 97 enlisted men accounted for the majority of the garrison. Key enlisted men included Ferdinand Bryant, Ordnance Sergeant since 15 October 1898; Cyrus F. Dugger, Commissary Sergeant since 17 March 1898; Henry Donaldson, Post Quartermaster Sergeant since 30 June 1896; and Charles Gell, Hospital Steward since 24 November 1897.[47]

Brevet Lt. Col. John A. Kress also remained in command of the Powder Depot, with twenty-four enlisted men. First Class Private George F. Kettler was discharged on January 5, accounting for the decrease of one enlisted man from December 1899.[48]

Meanwhile, in the Philippines the 38th and 49th U.S. Volunteer Infantry regiments participated in numerous combat actions during the first two months of 1900. In accordance with orders from Headquarters, 1st Division, 8th Army Corps, dated 4 January 1900, Brigadier General Loyd Wheaton's Expeditionary Brigade was organized in early January 1900. The 38th Volunteer Infantry, which had been organized at Jefferson Barracks became a part of this brigade. Wheaton's brigade conducted an expedition into Cavite Province from 4 January to 31 January 1900.

Col. George S. Anderson, commanding the 38th Volunteer Infantry, received orders from General Wheaton to proceed on 10 January to Talisay, with his regiment. Wheaton ordered Anderson to attack any enemy found and to clear the country around the northern shore of Lake Taal of all armed bodies of insurgents. No armed insurgents could be found, and on 12 January the 38th transferred to the command of Brigadier General Theodore Schwan.[49]

While a part of General Schwan's force, the 38th did participate in several minor engagements. On 20 January, approximately 240 men of the 38th Volunteer Infantry stationed at Lipa scouted to Oila. They dispersed a small hostile band near Oila, wounding two, with no casualties suffered.

On 25 January, Major Willard A. Holbrook, with two companies of the 38th Volunteer Infantry, while scouting the base of the mountains east of Lipa surprised and dispersed a small party of about twenty-five insurgents. Then on the same day his force had a sharp skirmish with about fifty insurgents near San Benito.

On 27/28 January, Major Charles H. Muir, with three companies of the 38th Volunteer Infantry, while scouting to San Luis and Taal, encountered and defeated a small hostile force. Six insurgents were killed, eight wounded and thirty-three prisoners taken. Major Muir and two enlisted men were slightly wounded. Again on 2 to 4 February, Major Muir's men drove the insurgents from their entrenchments, killing two and wounding two. Muir's force did not suffer any casualties.[50]

On 28 February 1900, Col. William H. Beck, 49th U.S. Volunteer Infantry, reported the capture of Lt. Col. Tomas Aguinaldo of the insurgent Army, near Bacon, Philippine Islands.[51]

There was little change in the Jefferson Barracks garrison in February and March 1900. Capt. Cabell remained in command and 2nd Lt. Guiney remained the only other officer of the line.

The St. Louis Powder Depot continued to be commanded by Brevet Lt. Col. Kress of the Ordnance Department with twenty enlisted men, two sergeants, four corporals, twelve 1st Class Privates and two 2nd Class Privates in February. 1st Class Pvts William F. Kettler, John G. Enders and John P. Greavey and 2nd Class Privates Michael Driscoll and Frederick Geiser were discharged in February. (PR, Feb. 1900) In March 1900, Kress was promoted to the permanent rank of Lieutenant Colonel. He commanded twenty-two enlisted men.[52]

April 1900 witnessed some change to the composition of the Jefferson Barracks garrison. First, on 2 April Major Charles L. Cooper arrived in command of the 1st Battalion, Troops A, B, C and D, 5th Cavalry. The four troops of the 5th Cavalry soldiers, totaling 352 men, more than doubled the strength of the garrison, bringing the total enlisted strength to over 450 men. Major Cooper relieved Capt. Cabell as commanding officer of Jefferson Barracks, on 2 April Cooper was a Civil War veteran having served as a private in Company B, 71st New York Militia, from May 27 to 2 September 1862. He then served as a private in Company A, 21st New York State Militia, from 27 June to 6 August 1863. He received a commission as a 2nd lieutenant in the 127th U.S. Colored Infantry on 5 September 1864, and was promoted to first lieutenant on 5 March 1865. He honorably mustered out on 20 October 1865. On 28 July 1866, he was commissioned a 2nd lieutenant in the 39th Infantry and promoted to 1st lieutenant on 5 October 1867. He was assigned to the 10th Cavalry on 31 December 1870 and served as regimental adjutant from 21 December 1882, until 15 September 1883. He was promoted to captain on 15 September 1883; to major in the 5th Cavalry on 5 July 1898; to lieutenant colonel in the 15th Cavalry on 17 February 1901; transferred to the 14th Cavalry on 7 March 1901; and became colonel of the 5th Cavalry on 30 January 1903.[53]

Ten additional 5th Cavalry officers arrived on 2 April. As no Post Returns exist accounting for the officers and the number of enlisted men at Jefferson Barracks from January through May of 1900, it is not possible to list names and numbers.[54]

It did not take long for the men of the 5th Cavalry to take advantage of the new rifle range at Arcadia. Troop B departed Jefferson Barracks for Arcadia on 26 April, arriving on 30 April. They did not return to Jefferson Barracks until 31 May.[55]

Lt. Col. Kress remained in command of the Powder Depot and the twenty-four enlisted men assigned to it. Kress also served as Quartermaster for the Powder Depot.[56]

Although a date for departing Jefferson Barracks for the rifle range at Arcadia cannot be found, Troop M, 6th Cavalry, must have participated in their annual target practice in May 1900, as it is known that Troop M began their return march on 27 May and arrived at Jefferson Barracks on 31 May.[57]

During April 1900, two units that had left Jefferson Barracks for service in the Philippine Islands, the 3rd U.S. Cavalry and the 49th U.S. Volunteer Infantry, saw active service. The 3rd Cavalry, as of 28 April 1900, had been split up by troops and occupied nine separate stations in Union, Ilocos Norte and Ilocos Sur Provinces. The 49th Volunteer Infantry, also split by company, occupied seven stations in Cagayan and Isabella Provinces.

The 3rd Cavalry suffered two casualties in April. Pvt. Charles A. Harris, Troop A, was shot in the head and killed near Badoc on 19 April, and Sgt. Edward R. Cooper, Troop F, suffered a bruised left side, shoulder and head when he was wounded by a spear near Batac on 25 April.[58]

April 1900 saw several of the larger clashes between the insurgents and the units that had been at Jefferson Barracks directly before moving to the Philippine Islands. Capt. George A. Dodd, Troop F, 3rd Cavalry, struck 200 insurgents near the District of Cullenberg. Eighty of these insurgents carried rifles, the remainder were armed with bolos. The fight lasted an hour with fifty-three insurgents killed and forty-four captured. Six days later, fifteen men of Troop A, 3rd Cavalry, defeated a large force of insurgents, estimated at 200, two miles south of San Nicolas. The Americans suffered no casualties.[59]

Capt. Dodd's Troop F, 3rd Cavalry, encountered 325 insurgents near Batac on 25 April. In an hour's fight twelve insurgents were killed and five captured, with one cavalryman wounded.[60]

Major Cooper remained in command of Jefferson Barracks during May. Troops A, C and D performed the usual garrison duties during the month. Little changed at the post during May 1900. Lt. Col. Kress commanded the Powder Depot. That organization had one fewer assigned as 1st Class Private Michael O'Connor transferred to Sandy Hook Proving Ground in May.[61]

Members of the Grand Army of the Republic traveled to the Jefferson Barracks National Cemetery by train and steamboat on 30 May for ceremonies to honor their dead comrades. Graves were decorated in the morning and a parade took place in the afternoon.[62]

In the Philippine Islands, Major General Elwell S. Otis relinquished command of the Division of the Philippines to Major General Arthur MacArthur on 5 May 1900. Also during May, the 38th Volunteer Infantry reported being involved in three engagements, and the 49th Volunteer Infantry reported one engagement.[63]

In June, Troop B, 5th Cavalry performed the usual garrison duties, while Troops A, C and D left on 4 June for their annual target practice at the Arcadia Rifle Range. They arrived on 7 June, set up camp and participated in target practice for the remainder of the month. Troop D returned to Jefferson Barracks on 28 June, although thirty-seven enlisted men of the company who had no horses returned to the post on 25 June.

Troop M, 6th Cavalry was relieved from duty at Jefferson Barracks on 19 June and departed the Post on 21 June under the command of Capt. DeRosey C. Cabell, en route to San Francisco. 2nd Lt. Patrick W. Guiney and twenty-seven enlisted men of Troop M departed the next day at 11:40 a.m. en route to Portland, Oregon, with a stock train composed of 122 horses. The ultimate destination of Troop M was China.[64]

Major Cooper commanded the post and the 1st Battalion, 5th Cavalry. The garrison consisted of eleven officers and 361 enlisted men, ten recruits and four casuals, plus four general prisoners after the departure of Troop M, 6th Cavalry. The post also employed twenty-two civilians.[65]

Major Surgeon Marshall W. Wood served as the post medical officer and Capt. Walter Allen, U.S. Volunteers, served as Post Quartermaster, Commissary and Ordnance Officer. Ferdinand Bryant, Cyrus F. Dugger, Henry Donaldson and Charles Gall remained at Jefferson Barracks in their respective posts as senior non-commissioned officers.[66] There were no changes at the Powder Depot.[67]

Major General MacArthur, commanding the Division of the Philippines, issued an amnesty proclamation on 21 June 1900. This proclamation, from the President of the United States, offered amnesty with complete immunity for the past and liberty of action for the future, to all persons who have been in insurrection against the United States, and who will, within 90 days, formally renounce all connection with such insurrection and accept the sovereignty and authority of the United States in and over the Philippine Islands.[68] Despite this offer of amnesty, resistance to U.S. authority continued unabated.

Also in June 1900, a future commanding officer of Jefferson Barracks, Walter C. Short, saw action in the Philippines. Major Short, in command of a detachment of the 35th Volunteer Infantry, engaged about forty insurgents near Norzagaray.[69]

July 1900 witnessed more changes in the personnel assigned to Jefferson Barracks. Troops A and C, 5th Cavalry, returned from their annual target practice at Arcadia on 6 July. Troops A, B, C and D, 5th Cavalry performed the usual garrison duties at Jefferson Barracks until 17 July. Troop A then proceeded by rail to Fort Huachuca, Arizona Territory, arriving on 22 July. Troop C proceeded by rail to Wilcox, Arizona Territory, then marched the final twenty-seven miles to Fort Grant. Troop D proceeded by rail to Fort Wingate, New Mexico, arriving on 21 July. Major Cooper relinquished command of the post to 1st Lt. Herschel Tupes, Company C, 1st Infantry, on 18 July, and left for Fort Grant. Company B, 1st Infantry arrived at Jefferson Barracks from Fort Leavenworth, Kansas, on 17 July.

This contingent of the 1st Infantry consisted of two officers and sixty-seven enlisted men. Acting Assistant Surgeon George Newloor, U.S.A., accompanied the 5th Cavalry to their new stations in the Arizona Territory, and acting Assistant Surgeon A.A. Von Clossman was relieved from duty on 9 July. Thus, only five officers remained on duty at Jefferson Barracks. In addition to 1st Lt. Tupes, 2nd Lt. William M. Parker, Company B, 1st Infantry; Major Surgeon Marshall W. Wood, Post Surgeon; Capt. Walter Allen, Post Quartermaster; and Acting Assistant Surgeon W.R. Van Tuyle, U.S. Volunteers, made up the officer corps at Jefferson Barracks. 1st Lt. Lambert W. Jordan, Jr., Company B, 1st Infantry, was on leave, and Capt. Charles G. Starr, Company B, 1st Infantry, was on detached service in the Philippine Islands serving as Lieutenant Colonel of the 11th U.S. Volunteer Cavalry and Inspector General of the 8th Army Corps. The latter two officers were assigned to Jefferson Barracks, but absent.[70]

August 1900 saw more changes in the personnel assigned to Jefferson Barracks. 1st Lt. William S. Guignard, 4th Artillery and ten enlisted men of Troop B, 8th Cavalry, joined on 11 August from Fort Riley, Kansas. They returned to Fort Riley on 30 August. Guignard commanded the post from 14 August to 28 August. Guignard had graduated from the U.S. Military Academy in 1896. Two officers, 1st Lt. Lambert W. Jordan and 2nd Lt. Edwin E. Carroll, and 128 enlisted men of Company B, 1st Infantry, left the post on August 13 for the Presidio of San Francisco. Finally, Capt. Harold L. Jackson and eighty-two enlisted men of Company B, 1st Infantry, joined from Fort Leavenworth on 28 August.[71]

Capt. Jackson assumed command of Jefferson Barracks upon his arrival on 28 August. Jackson had served as a private and corporal in Company F, 13th and 15th Infantry, from 1 April 1885 to 5 March 1889. He had received a commission as a 2nd lieutenant in the 15th Infantry on 11 February 1889. He had been promoted to captain in the 1st Infantry, on 25 May 1899. Major Surgeon Wood, 1st Lt. Tupes, Capt. Allen and 2nd Lt. David A. Lindsay of Company L, 1st Infantry, who had joined on August 31, made up the officer corps assigned to Jefferson Barracks. Acting Assistant Surgeon D.W. Van Suple accompanied Company B, 1st Infantry, to San Francisco.[72]

The garrison consisted of 214 enlisted men and recruits, plus three general prisoners, and seventeen civilian employees. This was the count as of 31 August.[73]

Lt. Col. Kress remained in command of the St. Louis Powder Depot at Jefferson Barracks. His command consisted of twenty-four enlisted men.[74]

September 1900 saw little change in the officer corps assigned to the post. Capt. Jackson remained in command. 1st Lt. Tupes had been sick in his quarters since August 14, then was transferred to the Army and Navy Hospital in Hot Springs, Arkansas, on 7 September. Acting Assistant Surgeon Van Tuyle replaced Surgeon Wood while the latter was on leave for 50 days.[75]

The garrison decreased in strength from the previous month, with a total enlisted strength of 126. However, when recruits are taken into account the total rose to 261. A total of 52 recruits transferred to permanent stations during the month. Thirty-six of these recruits were for the Hospital Corps at Fort McDowell, California.[76]

October 1900 witnessed few changes in the composition of the Jefferson Barracks garrison. Capt. Jackson commanded a garrison consisting of two other officers and Acting Assistant Surgeon Van Tuyle, 96 enlisted men, 108 recruits, four casuals and two general prisoners. A total of 98 recruits transferred to permanent stations. Twenty-four of these recruits belonged to the Hospital Corps and went to Fort McDowell, in the care of Hospital Steward Edward F. Costine.[77]

Capt. Harold Jackson remained in command of Jefferson Barracks until 30 November, when Lt. Col. Henry Jackson, 5th Cavalry, arrived and assumed command. Surgeon Wood returned from leave on 22 November and Acting Assistant Surgeon Van Tuyle transferred to Fort Thomas, Kentucky, on 5 November. This left the Post without a medical officer for 17 days. Enlisted men at the post numbered 93, plus 141 recruits, two casuals and two general prisoners.[78]

Lt. Col. Jackson had served as a private and corporal in Company A, 14th Illinois Cavalry, and as Sergeant Major of the 5th U.S. Colored Cavalry from 28 December 1863 to 13 May 1865. Jackson had been commissioned a 2nd Lieutenant in the 5th U.S. Colored Cavalry on 14 May 1865, and promoted to 1st lieutenant on 28 December 1865. He honorably mustered out on March 16, 1866, then received a commission as a 2nd lieutenant in the 7th Cavalry, on 28 July 1866. He was promoted to 1st lieutenant on 31 July 1867; to captain on 25 June 1876; to major in the 3rd Cavalry, on 27 August 1896; to lieutenant colonel in the 5th Cavalry on 23 January 1900; and finally, to colonel of the 3rd Cavalry, on 29 April 1901. He retired on 31 May 1901.

The garrison was practically devoid of enlisted men from 5 November 14 November, while Company L, 1st Infantry, engaged in their annual target practice at Arcadia. Fifty-one recruits transferred during the month.[79]

Lt. Col. Jackson remained in command of Jefferson Barracks in December 1900, but the personnel he commanded did change somewhat. Troops F and H, 5th Cavalry, left San Juan, Puerto Rico, aboard the transport *Crook* on 15 December and arrived at Newport News, Virginia, on 21 December. The same day the units boarded a train for Jefferson Barracks, arriving on 23 December. This troop movement brought two officers, Capt. George H. Paddock and Capt. Charles H. Watts, and 162 men to Jefferson Barracks. Company L, 1st Infantry, two officers and eighty men departed Jefferson Barracks the day after Christmas for Fort Leavenworth, Kansas. Twenty-three recruits also transferred to their permanent units. Thus, the Jefferson Barracks garrison consisted of six officers and 239 enlisted men, including recruits, casuals and general prisoners. The St. Louis Powder Depot at Jefferson Barracks remained under the command of Lt. Col. Kress, whose command consisted of 24 enlisted men.[80]

The water supply at Jefferson Barracks had been a source of concern for years. In addition to a lack of water, what water the post had was filthy with sediment and bacteria, causing a great deal of illness. Artesian wells, filtration beds, distillation plants, deep wells and many other means had been suggested and tried, but without success. It got to be so bad that during 1900, filters were installed in all barracks and quarters. Finally, the entire water supply was boiled and filtered at the Mess Hall and furnished to everyone except the general prisoners.

In June 1900, the Quartermaster Department approved large contracts for grading, road work, sewers, water systems and the construction of an administration building and an addition to a storehouse. All of this work was completed in December, except the road repairs, for which a new contract had to be let. In other construction, an ordnance storehouse was built with funds from fiscal year 1900.[81] Deputy Quartermaster-General, Lt. Col. Daniel D. Wheeler was in charge of all the construction at Jefferson Barracks.[82]

During the second half of 1900, fighting in the Philippines continued unabated. According to official figures during the thirteen months that the insurgency had been waged, there were 1,026 engagements, 245 Americans had been killed, 490 wounded and 118 captured. The Filipinos had suffered 3,854 killed, 1,193 wounded and 6,572 captured.[83]

During the year 1900, the U.S. Army consisted of 2,535 officers and 68,221 enlisted men in the Regular Army and 1,548 officers (233 of whom were Regular Army officers holding volunteer commissions) and 31,079 enlisted men in the volunteer force. Of these, 2,367 officers and 71,727 enlisted men served in the Philippine Islands.[84]

The units that had served at Jefferson Barracks - the 3rd Cavalry and the 6th Infantry - and the volunteer units organized at Jefferson Barracks - the 38th and the 49th U.S. Volunteer Infantry - were serving in the Philippines. These units certainly saw their share of action during the second half of 1900. According to official reports of engagements in the Philippine Islands for July through December 1900, elements of the 49th Volunteer Infantry engaged insurgents on at least twenty-six separate occasions; the 38th Volunteer Infantry, twenty-five times; the 3rd Cavalry, fifteen; and the 6th Infantry, ten times.

Each of these units suffered casualties during the latter half of 1900. In an engagement on 6 July, the 38th Volunteer Infantry had six men wounded, and on 23 July another private was wounded. All seven wounded survived. The 49th Volunteer Infantry had a musician wounded on 18 December, and Corporal Bunn of Company I was killed in action on the last day of the year. The 3rd Cavalry lost Sgt. Matthew Similia, who was killed in action on 9 September. In this same engagement, Privates Ernest A. Musseler, James G. Lyons, and Otto Schott received wounds. Two weeks later, on 23 September, the 3rd Cavalry had one private killed and two wounded, and on 7 October Pvt. McMahon, Company H, was wounded. Corporal Ditman of the 6th Infantry was killed in action on August 6. Two privates were killed and two more wounded on 30 July, and on 1 October, Lt. Hayden Y. Grubbs was killed and four more men were wounded.[85]

In early December 1900, Col. George S. Anderson, who organized and commanded the 38th U.S. Volunteer Infantry at Jefferson Barracks, received command of the mobile troops in the province of Iloilo. His command consisted of troops from Light Battery G, 76th Artillery; 18th Infantry; 26th Infantry; and 1st and 3rd Battalions, 38th Volunteer Infantry.[86]

1901

The new year, 1901, began much the same as 1900 had ended. Lt. Col. Henry Jackson, 5th Cavalry, commanded the post, which consisted of Troops F and H, 5th Cavalry, and recruits, eight officers and 289 enlisted men. Thus, the garrison consisted of 155 5th Cavalry troopers, 118 recruits, fourteen enlisted men on the General

Staff, and two general prisoners. In addition to Lt. Col. Jackson, Capt. Paddock, and Capt. Watts (all 5th Cavalry officers), Major Marshall W. Wood served as Post Surgeon; 1st Lt. Alonzo Gray, Troop H, 5th Cavalry, joined on 21 January; Capt. Walter Allen served as Post Quartermaster, Commissary and Ordnance Officer; 2nd Lt. Albert N. McClure, Troop F, 5th Cavalry, joined on 13 January; and Acting Assistant Surgeon Francis M. McCallum made up the officers at Jefferson Barracks.[87]

The primary enlisted men at the post consisted of Signal Corps Sgt. James E. Davis, who had been at Jefferson Barracks since 19 October 1899; Ordnance Sergeant Ferdinand Bryant, at Jefferson Barracks since 15 October 1898; Commissary Sergeant Cyrus F. Dugger, at the Post since 17 March 1899; Quartermaster Sergeant Henry Donaldson, at the post since 20 June 1896; and Hospital Steward Charles Gall, at Jefferson Barracks since 24 November 1897.[88]

Lt. Col. Kress remained in command of the Powder Depot. Kress commanded twenty-two enlisted men in January 1901. This number represented a decrease of two due to the discharge of Cpl. Samuel Schling and 1st Class Pvt. John Kolb at the expiration of their terms of service.[89]

Lt. Col. Henry Jackson remained in command of Jefferson Barracks through May 1901. However, the units present at the post did change. Company I, 1st Infantry, three officers and ninety-eight enlisted men arrived and took station on 26 February. The next day Troop F, 5th Cavalry, two officers and eighty-seven enlisted men; and Troop H, 5th Cavalry, three officers and eighty-three enlisted men departed Jefferson Barracks. Troop F took station at Fort Huachuca, Arizona Territory; and Troop H took station at Fort Wingate, New Mexico.[90]

1st Lt. William T. Mercy and 2nd Lt. Joseph W. Beacham, Company I, 1st Infantry, joined the post, while Capt. George H. Paddock and Capt. Charles H. Watts departed with the 5th Cavalry troops. Paddock then received orders to report to the Presidio of San Francisco. Capt. Frank Carrington reported on 26 February, but departed the next day on detached service to Fort Leavenworth.[91]

During most of February 1901, the garrison consisted of nine officers and 338 enlisted men, of which 144 were recruits. During March, the garrison consisted of six officers and 157 enlisted men. The decrease in enlisted personnel was due to the transfer of most of the recruits. Only twenty recruits were present during March. A detachment from Company H, 10th Infantry, arrived from Fort Niobrara, Nebraska, on 24 March. The detachment consisted of one officer, 2nd Lt. Henry Watterson, Jr. and twenty enlisted men.[92]

Capt. James B. Erwin, Acting Inspector General, Department of the Missouri, conducted the annual inspection of the Post on 30 and 31 March. No major deficiencies were noted.[93]

Acting Assistant Surgeon Justin M. Wheate joined on 21 March. Capt. Walter Allen, U.S. Volunteers, held several duties, serving as Post Quartermaster and Commissary Officer, Post Exchange Officer and Signal Officer. 1st Lt. Alonzo Gray also served in numerous roles. Lt. Gray served as Mess Officer, Range Officer and commander of the Recruit Detachment. He left the post on 28 March in charge of the recruits being transferred to permanent duty stations.[94]

The post flag was lowered to half-staff on 14 March when the post received news of the assassination of President William McKinley. At dawn the next morning, thirteen guns were fired. This was repeated every thirty minutes throughout the day. At sundown on 15 March the forty-five-gun salute to the Union was fired. Troops assembled at 10:00 a.m., when an order of General Nelson Miles, General-in-Chief of the Army, was read, and after a review parade a holiday was observed for the remainder of the day.[95]

Company I, 1st Infantry performed the usual garrison duties until 9 April at which time they departed for San Francisco. They arrived on 14 April and departed the next day on the U.S. Army transport *Logan* bound for the Philippine Islands. 2nd Lt. Joseph W. Beacham left with Company I, leaving Lt. Col. Henry Jackson, Major Surgeon Marshall W. Wood, Capt. Walter Allen and Acting Assistant Surgeon Justin M. Wheate as the only officers at the post.[96]

Lt. Col. Henry Jackson received a promotion to colonel of the 3rd Cavalry on 29 April 1901. He continued to command Jefferson Barracks, but served on detached service on court martial duty at Fort Reno, Oklahoma Territory from 16 May to 20 May. Col. Jackson retired at noon on 31 May 1901.[97]

The day before Col. Jackson's retirement, on 30 May, Memorial Day celebrations began in St. Louis with the decoration of the statues of prominent men throughout the city by committees from the various Grand Army of the Republic posts. A procession made up of members of the Grand Army, as well as Spanish-American War and Philippine War veterans associations marched through the downtown streets. After the parade, the different organizations held exercises in the cemeteries where the dead are buried. The principal exercises were held at Jefferson Barracks National Cemetery, where the graves of thousands of veterans are located.[98]

With the retirement of Col. Jackson, 1st Lt. Henry Watterson was promoted on 2 February, and transferred to the 26th Infantry, took command of Jefferson Barracks. The post consisted of the fewest number of troops present in quite some time. Only two officers beside Watterson - Marshall W. Wood and Walter Allen - remained at the post along with sixty-two enlisted men. The Post also employed twenty-one civilians. At the north end of the post, Lt. Col. John A. Kress remained in command of the St. Louis Powder Depot. His command consisted of twenty-four enlisted men.[99]

Not many changes took place in June 1901. Capt. and Assistant Surgeon Francis A. Winter joined as Post Surgeon on 29 June, as Major Marshall Wood had been relieved on 10 June. Capt. Walter Allen received his honorable discharge on 30 June.[100]

After almost three months with an unusually small garrison, the 1st Squadron of the 11th Cavalry arrived from Fort Ethan Allen, Vermont, on 24 July. This swelled the ranks of the garrison by seven officers and 301 enlisted men, bringing the total garrison to nine officers and 455 enlisted men. Included in this number were 120 recruits, 97 of whom represented Coast Artillery recruits. Major James B. Hickey, 11th Cavalry, took command of the post.[101]

Hickey had joined the military as a Surgeon's Steward in the U.S. Navy on 4 April 1864, and served in that capacity until 15 May 1865. He then attended the U.S. Military Academy, graduating 1 July 1871. He served as a 2nd lieutenant in the 8th Cavalry, was promoted to 1st lieutenant on 23 April 1879, and to captain on 20 January 1890. He served as a major and Acting Adjutant General of Volunteers until 5 September 1899. He was promoted to the permanent rank of major in the 11th Cavalry on 2 February 1901.

No significant changes took place during August. Major Hickey remained in command of a garrison that consisted of fifteen officers and 450 enlisted men.[102] This was a gain of six officers.

A detachment of twenty men left the post on 10 August to take station at Fort Crook, Nebraska. 1st Lt. Guy Cushman, 11th Cavalry, commanded this detachment. Many recruits also departed during the month to join their permanent organizations. Lt. Cushman commanded forty Coast Artillery recruits sent to Fort Washington, Maryland, on 21 August. 2nd Lt. Fred H. Turner, 23rd Infantry, commanded sixty Coast Artillery recruits sent to Fort Caswell, North Carolina, and Sgt. Murray, Troop C, 11th Cavalry, was in charge of twenty-nine Coast Artillery recruits bound for Fort Morgan, Alabama, that left on 21 August.[103]

It is also interesting that Troops A and D, 11th Cavalry, left by rail for their annual target practice near Arcadia, Missouri. They completed target practice and re-joined the post on 31 August. This is the first mention of troops taking the train to target practice and not marching to Arcadia.[104]

It appears that Post Quartermaster Sergeant Henry Donaldson, who had held his position at Jefferson Barracks since 30 June 1896, was no longer at the post. He was not listed on the Post Returns and Major Hickey was detailed as a member of a board to examine non-commissioned officers for the duty of Post Quartermaster Sergeant.

September 1901 saw a significant increase in the size of the garrison at Jefferson Barracks. The 3rd Squadron, Troops I, K, L and M, 4th Cavalry, arrived at 6:00 a.m. on 11 September. Major Frank A. Edwards commanded this contingent of eight officers and 280 enlisted men.[105]

Troops B and C, 11th Cavalry, under the command of Capt. Edward M. Leary, proceeded by rail to Arcadia on September 8 for target practice. They returned on 23 September, and Troops I and M, 4th Cavalry, left by rail the same day for target practice. 1st Lt. Charles T. Boyd commanded these troops.[106]

Recruits continued to leave Jefferson Barracks for their permanent duty stations. On 4 September, forty-four Coast Artillery recruits under the command of 2nd Lt. William G. Meade, 11th Cavalry, left for Fort Dade, Florida. 2nd Lt. John Symington, 11th Cavalry, commanded forty-two Coast Artillery recruits that departed on 18 September for Fort Severn, Georgia. On 21 September, thirty Infantry recruits, commanded by 1st Lt. Charles S. Haight, 4th Cavalry, went to Fort Sheridan, Illinois, and on 27 September, fifty-seven Coast Artillery recruits under 2nd Lt. George H. Baird, 11th Cavalry, left for Fort Dade, Florida.[107]

The size of the garrison at Jefferson Barracks remained steady in October, with seventeen officers and 730 enlisted men.[108]

Troops L and K, 4th Cavalry, under the command of Capt. Harry C. Benson, Troop K, 4th Cavalry, took part in target practice between 9 October and 25 October. Again, the travel to the target range near Arcadia was by rail.[109]

The number of recruits transferred during October increased. Fifty Field Artillery recruits, under the command of Capt. John T. Haines, 11th Cavalry, transferred to Vancouver Barracks, Washington on 1 October. Fifty more Field Artillery recruits, under the command of 1st Lt. Frank T. Amos left for Fort Walla Walla, Washington, also on 1 October; and thirty-one Field Artillery recruits, commanded by 1st Lt. and Squadron Adjutant Frederick T. Arnold, 4th Cavalry, left for Fort Leavenworth, Kansas, on 13 October. Finally, 121 Coast Artillery recruits, under the command of Capt. Edward M. Leary, 11th Cavalry and 2nd Lt. Charles J. Naylor, 4th Cavalry, transferred to Key West Barracks, Florida, on 22 October.[110]

A new practice started during October, when units began reconnaissance marches around the area. Troop B, 11th Cavalry, Capt. Leary commanding, went on reconnaissance to Webster Groves, Missouri, on 11 October, marching twenty miles. On 16 October, Troop C, 11th Cavalry, under 1st Lt. Amos, marched sixteen miles on reconnaissance to Butler Lake, Missouri. Then on 28 October, Troop A, 11th Cavalry, under Capt. Haines, and Troop D, 11th Cavalry, under Capt. Melvin W. Rowell, went on reconnaissance to the Meramec River.[111]

Sgt. Louis Main received an appointment as Post Quartermaster Sergeant on 11 October. In November, Henry Donaldson is once again listed as Post Quartermaster Sergeant and Sgt. Main is listed as Sergeant Major of the 11th Cavalry.[112]

Lt. Col. John A. Kress remained in command of the St. Louis Powder Depot at Jefferson Barracks throughout 1901. However, in October Kress was relieved of his command, but ordered to return to the Powder Depot once each month. His command consisted of twenty-two to twenty-eight enlisted men during this time period.[113]

Again, there was little change during November 1901. Major Hickey was still in command of a garrison that listed fifteen officers and 703 enlisted men. 1st Lt. Guy Cushman transferred, at his own request, from Troop B to Troop G, 11th Cavalry, and was ordered to his new duty station, leaving on 28 November.[114]

Only fifty-seven recruits transferred during the month: fifty Coast Artillery and seven Field Artillery recruits. The Coast Artillery recruits went to Fort Clark, Texas, and the Field Artillery recruits to Fort Riley, Kansas.[115]

A major change in personnel took place early in December. The 1st Squadron, Troops A, B, C and D, 11th Cavalry, with Major James B. Hickey commanding, left Jefferson Barracks at 3:00 p.m. on 7 December en route to San Francisco. The contingent included twelve officers and 305 enlisted men, one contract surgeon, Alva R. Hall, six hospital Corpsmen, nineteen Infantry privates, forty-five Coast Artillery recruits and one veterinary surgeon.[116]

Companies B and D, 124 enlisted men of the 1st Battalion Engineers, under the command of Capt. George A. Zinn, arrived at the post at 8:00 a.m. on 26 December. They had left the Philippine Islands on 18 October, arrived in New York at 1:45 a.m. on 23 December, and then traveled by rail to Jefferson Barracks.[117]

With the departure of Major Hickey, Major Frank A. Edwards, 4th Cavalry, took command of Jefferson Barracks. Frank Augustine Edwards joined the Army as a 2nd lieutenant in the 1st Cavalry on 1 October 1873. He was promoted to 1st lieutenant on September 7, 1879; to captain on 9 March 1891; to major in the 12th Cavalry on 28 February 1902; and then transferred to the 4th Cavalry on 13 April 1901.[118] The garrison consisted of Edwards and eleven officers and 421 assigned enlisted men, sixty-four recruits, seventeen casuals, and nineteen general prisoners.[119]

On 20 December, governors, congressmen and other distinguished representatives of Missouri, Nebraska, Kansas, Arkansas and other states of the Louisiana Purchase territory attended the groundbreaking ceremonies for the Louisiana Purchase Exposition in St. Louis. The ceremonies were of a character befitting the importance of the occasion. They were preceded by a parade of civic and military organizations, including several troops of cavalry from Jefferson Barracks. The procession formed at Grand Avenue and Lindell Boulevard, in the western section of the city and marched to the site of the World's Fair in Forest Park. The entire route was elaborately decorated with flags and bunting. Arriving at Forest Park, the exercises of the day were opened with an address by Mayor Wells. The oration of the day was delivered by Congressman James A. Tawney of Minnesota, chairman of the World's Fair Committee of the House of Representatives. The ceremony of breaking ground was performed by former Governor Francis, president of the exposition.[120]

The fighting in the Philippine Islands continued throughout the year 1901, but clashes with insurgents were less frequent. During the fiscal year 1901, May 1900 to 30 June 1901, the number of troops in the Philippines decreased from 2,367 officers and 71,727 enlisted men to 1,111 officers and 42,128 enlisted men. Casualties during this period amounted to 3,854 insurgents killed, 1,193 wounded, 6,572 captured and twenty missing. These numbers occurred during the more than 1,000 contacts between U.S. troops and the insurgents.[121]

The two volunteer regiments organized at Jefferson Barracks, the 38th and 49th U.S. Volunteer Infantry, returned to the United States in June 1901. The 38th had arrived in Manila on 26 December 1899. Headquarters and Companies A, C and D departed Manila on board the U.S. Army Transport *Thomas* on 27 May and arrived in San Francisco on 26 June. The 2nd and 3rd Battalions, 38th Volunteer Infantry departed Manila on board the U.S. Army Transport *Logan* on 31 May and arrived in San Francisco on 25 June. All of these troops mustered out of U.S. Service on 30 June 1901. Company B, 38th Volunteer Infantry departed Manila on board the *Thyla* on 1 June, arrived in San Francisco 1 July, and mustered out on 5 July.[122]

Four companies of the 49th U.S. Volunteer Infantry also departed Manila on board the U.S. Army Transport *Thomas* on 27 May, and arrived in San Francisco on 26 June. Headquarters and the other eight companies of the 49th Volunteer Infantry departed Manila on board the U.S. Army Transport *Grant* on 2 June, and arrived at San Francisco on 24 June. All members of the 49th mustered out of Federal service on 30 June 1901.[123]

According to the records, compiled from the field returns of the 38th U.S. Volunteer Infantry, the 38th had fifty-four officers on its rolls when it reached Manila on 26 December 1899. Six officers were discharged and forty-eight returned to San Francisco to be discharged. The 38th had 1,530 enlisted men on its rolls when it reached Manila. Of this number, 453 were discharged in the Philippines, eleven were killed or died of wounds, forty-eight died of disease, twenty-eight deserted, two drowned and 962 returned to be mustered out.[124]

The 49th U.S. Volunteer Infantry had fifty-six officers on its rolls when it reached Manila on 2 January 1900. Of these officers, three resigned, five were discharged and forty-eight returned to the United States to be mustered out. The 49th listed 1,583 enlisted men on its rolls when it was organized. Of that number, 453 received discharges, eleven were killed or died of wounds, thirty-seven died of disease, ten deserted and 1,072 returned to the United States to be mustered out.[125]

The most important single military event of 1901 in the Philippines took place in mid-March when Brigadier General Frederick Funston, with four other officers and eighty-one Macabebe scouts, captured Emilio Aguinaldo. (Funston would later serve at Jefferson Barracks).

Funston hatched the scheme to capture the principal Filipino leader. From captured Filipino documents Funston knew that Aguinaldo had called for guerrilla replacements in his headquarters area, and that these replacements were expected to arrive over a period of time in small numbers. Funston's scheme involved the Macabebe scouts posing as replacements bringing in the five officers as prisoners to Aguinaldo's headquarters. The Macabebe scouts, from Pampanga Province, had always been mercenaries. After fighting against the Tagalogs for Spain, they had switched their allegiance to the United States. Indistinguishable in appearance and language from other Filipino Malays, they possessed a proclivity for the rape, torture and robbery of their countrymen that Americans had always had a difficult time restraining.

Funston and the other four officers were to accompany the Macabebes in the guise of prisoners. The story was that they had been captured during the march.

Just after midnight on 14 February, the party, after sailing around the southern tip of Luzon on the gunboat *Vicksburg,* secretly landed at Casigerian Bay, then proceeded overland 100 miles through wild, unknown country. The *Vicksburg* was to return for them on 25 March.

Even on half rations the expedition ran out of food in a week. They finally reached Aguinaldo's headquarters at Palonan. Three members of the expedition, Segovia, Placido and Segismundo, walked straight into Aguinaldo's headquarters on the second floor of a little house overlooking the village square. Aguinaldo and two of his officers were in the room. Segovia nodded to the ranking Macabebe officer, Gregorio Codhit, watching him from below. Codhit turned to his men and shouted, "Now is the time, Macabebes. Give it to them." They fired wildly killing two men and badly wounding the leader of the band, who had gotten in the way.

When Aguinaldo heard the shots, he believed that his men were celebrating the arrival of the reinforcements. He leaned out the window and shouted, "Stop that foolishment, don't waste your ammunition." At that moment Placido, a burly man, grabbed Aguinaldo from behind and Segovia began shooting. One of Aguinaldo's bodyguards was hit three times and the other fled. Struggling to draw his revolver, Placido threw Aguinaldo to the floor and held him down. "You are a prisoner of the Americans," Placido explained, while sitting on Aguinaldo.

Meanwhile the Macabebes, who outnumbered the entire Filipino force in Palanan had taken over the town and the Americans had entered. When Funston encountered Segovia, spattered with the blood of his victim, Segovia said, "It is all right. We have him." Funston hurried upstairs and found Aguinaldo almost in a state of shock. "Is this not a joke?" Aguinaldo mumbled in Spanish. Funston introduced himself, and Aguinaldo seemed to relax. It was all over.

After a day of rest, the expedition returned to the coast without incident and was met on schedule by the *Vicksburg*. She cruised around the island, steamed up the Pasig River and docked near "The Palace" on the morning of March 28. Funston, Aguinaldo and the others came ashore. Aguinaldo was put in a private room under a heavy guard. General MacArthur, who had just awakened for breakfast, descended in a dressing gown to greet Funston, another, he thought, in a long list of men who had set out on wild-goose chases after the Philippine president. "Where is Aguinaldo?" he asked dryly. "Right in this house," Funston replied.[126]

Aguinaldo took the "Oath of Allegiance" to the American government on 19 April and followed that with a proclamation, which MacArthur published in all dialects throughout the islands "...There has been enough blood, enough tears, enough desolation...I cannot refuse to heed the voice of a people longing for peace...By acknowledging and accepting the sovereignty of the United States throughout the Philippine Archipelago...I believe that I am serving thee, my beloved country...."[127]

Frederick Funston, 36 years of age, was a curious individual. He was 5' 5", red-haired and muscle-bound, an incurable romantic, adventurous, with an adulation of the Anglo-Saxon legend, and slightly intellectual. He had joined a botanical expedition to California's Death Valley ten years before the war. From there he drifted to Alaska. Before the United States declared war on Spain, Funston fought with the rebels in Cuba against the Spanish. He was wounded and contracted malaria. He returned to Kansas and after the explosion of the *Maine* received a commission as colonel of his Kansas regiment, was posted to the Philippines, and was soon promoted to brigadier general of volunteers.

Funston, who had no permanent rank in the Army, received a commission as a brigadier general in the Regular Army on April 1, 1901. He received the Medal of Honor on 14 February 1900, for most distinguished and gallant action at Rio Grande de la Pampanga, Luzon, Philippine Islands on 27 April 1899, in crossing the river on a raft, and by his skill and daring enabling the general commanding to carry the enemy's entrenched position on the north bank of the river and drive him with great loss from the important and strategic position of Calumpit.[128]

After the capture of Aguinaldo many of the other rebel leaders came in to surrender. On 16 April 1902, Miguel Malvar, the last of the principal insurgent leaders, surrendered with his exhausted, famished troops. That date marked the practical end of the insurrection, although it was not officially terminated by edict of President Theodore Roosevelt until 4 July 1902.[129]

It proved to be a costly war, not only in terms of dollars, which came to over $600 million, but in terms of American and Filipino lives. The graves of 4,234 Americans from this conflict are in the Philippines, and hundreds more Americans later died in the United States of service connected diseases. The number of American soldiers wounded came to 2,818. On the other side, 16,000 Filipinos had been killed and their corpses physically counted by the Americans. The total probably exceeded 20,000. Another 200,000 civilians died of disease and pestilence.[130]

1902

The year 1902 started as 1901 had ended. Major Frank Edwards remained in command of the 3rd Squadron, 4th Cavalry and the post. In addition to the 4th Cavalry contingent at the post, Companies B and D, 1st Battalion of Engineers also remained at Jefferson Barracks. The 4th Cavalry consisted of ten officers and 223 enlisted men, while the Engineers numbered two officers and 156 enlisted men. There were also 180 recruits, 131 of which were Coast Artillery, and twenty-three casuals, providing a total of 426 men.[131]

Not included in this number were the twenty-five prisoners being held at Jefferson Barracks. One of these prisoners was a man named George Larison. Larison, wanted for over a year for desertion while on duty in Puerto Rico in 1899, walked into the office of Sheriff Minie of Shelby County, Illinois, and surrendered on 26 January. He had previously been arrested near his old home and taken to Jefferson Barracks, where he escaped within a few hours. He was again taken to Jefferson Barracks.[132]

Losses during January included eighty-seven recruits, twenty-nine Field Artillery and fifty-eight Coast Artillery, recruits transferred to permanent duty stations. Also, the non-commissioned staff of the 1st Battalion of Engineers transferred to Fort Leavenworth where Major Smith S. Leach, Corps of Engineers, had assumed command of the 1st Battalion and established its headquarters at that post.[133]

At Jefferson Barracks, Companies B and D continued to perform the usual garrison duties and were instructed in close and extended order infantry drill and in small arms firing. The 4th Cavalry troopers performed the usual garrison duties during January.[134]

A prime example of the horrors of war came to light in St. Louis in January, when a story appeared in the 21 January 1902, issue of the *Daily Herald*. 2nd Lt. James H. Bradford, Jr., 17th Infantry, son of the late Lt. Col. James H. Bradford, Sr., mysteriously disappeared in San Francisco in late 1901. The War Department could not find any information as to his whereabouts until a few days before the newspaper article came out. Young Bradford was found living in a St. Louis boarding house, eking out a living as a teacher and wheelwright under an assumed name. An investigation showed that the young man had lost his mind, and his condition was attributed to the fact that he had a severe attack of jungle fever while serving in the Philippines.

February and March 1902 passed much as January. Major Edwards commanded the post with the 3rd Squadron, 4th Cavalry and Companies B and D, 1st Battalion of Engineers, plus recruits making up the garrison. The 4th Cavalry contingent consisted of ten officers and 282 enlisted men in February and nine officers and 315 enlisted men in March. The Engineer contingent consisted of two officers and 150 enlisted men in February and six officers and 139 enlisted men in March. The garrison had 197 recruits in February and 93 recruits in March. The number of recruits transferred to permanent duty stations in February came to 123 and 172 in March. 1st Lt. Guy V. Henry with a detachment of troops from Troops I and M, 4th Cavalry, joined the post from Fort Logan H. Roots, Arkansas, on 14 March.[135]

In addition to the usual garrison duties, Companies B and D, 1st Battalion of Engineers received practical instruction in infantry drill regulations, Butts' manual, and hospital drill regulations.[136]

The 4th Cavalry troops from Jefferson Barracks left on 2 March and served as an escort of honor for Prince Henry of Prussia. They returned on 3 March.[137]

A fire broke out in the quarters of 1st Lt. Ben H. Dorcy, 4th Cavalry, at 10:20 p.m. 17 March. The Post Quartermaster estimated damage at $413.[138]

April 1902 saw numerous changes in Post personnel. These changes took place on 10 April when Companies B and D, 1st Battalion of Engineers, seven officers and 134 enlisted men commanded by Capt. George A. Zinn, transferred to Fort Leavenworth, Kansas. On the same day, Headquarters Field and Staff and a detachment of the Band, five officers and twenty enlisted men of the 8th Cavalry commanded Col. Louis H. Rucker, arrived from Fort Reno, Oklahoma Territory. (PR, April 1902) Col. Rucker relieved Major Edwards in command of the post. Rucker, then received an appointment on 18 April as a brigadier general and retired the next day. Even though retired, Rucker remained in command of Jefferson Barracks through March 1902.

 Rucker, from Illinois, joined the military as a private in the Chicago Dragoons on 19 April 1861. He served as a private, a sergeant and 1st sergeant of Company G, 8th Illinois Cavalry from 14 September 1861, to 9 February 1864, when he received a commission as a 2nd lieutenant in the 8th Illinois Cavalry. He was promoted to 1st lieutenant on 26 November 1864. Rucker honorably mustered out of volunteer service on 21 April 1865. He then received a commission as a 2nd lieutenant in the 9th Cavalry on 28 July 1866. He received a promotion to 1st lieutenant on 31 July 1867, then served as regimental adjutant from 25 August 1872, to 20 March 1879, when he was promoted to the rank of captain. Rucker transferred to the 4th Cavalry as a major on 13 January 1897. He transferred to the 6th Cavalry on 2 January 1900. He became a lieutenant colonel on 2 February 1901, and a colonel in the 8th Cavalry on 17 September 1901.[139]

Troops K and M, 4th Cavalry; three officers: 1st Lt. Dorcy, 2nd Lt. Anton Jurich, Jr., and Capt. Harry C. Benson, commanding; one contract surgeon: Aron Clossman; 131 enlisted men and two civilian employees left for annual target practice at Arcadia on 23 April.[140]

At the end of April, a detachment of the 8th Cavalry consisting of 1st Lt. Albert A. King, Troop F; Harry F. Steele, Veterinary Surgeon; twelve enlisted men and two pack trains joined the post. Capt. William F. Flynn, 8th Cavalry Quartermaster, had joined on 10 April. Capt. Flynn became the Post Quartermaster.[141]

Seventy-eight recruits were posted to Jefferson Barracks during April and 88 recruits transferred to permanent stations. Of the recruits transferred, fifteen were Cavalry recruits, twelve for Field Artillery and sixty-one for Coast Artillery.[142]

During April Jefferson Barracks received pack trains from Cuba. This was caused by the abandonment of U.S. posts throughout the Department of Cuba. A good example of one such instance was the 21 April shipment on the steamship *Uto* of 220 animals at $25 each; fifty attendants at $30 each; 7,500 pounds (estimated) public property

Gun taken from Spanish ship *Oquendo*. This gun remains located behind #1 Grant Road.

Brigadier General Frederick Funston

Funston hatched the scheme to capture Philippine leader Emilio Aquinaldo in 1901. Funston was the first choice of President Woodrow Wilson to command the American Expeditionary Force in World War 1 until he died suddenly of a heart attack. Funston received the Medal of Honor on February 14, 1900, for most distinguished and gallant action at Rio Grande de la Pampanga, Luzon, Philippine Islands on 27 April 1899.

Col. Louis H. Rucker

Col. Rucker arrived from Fort Reno, Oklahoma Territory, on 10 April 1902, and assumed command of Jefferson Barracks. On 18 April Rucker was appointed a brigadier general and retired the next day. Although officially retired Gen. Rucker remained in command of Jefferson Barracks.

at $2 per 100 pounds and 8,800 pounds [estimated] forage at 50 cents per 100 pounds, total value $7,194. This load left from Santiago de Cuba to Mobile, Alabama and on to Jefferson Barracks.[143]

In May 1902, the garrison at Jefferson Barracks again changed. First, on 2 May Troops F and G, 8th Cavalry, with Capt. Joseph A. Gaston commanding, arrived from Cuba. This included fourteen officers and 134 enlisted men. Then at the end of the month, on May 28, Major Henry W. Sprole brought Troops F and H, Field and Staff, Non-commissioned Staff, 8th Cavalry Band and a detachment of the hospital corps to Jefferson Barracks from Cuba.[144]

Lightning struck Cavalry Stable No. 4 at 10:40 a.m. on 24 May. The stable was totally destroyed, but the horses were saved.

Louis H. Rucker commanded a garrison that consisted of twenty-six officers and 527 enlisted men. Add to this number 116 recruits and six casuals and Jefferson Barracks had the largest garrison it had since 1899. Also during May, sixty-three cavalry recruits and four Field Artillery recruits transferred to permanent stations. Twenty-one of the cavalry recruits were colored recruits sent to Fort Robinson, Nebraska.[145]

A rather unusual and different type of commemoration took place for Memorial Day on 30 May. First, the graves of 16,000 soldiers were decorated, then despite threatening weather, the Commodore Foote Association of Naval veterans boarded the steamer *Hill City*. On the way to Jefferson Barracks, the Naval veterans cast adrift floral models of the steamers *Cairo* and *Louisville*, in memory of the sailors who lost their lives in the Civil War.[146]

Little changed in June. Troops I and L, 4th Cavalry, left on 11 June for their annual target practice at the Arcadia Range. They arrived at Arcadia at 12:30 p.m. on 15 June meaning that they must have marched to the range, not traveled by train as had been done earlier. Troops K and M, 4th Cavalry, completed their target practice on 16 June and arrived at Jefferson Barracks on 19 June. During their march, they received instructions in advanced guard, rear guard and road sketching.[147]

Lt. Col. John A. Kress officially remained in command of the St. Louis Powder Depot, although he served as temporary commander of the Allegheny Arsenal in Pennsylvania. He made monthly visits to the Depot. His command consisted of twenty-three or twenty-four enlisted men through the first half of 1902.[148]

The post also employed forty-nine civilians. Their pay ranged from one clerk who made $133.33 per month to four laborers who received $20 per month.[149]

As the second half of 1902 began the Jefferson Barracks garrison still consisted of the 3rd Squadron, 4th Cavalry, Troops I, K, L and M; and Troops E, F, G and H, 8th Cavalry, a total of sixteen officers and 310 enlisted men. The post's General Staff consisted of two officers and twenty-two enlisted men and there were 241 recruits, 232 of which were Mounted Service recruits. One officer and nine enlisted men were listed as casuals, plus fifteen general prisoners. The officer was Henry W. Sprole, who had been promoted to lieutenant colonel and transferred to the 1st Cavalry.[150]

Detachments from Jefferson Barracks participated in several celebrations during July. Troop E, 8th Cavalry, participated in the 4th of July celebration at St. Charles, Missouri. Also, Troop G, 8th Cavalry, and Troop K, 4th Cavalry, marched to the St. Louis Fair Grounds on 25 July, where they participated in drill and field exercises with the 1st Regiment of Missouri National Guard. They returned the next day. Troops I and L, 4th Cavalry, remained at the Arcadia Target Range.[151]

Col. Kress returned from temporary command of the Allegheny Arsenal, which had been abandoned. His command consisted of twenty-three enlisted men.[152]

The units making up the Jefferson Barracks garrison remained unchanged for the remainder of 1902, and Col. Louis H. Rucker remained in command. Troops I and L, 4th Cavalry, completed their annual target practice and rejoined the post on 7 August.[153]

Jefferson Barracks received a visit from Department Commander, Major General John C. Bates on 6 August. He reviewed the troops and inspected the Post before departing the same day.[154]

Several items of a general nature affecting Jefferson Barracks came to light in Major General Bates' annual report to the War Department for fiscal year 1902, filed 30 June 1902. In his report on the sanitary conditions at the post, Bates reported that malarial fever remained prevalent at the post, more so than at any other post in the Department. On the recommendation of Post Surgeon, Capt. Francis A. Winter, who believed that malarial fevers were transmitted by mosquitos, energetic measures were taken to exterminate them as nearly as practicable.[155]

In another section of General Bates' report, he stated that eight troops of cavalry garrisoned Jefferson Barracks. These troops served as instructors for recruits. Bates did not feel that Jefferson Barracks was well adapted for mounted troops and therefore recommended that the post be converted to an Infantry garrison.[156]

At the time of Bates' report to the War Department Jefferson Barracks still maintained the General Mess, one of only thirteen posts in the country that had not converted to the Company Mess system. Major General John R. Brooke remarked that he did not believe in General Messes, as they were unsatisfactory, impracticable in camp and field. He went on to recommend that suitable company messes with both steam and range cooking be installed at all posts. General mess halls should be converted into well-equipped gyms or used for other necessary purposes.[157]

In the same vein, Volume I of the Fiscal Year 1902 Report stated that Section 38 of the Act of 2 February 1901, prohibits the sale of beer and light wines in Post Exchanges. After asking for and receiving a great number of reports on the subject, the Secretary of War, Elihu Root, had become convinced that the general effect of prohibiting the use of beer and light wines within the limited area of an Army Post was to lead the enlisted men to go off the post in order "to frequent vile resorts which cluster in the neighborhood, to drink bad whiskey to excess, and to associate intimately with abandoned men and more abandoned women; and that the operation of the law is to increase drunkenness, disease of the most loathsome kind, insubordination and desertion, and moral and physical degeneration ...." Root and most department commanders continued to push for the repeal of this act.[158]

Also, in Volume I of the report is an Ordnance Department report on small arms that not only held significance for Jefferson Barracks but for the entire army for years to come. It states that the Ordnance Department had produced a rifle which it considered an improvement upon the then current service rifle, the Krag-Jorgenson. The report goes on to state that "it is clearly superior to the present rifle in many respects. It is a bolt gun, caliber .30, having a clip magazine under the chamber instead of at the side, and therefore better balanced than the present gun. It continues the 220-grain bullet, but increases the charge of powder from 37.6 grains to 43.3 grains. It gives an initial velocity of 2,300 feet per second as against 2,000 of the present rifle, a striking energy at 1,000 yards of 447.9 foot-pounds as against 396.2 for the present rifle. It has a flatter trajectory and weighs about a pound less." The head of the Ordnance Department had authorized the production of 5,000 rifles for issue and practical trial. This rifle was ultimately adopted for general Infantry usage, as the Model 1903 Springfield, arguably the finest rifle ever produced.[159]

On 15 August, Jefferson Barracks held a Field Day. During Field Day, each individual unit was judged on exercises involving running, jumping and other elements of horsemanship. Points were awarded for each exercise with first, second, etc. being named. Troop K, 4th Cavalry came in first and Troop I, 4th Cavalry second.[160]

An event of another kind took place during the night of 28 August, when six long term prisoners were caught sawing through the roof of their guardhouse. 2nd Lt. Anton Jurich, Jr., 4th Cavalry and Officer of the Guard, frustrated the attempted breakout. If allowed another ten to fifteen minutes, twelve prisoners would have been on the roof of the guardhouse ready to lower themselves with ropes at the first opportunity.[161]

Another Field Day was held on 25 September. This time Troop F, 8th Cavalry, earned the most points.[162] Troop K, 4th Cavalry, took first place at the 28 November Field Day.[163]

In October, the 3rd Squadron, 4th Cavalry marched to St. Louis on the 6th. On 7 October, the Squadron took part in the Veiled Prophet Parade and then returned to Jefferson Barracks.[164]

A report contained in the Annual Report to the War Department for the fiscal year ended 30 June 1903, written by Jefferson Barracks surgeon, Francis A. Winter, addressed the problem of malarial fever at Jefferson Barracks. In his report, written 4 October 1902, Winter said that Jefferson Barracks had a very unsavory reputation in the past as a malarial locality, and that the prosecution of a mosquito crusade to eradicate the pest during the past summer had improved the sanitary conditions of the post. Winter went on to say that the summer of 1902 showed a marked decrease in the percentage of the command sick with malarial fever. Winter hoped that a continuation of the systematic measures already taken to eradicate the mosquito would result in continued improvement.[165]

In November 109 horses were received from the Quartermaster and assigned to troops of the 8th Cavalry. With the addition of these horses, horses previously attached to the 8th Cavalry could be returned to the 4th Cavalry Troops.[166]

The only event of importance in December took place on 5 December when the Field Artillery Inspector for the Department of the Missouri arrived for the annual inspection. He departed the post on 9 December.[167]

Chapter 4: Jefferson Barracks and the Army Reorganize

The year 1903 began as 1902 had ended. Col. Rucker remained in command of a garrison that included twenty-seven officers and 580 enlisted men. The 3rd Squadron, 4th Cavalry and 2nd Squadron, 8th Cavalry, made up the bulk of the officers and men, along with 156 recruits, 117 of which were white mounted service recruits. There was one officer and eleven enlisted men listed as casuals and twenty-one general prisoners.[11]

January 1903 did see the passage of Public Law 57-33, commonly referred to as the Dick Act that had far-reaching effects not only for Jefferson Barracks and the State of Missouri, but for the entire country and the Army. Passed on 21 January 1903, The Act clarified the concept of a universal militia. It divided the militia into two groups. The first group consisted of the organized militia, known as the National Guard, which was defined as the regularly enlisted, organized and uniformed active militia of the several states and territories. The Reserve Militia, which consisted of all able-bodied male citizens 18 to 45, made up the second group. For the first time, the Dick Act provided that general military stores, as well as arms and equipment, were to be offered to militia units that drilled at summer encampments of not less than five days. The militia units were to be periodically inspected by Regular Army officers and Regular officers were detailed to the militia. In addition, National Guard officers became eligible to attend Regular Army schools and Guardsmen received full pay and allowances while on maneuvers with the Regular Army. This Act was the first in a series of bills from the establishment of an enlisted Army Reserve, in 1912, through the sweeping National Defense Act of 1916 and its 1920 Amendments that laid the groundwork for the Army's contemporary Reserve components.[11]

Following the passage of the Dick Act, Secretary of War Root achieved another of his objectives when Congress passed the General Staff Corps on 14 February 1903. With the new National Staff of forty-five officers, the Army was able to formulate cohesive continuing military policies for the first time and take those planning steps which are essential for a successful mobilization.[11]

This act abolished the separate office of General Commanding the Army; provided for a Military Chief of Staff to the President, who, acting under the direction of the President, or of the Secretary of War representing him, should have supervision not only of all troops of the line, but of the special staff and supply departments which had until then reported directly to the Secretary of War; and it created for the assistance of the Chief of Staff a corps of forty-four officers who were relieved of all other duties.

A board was convened in March to recommend selections for the new corps. It consisted of Generals Samuel B.M. Young [a Jefferson Barracks alum], Adna Chaffee, John C. Bates, Tasker Bliss, Wallace F. Randolph and Major Henry A. Greene, recorder. The board function was to recommend forty-two officers for the General Staff. The President selected the three general officers without action of the board.[11] Major General Samuel B.M. Young, who served with the 3rd Cavalry at Jefferson Barracks in September 1891, became the first Chief of Staff of the Army.[11]

February and March 1903 saw little change in the composition of Jefferson Barracks. Col. Rucker remained in command of the 4th and 8th Cavalry Troops at the Post. Their numbers did increase from 449 enlisted men in February to 552 in March. The Mounted Service recruits provided the majority of the remainder of the garrison, 131 in February and 110 in March.[11]

Major Frank A. Edwards, 4th Cavalry, relieved Col. Rucker in command of Jefferson Barracks on 22 April. The 4th Cavalry and 8th Cavalry Troops performed the usual garrison duties until April 27. The next day, April 28, they left the post and marched to the Fair Grounds in St. Louis where they went into camp. They were there to participate in the Dedicatory Ceremonies of the Louisiana Purchase Exposition. Col. George S. Anderson, who had commanded the 38th U.S. Volunteer Infantry when it organized at Jefferson Barracks in 1899, commanded the troops at the Fair Grounds. Anderson had recently been promoted to colonel and assigned to command the 8th Cavalry.

The garrison had grown to 800 enlisted men. Most of this increase came in the form of 244 recruits at the Post.[11]

In addition to the troops from Jefferson Barracks, the entire brigade of the Missouri National Guard (except the 1st Regiment from St. Louis which performed guard duty at the Fair Grounds) mobilized in St. Louis on April 29 to take part in the great military parade and other exercises attending the Dedicatory Ceremonies of the Louisiana Purchase Exposition held on April 30 and the 1st and 2nd of May 1903. Due to the expenses involved, each company was only allowed fifty men. Thus, approximately 1800 Missouri National Guardsmen participated.

To this was added a Battalion of Engineers, two additional Troops of the 8th Cavalry, four Battalions of Field Artillery, two Battalions each of the 3rd, 20th and 22nd Infantries, and bands of the 4th and 8th Cavalry, 3rd, 20th and 22nd Infantries and the 9th Band of the Artillery Corps. The Regular Army troops assembled for the dedicatory ceremonies, organized as a division under the command of Major General John C. Bates, commanding the Department of the Missouri, numbered 173 officers and 3,343 men.

The command (except for the Cavalry from Jefferson Barracks, which was in camp) was comfortably quartered in the Educational Building on the Fair Grounds. The officers and men messed in the same building under the very satisfactory management of Lt. Col. Abiel L. Smith, Chief Commissary of the division.

The troops made an excellent appearance and on several occasions, when not occupied with other duties, engaged in military athletics, which were well received.[11]

The parade was the largest military parade since the Civil War. Major General Henry C. Corbin, Adjutant General of the Army, reviewed the parade. The troops from Jefferson Barracks were equipped with the first issue of the new full dress (mounted) uniform, consisting of the new bell cap, a dress coat, olive drab breeches, leggings, and tan shoes. Breast cords were worn for the first time.

An unintended result of the dedicatory ceremonies took place at Jefferson Barracks. While the post was virtually deserted fourteen prisoners escaped. The purported leader of the escape, a man named Frank A. Detterman, 37th Volunteer Infantry, hit the sergeant of the guard with the ball of his ball and chain. Nine of the prisoners were re-captured, including Detterman. The remainder of the escaped prisoners remained at large.

Major Edwards commanded Jefferson Barracks until 29 May, when Col. Anderson relieved him. The troops returned from the Fair Grounds on 3 May. The 3rd Squadron, 4th Cavalry, left on 7 May for their annual target practice. They arrived at Arcadia on 10 May and participated in target practice for a month. The 2nd Squadron, 8th Cavalry, Troops E, F, G and H, remained at Jefferson Barracks and performed the usual garrison duties.[11]

A different type of event took place near Jefferson Barracks on 6 May when Dong Gong, a Chinese man with leprosy escaped from confinement at the Quarantine Hospital, about two miles below Jefferson Barracks. Gong had been confined at the hospital for a year and a half. Dr. Woodruff, Hospital Superintendent, at once ordered a search for the dangerous patient. Woodruff stated that Gong's condition had not changed materially since his ostracism from society, but he was too dangerous to be left at large. [As of the publication of this article, Gong had not been located.][11]

June and July 1903 proved to be an almost carbon copy of May. Col. Anderson remained in command with the 3rd Squadron, 4th Cavalry, and the 2nd Squadron, 8th Cavalry, making up the bulk of the garrison. The 3rd Squadron, 4th Cavalry, remained at Arcadia and the 2nd Squadron, 8th Cavalry, performed the usual garrison duties.[11]

Extensive flooding in Missouri and Kansas in June brought a request for assistance from Mr. F.G. Niedringhaus of St. Louis. In compliance with a telegraphic communication from the War Department to provide all possible assistance, the Jefferson Barracks Quartermaster provided seventeen common tents, eight wall tents and seventeen gold-medal tents for use by flood sufferers, and the Depot Quartermaster in St. Louis furnished twelve hospital tents.[11]

Also in June, Sgt. Klein, steward of the General Mess, took off with several thousand dollars of mess funds. Sgt. Klein was never apprehended and the shortage of funds had to be made up from savings in ration funds.[11]

During June, the 8th Cavalry lost one of its oldest soldiers, Regimental Quartermaster Sgt. Kennedy. Sgt. Kennedy died and was buried in the Jefferson Barracks National Cemetery.

A couple of items in General Bates' 1903 Annual Report to the War Department directly concerned Jefferson Barracks. The first item described the Jefferson Barracks hospital as "a very old structure. The internal arrangements are antiquated, and the location of the kitchen and dining room in the basement is extremely objectionable. The plumbing is decidedly old style, though fairly efficient. The building does not fit with the remainder of the post." General Bates recommended the construction of a new hospital[11]

The second item came from the Inspector of small-arms practice, via General Bates, and concerned the target range at Arcadia. The Inspector recommended the construction of a new rifle pit which would have a rubble masonry retaining wall and a cement floor. The rifle pit currently in use had a wooden post retaining wall and a dirt floor, which often became unusable after a heavy rain. This condition was exacerbated due to the fact that the pit was located at the foot of a hill. The Inspector went on to report that as long as Jefferson Barracks was maintained, permanent improvements had to be made, including roads and several necessary bridges. He also considered the water supply unsatisfactory and recommended either an artesian well be sunk or that water be piped from springs in the vicinity. Although the reservation was fenced, the fence posts had been placed at 15-foot intervals which allowed the wire to sag, allowing cattle and hogs entrance. Apparently, the current appropriations could not come close to covering the cost of the above improvements, therefore, the Inspector-General recommended and desired a special appropriation.[11]

The 3rd Squadron, 4th Cavalry, returned from Arcadia on August 3, and the 2nd Squadron, 8th Cavalry, left for Arcadia on August 5. Troop K, 4th Cavalry, departed on 31 August for West Point, Kentucky, to attend maneuvers.[11]

One significant change that occurred in August was the promotion of Lt. Col. John A. Kress, long-time commander of the St. Louis Powder Depot. He was promoted to colonel on 1 August, to brigadier general on 16 August, and then he retired on 17 August 1903.[11] Major William A. Schunk, 8th Cavalry, was detached to temporary command of the Powder Depot. His command consisted of twenty enlisted men.

On 8 August, Major General Samuel B.M. Young assumed command of the Army. A week later, he relinquished that command and retired from the active military after 40 years of service.[11]

Major Frank A. Edwards took command of Jefferson Barracks again on 23 September, relieving Col. George S. Anderson, who had been ordered on detached service at Chicago and West Point, Kentucky. Edwards also took command of the St. Louis Powder Depot on 18 September. Several officers joined the garrison in September. 1st Lt. Llewellyn P. Williamson, Assistant Surgeon, joined on 25 September from San Francisco; 1st Lt. William B. Renziehausen, commanding Troop M, 4th Cavalry, joined on 17 September from Fort Leavenworth; and 2nd Lt. Alexander M. Milton, Troop L, 4th Cavalry, joined on 11 September from the U.S. Military Academy after graduation leave.[11]

Troop I, 4th Cavalry, left on 25 September for maneuvers at West Point, Kentucky, joining Troop K. The 2nd Squadron, 8th Cavalry, attended annual target practice at Arcadia from 1 September until 12 September. Then on 25 September, they moved to West Point, Kentucky, for maneuvers.[11]

Major Edwards remained in command of Jefferson Barracks during October, but was relieved of command of the Powder Depot on 6 October, when Capt. James B. Hughes, 4th Cavalry, took command. Troop I, 4th Cavalry, and Troops E, F, G and H, 8th Cavalry, returned from detached service at West Point, Kentucky, on 17 October. Troop K, 4th Cavalry, remained at Camp Young, West Point, until 7 November. Troop K furnished scouts and troops participating in the maneuvers. Since 15 October, the Troop repaired fences and performed other repairs to property damaged by troops during the maneuvers.

It seems that not everything during the maneuvers was work related. Troop K played several baseball games while at West Point. On October 2 Troop K beat the 7th Cavalry team 9 to 1. On 4 October, they lost 19 to 11 to a team composed of players picked from the 1st, 3rd, and 20th Infantries. Then on 7 October they beat a team of players picked from the 3rd and 20th Infantries, 7 to 4. and lost again, 12 to 8, on 11 October to the team that had beaten them 19 to 11.[11]

During October, Troops L and M, 4th Cavalry, commanded by 1st Lt. George M. Lee, left on the 17th for Fort Logan H. Roots, Arkansas. Lee returned to Jefferson Barracks on 18 October. He left again on 20 October for detached service in Des Moines, Iowa.[11]

Jefferson Barracks had three commanding officers during November. Major Edwards relinquished command to Major Charles B. Ayers, 8th Cavalry, on 3 November. Edwards had been ordered on detached service to Rome, Italy, as Military Attache. Ayers commanded the post from 3 November to 25 November, when Col. Anderson returned from detached service and resumed command.[11]

As of 7 November, the troops assigned to Jefferson Barracks had all returned. The garrison then consisted of twenty-five officers and 504 enlisted men, plus 178 recruits, 13 casuals and 43 general prisoners.[11]

The only significant changes in December were in the number of troops, increasing to 758 enlisted men. Cavalry recruits continued to provide the single largest number of personnel, 203 in December. The recruits had their own barracks and their own personnel. 2nd Lt. Frank E. Davis, 8th Cavalry, was in charge of the Recruit Detachment.[11]

The principal enlisted men at the post throughout 1903 remained relatively unchanged. Jeremiah James, Ordnance Sergeant, had been at the Post since 26 December 1901; Otto Kraatz, Post Quartermaster Sergeant, since 22 February 1902; George Gibbens, Sergeant in the Hospital Corps, since 29 November 1902; William C. Dougherty, Signal Corps, joined 11 December replacing Henry Drum, who transferred to Fort McDowell, California in December. Drum had been at Jefferson Barracks since 6 November 1902.[11]

Capt. Hughes remained in command of the St. Louis Powder Depot at Jefferson Barracks. His command consisted of nineteen enlisted men.[11]

Toward the end of 1903, the War Department granted a right of way, 70 feet by 700 feet, through Jefferson Barracks to the St. Louis and Iron Mountain Railroad for the erection of a new depot. The old depot stood about 200 yards to the south, where the World War II swimming pool was later located.[11]

Early in the new year, on 15 January, General Order No. 15 rearranged the Army's military commands. The United States was organized geographically into five military divisions, each of which was subdivided into two or more military departments. A major general commanded each division, with a brigadier general in command of each department.

The great stretch of country drained by the Ohio and Missouri rivers, the upper Mississippi valleys, and the states along the Canadian border from Lake Erie to western Montana comprised the Northern Division, which was divided into the Department of the Lakes, the Department of the Missouri, and the Department of Dakota.[11]

The states of Iowa, Nebraska, South Dakota, Wyoming [except for Yellowstone National Park], Kansas, and Missouri made up the Department of the Missouri. These states contained military installations at Jefferson Barracks; Fort Crook, Nebraska; Fort D.A. Russell, Wyoming; Fort Des Moines, Iowa; Fort Leavenworth, Kansas; Fort Mackenzie, Wyoming; Fort Meade, South Dakota; Fort Niobrara, Nebraska; Fort Riley, Kansas; Fort Robinson, Nebraska; and Fort Washakie, Wyoming.[11]

On 14 January, General Order No. 9 ordered another significant event that directly affected Jefferson Barracks when the section of the post which had been set aside in 1840 for use as a powder depot was turned over to the Quartermaster Department. This included all buildings, furnishings, and supplies contained in the approximately 150 acres of the northwest portion of the military reservation. The buildings included seven powder magazines, one set of officers' quarters, three small double cottages, three single cottages, and a stable. The transfer order provided that an ordnance sergeant be detached as storekeeper of the 2,240,000 pounds of nitre then in storage. He had the privilege of living quarters on the grounds. The powder from the magazines had already been shipped to the Rock Island Arsenal.[11]

At the time of its closing, the St. Louis Powder Depot consisted of one officer, Capt. James B. Hughes, 4th Cavalry, commanding, and sixteen enlisted men.[11]

Major Charles B. Ayers, 8th Cavalry, took command of Jefferson Barracks on 23 January, when Col. George S. Anderson left on leave. His command remained the 2nd Battalion, 8th Cavalry, and the 3rd Battalion, 4th Cavalry, a total of twenty-four officers and 543 enlisted men. Add to this one officer, 1st Lt. Theodore B. Taylor, 11th Cavalry, who was attached to Troop K, 4th Cavalry for duty; 265 Cavalry recruits; twenty-one Field Artillery recruits; fifteen casuals and twenty-eight general prisoners, for an aggregate total at Jefferson Barracks of twenty-five officers and 872 enlisted personnel. It should also be noted that all of the men carried on the rolls as casuals were either awaiting trial or charges.[11]

In late January, the presence of smallpox among the troops at Jefferson Barracks resulted in the vaccination of all personnel in the 4th and 8th Cavalry regiments. 2nd Lt. Frank E. Davis, 8th Cavalry and Squadron Quartermaster, was moved to the county quarantine station suffering from the disease. 1st Lt. Alexander B. Coxe, 1st Lt. John Watson and 2nd Lt. Frank Keller, all in the 8th Cavalry, were exposed to the disease and placed in quarantine as of 21 January.[11]

Since Jefferson Barracks was one of three primary recruit depots in the country, [Columbus Barracks, Ohio, and David's Island, New York, were the other two] a description of the training is in order. Jefferson Barracks had 265 Cavalry recruits in January 1904. This number increased to 373 in February.[11]

There were three categories of recruits at the depot: those who had been there less than fifteen days, those with fifteen to thirty days at the post, and those that had re-enlisted. The schedule that provided order to the lives of the first two groups started with reveille at 5:30 a.m. In the mornings, recruits had three drill periods at which they learned to stand at attention, turn the Army way, march, and salute. The advanced group drilled more, but continued to have readings of the Articles of War, as well as assorted lectures on other introductory subjects. In the afternoon, physical exercises and games kept them occupied. There were also daily formations as recruits graduated to the other sections, which also meant moving to different barracks. Although the advanced recruits could expect to work in fatigue details around the post, most of the more unpleasant duties fell to the older soldiers in the last section.[11]

A detailed account of Cavalry recruit training came from William L. Banks, 10th Cavalry. A sergeant would take charge of about six recruits. Training began bareback. First, recruits had to learn to mount and dismount properly. Once that had been practiced and accomplished, they had to learn to keep their balance with the help of stirrups on the blanket, held in place by a circingle [a large webbed belt on the horse's back] as the horse walked around a ring. From a walk, they progressed to a trot, then to a gallop. After the recruits mastered these basics, the sergeant issued them saddles, and they went through the entire process again until they did it well. Finally, he taught them the rudiments of mounted drill, i.e., staying together in fours, and the various maneuvers. Then they were, perhaps, ready for an exciting ride down a steep, sandy bridle path. Ideally, training would progress from the individual through the squad and on to the regiment with simulated combat conditions.[11]

Another important part of training was physical fitness. This training had developed to a high level in the 1890s, so much so that Nelson A. Miles, General-in-Chief of the Army, referred to the Army of those days as a "corps of athletes." Soldiers, not just recruits, went through a daily routine of calisthenics, with Infantrymen also doing bayonet drills and various exercises with rifles, while the Cavalry and Field Artillery had their workouts with horses. The Army encouraged athletics and even provided expense money for competitors to visit other posts.[11]

Col. Anderson returned from leave and relieved Major Ayers on 16 February. The composition of the garrison did not change except for an increase in numbers, to twenty-seven officers and 923 enlisted men. The only event of significance took place on 26 February, when under the authority of the Secretary of War, the 8th Cavalry Band, twenty-eight enlisted men, left the Post for Fort Sill, Oklahoma Territory, for temporary duty.[11]

The Department of the Missouri changed commanders on 23 February. Brigadier General Theodore J. Wint relieved Brigadier General Eugene A. Carr. Carr had previously served at Jefferson Barracks and had been breveted to lieutenant colonel for gallantry and meritorious service at the Battle of Wilson's Creek, Missouri, on 10 August 1861.[11]

March 1904 witnessed few changes to the Jefferson Barracks garrison. Col. Anderson remained in command of a garrison consisting of twenty-eight officers and 817 enlisted men. Lt. Col. Samuel W. Fountain reported for duty with the 3rd Squadron, 4th Cavalry, on 18 March. Fountain became the second ranking officer at the post.[11] Fountain had joined the Army as a private in Company K, 140th Ohio Infantry on 2 May 1864. He attended the U.S. Military Academy after the Civil War, graduating in 1870.[11]

On 1 March 1904, a battalion of Philippine Scouts, 424 officers and men commanded by Capt. William H. Johnson, 16th Infantry, received orders for duty at the Louisiana Purchase Exposition in St. Louis. Although they encamped at the fairgrounds, Jefferson Barracks provided subsistence and medical care for the Scouts.[11]

Although the Jefferson Barracks garrison decreased in numbers to twenty officers and 673 enlisted men in April, two troops [L and M] of the 11th Cavalry joined the post on 25 April. The 11th Cavalry had departed Manila, Philippine Islands, on March 15. Capt. Powell Clayton, Jr., commanded the 11th Cavalry troops when they arrived.[11]

The 2nd Squadron, Field and Staff, 8th Cavalry, left for their annual target practice at Arcadia on 24 April, under the command of Major Ayers. The troops once again traveled overland to Arcadia instead of via rail.

Target practice made up a significant part of a unit's field training. In the two decades prior to the Spanish-American War, the Army developed an intensive, highly competitive marksmanship program but, like training in general, it declined during the period 1898 to 1902. The increased range of small arms and the fact that fewer recruits were familiar with weapons prompted Secretary of War Elihu Root to emphasize the importance of marksmanship in 1903. That year, the Army sponsored a national meet and was embarrassed to have National Guard teams outscore Regular Army teams. Few soldiers reached that level of competition, but there were monthly pay increases of $3 per month for all those who achieved the level of expert; a sharpshooter earned $2 per month; and a marksman, $1 per month.[11]

In its continued support in the community, the 3rd Squadron, 4th Cavalry, commanded by Lt. Col. Fountain marched to St. Louis on 30 April to participate in the opening ceremonies for the Louisiana Purchase Exposition. They returned the same day.[11]

An interesting article appeared in *Guide to St. Louis and World's Fair 1904* by the Greeley Printery of St. Louis. The article described Jefferson Barracks as follows: "A military post of importance, is situated ten miles south of St. Louis, and can be reached by trolley car, train or steamboat. It is a point of historic as well as contemporaneous interest. Both the North and the South may boast of famous men who served at Jefferson Barracks. Among some of those who were officers, there may be named General Robert E. Lee, General Winfield Scott Hancock, General Albert Sidney Johnston, (whose death on the field is claimed by the historians to have turned the tide at Shiloh and hastened the end of the Confederacy), General Jubal A. Early, and last, but not least, Ulysses S. Grant. General Jacob Smith, who attained fame by his conduct in the Philippine disturbances, was one of the recent commandants of the Barracks. Aside from the historic interest attached to the place, the Barracks is a delightful place to spend a day. The scenery is beautiful. The river flows majestically along at the foot of the bluff of the Reservation, and a view of many miles can be had on a clear day. The National Cemetery is on the Reservation and is a pleasant place to visit. A Market or Laclede car, east on Market St. in front of the Station, will take you to Broadway in fifteen minutes. Here you transfer south. The Broadway car takes you direct to the Barracks." The next article in the guide is on the Anheuser and Lemp breweries.

Col. Anderson remained in command of the twenty officers and 178 enlisted men that comprised the Jefferson Barracks garrison during May 1904. The 8th Cavalry troopers remained at Arcadia throughout the month. The Field, Staff and Band, 3rd Squadron, 4th Cavalry participated in the Memorial Day exercises of the G.A.R. at the Louisiana Purchase Exposition. They marched thirty miles to St. Louis and back.[11]

On 31 May, a battalion of cadets from West Point visited the Exposition, making Jefferson Barracks casual headquarters. Various other units assigned to duty at the Exposition used the post as a base for equipment and supplies.[11]

Recruits continued to come to Jefferson Barracks for training and be transferred to units throughout the country. In May, two groups of recruits transferred to Angel Island, California, and one group to Fort Des Moines, Iowa and Fort Riley, Kansas.[11]

The 8th Cavalry troops returned from Arcadia on 4 June, and the 3rd Squadron, 4th Cavalry, commanded by Lt. Col. Fountain left on 13 June for Arcadia.[11]

It is interesting that according to the Chief Commissary of the Army, Jefferson Barracks had purchased all needed fresh beef in St. Louis for the previous six months. The price paid for this beef was 5.17 cents per pound, the lowest of any post in the Department of the Missouri. Fort Mackenzie, Wyoming, paid the highest price of nine cents per pound.[11]

In the reports of the Department of the Missouri for Fiscal Year 1904, the subject of inadequate guardhouse facilities was raised. The crowding of prisoners and consequent insufficient air space, the lack of bathing facilities, and the absence of water-closet conveniences were the reported unsanitary conditions at the Jefferson Barracks guardhouse. The barracks for quartering recruits at the post also were reported as being frequently taxed to capacity.[11] During June, the last month covered by this report, forty-six general prisoners were confined in the guardhouse and 258 recruits were in training.[11]

On 21 July, Troops L and M, 11th Cavalry, proceeded to Arcadia by rail and on 24 July the 3rd Squadron, 4th Cavalry, returned from Arcadia. 1st Lt. Edward R. Tompkins commanded the 11th Cavalry contingent. Col. Anderson paid a visit to the Rifle Range on 9 and 10 July[11]

The number of enlisted men at the Post increased during July to 887. Most of this increase can be credited to the 345 recruits at the post.[11]

Again in July Jefferson Barracks troopers took part in ceremonies at the World's Fair by marching in the 4th of July parade.

In August, the number of troops at Jefferson Barracks reached its highest number in quite some time with twenty-nine officers and 945 enlisted personnel. The 4th Cavalry numbered ten officers and 246 enlisted men. The 8th Cavalry numbered thirteen officers and 272 enlisted men, and the 11th Cavalry had two officers and 117 men. There were also 288 recruits, seven casuals, and fifty-two general prisoners present.[11]

The Field, Staff, and Band, 2nd Squadron, 8th Cavalry and 3rd Squadron, 4th Cavalry, took part in the Philippine celebration at the World's Fair on 13 August. The next day Troops L & M, 11th Cavalry, commanded by Lt. Col. Fountain, left by rail for the Ohio State encampment at Armitage, Ohio. They returned on 24 August.[11]

The biggest event of the month and probably for several years took place on 17 August when the Chief of Staff, Lt. General Adna R. Chaffee and Brigadier General Grote Hutcheson arrived for an inspection tour of the post. They left the same day.[11]

No significant changes or events took place in September. The primary units remained unchanged, with thirty-two officers and 833 enlisted personnel comprising the garrison.[11]

October, however, saw the first major change in personnel since the arrival of Troops L and M, 11th Cavalry, in April. In compliance with General Order No. 98 and General Order No. 134, Troops I, K, L and M, 4th Cavalry, left Jefferson Barracks at 3:00 p.m. on 14 October, to take station at the Presidio of Monterey, California. They arrived on 19 October. The next day, 15 October, Troops L and M, 11th Cavalry, left Jefferson Barracks and proceeded by rail to Fort Des Moines, arriving October 16. Lastly, on 27 October, the 3rd Squadron, Troops I, K, L and M, 9th Cavalry, arrived from the Presidio of San Francisco, California, and took station at Jefferson Barracks. Lt. Col. Edward A. Godwin commanded the 9th Cavalry troops. The Jefferson Barracks garrison then consisted of the 2nd

Squadron, 8th Cavalry, fifteen officers and 270 enlisted men; the 3rd Squadron, 9th Cavalry, seven officers and 244 enlisted men; twenty-three Hospital Corpsmen; two Signal Corpsmen; three Ordnance Department men; thirty-three Cavalry recruits; eighty-four Field Artillery recruits; ten casuals; and fifty-six general prisoners. The aggregate total was twenty-seven officers and 662 enlisted men.[11]

Again, in October troops from Jefferson Barracks participated in ceremonies at the World's Fair. The Field, Staff, Band and 2nd Squadron, 8th Cavalry, marched to the fair grounds on 11 October to take part in the Missouri Day parade. On 19 October Troops E and H, 8th Cavalry, participated in the District of Columbia Day parade.[11]

The only significant events in November also involved ceremonies at the World's Fair. Troops E and G, 8th Cavalry, commanded by Capt. Ellwood W. Evans marched to St. Louis to serve as escort to Prince Fashimi, Lt. General of the Japanese Army. Then on 25 November, Troop F, 8th Cavalry, again commanded by Capt. Evans, marched to St. Louis and remained on duty at the World's Fair until 27 November, escorting the President of the United States, Theodore Roosevelt. On the 26th, the Field, Staff, and Troops E, G and H, 8th Cavalry, and the Field, Staff, and Troops I, K, and L, 9th Cavalry, marched to St. Louis and participated in a parade for the President.[11]

The year 1904 ended on a quiet note, except for a fire on the night of 13 December that destroyed the center tower and west wing of Barracks No. 29. Troops E and H, 8th Cavalry, occupied the area destroyed.[11]

Col. Anderson remained in command of Jefferson Barracks. The post garrison consisted of twenty-five officers and 708 enlisted men.[11]

Chapter 5 - The Quiet Before the Storm

As our look at the year 1905 begins, it is perhaps a good time to briefly examine the overall strength of the United States Army. This will make it possible to ascertain how the troop strength at Jefferson Barracks fits into the overall strength of the Army. As of 28 November 1904, the Army consisted of approximately 3,744 officers and 56,439 enlisted men, a total of 60,183. An additional 3,167 men served in the Hospital Corps, excluded from classification as part of the enlisted force of the Army by the Act of Congress dated March 1887. Also, 21 officers and 549 men served in the Puerto Rico regiment, and 100 officers and 3,978 enlisted men served in the Philippine Scouts. Of these numbers combined, 2,820 officers and 42,682 enlisted men served in the United States; 739 officers and 11,164 enlisted men served in the Philippine Islands; 5 officers and 133 enlisted men served in the Hawaiian Islands; and 53 officers and 992 enlisted men served in Alaska.[1]

At Jefferson Barracks, Col. George S. Anderson remained in command of the 8th Cavalry and the post. The garrison consisted of the 8th Cavalry, Field and Staff, Band, and Troops E, F, G and H, a total of 16 officers and 266 enlisted men; and the 9th Cavalry, Troops I, K, L and M, nine officers and 250 enlisted men. Recruits numbered 194 Cavalry and 29 Foot Service. There were also fourteen officers and fourteen enlisted men on casual status, nineteen Hospital Corpsmen, two Signal Corps members, three Ordnance Department enlisted men and sixty-three general prisoners. The aggregate strength at Jefferson Barracks came to thirty officers and 766 enlisted men. [2]

In addition to Col. Anderson, the senior officers at the post included Lt. Col. Edward A. Godwin, commanding the 3rd Squadron, 9th Cavalry; Major William B. Banister, Post Surgeon; Major Charles G. Ayers, commanding the 2nd Squadron, 8th Cavalry; Captain Stephen L.H. Slocum, 8th Cavalry, Post Adjutant and Recruiting Officer; Captain Malvern H. Barnum, 8th Cavalry, Post Quartermaster; and Captain Charles T. Sawtelle, Jr., 8th Cavalry, Post Commissary Officer.[3]

Col. Anderson remained in command of Jefferson Barracks until 15 February, when Lt. Col. Godwin relieved him. The 2nd Squadron, 8th Cavalry, left Jefferson Barracks at 5:00 p.m., on 15 February, en route to San Francisco and the Philippine Islands. Capt. Barnum, Post Quartermaster, commanded the 8th Cavalry troops as Col. Anderson and Major Ayers remained at Jefferson Barracks on casual status as witnesses in a General Court Martial proceeding. In addition to these two senior 8th Cavalry officers, Capt. Slocum, Capt. Ellwood W. Evans, Capt. Charles T. Sawtelle, Jr., Capt. Rush S. Wells, 1st Lt. Osman Latrobe, Jr., 2nd Lt. Sebring C. Megill and Regimental Sergeant Major Charles H. Whitehurst, 8th Cavalry, remained at the post as witnesses in the court martial. Capt. Benjamin A. Poore, 6th Infantry, arrived at Jefferson Barracks as a witness in the same court martial.[4] Col. Albert L. Meyer, 11th Infantry, served as president of the General Court Martial, while Major Homer W. Wheeler, 11th Cavalry; Capt. William E. Welsh, 30th Infantry; Capt. Ralph R. Stogsdall, 30th Infantry; Capt. William Kelly, Engineer Corps; 1st Lt. Samuel Ansell, 11th Infantry; 1st Lt. Edward Davis, 11th Cavalry; 1st Lt. William A. Carleton, 30th Infantry; 1st Lt. James E. Shelly, 11th Cavalry; 1st Lt. Casper W. Cole, 9th Cavalry; 1st Lt. Augustus B. Warfield, Artillery Corps; and 1st Lt. Warren Hammin, Engineer Corps, all arrived at Jefferson Barracks to serve as members of the General Court Martial.[5]

With the departure of the 2nd Squadron, 8th Cavalry, the only regular troops remaining at Jefferson Barracks were the 3rd Squadron, 9th Cavalry, some 235 enlisted men.[6] Lt. Col. Godwin applied to higher headquarters for more troops and Major General John C. Bates recommended that the 30th Infantry at Fort Crook, Nebraska, be sent to Jefferson Barracks. However, the Military Secretary disapproved the request and made a recommendation stating that Jefferson Barracks was to be converted into a recruit depot.

During February 1905, the Jefferson Barracks garrison consisted of fourteen officers and 457 enlisted men. Included in this number were 192 recruits.

Under instructions from the War Department dated 15 February 1905, Jefferson Barracks, along with Fort Slocum, New York and Columbus Barracks, Ohio, were designated the three primary recruit depots in the country. These instructions also changed the recruiting procedure. In addition to mandatory physical examinations by Army doctors, the recruits were required to stay at a recruit depot for instruction until they were deemed ready and fit to join a Regular Army unit. This had been the Army way for recruits until 1894, when the Army had begun to ship recruits directly from recruiting stations to their respective units. This policy proved to be, as one officer bluntly put it, "a complete and dismal failure." In 1905, a recruit could expect to spend twenty-five days learning to be a soldier at a depot before he went out to his unit.[7]

The recruits at depots were organized into provisional companies for instruction and administration with three officers of the general recruiting service assigned to duty with each company. At Jefferson Barracks, sixteen sergeants and twelve corporals were detailed from regiments serving in the United States for duty with the recruit companies for instruction.[8]

It should be noted that prior to 15 February 1905, it was found necessary to discontinue Jefferson Barracks for prison purposes.[9] This would explain the drop in the general prisoner population from sixty-three in January 1905, to four in February.

In February, Jefferson Barracks provided the venue for an interesting court martial. Lt. Albert J. Mohn, 4th Cavalry, had been charged and convicted on charges of false muster, but he had appealed the ruling stating that his brother officers wanted to oust him from the Army. He received a new trial that took place at Jefferson Barracks. His original trial had taken place on 14 October 1904. He had been found guilty and fined $25 pay a month for six months. He was detailed at Jefferson Barracks when his troop was sent to Monterey, California a few days later. The charge faced at Jefferson Barracks was that rather than report some of his men absent and subjecting them to punishment, he reported all present. Lt. Mohn asserted that he could produce sufficient evidence to warrant the dismissal of the charge, or at least a reduction of the fine.

Lt. Mohn further declared that he was found guilty unjustly because of a cabal among his brother officers to oust him from the Army because he was not a West Pointer. The verdict of the new trial cannot be found, but according to Post Returns, Lt. Mohn was returned to duty at Jefferson Barracks.[10]

March and April 1905 saw little change in the garrison at Jefferson Barracks. Lt. Col. Godwin remained in command. In March, the garrison consisted of nineteen officers and 482 enlisted men, and in April, eighteen officers and 485 enlisted men.[11]

Under the provisions provided for the new recruit depot detachments, various units began arriving for duty with the recruit companies in March: 1st Lt. John S.E. Young, 5th Cavalry, arrived March 29; 2nd Lt. Daniel D. Gregory, 1st Cavalry, arrived 30 March; 2nd Lt. Nelson A. Goodspeed, 3rd Cavalry, arrived 21 March. Six 1st Cavalry, one 2nd Cavalry, and twelve 15th Cavalry enlisted men arrived for duty with the recruit companies.[12]

In March, there were 177 Cavalry recruits and twenty-four Field Artillery recruits, but in April the numbers increased dramatically as the role of Jefferson Barracks as a recruit depot took effect. In April, there were 303 Cavalry recruits and twenty-nine Field Artillery recruits at the post.[13]

Other changes were in the works. With a $500,000 appropriation, Post Exchanges, schools and libraries were being built. At Jefferson Barracks construction of a Post Exchange building was completed on 30- March, at a cost of $36,928.[14] In addition to the aforementioned buildings, the appropriation also covered the costs incurred for gymnastic equipment, approximately $1,600 for a post the size of Jefferson Barracks, and for bowling alleys, approximately $700.[15]

Also in April, annual target practice began again at the Arcadia Rifle Range. 1st Lt. James E. Fechet, 9th Cavalry, conducted fifty-seven enlisted men of Troop K and two enlisted men from Troop I, 9th Cavalry, to target practice, leaving Jefferson Barracks on 17 April.

Several new officers arrived in April for duty with the recruit companies. Capt. Percy E. Trippe, 12th Cavalry; Capt. Edwin M. Suplee, 14th Cavalry; 1st Lt. William L. Luke, 11th Cavalry; and 1st Lt. Eugene J. Ely, 10th Cavalry; all arrived in April. George W. Pridleau, Chaplain of the 9th Cavalry, reported on 12 April.[16]

The only change of significance in May took place in the number of recruits handled at the post, with 458 Cavalry recruits and thirty-two Field Artillery recruits. Two officers and sixty enlisted men from Troop I, 9th Cavalry, left the post on 19 May for their annual target practice, and Troop K returned on May 29. One hundred and thirty recruits transferred to their units during the month. The next significant transfers were the sixty-eight enlisted men going to the 6th Cavalry at Fort Keogh, Montana, on May 10 and thirty-seven men to the 5th Cavalry at Fort Huachuca, Arizona Territory, on 24 May.[17]

Probably the most significant event to take place in June was the promotion of Edward A. Godwin to the rank of colonel on the 22nd of the month. Col. Godwin relinquished command of the 9th Cavalry, as his promotion to colonel had been accompanied by a transfer to command of the 14th Cavalry. Godwin remained in command of Jefferson Barracks through the end of September as the 14th Cavalry was due to rotate back to the United States from the Philippines in a few months.[18]

Of significance but not directly affecting Jefferson Barracks, the Headquarters of the Northern Division of the Army moved to St. Louis on 10 June. At the same time, Brigadier General Theodore J. Wint relieved Major

General John C. Bates in command of the Northern Division. Major General George M. Randall succeeded Wint on 25 July 1905.[19]

It appears that all the events during June were routine. Troop L, 9th Cavalry, left for Arcadia for their annual target practice on 19 June, and returned from Arcadia on 27 June.[20] It should also be noted that $1,000 was expended on improvements to the Arcadia range. This money was used for five closets for sinks, for grading the range, for a fence, and for a new road to the range.[21]

During June, 529 Cavalry recruits and thirty-seven Field Artillery recruits trained at Jefferson Barracks, and 283 recruits transferred to their permanent units. The largest contingents were eighty-four men for the 1st Cavalry at Fort Clark, Texas and sixty-two men for the 13th Cavalry at Fort Riley, Kansas.[22]

July, August and September proved to be carbon copies of June. Troop M, 9th Cavalry left for Arcadia on 19 July. A total of 648 recruits were in training during July, 506 in August, and 468 during September. The number of recruits transferred in August came to 416, with 323 in September. The largest contingents were 107 men in August to the 4th Cavalry at the Presidio of San Francisco and eighty-three recruits in September to the 12th Cavalry at Fort Oglethorpe, Georgia.[23]

During July, yellow fever had become epidemic at Jackson Barracks, just outside of New Orleans, Louisiana. The commander of the post, Major Charles J. Bailey, had requested that the soldiers and officers at Jackson Barracks be moved to Chickamauga Park, Georgia, because the disease had gotten so bad. On 25 August, soldiers from Jefferson Barracks captured a steamer, the *Alma Eva*, which was said to be carrying yellow fever refugees. The vessel was detained at quarantine outside of St. Louis.[24]

On 30 September, Col. Godwin left for the Presidio of San Francisco, as his new regiment, the 14th Cavalry, was due to arrive at that post from the Philippines. Lt. Col. Herbert E. Tutherly succeeded Godwin in command of Jefferson Barracks.

Tutherly commanded a garrison that consisted of eleven officers and 715 enlisted men. Of these 715 enlisted men, 252 belonged to the 3rd Battalion, 9th Cavalry, and 353 were recruits in training. A total of 274 recruits transferred to their permanent units during October. Most of these men transferred in one- to six-man groups, except for the fifty-one men who went to the 3rd Cavalry at Fort Snelling, Minnesota.[25]

In November, a new School of Instruction began at Jefferson Barracks. On 24 July, Col. Godwin had requested authority from the Military Secretary to organize a band and suggested it be used as a School of Instruction. The band was authorized, and instruments ordered on 8 November.[26]

There were 376 recruits training at Jefferson Barracks during November and 282 transferred to their permanent units.[27]

At the end of the year 1905, Lt. Col. Tutherly commanded a garrison of fifteen officers and 710 enlisted men. Of these enlisted men, 251 served in the 9th Cavalry and 429 were recruits in training. Senior officers at the post included Major Augustus C. Macomb, commanding the 3rd Squadron, 9th Cavalry since his arrival on 17 October; Major William B. Bannister, Post Surgeon; and Capt. William C. Cannon, Post Quartermaster.[28]

Many improvements had been made on the post during 1905. In addition to repairing the fire damage to Building No. 29, modern plumbing had been installed at a cost of $2,727. The Post Exchange was constructed and two wings were to be added. The old Post Exchange building became a barracks, to be converted to a gymnasium. A new Post Bakery and coal sheds were also erected. Adequate and satisfactory water had always been a problem. To solve this problem, a second steel tank with a capacity of 150,000 gallons was erected near the west gate at a cost of $12,900.[29]

1906

The new year dawned just as 1905 had ended. Lt. Col. Tutherly commanded the Jefferson Barracks garrison, which consisted of the 3rd Squadron of the 9th Cavalry, nine officers and 256 enlisted men, and a total of 492 recruits for the Cavalry, Field Artillery, Coast Artillery, and Infantry, with one recruit each for the Signal Corps and Hospital Corps.[30] These numbers changed only slightly during the first six months of 1906.[31] During January, 309 recruits transferred to their permanent stations; in February, 243; in March, 345; in April, 112; in May, 400; and in June, 223.[32]

Two human interest stories involving soldiers at Jefferson Barracks appeared in the *St. Louis Post-Dispatch*. The first appeared on 3 January 1906. It was about soldier F.J. Edwards, who had been arrested in East St. Louis on

15 October 1905. Edwards' wife, 19-year-old Helen Edwards (nee Tebeau) told her sad story. The couple had been married for only four days when Edwards received orders to transfer with his troop to Des Moines, Iowa. Edwards had deserted from his post at Jefferson Barracks because he could not bear to be separated from his bride. He obtained a seven day leave. When he returned to St. Louis to see his wife, he said that he understood that he was to obtain a discharge or a transfer to St. Louis, and so did not return to Iowa as he expected one of those things to happen. Edwards believed that a former suitor for his wife's hand was responsible for his arrest.

Edwards obtained employment as a fireman at the powerhouse of the East St. Louis and Suburban Electric Line and he lived with his wife at 1707 Kansas Avenue. Policeman Hanson said a man approached him on Broadway, told him Edwards was a deserter, gave him his address and told him where Edwards worked. Hanson arrested Edwards at the powerhouse and Edwards was locked up at the East St. Louis Police station.

Mrs. Edwards started for Jefferson Barracks as soon as she learned of her husband's arrest, to intercede with the Jefferson Barracks commander for him. She telephoned home that the colonel was not at the Barracks, but said she would stay until Wednesday to see him when he was due to return.

Edwards said that the officers at the Barracks knew his whereabouts and did not care to have him apprehended. He was 32 years old. The outcome of this story is unknown. Therefore, we do not know if love conquered all.[33]

The other story appeared in the *St. Louis Post-Dispatch* on 10 January 1906, and had a much sadder ending. F.C. Luckey, a 28-year-old member of the Hospital Corps at Jefferson Barracks, ended his life by swallowing poison. Luckey had been transferred from Fort Riley, Kansas, at the end of December 1905. His comrades at Jefferson Barracks knew little of his past, but said he appeared morose.

After attending a lecture in the hospital Monday afternoon, Luckey went upstairs to the dormitory and went to bed. Half an hour later, Sgt. George Lewis passed the room and was startled by Luckey's heavy breathing. Major Bannister, Post Surgeon Dr. Davis, Lt. Pyles, Lt. Powell and members of the hospital staff worked over Luckey, but he died six hours after his condition was discovered.

Luckey's comrades believed that in being transferred to Jefferson Barracks, he was compelled to leave his sweetheart and many friends in Fort Riley, where he had spent several years.

The Department of the Missouri with headquarters in St. Louis received a new commander in January 1906. Word was received that Major General Henry C. Corbin would succeed General John F. Weston, who had recently relieved General John C. Bates in command of the Department of the Missouri. General Corbin was best remembered in St. Louis as Grand Marshal of the great military parade on April 30, 1903, marking the dedication of the Louisiana Purchase Exposition.

General Corbin, a native of Ohio, joined the Union Army as a second lieutenant of the 79th Ohio Volunteers. He remained in the Army of the Cumberland until the close of the Civil War, when he was breveted to brigadier general of Volunteers. Corbin remained in the Army and for the next ten years he participated in the Indian campaigns in the West. General Corbin was at President Garfield's side when the President was assassinated. General Corbin came to his new post from command of the Philippine Division of the Army. General Leonard Wood succeeded Corbin in the Philippines.[34]

In March 1906, the War Department mandated an Army-wide systematic training program with an emphasis on realism. While traditional training was to be continued, commands were expected to conduct rigorous field training to include regular practice marches and tactical problems.[35] Possibly as a result of this new directive, the 3rd Squadron, 9th Cavalry, participated in a practice march to the World's Fair Grounds in St. Louis on 24 March, and returned the next day. They traveled thirty-six miles. Then on 27 March, the same units marched to the Missouri River and back, traveling twenty-two miles in one day.[36]

A federal murder trial, the first murder case to be tried in the Federal Court in St. Louis, began on 22 March. Emmet McCoy, a 9th Cavalry trooper at Jefferson Barracks, went on trial in the U.S. Circuit Court, charged with killing Alexander Baskerville, a fellow trooper, in a duel on horseback. It was charged that on the night of 7 December 1905, when both men were on picket duty, they quarreled over the wearing of a sample Army overcoat sent to the Barracks for testing, and that McCoy shot Baskerville. Baskerville, of Troop L, died at 6:40 p.m. in the Post Hospital.[37] A number of officers were summoned as witnesses in the case.

The most significant and regular duty performed by the officers at Jefferson Barracks involved escorting recruits to their permanent duty stations around the country or to the rifle range at Arcadia. Troops K and M, 9th

Cavalry, marched to Arcadia on 23 April, returning on 29 May. 1st Lt. James E. Fechet, 2nd Lt. Beauford R. Campo and 2nd Lt. Edwin L. Cox accompanied the troops to Arcadia.[38]

Troops I and L, 9th Cavalry, marched to Arcadia on 2 June. Capt. Alvarado M. Fuller, 2nd Lt. Joseph V. Kuznik, 2nd Lt. Thomas B. Esty and Contract Surgeon Caspar A. Byars accompanied the troopers to Arcadia.[39]

In his report to the War Department, Brigadier General Theodore Wint, commanding the Department of the Missouri, reported that, as of 30 June 1906, the 3rd Squadron, 9th Cavalry, at Jefferson Barracks was well drilled and in generally good condition, except that their brasses were not in good condition and letters and numbers were missing from the hats of a great number of the men. Wint's report went on to state that the buildings were in good condition and stores were well cared for and in ample supply. The report of the Medical Department contained in Wint's report stated that the Post Hospital was an old building, inadequate for the requirements of the post, but neat and clean. An appropriation had been made for a new hospital.

One negative contained in the report dealt with the Arcadia Rifle Range. Wint reported that the field capacity of the range was not utilized and, as a consequence, an unnecessary length of time was being expended in completing the season's practice.

The only other negative contained in Wint's report had been a constant for years. The high prevalence of malaria at the post. The Medical Department reported 289.4 cases per 1,000 personnel.

Taking the Army as a whole, not just Jefferson Barracks, venereal disease proved once again to be the most important disease affecting the efficiency of the Army. Venereal disease was a major problem during all of the 19th century (see Volume I). Venereal diseases ranked first in hospital admissions, discharges and non-effective with rates of 200.34 per 1,000 for admissions, 341 per 1,000 for discharges, and 12.47 per 1,000 for non-effective. This in turn amounts to 19 percent of all admissions, 15 percent of all discharges and 30 percent of all non-effective for disease. During the 1906 fiscal year, there were constantly 710 men on sick report for venereal disease, equal to the loss for an entire year of service of about eleven full companies of Infantry. These figures represented a totally unsatisfactory condition.[40]

After venereal disease, the most prevalent disease causing admission to the hospital was malarial fevers with an admission rate of 88.85 per 1,000; then diarrheal diseases with an admission rate of 84.67 per 1,000, although this rate showed a marked improvement from the 108.36 of the previous year. Alcoholism was next in order, with an admission rate of 29.65 per 1,000.[41]

As a cause of death tuberculosis topped the list with a rate of 0.68 per 1,000; pneumonia was second at 0.32, down markedly from the 1904 rate of 0.65; typhoid fever was third at 0.29, down from 0.30 the previous year.[42]

As a cause of discharge for disability, venereal diseases ranked at the top with a rate of 3.41 per 1,000; tuberculosis was second at 2.69; defects of vision ranked third at 2.29; and diseases of the heart were fourth at 1.83 per 1,000.[43]

In the Department of the Missouri, Fort Riley had the lowest admission rate, while Jefferson Barracks had the highest non-effective rate. This can be accounted for by the fact that Jefferson Barracks was a rendezvous for recruits whose admission rate is always higher than that for seasoned soldiers.[44]

During the fiscal year ending 30 June 1906, Jefferson Barracks had been supplied with material to standardize the post telephone system. The department's telephone system comprised 179 telephones and 76.5 miles of line, of which 27 miles had been constructed during the current year. [This is the first mention of telephones being in use at Jefferson Barracks.][45]

According to a report prepared by the Office of the Military Secretary, Jefferson Barracks had 3,722 recruits shipped to the Recruit Depot during the fiscal year ending 30 June 1906. Of this number, forty failed to report and 151 deserted after reporting.[46] During that fiscal year, the daily average number of recruits at Jefferson Barracks was 480, and the average number sent to organizations monthly came to 303.[47]

The report of the Military Secretary goes on to state that Lt. Col. Tutherly, commanding Jefferson Barracks, did not believe that it was practicable to add materially to, or change for the better, the system of instruction followed at the Jefferson Barracks Recruit Depot. He did recommend, as worthy of a trial, that exceptionally good men be assigned for short periods to detached duty from time to time in the vicinity of their homes, for the purpose of inducing their comrades to apply for enlistment, and suggested that a bonus of a small sum for each recruit obtained might be given to these men. Tutherly said this experiment, except for the bounty, was very successfully employed by one of the recruiting officers on last year's detail.[48]

This report also cited the enlistments for the St. Louis recruiting station. It appears that a total of 1,235 persons applied for enlistment in St. Louis, but of these only 384 were accepted, meaning 851 applicants were rejected.[49]

The last, but certainly not the least, important topic to be covered in the War Department report had to do with pay. As of June 1906, the pay rate of officers had not changed since 1870. As an example, the pay rates for the three junior grades of officers stood at $1,400 per year for second lieutenants; $1,500 a year for a first lieutenant; and $1,800 a year for a captain. For each five years of service up to twenty years, ten percent was added, which was known as longevity pay. A study showed that these salaries did not meet ordinary expenses.[50]

Like officers, the pay of the enlisted men was small compensation for their services. This applied to all grades, but particularly to non-commissioned officers. While the enlisted man was fed, clothed, and housed by the government, he believed he should get paid more than $13 per month, which was the pay of a private. A corporal made $15 per month and a sergeant $20. The report goes on to state that the small difference in pay between the grades meant that it was difficult to find the right kind of men for the noncommissioned grades.[51]

The second half of 1906 began exactly as the first half ended. Lt. Col. Tutherly continued in command of the post and the Recruit Depot. The 3rd Squadron, 9th Cavalry, provided the troops of the line at the post and 400 recruits trained in the Recruit Depot. The number of recruits transferred during July came to 198.

Lt. Col. Tutherly began a two month leave on 8 August. Lt. Col. Robert K. Evans arrived and assumed command on 24 August. Tutherly returned from leave and then retired on 1 October. Capt. Alvarado M. Fuller commanded in the interim between 8 August and 24 August. Also leaving in August were Capt. Cornelius C. Smith, 14th Cavalry, who transferred to the Division of the Philippines on 22 August and 1st Lt. John S.E. Young, 9th Cavalry, who left on 18 August, being detailed as an instructor at North Carolina College in Raleigh.[52]

Six recruit companies organized on 10 August and were assigned numbers from fourteen through nineteen, inclusive. As a recruit depot, Jefferson Barracks received candidates for enlistment from the recruiting stations in nearby states. Upon arrival, these men were given a thorough physical examination and had the necessary papers for enlistment completed. A complete set of clothing was then issued to the recruit and he was assigned to one of the six recruit companies. He then received twenty-five days of intensive training.[53] The six recruit companies served the General Service Infantry recruits, but there were also Cavalry, Field Artillery, and Coast Artillery recruits at the depot. During August, there were 185 General Service Infantry recruits, 118 Cavalry recruits, 31 Field Artillery recruits, and 120 Coast Artillery recruits for a total of 454 recruits.[54]

September 1906 mirrored August with Lt. Col. Evans in command. A total of sixteen officers and 744 enlisted men composed the Jefferson Barracks garrison.[55]

On October 4, the 3rd Squadron, Troops I, K, L and M, 9th Cavalry, left Jefferson Barracks by rail for their new station at Fort Sheridan, Illinois. This left no troops of the line at Jefferson Barracks and the post became exclusively a recruit depot.[56]

Lt. Col. Evans now commanded a garrison of six Regular Army officers and 521 enlisted men, of which 489 were recruits. In addition to Evans, the officers at Jefferson Barracks included William B. Bannister, Post Surgeon; 1st Lt. Will L. Pyles, Medical Department; 1st Lt. William A. Powell, Medical Department; 1st Lt. John Bosley, Medical Department; Capt. William T. Littlebrandt, 12th Cavalry; Capt. John T. Geary, Artillery Corps; 1st Lt. Francis T. McConnell, 17th Infantry; 1st Lt. William L. Luhn, 5th Cavalry; 2nd Lt. John R. Musgrove, 2nd Light Artillery; and 2nd Lt. Nelson A. Goodspeed, 3rd Cavalry. In addition, 1st Lt. Wilson G. Heaton, 13th Cavalry; 1st Lt. Clarence G. Bunker, 1st Light Artillery; 1st Lt. Daniel D. Gregory, 5th Cavalry; 2nd Lt. Edwin J. Ely, 15th Cavalry; and 1st Lt. Allen Parker, 26th Infantry, were absent conducting the 243 recruits from Jefferson Barracks to their permanent duty stations.[57]

November and December 1906 mirrored October after the departure of the 9th Cavalry troops. Present for duty were seven officers and 467 enlisted men in November and nineteen officers and 634 enlisted men in December. There were 185 recruits transferred in November and 139 in December.[58]

The War Department transferred the State of Missouri to the Department of Texas on 19 October. The department commanders during the year included Brigadier General Theodore Wint, 1 July to 1 October 1906; Col. Edward S. Godfrey, 1 October to 4 October; Major General Adolphus W. Greely, 4 October to 29 October; Wint again from 29 October to 30 May 1907; and Brigadier General Edward S. Godfrey, 30 May to 30 June 1907.[59]

First United States Cavalry
This detachment of U.S. Regulars stationed at Jefferson Barracks, accompanied by a mounted band, took part in the Fourth of July demonstration at the 1904 World's Fair Exposition in St. Louis.

16th Recruit Company on parade at Jefferson Barracks.

15th Recruit Company barber shop in early 1900s.

The headquarters of the Northern Division changed on 14 November 1906, from St. Louis to Chicago, Illinois, under the provisions of paragraph 2, General Order No. 139, War Department, series 1906. Under the aforementioned provisions Major General Adolphus W. Greely relieved Lt. General Henry C. Corbin in command of the Northern Division.[60]

General Frederick Funston succeeded General A.W. Greely in command of the St. Louis headquarters of the U.S. Army in November. You will remember Funston from his exploits in capturing Emilio Aguinaldo during the Philippine War. Funston was expected to occupy the home at Jefferson Barracks formerly used by Brigadier General John A. Kress, retired. Former commandants of the Army division, of which St. Louis was the head, resided at hotels in the west end of the city.

The reader can get a good idea of what this old house looked like from the newspaper description given in the article about Funston: "The home formerly occupied by General Kress is a tasteful structure with wide verandas, overlooking the Mississippi River. It is somewhat old, having been built in 1876 for the use of the ordnance officer in charge of the Powder Depot near Jefferson Barracks. It is on the military reservation, south of the Post Hospital. The residence contains 12 rooms. The grounds form one of the most beautiful features of the place, being ornamented by fine shade trees and flower beds. The house is approached by walks and a magnificent driveway. During the past year the house has been occupied by Lieutenant Colonel von Schrader, Depot Quartermaster."[61]

The system of personal identification also changed in November. General Order No. 68, War Department, dated 7 April 1906, directed that the fingerprint system of personal identification be put into operation in the Army on 1 September 1906, or as soon as practicable thereafter. Prior to this, personal identification was an outline figure card system. However, the new system did not begin until 1 November and then only at the three recruit depots, including Jefferson Barracks.[62]

1907

As the year 1907 began, Lt. Col. Robert K. Evans, 5th Infantry, remained in command of the Jefferson Barracks Recruit Depot. His command included twenty-one officers and 679 enlisted men.[63] The recruits were divided among the 15th, 16th, 17th, 18th and 19th Recruit Companies, with a total of 223 recruits; 142 white Cavalry recruits; 14 Field Artillery recruits; 110 Coast Artillery recruits; 117 white Infantry recruits; 1 Hospital Corps and 1 Signal Corps recruit; 8 colored Infantry recruits; and 17 colored Cavalry recruits, for a total of 633 recruits. During January 306 recruits transferred.[64]

An interesting news article in the 19 January 1907 issue of the *St. Louis Globe-Democrat* brought to light the mysterious disappearance of thousands of dollars shipped to Iowa from St. Louis during the Black Hawk War and the 1804 treaty with the Sac and Fox Indians in St. Louis.

The question was what had become of the thousands of dollars in gold eagles and double eagles sent from St. Louis seventy-five and one hundred years ago to pay the Sac and Fox Indians for the lands which they had ceded to the United States, millions and millions of acres, and to pay the U.S. troops commanded by Col. Zachary Taylor at Fort McKay during the Black Hawk War. Most of these troops had come from Jefferson Barracks in 1832.

The belief that this golden treasure had lain buried in various parts of the state of Iowa led hundreds of people to dig industriously for more than half a century. The article went on to state that the recent discovery of $45,000 in gold in one part of the state and a map giving the whereabouts of $9,000 of Black Hawk's fortune in another had set hundreds all over the state searching the records and digging the ground. After a lapse of a century the fortune, for the first time, seemed about to be discovered.

That the gold, aggregating well over $100,000, was sent from St. Louis to the Northern Indians before and after the Black Hawk War, is undeniable. A map found with an old letter purportedly showed where the gold had been buried. The article stated that dozens of treasure hunters were at work digging in the various parts of the neighborhood shown on the map in search of the money. All, however, came to naught as no gold was ever found. [Do you suppose that this gold is still buried in Iowa? It would certainly be worth a great deal more today given the current value of gold.]

Jefferson Barracks received a visit from Secretary of War William Howard Taft on 22 January. Secretary Taft served as the chief speaker at the banquet when the Spanish-American War veterans held their reunion at Jefferson Barracks on the evening of 22 January. Col. Michael Adami was in charge of the program and acted as toastmaster. Several other prominent men delivered addresses.[65]

February through June 1907 witnessed few changes in the Jefferson Barracks garrison. Lt. Col. Evans remained in command. Twenty officers and 779 enlisted men comprised the garrison personnel in February. The low point in personnel came in April with only thirteen officers and 386 enlisted men. By the end of May nineteen officers and 618 enlisted men made up the garrison and in June 731 enlisted men belonged to the garrison. In February, 305 recruits were forwarded, but in March only thirty recruits were forwarded, all as permanent party at Jefferson Barracks. In April, 399 recruits transferred, but in May only sixty-seven recruits transferred.[66]

Sometimes we forget that officers and men in the military have some semblance of a life outside the military. The fact can be seen when on 10 April, Miss Catherine Luhn, daughter of Major and Mrs. Luhn got married at Jefferson Barracks to Lt. James Fachet, U.S. Army. A favorite feature of the wedding was a brilliant military reception held at the post. Lt. Fachet and his bride were to depart soon for duty in the Philippines.[67]

In May, Lt. Col. Evans went on detached service to the National Rifle Match. Capt. William T. Littlebrandt, 12th Cavalry, took command of the depot and remained in command until 15 July.[68]

On 25 May Elmer Martin, who was awaiting trial at Jefferson Barracks for desertion from the Coast Artillery at Fort Barramcas, Florida, was killed by Sentry Joseph Cothran. Martin had escaped from Cothran, who later found Martin hiding in the woods. Cothran said that Martin refused to surrender and that he then fired resulting in Martin's death. Edward V. Anderson, who was also awaiting trial for desertion, escaped with Martin and had not been apprehended at the time of the newspaper article reporting Martin's death.[69]

Perseverance and determination can often overcome great obstacles. A case in point is that of a young 22-year-old Kansas man who was determined to be a soldier. In June, Charles L. Dagan of Keats, Kansas, enlisted in Kansas City and left with a squad of men for Jefferson Barracks. Dagan was probably the shortest man in the Army. His height was 5 feet 2 inches, which was two inches below the minimum for acceptance in the Army. Dagan was accepted only on the recommendation of President Theodore Roosevelt, to whom he wrote a letter explaining his situation, after he had been rejected on account of his height at the auxiliary recruiting station at Topeka, Kansas.

Dagan had entertained the hope of becoming a soldier for a number of years. When he went to the recruiting station to enlist, he passed a rigid examination except for his height, but the news that he could not become a soldier for this reason did not deter him. He had decided to become a soldier and promptly wrote to President Roosevelt explaining his situation. He made an earnest appeal to the chief executive, and the frank and earnest manner in which he couched his plea seemed to strike the president as that of a man who would make a good soldier.

This was probably the first instance of an acceptance of an application for enlistment in the Army when a discrepancy of two inches in the required height existed. But, being of almost perfect build [excepting his height] and weighing 130 pounds, he was accepted on the recommendation of the President of the United States. Dagan hoped to become a cavalryman and was sent to Jefferson Barracks where he was assigned to a Cavalry regiment and prepared for duty in the Philippines, which he also desired.[70]

A number of changes in officer personnel took place during the first half of 1907. Major Alfred E. Bradley, Medical Department, arrived for duty on March 27 and Major William B. Bannister transferred to San Francisco en route to the Philippine Islands on 30 March. Capt. William C. Cannon, QM Department, transferred on 7 March, and Capt. Lester W. Cornish left for his home on 11 March, awaiting retirement.[71] On 3 April, 1st Lt. James D. Fife, Medical Department, transferred. 1st Lt. George B. Rodney, 5th Cavalry, reported to Jefferson Barracks for duty with the 15th Recruit Company on 2 May.[72]

An interesting personage was laid to rest in the Jefferson Barracks National Cemetery on 2 February, when Samuel Allen, a 102-year-old former slave, was interred. Allen, born at Harper's Ferry, Virginia, died in a hovel in what was known as Paradise Alley. Allen was known in the vicinity of Paradise Alley as "The Governor" and, despite his age, he was a man of unusual activity. Allen had witnessed the execution of John Brown, about whom he loved to tell stories. He also loved to tell stories about his Army record, as he had served in the Army of the Republic during the Civil War. He was buried with full military honors.[73]

In the annual report to the War Department for the fiscal year ending 30 June 1907, the Quartermaster General reported that based on estimates supplied by the Surgeon-General of the allotments from the appropriations for construction and repair of hospitals, $74,552 had been appropriated for construction of a new hospital at Jefferson Barracks complete with plumbing and electrical wiring. Contracts had been entered into for the construction of this modern hospital.[74] The Quartermaster General also reported that an appropriation of $1,192 had been approved for the construction of a photograph gallery at the Post.[75]

In Volume I of the War Department Annual Reports for Fiscal Year 1907, it was reported that enlistments in St. Louis had been 514, with 977 applicants rejected. Of the 514 accepted, 38 applicants were then rejected at Jefferson Barracks.[76] At Jefferson Barracks, 2,487 men enlisted with 172 applicants rejected.[77] Of the applicants accepted at recruiting stations, 153 failed to report to Jefferson Barracks and 90 left before formal enlistment.[78]

Army-wide 20,410 men enlisted during fiscal year 1907. Of this number 7,384 were re-enlistments and 13,026 were original enlistments. Of these enlistments, eighty-six percent were native-born men.[79]

As also reported for fiscal year 1906, venereal diseases were again by far the most prevalent diseases affecting the efficiency of the Army during fiscal 1907. There were consistently 739 men on sick report for this class of afflictions, equal to the loss of about eleven full Infantry companies for the entire year. Malarial fevers ranked second, and materially increased in incidence from fiscal 1906.[80]

As in all previous years, desertion also remained a major problem. In fiscal year 1907, 4,522 men deserted from the enlisted force of the Army. That was 5.6 percent of the whole number of enlisted men in the Army. However, the 1907 percentage had dropped from 7.4 percent in 1906.[81]

Low pay was listed as the number one cause of desertion, especially when compared to much higher wages in civilian life. The daily pay of a private in his first enlistment was $0.429, plus a clothing allowance of $0.527, and value of rations of $0.1518, for a total daily earnings of $0.7325.[82]

In contrast, it had been ascertained through official reports from all posts in the Northern Division that the minimum daily wages for unskilled labor ranged from $1.50 per day at one post to $3.50 at another; the average minimum daily wage at posts throughout the Northern Division was $2.70 per day.[83]

The report went on to state that it was believed that the time had arrived when the pay of the Army should be increased. It recommended that pay at enlistment should increase to $15 per month. If the enlistee becomes a marksman, sharpshooter, or expert rifleman, his pay would increase a dollar a month for each classification. A first class private's pay should increase by $4 per month, to $19, plus the increase for marksmanship.[84]

As regards re-enlistment, the commanding officer at Jefferson Barracks recommended to the War Department that a bounty of $100 be paid to each soldier who re-enlisted in his own organization upon discharge by expiration of term of service. He stated that there were two reasons why this was in the interest of the service: "First, it is assumed that it costs the government on an average at least $300 to deliver a recruit to his organization. At present, and for some years past, the number of re-enlistments has been very small. Hence, for every soldier who re-enlists in his old organization, the Government makes a savings of $200. Second, it is greatly in the interest of the service to keep disciplined, instructed and drilled men in the organization rather than to have a stream of green, non-disciplined recruits chasing each other through the Army as the regiments go to or return from foreign service."[85]

In another report on the health and morale of the Army, it was stated that from the lowest rank up, it was practically unanimous in its desires to have the canteen re-established. Even many officers who, on principle, were opposed to the use of intoxicating liquors, realized that such use cannot be prevented and that the sale of beer at post exchanges would be the lesser evil.

In considering the subject, three time periods were discussed. The first time period was from 1881 to 1890, which covered the time prior to the establishment of post exchanges, when post traders were authorized. The second period was when the canteen was in operation, and the third period since the abolition of the canteens. When the canteen was in operation there were fewer desertions, fewer fines and forfeitures imposed by sentence of courts martial, less alcoholism and less venereal diseases than prior to its establishment. Since abolition of the canteen, venereal diseases have increased, and desertions have increased somewhat. The report goes on to state that a careful consideration of the whole subject, together with the views of department commanders, provide convincing evidence that the abolition of the canteen had resulted in injury to the service. The morals and discipline of the Army had suffered as a consequence.[86]

Despite the overwhelming concurrence of the Army's ranking officers, the re-establishment of the canteen system had to wait. This was probably due, at least in part, to the pressure of the temperance movement throughout the country.

July 1907 saw virtually no change at Jefferson Barracks from the previous month. Lt. Col. Evans returned from detached service at the National Rifle Match on 15 July, and resumed command of the post. The garrison consisted of seventeen officers and 663 enlisted men.[87]

On 10 August, Evans again left on detached service, and Capt. Littlebrandt took over command of the post. 1st Lt. Wilson G. Heaton, 13th Cavalry, transferred on 4 August, and 1st Lt. Thomas L. Brewer, 21st Infantry, reported for duty on 21 August. The garrison consisted of seventeen officers and 664 enlisted men. Two hundred thirty-nine recruits transferred during the month.[88]

Lt. Col. Evans returned and resumed command on 5 September. 1st Lt. Eugene J. Ely, 5th Cavalry, transferred on 3 September, and Major Willoughby Walke, Artillery Corps, reported for duty on 28 September. Evans' command consisted of nineteen officers and 725 enlisted men in September. There were 201 recruits transferred during the month.[89]

In October, Evans again left on detached service, this time to Washington, D.C., and Major Walke assumed command on 30 October. 1st Lt. Albert A. King, 8th Cavalry, reported for duty at the Jefferson Barracks Depot on 2 October, and 2nd Lt. Nelson A. Goodspeed, 3rd Cavalry, transferred on 30 October. The Post Commissary Sergeant, Paul L. Spaney, who had been at Jefferson Barracks since February 3, 1906, transferred to Manila, Philippine Islands, and Andrew J. Merrill arrived on 20 October, to assume the duties of Post Commissary Sergeant.[90]

A slight break from the rather monotonous routine took place during October, when President Theodore Roosevelt arrived in St. Louis by boat. The 15th Recruit Company, commanded by Capt. Gaston S. Turner, 7th Infantry, and the 17th Recruit Company, commanded by Capt. John T. Gray, Coast Artillery, served as honor guard for the president. Dressed in full dress uniform, they made a long march to the city. They returned to Jefferson Barracks on board the presidential steamer. As they got underway when President Roosevelt left, the companies presented arms as they stood on the railroad tracks east of the headquarters building.[91]

Another October event provided a break in the routine for 120 soldiers from Jefferson Barracks. President Roosevelt had ordered Lt. Col. Evans "to render every assistance possible" for the International Balloon Races to be held in St. Louis. The Jefferson Barracks soldiers provided police and ground duty at the Races, and were commended for their services.[92]

After months of planning, weeks of preparation, and hours of manual labor the week-long event kicked off on 20 October. This second competition for the Bennett Cup was organized by the Aero Club of America under the rules of the International Aeronautics Federation, and was conducted under the auspices of the Aero Club of St. Louis. The first five days of the week were devoted to aeronauts. On Monday, nine balloons: three American, three German, two French, and one English were to ascend for the long-distance race for the Bennett Cup.

Tuesday featured a contest for aeroplanes heavier than air, with total cash prizes of $2500. On Wednesday, there was a contest for air ships and vehicles lighter than air, with total prizes of $2500. On Thursday, the contest of flying machines for the "Scientific American" cup was held, and Friday was a "free for all" day, in which any kind of aircraft that could get off the ground could participate in the contest to win the Lahm Cup.[93]

It is interesting to note that in late November, General George B. Davis, Judge Advocate General of the Army, stated that in his opinion the troops from Jefferson Barracks were not needed at the Balloon Races as no emergency existed sufficient for Federal interference. Davis held "that having regard to the mandatory requirements of law the use of troops from Jefferson Barracks at the recent balloon competitions at St. Louis was not warranted by law." Acting Secretary of War Oliver approved Davis' opinion.[94]

November 1907 was basically a re-run of the previous ten months of 1907. Major Walke remained in command of a garrison consisting of sixteen officers and 831 enlisted men. There were 318 recruits transferred to their permanent organizations during the month.[95]

1st Lt. O.G. Brown, Medical Department, arrived for temporary duty on 2 November and Capt. George W. Helms. 19th Infantry, arrived on 10 November and was assigned to the 19th Recruit Company. Capt. Howard L. Laurback, 23rd Infantry, transferred from Jefferson Barracks on 19 November.[96]

Lt. Col. Evans returned to command on 3 December. Lt. Col. Robert N. Getty, 7th Infantry, reported for duty on 19 December and relieved Evans in command the next day. Lt. Col. Evans returned to his regiment.

Getty's command consisted of eighteen officers and 843 enlisted men. Of this number 800 were recruits. The number of recruits transferred during December came to 184.[97]

Three new officers reported for duty in December. Capt. Charles J. Symmonds, 12th Cavalry, reported on 21 December; 1st Lt. Clarence L.R. Cole, Medical Department, reported on 23 December; and 1st Lt. Lewis Forester, 5th Cavalry, reported on 30 December. In the senior non-commissioned officers, First Class Sergeant George C. Young, Signal Corps, reported on 12 December.[98]

1908

As the year 1908 began Lt. Col. Robert N. Getty, 7th Infantry, commanded a garrison of twenty-two officers and 783 enlisted men. Of the enlisted men, 739 were recruits. Among the recruits were twenty-nine colored Cavalry recruits. The most recruits ever transferred in a month departed Jefferson Barracks during January, when 877 recruits left the post.[99]

February through April 1908 saw little change in the Jefferson Barracks depot garrison. Routine training of recruits remained the primary activity with little to break the monotony.

In February, the garrison consisted of twenty-two officers and 890 enlisted men. One officer, 1st Lt. John B. Hasson, 6th Cavalry, transferred on 4 February; and Capt. Marcus D. Cronin, 25th Infantry, reported for duty on 9 February. There were 722 recruits transferred to their permanent organizations.[100]

In March, Getty's command consisted of twenty officers and 722 enlisted men. The only change in the officer corps took place on 14 March, when Capt. William T. Littlebrandt transferred.

A good example of the transfer of recruits can be seen from the March returns. On 3 March, eighty-five recruits transferred to the 19th Infantry at Fort Bliss, Texas. The next day thirty-nine recruits transferred to the 19th Infantry at Fort McIntosh, Texas; and sixty-eight Coast Artillery recruits transferred to Fort Caswell, North Carolina. On 5 March, seventeen recruits transferred to Company D, 2nd Field Artillery at Fort D.A. Russell, Wyoming; and on 6 March seventy-six recruits transferred to the 8th Cavalry at Fort Robinson, Nebraska. On 9 March one hundred and seventeen recruits transferred to the 6th Field Artillery at Fort Riley, Kansas; and the next day forty-six recruits went to the 33rd Coast Artillery at Fort Columbia, Washington. Forty-six Infantry recruits transferred to service in Cuba, via Fort Monroe, Virginia; and fifty-one recruits transferred to the 13th Infantry at Fort Leavenworth, Kansas, on 13 March. On 24 March, one hundred and five recruits transferred to the Coast Artillery at Fort Flagler, Washington; thirty-eight transferred to the 9th Infantry at Fort Sam Houston, Texas, on 25 March; and seventy-five colored Cavalry recruits transferred to the Philippine Islands via Fort McDowell, California, on 26 March.[101]

In April, the post's enlisted personnel increased by 190 to 912 enlisted men. The officer corps at the post remained unchanged except for the transfer of 1st Lt. Davis C. Anderson, 6th Infantry, who transferred on 16 April.[102]

Also in April, the nation's first federal military reserve was established with the passage of Senate Bill 1424 on 23 April. The bill authorized the Army to secure a reserve corps of medical officers who could be ordered to active duty by the Secretary of War during time of emergency. These reserve doctors would be commissioned as first lieutenants and rank below all other officers of like grade. The bill also provided for the commissioning of contract physicians in either the Regular Army or the Medical Reserve Corps, depending upon their age. The bill passed the House 126 to 15.[103]

In May, the enlisted personnel again increased, to 969. The officer corps remained unchanged except for the addition of Dental Surgeon John R. Ames, who arrived on 18 May. Four hundred forty-two recruits transferred during the month.[104]

Again, little changed during June with nineteen officers and 924 enlisted men comprising the garrison. Capt. William A. Powell, Medical Corps, transferred on 27 June. Five hundred four recruits transferred to permanent organizations.[105]

War Department Reports for the fiscal year ending 30 June 1908, showed that at the recruiting station in St. Louis, 1,265 applicants were accepted and 2,256 rejected. Of those accepted, the Jefferson Barracks Recruit Depot rejected 179. Of the recruits sent to the Jefferson Barracks Depot, 265 failed to report and 252 reported, but left before enlistment. At Jefferson Barracks 7,503 men enlisted and 978 were rejected.[106]

During the 1908 fiscal year, the overall health of the Army made steady and progressive improvement. Venereal diseases were again the most prevalent item effecting the efficiency of the Army. Next in order of importance were malarial fevers, diarrhea, enteritis, bronchitis and influenza. Tuberculosis ranked first as a cause of death, followed by pneumonia, cerebro-spinal fever, typhoid fever and heart disease. Tuberculosis also ranked first as a cause of discharge for disability, followed by venereal disease and insanity.[107]

In July, the number of enlisted personnel fell to 743. This was due to the large number of recruits transferred during the month, 711. The officer corps remained unchanged.[108]

August saw the number of enlisted personnel jump back up to 970. The officer corps went back to twenty when 1st Lt. Armin Mueller, Medical Reserve Corps, reported on 12 August. Mueller remained only until September 27 when he departed for the Army Medical School. Only 373 recruits transferred during the month.[109]

Gideon Six hundred thirty-three recruits transferred in September, leaving 659 enlisted men at Jefferson Barracks. Lt. Col. Getty and eighteen officers remained on duty at the post.[110]

The remainder of 1908 saw a steady increase in the number of enlisted personnel at Jefferson Barracks, with 752 in October; 1064 in November; and 1194 in December. Four hundred and eleven recruits transferred in October, only 135 in November and 343 in December.[111]

1909

To begin the year 1909, Lt. Col. Robert N. Getty, 7th Infantry, remained in command of the post, which consisted of twenty officers and 1354 enlisted men, the largest number of enlisted men in many years. Major Alfred E. Bradley served as Depot Surgeon, with Major Robert N. Winn, Capt. John C. Gregory and Capt. J.I. Mabee also serving as physicians at the post. Capt. Ola W. Bell served as Quartermaster and Prison Officer, Capt. Gaston S. Turner as Adjutant and Signal Officer; and Capt. Francis J. McConnell as Commissary, Mess and Exchange Officer. The Recruit Company commanders were 1st Lt. George B. Rodney, 5th Cavalry, commanding the 15th; 1st Lt. Albert A. King, 8th Cavalry, commanding the 16th; Capt. Charles J. Symmonds, 12th Cavalry, the 17th; Capt. Thomas L. Brewer, 23rd Infantry, the 18th; and Capt. George W. Helms, 19th Infantry, the 19th. Capt. Turner relieved Capt. Clarence G. Bunker, Coast Artillery Corps, as commander of the 14th Recruit Company on January 1. Also on duty at Jefferson Barracks were Major Willoughby Walke, Coast Artillery Corps; 1st Lt. Louis Foerster, 8th Cavalry; 1st Lt. C.A. Mitchell, Coast Artillery Corps, who reported January 20; 1st Lt. Gideon H. Williams, 28th Infantry, who reported on 7 January; 1st Lt. J.F. Walker, Coast Artillery Corps, on indefinite leave; 1st Lt. C.S. Blakely, 3rd Field Artillery; 1st Lt. John C. Fairfax, 21st Infantry; and Dental Surgeon John R. Ames. Capt. Allen Parker, 21st Infantry, departed 2 January; Capt. John T. Geary, Coast Artillery Corps, departed on 7 January; and 1st Lt. John R. Musgrave left on 10 January.[112] All twenty of these officers served on detached service from their regular units. In 1909, twenty-seven percent of the line officers served on detached service. This created a shortage of line officers and with the newly created Coast Artillery Corps' rapid expansion the shortage became more acute. By January of 1910, the War Department had to create a special examination to commission more civilians to fill the officer shortfall.[113]

The senior non-commissioned officers remained unchanged: James S. Ruby had served as Ordnance Sergeant since 9 October 1906; John G. Geisler as Post Quartermaster Sergeant since 28 June 1907; Andrew J. Merrill served as Commissary Sergeant since 20 October 1907; John Wikander also served as Commissary Sergeant since 31 October 1907; and Charles H. Hunter as Quartermaster Sergeant since 30 June 1908.[114]

In January, meningitis was discovered at Jefferson Barracks. Major Percy M. Ashburn, Medical Department, stationed at Fort Banks, Massachusetts, received orders to proceed to the post to assist in the investigation of the origin and spread of cerebro-spinal meningitis. Major Alfred Bradley, Post Surgeon, maintained that there was not an epidemic of the disease at Jefferson Barracks as only four cases in six weeks had been diagnosed. As no additional information can be found regarding this disease the efforts to control the spread and find a cure must have been successful.[115]

In February, the number of enlisted men at Jefferson Barracks increased to 1404, but each succeeding month the number decreased until by July only 812 enlisted men served at the Jefferson Barracks Recruit Depot.

In January, 394 recruits transferred to permanent organizations. In February that number decreased to 283. In March 89 recruits transferred and in April only 64. In May, the total transferred increased to 396.

In May, two additional recruit companies, the 20th and 23rd, were formed. This brought the total of recruit companies at Jefferson Barracks to eight. The 17th Recruit Company and the newly created 20th Recruit Company transferred to Fort McDowell, California, on 30 May. By the end of July 1909, the recruit companies at Jefferson Barracks included the 14th, 15th, 16th, 18th, 19th, 23rd, 24th Band and 27th.[116] The 24th Band Recruit Company organized in June, and in July the 27th Recruit Company formed.

Col. Cunliffe H. Murray, 14th Cavalry, relieved Lt. Col. Getty on May 19. Colonel Murray remained in command only until 15 July, when Lt. Col. William A. Mann, 6th Infantry, took command. Lt. Col. Mann commanded the post for the remainder of 1909.[117]

An interesting footnote took place in July, when the last of General John C. Fremont's Pathfinders died. John Stundon, 87, had been living on a farm near Marysville, Missouri. Also known as Pat White, Stundon had joined the famous explorer at Jefferson Barracks in 1843.[118]

Robert Nelson Getty was born at Fort Hamilton, N.Y., 17 January 1855. Upon graduation from West Point in 1878, he was assigned to the 22nd Infantry with that unit at Fort Wayne, Michigan, and Fort Griffin, Texas, until June 1881. He then served tours of duty at San Antonio, Texas, Forts Garland and Lewis, Colorado; at Camp Merritt and Fort Keogh, Montana. He served with the 22nd in Cuba in 1898 and was awarded the Silver Star for gallantry. He served with the 1st Infantry in the Philippines from 1900 until his return to the states in April 1905 when he assumed command of the 1st Infantry. He returned to the Philippines in February 1906. Upon his return to the states in November 1907 he commanded the Recruit Depot at Jefferson Barracks until his third trip to the Philippines in July 1909. He served in numerous command positions until his retirement for age on 17 January 1919. Getty died at San Francisco, California, on 15 April 1941, as a retired brigadier general.

Lt. Col. William Abram Mann, 6th Infantry, born 31 July 1854 in Altoona, Pennsylvania, took command of Jefferson Barracks on 15 July 1909, and remained the post's commanding officer until 12 August 1911. Mann graduated from West Point in 1875, receiving a commission in the Infantry. He served with the 17th Infantry during the Spanish-American War and in the Philippines in the early 1900s. Mann commanded the 6th Infantry from 1907 to 1909. After leaving Jefferson Barracks, Mann was assigned the Army's General Staff. He served as Chief of Staff for the division based in Texas City, Texas, from 1913 to 1914. From 1914 to 1915 Mann commanded the 3rd Infantry and in 1915 became commander of the 1st Brigade, Dept. of the East and was promoted to brigadier general. He commanded the 2nd Cavalry Brigade during the Poncho Villa Expedition. In 1917 Mann headed the Army's Militia Bureau, receiving a promotion to major general. Mann became the first commander of the 42nd Infantry Division, nicknamed the Rainbow Division, made up of National Guard units from 26 states. Mann led the Division to France, but was found to be physically unfit for combat. Mann retired in 1918, living in Washington, D.C., until his death on 8 October 1934. He is buried in Arlington National Cemetery.

Old entrance to the National Cemetery.

Band plays for review parade ca. 1910.

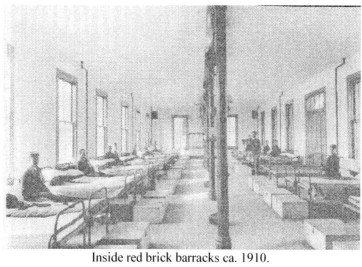

Inside red brick barracks ca. 1910.

In August, Mann's command consisted of eighteen officers and 852 enlisted men. The 19th Recruit Company and the 24th Band Recruit Company transferred to Fort Logan, Colorado, on 30 August.[119]

In September, the garrison consisted of nineteen officers and 774 enlisted men. One noteworthy event of the month involved one of the senior non-commissioned officers. Quartermaster Sergeant Charles Hunter, who had been at his post since 30 June 1908, deserted at Jefferson Barracks on 9 April. Civil authorities apprehended Hunter in St. Louis on 1 July and turned him over to military control at Jefferson Barracks on 2 July. Hunter remained in confinement until 21 August. He had been tried by General Court Martial, found guilty of desertion and sentenced to forfeit $30 pay per month for three months. Hunter also had to forfeit $50 to cover the reward paid for his capture and delivery to military control, but he retained his rank and had no other punishment.[120]

In October, Lt. Col. Mann commanded a garrison that consisted of eighteen officers and 674 enlisted men. Large numbers of recruits continued to be detailed to their permanent units, with a total of 355 departing during the month.[121]

Also during October, Major Willoughby Walke, Coast Artillery Corps, was relieved from duty at Jefferson Barracks and departed on the 19th.[122]

Twenty officers and 922 enlisted men made up the garrison's personnel in November. Only 92 recruits were forwarded during the month.[123]

One of the officers to be relieved of duty at Jefferson Barracks during November was 1st Lt. Walter C. Jones, 13th Infantry. It is not Jones himself that is of interest, but rather his assigned duties while at the post. Jones came to Jefferson Barracks to oversee the installation of a telephone system. From Jefferson Barracks, Jones proceeded to St. Paul, Minnesota, leaving on 17 November.[124] Also involved in the installation of the telephone system were Cpl. Lawrence L. Youchim, First Class Private John R. Evans and First Class Private Elmer E. Colebaugh, all of the Signal Corps. These men remained on duty at Jefferson Barracks.

Three hundred and five recruits were forwarded during December 1909.[125]

Lt. Col. Mann transferred from the 6th Infantry to the 3rd Infantry on 17 December, but remained in command of Jefferson Barracks.[126] The complement of officers at the post remained unchanged.

Construction at Jefferson Barracks had continued during 1909 with an addition to the main hospital building to accommodate 100 more beds, This project was completed at a cost of $110,388. A Post Office costing $2,459 and hospital steward's quarters costing $10,642 were also completed in 1909. On 30 June 1909, the first electric lights throughout the post were turned on.[127]

1910

Lt. Col. William A. Mann, 3rd Infantry, remained in command of Jefferson Barracks at the beginning of 1910. The garrison had a complement of nineteen officers and 945 enlisted men. Of the 945 enlisted men, 587 were unassigned recruits and five were military convicts. The number of recruits forwarded in January numbered 274.[128]

In addition to Lt. Col. Mann, Major Alfred E. Bradley served as Post Surgeon; Capt. John C. Gregory as Assistant Surgeon and Recruiting Officer; Capt. J. I. Mabee as Assistant Surgeon and Recruiting Officer; 1st Lt. Norman L. McDiarmid as Assistant Surgeon and Recruiting Officer; Major Oscar I. Straub, Coast Artillery Corps, served as Summary Court Officer; Capt. Charles J. Symmonds, 15th Cavalry, as Adjutant and Commander of the 14th Recruit Company; Capt. S. H. Ford, Quartermaster Department, served as Quartermaster and Commissary Officer; 1st Lt. C. H. Errington, 11th Infantry, served as Commissary and Mess Officer and was detailed as Post Treasurer; 1st Lt. Alden F. Brewster, 2nd Field Artillery, served as Prison and Signal Officer and as assistant to the adjutant; 1st Lt. C. S. Blakely, 3rd Field Artillery, as Post Exchange Officer and in charge of the Receiving Barracks; Capt. John Robertson, 27th Infantry, commanded the 23rd Recruit Company; Capt. Frederick W. Benteen, 7th Infantry, commanded the 27th Recruit Company; 1st Lt. G. B. Rodney, 5th Cavalry, commanded the 15th Recruit Company; 1st Lt. Lewis Forester, 5th Cavalry, was on duty with the 27th Recruit Company; 1st Lt. James T. Walker, Coast Artillery Corps, commanded the 16th Recruit Company and served as Ordnance Officer; 1st Lt. Robert D. Goodwin, 4th Infantry, was on duty with the 15th Recruit Company; 1st Lt. C. A. Mitchell, Coast Artillery Corps, was on duty with the 18th Recruit Company; 1st Lt. Ralph D. Bates, Coast Artillery Corps, was on duty with the 23rd Recruit Company; H. G. Voorhies served as Dental Surgeon; 1st Lt. Henry A. Wiegenstein, 25th Infantry, commanded the 18th Recruit Company; and 1st Lt. Ferdinand Schmitter, Medical Corps, transferred to Fort Slocum, New York.[129]

The senior non-commissioned officers included James S. Ruby, Ordnance Sergeant, since 9 October 1906; John R. Callaghan and Daniel O'Connell, Commissary Sergeants since 6 May and 27 June 1909 respectively; and William Day, Post Quartermaster Sergeant since 17 May 1909. Quartermaster Sergeant John G. Geisler transferred to Fort Ward, Washington, in January.[130]

In February, the number of enlisted men at the post decreased to 614 as only 272 unassigned recruits remained at the Post. The number of officers remained at nineteen with Lt. Col. Mann in command. Three officers; 1st Lt. Norman L. McDiarmid, 1st Lt. Alden R. Brewster and 1st Lt. Ralph D. Bates were relieved of duty at Jefferson Barracks during February. 1st Lt. Walter J. Buttgenback, Coast Artillery Corps and Major Jay Ralph Shook arrived for duty.[131]

In March, the number of enlisted men at the post increased dramatically to 1,113 with the addition of 758 unassigned recruits. Only 75 recruits transferred during the month. Sergeants J. O. Danbenberger, 16th Recruit Company, and James T. Bloomer, 27th Recruit Company, escorted nineteen recruits for the 30th Infantry and thirty-six for the 1st Cavalry to the Presidio of San Francisco. Sergeant Capell, 18th Recruit Company, escorted twenty Hospital Corps recruits to Fort D.A. Russell, Wyoming.[132]

One officer, 1st Lt. Leo C. Mudd, Medical Reserve Corps, arrived for duty at Jefferson Barracks on 9 March. 1st Lt. James F. Walker, Coast Artillery Corps, was assigned to duty with the 170th Company and left on 31 March. 1st Lt. Robert D. Goodwin, 4th Infantry, left on 21 March, detailed as Judge Advocate of the Department of California at San Francisco.[133]

During April 1910, the number of officers increased to twenty-one with the addition of 1st Lt. Dennis P. Quinlon, 5th Cavalry, on 24 April; and 1st Lt. Otis R. Cole, 25th Infantry, on 19 April. Six hundred sixty-seven unassigned recruits made up the bulk of the 1,055 enlisted men at the post.[134]

There were few changes in May 1910. The officer corps consisted of twenty-one officers, with the addition of Major Deane C. Howard, Medical Department, who arrived on 21 May; 1st Lt. Henry C. Pillsbury, Medical Department, also arrived on 21 May; 1st Lt. Ray W. Bryan, Medical Department, who arrived on 29 May; and Capt. Samuel B. McIntyre, 19th Infantry, who arrived on 1 May and was assigned command of the 16th Recruit Company on 5 May. Lt. Col. A. E. Bradley, Post Surgeon, was relieved from duty at Jefferson Barracks, and ordered to proceed to San Francisco, which he did on 25 May, after being granted a one-month leave.[135]

In May, the number of enlisted personnel at the Jefferson Barracks Recruit Depot stood at 1,085. There were 717 unassigned recruits, thirteen casuals and four military convicts. Sgt. Kastler, Sgt. Denton, Sgt. Neal, Sgt. Dunn and Cpl. Snyder served as escorts for the fifty-seven recruits transferred during May.[136]

From June 1910 to the end of the year, the Jefferson Barracks garrison performed their usual duties. The only changes that took place involved the transfer of recruits and some officers. New officers transferred to Jefferson Barracks took the place of those that departed. In June, the garrison consisted of twenty-two officers and 850 enlisted men; in July, twenty-two officers and 728 enlisted men; in August nineteen officers and 808 enlisted men; in September, eighteen officers and 863 enlisted men; in October, twenty officers and 812 enlisted men; in November, twenty officers and 921 enlisted men; and in December nineteen officers and 1,081 enlisted men.[137]

A total of 2,510 recruits transferred to their permanent units during 1910. The number of recruits transferred varied by month from a low of fifty-six in May to a high of 359 in October.[138]

The construction program at Jefferson Barracks continued during 1910 with an isolation building completed for the hospital. A new post laundry was also completed during the year.[139]

Thirty-three bodies from the burial ground at old Fort Bellefontaine were transferred to the Jefferson Barracks National Cemetery. Among the remains transferred were those of Col. Thomas Hunt, who commanded Fort Bellefontaine in 1808, and those of a two-year-old girl who had died at Fort Bellefontaine on 23 November 1806, while her father, Zebulon Pike, was on the expedition which resulted in the discovery of what was later to be called Pike's Peak.[140]

1911

The end of the year 1910 and the beginning of the new year 1911 saw no changes from the routine at Jefferson Barracks. Lt. Col. William A. Mann remained in command of a garrison consisting of eighteen officers and 1,257 enlisted men. Of the enlisted men, 1,204 were recruits assigned to the 14th, 15th, 16th, 18th, 23rd and 27th Recruit Companies or were unassigned recruits.[141]

Three officers: Capt. James J. Mabee, Medical Department; 1st Lt. Lewis Foerster, 11th Cavalry; and Capt. Samuel B. McIntyre, 19th Infantry, were relieved of duty at Jefferson Barracks during the month.[142] Five hundred thirty-eight recruits transferred during January, the largest number in over a year.

The Recruit Depot received its yearly inspection from the Inspector General's Office in January. Major L. S. McCormick of that office inspected the post between 19 January and 26 January.[143]

In February, the number of enlisted men decreased to 1,052 and officers to seventeen. The decrease in enlisted men came about due to the transfer of 695 recruits. Two officers: Capt. Guy V. Rukke, Medical Corps; and 1st Lt. Thomas M. Knox, 1st Cavalry, arrived to replace the officers transferred in January.[144]

On 20 March, Lt. Col. Mann received a promotion to colonel of Infantry to date from 3 March, relieving him from duty with the 3rd Infantry. A total of twenty officers served at Jefferson Barracks during the month of March. 1st Lt. Guy L. Qualls, Medical Reserve Corps, arrived on 7 March. Capt. William H. Peck, Coast Artillery Corps, arrived on 25 March and was assigned to the command of the 18th Recruit Company. Capt. Edward R. Stone, 14th Infantry, was relieved from duty at Jefferson Barracks and left the post to join his unit on 27 March.[145]

Jefferson Barracks also lost one of its senior non-commissioned officers in March when Commissary Sergeant John R. Baker was promoted to Post Commissary Sergeant and ordered to St. Louis for duty in the purchasing commissary. Baker had been on duty at Jefferson Barracks since 27 April 1908, most recently with the 23rd Recruit Company.[146]

During the first part of 1911, the old order of conditions still prevailed at Jefferson Barracks. Recruits were assigned to sections of twelve men, and performed a series of progressive drills, totaling thirty-six drills. All sections, regardless of their degree of progress, had to attend all parades. This made for a rather ragged formation, which became even more undesirable by having the Coast Artillery recruits drilled in blue trousers, interspersed with other recruits dressed in olive drab.[147]

At the same time, it must be pointed out that the Army placed a tremendous importance on the perfection of all enlistment papers. Officers, non-commissioned officers and other enlisted personnel with clerical ability found much of their time devoted to paperwork.

In April, the number of enlisted personnel at the Recruit Depot again dropped, this time to 915. The officer complement remained the same, with Col. Mann still in command. The number of recruits transferred during the month came to 642.[148]

In the spring of 1911, a young farm boy from Kansas arrived at Jefferson Barracks. This young man would go on to command the greatest American Army in history during World War II. Dwight D. Eisenhower received an appointment to West Point and came to Jefferson Barracks to take the entrance examination.

The farm boy was completely unprepared for the wonders of the big city. Later in life Eisenhower reminisced that one night while at Jefferson Barracks he left the barracks with another applicant and they wandered around the city. Eisenhower stated, "We walked the streets for a time. Thinking we'd see more of the city, we took a streetcar and, riding it to the end of the line, found ourselves at a car barn in East St. Louis, on the eastern side of the Mississippi River. Now we had a problem. No more streetcars were running. We saw no sign of any kind of transportation and we were lost. A heavy fog lay over the city and we could not orient ourselves by the stars. We did think that by following the tracks we would soon reach the river. This ruse failed when we came to a point where the line branched and we had no idea which one to take.

Fortunately, in a nearby building, we saw a dim light. There we hoped to find a friendly soul who would set us on the right road to the city. We knocked on the door and soon heard someone in the room moving toward us.

The door, which was massive, began to open slowly and the first thing we saw was the muzzle of a revolver.

A voice said, 'Who are you?'

We stammered that we just wanted help in getting back across the river. The man, who proved to be a bartender, apparently decided we were harmless young fellows, and he let us in, lowered the revolver, and gave us explicit instructions.

We were within a block of the bridge. We crossed it at double-time, hoping to catch the final car for the Barracks which we had been told left the St. Louis side of the river at 1:00 a.m. We made it but we had not yet solved the problem of avoiding discovery upon reaching the Barracks; and because we had violated instructions to be in by taps, we were afraid we would be barred from completing the examination.

At the main gate, a guard would have taken our names, of course. We decided to avoid it. Instead we went down along the wall through the darkness, under the trees, to find a spot where we would be undetected as we scaled the wall. I have often thought that we were fortunate. The nation was at peace and there was no thought of subversion, sabotage, and so on. Security was lax and we got over the wall undiscovered and sneaked into the building. So far as I know, no one ever learned of our silly escapade."[149]

Again, in May the number of enlisted personnel at Jefferson Barracks dropped, this time to 755, the lowest total in over a year. Six hundred sixty recruits transferred to their permanent units.[150]

In June, the number of enlisted men increased to 934. Only 281 recruits shipped out.[151]

In July, the Jefferson Barracks personnel consisted of twenty-one officers and 1,356 enlisted men. Only 156 recruits transferred.

Two officers: Capt. Thomas F. Ryan, 13th Cavalry, and 1st Lt. Olney Place, 13th Cavalry, were detailed for General Recruiting duty and arrived during July. Ryan took command of the 16th Recruit Company, and Place was assigned duty with the same company.[152]

Capt. Charles J. Symmonds, 12th Cavalry, was relieved from duty at Jefferson Barracks and ordered to join his proper station. He departed on 1 July on a four-month leave, after which he was to join his unit. Capt. John Robertson, 27th Infantry, was also relieved from duty at Jefferson Barracks, and after a one month and five-day leave was ordered to report to the Army School of the Line at Fort Leavenworth, Kansas. Robertson left on 10 July.[153]

Col. Mann left Jefferson Barracks on 12 August after being relieved by Major Oscar I. Straub, Coast Artillery Corps. Straub received a commission as lieutenant colonel in the Coast Artillery Corps on 28 July, which he accepted on 21 August.[154]

Lt. Col. Straub commanded a garrison of twenty officers and 1,311 enlisted men. Six hundred and sixty-six recruits transferred during the month.[155]

Col. William T. Wood, Infantry, replaced Straub as commander on 20 September. Col. Wood took command of a garrison consisting of twenty officers and 1,270 enlisted men. Five hundred eighteen recruits transferred during his first month of command.[156]

Col. Wood, familiarly known as "Stumpy," had a remarkable understanding of young men and an equally remarkable fellow-feeling for them. As a result, Wood gave particular attention to the amusement facilities at the post. Wood maintained the proper emphasis on training and the aforementioned paperwork, but they became secondary to the encouragement of recruits. Col. Wood was particularly anxious that a recruit's first impression of the Army should be favorable and he knew that first impression took place at the Recruit Depot. He took immediate steps to make the first impression of Jefferson Barracks favorable and lasting. He installed a moving picture show where the best movies were played. Community singing with good instrumental music became popular. He installed a roller-skating rink and purchased 500 pairs of skates. In addition, he had a race track built at the west end of the parade grounds and laid out a baseball diamond. He brought the post to the forefront of popular attention in St. Louis by having soldiers participate in innumerable civic activities. Wood also had amateur theatricals performed by members of the command and hired performers to come out from the city. The money for these entertainments came from a liberal post exchange counsel.

Monthly field days were held with prizes for all participants and special events provided for recruits. Enthusiasm reached a high pitch in athletics and other forms of amusements. The only serious drawback was having ample seating for the audiences that attended, a fact that provided evidence of the success of Wood's efforts.[157]

Few changes took place during the final three months of 1911. Col. Wood remained in command of the Recruit Depot which maintained a garrison strength of eighteen to twenty-one officers and between 1,223 and 1,428 enlisted men. The permanent party continued to provide training for the recruits and perform the routine garrison duties.[158]

By 1911, the military service offered a career. On 2 November 1911, William A. Banks, who had turned nineteen about three weeks earlier, walked into the recruiting station in Lexington, Kentucky, and signed up. During the fiscal year from July 1, 1911 to 30 June 1912, Banks was one of 1,827 who applied at that particular station. He was one of the 496 applicants accepted. Officially, Banks was designated a "colored" recruit, one of the 2,672 African-Americans who made up 6.6 percent of all enlistments during the fiscal year. As noted in Volume 1 of the *History of Jefferson Barracks,* African-Americans had almost always been present at Jefferson Barracks since the end of the Civil War.[159]

The statement of Secretary of War Redfield Proctor in 1889 still held true: "To the colored man the service offers a career, to the white man too often only a refuge." At a time when race relations were deteriorating in American society, the Army still maintained two segregated Infantry and two segregated Cavalry regiments and permitted a few black troops to serve in the Signal Corps and the Hospital Corps. The Navy, however, took steps to curtail recruitment of African-Americans and downgraded the jobs available to those who were able to enlist.[160]

At the time, discipline in the Army remained a major problem. "Discipline," Capt. George H. Shelton warned that the Army was strict about what seemed "little things" to civilians. While this policy might appear harsh, the soldiers' rights were protected, and they need not fear the military code as long as they did "their duty in the right spirit." Once in the Army, a man soon learned a good deal about military justice. First, Alfred Reynolds, author of the Army publication, *The Life of an Enlisted Man in the United States Army,* warned there were many seemingly trivial matters that could result in a court-martial, and one's chances of being tried were high. From 1908 to 1911, for example, an average of 58.25 percent of enlisted men were court-martialed in the lowest summary courts, while another six percent had to appear before general courts-martial.[161]

1912

As the year 1912 began, Col. William T. Wood remained in command of Jefferson Barracks. His garrison personnel included twenty-one officers and 1,375 enlisted men. The Hospital Corps made up the largest single unit of permanent party, numbering fifty-three. Major Deane C. Howard was the ranking medical officer. Capt. Guy V. Rukke, Capt. Henry C. Pillsbury, Capt. Ray W. Bryan, 1st Lt. Francis X. Strong, and 1st Lt. John A. McAlister, Dental Surgeon, made up the remaining medical officers.[162]

February and March 1912 provided an almost carbon copy of January. Six hundred twenty-five recruits transferred in January; 513 in February; and 301 in March.[163] The number of enlisted men increased to 1,501 in March. The officer contingent increased to twenty-two in March with the addition of Capt. James Hanson of the Quartermaster Department, who arrived on 26 March.[164]

Jefferson Barracks gained national attention in March 1912 in connection with aviation. On 1 March, a cold Friday afternoon, as hundreds of soldiers stood at the edge of the parade grounds with their baggage preparing to entrain for new assignments, the sound of a six-cylinder engine caught their attention. Looking up in the direction of the sound, the sight of a flying machine moving directly towards them through the clear sky aroused their interest. To some it was a sight of wonderment, for others it was the first flying machine they had ever seen. With compelling curiosity, the soldiers continued to observe the aircraft as it passed overhead and gracefully banked into a wide circle over the Mississippi River. Before completing its 180 degree turn, the plane began a gradual descent to 1500 feet. After passing over the field a second time the pilot circled once again and lined up with the center of the parade ground. In minutes the news that a flying machine might land at the Barracks spread through the garrison like wildfire. Excitement mounted as the machine reached the approximate center of the drill field and an object seemed to separate from the plane and tumble towards the earth. Great apprehension gripped the onlookers, shouts and finger pointing caused every soldier's attention to focus on the unfolding spectacle. The object seemed to fall a great distance before a huge umbrella of white material suddenly blossomed. Hundreds of spectators watched in amazement as the open parachute slowly descended onto the parade ground. The crowd was unaware they were witnessing the world's first successful parachute jump from an airplane. As soon as the jumper touched ground and recovered himself from his hard landing, he was immediately surrounded by the excited crowd with shouts of congratulations and backslapping.

The daredevil parachutist was young Albert Berry from St. Louis, who had performed aerial exhibits by leaping from hot air balloons at state fairs across the country. His father was Capt. John Berry, an internationally famed balloonist.

Although apt in his field as a jumper, the leap from an airplane was an unusual experience which called for great courage and skill. Because of his experience as a daredevil parachute jumper, Albert Berry was approached by an early aviation enthusiast, Thomas Wesley Benoist, with a fascinating plan to bring attention to his new airplane designs. Benoist was a builder and designer of aircraft. Later in his career, he was noted for advanced aircraft design. His Benoist "Flying Boat" was used to establish the first commercial airline in the United States. Thomas Benoist died in a streetcar accident in Sandusky, Ohio, when he was hit a by a utility pole during a sharp turn, at the height of his career in 1917.

Thomas Benoist had been a member of the Aero Club of America, whose members included early pioneers such as Albert Lambert [for whom Lambert-St. Louis International Airport is named]; William Robertson, who helped organize the First Missouri Air National Guard unit; Arch Hoxsey, who took President Theodore Roosevelt for his first airplane ride in 1910 from Kinloch Field; and many others famous in aviation history.

Benoist's chief pilot, Anthony (Tony) Jannus, had achieved fame for his flights of endurance and distance, and was also the pilot to inaugurate Benoist's airline flights. Because of Jannus' ability, he was selected to pilot the craft from which Berry would make his now famous jump.

Parachute jumping, which dates to 1783, was still in the early stages of development. New methods and means by which parachutists could leap from balloons were constantly being devised. At the time of Berry's history-making jump, the latest development in the use of a parachute called for the chute to be folded and held in the jumper's arms. He then threw the parachute clear in order for the rushing air to open the canopy. Many times this would end with tragic results.

The method which Berry used was to place the folded parachute in a large cone shaped tin container which was secured to the underside of the fuselage with the opening facing the rear behind the landing gear. The parachute was confined in place by rubber bands stretched across the wide end of the cone. The lines were then brought forward and secured to the axles of the wheels. At the time of exit from the plane, Berry first had to leave his seat, climb down to the wheels and secure the line from the parachute to himself. As he dropped into space the weight of his body pulling the parachute would break the rubber bands allowing the material to pull free. The rip cord was not developed until 1914, some two years later, which would allow for a confident free fall to be accomplished.

The aircraft was of a Benoist design and named after its builder, with a modified engine mounted aft of dual seats which would allow the craft to carry a passenger. The machine would be equipped with wheels instead of skids, which were commonly used at that time. It would also be fitted with an up-to-date series of cable controls to maneuver the aircraft in flight.

Benoist's plan was to demonstrate the efficiency of airplanes in time of war. If the exhibition was executed as planned, favorable comments from the military at Jefferson Barracks could be added assets when endeavoring to obtain a government contract to manufacture planes.

The date and preparation for the exhibition was set twice for late February, but had to be cancelled both times due to unfavorable weather conditions. To maintain a continued interest in the project, it was agreed to execute Benoist's plan at the first opportunity.

On Thursday night, 28 February, the weather began to show signs of coming to terms, although the temperature remained in the 20s. The winds had calmed considerably. By Friday morning, 1 March, the weather and winds were holding favorably, and were predicted to hold through the day. By 1:00 o'clock that afternoon, the mechanic and Tony Jannus had completely checked out the machine, while Berry and Benoist worked on the apparatus which was to hold the parachute. When all was in readiness, Albert Berry and Tony Jannus climbed aboard the biplane and took to the air. The unusual costume worn by Berry is worth mentioning. His head piece resembled a football-style helmet with automotive-style goggles. He wore a heavy rubber knee-length coat, Cavalry trousers and boots, and a long stocking cap pulled down over his ears. Jannus was similarly dressed for the sub-zero weather aloft.

After circling above Kinloch Field until 2000-feet altitude was gained, they then took up a heading toward Jefferson Barracks seventeen miles away. The flight, which took twenty minutes, was extremely cold but smooth and there was great relief when the target area was sighted at approximately 2:00 p.m. The biplane passed over the drop zone at 2000 feet and swung into a 180-degree turn over the river, while gradually lowering altitude to 1500 feet. After a second pass over the field, the plane lined up and headed toward the center of the drill field. Berry left his seat beside Jannus and climbed down to the axle. Holding on with the aid of a rope and one hand, he secured the line from the parachute to himself. He mentally gauged air speed and wind fracture, and he cut himself loose at the appropriate time and hurled into space.

Berry remarked after his extraordinary jump, "Ordinarily a parachute will open when one jumps from a balloon at about 200 feet, but my drop was 500 feet and I had been afraid I would have fallen out of the rings. I am glad I took the chance and delighted it was attended with such success." The rings Berry mentions was a belt-type affair which circled his waist, and with the sudden shock at the opening of the canopy, he felt he could have slipped through. The harness-type arrangement as we know it today was a later development.

As many hearty souls residing on the reservation as could then gathered around the jumper extending their congratulations.

Thomas Benoist, who had traveled by automobile from Kinloch Park Flying Field, which was the center of flying activity around St. Louis, arrived too late to witness Berry's historic jump.

Meanwhile, Tony Jannus, at the controls of the Benoist biplane, continued circling the drill field watching Berry's descent. In fact, he was so intent on watching the drop that he almost lost control of the plane in a steep spiral, but he recovered in time. After his passenger touched ground safely, Jannus circled once more before landing on the parade ground.

Col. William T. Wood, Post Commander at Jefferson Barracks, had received a letter from Benoist stating his intentions and asking permission for the landing at his base. After the delays due to weather, Wood had forgotten the request and so missed the entire affair. The original plan called for Berry to deliver a message to the Post Commander stating that an enemy had attacked Kinloch, and requested that a military observer be sent immediately. The plane would then land and take on the observer and return to Kinloch to assess the activities. Col. Wood asked Berry to repeat his performance but Berry was chilled to the bone and Jannus refused altogether. The episode had unnerved the daring pilot.

On Jannus' return flight to Kinloch Flying Field, he lost his bearings in the darkening hours. He realized his error when he spotted the Missouri River. Correcting his mistake, he flew on to Kinloch. The flight required almost thirty minutes. Albert Berry returned to St. Louis by automobile with Tom Benoist.

The major contribution of this event to aviation history led directly to the famous airborne troops active during World War II, and in great measure to the safety of aircraft pilots and passengers the world over.[165] When one considers the duty of soldiers during peacetime, one only need look at Jefferson Barracks as a prime example of this routine, monotonous duty. Despite the thrill of Berry's successful parachute jump the previous month, duty at Jefferson Barracks was anything but thrilling. Permanent party spent the vast majority of their time teaching new recruits the rudimentary skills of becoming a soldier. This routine duty was relieved on occasion by orders to escort recruits to new duty stations, but for the most part, duty at Jefferson Barracks remained routine and boring.

During April, the Jefferson Barracks garrison numbered twenty-one officers and 1,403 enlisted men. Capt. Stanley H. Ford, Quartermaster Department, was relieved and departed the post on 3 April. Permanent party escorted 531 recruits to new duty stations.[166]

In May, the number of enlisted men decreased to 1,021 and 809 recruits transferred. The officer corps remained unchanged.[167]

The number of enlisted men at Jefferson Barracks remained around 1,000 or slightly below for the remainder of 1912. In June, the number stood at 1,076; in July at 995; in August at 890; in September at 918; in October at 960; in November at 831; and in December at 843.[168]

New construction at Jefferson Barracks continued during 1912. Designated Mess Hall No. 1 and nicknamed "The White Elephant," Atkinson Hall was named in honor of Brigadier General Henry Atkinson, the first commander of Jefferson Barracks. It was built at a cost of $90,432. A number of other buildings, including a building for storing mail wagons were also completed during the year.[169]

A lovers' triangle claimed the lives of two young people in August. It seems that Pearl Leroy drank carbolic acid because her love for Frank Kehoe, a soldier at Jefferson Barracks, was not returned. William Toenyes, a drill master at Jefferson Barracks, then ended his life beside her grave on 20 August. Toenyes told of his love for the girl in a letter to a city detective, stating where his body could be found. Toenyes is buried at Jefferson Barracks National Cemetery.[170]

The Memorial Day observance at the Jefferson Barracks National Cemetery included something new in 1912. Thousands of roses were scattered on the Mississippi River opposite the National Cemetery by the Sons of Veterans and the Ladies Auxiliary at the memorial ceremonies on 27 May. The flowers were thrown upon the waters from the steamer *Gray Eagle*, on which the trip to the Barracks was made, while the guns of the USS *Isle de Luzon*, the training ship of the Missouri Naval Reserve, boomed a salute.[171]

The organization of the Army, or at least the Army's defense capabilities, changed for the better during 1912. The Palmer Plan, proposed to Congress in detail in 1912, organized the mobile land forces of the United States into three distinct parts. The first was the Regular Army, which would be ready for immediate use as an expeditionary force or for the first stages of a defensive war while the citizen-soldier, the traditional backbone of the nation's military, was being mobilized. The second force was an army of citizen-soldiers organized into units and ready to reinforce the Regular Army in time of war. In 1912, this was the National Guard. The third force was an army of volunteers turned citizen-soldiers.

14th Recruit Company Band ca. 1915.

Unloading hay into the second story of the old stable ca. 1910. This building also served as a tank repair station in the 1920s, a guest house for new recruits in the early days of World War II, a pub called "The Red Roof Inn," and is currently used as the Visitors' Center for Jefferson Barracks St. Louis County Park.

Dwight D. Eisenhower as he looked in June 1911 when he came to Jefferson Barracks from his home in Kansas for his physical and entrance exams for the U.S. Military Academy.

Albert Berry (standing) and Anthony Jannus (pilot) made their historic parachute jump onto the parade ground at Jefferson Barracks on 1 March 1912.

The proponents of a federal reserve force were strengthened in February 1912, when Attorney General George W. Wickersham ruled that "the militia, while in U.S. service, might pursue an invading force beyond the U.S. Boundary as part of repelling an invasion, but in general the militia cannot be employed outside of the United States."

In light of the Wickersham opinion, and persuaded by the exhortations of Secretary of War Henry Stimson and General-in-Chief Leonard Wood, Congress created a Reserve Army under provisions of Section Two of the Army Reserve Appropriations Act of 24 August 1912. This was accomplished by changing the term of Regular Army enlistment to seven years, with three or four years to be served with the colors and the balance to be a furlough to the Army Reserve. This was the first provision for a federal reserve outside of the Medical Department's Medical Reserve Officers.[172]

Although pleased by the creation of the Army Reserve through the Act of 1912, Wood continued to press for a more comprehensive federal reserve force. By 31 August 1913, the Army Reserve consisted of only eight men, and Wood observed that men would not enlist in the Army Reserve under present conditions. He wanted pay for Reservists, noting that "we cannot secure valuable service for nothing."[173]

1913

As the new year 1913 began, the commanding officer, William T. Wood and other officers and units at Jefferson Barracks remained unchanged. As one of the Army's three primary recruit depots, Jefferson Barracks contained the 14th, 15th, 16th, 18th, 23rd and 27th Recruit Companies. Capt. Jennings B. Wilson commanded the 14th Recruit Company; Capt. Dennis Quinlan the 15th; Capt. George E. Houle the 16th; Capt. Francis H. Lomax the 18th; Capt. Charles C. Farmer the 23rd and Capt. Alexander M. Wetherill the 27th.[174]

The garrison consisted of twenty-one officers and 981 enlisted men with 688 of the enlisted men being unassigned recruits. Two hundred seventy-five recruits transferred to their permanent organizations during January. The largest was a contingent of eighty Infantry recruits who left for the Presidio of San Francisco on January 9 under the charge of Sgt. Benjamin A. Brinkley, 27th Recruit Company.

In February, the garrison consisted of twenty officers and 1,111 enlisted men, of which 810 were unassigned recruits. Only 121 recruits transferred to their permanent units during the month. The largest contingent of fifty Cavalry recruits transferred to the 2nd Cavalry at Fort Bliss, Texas, under the command of 1st Lt. John R. Starkey, 2nd Field Artillery, on February 7. Starkey replaced Capt. Quinlan in command of the 15th Recruit Company on February 13. Quinlan had transferred from the 5th Cavalry to the 12th Cavalry and left Jefferson Barracks on that date.[175]

In March, the number of recruits decreased to 855 as a result of 655 recruits being transferred. The largest contingent of 116 Infantry recruits transferred on 1 March to the 1st Infantry at Honolulu, Hawaiian Islands, under the command of 1st Lt. Julius C. Peterson, Coast Artillery Corps. Another 143 Coast Artillery Corps recruits transferred on March 1 to Fort McDowell, California, also under 1st Lt. Peterson.[176]

A large group of recruits being transferred to San Diego, California, ran into problems at Pueblo, Colorado. Public health authorities in Pueblo discovered two soldiers with measles on the troop train passing through that city. The two had to be hospitalized and the train had a two hour wait, while health authorities threatened to quarantine 100 more soldiers. The problem was solved by keeping the troops in a body and marching them through the city streets accompanied by a health officer who prevented them from visiting any public places.[177]

Col. Adam Slaker, Coast Artillery Corps, arrived at Jefferson Barracks on 2 April 1913. The next day Slaker relieved Col. William T. Wood in command of the post. Wood was placed on the retired list on 3 April.[178]

Col. Slaker took command of a garrison that consisted of twenty officers and 898 enlisted men, of which 579 were unassigned recruits. Three hundred twenty recruits transferred during the month. The largest contingent of sixty-eight Cavalry recruits left for the 1st Cavalry at Fort Yellowstone, Wyoming, under the charge of Sgt. Oscar Chapert, 16th Recruit Company.[179]

In May, Slaker's command dwindled to 788 enlisted men, of which 462 were unassigned recruits. Five hundred recruits transferred during the month, the largest contingent of Coast Artillery Corps recruits transferred to Fort Adams, Rhode Island, under the charge of Sgt. Jacob Miller, 16th Recruit Company.[180]

Several enlisted men who had deserted were apprehended or surrendered in the area during May. William T. Bordeaux, a horseshoer in Troop F, 11th Cavalry, was apprehended at Belleville, Illinois, on 16 May and turned over to military control at Jefferson Barracks the next day. Pvt. James Gilmore, Co. B, 7th Infantry; Pvt. Lester Schefferling, Battery E, 4th Field Artillery; Pvt. Ernest B. Smith, Co. A, 9th Infantry; and Pvt. Howard W. Watson,

Co. 10, Coast Artillery Corps were apprehended at Jefferson Barracks and Pvt. Eddie Reveis, Co. G, 9th Infantry, surrendered in St. Louis. Pvt. Robert Roper, Co. 156, Coast Artillery Corps, was apprehended at Taylorville, Illinois, on 20 May and turned over to military control at Jefferson Barracks on 21 May.[181]

In June, the Jefferson Barracks garrison consisted of nineteen officers and 856 enlisted men, with 524 of these men being unassigned recruits. Two hundred ninety-seven recruits transferred during the month, the largest contingent was sixty-three Cavalry recruits who transferred on June 6 to the 4th Cavalry at Fort McDowell, California, under the command of Lt. Col. Thomas W. Griffiths, Infantry.[182]

In July, the number of enlisted men increased to 969, of which, 636 were unassigned recruits. Major James M. Kennedy, Medical Corps, arrived for duty at Jefferson Barracks on 21 July. He was appointed surgeon and recruiting officer. Capt. Frederick G. Lawton, Quartermaster Corps, arrived on 15 July and was detailed as Post Quartermaster. Two officers were relieved from duty at Jefferson Barracks during July: Major Deane C. Howard, Medical Corps, was relieved on 15 July and left on 27 July; and Capt. James Hanson, Quartermaster Corps, was relieved of duty on 27 May, and left the post on 24 July.[183]

Also in July, several enlisted men who had deserted from the Army were returned to military authority at Jefferson Barracks. Pvt. Lamont R. Burr, Troop B, 12th Cavalry, was apprehended at Jefferson Barracks, while Pvt. Robert Cooper, Co. I, 20th Infantry; and Pvt. James Griffiths, Troop C, 14th Cavalry were apprehended in St. Louis. Pvt. James O'Brien, Co. G, 9th Infantry and Pvt. Bert C. O'Brady, Battery B, 3rd Field Artillery, surrendered at Jefferson Barracks and Pvt. Dell C. Prater, Co. 61, Coast Artillery Corps, was apprehended at Havana, Illinois. All of these men were held in confinement at Jefferson Barracks awaiting charges and trial.[184]

August and September 1913 passed much as the first seven months of the year. The troops performed routine garrison duties and the recruits received their training from the post's permanent party personnel. In August, 366 recruits transferred and in September 641.[185]

Col. John H. Beacom, Infantry, relieved Col. Slaker in command of Jefferson Barracks on 3 October. Col. Beacom, from Ohio, graduated from the U.S. Military Academy in 1882 and was commissioned a second lieutenant in the 18th Infantry. He transferred to the 3rd Infantry on 19 April 1883. Beacom received a promotion to first lieutenant on 20 January 1888, and to captain, 6th Infantry on 26 April 1898. He became Assistant Adjutant General of the 7th Army Corps on 12 May 1898 and lieutenant colonel of volunteers on 27 August 1898. He received an honorable discharge from volunteer service on 22 April 1899. Just two weeks later Beacom transferred to the 42nd U.S. Volunteer Infantry, which he organized at Fort Niagara and saw service in the Philippine Islands with that unit. He received an honorable discharge from volunteer service on 27 June 1901. Beacom served as Military Attache at the American Embassy in London from October 1903 to January 1907. While on active duty, Col. Beacom died suddenly in Mexico on 17 September 1916. Commenting on his "deplorable loss" to the military, General John J. Pershing wrote,"[He] was one of the ablest officers in our Army. His services..., have been of the highest order and second to none."[186]

Beacom took command of a garrison consisting of twenty-one officers and 860 enlisted men in October 1913. There were 536 recruits in training at the post, and 457 recruits transferred during his first month on the job. They consisted of 255 Infantry, 73 Coast Artillery, 54 Field Artillery, 50 Cavalry, 18 Quartermaster Corps, and 7 Engineer recruits.[187]

In November, Col. Beacom's command increased to 1,025 enlisted men, which included 690 unassigned recruits. Four hundred twenty-two recruits transferred during the month. Recruits transferred to the east, west, and south, going to such places as Plattsburg Barracks, New York; Fort Warren, Massachusetts; Texas City, Galveston, and El Paso, Texas; Fort Morgan, Alabama; Fort Sill, Oklahoma; and Fort McDowell, California.[188]

December 1913 witnessed the largest contingent of enlisted men at the post during the entire year, with 1,464 enlisted men present. This was even after 568 recruits transferred during the month. One contingent of fifty Infantry recruits transferred to the 10th Infantry in the Canal Zone in Panama. Sgt. Frederick Wollman, 16th Recruit Company, was in charge of those recruits. This was the first time that recruits from Jefferson Barracks had been sent to the Canal Zone.[189]

During 1913, relations between the Regular Army and the National Guard became strained. The Army, under General Leonard Wood, made a strong effort to develop better relations, as well as develop another source for citizen soldiers through the establishment of summer training camps. General Wood began this program with two camps for college students in 1913. Regular Army officers and enlisted men served as instructors for 245 students from ninety colleges and universities. The students paid their own way for six weeks of training. The next year there were more camps, and by 1915, businesses and professional leaders were invited. In 1916, over 16,000 students attended sixteen one-month camps and six two-week courses. [One of the instructors in 1916 was newly promoted Capt. George C. Marshall] In the early 1920s these camps, or camps modeled on these earlier efforts, came to be called Citizen's Military Training Camps or C.M.T.C. Jefferson Barracks hosted its first C.M.T.C. in 1921.[190]

Chapter 6 - 1914: World War I Begins in Europe

The year 1914 would prove to be monumental. At Jefferson Barracks Col. John H. Beacom, Infantry, remained in command. The post remained a Recruit Depot with the 14th, 15th, 16th, 18th, 23rd and 27th Recruit Companies comprising the principal units. Eighteen officers and 1,338 men made up the personnel under Col. Beacom's command.[1]

Permanent party performed routine garrison duties during the month. The total number of recruits forwarded during January came to 970. Of these, 481 recruits went to the Infantry, 236 to the Coast Artillery, 137 to the Cavalry, 88 to the Field Artillery, 13 to the Quartermaster Department, 12 to the Engineers and 3 to the Hospital Corps. The largest single shipment consisted of 153 Coast Artillery recruits that left January 26 en route to the Philippine Islands, under the command of Capt. George E. Houle.[2]

Little did Col. Beacom or any of the other officers or men suspect in January 1914 that events in Europe would soon dramatically change the routine at Jefferson Barracks and throughout the United States. Those events remained more than seven months in the future, but they would forever alter the way the Army and Jefferson Barracks conducted business. During February 1914, Col. Beacom commanded a garrison that consisted of nineteen officers and 1,119 enlisted men. 1st Lt. George L. Kelcher, 26th Infantry, had been detached for General Recruiting duty and ordered to Jefferson Barracks. He arrived on February 5 and was assigned to duty with the 15th Recruit Company. Kelcher represented the only change in the Jefferson Barracks officer corps during the month.

A total of 663 recruits were forwarded during February. The largest contingent was 176 Infantry recruits who were forwarded to the 2nd Infantry at Fort McDowell, California, under the command of Capt. George W. England, Infantry.[3]

March saw little change. 1st Lt. Julius C. Peterson, Coast Artillery Corps, was relieved from duty at Jefferson Barracks on 13 March and departed the same day. He was replaced by 1st Lt. John G. Donovan, Coast Artillery Corps, who arrived on 19 March.

A total of 641 recruits transferred during the month. The largest single group was 125 Infantry recruits going to Fort McDowell. 1st Lt. Walter W. Merrill, 6th Field Artillery, commanded these recruits.[4]

The only change in April was a slight increase in enlisted personnel to 1,281. A total of 664 recruits transferred during the month.[5]

May saw little change. The garrison consisted of a total of nineteen officers and 1,265 enlisted men. During the month, Col. Beacom went on leave for twelve days, leaving Capt. George E. Houle in command in his absence. Six hundred and eighty-four recruits transferred during the month.[6]

In June 1914, Col. Beacom commanded a garrison of nineteen officers and 952 enlisted men, which was the lowest number of enlisted personnel at Jefferson Barracks since October 1913.

A total of 657 recruits were forwarded during the month. The largest contingent of recruits, 125, went to the 2nd Infantry at Fort McDowell, under the command of Capt. A.E. Williams, Cavalry. Another 100 Infantry recruits went to Texas City, Texas, under the command of 1st Lt. F.H. Burr, Infantry. The recruits traveling the farthest were forty-four recruits destined for the 10th Infantry in the Canal Zone in Panama. Sgt. Edward Schooler, 27th Recruit Company, was in charge of these recruits.[7]

July 1914 saw little change in the garrison. Col. Beacom remained in command of a garrison consisting of twenty officers and 980 enlisted men. Only 456 recruits were forwarded during the month.[8]

As mentioned previously, desertion had always been a major problem in the Army. During July, there seemed to be an inordinate number of deserters apprehended or who surrendered. Most did not get too far from Jefferson Barracks. Pvt. Louis Barbee, Coast Artillery Corps, was apprehended at Kinnundy, Illinois on 17 July and turned over to military control at Jefferson Barracks on July 18 to await trial on charges of desertion. Pvt. John C. Byrd, Coast Artillery Corps, surrendered at the recruiting station in St. Louis on 28 July and was turned over to military control at Jefferson Barracks the next day. He was held in confinement awaiting charges. Pvt. Earl D. Connor, Signal Corps, was apprehended at Mount Vernon, Illinois, on 9 July and was turned over to military control at Jefferson Barracks the next day. He was held in confinement awaiting trial for desertion. Pvt. Raymond J. Daum was apprehended in Sullivan, Illinois, on 27 July and turned over to military control at Jefferson Barracks on 28 July. He was held in confinement awaiting charges. Pvt. James Green, 9th Infantry, was apprehended in St. Louis on 18 July and turned over to authorities at Jefferson Barracks the same day. He was held in confinement awaiting charges.

Pvt. Edwin F. Jones, 3rd Battalion of Engineers, Company G, was apprehended in St. Louis on 27 July and turned over to military authorities at Jefferson Barracks on 28 July. He was held in confinement awaiting charges. Pvt. Thomas H. Johnston, Company K, 26th Infantry, was apprehended at Chaffee, Missouri, on 7 July and turned over to military control at Jefferson Barracks on 9 July. He was held in confinement awaiting charges. Pvt. John Keogh, Quartermaster Corps, was apprehended at Jefferson Barracks on 1 July. He was held in confinement awaiting trial for desertion. Pvt. Clifford G. Karrelmeyer, Company B, 7th Infantry, was apprehended at Hermann, Missouri, on 11 July and turned over to military control at Jefferson Barracks the same day. He was held in confinement awaiting the result of his trial. Pvt. Joseph F. Ledoux, Coast Artillery Corps, was apprehended at Jefferson Barracks on July 10 and held in confinement awaiting trial. Pvt. Walter B. McKay, Troop H, 12th Cavalry, surrendered at the recruiting station in Memphis, Tennessee, on 29 July and was turned over to military control at Jefferson Barracks on 31 July. He was held in confinement awaiting charges. Pvt. Roy A. Barnell, Troop H, 15th Cavalry, surrendered at the recruiting station in Champaign, Illinois, on 11 July and was turned over to military control at Jefferson Barracks on 15 July. He was held in confinement awaiting trial by general court martial.[9]

Not everything at Jefferson Barracks involved training and military activities. From the top down, officers and higher ranking non-commissioned officers knew that the morale of the troops had to be a priority. On 18 July 1914, the 27th Recruit Company held a "Good Time Party" in an effort to promote morale and establish camaraderie among the trainees. Sgt. Anthony Julis served as chairman of the event and all 27th Recruit Company personnel received invitations sent by Sgt. Edward Schooler and Pvt. William Thompson. Sgt. John S. Lowell and Pvt. James Gibbs prepared supper, a magnificent feast. Sgt. James Hayes took care of the refreshments and Cpl. Otis W. Haynie, Artificer James R. Stewart and Pvt. John H. Schroeder decorated the hall. The evening program included music, such as "Dreams of the Retirement," a waltz; "How Did the Joker Get into the Pinochle Deck?" a two-step; and "Turn the Switch and Call Outside," a tango. After the musical interlude, supper was served, with music playing the entire time. The program featured "The Act of Hypnotism" introduced by Sgt. Julis, followed by ten additional waltzes, tangos and two-steps. The General Order of the Day included "Tonight to exercise the greatest happiness. Between 8 o'clock and 1:00 a.m. dance, sing, laugh and drink all you can, and allow no one to leave the party until everything is over, unless he has the proper authority." That "a little nonsense now and then is relished by the best of men," and "that all growling, anger and things of that sort is [sic] strictly prohibited. All persons found in this state will be arrested and punished as the court martial directs." The last page of the evening program contained the poem "Good Old Jefferson Barracks."[10]

Good Old Jefferson Barracks
Near the lonely railroad station
On the Iron Mountain line,
Stands old Jefferson Barracks
With its solder boys so fine.

Strict are rules and regulations,
As it frowns down from the height;
The married men stay twice a week,
Where the single ones go every night.

There's a lot of noise and grumbles
Of the permanent party there;
They like to go to some other place,
Which direction they do not care.

Then comes the day when they depart
To the better land they know;
But finding all not as they thought it was,
Again disgusted, back want to go.

Dreaming of the good old Barracks,

With their loved ones standing beside,
For they know not but some other fellow
Is kissing his girl this evening tide.

Now he ponders for good old Barracks
On the Iron Mountain line,
Again he'd like to be a member
Of those soldier boys so fine.

Yes, this is our good old Barracks,
In the grand old state of Mo.
The best one out of its outfits
Is the twenty-seventh Co.

In August 1914, Col. Beacom's command included twenty officers and 1,150 enlisted men. The only change in the officer complement took place on 7 August, when Capt. Henry C. Pillsbury was relieved of duty at Jefferson Barracks. A total of 490 recruits transferred to their permanent organizations during the month. Ten deserters either surrendered or were apprehended during the month.[11]

August 1914 passed much as any other month had passed at Jefferson Barracks. However, events in Europe took place that would change forever the complexion of the Army and the routine at Jefferson Barracks. On the night of 1 August 1914, as the first step in the long-prepared strategic move against France, German troops entered Luxembourg. It was a small-scale operation with the objective of occupying a rail and telegraph junction. The next day, 2 August, German military patrols crossed the French frontier for the first time since 1871, and there were several skirmishes. At Joncherey, near the German-Swiss border, a French soldier, Cpl. Andre Peugeot was killed, the first French victim of a war that was to claim more than a million French lives.[12]

At 7 o'clock on the evening of 2 August 1914, Germany delivered a 12-hour ultimatum to Belgium. German troops must be given free passage through Belgium. The Belgians refused. By the Treaty of London in 1839, Great Britain, Austria, Prussia, France and Russia had agreed that Belgium should be an independent and perpetually neutral state. On 3 August 1914, Germany declared war on France, and German troops crossed into Belgium.[13]

These events had been set in motion on 28 June 1914, when Archduke Franz Ferdinand, heir to the Hapsburg throne (Austro-Hungarian Empire), was assassinated in Sarajevo. Among those gathered to watch the Archduke and his wife drive through the city to the governor's residence that day was a 19-year-old Bosnian Serb, Gavrilo Princip, who had a pistol. Princip was one of six conspirators present in the streets that day who dreamed of the moment when Bosnia would be free of Austrian subjugation.[14]

By midnight on 4 August 1914, five empires were at war: the Austro-Hungarian Empire against Serbia; the German Empire against France, the British Empire and Russia; the Russian Empire against Germany and Austro-Hungary; and the British Empire against Germany.[15]

Before all was said and done, more than nine million soldiers, sailors and airmen would be killed as well as another five million civilians. The make-up and routine of the United States Army and Navy would never be the same.

By the end of August, the British Expeditionary Force was fighting the Germans at the Battle of Mons in Belgium and the French were fighting the Germans at Charleroi in Belgium. A total of 500,000 Germans and 336,000 French and British soldiers had clashed on the Western Front.[16]

When war began, the belligerents showed little interest in the United States. Aside from their naivete about military matters, their dependence on an anachronistic volunteer system, and an apparent incompetence of commanders, the United States had a very small Regular Army. At just under 98,000 men in 1914, it was about sixteen percent of the peacetime strength of the German Army [620,000] less than eighteen percent of the French Army [600,000] just over thirty-eight percent of the British Army [250,000]and not quite seventy percent of the Swiss Army [40,000] In 1912 the American military attache in St. Petersburg had reported that neither the Russians nor any other European officers comment on American military affairs, as there was a "universal belief that our Army is not worthy of serious consideration."[17]

While events in Europe would affect the army as well as civilians in the United States before too long, September 1914 dawned much as every other month during 1914 at Jefferson Barracks. Col. Beacom had two fewer officers than during the previous month, but his enlisted personnel had increased to 1,294, of which 1,195 were recruits in training. A total of 636 recruits transferred to their permanent organizations during the month. The largest contingent was 165 Coast Artillery Corps recruits who transferred to Fort McDowell on 24 September under the command of Capt. F.M. Jones, Cavalry.[18]

An event of major significance took place on 3 September in the North Sea when a German submarine, the *U-21*, sank the British cruiser HMS *Pathfinder*. This was the first warship sunk by torpedo fire; 250 sailors died. The submarine was a new and virulent weapon of war.[19]

On the very same day that the Germans had their submarine success, a British pilot, Lt. Dalrymple-Clark, carried out the first British bombing raid of the war, over land, near the Franco-Belgian border. According to the official report, he "expended one bomb on about forty Germans, some evidently hurt."[20]

On 5 September, the Battle of the Marne began. It lasted four days and marked the end of any chance of a rapid German victory in the West. The battle pitted 1,275,000 Germans against 1,000,000 French and 125,000 British.[21]

On 22 September, the British made their first air raid on Germany, attacking Zeppelin sheds at Cologne and Dusseldorf. The German submarine, *U-9*, torpedoed three British cruisers: the *Aboukis, the Cressy* and *the Hogue*, causing the deaths of 1,459 sailors.[22]

The number of recruits at Jefferson Barracks increased to 1,403 in October 1914, dropped to 1,095 in November, and then increased to 1,560 in December, the highest number of recruits for any month during 1914. The number of officers at Jefferson Barracks remained at nineteen or twenty for the remainder of the year.[23]

A total of 795 recruits transferred during October. The largest single shipment was 255 Infantry recruits sent to Fort McDowell on 21 October, under the command of Capt. George E. Houle.[24] In November 818 recruits transferred. Another 255 Infantry recruits went to Fort McDowell on 27 November, under the command of 1st Lt. George C. Keleher.[25] A total of 677 recruits transferred during December. Again, Fort McDowell received the largest single contingent when 265 Infantry recruits left Jefferson Barracks on December 28, under the command of 1st Lt. Talbot Smith. Fort McDowell received another fifty-one Infantry recruits and twenty-one mounted Field Artillery recruits during the month. It should be noted that the final destination of many of these recruits was the Philippine Islands.[26]

Although the construction of new facilities at Jefferson Barracks had slowed during 1914, a dairy barn for forty cows was built during the year. This proved to be a real asset in the days to come as it greatly simplified supplying milk to the post personnel.[27]

1915

With war now raging in Europe, Jefferson Barracks opened the new year, 1915, with as yet little change in routine. Col. John H. Beacom remained in command. The garrison consisted of twenty officers and 1,596 enlisted men. Of these, 1,491 were recruits. The largest contingents of permanent party men belonged to the Hospital Corps [55], and the Quartermaster Corps [one officer, four sergeants and forty-two enlisted men].

The only change in the officer corps took place on January 6, when 1st Lt. John R. Starkey was relieved of duty at Jefferson Barracks and departed.[28]

During the month, 743 recruits transferred to their permanent organizations. Two groups of over one hundred recruits transferred: one group of 128 Coast Artillery Corps recruits left Jefferson Barracks on 2 January for Fort Winfield Scott, California, under the command of Capt. George W. England; and the other, a group of 111 Infantry recruits departed on 18 January for duty with the 17th Infantry at Eagle Pass, Texas, under the command of 1st Lt. John G. Donovan.[29]

There were also 106 enlisted men attached or carried on casual status and twenty-six general prisoners. Sixty-two enlisted men received a dishonorable discharge at Jefferson Barracks during the month.[30]

Another first took place in the war in Europe during January. On the night of 19 January, the Germans launched their first bombing raid on Great Britain, when two Zeppelins crossed the North Sea to the Norfolk coast. Four civilians were killed in the attack: two at Yarmouth and two at King's Lynn.[31]

In the English Channel, the first British merchant ship to be torpedoed without warning was sunk by a German submarine on 30 January. On 1 February, an American diplomat in Paris, John Coolidge, noted in his diary: "Another little merchant ship has just been sunk by the Germans, just at the mouth of the Mersey, which gives us all a horrid feeling. The Germans are so angry at not getting ahead that they leave nothing undone."[32]

That day, the German Chancellor agreed to the German Imperial Navy's request to launch submarine warfare against all ships, including neutral ships, that were bringing food or supplies to the Entente Powers.[33] The German use of unrestricted submarine warfare constituted one of the primary reasons that the United States would declare war on Germany just over two years later. The Germans made this new war policy public on 5 February. Five days after the German declaration, the United States warned the German government that the proposed submarine warfare constituted an indefensible violation of neutral rights, and that Germany would be held to 'strict accountability' if an American vessel or the lives of American citizens were lost as a result of the new policy. The United States would take any steps that might be necessary to safeguard American lives and property. What those steps might be was not explained.[34]

Little changed in February 1915. The number of enlisted men at the post climbed to 1,627. A total of 916 recruits transferred; the largest number in any month. Again, Fort McDowell was the destination for many of the recruits, receiving a total of 564 during the month.[35]

On 26 February, another first took place in the war in Europe when the Germans used flame-throwers for the first time against the French in trenches near Verdun. This was the first of an estimated 653 flame-thrower attacks.[36]

The month of March 1915 was much like the previous month. The number of enlisted men dropped to 1,373, probably due to the record number of recruits that transferred, 1,145. The number of officers remained at twenty-one as Capt. Guy V. Rukke, Medical Corps, was relieved of duty at Jefferson Barracks on 30 March. He was replaced by Capt. Charles E. Freeman, Medical Corps, who had arrived on March 8 and had been appointed recruiting officer.[37]

In April, the size of the Jefferson Barracks garrison decreased to nineteen officers and 1,057 enlisted men. Only 667 recruits transferred to their permanent organizations.[38]

During April, yet another first in warfare took place. On 22 April, poison gas was used for the first time in World War I. That evening, near Langemarck in the Ypres Salient, the Germans discharged, within five minutes, 168 tons of chlorine gas from 4,000 cylinders against two French divisions, one Algerian and the other Territorial, and against the adjacent Canadian Division, over a four-mile front.[39]

May 1915 again saw little change at Jefferson Barracks. Col. Beacom's command numbered twenty-one officers and 1,091 enlisted men, with 729 unassigned recruits. Only 406 recruits transferred. The garrison performed the usual garrison duties.[40]

There were also fifty-two enlisted men apprehended or surrendered from desertion, held in confinement or dishonorably discharged during the month.

The only event not of a routine nature took place between 9 May and 15 May. During this time, Lt. Col. Andre W. Brewster, Inspector General's Office, arrived at Jefferson Barracks and performed an annual inspection of the post and personnel.[41]

In May, an event took place that has always been cited as a major cause for the United States entry into World War I. On 1 May, the *Lusitania* sailed as planned, but left her berth two and a half hours late. On 6 May, the *U-20* commanded by Capt. Walther Schweiger sank two British merchant ships without warning. Four torpedoes had been fired, three were left. That evening Captain William Turner of the *Lusitania* received a wireless message from the British Admiralty: 'Subs active off south coast of Ireland.' Four further warnings were sent that night and early the following morning.

At noon on 7 May, the *U-20* sighted the cruiser *Juno*, but as the *Juno* was zigzagging and going at full speed, Capt. Schweiger gave up the chase. An hour and a half later, he sighted the *Lusitania*. A single torpedo was fired without warning. hitting the *Lusitania* which sank in eighteen minutes. Of the 2,000 passengers and crew on board, 1,198 drowned, among them 128 Americans.[42]

Stunned by the sinking of the *Lusitania*, law partners Grenville Clark and Elihu Roots, Jr., son of the former U.S. Secretary of War, determined to do something to demonstrate a firm national policy against Germany. Enlisting the aid of Theodore Roosevelt, Jr., they approached Gen. Leonard Wood, Commander of the Army, with the idea of adapting the youth summer camps to camps for men in their 20s and 30s. Wood was supportive. If Clark and others could sign up at least 100 professional and business men for the camps, Wood would provide the officers and equipment. When recruiting for the businessmen's camps went well, Wood was able to have the adult camps included under War Department General Order No. 38, of 22 June 1915, which authorized that summer's college camps. Approximately 1,200 men assembled at Plattsburg, New York, for the first businessmen's camp. Compressing the five-week program into four weeks, the men started their day with calisthenics at 5:45 a.m., followed by drill until noon. After lunch, there was specialized instruction in the arms of the service - cavalry, signal, and engineering. The men at Plattsburg tackled the training with enthusiasm and at the end of camp formed the First Training Regiment.

Determined that Plattsburg would not be a one-time phenomenon, Clark worked with members of similar businessmen's camps and with the advisory Board of University Presidents of the National Reserve Corps to form the Military Training Camps Association of the United States [MTCA]. The stated purpose of the MTCA was to encourage reasonable military training for citizens through federal training camps, and the group's efforts later played an important role in the "90-day wonder" commissioning camps of World War I.[43]

Again, in June, there was little change at Jefferson Barracks. Beacom's command numbered twenty-one officers and 1,112 enlisted men, with 752 unassigned recruits. The number of recruits forwarded to permanent organizations came to 436.[44]

In July, the number of recruits forwarded remained rather low at 492. The largest single group forwarded during the month was 113 Colored Infantry recruits who were forwarded to Fort McDowell on 23 July under the charge of Sgt. George E. Davis, 16th Recruit Company.[45]

During July, the Jefferson Barracks garrison consisted of twenty-two officers and 1,015 enlisted men with 668 unassigned recruits. The one additional officer was 1st Lt. Augustus B. Jones, Medical Corps, who arrived on 16 July. Less than one month earlier Lt. Jones had been commissioned a 1st lieutenant in the Medical Corps from the Medical Reserve Corps.[46]

In August, few changes took place. The officer corps lost two men when Capt. Harry G. Humphreys, Medical Corps, was relieved of duty at Jefferson Barracks on 10 August, and 1st Lt. John A. McAlister, Dental Service, was relieved on 19 August.

The garrison had 1,186 enlisted men assigned with 832 unassigned recruits in August. The number of recruits forwarded during the month dropped to only 379. Ninety-eight of these, or slightly over 25 percent, went to Fort McDowell, under the charge of Sgt. Charles M. Watkins, 23rd Recruit Company.[47]

The wife of Lt. Francis Burr was shot on the night of 7 August while riding as a passenger in a car driven by her husband. Col. Beacom explained that Dan H. Schremesel, a lance corporal, and Hora G. Woodruff, a private, had been detailed to investigate several shots which had been fired on the reservation and had come upon the automobile in which Lt. Burr and his wife were riding. A command to halt was ignored because, Burr said, it was not heard. Then Schremesel ordered Woodruff to shoot at a tire. Mrs. Burr was shot, but the bullet was removed and she recovered. Col. Beacom stated that no arrests had been made, as both enlisted men believed that they were acting within their rights.[48]

Again, in September the number of recruits forwarded dropped, this time to 290. The largest single group was eighty Infantry recruits forwarded on 24 September to the 11th Infantry at Douglas, Arizona, under the charge of Sgt. Arthur V. Burnett, 23rd Recruit Company.[49]

Col. Beacom's command consisted of nineteen officers and 1,399 enlisted men with 1,050 unassigned recruits. There were seven enlisted men who surrendered or were apprehended for desertion during the month, nineteen awaiting charges or on trial for desertion, at least thirty-two men in confinement, and seven who received dishonorable discharges during the month.[50]

October 1915 passed much as the previous month had passed. The garrison of nineteen officers and 1,099 enlisted men performed the usual routine garrison duties and recruits, 748 in number, continued to receive training.

A total of 650 recruits transferred to permanent organizations during the month. Sgt. Robert Bell, 23rd Recruit Company, led the largest contingent of recruits, seventy-nine Cavalry recruits for the 8th Cavalry at Fort Bliss, Texas. They departed Jefferson Barracks on 27 October.[51]

Tragedy struck a young recruit from New Orleans during the night of 7 October. Joseph B. Cox, a recruit at Jefferson Barracks, was killed by an Iron Mountain train between the Barracks and St. Louis while returning to his quarters from the city. Cox's body was found early the next morning by a train crew and officials were notified.

Cox had enlisted from 123 South Miro Street in New Orleans a few months previously and had been stationed at the Barracks for a short time.[52]

After two years of being in command of Jefferson Barracks, Col. John H. Beacom was assigned to command of the 6th Infantry Regiment and departed the post on 27 November. Capt. Andrew E. Williams, Cavalry, took command of the post upon Beacom's departure. Williams had been in command of the 18th Recruit Company.[53]

During November, the garrison consisted of seventeen officers and 1,237 enlisted men with 874 unassigned recruits. Only 318 recruits were forwarded during November. Cpl. John M. Collins took eighty Infantry recruits for the 21st Infantry at Vancouver Barracks, Washington, on 11 November. This was the single largest group forwarded. The next largest group was sixty-three Coast Artillery Corps recruits forwarded to Fort Warren, Massachusetts, under the charge of Sgt. Aaron Kaplan, 15th Recruit Company, which left on 1 November.[54]

In the World War, a new war zone opened on 14 November. Although it is probably one of the least remembered of the war, on that day, in the deserts of Italian Libya, which before 1912 had been part of the Ottoman Empire, the Senussi tribesmen revolted against the Allies. Supported by Turkey, the Senussi opened fire on a British-Egyptian border post at Sollum.[55]

Capt. Williams remained in command of Jefferson Barracks until the arrival of Lt. Col. William L. Kenly on 30 December 1915. Kenly, from Maryland, had graduated eleventh in his class at West Point in June 1889. He had been commissioned a 2nd lieutenant in the 4th Artillery upon graduation and became a 1st Lt. in the 1st Artillery on 29 June 1896. He served at Jefferson Barracks in 1898 and was made a captain of the Artillery Corps on 2 February, 1901.[56] On 3 September 1917, Kenly, who by then was a brigadier general, became the first Chief of the Air Service of the American Expeditionary Force in France. Kenly returned to the United States to become Director of Military Aeronautics from 20 May 1918 to 28 August 1918. During that period, Kenly was also titular head of the newly established United States Army Air Service.

Lt. Col. Kenly's new command at Jefferson Barracks consisted of twenty officers and 1,314 enlisted men with 959 unassigned recruits. One of the largest turnovers ever in officer personnel at Jefferson Barracks took place in December 1915. In addition to Kenly, new officers who arrived at Jefferson Barracks in December 1915 included: Capt. Frank W. Chilton, Medical Corps; Frederick R. Wunderlich, Acting Dental Surgeon; Capt. William W. McCammon, 22nd Infantry; 1st Lt. Odione H. Sampson, 28th Infantry; Capt. James D. Watson, Coast Artillery Corps; 1st Lt. George I. Gunchel, Dental Service; and Ben H. Sherrad, Acting Dental Surgeon. Those relieved from duty at Jefferson Barracks and who departed in December included Capt. Alexander M. Wetherill, Infantry; Capt. Francis H. Lomax, Coast Artillery Corps; 1st Lt. Francis H. Burr, 28th Infantry; 1st Lt. Talbot Smith, 5th Cavalry; and 1st Lt. George C. Keleher, 26th Infantry.[57]

Three hundred fifty-two recruits were forwarded during the month. The largest contingent was fifty-eight Cavalry recruits sent to the 9th Cavalry at Fort McDowell, under the charge of Sgt. George Stainway, 23rd Recruit Company.[58] Eighteen enlisted men received dishonorable discharges during the month.

Athletics has been and always will be a morale builder and a diversion from normal duties in the military. Boxing has always been a favorite with soldiers. On the night of December 23 just such a boxing match took place at Jefferson Barracks. Veteran boxer Eddie Lennon fought Harry Kabakoff. Kabakoff was declared the winner when referee Eddie Randall stopped the fight in the sixth round and awarded the match to Kabakoff. Randall charged that Lennon persisted in holding and hitting in the clinches despite several warnings. To many of the fans present, it appeared that Randall had erred, as Lennon seemed to be battling Kabakoff at his own style on even terms with the boy wonder, Kabakoff. Willie Colonna made his debut as a professional by boxing "Kid" Van to a draw in the semi-windup.[59]

There were also several new developments in the World War. The Germans released phosgene gas, ten times more toxic than chlorine gas, on 19 December against the British forces in the Ypres Salient. A thousand soldiers were gassed and 120 killed. However, a strong wind that day blew the gas cloud far to the rear, and due to a curve in the line, some of the gas blew along the German trenches.[60]

Another new development, trench foot, proved especially debilitating. Men standing in slime for days in field boots or puttees lost all sense of feeling in their feet. Their feet began to swell, then go "dead," then suddenly to burn as though touched by red hot pokers. When the "reliefs" went up scores of men could not walk back from the trenches, but had to crawl, or be carried by their comrades. Battalions lost more men from the fighting line from trench foot than from wounds. A cure was eventually found; rubbing the feet with oil two or three times a day.[61]

Col. John H. Beacom, Infantry, commanded Jefferson Barracks from 3 October 1913, until 27 November 1915.

Designated Mess Hall No. 1 and nicknamed "The White Elephant," Atkinson Hall
was named for Brigadier General Henry Atkinson, the first commander of Jefferson Barracks.
It was built at a cost of $90,432 in 1912. Note the long line of soldiers
waiting for chow. It had a capacity of 4,000.

Major General William L. Kenly served as the first Chief of the Air Service of the American Expeditionary Force during World War I. Lt. Col. Kenly took command of Jefferson Barracks on 30 December 1915. Kenly had served as a 1st lieutenant at the post in 1898. Kenly remained in command until relieved on 8 November 1916.

Jefferson Barracks Baseball Club

One of the first baseball teams ever organized by the Army Standing, left to right: Lindsey, right field; Getty, center field; Thomason, manager, captain & shortstop; Clinton, pitcher; Haigh, first base. Sitting: Smith, third base; York, shortstop; Lewis, catcher; Teary, second base; Gallagher, left field. Two of these men were killed at Wounded Knee.

Jefferson Barracks baseball team ca. 1909.

1916

Lt. Col. William L. Kenly commanded a garrison consisting of twenty-four officers and 1,092 enlisted men, with 739 unassigned recruits. As one of three primary recruit training posts in the country, the Jefferson Barracks garrison consisted of numerous units. The Hospital Corps had fifty-four enlisted men and the Quartermaster Corps had one officer, four Quartermaster sergeants and forty enlisted men. The recruit training companies were the 14th (Band) with twenty-four enlisted men; the 15th with two officers and forty-four enlisted men; the 16th with two officers and forty-six enlisted men; the 18th with one officer and forty-five enlisted men; the 23rd with one officer and forty-five enlisted men; and the 27th with two officers and forty-five enlisted men.[62]

A few changes did take place in the officer corps in January. 1st Lt. Walter W. Merrill, 6th Field Artillery, was relieved of duty at Jefferson Barracks and left on 21 January. Capt. Ralph C. Caldwell, Cavalry; 1st Lt. George W. Harris, 28th Infantry; and 1st Lt. Robert L. Collins, 8th Cavalry; were detailed for the General Recruiting Service and arrived at Jefferson Barracks on 10 January, 8 January and 2 January respectively.[63]

A total of 670 recruits were forwarded during January. The largest group was seventy Infantry recruits sent to the 12th Infantry at Nogales, Arizona, under the charge of Sgt. Robert Baker, 27th Recruit Company.[64]

There were few changes, except for the number of troops, during February. The officer corps remained at twenty-four, with 1,000 enlisted men, of which 648 were unassigned recruits. Capt. Charles E. Stodter, 7th Cavalry, arrived on 22 February to take over the duties of Executive Officer and Capt. Andrew E. Williams, Cavalry, who had been Executive Officer, was relieved of duty at the post and departed on 26 February. The number of recruits forwarded during the month was only 360.[65]

March 1916 would see the beginning of changes in numbers and disposition of troops in the Army, but little change occurred at Jefferson Barracks during the month. A total of 413 recruits transferred to their permanent organizations during March. Two of the more interesting groups forwarded were forty Cavalry recruits for the 13th Cavalry and twenty-five Infantry recruits for the 16th Infantry, both at Columbus, New Mexico, under the charge of Sgt. William R. Surles, 18th Recruit Company.[66]

The transfer of troops to Columbus, New Mexico, is interesting because in the early morning of 9 March 1916, Pancho Villa led 500 men in an attack on Columbus. Since troops of the 13th Cavalry were at Columbus, the small battle that ensued precipitated the greatest crisis in Mexican-American relations since the revolution in Mexico which toppled Porfirio Diaz five years earlier.[67] Within a week, the War Department dispatched troops under Brigadier General John J. Pershing across the border in pursuit of Villa. Pershing sent two columns in an enveloping movement into the mountains of Chihuahua. He lived up to his reputation as a tough, hard-driving commander as he pushed his troops to the limits of their capacity. He was a Cavalryman, and most of his troops were Cavalry: the 7th, 10th, 11th and 13th Regiments, along with the 6th and 16th Infantry Regiments and two Field Artillery Battalions from the 6th Field Artillery. With support elements, Pershing's force numbered around 10,000 men.[68]

While Pershing kept his troops busy in Mexico, there was a massive build-up on the border. By the end of August 1916, 48,000 regulars - sixty-seven percent of the entire Army - and more than 111,000 National Guard troops were in camps scattered along the Mexican border. Although President Wilson had called out the Arizona, New Mexico, and Texas National Guards in May, he waited until summer to call out the remainder of the Guard.[69]

In Europe, the war at sea had become a war with few restrictions on either side by the end of March. On 28 March, the Reichstag in Berlin voted for immediate unrestricted submarine warfare. On 30 March, a German submarine in the Black Sea sank the Russian hospital ship *Portugal*, stating that she had mistaken her for a troop transport. When the U.S.-bound liner *Cymric* was sunk in early May, it brought the total unarmed liners sunk since the *Lusitania* to thirty-seven.[70]

In April, more recruits from Jefferson Barracks transferred to units in Columbus, New Mexico. Sgt. Carl Witcher, 18th Recruit Company, departed Jefferson Barracks on April 7 with twenty-eight Cavalry recruits for the 5th Cavalry at Columbus. More recruits also headed to forts in Texas. Cpl. Duncan W. Wing, 16th Recruit Company, departed on 6 April with ten Coast Artillery Corps recruits bound for Fort Crockett, Texas, and the next day Cpl. James C. Anderson, 15th Recruit Company, departed with thirty-five Infantry recruits for the 7th Infantry at Fort Bliss, Texas. On 17 April, Cpl. John C. Miller, 15th Recruit Company, left with forty Quartermaster recruits for Fort Sam Houston, Texas. Sgt. LeRoy Ayres, 16th Recruit Company, took sixty Cavalry recruits for the 3rd Cavalry at Brownsville, Texas, and five Cavalry recruits for the 3rd Cavalry at Fort Ringgold, Texas on 22 April. That same day Sgt. John J. Gardner, 23rd Recruit Company, took seventy more Infantry recruits for the 7th Infantry at Fort Bliss. This brought the total number of recruits transferred to Texas to 220, with another forty to Columbus, out of 373 recruits transferred during April.[71]

The Jefferson Barracks garrison, Lt. Col. William Kenly commanding, consisted of twenty-two officers and 1,266 enlisted men. The post was home to 924 unassigned recruits in training.[72]

Lt. Col. Kenly's command changed only slightly in May 1916. Twenty-one officers and 1,091 enlisted men with 741 unassigned recruits made up the garrison. Of the 584 recruits transferred during the month, 350 went to posts in Texas.[73]

In June 1916, the number of unassigned recruits jumped to 1,227 bringing the total of enlisted men at Jefferson Barracks to 1,573. Only 248 recruits transferred during the month and none of those went to posts in Texas or New Mexico.[74]

Meanwhile, in Mexico, Gen. Pershing continued to pursue Villa with scant success. Basically, Villa made a mockery of the campaign and continued to threaten American towns near the border. The Mexican government demanded that Pershing be withdrawn.[75]

Under pressure from events along the Mexican border, Congress acted on compromise legislation, which passed the Senate on 17 May and the House on 20 May. President Wilson signed the National Defense Act of 1916 into law on 3 June. The bill, more than one hundred pages in length and containing 128 sections, defined the army as the "Regular Army, the Volunteer Army, the Officers' Reserve Corps, the Enlisted Reserve Corps, the National Guard while in the service of the United States, and such other land forces as are now or may hereafter be authorized by law." The Guard retained its traditional role as the nation's first line behind the regulars, but in return, Guardsmen took two oaths - one to the state and one to the Federal government, which meant that, once called up, they had to go abroad if necessary. In this comprehensive act, Congress provided for increases, over a five-year period, in both the Army and the National Guard, as well as for a reserve force to include a training program in the Reserve Officers Training Corps. Finally, Congress gave the Federal government powers to regulate industry and transportation in a national emergency.[76]

Jefferson Barracks continued to increase in strength during July 1916. The officer corps increased to twenty-six, and the enlisted strength to 1,908. There were 1,557 unassigned recruits. Lt. Col. Kenly departed for detached service at Washington, D.C. on 15 July and Capt. Charles E. Stodter, 7th Cavalry, assumed command in Kenly's absence.[77] Charles Ezra Stodter had graduated from West Point in June 1896 and had been commissioned a second lieutenant in the 9th Cavalry.[78]

The exodus of recruits from Jefferson Barracks to posts in Texas increased during the month. A total of 241 recruits were sent; the largest group of 170 Cavalry recruits went to the 14th Cavalry at Del Rio, Texas, on 13 July under the command of Capt. F.M. Jones, Cavalry. Another 190 recruits transferred to posts in Arizona. One hundred and forty of these went to the 22nd Infantry at Bisbee, and fifty to the 1st Cavalry at Douglas, Arizona. Thus, 431 recruits of the 566 transferred during the month went to Texas or Arizona.[79]

Lt. Col. Kenly returned to command at Jefferson Barracks on 31 August 1916. He assumed command of twenty-one officers and 1,524 enlisted men. A total of 1,038 recruits transferred to their permanent organizations during the month. Of these recruits transferred, 558 went to posts in Texas, eighty to Arizona, and ten to Columbus, New Mexico. The largest shipment included 190 Infantry recruits sent to the 30th Infantry at Eagle Pass, Texas, on 14 August, under the command of 1st Lt. O.H. Sampson, 28th Infantry. Another 130 Cavalry recruits were sent to the 3rd Cavalry at Mercedes, Texas, on August 3, under the command of Capt. John M. Craig, 22nd Infantry.[80]

September and October 1916 remained fairly unchanged. Col. Kenly, who had been promoted to colonel on 8 July and accepted on 9 October, remained in command. His command consisted of twenty-two officers in September and twenty-one in October. In September, there were 1,516 enlisted men at Jefferson Barracks, with 1,129 unassigned recruits and in October the count was 1,498, with 1,093 unassigned recruits.[81]

In September, out of 573 recruits forwarded, 328 went to units in Texas and seventy-five to Douglas, Arizona. In October, 536 recruits departed Jefferson Barracks, with 225 to the 11th Infantry and seventy-five to the 35th Infantry, both at Douglas, Arizona. Another 165 recruits went to posts in Texas and 31 to Columbus, New Mexico.[82]

Col. Kenly was relieved from duty with the General Recruiting Service and as commanding officer of Jefferson Barracks on 8 November. Charles Stodter, who had been promoted to major on 8 October, served as commanding officer from 8 November to 19 November, when Col. George LeRoy Irwin, 4th Field Artillery, arrived and assumed command of the post.[83] Irwin had graduated from the U.S. Military Academy in June 1889, and received a commission as a second lieutenant in the 2nd Artillery. As a first lieutenant in September 1897, he served with the 5th Artillery, was promoted to captain in the 2nd Field Artillery on June 6, 1907; to major on 14 January 1910; to lieutenant colonel on 18 November 1914; to colonel on 1July 1916; and to brigadier general on 5 August 1917. General Irwin commanded the 161st Field Artillery Brigade from August to December 1917, then assumed command of the 41st Division on 10 December 1917, and arrived in France with the Division on 27 December 1917. In World War I, Irwin also commanded the 2nd Field Artillery Brigade, the 57th Field Artillery Brigade and the Artillery of the 32nd Division and the 9th Division. Irwin was awarded the Distinguished Service Medal "For exceptionally meritorious and conspicuous services. He commanded with ability the 57th Field Artillery Brigade during the Marne-Aisne, Oise-Aisne and Muese-Argonne offensives...."[84]

Jefferson Barracks, its units and men were all new to Col. Irwin, but little had changed. Including himself, the officer corps consisted of twenty officers. Major Stodter served as Executive Officer with Major William A. Wicklive, Major James M. Kennedy, Major Henry F. Pipes, Capt. Frank W. Pyles, Capt. Charles E. Freeman, Capt. Frank W. Chilton and 1st Lt. Augustus B. Jones, all of the Medical Corps, serving as surgeons and recruiting officers. Capt. John M. Craig served as Post Adjutant, Signal and Engineer Officer and commanded the 14th Recruit Company. Capt. William McCammon, Jr., was the Post Exchange and Mess Officer. The remaining officers served in some capacity with the Recruit Companies.[85]

The Jefferson Barracks garrison that Col. Irwin took over also consisted of 1,451 enlisted men, with 1,035 unassigned recruits. The largest unit on the post was the Hospital Corps with fifty-five enlisted men, followed closely by the Quartermaster Corps with fifty-two enlisted men. Of course, this is to be expected as all the recruits needed physicals and original issue of uniforms and equipment; and since Jefferson Barracks was a training depot, numerous recruits got injured during training requiring medical treatment.[86]

As in most months since "Poncho" Villa's raid at Columbus, New Mexico, the majority of the 278 recruits forwarded during November went to posts in Texas, with sixty-nine going to Columbus. A total of 632 recruits transferred during November.[87]

Just like civilians, the soldiers at Jefferson Barracks had a festive time at Thanksgiving, with a typical holiday dinner. Under the supervision of the Mess Officer, Capt. William W. McCammon, Jr., and the Mess Steward, Quartermaster Sergeant James F. Crosson and Chief Cook William Stone, the Mess Sergeants and their assistants prepared the Thanksgiving Day Dinner of roast turkey with oyster dressing, mashed potatoes with giblet gravy, succotash, cold sliced ham, cole slaw, bread, puree of green peas, with sweet and dill pickles and olives. For dessert, the cooks prepared hot mince pie and pumpkin pie. Coffee and cigars topped off this fabulous meal.[88]

The last month of 1916 passed as most every month of the year. Col. Irwin remained in command of Jefferson Barracks. The recruit depot contained 1,468 unassigned recruits undergoing training before being shipped to their permanent organizations and duty assignment. A total of 424 recruits shipped out during December. One hundred and seventy-five of these recruits went to Douglas, Arizona, under the command of Capt. W.W. McCammon, Jr.[89]

Jefferson Barracks was also home to twenty-three officers and 1,890 enlisted men. These officers and men performed normal, routine garrison duties during the month.[90]

Just as at Thanksgiving, Christmas dinner proved to be a fantastic repast. Chief Cook William Stone, 18th Recruit Company, and his two Shift Chiefs, John Goodman and John L. Wilson, both of the 16th Recruit Company, supervised Charles Pinnick, Benjamin C. Hoyel, John C. Hildreth, Frank Eppinger, Anthony Mosblech, Thomas Lafferty and George E. Milne, in the preparation of the meal. After oyster soup, roast turkey with sage dressing and giblet gravy, mashed potatoes and creamed peas, bread and butter made up the entree. Hot minced pie and assorted cakes were served for dessert. Coffee and cigars finished the Christmas dinner.[91]

During 1916, a most welcome addition to the facilities was finished. Capt. McCammon, Post Exchange Officer, had conceived the idea of a swimming pool and supervised its construction. John B. Steel, a civilian construction assistant, took a great interest in the project and planned and supervised most of the work. The pool, fifty feet by one hundred fifty feet and holding 300,000 gallons of water, cost $5,000, which came from mess funds. Soldiers and prisoners labor was used for construction.

In Europe, World War I continued to rage with no end in sight. The year 1916 had witnessed two major battles in Europe, the Somme and Verdun. After 4½ months, the Battle of the Somme had no conclusive victor. However, the death toll for both sides reached unprecedented levels. The British dead on the Somme amounted to 95,675, and the French total stood at 50,729. The German total was even higher, at 164,055. When the battle ended, the British front line had moved forward six miles, but was still three miles short of Bapaume, the first days' objective.

The death toll at Verdun stood at 650,000 men. When added to the death toll of the Somme, it made a five-month death toll of 960,459 men. It was an average of more than 6,600 men killed every day, more than 277 per minute, nearly five men every second.[92]

Alistair Horne, a historian of Verdun, wrote "Neither side 'won' at Verdun. It was an indecisive battle in an indecisive war; the unnecessary battle in an unnecessary war; the battle had no victors in a war that had no victors."[93]

Chapter 7 - War Comes to the United States - 1917

The World War had been in progress since 28 July 1914, when the *Lusitania* had been sunk and the specter of war loomed on the horizon of the United States. While the pacifists were still in the majority and Woodrow Wilson was re-elected on a "keep-us-out-of-war" platform in 1916, the clamor for preparedness grew more and more persistent. More and more recruits passed through Jefferson Barracks until the post again became literally a beehive of activity. Time was found, however, to construct an officer's swimming pool, which proved to be one of the post's luxuries through World War II.

Col. Irwin remained in command of the Jefferson Barracks Recruit Depot. Although his command would soon be enlarged beyond anyone's expectations. In January 1917, everything remained just as the year 1916 had closed. Officers and troops performed the usual routine garrison duties.

The call for preparedness resulted in stepped up recruiting, which brought more new soldiers to Jefferson Barracks for training. Many postcards like the following were sent from Jefferson Barracks by these new recruits.

Postmarked 2 February 1917, this card went to Mr. Alfred Baschen of Emerald Avenue, Chicago Heights, Illinois. On the back is written: "Hello All - This is the entrance to the barracks on the Miss R. someplace. Passed stiff exams this morning & took oaths. Will probable [sic] stay here a week & then go south. Talk about host. Yours Red."

Officials at Jefferson Barracks made a gigantic blunder when they sent a telegram on February 19 to Alexander Miller of Leavenworth, Kansas, advising him that his son, George 'Bud' Miller, a black soldier at Jefferson Barracks, had died and that his body was to arrive on the Missouri Pacific.

Accordingly, funeral arrangements were made and the Leavenworth Home Guards, a black company, was notified to prepare for a military funeral. When the casket arrived, and was later opened it was found that a mistake had been made. A wire to Jefferson Barracks brought the information that "Bud" Miller was eating three meals a day and was in perfect health. The Jefferson Barracks officials in some unaccountable mistake had wrongly identified the dead soldier and sent the body to Leavenworth. The casket was returned to Jefferson Barracks [We don't know who the dead soldier really was][1]

Also in February, Germany took another step that brought the United States closer to entering the war. On January 9, the Kaiser had presided over a Crown Council that debated the long-standing question of unrestricted submarine warfare. Now the Kaiser hesitated no longer. Unrestricted German submarine warfare against all shipping, regardless of the flag it flew and whatever cargoes it carried, was to begin 'with the utmost energy' as of 1 February. During January 1917, the last month in which restrictions were in force, German submarines sank fifty-one British, sixty-three other Allied, and sixty-six neutral ships. This came to more than 300,000 tons, of which a third was British. With American merchant ships as acceptable targets, those figures would substantially increase.[2]

Germany notified the United States that it would permit only one ship per week to sail between the U.S. and England. This meant revocation of the freedom of the seas.

As Germany moved toward an intensification of the war at sea, the recently appointed German Foreign Minister, Dr. Alfred von Zimmermann, worked out a scheme whereby, if unrestricted submarine warfare were to bring the United States into the war, Germany could win the support and active alliance of Mexico. With Germany's generous financial support, he explained in a coded telegram to the German minister in Mexico City on January 9, Mexico would 'reconquer' the territories it had lost seventy years earlier during the Mexican War: Texas, New Mexico and Arizona. Germany and Mexico would "make war together, make peace together."

On 23 January, while the Zimmermann telegram was still a closely guarded secret, the German Ambassador in Washington, Count von Bernsdorff, who was hoping to keep the United States out of the war, asked Berlin for $50,000 to influence individual Congressmen. As a result of skillful British cryptography, the Zimmermann telegram was decrypted in London two days before it was received in Berlin. But on February 2, less than two weeks after von Bernsdorff's attempt to buy American neutrality, the German submarine *U-53* (in one of the first actions of unrestricted submarine warfare) sank an American cargo ship, the *Housatonic*, carrying a cargo of grain. In Berlin, Zimmermann told the American ambassador, "Everything will be alright, for President Wilson is for peace and nothing else. Everything will go on as before."[3]

The Zimmermann telegram was published in the United States on 1 March. Many Americans, alarmed at the prospect of the United States entering the war, denounced the telegram as a fake, but two days later Zimmermann confirmed that it was indeed genuine.[4]

With unrestricted submarine warfare in effect for two months and the revelation of the Zimmermann telegram, President Wilson went before Congress on 2 April 1917 and asked that a state of war be declared to exist between the United States and Germany. On 4 April, the United States Senate voted in favor of war, 82 to 6. Two days later, on April 6, the House of Representatives voted for war, 373 to 50. That day, 6 April 1917, the United States declared war on Germany.[5]

There was a related incident involving a soldier who had enlisted in the Coast Artillery at Jefferson Barracks on 6 December 1913. He was being sought by Federal officials as a supposed German agent. Louis Hollweg had enlisted at Jefferson Barracks under the name of Louis Tettenhausen and had been sent to the Philippine Islands. While stationed in the Philippine Islands he had been sentenced to eighteen months at Alcatraz Island for disobedience, embezzlement, and fraud and was dishonorably discharged. Hollweg was released 4 October 1916, on parole, but the parole was revoked ten days before it was to expire on 15 February 1917. Officers would not reveal why or what had led to the revocation, but did reveal that Hollweg, aka Tettenhausen, was being sought as a suspected German agent.[6]

Immediately after the declaration of war on 6 April, Jefferson Barracks was designated as a clearing house for recruits from twelve mid-western states and was ordered to ship 15,000 recruits to the Mexican border for mobilization and training. This meant an expansion of post facilities. Modern fireless cookers, steam tables and other mess hall equipment was installed that made it possible to feed 5,000 meals in twenty minutes. Temporary buildings began to spring up almost overnight around the post.

Jefferson Barracks enjoyed one facility that proved of great importance under the strained circumstances. A dairy barn, 32 feet by 205 feet, had been built in 1914. The barn held forty milk cows that provided milk for the troops.[7]

Immediately after the declaration of war, young men flocked to recruiting stations to enlist in order to fight "the Hun." The stories of the lengths some of these young men went through to enlist provide a glimpse into the depths of their patriotism.

Carroll E. Campbell of Newell, North Dakota, an 18-year-old farm hand, walked 140 miles in four days to Bowman, North Dakota and then spent three days on a train to get to the nearest recruiting station at Aberdeen, North Dakota, in order to enlist in the Army. When he arrived at the recruiting office, he had just 15 cents in his pocket. The Army accepted Campbell and he was sent to Jefferson Barracks for duty in the Infantry.[8]

Also at Aberdeen, William and Harry Pinkerton, twin sons of Mrs. W.A. Pinkerton, answered the call to duty of their country. They joined Campbell and were sent to Jefferson Barracks.[9]

By the middle of April, the age limit for recruits had been raised from thirty-five to forty years of age. This was done in order that veterans of the Spanish-American War could enlist. Levi T. Koch, aged 39 years and one month, proved to be one of the first to take advantage of this new age limit. Koch had been the general blacksmith and a rancher in Athboy, North Dakota. On hearing that men up to forty were being accepted, he promptly enlisted and was sent to Jefferson Barracks for service in the Coast Artillery Corps. Besides being the oldest man accepted from Aberdeen, Koch was one of the best physically developed men who applied at the recruiting station. He was six feet two inches tall and weighed 205 pounds.[10]

The stream of recruits passing through Jefferson Barracks continued to grow in size. As soon as the new recruits passed their physicals, and were equipped and prepared for shipment, they were loaded onto trains and moved by night to outlying camps. The number of temporary barracks and hospital buildings on the post steadily increased. More than 100 were built during the first months of the war.

One large group of new recruits to leave Jefferson Barracks in April was a group of 230 colored troops that had enlisted to fill the ranks of the Regular Army colored regiments. This group of 230 colored troops left Jefferson Barracks by train for San Francisco, California. From there these new troops being sent to the 9th Cavalry were to go to Hawaii, and those going to the 25th Infantry were sent to the Philippine Islands.[11]

Troops leaving Jefferson Barracks for the Mexican border as part of the Poncho Villa Expedition.

George LeRoy Irwin commanded Jefferson Barracks from 19 November 1916, until 1 July 1917. During World War I Irwin participated in the Aisne, Marne, Oise-Aisne, and Muese-Argonne campaigns, for which he won the Croix de Guerre with palm, and was made an officer of the French Legion of Honor.

View of No. 1 Grant Road (background) and two red brick barracks buildings.

By arrangement with Major George W. Goode, recruiting officer of the United States Army Recruiting Station at 222 North Third Street in St. Louis, a *Post-Dispatch* staff writer was permitted to enlist in the Army for the purpose of writing an article on the first days of a recruit's life. What follows is that writer's article which provides an excellent description of what a new recruit faced at Jefferson Barracks.

The article is entitled *From Recruit to Rookie*. A few hours later I returned to the recruiting office and presented myself for enlistment. Five soldiers, who had not been informed of the arrangement or my purpose, sat at desks in the large office adjoining that of Major Goode. One advanced and greeted me cordially. Informed that I desired to enter the army, he requested another soldier, seated before a typewriter, to take "the gentleman's application."

He took my name, address, age, place of birth, and vocation which he transcribed with much satisfaction, but with some difficulty, on the machine. [The recruiting officer talked the reporter into applying for the Signal Corps, which would pay up to $75 a month.]

I was required to sign the application and was told to take a few hours in which to arrange my affairs and return at 4 o'clock for my first physical examination....

At 4 o'clock I reappeared at the station and was conducted into a room farther down the hall, where nude applicants were being put through the paces of the physical examination. I soon joined them. Major Goode sat at a table making the record, a sergeant conducted the examination, directing the aspirants by example. A simple vision test was made, after which we were weighed and measured. The sergeant's commands were clear and compelling.

"Bend forward, legs rigid, try to touch the floor with finger tips! Extend right leg forward, resting on left foot, and work the other foot at ankle from side to side! Now, up and down! Same action with other foot! Stand erect, legs together, bend forward, touching knees to floor, and spring up quickly! Stand erect, arms extended forward! Work hands from side to side and up and down at wrists!! Stand erect! Hop across the room on one foot and back on the other!"

During these and a few simple movements, the sergeant watched each man critically and called out to Major Goode any defects he noted, such as "slight varicose vein in lower left leg; deformed small toe on left foot; enlarged joint of great toe on right foot," not the slightest defect escaping him.

This concluded the first examination, and a period of an hour ensued while our papers were being made out by the sergeant and countersigned by Major Goode. In the interim the applicants lounged in an anteroom and dropped into discussion of their reasons for quitting civil life. Five young men, all in their teens, had previously been examined and were waiting to be sent to Jefferson Barracks....

...the sergeant called each to take examples of our handwriting. We were required to write: "In case of fire or disorder, give the alarm." Our papers were then sealed in envelopes addressed to the commanding officer at the barracks, and we returned to the waiting room. At 5 o'clock, the sergeant appeared at the door and announced that he would take us to supper and then to the barracks....

After partaking of a 35-cent lunch at a restaurant, we boarded a street car for the barracks. In less than an hour we arrived there and marched straight to the receiving barracks.

We were received by a sergeant, who made a record of our clothes and other possessions. Then he gave a brief lecture on care of quarters and general conduct and informed us of the next steps we were to take. When he had finished we were each given a towel and made to take a shower bath in the basement. After the bath, we returned to the receiving room, where two barbers administered haircuts and shaves. Then each received two blankets and a pillow and were shown our bunks, in a farther room on the same floor.

It was nearing 9 o'clock, when all lights were turned out, and we retired. The bunks in this room are double-deck affairs, made of iron, with a soft mattress and were scrupulously clean. The refreshing bath and cool air from open windows soon induced sleep.

At 5:45 next morning we were roused by a clanging gong. All turned out, received a towel and went to the washroom in the basement. After the toilet, we lined up in front of the barracks, fully a hundred, and marched to breakfast in the messroom, a block distant. We presented a motley, straggling appearance beside the nattily clad troops.

Breakfast consisted of corn flakes and milk, liver and bacon, bread and butter and coffee.

After breakfast, we returned to the receiving barracks and were released for a few hours leisure on the parade ground, where most of the crowd diverted themselves with football and baseball. Our numbers kept swelling with applicants from the 12 middle western states which enlist through Jefferson Barracks, who arrived by every car and train.

A few hours of play and we were sent to examination barracks. There a sergeant conducted a preliminary examination and a surgeon went over us more carefully, giving particular attention to heart and lungs. All were innoculated with typhus serum and then required to take the soldier's oath of allegiance, where I stepped aside for a moment. [The reporter had been warned by Major Goode not to take the oath unless he wanted to stay in the Army.] Bortillon measurements followed and each was photographed. This record completed, we returned to our barracks and later to lunch, which consisted of fried halibut, boiled potatoes, stewed corn, cream sauce, bread and tapioca pudding.

The remainder of this, the second day, was spent in and out of the barracks, where daily papers, magazines and books were furnished for those who cared to spend their leisure time reading. We had sliced bologna, potatoes au gratin, ginger cake, syrup and coffee for supper and attended the free picture show in the post hall at night, returning to quarters before 9 o'clock.

The same clanging roused us promptly at 5:45 next morning, the third day. For breakfast, we had oatmeal and milk, fried bacon, brown gravy, boiled potatoes, bread, syrup and coffee.

At 9 o'clock, we were measured for uniforms and taken to the Quartermaster Depot. Each received two pairs of breeches, one coat, one shirt, one hat, one cap, one belt, three suits of underwear, two pairs of shoes, six pairs of socks, one pair of leggins and a kit containing comb and hair brush, shoe brush and polish, razor, shaving brush and soap, two towels, one wiskbroom and one "housewife," which is a case containing needles, thread, buttons, scissors and safety pins.

The shoes were fitted while wearing a leather sandbag weighing 40 pounds strapped to the shoulders – the weight a soldier must carry on the march.

We returned to the receiving barracks, where each was given an identifying number for the record, and this number was then stamped with indelible ink on each article of clothing. We were urged to retain the civilian apparel or send it home. All save two in our crowd sold it to the Government, after appraisal there and then by the Sergeant....

All civilian clothes were then taken to be fumigated, and each man was assigned to one of the five companies. Passing out of receiving barracks, we received a copy of the soldiers' handbook of instructions, on all phases of military life.

Sixteen of our crowd went to 27th Company. At company barracks storeroom each received for permanent possession three blankets, two sheets, pillow and case, mattress, and case bag for soiled linen and an overcoat.

A sergeant...introduced himself as our commander and instructor for the ensuing 25 days, and with the command, "Follow me," led us to the company squad room. He informed us with ominous emphasis that the beds in the squad room were for sleeping purposes; that when we retired it was to sleep and not "to lay there and giggle and squirm and tell funny stories be no "foolishness or skylarking or the like" in the squad room or barracks at any time.

"And when that bell rings in the morning," he added, solemnly weighing each word, "it means one thing: get out of that bunk as quick as you can–we do no coaxing here–dress, make your bed, go downstairs and wash your face and hands, and get out on the parade grounds, in 15 minutes."

"I have my doubts," he continued...., "that all of you are paying strict attention to what I am saying, but I'll warn you now; you'll rue the day when you break one of these orders."

This last brought us all to attention, and we received a barber ticket, for one dollar in trade, and a tailor ticket, for seventy-five cents in trade. Closer attention also was given lessons in regulation bed dressing, the most difficult part of which was placing the mattress in its case, which the sergeant, and old hand at this, deftly executed by placing the mattress on his head and letting it slip from this position into the case which he held open. Nearly all the men got hopelessly involved in trying to perform this seemingly simple feat, but unfortunately managed it just as the sergeant was about to deliver a scathing lecture on "solid ivory."

One recruit had the temerity to ask the sergeant for a piece of string. The scene that followed recalled the tragic incident of poor little Oliver Twist asking for more gruel. He wanted the string to fasten his identifying number to the clothes chest.

"Now, ain't that too bad," sighed the sergeant, with mock commiseration. "The poor boob ain't got no string, and worse still, we ain't got no nurses in the Army to get him a piece of string. Oh-h-h, now, ain't it terrible when a poor boob ain't got no string!"

"Now, men, listen to me: Don't ever do a thing like that. Don't ever ask your officer or the Colonel, for instance, for a piece of string or the like; don't ever ask anybody to do something for you that you can do yourself, or you might rue the day of your laziness."

We had come to respect this sergeant.

A trip through company barracks followed. He explained each room and its purpose; which rooms to enter, which to avoid, and how to enter them, and we were taught how to clean cuspidors.

"These things is privileges," he explained, pointing to a cuspidor, "and if you want to get along in the Army, never take liberty with a privilege. When you want to use a cuspidor, spit in it, not at it; it ain't a target; if you miss the cuspidor, men, you'll find yourself on your knees with a scrub brush. You must not heave big gobs or cuds or throw matches or cigarette butts on them nice floors or that fine grass outside."

The sergeant released us with a sigh of misgiving and we had dinner of split-pea soup, German pot roast, canned tomatoes, browned potatoes, gravy, bread and rice pudding. Then we were taken by the same Sergeant to the rear of company barracks for rudiments of drill, or foot movements. An hour of this was enough for the men and almost too much for the sergeant, "which was little enough, to say the least."

Passing through company barracks to the squad room, he stopped suddenly in front of a door.

"See that door, men?" he warned. "Stay away from there unless you have orders to go there. That's the commanding officer's office. I can't make this command too strong, men–STAY AWAY FROM THAT DOOR!~"

Pointing through the barracks door, across the parade grounds, he said: "Them's the officers' quarters. Whatever you do, men, and I'm telling you fair, don't go over there and parade up and down in front of them houses to show off your new uniforms."

Supper consisted of chile con carne, biscuits and butter, apricots and coffee. Another evening at the movies and the second day passed.

The first duty on arising the third day was to dress the bed for inspection and we went about this important detail clumsily and ill at ease, for we could not quite shake off the forebodings created by the sergeant's "rue the day." It was necessary to observe closely the manner in which members of the "permanent party," or permanent members of the company on recruiting duty, folded and tucked their sheets and blankets before we left the bed for the morning toilet, and it was plain that many had their doubts that the beds would pass inspection, for they appeared uneasy even after the final pat of the pillow.

After breakfast the first of four one-half-hour rudimentary drills, to be given that day, took place in platoons on the parade grounds, under the direction of our sergeant. He was much refreshed, apparently, after the night's rest, but was quite as impressive in his commands as the day previous. Between drills, he lectured on general orders and post regulations. A Captain talked half an hour just before dinner, on Army life and its requirements of the men and how they could profit by good behavior.

At dinner, we were thoroughly hungry, as the morning had been an active one in the cool, fresh air. Succotash was on the menu and it was good. We ate our fill but one unfortunate evidently over estimated his capacity for this delectable dish and filled his plate a third time, heaping full. He ate a small portion of the last helping and was about to rise and leave the remainder in the dish, but that was a mistake, a serious blunder, we soon learned.

A heavy hand pushed him back on the stool and a sergeant–another one–eyed him critically.

"Don't you like succotash?" he inquired of the recruit.

"Yy-y-es," the recruit faltered.

"Why don't you eat it, then?"

"Got enough."

"Why did you heap your plate up, then?"

"I thought I wanted it, but I"--

"Oh-h-h, I see. You thought, did you? Well, just eat that succotash, every bit of it. You can't get away with that civilian foolishness here. We waste nothing in the Army"--

We were required to stand by while the unlucky recruit, with some difficulty, got away with the dish.

"....If we didn't do that," the sergeant explained, "those men would waste more food than they eat. They may eat all they like of any and all dishes, but they must not leave a big gob of perfectly good chow...to be thrown to the hogs."

One of our recruits went to the sergeant's office in the receiving barracks to get his first papers.

"Who sent you here for your first papers?" demanded the sergeant.

"That guy out there," answered the recruit, pointing to a soldier lounging on the parade ground.

"Guy?" queried the sergeant, struggling to contain himself.

"Uh huh; he told me."

"Now, stand right where you are and look me in the eye," commanded the sergeant. "I'll give you to understand that there are no guys in the United States Army–you find them things only in civilian life. You are a soldier and a man, and the soldier who sent you here is a man–a man, MAN! You ought to be ashamed of yourself, calling a soldier a guy. GET OUT OF THIS OFFICE! Your first papers haven't come back from the examining barracks."

"Guy, guy, GUY!" the Sergeant fumed, pacing the floor. "The nerve of him. He thinks he's still a civilian."

At Jefferson Barracks, there are several sergeants who enlisted as privates...and fought through the Spanish-American War, and there are others who have seen service in Mexico, Cuba, Central America and the Philippines. These men are in love with Army life and intend to stay with the colors in their remaining days or until forcibly retired. They are of the type who understand that to get the most out of life is to make the best of his trying situations.

One of these men, Sergeant William Levin of 27th Company, was a newsboy in St. Louis 25 years ago. He entered the Army in 1898 and participated in the Philippine campaign. Army life today, even at barracks or post, is much easier on the man than when he entered the service. In the Philippines, for instance, the soldiers slept on the ground for months, or until Miss Helen Gould, now Mrs. Finley J. Shepard, sent them thousands of cots, he said. This type is still called the Helen Gould cot and is used at the barracks to accommodate men in tents when quarters are crowded.

[Sgt.] Levin....has charge of the receiving room, lectures the applicants, appraises their civilian clothes, cares for their valuables, prepared them for examination by the surgeon, keeps a complete record of their first steps and acts as general adviser before they take the oath of allegiance....

"Many men come to the Army as a last resort," he explained, "broken in spirit and purse....As a rule, they have no regular habits, never restrain themselves and know nothing of hygiene. We like to get hold of a chap in this pitiful state, just to witness the transformation that takes place when he wakes up."

"The bath is a marvelous rejuvenator, and the sense of feeling clean and fresh immediately generates hope of better things. New clothing adds buoyancy to the depressed spirit, and a day's drill accomplishes wonders in the shiftless man.

"Not until the recruit becomes strictly amenable to discipline does he fully appreciate the value of military training in the fullest sense, and he soon learns that to get the good out of life he must become a useful and necessary part of the harmonious system."

"The recruit might first surrender to little mental rebellions against the strict order of things, but he soon learns that it is all for his benefit. We never coddle the man; it is a mistake to do so, even in civil life. We command them, and, after they have come to their senses they obey with a pleasure that must be experienced to be appreciated."

"It requires at least 10 days for a recruit to get wise to the fact that becoming a soldier is not a joke, and 15 days more to be of actual usefulness to the Army, and we never send them away to join their companies until we have satisfied ourselves that they have conquered their old habits and fully realize the responsibility of a soldier. We find very few really bad men, and some of the most efficient among us came to the Army in a frightful state of mind. The more intelligent a man is, the less difficult he is to handle, of course, and the more easily is he amenable to discipline, however rigid it might be. As in civilian life, he is usually the man who gets ahead."

"We never impose upon or humiliate a man because of his ignorance or otherwise. On the contrary, every effort is put forth to establish him in the good graces of himself, and the man behaves half way right in the army finds the life surprisingly pleasant and profitable."

Levin is one of a score of sergeants who have been recommended for commissions by their companies, and likely would be made a Captain should the Government's plan to elevate noncommissioned officers materialize.

Foot movements are taught the first five days, handling the rifle the next five days and marching with the rifle and guard duty after that. With 25 days of training, the men are ready to be sent away for regular service. In the period after their fifth day, they must attend five lectures a week, delivered by an officer, touching every phase of the life they are entering.[12]

On 1 April 1917, the Regular Army, including the Philippine Scouts numbered 133,111. There were 80,446 National Guardsmen, plus 101,174 Guard members still in State service.[13]

President Wilson authorized the organization of twenty-seven new regiments of Infantry on 14 May 1917, and Congress passed the draft bill on 24 May.

Also in May, it was learned that women nurses of the United States Army Nurse Corps were to be sent to France with the American Hospital Corps units. Miss Dollie Belle Schmitt, a nurse at the Fort Bliss, Texas, post hospital was ordered to St. Louis for service in France with the Base Hospital No. 21, which mobilized at Jefferson Barracks.[14]

Jefferson Barracks provided new recruits for many different elements of the Army. In the preceding pages have been mentioned the Infantry, Coast Artillery Corps, and Hospital units. An article in the Grand Forks, North Dakota *Herald* of 24 May 1917, shows that an Aviation Squadron was also formed at Jefferson Barracks. The article states that six young North Dakota men: John C. Jennison, Sandy Green, Harry E. Scouton, Chester A. Coles, Harlan McGlern and Harold L. Barnes were with an Aviation Squadron that was expected to leave Jefferson Barracks soon. A joint letter home from the six men also stated that war preparations were in full swing at Jefferson Barracks with about 7,000 men in training.

Jefferson Barracks also sent men to assist other posts in their preparations for war. Fort Snelling, Minnesota, began a course for sixty enlisted men of the Army Medical Department. The camp hospital had three hundred beds and thirty regulars from Jefferson Barracks arrived to act as hospital stewards.[15]

By the end of May 1917, the impetus to move recruits forced a change in the time spent at Jefferson Barracks. Before May, a recruit would be kept at Jefferson Barracks for at least one month, but by the end of May that month had been trimmed to one week of training before being sent to Infantry, Cavalry, or Coast and Field Artillery regiments of the Regular Army.[16]

The following letter written at Jefferson Barracks on 11 May 1917 provides a glimpse of how patriotic young men made their way to Jefferson Barracks and how they were treated on their journey. The letter is entitled "Letter From Ellington Boys In U.S. Army."

"We have been faring nicely since we left Ellington, Sunday. When we got to Leeper, Mr. Radke invited us all, including the recruiting officer and wife to a banquet at the Ozark Hotel. We all used our best manners but notwithstanding all our care, John Tubbs and I (Warmack) got the butter knife on the floor and Victor Olson got pepper in his nose while he had his mouth full of potatoes and he sneezed potatoes all over the room. After the banquet, we went to church at the Union church where Rev. McPheeters preached on "War and Patriotism." He certainly preached a fine sermon and said all kinds of good things about us because we were going to enlist.

Ben Goodman came down to Leeper, stayed around with us and gave us some much needed instructions for he has seen three years service in the Army.

We went to Poplar Bluff on No. 9 and were examined immediately after arriving. We all passed except Victor Olson and John Tubbs.

Glen Piles found out that he was 12 pounds light according to his height and he ate all the salt and tried to drink all the water trying to bring his weight up.

We got to bed Sunday night about 8:30 and had to get up at 5:30 in order to get breakfast and catch the Sunshine Special for St. Louis. There were 48 in all from Poplar Bluff Monday morning.

We got to St. Louis about 11:00 and were met at the station by a man in uniform and taken to the recruiting station on 3rd and Olive where we stood the next examination which we all passed. They got through with us about 6:30, then we were taken to the Merchant's Restaurant on 12th and Olive and given supper. We also had dinner there. After supper, we were taken to Jefferson Barracks arriving here about 10:00 o'clock.

We slept in the skating rink Monday night with about 1,000 other men. We didn't sleep much for there was too much noise.

Tuesday, we stood the examination here which consisted of nearly everything, eyes, nose, teeth, feet, throat, lungs, ears, heart and other things too numerous to mention. We also were vaccinated....and had our fingerprints taken. Tuesday evening, we were measured and Wednesday we got our uniforms. We have been strutting around here since, except when part of us had our turn in the mess hall.

We saw Frank Payne, Roy Chitwood, John McMury and Luther Flowers. Bill Darr is a sergeant here and is issuing clothes to the recruits. Wesley Praul has stood the examinations and is now ready for his uniform.

Recruits are arriving here by the thousands and soldiers leaving the same way. We haven't been drilled very much and about all the orders we have is to stay at quarters and listen for our names to be called, and we are expecting to leave any time.

We all appreciate the letter that Mrs. A.L. George sent to us and we wish to thank her for remembering us so kindly.

We have been separated, some of us are in one company and some in others. Fred, Jess, Winfred and I are in 16th Co. Leslie is in 27th and Glenn is in the 18th Co.

I could write more but I guess this is rather lengthy now.

Signed   Roy Warmack
           Leslie Stokeley
           Fred Santhuff
           Winfred Thurman
           Glenn Piles
           Jesse Stogsdill"

The city of St. Louis rallied behind the brave young men who answered the call to arms after 6 April. The *Charlotte Observer* of 6 June 1917 bears witness to this: "At the Union Station in St. Louis Wednesday, I saw 375 rookies on their way to Jefferson Barracks and I wish you could have heard the mighty shout that went up from the immense throng in the great station when the men, under command of a United States Army officer, came through to take an Iron Mountain train to the post.

The men were not in uniform. Some were well dressed, apparently, business men, clerks, bookkeepers and the like, while others were poorly dressed, some in overalls and a good many without coats.

In every instance, these men carried a bundle under their arms and many waved "good-bye" to friends and loved ones in the great crowd.

These men had been recruited in Missouri from all walks of life. Some had been in the service before, but though they had just taken the oath, they seemed to hold their heads a bit higher, and step a little more briskly, and stand a little more erect than perhaps they did the day before, but the most interesting fact to me was the mighty cheer that went up when they appeared. They must have felt good that their service was appreciated even before they reached camp or donned uniforms.

And they were strong, robust men, too, and I suspect they will give a most excellent account of themselves when they reach the trenches in France–or Germany."

Another article in the 19 May 1917 edition of the *St. Louis Post-Dispatch* provides evidence of the patriotic spirit of St. Louisans during the early stages of mobilization for World War I:

"Not since the days of the World's Fair in 1904 has Forest Park presented such a military aspect as it will tomorrow afternoon when there will be a general review of Army and Navy forces there.

This pageant to celebrate the probable enlistment to war strength of the new 5th Regiment will be staged just south of the Jefferson Memorial building, and will begin promptly at 3 p.m.

Governor Frederick D. Gardner will review the troops half an hour later. He is to be accompanied by his military escort. The Governor will remain in the city only for the day.

Major E.J. McMahon, who has charge of the military review, will issue his formal instructions this afternoon. Many civic and business organizations which have uniforms will assemble at Forest Park and participate in the fete.

The United Railways has made provision to run additional through cars to Forest Park to accommodate the crowds. An elaborate program of fancy drills has been arranged.

Scores of brass bands have been engaged and there will be concerts in various sections of the reviewing ground until nightfall.

The whirlwind campaign for enlistments in the 5th Regiment has greatly pleased the Business Men's Recruiting Committee, which met yesterday afternoon at the Chamber of Commerce.

Former Judge Selden P. Spencer, who in the absence of Mayor Henry W. Kiel is acting chairman of this committee, last night said if the new regiment is recruited to war strength by June 1, all records for enlistments in this country will have been broken.

There will be a flag raising at noon today at the plant of the United States Incandescent Light Company, Ewing and Clark Avenues. George Williams will make the principal address. Recruiting officers of the 5th Regiment will be on hand in quest of enlistments.

The contest for a gold watch donated by *The Republic* as a prize for the young woman securing the most recruits for the new regiment, has occasioned a keen competition. Each recruit counts 1,000 votes.

Miss Eugenia Nichols, 6195 Delmar Avenue, in the last two days has advanced from second to first place. She now has 34,000 votes, while Miss Ansella Bell, 4279 Olive Street, is second with 32,000 votes. Miss Ruth Mayberry, Webster Groves, continues to remain in third place, with 23,000 ballots to her credit. Miss Eva Mitchell, Webster Groves, has 13,000 votes; and Miss Georgia Shiflette, 4132 McPherson Avenue, 12,000.

By the middle of May, Jefferson Barracks seemed to be overflowing with new recruits. Other quarters needed to be found. A new regiment of engineers was quartered on two U.S. River Boats. Col. Curtis McD. Townsend obtained four "quarter boats" to use as quarters by the new regiment from the Government's river fleet. The river boats were used as quarters until the men of the new regiment were mustered into the Army. As of May 19, there had been 327 men accepted and 1,200 applications filed. Of those accepted, 177 were from St. Louis and 150 from Kansas City.[17]

With the rapid expansion of the Army, the need for qualified officers became acute. The *St. Louis Post-Dispatch* reported on 6 May 1917, that eighty-seven men had passed the examinations for entrance to the Officers' Training Camp at Fort Riley, Kansas, on May 5. That same day the Examining Board reported that it had been deluged with applications from men seeking commissions. The total of applications was brought to more than 1,700 with other applications still not opened.

Major George W. Goode and Capt. Wallace Craigie found themselves so swamped with clerical work that A.T. Perkins of the St. Louis Union Trust Company, chairman of the campaign to recruit officers, volunteered to furnish several bank clerks to assist them.[18]

In yet another article, it was reported that at the rate St. Louis was recruiting men it could supply the 2,500 men needed for the Officers' Reserve Training Camp at Fort Riley, which had opened the second week of May 1917. Major Goode, in charge of the Examining Board at Third and Olive streets, reported that he had received 1,708 applications and examined 638.[19]

The Officers' Reserve Corps provided a total of 89,476 officers during World War I, of whom 57,307 received commissions through the 90-day Officers' Training Camps.[20] In Missouri, all candidates for Officers' Reserve Training Camp had to file their applications at Jefferson Barracks between 15 June and 15 July. The War Department cautioned that any applications filed before or after those dates would be returned.[21]

Of course, with the rapid expansion of the number of trainees at Jefferson Barracks and other training posts came many unwanted side effects. The War Department's committee on training camp activities, headed by Raymond D. Fosdick, began work on safeguarding the health and morals of officers and men of the new Army. A committee spokesperson stated that at the committee's request local authorities at San Antonio and El Paso, Texas, had taken steps to rid the cities of moral hazards for the troops. The spokesperson went on to state that the committee's agents had begun work on cleaning up the area around Jefferson Barracks. Under the terms of the new Army law, the War Department had been given broad authority to take drastic action to rid the vicinity of the training camps of moral dangers unless local authorities working in co-operation with the committee do it voluntarily.[22]

In response, Col. Irwin, commanding officer at Jefferson Barracks, issued an emphatic denial of reports sent to Washington concerning illegal sales of liquor and lax moral conditions near Jefferson Barracks. Col. Irwin stated that "drunkenness and immorality positively do not exist here." Irwin denounced the reports as part of an organized campaign to discourage enlistments.[23]

Col. Irwin remained in command of Jefferson Barracks until 1 July 1917, when he transferred to Sparta, Wisconsin, to take command of the 8th Field Artillery Corps. During his stay at Jefferson Barracks, Col. Irwin had impressed everyone with his efficiency, which was to soon be demonstrated on the battlefields of France. On 5 August, Col. Irwin was commissioned a brigadier general and assigned to the 57th Artillery Brigade for overseas duty.

He participated in the Aisne, Marne, Oise-Aisne, and Meuse-Argonne campaigns, for which he won the Croix de Guerre with Palm, and he was made an officer of the French Legion of Honor. On his return to the United States, he rose to the rank of major general in command of the Panama Canal Department. He died on board the steamship *Virgilio* at Port of Spain, Trinidad, on 19 February 1931.

Major Charles E. Stodter succeeded Col. Irwin in command. Stodter had served as a captain in the 9th Cavalry in Cuba and the Philippines; as senior instructor in the Army War College; and had been on recruit duty at Jefferson Barracks since February 1916. Major Stodter was appointed colonel, unassigned, on 18 August 1917, and turned over command of Jefferson Barracks to Capt. William B. Cowin, who served only one day and then he turned over command to Capt. Kenzie B. Edmunds. Edmunds remained in command until the arrival of Col. Cunliffe H. Murray on 4 September 1917. Col. Murray had previously commanded Jefferson Barracks in 1909. Col. Stodter served overseas during World War I, and was Inspector General of the Third Army Corps at Neuwid, Germany, during the occupation period.[24]

Col. Murray was born 26 August 1852, in South Carolina. He entered the U.S. Military Academy in 1873 and graduated 15 June 1877. He received an appointment as a 2nd Lt. in the 4th Cavalry at the Presidio of San Francisco. Murray was promoted to 1st Lt. 2 September 1879, and to captain 15 April 1890. During the war in the Philippines Murray served as Aide-de-Camp to Major General Elwell S. Otis from 13 August 1898, until 10 February 1899, and as Inspector-General of Volunteers from 11 February until 30 June 1899. He then served as Secretary to the Military Governor of the Philippines from 1 July 1899 to 4 May 1900. After his return from the Philippines Murray served in Washington, D.C. as Inspector-General and Assistant Adjutant-General in the Department of the Lakes before retiring.[25]

Governor Frederick D. Gardner of Missouri announced on 29 June that he had received a letter from Prosecuting Attorney Ralph stating that an inquiry had proven that the report of immoral conditions near Jefferson Barracks was a "gigantic hoax."[26] Then on 10 July, Missouri Attorney General Frank W. McAllister sent a report to Governor Gardner relative to conditions at Jefferson Barracks and suggested that the governor ask the War Department to establish a war zone of 500 yards around Jefferson Barracks. If acted upon, no alcohol could be sold within 500 yards of the post. Governor Gardner announced that he would make the request. McAllister went on to state that "conditions are not bad now, but some time ago immorality was said to exist and complaint was made that saloons were selling liquor to soldiers." Five saloons would be closed if the war zone was established.[27]

Not all of a new soldier's entertainment came from a saloon. Sports, even in times of war, played a major role. During the summer of 1917, Jefferson Barracks fielded a baseball team that proved to be one of the best in the area. The *Belleville News Democrat*, dated 29 September 1917, reported on the "Soldier Nine From Jefferson Barracks Here." The Jefferson Barracks team, composed mostly of baseball professionals who had enlisted in the Army, traveled to Belleville to take on the champion Belleville B's at North End Park.[28]

The B's defeated the Jefferson Barracks team by a score of 7 to 4, coming back from a 4 to 3 deficit in the final two innings. The Jefferson Barracks team asked for a rematch, to be played a week later.[29]

In August, Dr. Julius L. Bisckof, a Belleville dentist, spent seven days at Jefferson Barracks taking tests. In early September, Dr. Bisckof received notification that he was one of fourteen dentists out of 1,200 who took the tests to be accepted and commissioned in the Regular Army. Dr. Bisckof and the other dentists headed up a new branch of plastic dentistry and oral surgery. Dr. Bisckof was the first Belleville resident to receive a commission in the Regular Army during World War I.[30]

Col. Murray co-operated in the organization of a soldiers' entertainment service set up by the Y.M.C.A., the Knights of Columbus, the Red Cross, and other organizations in St. Louis. Theaters, ball parks and amusement places of various kinds extended an enthusiastic welcome to all men in uniform, and many notable actors, actresses, and musicians gave free performances at the Barracks.[31]

In November 1917, a trial took place at Jefferson Barracks that might just have been one of the first of its kind. On 16 November, Robert Henry Franke, a conscientious objector who resided at 2658 Shenandoah Avenue, charged with desertion from the Army for failing to answer a draft summons, was tried under martial law before a military court at Jefferson Barracks. The penalty for desertion in time of war was death. Franke's attorneys, Kurt von Reppert and Chester H. Krum, contended that Franke could not desert from an Army in which he had never served. At the conclusion of the attorney's arguments the Judge Advocate, representing the government, asked for conviction and imprisonment for the duration of the war.[32]

During the trial Franke sat beside his counsel, staring out the window at the parade ground in a detached manner. He showed little or no interest in the proceedings and while in the courtroom did not speak to his attorneys. The military court at Jefferson Barracks found Franke guilty.

On 15 December 1917, men who were draft eligible could no longer enlist to avoid being drafted. This created a frenzied rush all over the country to beat the draft. In Chicago, almost 5,000 young men attempted to enlist to beat the deadline. Of these between 3,000 and 4,000 were accepted, and all of them were sent to Jefferson Barracks so that the recruits could be sworn in by 15 December, the last day. Applicants at Kansas City, as at other recruiting offices in the midwestern states covered by Jefferson Barracks, were given a preliminary examination at the recruiting office, then sent to Jefferson Barracks where Army medical officers made the final physical examination and the men were sworn in. A special train car had been chartered each night of the final week to take the successful applicants to Jefferson Barracks. Fifty-six men entrained on Monday night, forty-two on Tuesday, fifty-three on Wednesday and another car was scheduled for Thursday.[33]

When the doors opened at the recruiting office on 13 December, two hundred men stood in line. The line grew during the day to nearly 300. They had to be accepted by 9:30 p.m. that night in order to get on the train for Jefferson Barracks.[34] It is interesting to note that 1,683 men from Kansas City were accepted for enlistment in the Army during the first 15 days of December.[35]

In another case of beating the deadline, Raymond O. Upper, from Dallas, Texas, who had a wife and five children enlisted in the Army. Upper, a bridge foreman, explained that he could make more money in civilian life, but was willing to sacrifice a little money to render service to his country. Upper was assigned to duty at Jefferson Barracks.[36]

Another interesting story of a recruit sent to Jefferson Barracks is that of Alex Schnaible. Schnaible, it seems, had fifty-two relatives in the German Army. If Schnaible got his way, he would fight them from one of Uncle Sam's aeroplanes. [We don't know if he accomplished this or not.][37]

At Kansas City's recruiting office, it was announced that the final day to enlist to beat the draft was 13 December. Almost all of the men who enlisted on this date were sent to Jefferson Barracks.[38]

By 15 December, Jefferson Barracks was taxed to capacity with more than 12,000 recruits, the largest number to that time ever stationed at Jefferson Barracks at one time. A continuous stream of recruits poured into the Barracks, among them 500 from the St. Louis recruiting office.

Col. Murray stated "that although the post was taxed to capacity, all the recruits would be properly equipped and cared for. They will be assigned to regiments and sent out as fast as possible. Yesterday, 3,000 recruits arrived at the Barracks. This is the largest number in one day in the history of the post. Tuesday and Wednesday the numbers received were 1,500 and 2,600 respectively. The 500 Army recruits accepted at the St. Louis office yesterday made a new record for a days work here."[39]

In St. Louis, the registering of recruits at the St. Louis office stopped at 4 p.m. on 14 December, as it was deemed there would not be sufficient time for men applying after that hour to complete their applications before the noon 15 December deadline. Outlying recruiting stations in the St. Louis District stopped even earlier. The men recruited in St. Louis on 14 December were kept at the 1st Regiment Armory that night and sent to Jefferson Barracks on the morning of 15 December. Since 1 December, when the campaign for recruits started, 9,000 recruits had been received at Jefferson Barracks.[40] On the final day, trains from Alabama, Kansas, Illinois, Minnesota, and both North and South Dakota brought new recruits. Six hundred of the new recruits had to sleep in blankets on the Y.M.C.A. gym floor the night of 14 December.[41]

During the year 1917, Jefferson Barracks had furnished more than its quota of the 1,189,000 men that the United States had under arms. It was one of the six largest recruiting depots in the United States.[42]

How did Jefferson Barracks handle the massive influx of recruits? Col. Murray explained that the number of recruit companies did not change, but more recruits were attached to them. As an example, on the last day of 1917, the 16th Recruit Company consisted of sixty-three permanent party personnel and 2,313 recruits.

While recruits were flocking to Jefferson Barracks and other recruit depots, the first contingent of American troops, some 14,000, disembarked at St. Nazaire, France, on 26 June 1917. These men would have no effect on the battlefield. They were in France to make preparations for the thousands of American troops to follow. On 4 September 1917, four American troops were killed during a German air raid on a British base hospital, the first American fatalities in France. The following day two Americans, both engineers, were killed by German shellfire while repairing a light railway track at Gouzeacourt. These were the first of thousands more to be killed.[43]

The first American troops went into action on the evening of 2 November 1917, when an American Infantry battalion took over for French troops at Barthelemont. At 3 o'clock the next morning, one of its isolated outposts was shelled in an hour-long artillery bombardment, after which a raiding party of 213 Germans attacked. The Americans were outnumbered 4 to 1 and three Americans were killed: Corporal Gresham and Privates Enright and Hay.[44]

1918

On 1 January 1918, General Pershing, commanding the American Expeditionary Force (AEF) in France, successfully opposed an urgent request from Great Britain's Prime Minister David Lloyd George that America send over as many surplus troops as possible, and incorporate them immediately on their arrival into British and French units. Lloyd George argued that the Germans were planning "a knock-out blow to the Allies" before a fully trained American Army was ready to take its place in the line during the summer of 1918. Pershing disagreed: "I do not think the emergency now exists that would warrant our putting companies or battalions into British or French divisions," he telegraphed the Secretary of War in Washington "and would not do so except in grave crisis." Pershing did accept a request from French Marshall Petain that four black regiments that were already in France should serve as integral parts of French divisions. They did so for the remainder of the war, and served with uncommon valor.[45]

On 18 January, a full American division, the First, entered the front line in the Ansauville sector of the St. Mihiele Salient. It had been sent there to gain experience in holding the line, and took no offensive action. As soon as the Germans discovered that Americans were opposite them, they attempted to demoralize the Americans by launching a raid on an American listening post killing two, wounding two, and capturing one. They then ambushed an American patrol in No-Man's Land, killing four, wounding two, and capturing two.[46]

At Jefferson Barracks, Col. Murray announced on 2 January that the 16,000 recruits currently at the post would be moved to training camps at a rapid rate during the coming week. Murray stated that 686 recruits had departed the day before and that, as fast as recruits departed, the men quartered at the Central and Railroad Y.M.C.A. buildings and at the Armory would be moved to the Barracks. The recruits at the Armory were under a quarantine order to keep the public away as a case of scarlet fever had been discovered there. He added that the quarantine would remain in effect for some time.[47]

In St. Louis on 4 January 1918, Major General William M. Wright, commander of the 35th Division which included many former Missouri National Guardsmen, stated that he did not believe that his officers and men were developing as rapidly as they should. "The division is not acquiring the punch it should" he said. "It is not going with the speed and spirit it must have. It drags in place. It is going ahead, improving constantly, but not as rapidly as it should."

"To go into this most terrible of wars, every man has got to be a Crusader, a cheerful, capable, earnest Crusader, physically fit, willing to give the last ounce that is in him and ready to die. You cannot acquire that spirit in a half-hearted manner. It takes all of a man, and this division has got to acquire it. The failure of the men to mature and ripen into soldiers as they should is due to the scattering of incompetent officers and non-commissioned officers in the division, and I am endeavoring to eliminate every officer and non-commissioned officer who is not efficient." Wright went on to say that it was the duty of competent officers to report those officers who were not capable. For every inefficient officer who goes into action, there will be a toll of death four times as heavy as if the officer was capable, competent and efficient. Wright praised the 35th's enlisted men as being as good as any, in physique, intelligence and capacity for learning.[48]

The 35th Infantry Division was constituted 18 July 1917, and organized 25 August 1917, at Camp Doniphan, Oklahoma, from National Guard units from Missouri and Kansas. The Division consisted of the 137th and 138th Infantry Regiments that made up the 69th Infantry Brigade, and the 139th and 140th Infantry Regiments that made up the 70th Infantry Brigade. Major General William M. Wright became commander of the 35th Division when it organized on 25 August. Brigadier General L.G. Berry relieved Wright on 18 September 1917, but Wright returned to command on 10 December 1917. It went overseas in May 1918 and upon arrival in France was garrisoned near the front in Alsace. It received limited training from the French Army. The 35th Division saw combat in the Meuse-Argonne offensive where it collapsed after five days of fighting. Major General Peter E. Traub commanded the Division during the Meuse-Argonne combat where it suffered 7,296 casualties. The 35th Division returned to the United States in April 1919 and was deactivated at Camp Funston, Oklahoma, on 30 May 1919.

In St. Louis, officers in charge of the Army Recruiting Office at Third and Olive were amazed at the lack of interest shown by St. Louisans in the Gas and Flame Regiment, officially designated as the 13th Engineers. Only about twenty men enlisted in this branch of the service, although the regiment was organized early in November and the inducement of active service in France was held out to men wishing to enlist.

"Applicants for this unit," Major Goode, in charge of recruiting, said, "have been few and far between. The average man seems to have a natural disinclination to being gassed...."

It was the duty of Gas and Flame men to operate the mechanical devices used in making gas and flame attacks.[49]

Also in St. Louis, a teacher in the Jefferson School, Miss Mary Irwin McDeamon of 456 North Newstead Avenue, left for Washington, D.C., the night of 3 January. Women could not join the service during World War I, but

Miss McDeamon went to Washington to work with the Department of Training Camp Activities, which had been authorized by the Government and financed by the Rockefeller Foundation.[50]

Two other St. Louis women also did their part to aid in the outcome of World War I. Miss Leslie La Beaume of 4710 Westminster Place and Miss Angelica Lockwood of 5710 Cates Avenue left St. Louis on 15 January to serve in the American Fund for French Wounded. Miss La Beaume was to drive an ambulance while distributing supplies to the military in and around the Paris Headquarters of the organization. It should also be noted that Miss Lockwood's brother, Preston, had been a Rhodes scholar at Oxford and was serving in the French Army.[51]

St. Louis and Barnes Hospital did their part with the AEF in France. Dr. J.S. Young, formerly of Barnes Hospital, served with Base Hospital Unit No. 18 of the AEF. Dr. Young, in letters to friends in St. Louis, wrote that the only thing lacking for the comfort of the men of the unit was music. He asked all St. Louisans to send discarded records to them. The men also wrote their families asking for talking machines and records.[52]

By January 1918, 150 young men had graduated from a free school for radio operators conducted by St. Louis University under the auspices of the War Department. The school, which opened in September 1917, trained drafted and enlisted personnel in the Army, Navy, and Marine Corps to become competent wireless or land telegraph operators.

Capt. A.G. Thompson, wireless expert in charge, stated that upon graduation the drafted men automatically transferred from the National Army to the Signal Corps of the regular forces, where they ranked as a high private. Thompson also stated that advancement opportunities and commissions were more rapid and easier to obtain in the Signal Corps.[53]

St. Louis was not without patriotic young men who wanted to become a part of the Signal Corps' new aviation section. On 9 January 1918, the names of ninety-seven young men from St. Louis City and St. Louis County were released. These young men had enlisted since December 1 and successfully passed the physical and mental examinations given by the Aviation Examining Board at Barnes Hospital. During this period, the St. Louis board had examined almost 300 candidates from Missouri, Illinois, Iowa, and Arkansas.

Seventy-two of the St. Louisans were seeking commissions in the Flying Division. Twelve candidates wanted to become balloon pilots and thirteen wanted to become ground officers in the Non-Flying Division. The ground officers were the skilled technical men who supervised the maintenance and repair of the machines and radio communications.

Among the St. Louisans accepted were two *Post-Dispatch* reporters: John T. Rogers and Sam J. Shelton. Another man accepted for the Flying Division was Frank H. Robertson, 4905 Argyle Avenue. Robertson's case is a bit unique. He passed a good examination in every respect, but, being under weight, he was permitted by the examiners to drink water while standing on the scales until he reached the required 110 pounds.[1]

In other war activity, the St. Louis Public Library received and distributed books for soldiers and purchased and circulated books on military organization and instruction; collected money for the War Library Fund; provided space in the branch libraries for work in connection with the draft; furthered the Liberty Bond and Thrift Stamp campaigns; gave space to the Red Cross committees to solicit memberships; and aided the food conservation campaign.[55]

By the middle of January, Col. Murray was able to say that the overcrowding of men at Jefferson Barracks due to receiving around 17,000 men by December 15, was rapidly being relieved. About 7,500 men had been shipped out by 13 January, and of the 9,500 remaining men, 1,800 were ready to be shipped, and more were to move out each day.

Col. Murray also emphatically denied reports which had been circulated that men were dying at the Barracks at the rate of six to eight per day. Murray stated that since 1 December 1917, there had been five deaths at the Barracks. One was an officer who had been taken from a train suffering from blood poisoning and was beyond medical help when received. Three died from pneumonia and one of these had it when he arrived. The cause of death in the other case was scarlet fever and bronchitis.

The sick report, he stated, was steadily shrinking and the proportion of sick was not greater at the time than among the same number of people in civilian life. There were thirty medical officers and twelve nurses on duty at Jefferson Barracks. There were between sixty and seventy cases of measles in the hospital. To prevent the spread of the disease, mingling of men from different companies was discouraged and recreational activities at the Y.M.C.A. and the Knights of Columbus buildings at the post had been suspended.

Murray explained that it was not uncommon for such a large number of men "coming from cities, villages and farms in twelve states" that there should be considerable sickness, partly because many of them would bring disease to the post. There was medical inspection every day, and all who were ill received adequate treatment.

All the men, Murray declared, were housed warmly and there were blankets for all. Some men had to sleep on the floors, but all were protected from the cold.[56]

The *Post-Dispatch* reported that besides Col. Murray, there were eight officers at Jefferson Barracks: a major, an adjutant, assistant adjutant, and five company officers. The recruits were divided into five companies, each under the command of an officer and each having twenty noncommissioned officers. At one time, there were 3,000 men in each company, nearly a regiment's war-time strength.[57]

Jefferson Barracks and St. Louis seemed to again be a beehive of activity regarding the prosecution of World War I on the homefront. On 16 January Secretary of War Baker requested an additional appropriation of $623,500 for an Army Supply Depot in St. Louis. Congress had previously appropriated $300,000 in its last session. Secretary Baker explained that the depot was needed for storage of great quantities of army supplies which were to be distributed in St. Louis. Chairman Shirley of the House Appropriations Committee said that the estimate would be included in the sundry civil appropriation bill.

The Surgeon-General's office requested that Representative Dyer obtain information about a suitable building in St. Louis for an Army hospital. It was observed that a large hotel or similar building with minimum fire risk would be considered. The building was to be leased for the period of the war and for one year after the cessation of hostilities. The West End Hotel, the old University Hospital and the Park Hotel were suggested.[58]

St. Louis University provided information in the middle of January that named 843 St. Louis University graduates and former students from the academic department then in the service. Of the 843 listed, 413 had obtained commissions. The medical and dental departments provided the names of 500 additional men in the service. The University estimated that 2,000 graduates and former students were then serving in the armed forces.[59]

St. Louis industrial plants joined in the World War I activities. On 16 January, the War Department announced the awarding of a contract to a St. Louis firm for 1,350,000 rifle breech stocks. A St. Louis firm also received contracts to furnish packing boxes for the stocks and for 100,000 small ammunition boxes. Names of the firms were withheld due to War Department rules.[60]

Just prior to the War Department's awarding of the above contracts, the War Department had been reluctant to place contracts in St. Louis because of reported freight congestion. Following the receipt of recent telegrams from E.J. Troy, Secretary of the Manufacturer's Association of St. Louis, showing that traffic conditions were no worse in St. Louis than in other manufacturing centers, Representative Dyer of St. Louis succeeded in getting the War Department to change its attitude.[61]

The following letter written by a young recruit at Jefferson Barracks, Alf, to his sister, Eda, provides a glimpse of what it was like to be a recruit at Jefferson Barracks in early January 1918.

Dear Sister Eda

Just got your letter today almost a week after you mailed it and was certainly glad to hear from you. The mail service down here is not very good on account of the large number of men here, they are using the Y.M.C.A. as an auxiliary P.O. and we get all our mail there, waiting in line according to alphabetical order. Ten clerks from the St. Louis P.O. are running it, and the man in charge of the A. B. C. section is the slowest moving P.O. Clerk I ever saw. Also, received the sweater from home, nine days after it was mailed. I suppose the big snow had something to do with the delay, so I won't put all the blame on the P.O....Pa means good all right, but a man in uniform hasn't much use for silk shirts, he isn't allowed to wear one even if he wanted to, so I sent them right back as soon as I got them.

I expect to leave this place soon [for Texas], will probably leave in a few hours but everything is so uncertain down here that there is no telling just what's going to happen. They called our names for an outgo shipment last Sunday, and we thought sure we would go then, but here it is Thursday and we are still hanging around. My kit is all packed and labeled "Kelly Field, Texas" that is near San Antonio. In my kit are 2 extra suits, extra woolen underwear, 2 pair socks, 2 Army blankets, extra pair of shoes, extra O.D. shirt, shoe laces and all my personal belongings, such as razor, towels, handkerchiefs etc. strapped to the bag outside, is a drinking cup, pie plate and knife, table spoon and fork. But I'm almost certain that we leave today. Have not done a stroke of work since I've been here and my hands are so clean that I can hardly believe that they belong to me, and eat, gosh, I eat 2 or 3 times as much as I did at home and believe me everything here is on a wholesale scale. Yesterday was Wilson's birthday, that's what they say anyhow, so for dinner we had turkey, that is some of them did, as there was not enough to go around, I had to be content with about ½ lb beef. Noodle soup, celery, mashed potatoes, and I don't know what else the finish was a big piece of Raisin Pie which everyone eats with their hands, as style doesn't count for much down here. The tables seat 80 men, 40 to each side and crowded pretty close, so there is not room for an elbow worker. The coffee is the only thing that I did not like but I'm getting used to it now. The bread is fine, no wheatless days down here as we get it every day, and meat we get three times a day, for instance the other morning we had liver and onions for breakfast, but most of them grab for the cream of wheat or cornflakes. They serve some sort of a stew every day, beans only once or twice a week, but they are good. The other day we had bean soup and the beans on the side, that's what I call a windy combination. When I said bed, in that card I sent, I meant an Army mattress on the floor, that is called luxury down here. The barracks that I slept in for the last 5 nights is an upper room, steam heated in a brick barracks on the door is a sign, "Maximum Capacity 61 Men" Last night 207 men slept there, there was hardly a square inch that wasn't occupied. The mattresses are laid on the floor as close as they can get them, then we spread our blankets over them. The mattresses are just about big enough for one man, but we cram 7 men on to 4 mattresses. But its better than sleeping on a cot in one of the stove heated wooden barracks, 10 ft away from the stove and you freeze. 3 or 4 weeks ago they used to spread the mattresses on the floor in these wooden shacks, and generally when they woke up in the morning they would find them frozen to the floor. No wonder there is such an epidemic of colds down here, but things are a whole lot better now as the recruits are not coming in so fast. My pals here are a Carpenter from Dixon, Ill and a draftsman from Beloit, Wis, The draftsman quit a $125 job to come down here, he said he wants an outdoor job for a while. Men of all trades down here, was talking with a Railway Mail Clerk the other day. A Sergeant just came in now and said we are going to leave at 315, everybody cheered. Its 250 now so Ill have to cut this letter short. On the day we were examined, we stood in line from 930 in the morning till 12, when I was half way through the exam. At 12, we were told to go to lunch, put on our clothes and come back again at 1. At 1 we stripped again and was finally finished with the finger prints by 230. Was measured for the uniform the same day and the next day we got our outfit everything is done wholesale, 300 of us examined 300 of us discarding our old clothes, all in a little room, so you can imagine the mix-up I sold my overcoat and the coat of my suit for $1.00 the rest I sent home.

Everything they gave me fitted me pretty good except the trousers and coat, which were too small but I exchanged them later on. Will have to close this as we are going to leave in about 10 minutes.

Regards to all

      from your brother Alf

Excuse the pencil, my fountain pen ran dry

      Not all men in St. Louis became soldiers or worked in war industries, but provided services in different ways. William H. Danforth of 17 Kingsbury Place, President of the Ralston Purina Mills, accepted the position of general secretary of the Y.M.C.A. canteen work in France. Danforth was to sail for France in February, and served without pay. He also agreed to defray all his own expenses.

      The office was created at the suggestion of General Pershing, who requested the Y.M.C.A. take over the United States canteen work in France, releasing thousands of enlisted men and officers for combat duty.[62]

      Word was received in late January that a telegraph battalion of the Signal Corps that was recruited during the summer of 1917 had reached England on its way to France. The battalion was recruited from employees of the Southwestern Bell Telephone Company and contained eighty St. Louisans. The commanding officer of the battalion was Major Frank A. Montrose of the Beverly Apartments. Other St. Louis officers in the battalion included 1st Lt. Humphrey Sullivan, Adjutant, former publicity agent for Southwestern Bell; 1st Lt. Earl H. Painter, Supply Officer; and former St. Louis University football coach, 1st Lt. W.H. Spencer. The battalion contained seventy-six privates from St. Louis. The battalion spent thirteen weeks training at San Antonio, Texas and was composed of practical telegraph men and was fully equipped to construct and operate telegraph and telephone lines.[63]

      Not all of the enlistees for war duty from St. Louis were men. Miss Helen Day and Miss Caroline E.L. Ives left for New York on Saturday, 26 January, to enlist for six months in the canteen service, which was headquartered in Paris. Both young women took a surgical dressing course at Barnes Hospital and qualified as nurses aides. The work that the young women were to do consisted of meeting troop trains passing through Paris and serving hot lunches to soldiers.[64]

      Col. George K. Hunter, 5th Cavalry, relieved Col. Murray in command of Jefferson Barracks on 15 February 1918. Col. Hunter first saw action in the field during the Sioux Indian War of 1890 and 1891. He had been severely wounded during the charge up San Juan Hill during the Spanish-American War and was cited for gallantry in the

Philippines. Col. Hunter had been stationed at Jefferson Barracks in 1899, after returning from Cuba and before leaving for the Philippines. Major K. Edmunds commanded the post after the departure of Col. Murray and until the arrival of Col. Hunter.

Col. Murray, who was sixty-five years old, had been recalled from the retired list the previous fall to take command at the Barracks. Col. Murray went back into retirement and returned to his home in New Jersey.[65]

It was reported on February 3 by General Gorgos, Surgeon-General of the Army, that the War Department was in receipt of an offer from St. Louis and Washington University for a site for a projected national hospital for reconstruction of soldiers disabled in war.[66]

On 5 February, orders were received from Provost Marshal-General Crowder that 600 men, forming the remainder of St. Louis' quota of 4,377 men in the first draft quota, were to depart St. Louis beginning 23 February for service with the National Army at Camp Funston. About 3,800 of the original quota had already been sent to camp.

As a result of the order approximately one-half of the twenty-eight local wards which had not yet filled their quotas resumed the examination of men. The District Board had received instructions on Saturday, 2 February, to discontinue examination of men at once, but with the new orders from the Provost Marshal it was decided to examine enough men to complete the quota.[67]

In news of St. Louis area men in the Army, the *Post-Dispatch* reported on 11 February that three St. Louis men who were aboard the *Tuscania* when it was torpedoed off the coast of Ireland had safely arrived at an Irish port. Sgt. Dewitt Schwartz, a former Soldan High School student who enlisted in the Field Artillery on 7 April 1917, and later transferred to the 20th Engineers, and Privates Vernon Baldwin and G.H. Lewis, 138th Aero Squadron, were reported safe and sound in Ireland.

Will Jordan, the 20-year-old son of the editor of the Belleville and Pana, Illinois newspapers and a member of the 100th Aero Squadron, also survived the *Tuscania* disaster. However, two other Missourians on board the *Tuscania*, William G. Smith of Festus and Walter Alexander of Marshall were still listed as missing. Smith belonged to the Camp Travis detachment of Infantry, and Alexander was a member of the 100th Aero Squadron.[68]

On the recruiting front in St. Louis, Capt. Fred M. Eslick, in charge of the U.S. Marine Corps recruiting station at 7th and Pine, transferred to New Orleans in February, where he served as recruiting inspector of the Southern Division. While Eslick served in St. Louis, the sixty-eight Marine Corps recruits he enlisted ranked first for recruiting in the Central Division. Lt. Francis E. Turin succeeded Eslick. Lt. Wylie J. Moore, another St. Louis officer, transferred to active duty with the Marines in New York.[69]

St. Louis officers received praise from Major General Wright, Commander of the 35th Division at Camp Doniphan, Oklahoma. General Wright praised the officers of the 3rd Battalion, 138th Infantry, in his general orders complimenting the troops for their efficiency and excellent appearance. All the officers were from St. Louis. Major Norman B. Comfort commanded the battalion.

In commenting on the general order, Col. Conrad of the 138th Infantry stated, "It is indeed a compliment that one organization should be repeatedly reported for its excellent appearance and general efficiency. Such conditions indicate a high rate of discipline and training."[70]

One hundred and fifty-nine St. Louisans, comprising part of St. Louis' last contingent of the first draft call, departed from Union Station at 9 o'clock on 26 February, for training camp at Camp Funston, Kansas. These men had been scheduled to leave St. Louis the previous November, but their departure had been postponed several times as Camp Funston was unable to receive them. The remainder of the final 15 percent of the first quota was to depart on 4 March.

Draft boards in St. Louis County sent fifty-seven men to camp on the evening of 26 February. The Clayton District sent twenty-two men, the Kirkwood District sent 17, and 18 went from the Ferguson District.[71]

General Pershing sent a casualty list from France at the end of February 1918. On the list was David Hickey, the first St. Louisan killed in action in France. Hickey listed his sister, Mrs. Cecilia Ebeler, 5832 Garfield Avenue, as his closest relative. Hickey, who had attended Bates School, enlisted during the summer of 1917 and had been assigned to Battery E, 6th Field Artillery.[72]

St. Louis soldiers, 3,000 strong, passed in review on 28 February before Major General Wright, commander of the Missouri and Kansas 35th National Guard Division. The review and inspection of the 138th Infantry, an amalgamation of the old 1st and 5th Missouri regiments, took the entire morning.

The Infantrymen marched with precision. They carried the Joffre flag, which had been presented to the 5th Regiment when the Marshal of France was in St. Louis with former Premier Viviani.

Four thousand area men were to arrive by 10 March in order to fill the division. They were held at a detention camp for a week or more before being assigned to units.[73]

In Europe during February 1918, American troops participated in offensive action on the Western Front for the first time. On 13 February, at the Butte du Mesnil in Champagne, American artillery batteries took part in a 6-hour rolling barrage before a French attack that broke through German lines and captured more than 150 German prisoners. Ten days later, south of German-held Laon, two American officers and twenty-four of their men volunteered to take part with French troops in a raid on German trenches. The raid lasted half an hour, and twenty-five Germans were taken prisoner.[74]

Word was received on 1 March 1918, that two East St. Louisans who had enlisted at Jefferson Barracks four months earlier had arrived safely in France. After enlisting, Hal Sheets and Frank Orr went to balloon school in Omaha, Nebraska, for training and then to Garden City, Long Island. Both men served with a U.S. Balloon unit.[75]

Major Edmunds, in command of Jefferson Barracks, met with the Executive Committee in charge of the Municipal Athletic Association Carnival that was to be held at the St. Louis Coliseum on 2 March. They met to complete arrangements for the event. Major Edmunds said that Jefferson Barracks' officers would cooperate in staging the festivities and that the Barracks band would provide a musical program.

One of the spectacular features of the evening was the formation of a "human flag" by 380 Sunday School children and Boy Scouts. A patriotic rally was held to conclude the program. The event was given as a benefit for the Soldiers and Sailors Club, located at 1137 Olive Street.[76]

The last of the St. Louis quota of 4,377 men in the first draft, except for six men, departed on a special train for Camp Funston at 9 a.m. on 5 March. There were 163 men on the train, representing eleven wards. Ninety-five men had departed the previous evening and the remaining six went on the night of 5 March.[77]

A former Jefferson Barracks soldier received the Croix de Guerre for heroism during a German raid in the American sector. David A. Smiley, 21, of Hannibal, Missouri, and formerly of St. Louis, was one of six American soldiers decorated by Premier Clemenceau of France. Smiley enlisted soon after the declaration of war in April, and was sent to Jefferson Barracks. He was in one of the first contingents sent to France. Smiley served in the Field Artillery.[78]

Austin J. McNulty, of 3412 Franklin Avenue in St. Louis, received notice on 1 March that his son, Pvt. Edward H. McNulty, had been killed in action in France. He was the second St. Louisan killed in action.

McNulty served in the 18th Infantry in the Regular Army. He enlisted in 1916 and saw action on the Mexican border.

Two brothers of Pvt. McNulty also served in the armed forces. Philip was (at the time) a bugler at Jefferson Barracks, and Patrick was a yeoman on the USS *Leonidas*.

The last word which Austin McNulty had from his son was a letter dated 29 January. It follows: "Dear Dad - Received your last letter with the photos, and box also arrived. O.K. No use of me trying to explain how glad I was to get them on New Year's morning."

"Well, Dad, I am feeling fine and getting along fairly well. The weather is pretty damp and cold at present. You must be having pretty tough weather in the States, judging by the letters the boys receive from home."

"Received Aunt Flora's box of candy. I will drop her a line as soon as I find time and a little better place to write."

"Pat's girl in Philadelphia sent me a swell outfit, one of those sleeveless sweaters, a pair of woolen gloves, skull cap, a pair of sox, handkerchiefs and lots of candy and chewing gum, also smoking tobacco."

"It surely was a fine outfit. She packed the goods in two boxes. Nobody could have done better. My eyes almost popped out when I received those boxes."

"I also got a letter in the trenches at midnight. It makes a man feel good to receive a letter there. I have just come back from the trenches and have had all the luck a soldier could wish for...."

The letter serves as a good example of thousands of letters home from the young men serving in France and of the importance of the letters and boxes from home.[79]

Jefferson Barracks and Columbus Barracks, Ohio, furnished the majority of aviation recruits at Camp Kelly Aviation Field. Recruits arrived at Camp Kelly at the extraordinary rate of 1,000 per day to fill the places of men who already had qualified for the flying and mechanical needs of the aviation service and had been advanced further toward the front. As fast as men arrived, they were organized into squadrons, and their preparation for overseas service rapidly pushed.[80]

Certainly, not all St. Louisans who served in World War I did so in the Army or went through Jefferson Barracks. The U.S. Navy's youngest Petty Officer came from St. Louis. Coxswain Clarence E. Mattison, 16, commanded a gun crew on a merchant ship, and by 24 March 1918, had survived eight trips across the Atlantic to Europe through the most thickly infested U-boat waters.

A year earlier Mattison had been a messenger for the Western Union Telegraph Company. He quit his job and presented himself for enlistment at the Naval Recruiting Office. Only 15 years old, 5 feet 3 inches and 117 pounds, and with his mother's consent Mattison was accepted.

Mattison was sent to the Great Lakes Naval Training Station, but after only fourteen days he was shipped to the Atlantic seaboard where he was assigned to the battleship *Maine*. He then sailed on the battleship *Texas* where he became a crew member of a 5-inch gun. During target practice, his crew scored four hits in four shots in forty-three seconds, and in recognition of this record the entire crew was assigned to the armed guard service for duty on passenger liners and merchant ships.

What follows is Coxswain Mattison's story of his experiences in the Armed Guard. "My first trip in the armed guard was on the grain-carrier *Satsuma*, to which I had been assigned as sight-setter of a 3-inch gun. We made a three months' trip to France and African ports and a two months' voyage to Italy. On the first trip, while we were at St. Michael's Islands near the Straits of Gibraltar, we picked up a wireless message from a U-boat which appeared to have exhausted its torpedo supply and was calling to other submarines nearby to get after us.

"Our radio men soon mussed up their message, and continued to do so for four days. The U-boat kept on our trail, but out of range of our gun. On the fifth day, the U-boat slipped a wireless message through and three other submarines answered.

"At the same time, we sighted the freighter *Orleans* returning to the United States. We knew the U-boats were coming for us, and started a dash to escape. I suppose they came upon the *Orleans* first, for we saw an explosion and received an SOS from her. We could see her sinking. We could not go to her assistance, because the captain had strict orders to save his own ship at all costs. We had 8,000 tons of wheat aboard, and the Germans figured us a rich prize."

"Well, we made a run for it, and managed to get away from the submarines."

"We had more trouble on our return trip, when we ran into a terrific gale. All of our life rafts were washed overboard, and the life preservers of my crew, which were piled behind our gun, were also swept away by the sea. The ship, which picked up some of our floating life belts, reported in New York that we had been sunk."

"My next ship was the liner *St. Paul*, and I remained on her for four trips between Liverpool and New York. We were not troubled by U-boats, but on my last inbound trip we were caught by a gale soon after we had left Liverpool, and driven ashore. It was a close call."

"I then went aboard the tanker *Northwestern* and made two trips to France, Italy and Africa. On our last trip to the United States we were caught in a storm off the Irish coast. The ship was absolutely empty of cargo, so the captain ordered her tanks filled with sea water and that was the only thing which kept us afloat until we could run into Belfast. During the gale, which lasted 36 hours, we lost our convoy in a sea which the old-timers estimated was running 50 feet high."

"On the same trip, outbound, we picked up a French aviator whose hydro-airplane had been brought down by the enemy in the Mediterranean Sea. He was drifting helplessly when we came up. We carried him to an African port, along with his machine, and after we arrived, he broke up the machine and distributed the pieces amongst us as souvenirs."

"The young sailor will leave St. Louis Tuesday night and will go to an Atlantic port for assignment to another ship. Before he departs, however, he will act as best man at the wedding of his sister, Edna, who tomorrow night will become the bride of Lewis Gillrath. Certainly, we can see that it was not only extremely dangerous on land during World War I, but just as dangerous at sea."[81]

At the end of March 1918, the local Army Recruiting Station received notice that it was authorized to enlist men for the Tank Service, National Army. All men over or under draft age were eligible. The men who were accepted were sent to Jefferson Barracks, and from there they transferred to the Tank Service camp at Gettysburg, Pennsylvania.

The Tank Service was one of the most interesting and exciting branches of the service and new to the American Army.[82]

In June, the recruiting campaign for the Tank Service intensified when Lt. F.E. Cooter of the Tank Service arrived in Kansas City from Jefferson Barracks. Lt. Cooter was to conduct a Tank Service recruiting campaign in Kansas City for ten days as no new recruits for the service had been taken for several weeks.[83]

On the battlefields of Europe March 1918 witnessed a major setback for the Allied cause. At 5 o'clock in the afternoon of 3 March, the Russo-German Peace Treaty was signed at Brest-Litovsk. It appeared that soon troops from the Eastern Front could be moved to the Western Front.[84]

On the Western Front the Germans began, on 9 March, the preliminary phases of what was to be their biggest and most essential gamble of World War I: a massive offensive against British and French forces. Up to this time the primary military initiatives on the Western Front had been taken by the Allied powers - on the Somme, at Ypres, and at Cambrai. Each of these offensives had broken against superior German fortifications and defensive lines. In March 1918, the Germans wanted to break through the line of Allied trenches and secure victory before the mass of American troops, unbattered in battle, reached the war zone.[85]

In one of the preliminary artillery bombardments, one of the German targets was an Infantry Post in the Pasroy Forest. When it was hit on 7 March, it happened to be held by men of the American 42nd "Rainbow" Division. Ten Americans were killed in a single dugout.[86]

In the early hours of 21 March, the Germans launched an offensive that was intended to bring victory to German forces on the Western Front. The objective was to drive the British from the Somme, the French from the Aisne, and to threaten Paris as it had been threatened in 1914.[87]

At an emergency conference of generals and politicians on 26 March 1918, Marshal Ferdinand Foch was given overall command of all Allied Forces. His first act was to order the French Army, then holding the line at St. Mihiel, to move forward to Ameins. When General Petain expressed doubts as to the possibility of holding the line at Amiens and suggested a new line twenty miles further back, Foch cut him short with the words; "We must fight in front of Amiens. We must stop where we are now. As we have not been able to stop the Germans on the Somme we must not retire a single centimeter."[88]

Under an intermediate draft call, 295 St. Louis men, representing all twenty-eight St. Louis wards; eight men from the Kirkwood District of St. Louis County; and fifty men from southeast Missouri left Union Station during the night of 1 April 1918, bound for Camp Funston. This brought the total of drafted men from St. Louis City and County to 4,640. All of them sent to Camp Funston.

The intermediate draft call asked for 95,000 men from the entire United States. Missouri's quota was 1,140. An additional thirty-two men from Ferguson and Kirkwood districts in St. Louis County left by train on the morning of 2 April.[89]

A news article in the *Post-Dispatch* stated that "Union Station was crowded last night with relatives and friends of the drafted men who assembled to bid goodbye to the prospective soldiers. There was much cheering and singing as the men boarded the train. Groups from some wards paraded to the station, singing and shouting, accompanied by relatives, friends and spectators.

Considerable enthusiasm was aroused by the singing of Hal Greer, a vaudeville performer who had just finished an engagement at a St. Louis theater. He had been drafted and will depart tonight for his home in Colorado to report to his local board to be sent to camp. Some of his St. Louis friends were among those sent away last night, and with them he paraded through the street before train time singing popular songs. At the station, he took a position in the center of the intersection of Eighteenth and Market Streets, and sang for 10 minutes while the crowd which collected blocked car traffic.

One of the songs that Greer sang with good effect was, "What Are You Going to Do for the Boys?" which has been adopted as the official song of the Third Liberty Loan Campaign."[90]

Paul Werner, a moving picture machine operator in a theater at 1440 South Broadway, St. Louis, enlisted about 5,400 men for the Navy. Werner became the champion recruiter for the St. Louis District. Werner told a *Post-Dispatch* reporter that he had induced over 1,000 men to apply for enlistment in the Navy, of whom more than 700 had been accepted since the war began.

Werner served seventeen years in the Navy. On his uniform, which he wore daily, he had six service bars for participation in the Boxer Rebellion, the Battle of Manila, the Spanish-American War, the Philippine Insurrection and the second occupation of Cuba. Commenting on the fact that he served the recruiting office without pay, he said "But they have given me permission to add the time I spend recruiting to my former term of service, giving me the right to add one more service stripe to my coat sleeve." Werner started recruiting 6 April 1917, the day the United States entered the war. Werner lived at 4357 Delor Avenue. Half a block away, at the corner of Gravois Avenue and Morganford Road, he got permission to open a recruiting station in an old garage.[91]

Two St. Louis physicians, Capt. John F. Hardesty, 30, of 3206 California Avenue, and Lt. Harold A. Goodrich, 29, of Webster Groves, were reported missing in action in the official casualty list issued by the War Department on 14 April 1918. These were the first two St. Louisans reported among the missing since the United States entered the war.

Both doctors had been with the British forces in Flanders. Dr. Goodrich had been in active service in a frontline dressing station for nearly eight months. His mother received a telegram stating that he had been missing since 24 March.[92]

One of the largest demonstrations ever held at Jefferson Barracks took place on 18 April 1918. An estimated 80,000 people came in cars, boats, by rail, and on foot to celebrate All-American Day. A parade formed in which groups of foreign-born citizens marched under banners showing their nationalities: English, French, German, Serbs, Croatians, Austrians, Greeks, Poles, Russians, Italians, and naturalized citizens from all over the world, attested their loyalty to the United States. Banners read "We were born in ...; Americans now." Among the inscriptions on other banners were: "Birth by accident, citizenship by choice;" "Italians by birth, Americans at heart." Many of the contingents had their own banners.

The First Infantry Regiment, under the command of Major Norman B. Compton, led the parade. The 5th Infantry followed, commanded by Major Barangrove. Next in line of march came the Knights of Columbus Choral Club in white uniforms, the St. Louis Corps Sons of Veterans, Boy Scouts, two hundred girls of the Famous-Barr Drum Corps, the Navy League, Naval Scouts, Citizens of Foreign Birth, other civic organizations, and a battalion of pride stirring regulars. The program included an exhibition drill and several patriotic speeches.[93]

The Grandstand at Jefferson Barracks was completed on 30 April. It cost $8,455 and was paid for with Post Exchange funds. During the entire year thousands of recruits assembled at Jefferson Barracks and were shipped by the trainload to other military camps for training and organization.

Since the United States entered into World War I a little more than a year before, nearly 90,000 Army recruits had passed through Jefferson Barracks. Another 12,950 draftees were to be mobilized in early May. Col. George K. Hunter provided these figures during a discussion of health conditions at Jefferson Barracks.

A recent dispatch from Washington said that Jefferson Barracks had the highest sick rate of all the Army stations. Col. Hunter said this was misleading because it did not take into consideration the fact that Jefferson Barracks cared for many cases of soldiers who became ill while passing through St. Louis. Also, cases of illness among recruits attending trade schools in St. Louis were sent to Jefferson Barracks. "On the whole," Col. Hunter said, "health conditions are as good at Jefferson Barracks as at any Army Post."

Preparations were then being made at Jefferson Barracks to provide care for the drafted men who were to begin arriving about 1 May. About 600 additional tents were procured to help shelter the men. The first arrivals were to come from Illinois, with succeeding arrivals from Missouri, Iowa, and Kansas. Arrivals were to continue until 20 May.

Jefferson Barracks was not turned into a training cantonment, such as Camp Funston, but instead served as a receiving station for drafted men, just as it had been used for regular Army recruits. The drafted men were given their final physical examinations, uniformed and given preliminary drill instruction, remaining no longer than about ten days, after which they were sent to regular training camps.[94]

An excellent description of the massive offensive that started toward the end of March 1918 came from Lt. Robert Hale of St. Louis, formerly agency secretary of the Equitable Life Assurance Society, 612 Locust Street. Hale was in the French front-line trenches which came under the big German attack of March 21, but he came out "through a hail of shells" without injury. Hale wrote, "They kept us ducking all the time, but luck was with us. 15 March - was awakened early this morning by the heavy bombardment of a raid in another sector. Went up to the first-line trenches early. I saw another airplane fight at noon today. My glasses are indeed useful. The German trenches are only a few hundred yards away and are on two sides of our sector. Have some fragments of one of the shells that hit near us, which I will bring home as souvenirs."

"Our company has a little dog mascot which they call Verdun and it was there they found him. He has a great time chasing rats. This morning he went out through the wire and we were afraid the Germans would take a shot at him.

"March 20 - We moved up to the very front line and live in a deep, dark dugout. I have seen my first real fighting. The Germans made a raid on our company. They killed some of our men and captured others. We had some hard fighting for a while. The big shells were falling around us like hailstones and the earth trembled like an earthquake. Machine gun and rifle bullets were whistling close to our heads. We did not know how anyone lived through it. The French replied with their artillery, machine guns, etc. It was my first sight of hand-to-hand fighting. The Boche beat a hasty retreat under the cover of their barrage. It was pretty hot for us for a while."

"The shells are going over all the time and some land very close. A splinter from one just grazed my steel helmet yesterday."

Lt. Hale added that he was on his way to join his own troops and then "back after the Boches with the Americans!"

A few of the long-awaited, much-needed American troops went into action on 20 April 1918 in the St. Mihiel Salient. That day two companies, 655 officers and men who had been stationed at Seichepey for the last month, were caught in an attack by 2,800 German troops. The Americans, outnumbered by more than four to one, fell back with heavy losses. Entering Seichepey, the Germans destroyed all fortifications and then withdrew to their original front line. Eighty-one Americans were killed, over 200 were incapacitated by gas, 187 were wounded and another 187 were either missing or taken prisoner. General Pershing was angered by what he regarded, even though outnumbered, as bad American generalship.[95]

On 2 May 1918, a new construction phase began at Jefferson Barracks with the conclusion of a contract for emergency construction between the United States of America and the W.M. Sutherland Building and Contracting Company of St. Louis. Capt. Thomas B. Motz, Engineers, would supervise construction for the Army. He was appointed Constructing Quartermaster on May 4. Assisting Capt. Motz were Capt. Walter B. Phillips, Property Officer, who arrived on 17 May, and Capt. A. Houston Jones, Assistant Constructing Quartermaster, who arrived the next day, 18 May.

The buildings to be constructed consisted of additions to the Jefferson Barracks Hospital Complex. In all, forty-two buildings or additions to buildings were completed. Work began on clearing the construction site almost immediately after the contract had been signed. By the end of May, most of the important construction materials had arrived at Jefferson Barracks. The first buildings completed were the Comfort Station, completed on 17 July 1918, and an addition to the Post Office completed on 31 July.

In September, a garage for Hospital Corps trucks, a refrigeration plant for the General Mess, and a storage building for medical property were completed. On 6 October, Hospital Corps barracks and two buildings for nurses' quarters were completed, and in November six wards, a lavatory, a storage building for patient's effects, an addition to the Post Laundry, and four covered walkways were completed. By the end of 1918, another storage building for patient's effects, a Hospital Corps Mess and Kitchen, a Nurses' Mess and Kitchen, a ward Mess and Kitchen, a garage for Quartermaster Corps trucks, a garage platform, and a concrete culvert under the railroad tracks had also been completed.

The buildings constructed under the original authorization which called for Hospital Corps enlisted men's barracks, nurses' quarters, wards and kitchens were occupied by the Post Surgeon during the month of September 1918, at the time of the influenza epidemic. At that time, the buildings were not being entirely completed according to plans, but they were needed to take care of the sudden increase in hospital admittances. Other units were also occupied prior to completion and formal transfer to the Post Quartermaster.

By the end of April 1919, four additional Hospital Corps barracks, two Officer's Quarters, an Officer's Mess and Kitchen, a Psychiatric Ward, a heating plant for the Hospital Group, a power plant for the Post Laundry and additions to the Fire Station and the General Mess building had been completed.

The source of labor for these major construction projects came from various St. Louis local labor unions. The maximum number of men employed on the project was 412 on 2 July 1918. Hourly wages paid were 85 cents to $1.00 for bricklayers; 75 cents to 82.5 cents for carpenters; 75 cents to 87.5 cents for electricians; 81.25 cents to 87.5 cents for plumbers; and 45 cents for common laborers.

An additional major project in the original plans concerned the post water supply, oftentimes a problem throughout the history of Jefferson Barracks. An original authorization of $15,000 included removing the 150,000-

gallon steel storage tank from the north entrance of the reservation to a point directly west of the new hospital group, along with the necessary supply mains and connections to buildings, and with fire hydrants.

After a careful study of the general water situation at the post by competent hydraulic engineers, an additional allotment of $30,000 was made to revamp the entire water system, to furnish the post with the necessary water at sufficient pressure for all uses. This included the installation of a 200,000-gallon redwood storage tank and two electric driven pumps. The additional distributing system consisted of approximately 10,000 feet of six-inch and eight-inch cast iron pipe and twenty-four hydrants.[96]

The first of 13,000 drafted men who were to be mobilized at Jefferson Barracks before 20 May arrived on the afternoon of 2 May. Jefferson Barracks received more drafted men daily in numbers calculated to not overtax the capacity of the post. The men received physicals and were then distributed to various training cantonments.

Missouri's drafted men began arriving at Jefferson Barracks on 10 May. St. Louis was to send 551 men, most of whom were to arrive on 12 May. In order to provide ample housing, Col. Hunter acquired 800 tents, each large enough to house six men. Col. Hunter explained that the Post had two large mess halls that were capable of feeding all the men present on the post at any time.[97]

In early May, it was learned that St. Louis doctors Harold A. Goodrich and John F. Hardesty, who had been reported missing in Flanders, had been captured by the Germans. Reports from the War Department and the Red Cross to the men's relatives said that they were well.[98]

The sad news that two more St. Louisans had been killed in France was reported by the *Post-Dispatch* on 4 May. Mrs. Emma Carter received notice that her son, Corporal Fred C. Carter, had died of wounds received in action in France. Cpl. Carter had completed a 4-year enlistment on 22 September 1917, and upon re-enlistment had transferred from the 16th Infantry to a machine gun company. He had served two years in the Philippines and with General Pershing's expedition to Mexico.[99]

Word was also received that Pvt. Kenneth M. Copley of Webster Groves was accidentally killed in the airplane service in France on April 29. Copley's parents had received a letter from him five days earlier informing them that he had passed the examination for a lieutenancy and was expecting to receive his commission. Copley had been married just nine months previously.[100]

St. Louis draft boards sent 555 men to Jefferson Barracks on 12 May and three County boards sent fifty-seven men. Among the men to go to Jefferson Barracks was Kenneth R. Williams, an outfielder for the St. Louis Browns.[101]

A letter written home to St. Louis told of the maiming of Fred A. Renick of St. Louis. Joel H. Blackmer, son of Dr. R.C. Blackmer, 6778 Manchester Avenue, related the story of Renick's injury. Blackmer wrote that "Fred has fallen victim of an enemy shell. He was not–thank God–killed, but very badly wounded. It seems that during a violent attack on the 4th, the Germans were pouring a terrific barrage fire into a little French village and along the road leading thereto. Three ambulances were ordered to a post there. Fred, with two of his comrades, started out, although it was nothing less than running a death gauntlet. Going into the town a high explosive shell burst between Fred's car and Hancook's (a chap in his section), a piece of steel striking Fred above the right eye. Hancook applied a first-aid dressing and Fred, dazed but undaunted, continued on to the post. There he loaded his car with wounded, all the while under fire, and calmly started back through that rain of shells."

"He had gone less than one kilo when a shell struck his ambulance, blowing it to bits and killing the three wounded soldiers within. Fred suffered a maimed left hand, a shattered right arm (which has since had to be amputated), a broken shoulder and a fractured skull, besides numerous other body wounds. But, in spite of it all the brave fellow staggered away until aid came."

"But those of his comrades who have been able to visit him at the hospital say that he is very cheerful and in remarkably good spirits, considering....."

Renick was awarded the French Medal Militaire, the highest honor bestowed by France.[102]

An article in the *Post-Dispatch* of 18 May 1918, tells an astonishing story of how Jefferson Barracks turned all makes and models of civilians into soldiers. Entitled "Mill at Barracks Turns Out Soldiers Rapidly: Varied Array of Drafted Men go in at One End of Huge U and All Come Out at Other End Clad in Khaki."

"There has been created at Jefferson Barracks a great, smoothly running mill, and out of which emerge soldiers. The mill is also a huge preparator, that unerringly divides fit and unfit."

"The mill is in the shape of a huge U. Into one horn of the U can be seen entering farmer boys, mechanics, clerks and rich men's sons. Their dress is as varied as the localities from which they come. Stylish spring suits mingle indiscriminately with overalls and jumpers. Modish hats, battered caps and eervies bob up and down together as they pour into the mouth of the mill."

"But the stream emerging from the other horn of the U is different. It is composed solely of men dressed in the same kind of khaki shirts and breeches, the same kind of service hats, the same shoes and leggins, and each carries the same kind of a blue bag, filled with precisely the same articles. The distinctions have been erased. There are no more mechanics or clerks; no wealthy or poor—only soldiers."

"In the five days closing with Monday, sixty-five hundred drafted men from Illinois passed through the Barracks. All of them have passed through the great machine and have been accepted or rejected. If accepted, they have been outfitted, and all of both classes are gone. There is no delay; drafted men generally go out the third day, including the day of arrival."

"Present facilities for handling them are in strong contrast to those of last December, when 16,000 enlisted men were billeted in vacant buildings, at the Y.M.C.A., in hotels, and wherever room could be found for them. The hills around the barracks now are cities of white tents, that, with the new cantonment buildings, are ample for the average of 5000 men who are there."

"The accumulation of men will be cleared out today and tomorrow, but the stream will start again Friday, when 2,163 drafted men from Missouri begin to arrive. Among these will be 555 St. Louisans, who will go to the Barracks Sunday."

"The scene around the barracks is a moving one. Groups of men in civilian clothes constantly arriving; men in uniforms continuously pour out on to the parade ground with their blue sacks on their shoulders; occasionally a bugle call blares across the parade ground, which, with the constant tramping of men, is strikingly reminiscent of the "Gathering of the Clans" scene in "The Birth of a Nation.""

"About 13,000 drafted men from Illinois, Missouri, Kansas, and Iowa are to be sent through the barracks in the two-week period ending May 25. They are shipped out to fill up Army divisions in training camps. They do not receive any training at the Barracks."

A *Post-Dispatch* reporter, to get first-hand information on the transition of a drafted civilian into a soldier, yesterday went through the entire process, from the moment of arrival to that of departure, just as a drafted man would do.

"When the 'drafts,' as they are called, arrive in the railroad yards, they are being placed in charge of a non-commissioned officer. Then they go to the receiving barracks, where they undress. A preliminary physical examination is immediately given them to discover contagious diseases. The dressing room constitutes the mouth of the first horn of the U."

"Each man takes a shower bath, and his number is marked on his chest with blue chalk. He continues down the side of the U, and his name, age, etc., are written on the record card which he carries."

"At the next stop (if a pause of 30 seconds may be called a stop), a young wizard in khaki weighs the drafted man, measures his height, his chest and counts the number of missing teeth, and sends him on down the line with a slap on the back, before the bewildered "draft" grasps what it is all about."

"However, the next station has another surprise.

"Any scars?" snaps a tired looking individual behind a table. The reporter answered that there were none."

"Whatthell's that on your left temple? Right arm? Right leg? Left Leg?" flashed back the inquisitor, and in less than a minute the incoherent one is again on his way, now holding a diagram showing the nature and location of five tiny scars that he had forgotten he ever had."

"Then, as he plods on, wondering where this scar-detector had seen him before, his chin is firmly grasped by a young dentist, his mouth is opened, his teeth again inspected, and diseases of the mouth, if any, recorded on his card by the assisting clerk."

"He has reached the first elbow in the U, in the curve of which the specialists lie in wait. Next his arm is grabbed, and a vaccination site is sponged off with alcohol by a young man in a white apron, who does nothing else. The vaccination follows immediately, consuming perhaps 15 seconds, and he passes on into a dark room. Here a blond man looks into his throat, his ears and his nose while he says: "Sorry if I twist your head off, but we're rushed," and on he goes, with more damning facts on the record card."

"The whispering test for the hearing, and the chart-reading one for sight, which follows, are familiar to many, but not the ordeal which is next on the program. The latter is called the "neurologist's test," but a young man in a stage whisper at the door states that, "This is where they find out if you are nutty.""

"The neurologists' room is no place for a man with family secrets. The skeleton will be dragged from the closet, weighed, measured, ticketed and put in a filing cabinet where all the War Department may see. If your father ever was hit on the head and knocked unconscious; if your mother ever fell down the stairs; if you or your folks ever had fits, fainting spells or brain fever, the neurologist will find it out."

"Nothing is sacred to him. He taps the "draft" on his "crazy bone" with a rubber hammer, and then, after making him shut his eyes, tickles him in the ribs. When this is finished, and the "draft" is feeling that everything about his past, present and future is public property, he passes on to the bone and muscle test."

"This consists of nothing much except jumping up and kicking his heels together; wiggling his toes and fingers, flexing his knees and ankles; doing a course of calisthenics, and finally hopping first on one foot, and then, at a command, on the other, to a distant enclosure known as the "heart and lung room.""

"Turn your heads to one side and keep them there until you leave this room, and keep quiet," orders the attendant. "Don't breathe in the doctor's face," he later snaps at a refractory one, and adds: "That's why you keep your heads turned.""

"When all lenses, valves and wheezy pipes have been catalogued, the "draft" goes to the "bone specialist," who examines for deformities due to previous fractures or wrenches. There is one more physical test, and when the now hopeless "draft" is wondering whether he will be disgracefully rejected or shot at sunrise, he is pulled up before a small table, his record card inspected, marked "accepted," and he passes on to where a company of clerks are making out service records."

"While he waits, his metal identification tags bearing his name and serial number, are stamped by a machine and he passes on for the final "shot in the arm." This is the inoculation for typhoid, and consists of an injection at the back of the right shoulder. Another assistant swipes a stick wrapped in iodine-soaked gauze across the sore spot."

"If, however, the man has been rejected instead of accepted, he is not given this inoculation. Instead, the assistant makes a yellow streak down his back with the iodine swab, to indicate that he is not to be given a uniform, for the outfitting room is next. There is no significance in the yellow streak, it may be added."

"The "draft" is now back to the mouth of the second horn of the U. Here he gets his uniform, hat, mess kit and blankets. He also gets his insurance policy, if he desires. Every one of the 1431 men accepted Monday took out $10,000 life insurance policies, that is, an aggregate of $14,310,000."

"The only thing left is to either throw into the reclamation box or express home his civilian clothes, and the drafted man emerges at last, having spent from an hour and a half to three hours in the mill."

"Through this process long lines of white, young bodies shuffle ceaselessly, apparently without end, day after day. The line never ends or changes. It is the same on Sundays and week days. The clans keep shuffling through the mill, and ranks of khaki-clad soldiers continue marching away to the train, on the west bank of the Mississippi River."

Despite what anyone's perception might have been, St. Louis certainly did its part in winning the war. By the middle of May 1918, 45,732 young men from St. Louis had enlisted in all branches of the military service, including shipbuilding, the medical reserve, the Red Cross and Army Y.M.C.A. service. St. Louis offered one person for service in the U.S. fighting forces out of every seventeen of its population. St. Louis had also subscribed over $160,000,000 for war work. Enlisting in the Regular Army were 8,143; National Guard 316; National Army 1,379; Enlisted Reserve Corps 369; Training Camp for Officers 1,281; British Recruiting 894; Royal Flying Corps 42; Quartermaster's and Mechanical Repair Shops of the National Army 90; Marines 3,524, U.S. Navy 5,067; 12th U.S. Engineers 1200; 1st Regiment National Guard [138th Infantry] 1800; 5th Regiment National Guard [138th Infantry] 2000; 1st Missouri Field Artillery 900; Missouri Signal Corps 300; National Army [Selective Draft] 5,027; Medical Reserve Corps and Medical Units 1200; Aviation Service 500; Ship Building [enrolled but not all called] 9700; Intelligence, Ordnance, Quartermaster, Red Cross, Red Triangle, etc., directly connected with War and Relief Work 2000.

St. Louis and its surrounding counties in Missouri furnished the second most applicants for the Navy, regardless of size of population. Only New York furnished more. In December 1917, when the government asked St. Louis for 12,000 Navy recruits in 30 days, the Chamber of Commerce raised $9500 for handling the campaign, advertising, etc., and received more than the desired number in 15 days almost doubling the number in the month.

St. Louis led the entire nation in Marine recruiting. Prior to the draft the nation's volunteer quota was one percent of the population, making St. Louis' quota 8000. St. Louis supplied 9730 volunteers, an excess of 21.6 percent.

Ferguson perhaps held the honors for recruiting. Of its 1935 residents, 130 enlisted, or 7 percent of its population.

The first American regiment in France to receive service stripes for six months' service was the 12th Engineers which was a St. Louis regiment. The second ambulance corps to land in France was from St. Louis. This unit was outfitted by the St. Louis chapter of the American Red Cross at an expense of $60,000.

Every one of the 3,450 factories in the St. Louis district had a portion of their capacity turned over to war production. Yet there was capacity, labor, capital and housing for increased production. Diesel engines, necessary for ship and submarine construction, were built in large quantities in St. Louis by Busch-Salzer Diesel Engine Company.

The Y.M.C.A. educated 1,000 automobile mechanic recruits. Through the Railway Y.M.C.A. and a special hut built at Union Station 35,800 troops had been cared for by 12 May 1918 as they passed through the city.

In Liberty Loans, St. Louis subscribed $42,000,000 to the first loan when the quota was only $25,000,000. St. Louis subscribed $74,000,000 for the Second Liberty Loan. The maximum quota was $68,000,000. With a quota of $39,000,000 for the Third Liberty Loan, St. Louis exceeded $45,000,000. St. Louis was officially declared the first city with a population of over 500,000 to exceed its quota for sales of the Third Liberty Loan. The St. Louis Federal Reserve District was the first of the twelve districts in the United States to surpass its quota, and it was estimated that the district subscribed $176,000,000; its quota was $130,000,000. The St. Louis Red Cross raised $2,000,000; the quota was $1,000,000. St. Louis was asked to get 150,000 Red Cross members. The total secured was 242,000. Junior Red Cross members numbering of 102,000 were also secured.

As of 1 May, St. Louis had bought $7,161,618 worth of War Saving Stamps, making the largest percentage of its quota of any other American city. The State of Missouri held the same position, leading the United States in subscriptions, with sales of $16,500,000.

St. Louis also had the first Food Conservation organization in the United States, with many of its ideas adopted nationally. These ideas included the Conservation Normal School, Community Canneries, and Hoover Lunch Rooms.

Twenty-eight thousand St. Louis women registered to do knitting. More than five thousand worked daily on hospital garments and 12,000 made surgical dressings. The agencies conducting this work had supplied over one million articles to the Army in France, besides those sent to local barracks and camps in this country.[103]

Despite protestations to the contrary by Col. Murray, a committee composed of three ministers and three businessmen were appointed to investigate vice conditions at Jefferson Barracks. On 28 May, reports had been received that vice was rampant and that immoral women solicited soldiers on the barracks grounds. The report stated that the Post was open to all comers without challenge. The committee was appointed by the Episcopal Diocese of Missouri.[104]

The St. Louis Cardinals and Major League baseball did their part in helping the soldiers. Several companies of soldiers from Jefferson Barracks attended the Cardinals and Boston Braves game on 15 May. The soldiers presented an exhibition drill and the J.B. Band played before the 2:30 p.m. start time for the game. Also, twenty complete sets of baseball equipment were presented to the company commanders for use by the troops at the Barracks. The equipment was presented to the officers by Mrs. Nelson Cunliff, chairman of the Recreational Supplies Committee. The date for this give-away had been selected because it was bat and ball fund day, set aside by both Major Leagues as a time to help fund Clark Griffith's bat and ball fund for the soldiers in France. Twenty-five percent of the gross receipts at Cardinal Field were given to the fund in addition to a collection solicited from those who attended the game.

In Europe, the fighting continued unabated. The first offensive by American troops took place at Cantigny, from May 28 to 30. Although the 1st Division, commanded by Col. Hanson E. Ely, suffered 1,603 casualties with 199 killed in action, the battle boosted U.S. morale.

Notice was received on 12 June 1918 of the death of Pvt. Frank J. Michael, Co. D, 2nd Engineers, of Jennings. Four other St. Louisans: Cpl. William A. Falvey, Cpl. Edward E. Gray, Mechanic William J. Ward and Henry R. Markus were listed as severely wounded. These men had all passed through Jefferson Barracks the previous summer.

Mrs. Michael said that Frank was determined to enlist at the outbreak of the war. He had the true "American spirit," she said, with a quavering voice, "and I am proud to have him die for such a glorious cause. Nothing but the hand of God would have held him back. "The day he left," she added, "he put his arms around me and said "Mother, I am going to fight for my country and you."

"My father and mother left Germany to escape the hand of autocracy," Mrs. Michael said, "and my boy has fought and died to conquer that evil."

In a letter dated 26 May, Michael wrote his mother that he was glad he was one of the first to go over and expressed his confidence that Germany would be defeated. The letter said in part, "I have no desire to return home until we can all return victorious. I want to return to St. Louis...."

"Square Deal" was the rule at Jefferson Barracks sporting events. The American spirit of "Give the guy a square deal," or "I'll take one dyin' Chance" rules at the sporting events at Jefferson Barracks, where thousands of enlisted and drafted men, passing through from civilian life to military life, took time to play.

One such an entertainment, consisting of one-round and two-round boxing matches, took place on Thursday, 13 June 1918. It was arranged by Fred Fowler, the musical director of the Jefferson Barracks Y.M.C.A. Between 3,000 and 4,000 soldiers sat on the grass in the natural amphitheater near the "Y" building and cheered the volunteer pugilists.[105]

Major Charles B. Gartrell, Quartermaster Reserve Corps, succeeded Lt. Col. Robert R. Wood as Quartermaster at Jefferson Barracks on 15 June 1918. Gartrell was from Kansas City, Missouri. He had arrived at Jefferson Barracks in July 1917 to serve as assistant to Wood, who had been transferred to the 55th Infantry. Major Gartrell's advance came as a result of his part in establishing Jefferson Barracks' record as the fastest recruiting station in the United States Army. Its record was 120 men an hour, examined, clothed, insured, records completed and assigned to different arms of service.[106]

As of 16 June 1918, nine St. Louisans had died fighting in France. The first was David Hickey, 40, who died in action and was reported 26 February 1918. The next casualty was Harry F. McNulty, 19. McNulty had enlisted in the Regular Army in 1916, and served on the Mexican border. He was killed in action on 1 March 1918. Oscar Pfasterer, 17, former Yeatman High School student, enlisted in the Regular Army in May 1917. He was wounded 1 March and killed in action 27 April 1918, while acting as a fuse-setter in place of a comrade who had been killed. Harry F. Raymond, 26, enlisted in the Marine Corps in May 1917. Raymond died 19 April of wounds suffered several days earlier. Vincent J. Blahovec, 31, enlisted in the Regular Army in May 1917. He was reported killed in action on 17 May 1918. Alois A. Parg, 20, enlisted in the Regular Army in May 1916 and died from wounds 15 May 1918. Parg had served under Pershing in Mexico. William Brogan enlisted in the Field Artillery last year (1917). He was reported as killed in action 23 May 1918. Lt. Richard J. Anderson, 27, lawyer and former Washington University athlete, joined the Signal Corps in the spring of 1917. Lt. Anderson trained in aviation and died as a result of an airplane accident on 25 May 1918. Sgt. Ollie H. Johnningmeier, 31, enlisted in the Marine Corps in June 1917. He was reported as killed in action on 12 June 1918.[107]

As related earlier, American troops were in the thick of the action in France by June 1918, and with the action came news home almost daily of more area men killed or wounded in action. The *Post-Dispatch* reported on June 21 that a St. Louis Marine, Sgt. Vincent M. Schwab, 31, had become the tenth St. Louisan killed in action. Schwab came to the United States when he was nineteen and had two brothers in the German Army.

On that same day, it was reported that 1st Lt. John D. Filley, 40 Westmoreland Place, had died of wounds received in action. Four other St. Louisans were listed as having been wounded in action: Leonard L. Enghausen, William Seigel, Steve Halblaub and Henry H. Benninger.[108] The next day Pvt. Halblaub was reported to have died of his wounds.[109]

On Monday, 24 June, Cpl. Peter Scharnell, 23, a member of Company L, 18th Infantry, was reported as having died of wounds he had received on 26 May.[110] The next day, June 25, Pvt. Walter Dawe, 26, of 2924 North 22nd Street, was listed as killed in action; and Pvt. James Lavin, 25, was listed as being severely wounded.[111]

Word was received on 26 June that Privates John E. Saunders, 21, and Walter E. Swenson, 21, of the Marine Corps had been killed in action. This brought the number of St. Louisans killed in France to seventeen.[112]

Word was received on 27 June from Adjutant-General McCann, of the death of an eighteenth St. Louisan, Lt. Jerome L. Goldman who had left for France on 8 January 1918.[113]

The frequency of St. Louisans on the American casualty lists can be easily understood when you look at the position of United States troops in France during June 1918. At Chateau-Thierry, two U.S. divisions had been in the line when Germany mounted an offensive to capture that city. The American divisions attacked the German bridgehead and forced the Germans back across the river.

Also, on 3 June, American Marines were in action at Belleau Wood. As the American Marine Brigade went into action, Sgt. Dan Daly called out, "Come on, you sons o' bitches, do you want to live forever?" At the end of the day 1,087 Marines had been killed. When the question arose of an American withdrawal, an American officer is said to have declared with indignation, "Retreat, Hell! We just got here!" The birth of the modern Marine Corps is said to have taken place at Belleau Wood.[114]

Two U.S. Marines from St. Louis, John Steele and Clarence Weismantel, were among the wounded at Chateau-Thierry. In a letter home after being wounded Steele wrote, "Yep - I got between five Fritz balls and where they were going. I think the 'jarines' must have stopped one hundred tons of machine-gun bullets and shrapnel. Didn't stop them (the Marines), in fact the German fire didn't even slow up the 'jarines.' Result is, Fritz is about four miles closer home than he was before we took this smash at him...."[115]

Jefferson Barracks continued to process new recruits during July. Col. George K. Hunter, U.S. Army retired, commanded Jefferson Barracks. Under Hunter's command were eighty-five officers and 5,704 enlisted men. Things had slowed down a little since the frenetic days of December 1917 and the first few months of 1918. During July 1918, 11,576 troops were forwarded to training cantonments.

Another draft call in July brought a new group of draftees to Jefferson Barracks. Just as earlier enlistees and draftees, these men were processed, given physicals, received uniforms, and were transferred to training centers.[116]

On 3 July, word was received of two more St. Louis Marines killed in action in France. They were Pvt. Theodore C. Grant and Pvt. Walter A. May. This brought to twenty the number of St. Louisans killed in action in France.[117]

An interesting letter from 1st Lt. Richard L. Daly of St. Louis telling of the battle at the Chateau-Thierry Front was received by a friend in St. Louis. Daly was serving as acting captain of Battery A, 12th Field Artillery, in France. Parts of the letter follow: "He mentions the sad plight of the French refugees whom the Americans on their way to the front met fleeing from the Germans, and declares that their misery filled the men with a furious desire to avenge the suffering of the helpless civilians."

Lt. Daly received a commission at the First Officers' Training Camp at Fort Riley and was among the first St. Louis officers to be sent to France. He had been acting captain of his battery since his regiment started for the fighting line, and had been recommended for a Captain's commission. His letter is dated 9 June.

"Your letter of 12 May was handed to me on a spot formerly occupied by the Boche. He was very much in evidence in this locality before the arrival of the Americans, but he is on the run now, and we hope to keep him on the run until he cries 'Quits.'

"This is Sunday afternoon and a beautiful day. This has been the busiest week I have ever spent in my young life. Haven't had my clothes off since Thursday a week ago. Yesterday morning was the first time since Monday that I have had more than one hour's sleep at a time."

"Nobody is complaining. We are getting results. We have not only stopped the Huns, but have pushed them back five kilometers, in as many days. They were their star troops, too - the Prussian Guards. Their reputation didn't get them anywhere with the Americans, in fact, when it was discovered that the Prussian Guards were opposite us everybody gave his trousers an extra hitch and went after them with more determination than ever."

"Our regiment, and particularly this battery, took a prominent part in the attack. I have had the extreme pleasure of seeing quite a few prisoners in the last four days. One batch contained two officers who were possessors of the Iron Cross. I haven't heard the number of women and babies they killed to get the Cross."

"The Americans are certainly showing up strong. One of the French officers in our locality said he never heard such cannonading and marveled at the amount of stamina displayed by the Americans."

"What we saw on the way up here has turned all our hearts to stone. The poor residents of these villages have had a dreadful time, and the fact that our men witnessed the sad plight of the refugees removes all possibility of faint heart, even on the part of the most timid, and all are going at the Huns with the fury of madmen."

"Feeling fine. Sleeping out agrees with me. I should say, being in the Open agrees with me, as I haven't had much sleep."

Word was received in July regarding another St. Louis Marine, Sgt. Major John H. Quick. Unlike the dreaded notices of killed in action, this message told of the heroism of Sgt. Major Quick. He was awarded the Distinguished Service Cross for his heroic deeds in France. In the Spanish-American War, Sgt. Quick won the Congressional Medal of Honor at Guantanamo, Cuba, for voluntarily exposing himself to enemy fire to signal U.S. ships in the bay to cease firing. The shells had been dropping among our men in a concealed position and Quick was the man who dared to step out and stop the bombardment so the Marines could charge. Sgt. Quick served in the Boxer Rebellion, in China, in the Philippines, and helped put down rebellions in Haiti and Santo Domingo.

According to a dispatch from Washington, Sgt. Quick was the only American soldier possessing both of these awards.

About 700 men selected for the National Army from Wards One to Sixteen inclusive entrained at Union Station at 3:00 p.m., 15 July, for Jefferson Barracks. A like number from the remaining Wards entrained the next day for Jefferson Barracks.

A movement of 2,534 men was to begin on 22 July. When it was completed St. Louis had sent a total of more than 6,000 men to camp in July and had furnished more than 16,000 soldiers through the draft.[118]

Word reached St. Louis of the death of four St. Louisans from wounds received in action in France. Two of the men had been members of the 138th Infantry (St. Louis) Regiment. Word was also received on 22 July 1918, of the severe wounding of two other St. Louisans, one a member of the 138th Infantry. Killed were Pvt. Clifford A. Beard, 19, Company E, 138th Infantry; and Pvt. August C. Meltner, 24, Company H, 138th Infantry. This brought the total so far of St. Louisans killed in action to thirty-one. In addition, thirty-nine St. Louisans had been officially listed as severely wounded, and thirty-one slightly wounded.[119]

By the beginning of July, a million American troops were in France. Their supplies entered French ports at the rate of 20,000 tons a day.[120]

During the middle of July east of Chateau-Thierry the American 3rd Division blew up every pontoon bridge the Germans built across the Marne in its sector, gaining for itself the title "The Rock of the Marne." American infantrymen and machine gunners mowed the Germans down. The commander of the 3rd Division, General Joseph T. Dickman, wrote that by noon on 16 July, "there were no Germans in the foreground of the 3rd Division except the dead."[121]

The officers and soldiers at Jefferson Barracks had always assisted the St. Louis area whenever possible and in July 1918 they did so once again. This time as part of the Tuberculosis Society Benefit held on 20 July. The main feature of the days' events was two baseball games, the first game was for the army and navy championship and pitted the Jefferson Barracks team against the Great Lakes Naval Station team. The second game of the day was played between the St. Louis Cardinals and New York Giants.

A parade of soldiers, sailors, and marines through the downtown district marked the opening of the program. Both the Jefferson Barracks band and the Great Lakes Naval Station band took part in the parade. Several girls' drum corps formed among employees of various concerns and two male drum corps participated in the parade. There were also airplane flights along the parade route by pilots from Scott Field. The Cardinals game was stopped for a short time to permit a boy's marathon race to be run. Proceeds from the day's events went to the war fund of the St. Louis Tuberculosis Society for the care of tubercular soldiers and sailors.[122]

August 1918 passed at Jefferson Barracks in the same manner as the previous months of 1918. That is, if one disregards January and possibly February when the number of draftees combined with the leftover late enlistees from December 1917 made the post a beehive of activity. Jefferson Barracks still maintained a population of eighty-one officers and 4,245 enlisted men, plus 2,912 unassigned recruits, a much larger number than during pre-war years. As one might expect, the post hospital, Base Hospital #131, contained the largest number of permanent party: ten officers and 199 enlisted men. Each new recruit had to receive a physical examination and overseas inoculations.[123]

Sports, whether a person is participating or watching, has always been a popular and morale-building activity. As such, during August and September 1918 the St. Louis War Camp Community Service Board staged one of the most prestigious military baseball programs in the area. The Jefferson Barracks Army baseball team faced off against the Great Lakes Naval Training Station team. The series consisted of four games between the two service teams, the first of which was played in Alton, Illinois, on 31 August. The second game was played at Belleville, Illinois, on 1 September; the third in East St. Louis on Labor Day; and the final contest in St. Louis on 3 September.

The proceeds of the four games were given to the War Camp Community Service, and were used to promote sports for the entertainment of soldiers and sailors in St. Louis and its immediate vicinity.[124]

Each of the eastside communities planned special activities for the games and several wagers were placed as to which community could raise the most money. At Alton, Mayor Sauvage and his event committee planned to have Col. Hunter, commandant at Jefferson Barracks, throw out the first pitch with Lt. Wilson, local Navy recruiter, and Major Robbins, commandant at Scott Field, attending the game. Several flyers from Scott Field flew over the field and landed at Alton and Baseballs autographed by Mrs. Woodrow Wilson and Illinois Governor Lowden were auctioned to raise money for the fund.

In East St. Louis, the Alliance of Labor and Democracy handled arrangements and Samuel Gompers was to give a speech. Also, a building lot donated by the War Camp Community service was auctioned off.[125]

There was also a plan for an Inter-Camp championship. Capt. B.V. Ogden, athletic director at Camp Funston, Kansas, and Charles D. Cooper, executive secretary of the War Camp Community Service at Jefferson Barracks, planned to stage a baseball series between Camps Funston, Dodge, Grant, Custer, Tyler, Jefferson Barracks and the Great Lakes Naval Training Station.[126]

Coming as a complete surprise, Col. Hunter ordered the Jefferson Barracks baseball team disbanded for the 1918 season. Hunter's decision forced the planned Inter-Camp baseball championship to be cancelled.[127]

Track and Field also held center stage during September when it was announced on 5 September that the Western District tryouts for the National Amateur Athletic Union meet was to be held at Jefferson Barracks the next Saturday, 7 September. The regular track program called for 17 events. The servicemen were to take part in special events such as a gas-mask run, the first ever seen in St. Louis, a tug-of-war, 50-yard dash, 100-yard dash, 220-yard dash, mile run, and mile relay all in full equipment.

According to Fred Ward, president of the Western District of the A.A.U. and chairman of the Athletic Committee of the War Camp Community Service, both Jefferson Barracks and Scott Field were to enter 45-man squads. (P-D, 9/5/1918) It had been hoped that Kansas City would send representatives to the meet but word was received from Dr. Reilly, athletic director of the Kansas City Athletic Club, that he would not be able to send any men to the tryouts.[128]

As already noted in this chapter, the Jefferson Barracks hospital complex was undergoing a massive renovation and enlargement that began in May 1918. In late August 1918, acting Adjutant-General Peter C. Harris told the *Post-Dispatch* correspondent in Washington that if Congress passed a manpower bill that contained a provision for drafting 18 and 19-year-olds, then Jefferson Barracks would (in all likelihood) be converted from an Army Recruit Depot into a military hospital.

Since the United States had entered World War I, Jefferson Barracks had served as one of the largest and busiest receiving depots. All army recruits from the St. Louis, Chicago, Minneapolis and other central recruiting offices had been sent to the Barracks for final physical examinations and outfitting. Thousands of drafted men had also been sent to Jefferson Barracks for outfitting.[129]

Another St. Louisan, Cpl. Charles E. McCleary, was listed as killed in action in France. His mother received notice of his death on 2 August. He was the 36th St. Louisan killed in France. Cpl. McCleary, 9th Regiment, had enlisted two years earlier at the age of 16 and had served on the Mexican border.

McCleary had three brothers in the service, a cousin in the Navy, and two great uncles that had been killed in action at the Battle of Gettysburg.[130]

In Europe, a great Franco-American counter-offensive had been launched on the Rheims-Soissons Front. As a result, the published casualty lists daily contained the names of St. Louis area men. On August 6, eight St. Louisans, two East St. Louisans, and a Webster Groves man were listed. The next day, 7 August, Pvt. Theophilus Canary, was listed as killed in action, while eleven St. Louisans, five East St. Louisans, one University City man, one Alton man and one Madison, Illinois, man were listed as wounded.[131]

The 10 August casualty list contained the names of three more St. Louisans killed in action: Pvt. Paul Eason, Cpl. Edward W. Hite and Cpl. Thomas E. Burke. Pvt. James B. Howard was listed as missing in action.[132] The next day's list contained the name of Sasal Vinson as being killed in action and seven area men wounded.[133]

In early August details were received of a raid in which Companies E, F, G and H, 138th Infantry, killed about sixty Germans and took seven prisoners and several machine guns on the evening of 6 July. Company H, commanded by 1st Lt. William H. Leahy, was composed of the members of Company H of the old 1st and 5th Missouri Regiments of St. Louis. The *Post-Dispatch* obtained letters telling how two corporals in the company killed five Germans in the raid. One of the corporals, William T. Brennan, 22, of 5224 Janey Avenue in Jennings, killed three Germans with his pistol. The other corporal, Elmer E. Grupe, 20, of 3518 Humphrey Street, killed two Germans with hand grenades. The raid was made the previous Monday, 6 July, at 8:30 p.m. on German trenches in the Vosges Mountains.

Lt. Leahy was recommended for a captaincy by the Division Commander for "commanding the raid and exercising perfect control of the operation." Sgt. Albert E. Elsa, "who continued to direct the fire of the machine gun section for two hours after he was blinded by the explosion of a shell," was recommended for promotion to lieutenant.

Cpl. Hayward Patton, Company H, 138th Infantry, provided a detailed description of fighting in the Vosges Mountains on 6 July 1918. Patton, who lived at 5847 Maple Avenue, was one of the first three men to go 'over the top' in the raid. Patton was wounded by a machine gun bullet through the leg during the raid. He wrote that a replica of the German position was constructed from airplane photographs, then eight rehearsals of the attack were made. Patton goes on to recount how the happiest moment of his life was when the word was given and they went over the top. Not a man hesitated. He says that "we were abreast as we cleared our own wire, with the rest following behind as per instructions (in twos). We hadn't gone 30 feet when the fellow on my left went down, shot through the stomach. That left the Lieutenant and myself in the lead."

"Things were so badly torn up, we lost our way when we got past the German second line and went about three times as far as we should. The first German I saw rose right in front of me in a trench and fired two shots from an automatic revolver, then mine got him directly in the center of the forehead."

"He was a Lieutenant, and I should have captured him alive, but being the first I saw so close, and firing directly at me, I was too excited. We crossed into the German lines from here, following as best we could the communicating trench, to the third line, killing I don't know how many Germans."

Patton related that a machine gun emplacement was blown up with hand grenades, and "sulphur lemons" were tossed into dugouts where the Germans were hidden.

"It was getting dark then, and the ones who emerged presented a grotesque appearance. This sulphur spreads like liquid fire and burns terribly. It shines in the dark like radio light. As one fellow expressed it, 'their faces were lit up like a church.' When we got this bunch, we started back."

"We had gone about 100 yards, when six Germans arose from a trench on our right and fired one volley; then our bombs laid them low. They killed one prisoner, and wounded two of our men slightly. About 200 yards further on, while I had several prisoners, I saw a German Lieutenant emerge from a dugout, all dolled up in a gas mask, high boots, gloves and a can under each arm, presumably gas. 'Twas just as I started for him that I was hit and had to leave him for someone else."

Pvt. William G. McFarland, a member of Company G, which participated in the raid, but who had been gassed previously and did not participate in it, writes that some of the prisoners cried when they were told the Americans tortured all prisoners. The Germans are sick of war and would quit if they only could."

Pvt. McFarland's name has not appeared in the casualty list, but he states that he has been given permission to wear a wound stripe. He tells of being sent to Base Hospital No. 21, which was recruited in St. Louis and which is at Rouen. There he found some old friends, including William C. Stack, formerly an artist on the *Post-Dispatch*.

The first commissioned officer from St. Louis, 1st Lt. George A. Bilsbarrow, of the 138th Infantry died of wounds he received in action on 14 July. Bilsbarrow, 28, had been 1st Lieutenant of Company D, 1st Missouri National Guard Regiment.[134]

During September 1918, Col. Hunter commanded the Jefferson Barracks' garrison that consisted of seventy-one officers and 3,488 enlisted men. Activity at the Barracks remained unchanged as recruits were received, given physicals, outfitted and transferred to training cantonments.

Among the new arrivals at Jefferson Barracks during September were draft registrants qualified for special or limited military service. The State of Idaho furnished 190 such men and Kansas City sent twenty-seven men especially qualified as stenographers and typists.[135]

Also in September, local police arrested 106 men in a draft raid carried out on 3 September. Twenty-five of these men had been classified as deserters by local Exemption Boards. These men were sent to Jefferson Barracks for immediate induction into military service.

The next night police arrested thirty men suspected of being "slackers." These men were also sent to Jefferson Barracks.[136]

During September, quarters at Jefferson Barracks remained limited. With this in mind, the Board of Education, which had taken over housing matters from the Y.M.C.A., arranged to lease the Marne Apartment Building that was being constructed at 5524 Berlin Avenue (now Pershing Avenue), as a barracks for 300 drafted men. These men were being sent to Jefferson Barracks for special technical training.[137]

By the end of September 1918, the number of St. Louisans killed in action or dying of wounds in France stood at seventy-six. The number had been seventy-nine, but an inquiry by Congressman Igoe found that three St. Louisans had been erroneously reported as killed. One of these, Cpl. Thomas E. Burke, Company C, 16th Infantry, had been reported as killed on 21 July, but he had recovered from his wounds and was back with his company.[138]

In late August and in September, the scope of the war broadened. On 31 August, the British Naval Attache in Petrograd had been murdered inside the Embassy. On 2 September, the Bolsheviks initiated "Red Terror." In Petrograd alone, 512 opponents of the Bolshevik regime were executed. On 11 September, 4,500 American troops landed at Archangel.[139]

Half an hour after midnight on 25 September, only ten days after the end of the St. Mihiel offensive, thirty-seven French and American divisions launched a new and even more ambitious offensive. It was aimed at the Argonne Forest and along the Meuse River. As part of the preliminary bombardment that night, the AEF fired 800 mustard and phosgene gas shells, incapacitating more than 10,000 German troops and killing 278. Almost 4,000 guns were in action.

Among the American battery commanders was Capt. Harry S. Truman. "I fired 3,000 rounds of 75 ammo from 4 a.m. to 8 a.m.," he later recalled. "I slept in the edge of a wood to the right of my battery position on Friday night. If I hadn't awakened and got up at 4 a.m. I would not be here, because the Germans fired a barrage on my sleeping place!"[140]

After making significant gains of up to six miles on the Meuse-Argonne Front during the first three days of fighting, by 29 September, the 4th day of battle, the American troops were brought to a halt. Two factors precipitated the halt: the unflagging German defense and the incredible chaos that had developed in the American lines of supply and communications.[141]

The Jefferson Barracks garrison increased somewhat in October over September's numbers, with eighty-six officers and 5,370 enlisted men. There were 4,019 unassigned recruits at the post, and 1,843 recruits transferred to training stations. The Hospital Corps remained the largest organization on the post with 576 assigned corpsmen. The Quartermaster Corps had the second most personnel with six officers and 139 enlisted men[142]

A new scare reared its ugly head during October, when influenza struck Jefferson Barracks. According to Dr. C.E. Freeman, chief surgeon at the post, 500 cases of influenza were reported in the Barracks' hospital as of the night of 3 October. He stated that most cases were mild, but added that he had wired the Surgeon General in Washington to request twenty additional physicians. Dr. Freeman was also trying to hire fifty additional nurses. Graduate nurses would to be paid $75 a month.[143]

Thirty-one young St. Louis women who had completed a 240-hour nurses' aid course at Barnes Hospital went to work at Jefferson Barracks on October 5 and expected to work through the influenza emergency. The number of influenza cases reported at this time came to 1,320, with twenty-one deaths.

The nurses' aids lived at the Barracks, working eight to ten hours a day. They received $30 to $50 per month depending on experience. They were housed in new nurses' quarters which were not quite finished when they moved in.

Also during the influenza emergency, the Right Reverend Frederick F. Johnson, Bishop Coadjutor of the Episcopal Church for Missouri, volunteered and served as an assistant chaplain at Jefferson Barracks. The Reverend Samuel Dorrance, Post Chaplain, had been severely overworked since the epidemic began.[144]

On a lighter note, recruits used to like to write postcards not only to their parents, but to young ladies in hopes of getting a letter in return. A good example of this can be seen in a postcard sent from Jefferson Barracks on 14 October 1918, by Chester W. Quost, 27th Company, Group 644, Jefferson Barracks, Missouri, to Miss Josephine Roberts. "Dear Friend I am sending you a few lines to let you know I am getting along fine we have good eats and we have music every night & Moving Pictures (from) The fellow who used to work at the Butcher."

The first St. Louis African-American soldier to be killed in France was Calvin Hyde, 28, of 4232 Washland Avenue. Hyde was the 87th St. Louisan to be killed in France.[145]

Another draft class was called in October. St. Louis supplied 653 men and St. Louis County supplied sixty-two of the four hundred men called in Missouri. St. Louis County men included three from Clayton, twenty-three from Ferguson and thirty-six from Kirkwood.[146]

On 10 October, the American First Army under General Pershing finally succeeded in driving the Germans out of the Argonne Forest. However, there was still no breakthrough. Ammunition, food and other essential supplies could not get through due to the congestion on the roads. Pershing and his 1st Army fought on. They were not going to dissolve or accept that they were beaten by supply problems.[147]

Recruiting continued unabated right up to the magic hour of 11:00 a.m. on 11 November1918, when news of the armistice flashed around the country. Jefferson Barracks had performed a great job. It had sent an estimated

200,000 men of the 3,665,000 that were then under arms, and had contributed its full quota to the 1,200,000 American soldiers who saw service in France.

In order to accomplish this, many facilities had been added to the post. In all, 142 temporary buildings had been constructed in a little more than a year. Libraries, chapels and recreation buildings had been provided. Funds from the Post Exchange had supplied many accessories.

Following the armistice, activities at Jefferson Barracks drifted back to the routine. Attention was directed to the enlistment of replacements, disposal of surplus supplies and temporary buildings, and training and transportation of recruits to other posts. Vocational training for enlisted men on the post was also inaugurated.[148] Jefferson Barracks became a demobilization center for troops returning from overseas.

Col. Hunter continued to serve as commanding officer, although he was eligible for retirement with the rank of brigadier general after his forty years of service.[149]

However, just days prior to the armistice, more sad news reached St. Louis. In the push through the Argonne Forest, the 138th Infantry had been in the forefront with the 128th Field Artillery, the St. Louis Artillery unit, in support. Virgil C. Pentz, Roy E. Brem, Oscar Fiori, 1st Sgt. Irvin Schmitt, Lt. Clarence W. Schnelle, and James B. Faffern, all of the 138th Infantry, had been killed during the fighting in the Argonne Forest. Frederick Stange and John D. McCarthy of the 128th Field Artillery were also killed in action in the Argonne fighting. Notice was received of these deaths around the first of November.[150]

The next day, 2 November, the names of Major August Sauerwein, Capt. Clarence J. Sodemann, Roy E. Green, Sgt. Harvey A. Hogrebe, Charles W. Martens, and William Goodwin were also added to the list of men killed during the Argonne Forest fighting.[151]

Before the end of November numerous additional names would be added to the list of those killed in France. According to the bronze plaques erected along Kingshighway in St. Louis by the Gold Star Mothers in 1922, there were 1,179 St. Louisans who were killed in action or died of disease during World War I.[152]

The day after the armistice was signed it was learned that ten men from St. Louis were among the prisoners to be freed by the Germans. Relatives and friends learned this happy news in the *Post-Dispatch* of 12 November 1918.

It might seem 'too little, too late,' but on 20 November, Federal Judge Munger of the U.S. District Court in St. Louis instructed a jury to find that Jefferson Barracks was a military camp, and therefore was within the scope of a War Department regulation forbidding the sale of intoxicants within five miles of the camp, except in incorporated towns. The regulation defined a camp as a place where more than 300 soldiers were stationed and being trained at one time. A letter from Col. Hunter said that the number of soldiers at Jefferson Barracks since May 1918 had never been less than 1,500.

Sheriff Bopp of St. Louis County said that there were fifteen licensed saloons and a number of wine gardens outside of incorporated towns within a five-mile radius of Jefferson Barracks.[153]

The slowdown of activity at Jefferson Barracks could already be seen in December 1918. Figures for October 1918, the last full month for which figures are available, show 5,370 troops at the post. By the time the Post Returns for December 1918 were completed that figure was reduced to 1,341. Due to the fact that Jefferson Barracks became a mustering out station for returning veterans, the number of Hospital Corps personnel remained fairly high, 446, compared to 576 in October. Of course, the most drastic change in numbers was in training personnel. The number of officers also dropped from eighty-six in October to forty-six in December.[154]

Peace had returned and the Jefferson Barracks Christmas Dinner was held with much happier hearts in 1918 than in previous years. Capt. Adgate A. Lipscomb, Quartermaster Corps, was the Mess Officer, and Quartermaster Sergeant William A. O'Brien was the Mess Steward. Sergeants William Kattner, 28th Company; George Stainway, 23rd Company; Melvin T. Smith, 16th Company; and Frank Johnson, 27th Company, were the Mess Sergeants. William Stone served as chief cook with Charles Rinnick, 15th Company; Fred Wordelman, 15th Company; Frank T. Smith, 16th Company; James E. Murnane, 16th Company; Eddie Schnither, 23rd Company; Frank Trojan, 18th Company; George Milne, 27th Company; and Charles E. Green, 27th Company on the staff.

The year 1918 had come to an end and with it "The War to End All Wars" according to President Woodrow Wilson. It had been arguably the busiest year in the history of Jefferson Barracks. But what was to come for Jefferson Barracks and the Army? Would the United States maintain the vastly expanded Regular Army, go back to a small standing Army as before the country entered the war, or something in between?

New recruits arrive at Jefferson Barracks having enlisted at the beginning of World War I.

Soldiers awaiting shipment from Jefferson Barracks during World War I.

Recruits out for a conditioning march through the wood at Jefferson Barracks during World War I.

Headquarters Company in front of their offices ca. 1918.

Gun practice probably taken around World War I time period.

Riflemen squad around World War I.

Chapter 8 - Years of Peace: 1919 and the 1920s

Demobilization proceeded rapidly after the end of the war, and by 28 June 1919, two million six hundred eight thousand two hundred and eighteen enlisted men and 128,436 officers had been discharged. By the end of 1919, the United States Army consisted of only 130,000 regular troops, about the same number as in April 1917 when the U.S. entered the war. There were no special plans for strengthening the reserve corps, and in fact Army Chief of Staff Peyton C. March proposed a plan to Congress in 1919 for an expanded Regular Army of over 500,000 men, filled out in time of war by conscripts backed up by the National Guard.[1]

Congress was in no mood to provide for such a substantial increase in the standing army, and resisted the blandishments of the War Department. Congress sought a reasonable alternative to March's proposal. In October 1919, it found a man who was willing to offer such a plan. Col. John McAuly Palmer had been one of Pershing's proteges in the AEF, and he had returned to Washington as a member of the War Plans Division of the General Staff. Palmer's experience in France had strengthened his existing belief in the values of the citizen-soldier. Senator James J. Wadsworth invited Palmer to testify before the Committee on Military Affairs. Palmer was ready to offer his opinion.[2]

By the end of Palmer's two days as an expert witness, Senator Wadsworth was convinced that the outspoken colonel, who had castigated March's proposals, was the man to work on a Senate proposal for amending the National Defense Act of 1916. Palmer was loaned to the Committee and worked for eight months on the project. After much compromising with the House of Representatives, which had developed its own bill, many of Palmer's ideas were enacted into law in 1920.[3]

Following the armistice, Jefferson Barracks drifted back to routine except for activities as a demobilization center for returning overseas troops. This continued until 19 March 1919 when detachments of regulars began to arrive.[4]

Attention was directed to the enlistment of replacements, disposal of surplus supplies and temporary buildings, and transportation of recruits to other posts. Vocational training was inaugurated for enlisted men.[5]

Despite having been recalled from retired status and now being able to retire again, Col. George K. Hunter remained in command of Jefferson Barracks as 1919 began. His command continued to decrease in size with an aggregate of thirty-eight officers and 1,097 enlisted men present for duty. Jefferson Barracks did move 1,605 recruits to other posts during January 1919.

Some of the AEF veterans who returned to Jefferson Barracks for demobilization did not look fondly on the experience. The *St. Louis Post-Dispatch* reported in the middle of January that "Overseas Heroes Are Angry." There were 135 soldiers who had been wounded in France at Jefferson Barracks for demobilization. Veterans of Belleau Wood, Chateau-Thierry, Soissons, the Argonne and Champagne were among them.

When a visitor saw them, he found that most were reticent about their exploits, but eager to tell about what they considered "mistreatment" at Jefferson Barracks. This entailed having their clothing sterilized, their hair cropped and their overseas caps and puttees taken away.

"This here colonel ain't never seen any AEF soldiers before," declared an exceedingly "sore" youth from Oklahoma. "Any man that's been in France knows a cootie never goes above a man's collar. Ain't no more sense to cuttin' our hair off for cooties than there would be wearin' a gas mask on your elbow. They don't go there. I seen some trouble since I went to this war, but this is the rawest thing I ever saw pulled."

Such was the chorus, and it was with much difficulty that the thoroughly disgusted heroes were induced to change the subject from barbers to battles.

Col. Hunter said that army doctors at Jefferson Barracks had recommended the sterilizing of the men and their clothing, including the cutting of their hair. The overseas caps and puttees were taken away on an order from the War Department, but will be returned, the order having been revoked, Hunter said.[6]

Lt. Col. Charles E. Freeman served as Post Surgeon during early 1919 and was succeeded by Col. William D. Crosby. Both had graduated from the Army Medical College in 1906. Doctors V.P. Blair and S.J. Tamer, distinguished St. Louis surgeons, and Dr. E.P. Dameron, dental surgeon, were attached to the Jefferson Barracks medical staff and had charge of the overseas reconstruction surgical cases.[7]

By March, the garrison had increased in size to sixty-one officers and 1,212 enlisted men. The Hospital

Corps troops remained the largest section on the post with 264 enlisted men. Only eighty-four recruits transferred to other posts during the month.[8]

In April, Col. Hunter took leave and in his absence Col. Albert B. Sloan, Infantry, commanded the post. Sloan had entered the U.S. Naval Academy as a cadet in September 1880 and left in January 1883. He served as a captain in the 6th Missouri Infantry in July 1898, and was honorably mustered out on 10 May 1899. He then served as a captain in the 27th Volunteer Infantry in the Philippines from 5 July 1899 to 1 April 1901. Sloan then received a commission as a 1st Lieutenant in the 29th Infantry.

The garrison consisted of fifty-two officers and 1,834 enlisted men. The number of troops transferred during the month increased to 1,119.[9]

Col. Hunter returned from leave in May to command a garrison that consisted of forty-seven officers and 1,858 enlisted men. Even though the war had been over for six months, Jefferson Barracks maintained a fairly large number of recruits with 912 in May. The Medical Department at Jefferson Barracks consisted of twenty-five officers and 314 enlisted men. The Quartermaster Corps had six officers and 131 enlisted men. The number of recruits transferred during the month came to 1,409.[10]

The J.B. garrison consisted of fifty-one officers and 1,837 enlisted men in June. Troops moved to other posts during the month came to 1,457.[11]

Col. Hunter again retired in July 1919, and Col. Monroe McFarland, Infantry, took command on 29 July. McFarland had graduated from the U.S. Military Academy and received a commission as a 2nd Lieutenant in the 21st Infantry on 11 June 1888. He became a 1st Lieutenant in the 13th Infantry on 5 July 1895, and a Captain in the 18th Infantry on 26 March 1899. By 1919 Col. McFarland had thirty-one years of active service in the United States Army to his credit. He had distinguished himself as commander of the 5th Cavalry at San Juan Hill, Cuba. During World War I, McFarland served as a brigadier general in command of the 162nd Infantry Brigade of the 81st Division in France. He retired with the rank of brigadier general.

Col. McFarland took command of a garrison that consisted of fifty-six officers and 1,723 enlisted men. Little changed for the remainder of 1919. In August, there were forty-six officers and 1,611 enlisted men; in September, forty-four officers and 1,361 enlisted men; in October, thirty-six officers and 1,409 enlisted men; in November, forty-three officers and 1,327 enlisted men; and in December, forty officers and 1,525 enlisted men [12]

In July, a post cafeteria addition to the Post Exchange was completed. The $30,000 cost came from Post Exchange funds.

In early September, it was announced that the Army and Navy Aeronautics Corps would take part in a race on 26 September. Three Army and three Navy balloon crews were to take off from the grounds of the Missouri Aeronautical Society at Grand Avenue and Meramec Street.

Major Albert B. Lambert, who contracted for the laying of gas mains to furnish the gas supply for the Army-Navy Race and for the National Balloon Race that was to begin on 1 October, had determined that the gas supply furnished by Laclede Gas Light Company was of such a superior quality that he hoped that long distance records might be set. Col. McFarland was in charge of the Army-Navy contest, which was planned to be an annual event. A silver plate of sufficient size and value, to create a desire for possession, was designed as the prize.

Regular troops from Jefferson Barracks took part in an exhibition of machine gun firing in Forest Park on 1 September. The event took place in the southeastern corner of the park, 200 feet west of the Bates statue. The veterans firing the guns had previous experience firing machine guns at the Germans during World War I. They fired 30,000 rounds at targets on the banks of the River des Peres, 300 yards away.

The Jefferson Barracks Band gave a concert at 8:00 p.m. on Art Hill, and at the foot of the hill fireworks, including star shells, trench bombs, rockets and roman candles were set off. These events were to help stimulate army recruiting. The Army Recruiting Service planned and presented the Forest Park event.[13]

Probably the grandest event seen in St. Louis and Jefferson Barracks in the first twenty years of the 20th Century took place on 22 December 1919. General John J. "Blackjack" Pershing arrived in St. Louis at Union Station for a 13-hour stay in his native state. It was Pershing's first visit to the state since his return from France. After his stay in St. Louis, Pershing left by train for a visit to his home town of Laclede in Linn County, Missouri.

General Pershing arrived at Union Station from Chicago at 8:12 a.m. and left on another train for Jefferson Barracks, where he inspected the troops. A gathering of several thousand people greeted the general upon his arrival at Union Station. A reception committee boarded General Pershing's private car, but the general's 10-year-old son,

Warren, ran ahead of the committee and was the first to greet him. Miss May Pershing of Lincoln, Nebraska, sister of the general, was with the committee.

To Edward Hidden, chairman of the Mayor's reception committee, who first greeted the general in his private car, General Pershing said, "I am very happy to be back in my native state, where I first saw the light of day, I'd better not say how many years ago." [General Pershing was 59 the previous September.]

General Pershing was then introduced to Mayor Kiel, and said; "Mr. Mayor, I thank you for this splendid reception to the City of St. Louis."

The General was smiling all the time, but his real display of enjoyment began after he had settled down for breakfast in the dining car of the Barracks' train.

"I want to meet all these St. Louis people," he said, and getting up from his table, he walked through the dining car, meeting the members of the committee individually, to the neglect of a tempting array of Missouri corn pone, buckwheat cakes, maple syrup and coffee. He showed hearty relish for the meal when he did get to it, and called to his sister, "May, this is a regular Missouri breakfast."

He talked to the St. Louis newspaper reporters, saying after a few minutes that he was speaking more freely with them than he had done with newspaper men in New York or Washington. The Pershing presidential boom was mentioned, and the General declared "I wish the papers would forget that. If anybody starts a boom while I'm here, I'll institute suit against him."[14]

The General arrived at Jefferson Barracks at 9:00 a.m., and ignoring the waiting automobile, walked up the steps from the station. There were five companies of regulars and 750 recruits in the line of review. The general went to the left of the line, while the band changed its tune to "Out, Out, Marie," and passed along the line. He stopped before every man who wore the stripes of overseas service, and asked him what command he had served in. When he saw a wound chevron, he made a more detailed inquiry.

"89th Division," one man replied to his question.

"Missouri?" the general asked. "You ought to be mighty proud to have belonged to that gallant division."

The next man he questioned was from the 39th Division, and with a "Proud to meet you," the general passed on to a man from the 3rd Division, a Regular Army command.

To a member of the 1st Division the general asked, "You were wounded? All right now?" You went through the Argonne? You did great service."

To a man of the Tank Corps, the general said, "Yours was a picked outfit." Another man, of the 306th Supply Train, was told, "You did your duty as much as the combat men."

The 1st Division was "Pershing's Own," and to a man of this division, the general gave an especial smile, remarking, "There was no division in Europe that excelled the First."

"The Second was a crack division," the general remarked to a man from that division, which has been in hot rivalry with the First in the "who-won-the-war" controversy.

"How old are you?" the general asked a man who had served in the 20th Engineers. The man replied that he was now 18, and enlisted two years ago. "Did you have your mother's consent?" the commander asked. The soldier nodded affirmatively. "That's fine," said the general.

Passing the recruits, the general stopped only to point to their shoes, which were an assortment of dull leather, and to remark, "Let's have the shoes polished."

The troops then passed in review, before the reviewing party consisting of General Pershing, Mayor Kiel, Edward Hidden and Col. McFarland, with the General's staff behind him. The troops executed the command "Eyes right" as they passed the general, and they were then dismissed.

General Pershing turned to Col. Morten, Executive Officer at Jefferson Barracks, and said "You have a fine body of troops here. Don't you think your recruits are of very high grade?"

In army transport motor cars, the General and his party then drove about the barracks grounds for 10 minutes, after which they went to a reception of officers at the house of Col. McFarland.[15]

On the train ride, back to St. Louis from Jefferson Barracks, Warren Pershing, the General's 10-year-old son, rode in the cab of the locomotive. He wanted to ride down that way, but was told that his father's consent was necessary. "Oh, all right," General Pershing said, but remarked to Federal Manager Murphy of the Missouri Pacific Railway, "I'm afraid you will spoil this boy."

"Oh, no, I rode in with him from Kansas City, and he's the kind of a boy who won't spoil," was Murphy's reply, which brought a parental smile that even military dignity could not suppress. Warren was provided with a pair of overalls, and he and the engineer were great friends by the time they reached Kingshighway. In the cab with Warren was General Pershing's aid and nephew, Capt. Frank Pershing.

Military discipline did not prevent the Commander-in-Chief from gently chaffing a subordinate, Lt. E.H. Wright, assigned from Jefferson Barracks. Wright saluted the general at Union Station, and said, "Sir, I am at your service. Is there anything I can do?"

"Just look handsome, that's all you will have to do," instructed the general. Later, as he was leaving the Barracks, he turned to Lt. Wright and said, "Lieutenant, you did very well."

Just as the Jefferson Barracks Band struck up *The Star Spangled Banner* after General Pershing's arrival at the Coliseum for luncheon, an elderly man walked forward and grasped the general's hand. The handshake lasted so long that General Pershing was not able to come to attention until just before the band finished playing the anthem.

The elderly man was Brigadier General Samuel L. Woodward, retired, of 5710 Clemens Avenue, who was Captain of a Cavalry Company in which Pershing was a lieutenant in 1896. They had not seen each other since that year.

Several hundred children were assembled at Bates Street as the train passed by on its return from the Barracks. The children waved flags and cheered enthusiastically. On the return, Lt. Col. Burkham, chairman of the Executive Committee of the American Legion of St. Louis, presented a welcome on behalf of the Legion.[16]

The general returned the city's greeting with the same evidence of hearty enjoyment which he showed from the time of his arrival at Union Station that morning. He showed not merely the geniality of a public personage responding to a community welcome, but also the happiness of a homecoming soldier. The presence of his 10-year-old son, Warren Pershing, whom he had not seen since early fall, and of Miss May Pershing, his sister, added a personal element to the pleasure which he manifested. Warren and his aunt rode in the car next behind the General.

The drive started from the St. Louis Club, after an unannounced drive to the club from the Kingshighway crossing of the Missouri Pacific, south of the viaduct, where the general left the special train on which he had come from the Barracks.

The Lindell-Locust route was followed to Twentieth Street, and from there to Washington Avenue, Broadway, Olive Street, Twelfth Street and Locust Street, then back to Twentieth, where the line turned into Washington Avenue and proceeded west to the Coliseum at Washington and Jefferson Avenue.

While the drive was nearly on schedule, the weather was so sharp as to discourage long waiting outdoors. In spite of this condition, the crowds on Washington Avenue, east of Eighteenth Street, and on Olive Street, were such that ropes were stretched by the police to insure a passage for the automobiles.

The steps of the St. Louis Club were lined with school children, who cheered everyone entering or leaving the club. When the general came out at 11:45, they broke ranks and jostled Mayor Kiel and Ambassador Francis, who were on either side of the general, in their attempt to seize his hand. He walked laughingly through the juvenile jam, with the indulgent air of one who had been a school teacher himself.

In the general's car, decorated with flags and roses, the mayor, Ambassador Francis, and Edward Hidden rode with the guest of honor. With Warren Pershing and his aunt in the next car were John Kattel, a Boy Scout designated as Warren's host for the ride, and Miss V.A.L. Jones. Eight cars carried the committee. Sgt. Michael B. Ellis, St. Louis' greatest war hero and winner of the Congressional Medal of Honor, was in one of the cars behind the newspaper and motion picture photographers. General Pershing bestowed the Medal of Honor upon Sgt. Ellis at a mass meeting at the Coliseum at 7:30 p.m.[17]

Just three days after the excitement of General Pershing's visit the first peacetime Christmas in three years was celebrated at Jefferson Barracks. The usual lavish Christmas dinner of roast turkey, oyster dressing, cranberry sauce, candied sweet potatoes, creamed peas, bread and butter, with pumpkin pie, neapolitan ice cream and assorted cakes, nuts and candies was served. The cooks who prepared the meal included Charles Pinnick, 15th Company; Fred Wordleman, 15th Company; John Goodman, 15th Company; Frank Smith, 16th Company; Herold Fallis, 16th Company; Robert Jenkins, 18th Company; Cecil Van Zyle, 18th Company; Frank Eppinger, 23rd Company; Buckingham Waldo, 23rd Company; George Milne, 27th Company; Edward Janer, 27th Company; and Clem Craig, Quartermaster Corps.

The Mess Sergeants were William Kattner, 18th Company; George Steinway, 23rd Company; Melvin Smith, 16th Company; Frank Johnson, 27th Company; and Sigward Hansen, 15th Company.

Quartermaster Sergeant Alexander VanYanak supervised the preparation with Capt. Thomas P. Bernard, Cavalry, serving as the Mess Officer. The Chief Cook was William Stone, 18th Company, General Services Infantry, and the shift supervisors were John M. Wilson, 16th Company and Anthony G. Mosbleck, 23rd Company. [18]

Despite the brave and honorable service of African-American soldiers during World War I, racism in the army and throughout the country had not lessened after the war. A prime example of this can be seen in the case of two black soldiers detailed to escort a white prisoner, an alleged army deserter, from Fort Worth, Texas, to Jefferson Barracks.

The story appeared under the headline in the *Fort Worth Star-Telegram* "Negro Guards in Charge of White Prisoner are Relieved on Way to Jefferson Barracks." A white escort was provided Sunday instead of two negro sergeants for a white man, an alleged army deserter, on the remainder of his journey from Fort Worth to Jefferson Barracks, St. Louis, Mo. Department of Justice agents and the police, who had stopped the two negroes and their white prisoner here Saturday, released the white man Sunday afternoon, to Colonel Reed, commander of the old Camp Bowie detachment here. On advice from the Southern Department at San Antonio, Col. Reed provided a white soldier escort for the rest of the trip. Violence was feared if the negroes were permitted to resume their journey with the white soldier as their prisoner. They had brought him here from Nogales, keeping him with them in the Jim Crow car on the ride from El Paso. Officers took the trio to police headquarters for safe-keeping Saturday, when they heard threats from a crowd at the Texas & Pacific station. The negroes, armed with formal travel orders to Jefferson Barracks, resumed their journey to that point. The rest of their trip, however, will be in the nature of a vacation. They expressed pleasure at getting relieved of their charge. "They had been afraid of trouble all the time, they said."[19]

The next day the Fort Worth newspaper ran another story under the title "Another Case of Army Stupidity." "The two Negro sergeants who were stopped in Fort Worth on their way to Jefferson Barracks, St. Louis, Mo., with a white prisoner in custody, expressed pleasure when they were told they would be relieved of their charge, the prisoner, an alleged deserter, being sent on the rest of the trip with a white escort. The negro soldiers said they had been afraid of trouble all along. However, they had to obey orders. Their commanding officer at Nogales detailed them to take this prisoner, a white man, to Jefferson Barracks, and it was 'theirs not to reason why.' The Texas Jim Crow law required that they ride in the Negro coach, and the white prisoner, of course, was compelled to do likewise. In none of this were the negro sergeants responsible. According to all reports they conducted themselves very well, considering all the circumstances."

"But here is another illustration of a pig-headed policy in the Army that someday is going to cause trouble. Some weeks ago, the governor of Oklahoma requested that Federal troops be detailed for guard duty in the coal fields where a strike was in progress. Before the troops arrived, he learned that Negro troops were to be sent, and realizing what it would mean to have negro troops on duty in territory where white men were on strike, the governor cancelled his request. It was the common sense of the governor that averted trouble in that case. In the present case, it would appear that it was the common sense of the prisoner as well as the conduct of the negro sergeants that averted trouble, and at that it was averted by a narrow margin. When the trio were compelled to wait in the Texas & Pacific Depot while their train was being made up, a crowd gathered around. There were angry threats and persons in the crowd called upon the prisoner to make his escape. Had the prisoner made such an attempt a riot might have been the result, for it would have been the duty of the negro sergeants, under military regulations, to make every attempt to recapture him, even to the extent of shooting him if he refused to halt."[20]

Although the war in Europe had ended, a massive civil war raged on in Russia between the Bolshevik forces of Lenin and Stalin and the anti-Bolshevik forces. U.S. Forces in the form of the Siberian Expeditionary Force and troops from Great Britain, France, Italy, Czechoslovakia, Romania, Serbia, Japan, Latvia, and Finland all took part, as well as Russian Cossacks and Baltic Germans. Great Britain provided the Russian anti-Bolshevik forces with more than half a million rifles and 500 million rounds of ammunition.

In one of their last decisions before they left the Paris Peace Conference, the Allies decided not to continue with this new, distant and increasingly costly conflict. Before the Americans withdrew from Archangel and Vladivostok, 174 Americans had been killed in action or died of their wounds.[21]

The Peace Conference opened in Paris on 18 January 1919. For the Germans, the date was an insult as it was the anniversary of the day on which, in 1870, the German Empire had been proclaimed.[22]

On 28 June 1919, the Treaty of Versailles was signed between Germany and the 'Principal Allied and Associated Powers': The representatives of twenty-seven victorious powers appended their signatures to the 200-page document. Under the treaty, Germany was punished both territorially and financially. Her territory was reduced in both the east and west; her army, navy and air force were disbanded; and her responsibility for the war was expressed in the financial liability imposed on her to make reparations, especially to France and Belgium. Articles 42 to 44 forbade Germany from fortifying the German Rhineland or having any armed forces there. Article 80 forbade German union with Austria 'except with the consent of the Council of the League of Nations.' Articles 100 to 106 transferred the port of Danzig from German sovereignty and made it a Free City under the protection of the newly created League of Nations. Articles 119 and 120, in five lines, deprived Germany of all her colonial possessions. Article 170 forbade Germany from importing any arms, ammunition or war materials. Article 191 forbade her from building or buying submarines. Article 198 forbade her from having any military or naval air forces.

Germany was to be denied the ability to make war. Under Article 231 of the Treaty, she was forced to accept, along with her allies, "responsibility for the loss and damage caused as a result of the war 'imposed upon' the victors by the aggression of Germany and her allies". This was the war guilt clause, which served as a preamble to the reparations demands, and to which the German negotiators had particularly objected. While some Allied negotiators, including the British economist J.M. Keynes, thought the reparations clauses were too harsh, others praised them, led by Rudyard Kipling.[23]

The status of the United States Army became a question mark at the beginning of 1920. President Wilson was determined that the United States should join the League of Nations, while Congress and many people wanted nothing to do with the new organization. Wilson would fight his last, most pathetic and losing battle.

The basis for the organization of the army between World War I and World War II was the National Defense Act of 1920. The purpose of this Act was to establish an army structure based on the traditional principle that the citizen- soldier would be able to defend the nation under any possible foreseen conditions.

The National Defense Act of 1920 set the maximum authorized strength of the Regular Army at 17,717 officers and 280,000 enlisted men, but it was never that large until 1940, when the Selective Service and Training Act became law. Universal military service was rejected, and all services were required to depend solely on volunteers. Congress did not fully fund the Act, and until 1939 the actual strength of the Regular Army never exceeded 12,000 officers and 118,750 enlisted men. The Philippine Scouts, a force of 6,400, was also a part of the U.S. forces and was restricted to service in the Philippine Islands.

Included in the total number authorized by the Act were men who served in the Army Air Service (which became the Army Air Corps in 1925} and men who served in the Coast Artillery Corps (which manned fixed defenses at strategic locations). The regular services furnished advisers to the National Guard and Reserve Officer Training Corps (ROTC) units.[24]

Jefferson Barracks continued as a recruit depot with six recruit companies: the 14th, 15th, 16th, 18th, 23rd and 27th were all part of the General Service, Infantry.

Col. McFarland continued in command of the Post and Capt. G.C. Choulton, Army retired, served as adjutant. McFarland commanded a garrison that consisted of forty-four officers and 1,318 enlisted men, of which 540 were unassigned recruits. Naturally, with so many recruits, the Medical detachment made up the largest single element on the Post, with twenty-four officers and 123 enlisted men.[25]

The numbers did not change much during the remainder of 1920. In February, forty-two officers and 1,134 enlisted men comprised the garrison personnel. In March, forty officers and 1,104 enlisted men.[26]

During March, General Leonard Wood, the leading candidate for the Republican nomination for president, paid a brief visit to Jefferson Barracks. Wood arrived on 13 March to much less fanfare than a visit by such a heralded figure usually occasioned. He was on leave so his visit was not a formal affair. Col. McFarland and his staff met General Wood. He was accorded an informal demonstration and escorted around the Post. He displayed the greatest interest in the hospital, and spent much of his time passing among the patients, talking to many and plainly revealing his deep sympathy. Upon leaving Jefferson Barracks, Wood went to St. Louis where he made a speech outlining his presidential platform.[27]

In April, the post garrison decreased somewhat with only thirty-six officers and 754 enlisted men present for duty. This was primarily due to the fact that there were only 301 unassigned recruits. In June, there were only thirty-one officers and 772 enlisted men, and in July, thirty-five officers and 770 enlisted men.[28] In August, the number of officers decreased to thirty-three and the number of enlisted men increased to 926.[29] September and October remained almost unchanged, but in November there were thirty officers and 1,369 enlisted men.[30]

The final month of 1920 saw Col. McFarland in command of twenty-nine officers and 1,155 enlisted men. The number of recruits transferred during the month came to the astounding figure of 2,350. This was the most men ever transferred in any single month [31]

1921

The new year, 1921, began on a sad note when on January 1 Sgt. Paul Greer, 30, of the Quartermaster Corps at Jefferson Barracks was killed when the Ford Touring Car he was riding in overturned in the 9200 block of South Broadway while he and two other soldiers were returning to the Post. Pfc Frank Eppinger, 23rd Infantry, and Pfc John Goodman, 15th Infantry, were received injured, Goodman's serious. According to witnesses a rear tire came off and caused the car to roll over three times. Greer was dead at the scene from a crushed skull.[32]

Another Jefferson Barracks soldier, Pvt. Frank J. Bushy, 30, of the 18th Recruit Company, was found unconscious on the southbound Broadway streetcar that same day. Two St. Louis policemen who were on their way home boarded the car and discovered Bushy lying on a rear seat. There was a large welt on Bushy's head. The conductor told the officers that another soldier had put Bushy on the car at Broadway and Market street, then had gotten off the car a block later. Bushy was taken to a hospital. Bushy, who had discharge papers in his pocket for a D.K. Smith, said that he had several drinks downtown, but could not explain the welt on his head. Doctors pumped Bushy's stomach and during the morning he showed marked improvement, but when food was brought to him at noon attendants found him dead. Physicians at the hospital believed that alcoholism, due possibly to some form of poisoned whisky, caused Bushy's death.[33]

Jefferson Barracks served as a recruit depot with six recruit companies. However, things were about to change. Col. McFarland had been in command of Jefferson Barracks for more than a year and a half when he was relieved by Lt. Col. Charles E. Morton, 6th Infantry, on 13 February 1921.

Morton had lived at Jefferson Barracks as a boy. Another officer, Major T.P. Bernard, Post Exchange and Mess Officer, had also lived at Jefferson Barracks as a young boy.

Recruiting ceased on 7 February 1921, and Detached Enlisted Men's List personnel throughout the central Mississippi Valley assembled at the Jefferson Barracks Depot to await the resumption of recruiting. Jefferson Barracks was abandoned as a recruit depot, and the 6th Infantry, less two companies at Fort McPherson, Georgia, was ordered to garrison the barracks.[34]

Between 1 August 1906, the date of the organization of five recruit companies at the Post, and 7 February 1921, the date of discontinuance of recruiting, approximately 250,000 recruits passed through the Jefferson Barracks Recruit Depot.[35]

Lt. Col. Morton commanded for only one month before Col. John H. Parker, 6th Infantry, assumed command. Col. Parker won his first decoration, two silver stars, for gallantry at the battle of Santiago, Cuba. He later added the Distinguished Service Cross and the Distinguished Service Medal with three oak leaf clusters. He received his last decoration on 30 December 1922. The citation by General Pershing read as follows: "A bronze oak leaf is also awarded to Colonel Parker for extraordinary heroism in action near Gesnes, France, 29 September 1918. During the attack on the Village of Gesnes, he displayed great gallantry and fearlessness in leading and directing his front line with utter disregard for personal safety and urged his men forward by his personal example, all under heavy machine-gun, high-explosive gas-shell and shrapnel fire. He was abreast of his front line until he fell, twice wounded, but thereafter remained in active command for a period of five hours, when he was relieved by the lieutenant colonel of his regiment."

At the time that Col. Parker took command, the bodies of those killed in France were being returned for burial. It became a daily routine of the post to furnish escorts, buglers, and firing squads for those funerals. An impressive tribute was paid to St. Louis World War I dead in a public funeral on 21 April 1921, when a funeral for four St. Louis soldiers was conducted so that the entire population could participate in some way. This concluded a period of formal mourning that the city had entered the previous Friday at noon as a mark of gratitude and homage for the more than 500 of her sons that made the supreme sacrifice in France. The services began at noon with a two-minute period of silence, during which industry was to suspend business and citizens were to stand with bowed head. The bodies of the four men were then carried in a military funeral procession from City Hall to Twelfth Street. The Jefferson Barracks band, stationed on the City Hall steps, began to play a funeral march and the bodies were carried out of the City Hall Rotunda, where the public had been able to pay their respects, to caissons of Battery A, Missouri National Guard. The composition of the procession was almost entirely military. It was led by Col. John H. Parker, commandant of Jefferson Barracks, with a group of officers and Capt. Charles Vical, a French officer who was serving as an instructor at Washington University. Nine platoons of regulars, wearing overcoats and garrison hats and carrying rifles, followed behind the band. Next in line came about 500 men of the First Regiment, Missouri National Guard led by Lt. Col. Charles S. Thornton. Next in line came the flags of the American Legion posts and the banners of the G.A.R., Spanish-American War Veterans, Salvation Army, and a tricolor flag of France. This grouping of over fifty flags and banners was under a color guard of men in the uniform of the army, navy, and the marine corps, bearing rifles.

Four caissons carried the bodies of Pvt. Bollinger, Pvt. Linder, Cpl. Carter and Cpl. Alewell. A field gun proceeded and followed the four caissons. Mayor Kiel walked at the head of 164 honorary pallbearers. Then came the relatives of the four heroes and Gold Star mothers of other sons in 47 automobiles. The procession moved so slowly and was so long that it took one hour and thirty minutes to make the trip from City Hall to the Moolah Temple at 2621 Lindell Boulevard. The public lined both sides of the street the entire distance. After the ceremony at the Moolah Temple the bodies were put in four hearses and taken to locations at which more private services could be held.[36]

The public tribute mentioned above did not end the funerals for St. Louis men killed in France. The *St. Louis Post-Dispatch* reported on 15 June 1921, that the body of 1st Lt. John D. Filley, the first commissioned officer from St. Louis to be killed in the war, was to arrive that evening with the funeral the next day. Lt. Filley was wounded in the Battle of Chateau-Thierry on 6 June 1918, and died two days later at the age of 22. He received his training at Plattsburg and was one of the first to go overseas. He served in Company M, 23rd Infantry. Lt. Filley was laid to rest in Bellefontaine Cemetery.

The body of the first St. Louisan to make the supreme sacrifice in World War I arrived at Hoboken, New Jersey, in the middle of July. David Hickey, about 40 years of age, had lived on Garfield Avenue in St. Louis and worked in the mail room at the *St. Louis Post-Dispatch* and as a shoeworker. Hickey was wounded in action on 12 February 1918, and died twelve days later. He had served with Battery E, Sixth Field Artillery. Hickey is buried at Jefferson Barracks National Cemetery.

At about the same time the body of Oliver Guy Vassar, who was killed in action on 15 July 1918, arrived home. Vassar served in Company M, 39th Infantry Division. Vassar had been in charge of the first contingent of Selective Service men to leave University City.[37]

The bodies of area men who had been killed or died of disease in France continued to arrive in St. Louis throughout the remainder of 1921. The *Post-Dispatch* announced the arrival of six more bodies on 7 August. Among those arriving were the bodies of numerous men from around Missouri that were to be interred at Jefferson Barracks National Cemetery.

The funeral of a Medal of Honor recipient, Capt. Alexander Rives Skinker, took place on the afternoon of 11 September 1921. Capt. Skinker had commanded Company I, 138th Infantry Regiment, until his death during the Argonne battle. Services were held at Christ Church Cathedral with burial at Bellefontaine Cemetery.[38]

Col. Parker took a special interest in vocational training for his men. Parker wanted to see his men develop through practical education as well as physically. It was part of his philosophy that the Army should not only make soldiers of its men, but prepare them for useful and successful citizenship when they returned to civilian life. About a score of vocational training classes were organized, and regular hours, outside of military training hours, were set aside for study and instruction. This plan proved profitable, not only to the recruits, but also to the government. These classes provided training in removing and repairing buildings, installing plumbing and lighting, in automobile repair and in various technical trades. Men were taught brick and stone masonry, plastering, painting and carpentry in remodeling offices, quarters and barracks buildings, and even the technique of installing a three phase electrical system for the Post. A two-month course of instruction in recruiting duty was organized. Capt. Samuel G. Goodwin was in charge of athletic and entertainment activities. Capt. Goodwin organized dances and other social gatherings for the men.

Col. Parker kept in close touch with civilian activities in St. Louis, and many parades were given in the city. Co-operation in practically all public-spirited drives were given by post personnel. Col. Parker also had a road constructed around the Headquarters building in order that the beautiful view from the bluff would be readily accessible to automobile tourists visiting the post.

Capt. Harry E. Mitchell sponsored projects for landscaping and grounds beautification. Under his tutelage, many sidewalks and streets were built. Attention was given to arborage and floral adornment by utilizing the products from the post hothouse.

On 6 March, soldiers from Jefferson Barracks acted as an honor guard when the body of longtime Missouri Senator Champ Clark arrived in St. Louis from Washington, D.C., at 4:00 p.m. The special train bearing the body had been delayed for an hour when the terminal engine pulling the car bearing Senator Clark's body jumped the track and killed a yardman.

A torrential rain poured down unabated until the funeral procession reached city hall. The crowd became so dense shortly after the bier was placed for viewing in the city hall rotunda that those in charge were compelled to turn the catafalque in such a manner as to permit spectators to view the body from both sides. Jefferson Barracks soldiers aided the police in keeping the crowd on the move.

The soldiers honor guard stayed with Clark's body until it was returned to the train at 11:00 p.m. to await departure for Bowling Green. Burial was the next day in the Mound Cemetery.[39]

A new program in military preparedness began in 1921. By 1917 the Military Training Camp Association [MTCA] had gained sufficient political clout to influence Congress' approval of a full appropriation for training camps throughout the country. However, with the advent of war in April of that year, any possibility of holding summer camps was wiped out.

After World War I, the MTCA continued to lobby for military training camps, but even with its considerable influence it could not overcome the political realities brought on by the tide of isolationism and pacifist sympathies engulfing the nation by 1920. The MTCA had vigorously campaigned for a system of universal compulsory military training. Although the Senate passed a bill establishing universal military training, it was rejected by the House and failed to survive in conference. A compromise bill did provide for a summer training program for American youth: the volunteer, no-obligation Citizen's Military Training Camps [CMTC].

The legislation was a single, albeit long, paragraph of the 1920 Amendment to the 1916 National Defense Act, Section 47d, titled, 'Training Camps,' authorizing the Secretary of War, in broad terms, "to maintain, upon military reservations or elsewhere, schools or camps" for military instruction. One of the specific details in the section authorized round-trip travel allowances of five cents per mile, and a later amendment, a subsistence allowance of one cent per mile when transportation was furnished "in kind," i.e., when a train or bus ticket was issued by the army. The final sentence of section 47d put the General Staff to work determining what CMTC was to be and how it would work: "The Secretary of War is authorized further to prescribe the courses of theoretical and practical instruction to be pursued by persons attending the camps authorized by this section; to fix the periods during which such camps shall be maintained; to prescribe rules and regulations for the government thereof; and to employ officers, warrant officers and enlisted men of the regular army in such numbers and upon such duties as he may designate."

Early in 1921, the Army published Special Regulation No. 44b, dated 23 February 1921, establishing details on the conduct of the camps. The camps were to be 30 days in duration. The dates for camps scheduled for the nine United States Corps Areas were to be set by each corps commander, generally beginning in July or August. Attendance was voluntary and "without cost" to those attending, which also meant there was no pay other than reimbursement for transportation. The candidates were to be housed, fed and supplied with uniforms and necessary equipment just as any regular army recruit.

Initially, the complete CMTC course was designed to be of three summers' duration, with the first year designated as "Red," the second "White," and the third "Blue." Successful completion of the Blue course put a young man on the way to becoming a second lieutenant in the Officers' Reserve Corps. For 1921, the training would be limited, officially at least, to the Red course comprised of infantry drill, rifle marksmanship, guard duty, camping and marching, care of equipment, personal hygiene, military courtesy, athletic contests, and military ceremonies. In actual practice at many of the camps, military veterans and youths with some type of ROTC or other military training were treated as second or third-year men.

By the early spring of 1921, the general public was becoming aware of the new summer camp plan. In a headline reading "PICK WAR TRAINING CAMPS, Nine Corps Areas Expect to Instruct 9,800 Citizens in Summer" the *New York Times* reported a War Department announcement saying each corps area was to train approximately 1,200 men. "Of the three grades of camps, "red, white and blue," the first, it was said, will be emphasized because it should appeal particularly to men between the ages of 16 and 19 and demonstrate to parents the 'physical, moral and mental development that results from military training." The story went on to report on a list of sixteen camps that were under consideration as sites for the summer training.[40]

In 1921, 11,202 young men were accepted to become CMTC "pioneers." There were even a number, impossible to calculate, who had served in World War I. Rear Admiral Richard "Red" Patterson, an alumnus of the 1921 Plattsburg, New York, CMTC, said one CMTC company at Plattsburg Barracks was made up of older men, many of them vets, including Sam Drebbin, who had been a scout for General Pershing during the Mexican border fracas of 1916-1917.[41]

On 21 July 1921, General of the Army John J. "Black Jack" Pershing was appointed U.S. Army Chief of Staff, replacing General Peyton March. In his first two months as Chief of Staff, Pershing clearly demonstrated that he (and therefore the Army's General Staff) did not look on CMTC as a stepchild. In August, Pershing visited seven of the twelve camp sites. Back in Washington Pershing released a statement expressing his enthusiasm for the camps, and calling for attendance to be increased to 40,000 men the next year.[42]

It was announced on 12 July that the 6th Annual Tuberculosis Society baseball doubleheader was to be played on 27 July. The annual event pitted the army against the navy in a preliminary match before a St. Louis Cardinals game. Jefferson Barracks had furnished the army team each year and for the fourth time their opponent was the Great Lakes Naval Station from Chicago. In the second game of the day the Cardinals played host to the Philadelphia Phillies. The Cardinals donated a Ford car to be given away with one of the souvenir score cards for sale. It was also announced that about 25,000 other articles of all shapes, sizes, and description and every imaginable value, were given away as prizes for the purchase of a score card.[43]

Just prior to the game the players, accompanied by the two military bands and a contingent of sailors and soldiers, passed in review before the boxes occupied by the Governor, the Mayor and other guests of honor.[44]

On 24 July, the program for the Tuberculosis benefit had been completed. Prior to the games to be played at Sportsman's Park a parade and review of the service teams and their bands under the escort of a detail of United States Marines was to take place in downtown St. Louis. Missouri Governor Arthur M. Hyde, St. Louis Mayor Henry W. Kiel, the commandants of both Jefferson Barracks and the Great Lakes Naval Station, Acting President of the Tuberculosis Society Homer Hall and Chairman J.F. Oberwinder of the committee in charge of the games occupied the reviewing stand. Capt. Gilbert D. Jackson, U.S. Marines, in command of the St. Louis Marine Corps recruiting office, commanded the parade. A double color guard of marines, all of whom were decorated for gallantry at Chateau-Thierry and Belleau Wood, headed the parade line. After the service game the bands from each station presented a concert.[45]

As in all of the previous army/navy games for the Tuberculosis Society, the navy team defeated the army, this time by a score of 5 to 0. The highlight of the Cardinals game came in the 5th inning when the home team turned a triple play.[46]

Col. Hunter B. Nelson, 6th Infantry, relieved Col. Parker on 29 November 1921. Shortly after being relieved of command of Jefferson Barracks Col. Parker retired with the rank of brigadier general. Nelson had graduated from West Point in June of 1893 and received a commission as a second lieutenant in the 24th Infantry. With the advent of the Spanish-American War Nelson was promoted to first lieutenant in April 1898 and served with the 24th Infantry during the Santiago Campaign. Upon his return to the States Nelson served at Fort Douglas, Utah, then went to the Philippines in December 1899. He served at the Presidio of San Francisco and at Vancouver Barracks until being transferred to the 26th Infantry in September 1912. When the U.S. entered World War I, Capt. Nelson was serving in Hawaii and like many regular officers was quickly advanced several grades. In March 1918, he became lieutenant colonel of the new 41st Infantry Regiment, which was never activated for overseas duty. However, Nelson was ordered to France and in June 1918 was attached to the 328th Infantry Regiment, 164th Brigade, 82nd Infantry Division. Nelson was relieved of his command prior to the St. Mihiel Offensive and put in command of the German Officer's Prisoner of War Enclosure. Col. Nelson retired in December 1930.

Just a few days after the big game exciting news reached St. Louis. For the first time in 15 years, since the first squadron of the 9th Cavalry left the post, Jefferson Barracks was to be made the headquarters for regular army troops. Under general orders issued in Washington on July 26, the 10th Army Brigade, the 6th Infantry and the 60th Infantry were to be stationed at the post. The 6th Infantry, however, was the only active unit of the three. Only the headquarters organizations of the other two were to be stationed there as the units themselves were inactive.[47]

In the fall of 1921 a young boy, William Jay Smith, arrived at Jefferson Barracks. Smith's father was a bandsman in the 6th Infantry band. In the fall of that year, Smith's father was stationed at Camp Pike, near Little Rock, Arkansas. When the camp broke up that fall, the men were given a choice of transferring to a camp in the state of Washington or to Jefferson Barracks. Smith's father chose Jefferson Barracks mainly because it was closer to his home in the South. He had been born at Gaar's Mill, Louisiana, in 1891 and he enlisted in the Army in 1918.[48]

A great deal of information on the everyday life of soldiers and their families can be gleaned from Smith's writings. Smith describes Jefferson Barracks in 1921 as follows: "The garrison's 1702 acres were mostly wooded land with the headquarters building located at the highest point. Behind it a cannon from the Spanish-American War pointed out toward the river. The barracks buildings flanking headquarters and lining the parade grounds to the south, had been constructed at the turn of the century of the same uniform dark red brick. The buildings were all like so many firehouses one after the other - the same cement steps leading up to the same cement porch. The same iron railing circling each porch, all painted dark green, the companies with lettered designations, A, B, C, D, E, F along the parade ground, which was trim and immaculate, like a golf course.

The monotonous row of barracks was broken at one point by the ensemble of the guardhouse, the theater, which later served as a chapel, and the post exchange. Facing the company buildings and fashioned of the same dull brick were the officers' quarters. In the center of Officers' Row stood the Officers' Club with its tennis courts. The officers' quarters were indistinguishable from the company buildings. They were relieved by a little planting before them, and of course, differentiated from one another by the name of the occupant, each name white and placed on the top step just below the porch. These quarters were two-story duplexes with screened-in front porches separated from each other by green latticework; each had its bit of carefully tended lawn, its uniform garages behind. Off from the garages stretched the wild acres of the reservation with oak, hickory and sycamore trees.

Over a wooded area made up of sinkholes and limestone caves were spread the quarters of warrant officers, square brick structures or long wooden ones, the cantonment buildings constructed for troops during World War I and refashioned into quarters. Each set of quarters had its occupant and his rank designated in black and white lettering like the officers' - right down to the few meager privates who managed to live in quarters at all."[49]

Smith went on to point out that during his long residency at Jefferson Barracks during the 1920s and 1930s, all the soldiers and their families participated in an annual Thanksgiving dinner at Atkinson Hall, the huge mess hall located near the center of Jefferson Barracks. Built of concrete painted white, it stood out in contrast to the brick barracks surrounding it. When Atkinson Hall was first built shortly after Smith's arrival in 1921, the Old Mess Hall, known as "Cockroach Bogey," was abandoned and made available for entertainment. Entertainment at the time was simple; one form was roller skating. The old hall provided, if nothing else, a vast floor space, and someone had the idea to purchase 500 pairs of roller skates. Skating sessions were held on the main floor and later in the basement.[50]

The Post Mess Hall was the focal point of life at the Barracks as William J. Smith was to know it in the 1920s and 1930s, especially at Thanksgiving and Christmas. The married soldiers and their families along with their guests were invited to real feasts. There were the traditional holiday fixings - turkey with stuffing, sweet potatoes, cranberry sauce, mince and pumpkin pies - but there were always two items that made the meals special: the long pans of baked beans and the corn bread. The Boston baked beans, first boiled and then seasoned with brown sugar and molasses, ketchup, mustard and onions and baked with strips of bacon and ham, had, in their pans two or three inches deep and three feet long, the look of mahogany and an aroma that brought all the richness of the autumn wood right into the room. The corn bread, in accompanying pans, had the flavor of corn baked in husks and pulled from a flowing wood fire. The best cooks on the Post were Southerners, to whom cooking came naturally, and they had been brought up making the dishes that they served. Some of them went to their graves jealously guarding, even from their own families, the recipes for the barbecue sauce they offered the mess. Guests at these communal gatherings were always provided with a typed - often even a printed - menu. On one of these the Commanding Officer wrote: "When you think of an army post you must remember that we are really a small town," and then he listed all the services that made Jefferson Barracks a self-sufficient village, right down to the "Army finance officer - our banker."

Thanksgiving and Christmas meals were times all members of the garrison were brought together like one great family. The Post Chapel, a large frame building painted green, resembled in an odd way a great riverboat that had been beached in the woods. The Mississippi River, in any case, was never far away. It was a terrifying force, always ready to rise up beyond its banks, over the wasteland of the railroad tracks, right up to the entrances of the limestone caves in the hillside above, which had been blackened by the fires of hoboes who had spent the night. Smith's mother, when momentarily overcome by some trying situation, would say, "I'm going to walk to the river until my hat floats!" And Smith grew up thinking that was the way people coped with difficult situations in life. Smith said that he could see a great variety of hats of all shapes and sizes floating down that giant, mud-thick river, along with chicken coops and houses.

The faded blue-green Chapel consisted of one large auditorium with a stage so high that those seated below it could see only the feet of those standing above, unless they craned their necks up toward the ceiling. The Chapel had originally been an all-purpose theater and assembly hall during World War I. The beaver board that covered its interior was streaked with great wet spots that looked like fungi attacking it. Church services were held in a small alcove in the rear where there was an upright piano, and Sunday School classes occupied various corners of the rambling structure. One of the chaplains Smith knew was Chaplain Jones, an amiable man....

On Christmas Eve, the chapel, heated by potbellied stoves, would be packed with every married man on the post, from the highest rank to the lowest, and all his children big and small perched one on top of the other like fruit pouring from a horn of plenty, all the round faces straining to watch for the arrival of Santa Claus. (That role was always taken by the same hefty, pink-cheeked bachelor sergeant, an old army hand, who enjoyed every minute of it.) He would come into the hall, blowing, snorting, laughing and stride up to the stage, where he would stand, a giant of a man on a platform close to heaven, beside the great dazzling tree that seemed ready to burst blazing through the roof and carry us off through the sky. Beside him stood a wee, wizened private like a uniformed dwarf, calling out the names of each child as he made his way up - or was lifted up over the beaming faces - to the stage to receive his gift. On these communal occasions rank was forgotten: we were all one family, blessed with bounty.[51]

The woods on the reservation were a child's paradise. Smith and the other children on the Post knew every inch of these acres. They followed the fern-lined muddy streams to their swimming holes, fished for crawfish with strips of bacon fat, and on the banks built tree houses and lean-tos of sassafras in air blue with blueshells and heavy with the perfume of sweet william. On the edge of sinkholes on hot summer evenings, they played a game called "statues," which consisted of allowing yourself to be flung by whoever was "it" and holding whatever position you assumed.

The children gathered bittersweet, hazelnuts and persimmons in the fall and made their way to the Old Rock Spring (later called Sylvan Springs) to spend hours lying and drinking the clear water, watching waterbugs dart across the surface of the sandy pool.[52]

On the evening of 3 November 1921, after an almost 900-mile hike from Camp Jackson, South Carolina, with the men carrying full packs, the 6th Infantry Regiment marched into Jefferson Barracks. For the regiment, whose motto, "Remember your regiment," had been spoken by Lt. Col. Abner R. Thompson at the Battle of Okeechobee in the Seminole War, the return was something of a homecoming. The 6th Infantry had erected some of the first permanent buildings at Jefferson Barracks in 1827. The regiment was created in 1798, only to be disbanded two years later and, then reactivated in 1808. It served in many battles in the War of 1812 and then merged with five other regiments on what became its official birthday, 17 May 1815. After long years of Indian warfare, it always returned to Jefferson Barracks. It fought in a number of battles in the Civil War, marched to the Mexican border in 1914, and then on 4 November 1918, crossed the Meuse River in France and helped break the German line. The 6th Infantry was the first regiment to enter occupied territory after the Armistice in 1918, and afterward returned to Fort Gordon, Georgia.[53]

For the men of the 6th Infantry, the arrival at Jefferson Barracks that November evening was the end of a long journey and of a long and exacting day. They had left Jones Park in East St. Louis early that morning to pass in review, together with the American Legion, before the mayor of St. Louis, Henry W. Kiel, and his distinguished guests, General John J. Pershing and Marshal Ferdinand Foch. General Pershing was delighted to welcome the leader of the Allied Forces in World War I on his first visit to the United States. The men of the 6th Infantry entered Missouri over the Eads Bridge at 10:30 a.m. Because of a misunderstanding the regiment crossed the bridge too early and the soldiers had to stand in line for an hour and a half stretched from Broadway to Washington Avenue across the bridge. William Friendly, Secretary for Mayor Kiel, greeted Col. Hunter B. Nelson, commander of the 6th, from the steps of a limousine on Washington Avenue: "You have come to a land of plenty and you have not come under arms." When General Pershing later presented Col. Nelson to Marshal Foch, the Marshal said; "The fine, fresh appearance of his men after so long a march is characteristic of the American Army, and ...it is an honor to review such a splendid unit."[54]

The men of the 6th Infantry had looked less splendid when a *Post-Dispatch* reporter had visited them in East St. Louis on 1 November. It had recently rained and outside the "squatty, brown burrows" of their pup tents, alongside which "the higher tents of the company captains and lieutenants loomed big," the men were sloshing around in the mud preparing for the march "attired in uniforms of varying degrees of completeness, men all over the camps were busy washing those pieces of clothing they were not wearing in 100 metal tubs and on 80 scrub boards furnished by the city of East St. Louis....The officers too were getting their things cleaned, but it was their 'dog robbers' as the army refers to officers' servants, who do the worrying for them....The company field kitchens and muleless escort wagons for supplies were scattered about. Picket lines for the seventy-nine riding horses and 211 mules were established beyond the camp proper. Rags and puddles of soapy water were everywhere. Sparks flew from the farriers shed, where all the animals were being groomed; the rolling kitchens were getting a final gloss from a mixture of lampblack and vinegar. The men were also shining their howitzers, machine guns, and Stokes mortars, and greasing the hob-nailed shoes that had carried them over the Cumberland mountains.[55]

After the review parade, the nearly 800 men of the 6th were served a luncheon in Lafayette Park, where they assembled at 1:00 o'clock en-route to Jefferson Barracks. Members of the Federated Women's Club under the direction of Mrs. John S. Payne, and assisted by other women's organizations prepared the luncheon and served it to the companies as they filed past the band pavilion.

Judge Thomas L. Anderson, in voicing the welcome of the women of St. Louis to the regiment, said; "We are proud to welcome the men who constitute the regiment, which for 128 years has existed to defend our republic." Mrs. Frank V. Hammar, who served as chairman of the St. Louis Chapter of the Red Cross, expressed the welcome of the relief organization.

Chaplain H.R. Feld replied that, "We heartily appreciate the sincere and practical welcome accorded to us." He continued by saying that the men of the regiment felt as if they were coming home and hoped to be counted among the citizens of St. Louis and to be identified with the life and progress of the city.[56]

After leaving Camp Jackson, South Carolina, on September 2 the regiment marched at the rate of eighteen to twenty miles a day over rocks and mud, down cliffs and through rivers. The regiment had then spent two days in East St. Louis cleaning and polishing equipment and grooming horses and themselves.[57]

After their luncheon in Lafayette Park, the soldiers of the 6th Infantry marched the last few miles to their new home at Jefferson Barracks. The confusion incident to getting straightened out in new quarters at Jefferson Barracks prevented the 6th from celebrating the third anniversary of its crossing of the River Meuse on 4 November 1918, one of the outstanding feats of the A.E.F. Each regiment of the Regular Army customarily celebrates one day a year as "Organization Day," and that day for the 6th Infantry is November 4. Company commanders reminded the men of the significance of the occasion at retreat that evening.

It was a grateful lot of soldiers, who slept until the "late" hour of 6:00 o'clock on 5 November, in heated barracks. For two months since the regiment left Camp Jackson, the troops arose at 4:30 each morning, often after sleeping on the ground, wrapped in blankets and with "pup" tents for shelter. Officers, too, indulged themselves, as one officer admitted he stayed in bed until 7:15.

The soldiers spent the first full day at Jefferson Barracks removing straw from their blankets and cleaning all other equipment which had been visible during the parade the day before. The "mule skinners" quarreled over the best stables and the officers heatedly discussed the possession of desired quarters, as one officer expressed it.

The men received their October pay shortly after noon on November 5, and many looked forward to spending it that night, when the first real liberties were granted. There was to be great latitude in granting week-end liberty.

The officers already at the Barracks, which had been transformed from a Recruit Depot to an Infantry Post, entertained the thirty-four officers of the 6th Infantry at a reception and dance in the Administration Building on the evening of 5 November. The next evening a dance was held there for the enlisted men.

Companies I and M did not remain long at Jefferson Barracks, leaving soon for Fort Crook, Nebraska, headquarters of the 7th Corps Area.

With the arrival of about 800 soldiers of the 6th Infantry, there were about 1,000 soldiers at Jefferson Barracks. The remainder of the 6th Infantry, the 1st Battalion which had been left at Camp Jackson on guard duty, would join the Jefferson Barracks garrison before long.[58]

In the 1920s and 1930s, there was not much money anywhere, and the regular enlisted man was paid what seems like a pittance. A private received a base pay of $21 a month - plus clothing, food, and medical care. William Jay Smith's father made it to the rank of corporal and retained that rank for most of his twenty-seven years in the army. He was reduced - busted - several times to private, so that it was one step forward and one step back for him during all his years of service. A corporal's pay at this time was $42 a month. A corporal also received a food allowance - ration or subsistence money - amounting to $16 to $18 a month. If a noncommissioned officer lived off post, he had the right to purchase food at the Commissary, and this made a big difference. Freshly baked bread could be purchased for two cents a loaf, a whole side of bacon for fifty cents, a whole ham for just over a dollar. Also at the Commissary, which sold at wholesale prices canned goods could be purchased for five or six cents a can, a hundred-pound sack of potatoes for a dollar, a seven-to-eight-pound roast for sixty cents and chickens for thirty cents each.[59]

In addition, enlisted men could go to a picture show for five cents. The fare for the streetcar, which clanged along for about a mile through the woods, cost ten cents for adults and five cents for children. A ride on this streetcar, the " Dinkey" or "Toonerville Trolley," was a thrill in itself. At the end of Broadway next to the North Gate, it veered straight into the woods, a roller coaster ride through the wilderness. For ten minutes, there was no sign of civilization whatever. You could reach out and pick blackberries along the way. At night, the trip was even more mysterious as the owls haunted and darkness closed around the yellow jingling box of the trolley like a giant's palm....[60]

1922

For the second January in a row the new year began on a sad note. James M. Dickey, superintendent of the Jefferson Barracks National Cemetery, died suddenly on January 6, his birthday. He was at his home at the Barracks. Cause of death was attributed to heart disease. Dickey had been at Jefferson Barracks for six years and before his tour here had served as superintendent of the National Cemetery at Corinth, Mississippi, for 22 years. Dickey had served during the Civil War with the 4th New Hampshire Infantry.[61]

Still another Jefferson Barracks soldier lost his life in January 1922. Sgt. Clem Craig, Quartermaster Corps, died from a skull fracture at the Jefferson Barracks Hospital on 19 January. Craig drove a truck that took children to and from school. He had parked the truck on the east side of Broadway and was crossing the street to go to a bakery when a car driven by a Lieutenant from Scott Field hit him. The Lieutenant took Craig to the J.B. Hospital but he did not regain consciousness. Ironically, Craig's wife and son had been killed when the car they were in was struck by a train in Granite City the previous August.[62]

Lt. Col. A.R. Dillingham relieved Col. Nelson in early 1922. Dillingham served only temporarily until the arrival of Col. Halsey E. Yates on 21 March 1922. Col. Yates also succeeded Col. Nelson as commander of the 6th Infantry Regiment.[63]

On a more uplifting note, Lt. Col. Dillingham and the 6th Infantry participated in a ceremony on 11 February to bestow on Michael R. Ellis the Cross of Military Valor, awarded by the Italian Government. Ellis, who served as a sergeant in Company C, 28th Infantry, First Division, had been cited in divisional orders for valor in the Battle of Soissons, 18 July to 22 July 1918, when, in different exploits, he captured 44 prisoners and six machine guns. Ellis had already been awarded the Congressional Medal of Honor, one of two St. Louisans to receive the nation's highest award, for bravery during the Battle of Exermont on 5 October 1918. Ellis also won the Cross of the Chevalier of the Legion of Honor of France.[64]

Just as the Jefferson Barracks National Cemetery had come to be the final resting place for many area World War I soldiers, the Jefferson Barracks Hospital served to give hope to many others that had been disfigured during the conflagration. By the beginning of April 1922 only six men remained of the 163 that had come to the hospital in June 1919 from Cape May, Fort McHenry, and other eastern posts. During the almost three years that these men had been at Jefferson Barracks they had all undergone between 19 and 31 operations to restore their faces that had been disfigured during the war. Some had become discouraged by the numerous operations and the long process involved and had given up before the restoration had been completed.

One, Alexander Nesbit, whose nose and right eye had been claimed by shrapnel, departed at the end of March after 35 operations, most major surgery, for his home in Wyoming. His features had been almost totally restored.

The men had been sent to St. Louis where they had been told that Dr. V.P. Blair, a St. Louis surgeon, could possibly restore their faces after repeated operations covering a few months to several years. The men occupied a special ward in the south wing of the hospital. The ward was large, sunny, and equipped with a phonograph which was seldom not in use. Edward Harrington, W.H. Edrod, and Edward Lindstrom gathered around the phonograph to talk and listen. A studious L.M. Lauridsen spent a great deal of time reading with his friend H.A. Ecklund, who often could be seen playing solitaire. The two had met at a hospital in France in 1918 and had been together ever since.

All of these men through all of the procedures kept up a hopeful and light hearted spirit. Ecklund's case provides an insight into what all of these men had been through. He was advancing on 14 September 1918, the third day of the St. Mihiel offensive, when an "H.E." high explosive shell exploded in the air near him and tore off his nose and part of his right eyebrow. His brow had been restored by April 1922, and his nose had twice been built up almost to completion, when infection set in and necessitated destruction of the work already accomplished. Ecklund underwent twenty-eight operations, four since January 1922, when the third series began. Nevertheless, with an indomitable spirit, he maintained hope that by fall he would be back to normal. At that time, he wanted to enroll in a vocational school to study advertising.

A group of young St. Louis women gave a dance every Thursday night for the men in the south ward at the Red Cross headquarters at the hospital, and every Tuesday night the men were taken by the young ladies to dinner at some downtown hotel and afterward to a movie. Each of the men also spoke fondly of the good work done by the nurse, Miss Alice Price, and by Miss Elinore Williams, who ran the workshop. They had been with the men for two years.

Jefferson Barracks served to induct and train men to go to war, then to separate after the war, as a final resting place for many of those that gave the ultimate sacrifice and as a means of giving hope to some of those men shockingly disfigured from the war.

Jefferson Barracks was not the only military presence in the St. Louis area. The headquarters of the 102nd Division occupied the building at Third and Olive. Since the end of World War I, the number of men in the Army and Reserves had continued to decrease. On 24 April 1922, Jonathan N. Straat, Chief of Staff for the 102nd Division issued a memorandum informing the 102nd officers (and particularly its recruiting officers) that orders had been received authorizing the enlistment of noncommissioned officers and specialists for all organizations of the division. The memorandum went on to inform the officers of the best methods of recruitment. Personal solicitation was the preferred method, with local newspapers and postmasters also being good methods of recruitment. This was a major effort to bring the units of the 102nd Division up to their full peacetime quotas.[65]

If you go to the Jefferson Barracks National Cemetery today you will find Longstreet Drive by the first flag circle. Follow Longstreet eastwards and you will see a monument known affectionately as Miss Minnie. The dedication ceremony for Miss Minnie took place on 16 May 1922. An article in the Duluth, Minnesota *News-Tribune* the next day provides the story behind the monument.

"The Jefferson Barracks Monument."

"It is most fitting that Minnesota erect a monument to her soldiers who died while at Jefferson Barracks, Saint Louis, during the Rebellion. Governor Praus was especially happy in his reference to the high service soldiers render who die while engaged in their country's service even though they be not slain on the field of battle or expire from wounds received in conflict."

Among other things, he said:

"Service in handling supplies, digging trenches, making roads and doing guard duty were the lines of duty of Minnesotans in St. Louis. All this, if not as glorious, was just as arduous and often just as dangerous as actual fighting. It was service just as unselfish and as necessary as service in battle. Those who died from disease sacrificed as much and often suffered more than those who died in combat. Of the 164 Minnesotans buried at Jefferson Barracks, all, or nearly all, died of illness. In dedicating this monument to their memory, we want to show that we revere their memories, we appreciate their sacrifices, equally with any others who died for the preservation of the Union."

"The presence of Christopher Columbus Andrews, 92 years of age, at the unveiling yesterday of the monument at Jefferson Barracks stirred some Missouri G.A.R. veterans to recollections of the days when Andrews was commanding Union troops of Minnesota in the campaigns in the West. It is not easy to realize that Andrews has lived in the administration of every president except the first six, and has a tolerable knowledge of all our wars save the two with Great Britain and that with the Seminoles."

"Minnesota with Kansas and Oregon were the baby states of the Union when the Rebellion began, and the hardships of war came to this state and to Kansas in distressingly large measure, considering that they were far from the zones of the chief battles. The Sioux took advantage of the absence from this state of thousands of men and what that blood-thirsty nation did in the Minnesota Valley and elsewhere was appalling. Quantrell raided Lawrence in Kansas and its "Free Soilers" had added reason to hate the minions of Slavery."

158

 Louis Cooseman, from LeMay, was part of the Siberian Expeditionary Force that landed at Archangel in late August and September 1918.

 Col. John H. Parker, 6th Infantry, assumed command of Jefferson Barracks in March 1921 and remained in command until relieved on 29 November 1921. Parker retired shortly thereafter with the rank of brigadier general.

Citizen's Military Training Camp, (CMTC), ca. 1920s
This picture was taken on the south side of the parade ground looking toward the post gymnasium, now the Missouri Civil War Museum.

"It was at Jefferson Barracks that more than one distinguished Union general served. The best-known name associated with it is that of Grant."

"Minnesota does well to mark the resting places of its soldier and sailor sons. The legislature of this state has never been parsimonious about appropriating money for monuments, although it cannot be said it has ever been notably free in that direction. The work the Monuments Commission has done reflects great credit upon it. General Andrews has been unfailing in his devotion to the work. Considering his brilliant record as a soldier and his service as United States Minister to Sweden in the Grant administration, it is not too much to hope that the commonwealth of his adoption will in time raise a monument to his honor."

Certainly, one of the highlights of the year 1922 took place at Jefferson Barracks from 26 May to 28 May. when the post played host to a major horse show. The show, sponsored by the officers of Jefferson Barracks who were members of the Polo Association and the St. Louis Riding Club, proved to be the most ambitious sporting-social event undertaken at Jefferson Barracks in many years.

The post was all dressed up for the auspicious occasion with flags, pennants, and bunting, and the sweeping emerald gold field of the large parade ground provided a striking background, while horsemen and women galloped and cantered all around the field entertaining the packed grandstand and special boxes. The 6th Infantry band furnished music and soldiers acted as ushers and attendants distributing programs.

The military and civilian riding contests took place in categories such as showmanship, machine-gun going into action, three and five gate jumping, children's ponies, and numerous other classes. Winners received ribbons and in some adult contests received cash.

Festivities were marred during the second day by a severe injury to Major James A. Watson, who suffered a bad spill when Ned, his mount, failed to clear a four-foot brush jump. Horse and rider came down on their heads, but the horse regained his feet and, in jumping over Major Watson struck the back of the major's head. Major Watson quickly regained his feet, but collapsed in the arms of a soldier who had come to his assistance. He was taken to the post hospital. His injuries while serious were not life threatening. He suffered a fractured collar bone, deep scalp wounds, and a severely wrenched back.

A few minutes before this accident, Mrs. Watson, a contestant in the same event, was thrown from her mount at the third hurdle, when the horse shied at photographers and brushed her against one of the hurdle guards. Mrs. Watson was not injured and returned to the contest.

Major Watson was one of the chief promoters of the show, and with Mrs. Watson had devoted most of his spare time for several months to its arrangement. Proceeds from the show, which amounted to $3200, went to charity.[66]

Jefferson Barracks played host to a 15-day encampment for Reserve officers during late July and early August. The country around the Post was utilized for imaginary battle maneuvers. The primary object of the camp, which the officers were required to attend annually, was to give instruction in tactics and strategy. Thirty-five business and professional men of St. Louis were among the 114 reservists in attendance.

One of the examples of problems in troop action given the officers to work out was that of an attack by a hypothetical "blue" army, concentrated near St. Louis and moving past the Barracks on an imaginary "red" army entrenched at the Meramec River. To solve the problem the students were taken to the field in big trucks, shown the supposed theater of operations, provided with maps and instructed to "bring up their troops, prepare the necessary battle orders, place their detachments and show how they would proceed to their objective."

This was carried out in fine detail, to the precision of orders required and the requirement of placing all details, from field headquarters to battalion first aid stations. The solutions were written, then the instructors, who were 30 regular army officers, read and criticized them before the class.

The 6th Infantry, stationed at the Barracks, was used in other classes to demonstrate various phases of warfare. For example, a machine gun company showed how it would do its part in an attack. The entire regiment demonstrated an offensive. A one-pound gun actually threw a barrage as the infantry advanced. A small airplane and a blimp from Scott Field took part in the way airplanes proved useful during World War I. The public was invited to attend.[67]

Companies F and I of the 6th Infantry, which had been on duty at Fort Crook, Nebraska, returned to Jefferson Barracks on June 20, 1922. On September 15, 1922, Companies K and L arrived. The 6th Infantry Regiment was once again united at Jefferson Barracks.

The War Department announced on 24 July that the St. Louis region, including Jefferson Barracks, had been transferred from the 7th Corps Area to the 6th Corps Area, and would be under the direction of Major General James F. Bell with headquarters in Chicago.

The change gave General Bell a considerable additional force stationed in an area that contained numerous railway centers. While the reason for the change was not disclosed, it was generally understood to be in connection with the possible use of army troops during railway strikes that had become prevalent in the area.[68]

An interesting side note to activities at Jefferson Barracks during 1922 is an article that appeared in the Belleville *News Democrat* on 17 August. The article featured a picture of the Scott Field baby blimp which was to be a featured attraction in the flying circus given at Scott Field on 27 August. The baby blimp was used for instruction at Scott Field, which was the center of the army's lighter-than-air activities, but officers frequently used the craft on official business trips to Jefferson Barracks, passing over Belleville and St. Louis.

Word was received at the end of October that Martha Wade, 87, one of the few surviving Civil War nurses, had died from asphyxiation at her home in Valley Junction, Iowa. At the outbreak of the Civil War, Wade had enlisted in the Women's Nurse Corps, and had served at Jefferson Barracks for three and a half years, being discharged at the end of the war.[69]

It can be argued that the biggest event at Jefferson Barracks during 1922 was the Citizen's Military Training Camp that began on 1 August. During 1921 two camps had been held in the 7th Corps Area: one at Fort Snelling, Minnesota, and the other at Camp Pike, Arkansas. With a much larger appropriation in 1922, another camp had been added in the 7th Corps Area, at Jefferson Barracks. Even though Jefferson Barracks had been transferred to the 6th Corps Area, plans for the camp at Jefferson Barracks had already been finalized.

Recruiting for the 1922 camps had begun in April. An announcement from the office of Major Fred L. Lemmon, 7th Corps Area Recruiting Officer, stated that the CMTC combined the advantages of military training with the pleasures of an out-of-doors summer vacation. Any male citizen of the United States, whether by naturalization or birth was entitled to apply for the course. The training, given free to all accepted applicants, was planned to develop self-reliance and alertness, to promote physical and moral courage, and to increase health and vitality. Railroad fees and housing were furnished free to each student.

Athletics, physical training, target practice, and military instruction made up the life of the citizen-soldier while in camp. Abundant and excellent entertainment was furnished, and Saturday afternoons and Sunday were to be free.

The 7th Corps Area had room for 2700 applicants. Applications had to be received by 31 May.

Three courses of training were offered, the Red, White and Blue courses. The Red course, open to all fit citizens between the ages of 17 and 25, taught basic principles of military training, and fit men for service in the organized reserve.

The White course, open to citizens between the ages of 18 and 26 who had previous military experience equal to that given in the Red course, prepared specialists and noncommissioned officers for the organized reserve corps and the National Guard. Ex-soldiers with sufficient experience were eligible for this course.

The Blue course prepared noncommissioned officers and specialists for commissions in the officers' reserve corps. This course was open to men from 19 to 27.

Camps for the 7th Corps Area were held at Fort Snelling for residents of North Dakota and Iowa; at Fort Des Moines for residents of South Dakota and Nebraska; and at Jefferson Barracks for young men from Missouri and Arkansas.

The CMTC at Jefferson Barracks began on 1 August and ended on 30 August. Col. Halsey E. Yates, Jefferson Barracks commandant, served as camp commander. Lt. Col. W.H. Clendenin served as Executive Officer, Capt. Horace R. Fell as Chaplain, and Lt. E.P. Earle, 6th Infantry, was in charge of all recreational and educational activities.

The men were divided into three battalions with Companies A, B, C and D comprising the 1st Battalion; Companies E, F, G and H the 2nd Battalion; and Companies I, K, L and M the 3rd Battalion. Each company contained between seventy-two and eighty-three men for a total of 931 young men attending the CMTC at Jefferson Barracks in 1922. A total of eighteen men attended the Blue course and 194 took the White course with the remaining 719 men in the Red course.

Major E. Urrutia, Jr., commanded the 1st Battalion; Major J.A. Watson the 2nd Battalion; and Major George Stewart the 3rd Battalion. Each company had three company officers: a captain, a 1st lieutenant and a 2nd lieutenant. All the officers supervising training and otherwise taking part in the 1922 CMTC at Jefferson Barracks were Regular

Army or from the Officer Reserve Corps. The enlisted men who worked with the camp belonged to the 6ᵗʰ Infantry Regiment at Jefferson Barracks.

Military instruction and drill occupied much of a normal work day. From early morning reveille, the young men took part in assorted military instruction, whether it was Infantry, Signals, Aviation or whatever else happened to be on the agenda for that particular day. Some students took part in an hour or so of additional instruction after the noon meal, but for the most part afternoons were set aside for athletics and recreational activities. Baseball, softball, swimming and track and field constituted just a few of the activities offered.

William A. Borders of Kansas City and a member of Company E, Red Course, had this to say about athletics and entertainment at the camp:

"Few of us left our homes the latter part of July with the idea of a month of amusement before us. We knew, of course, that we would have some time for sports and the like, but little did we think that plans for our pleasure had been so carefully made. The camp circulars told us that many forms of athletics might be indulged in, that there would be swimming, dances, and all, but, to be frank, I did not believe them. I thought that there would be instead, voluntary means of entertainment into which no one would care to enter - but just think how I was mistaken! And you too, were widely misled if you happened to share my pessimistic opinion. Won't you admit as much?

By the end of our first five days in Jefferson Barracks, everything had been set in motion. We had drilled and drilled, it is true, but between our periods of work, we found ample time for play. And after only three days, there had been given for us an excellent dance, where those who were starving for pretty girls could, and were in fact, satisfied. [I know I was, anyway.] There had been for those individuals athletically inclined, all sorts and varieties of games, for when we arrived each company was fully supplied with hand balls, basket balls, base balls, weights and discs for throwing, baseball bats, more than was needed, in fact, for a rollicking good time in anything. Then the swimming pool, it must be mentioned; it is large and clean - the best things that can be said of any pool, but it has many other features, a long, wide water slide, floats, many diving boards; all that is necessary for perfection in the aquatic line.

Now, there were even other sports; for the movie fans, there were held nocturnal grandstand performances. Anyone could go there, and for an unusually low admission fee, see his favorite of the screen whether it be Charlie Chaplin, Doug or Mary, Theda Bara, or who. We had most of them here at one time or other. But if we did not care for the show, or felt rather lazy, it often times meant a trip to the canteen. We could go over there and play checkers or chess to our heart's content. Then we might saunter over to a chair and join the book worms, by reading some story or magazine article. After that, if it was not yet bed-time, there was always a quantity of Y.M.C.A. and Red Cross stationary, from which we could help ourselves; then we would usually go to our tents and wait expectantly for a letter from home.

It was all of these facts that helped in making the CMTC a phenomenal success. Everything that was attempted by those in authority was done correctly and fully, and not merely meddled with as is more than frequently the case. The dances, for example, were no small affair. They were real events. Every Saturday night promptly at eight-fifteen everyone knew a dance was beginning; a dance with an excellent orchestra of 6ᵗʰ Infantry fame, a dance with many fair eyed maidens from St. Louis, a dance that was attended and appreciated.

This is only typical. The right things were started at the first and they were continued until the last; because of this I feel sure that each boy who was a member of C.M.T.C. this year fully realized what has been done for him. And to realize is to be grateful!"

Edgar B. Eichman, Company M, White course, offered the following opinion of his month at Jefferson Barracks:

"It was sometime in May that I received, through the mail, an application to attend a Citizen's Military Camp to be held at Jefferson Barracks, Missouri, during the month of August 1922. Back in 1921, I received a similar application and, as curiosity killed the cat, I filled it out and went to Camp Pike, Arkansas. This year I filled out this application blank and sent it back to Col. Clendenin by return mail.

"About July 1ˢᵗ I began receiving literature and information relative to what a splendid time I would have at Jefferson Barracks, and needless to say I really expected a good time. July 20ᵗʰ, I received my final orders to travel to Jefferson Barracks, to arrive there not later than August 1ˢᵗ. Sometimes I would sit for hours, it would seem, and contemplate the pleasures of the vacation that was awaiting me at Jefferson Barracks. I would sleep in large brick barracks with showers in the basement, and rest upon good beds with springs in them and on good mattresses, and dine in unique little mess halls for each company, besides all sorts of athletics including baseball, swimming, boxing, etc., etc. Really I would be glad to quit my temporary vacation job at Montgomery Ward & Company to come to such a place for such an ideal vacation."

"August 1st, 9;00 o'clock at night found me at Jefferson Barracks. I was not sleeping in a spring bed on a soft mattress nor was I quartered in a brick barracks room with showers in the basement. I was to sleep on a cot in a tent with the cold, cruel ground as my floor, eat in a large crowded mess hall, drill hard and drill D—hard every day, do K. P. and serve on special details."

"Now it is time for the camp to disband and I have lots of things to say regarding the life as I found it in camp. As hard as I have drilled in the field, kissed by the rays of the Sun of the Sahara, and sweat till my shirt shed water like an umbrella on a rainy day, I have not regretted my stay in this camp. I would not take a large sum for the experiences encountered here. I am sure that the benefits derived have more than equaled the time and efforts invested. I lost one pound in weight, but gained one inch in chest expansion. My face is much brighter since my service here. Also, my duty here has shown me how to look upon men in a clearer light than I ever did before."

"During the course of the camp there were, of course, many things that did not agree with all of us at the same time. Taking into consideration all of the things that we disliked, I am sure that the good things more than outweighed the former."

"I have not regretted my month in Jefferson Barracks and hope that you have not either, "Buddy", and intend to be here to finish up with my Blue Course next year, and then if I qualify, to be a regular guy in the commissioned reserves."

"Yours until it is onion time in Bermuda and you will be my Valentine."

One of the fundamental and favorite activities of the military training was marksmanship, and Jefferson Barracks formed a Rifle Team that represented the Jefferson Barracks CMTC in a National Rifle Shooting Tournament at Camp Perry, Ohio. Contestants came from qualified cadets of the CMTC organizations of all the nine Corps Areas. Twelve student-cadets from Jefferson Barracks went to Fort Des Moines, then went to Camp Perry to compete with cadets from the various camps throughout the country in individual competition. Medals were given as rewards.

The twelve cadets selected from Jefferson Barracks were: Harry Minter, Mill Grove, Missouri; Harvey L. Humphrey, Branson, Missouri; James K. Mays, Fayetteville, Arkansas; Gaylord G. Weisner, Corning, Arkansas; Cecil T. Wallace, Ozan, Arkansas; Harold W. Busher, St. Joseph, Missouri; William M. Williamson, Pine Bluff, Arkansas; Charles Simpson, Monticello, Arkansas; Everett H. Smart, Joplin, Missouri; Ernest G. Blevins, DeQueen, Arkansas; William H. Ashcraft, Altheimer, Arkansas; and Roy G. Taylor, Willow, Arkansas.

Minter made a perfect score of 200 out of a possible 200. He was a member of Company M, White Course. Humphrey scored second with 198 points. He belonged to Company L. Weisner had 197 points and was a member of Company G.

Commencement exercises for the CMTC took place on 28 August. About 1500 civilians observed the ceremonies and competitive drills. Forty-one gold and silver medals were awarded for excellence and marksmanship. Winners of competitive drills received pecuniary awards.

In the regimental review, men of the Blue Course, third year men, were acting officers, and men of the White Course, second year men, were acting non-commissioned officers.[70]

Two men from each company received gold medals for marksmanship. Men without previous military training who received awards included Edward C. Utz, Faucett, Missouri; Harry Schineberger, Hopkins, Missouri; Olander Gresham, Liberty, Missouri; Donald L. Brock, Ozark, Missouri; William W. Burroughs, Marshall, Missouri; and Dean L. Sauceman, Westboro, Missouri.[71]

In closing the 1922 CMTC at Jefferson Barracks, Col. Halsey E. Yates, Camp Commandant, provided the following message:

"You young men of Arkansas and Missouri, who have completed thirty days intensive military training at Jefferson Barracks, have made one of the most important steps in your lives."

"You have learned obedience and discipline and you have learned how to accomplish things quickly yet efficiently. You have learned to keep yourselves physically fit at all times and under all conditions."

"You men, the future leaders of our nation and the pride of your country, will return to your homes better citizens and better, cleaner and quicker thinkers. You have been trained to become commissioned and non-commissioned officers. You men will, in time of war, be already trained and it will be you who will step forward when our brave old eagle of freedom first screams forth in anger at the approaching enemy."

"We will all look forward to the returning of you men next year. You have done nobly during your training period and you have accomplished much. You have worked when there was work to be done and when the recreation hour was at hand, you made the most of it."

"It is true that you were kept hard at work a large percentage of the time, but I have yet to hear you grumble. I repeat that you have done nobly. May you ever prosper."

Col. Yates arrived to take command of Jefferson Barracks on 9 March 1922. Yates had graduated from the U.S. Military Academy in 1899, and received a commission as a second lieutenant in the 5th Infantry Regiment. Col. Yates served in Cuba after graduation, then as an instructor at West Point. He then returned to Cuba and after that assignment went to the Philippines. After his tour in the Philippines, Yates returned to his birthplace of Lincoln, Nebraska, as commandant of cadets at the University of Nebraska. Col. Yates' next assignment sent him and his wife, Julie C. Nicholls of St. Louis, to Alaska, then on to the Presidio of San Francisco; Plattsburg, New York; Bucharest, Rumania as military Attache; and Fort Ontario at Oswego, New York. Col. Yates replaced Col. Hunter Nelson who was assigned to command of the 42nd Infantry at Camp Gaillard, Panama Canal Zone.[72]

Col. Yates' duties covered a wide range of obligations, and he was frequently absent from the Post. In the intervals of his absence, temporary command of Jefferson Barracks fell successively on Col. Thomas P. Bernard, Major Dean Halford, Col. Arthur P. Watts, Lt. Col. William H. Patterson, Capt. Louis R. Dougherty, Major George W. Maddox, Capt. William E. Hall, and Major Raymond C. Baird.[73]

A contract for a new Veterans Hospital at Jefferson Barracks was awarded on 5 July 1922. James Steward and Company of New York and St. Louis received a contract for the construction of seven buildings at a cost of $779,330. The new hospital was to have a capacity of 250 beds and was to be completed in eight months. Contracts for mechanical equipment were to be awarded within a few days, bringing the total cost of the institution up to $1,300,000.[74]

1923

There is very little to say about Jefferson Barracks for the year 1923. Col. Yates remained in command of the post for the entire year. Besides the 6th Infantry, the 14th Field Artillery was stationed at Jefferson Barracks.

The 6th Infantry conducted their annual target practice at the National Guard Range in St. Charles, Missouri, in 1923. The 2nd and 3rd Battalions of the 6th Infantry went to Camp Custer, Michigan, to take charge of the summer CMTC. No CMTC was held at Jefferson Barracks in 1923 and 1924. A detachment of the 6th Infantry performed guard duty at the Pulitzer National Air Races at Lambert Field in September 1923.[75]

During the second week of October, Master Sergeant Peter Barth, 6th Infantry, stationed at Jefferson Barracks, retired under the 30-year service clause with the unique distinction of having served his entire twenty-four years and ten months in the Army with the 6th Infantry.

MSgt. Barth's retirement was made the occasion of a general order by Col. Yates, commander of the 6th Infantry, outlining his career as an American soldier. Sgt. Barth enlisted in the 6th Infantry on November 8, 1898, and his foreign service during the Spanish-American War, the Philippine Insurrection, the Mexican Punitive Expedition and World War I earned him nearly six years of "double time," making his retirement possible with credit for thirty years of active service. Sgt. Barth retired with a notation of "character excellent" on all discharge papers, and according to the general order, with the respect and good wishes of both officers and enlisted personnel.[76]

The mystery of the disappearance of a young man from Twinsbury, Ohio, was solved on October 30. Robert C. Moe, 20 years old and a sophomore at Ohio State University, had mysteriously disappeared ten days earlier. The youth's father, the Reverend W.C. Moe, and University officials had been searching for young Robert Moe, when his father received a letter stating that he was in the U.S. Army stationed temporarily in St. Louis. Moe had arrived in St. Louis ten days earlier and signed up at Jefferson Barracks for service in the Hawaiian Islands. He was at Jefferson Barracks awaiting transfer.[77]

Gambling has always been endemic in the military, but on an Army Post in the 1920s, it was a way of life. Every company building had its day room where the men could play cards or shoot pool. Playing for money on the premises was against army regulations, but since the officers gambled at their officer's club, they closed their eyes to the whole thing. To attempt to do otherwise would probably have been impossible anyway, because as soon as a game was closed down in one place, another would immediately spring up elsewhere.

The stakes were often high in both poker and craps games. One of the top gamblers at Jefferson Barracks, a Bandsman who averaged $1,000 a month from poker, tried to get transferred to Schofield Barracks, Hawaii, because the stakes were said to be the highest anywhere. Every month the routine was much the same: the big winners in each company would move on to the basement of headquarters barracks near the stable for a final game.

If there were big winners, there were also big losers. "Jawboning" - living on credit - was an ancient tradition in the army, and most enlisted men jawboned from month to month, hoping each payday to recoup their losses. Loan sharks would advance them money at twenty-five percent interest. Or they could trade the canteen checks they drew for cash, but these would bring only half their value, and the little cash they received would soon disappear. They also would hock what was left of their civilian clothing at a pawnshop a few miles from the post, where it would usually remain unclaimed.

The men were paid in the morning and the poker games usually began at 10:00. William Jay Smith wrote that his father would appear at lunch time on ordinary days with great brown bags of commissaries and loaves of fresh bread. Unless he was on guard duty or unless there was a parade, as there always was on Friday afternoon, his main duties were frequently finished for the day.

On payday, his father never appeared at noon, never in the afternoon and sometimes not until late at night or early the next morning. [When the lights went out in the barracks, the poker and crap games would go on in the basements, in the tailor shops or in the latrines.] If his father did not appear until noon the following day, it was clear that something had gone wrong.

William Jay Smith states that the rent on their Smith Avenue house was $15 a month, and with the subsistence allowance they were able to scrape by - that is, if his father's monthly pay arrived home intact. But that was rarely the case. He would sometimes bring home as much as a hundred times his pay; at times, he would arrive without a cent. The reason was quite simply poker. Smith's father was an intense and devoted poker player. Gambling was a poison with him as it was with many other enlisted men.[78]

1924

The year 1924, like the previous year, offered the usual and monotonous routine of garrison life, at least for the 6th Infantry. There was a break in the routine as the entire regiment (with the exception of a small caretaking detachment) spent the summer of 1924 at Camp Custer, Michigan, overseeing CMTC training. For the second straight year, no CMTC took place at Jefferson Barracks.

Soldiers from Jefferson Barracks continued to use the National Guard Rifle Range in St. Charles for their annual target practice. Jefferson Barracks was represented at the Infantry's National Rifle Match at the U.S. Army Rifle Competition at Niagara, New York, by Lt. R.R. Street. This qualified Lt. Street to be a designated member of the Infantry's National Match team.[79]

Col. Halsey Yates relinquished command of the post to Col. David L. Stone on 2 September. Col. Yates left to assume command of Governor's Island, New York.[80]

Col. Stone, born David Lamme Stone on 15 August 1876, graduated from West Point in the Class of 1898 and received a commission as a second lieutenant in the 22nd Infantry. He was promoted to first lieutenant 2 March 1899. He became a captain in the 26th Infantry 20 April 1903, then transferred back to the 22nd, Infantry 6 May 1903. Stone was detailed as regimental quartermaster on April 3, 1908, at Fort Sill, Oklahoma, and served as constructing quartermaster from 20 April 1909, until 8 April 1912, when he was assigned to the 8th Infantry. Stone again transferred on 19 April 1912, this time to the 25th Infantry at Fort Lawton, Washington, and then went on to Hawaii. He again served as quartermaster from 1 September 1915, until 14 May 1917. Stone was promoted to major of Infantry 15 May 1917, and put in charge of building Camp Lewis at American Lake, Washington. He was made a temporary lieutenant colonel, 5 August 1917, and detailed as quartermaster 1 September 1917. He became division quartermaster at Camp Greene, North Carolina, on 15 December 1917, and then 3rd Division Quartermaster and G-1 in France. He was appointed a colonel in the National Army 11 May 1918, and served with the 3rd Division in World War I. He took part in the 3rd Division defense when attacked by Germans at Chateau-Thierry, in the pursuit of the German Army from the Marne River to the Vesle River, and the re-direction of the St. Mihiel Salient and Campaign in the Argonne Forest. Stone was relieved from the 3rd Division and assigned as G-1, 2nd Army, on 25

September 1918, and took part in the operations of the 2nd Army toward Metz in November 1918.

Stone was awarded the Distinguished Service Medal for exceptionally meritorious services. As Assistant Chief of Staff G-1, 3rd Division; as G-1 of that organization and later as G-1, 2nd Army, he performed his important duties with distinction. In the action from 5 June to 2 August 1918, near Chateau Theirry, and in the advance to the Ouigq River, he displayed tireless energy and an ability of an unusually high order in supplying troops under most difficult conditions. Aggressive and resourceful, he proved equal to every emergency.

Brigadier General Hugh A. Drum, Assistant Chief of Staff, arrived at Jefferson Barracks 13 December to inspect the post. Drum was looking toward establishing a CMTC at the post in the summer of 1925. At a luncheon of active and reserve officers at the Y.M.C.A., Drum stated that public support of the proposal would be helpful. Drum went on to say that he was open to convincing, but had not gone far enough into the matter to say whether the camp would be established here.

General Drum explained that Congress had appropriated enough money in 1924 to train 28,000 men in the citizens' camps. By decentralization, Drum had been able to get 34,000 out of 52,000 applicants trained. He hoped to accept 32,000 or more young men in 1925.

General Drum, in his luncheon address, said he liked to talk over "the fine accomplishments of the Missouri troops in the war with acquaintances in the 35th Division here and recalled that his Army career began as a second lieutenant at Jefferson Barracks in 1898."[81]

During the 1920s and 1930s, everything inside and out at Jefferson Barracks looked as if it had just been scrubbed and polished, for the very good reason that it no doubt had been. Nothing was left uncared for, right down to the lowliest mule. Indeed, the mules were the pride of the post. The stables were immaculate, and the mules were so combed and curried by the "mule-skinners" of Service Company that they looked as if they had been groomed for races rather than for their lowly duty of dragging equipment.[82]

1925

The year 1925 began and continued throughout much as the previous several years with routine and unexciting garrison duties being the norm. Col. David L. Stone remained in command the entire year with Lt. Col. George W. England serving as post executive officer. Other officers on Col. Stone's staff included Capt. N.D. Finley, Adjutant and Lt. Col. E.G. Bingham, Surgeon.

In June, 500 recruits from Camp Custer arrived at Jefferson Barracks for basic training. This training was conducted by the 6th Infantry officers and non-commissioned officers.

General Drum must have been impressed with Jefferson Barracks when he inspected the post the previous December, as CMTC returned to Jefferson Barracks after a two-year absence. Lt. Col. England was assigned to command the camp. Fifty-eight regular officers, including three chaplains, were assigned to the CMTC staff.

The CMTC reached its peak as an adjunct to military activity in 1925. The idea had grown in popularity as Chambers of Commerce and other civic organizations had taken an interest in its promotion. The reason behind the camps popularity can be found in the words of President Calvin Coolidge: "The CMTC are essentially schools of citizenship."[83]

In 1925, the CMTC was open to young men who were physically and mentally sound, between the ages of 17 and 24, in a four-year sequence of courses entitled Basic, Red, White, and Blue. All necessary expenses were paid by the government, and the camps were distributed throughout the country so as to make access easy in every section. Military instruction was given for the first year in the Infantry, but thereafter at the choice of the candidate in the Infantry, Cavalry, Artillery, Engineers, or Signal Corps. The schedule provided for military drill in the morning hours with afternoons devoted to physical training which was provided through a variety of sports. Evening recreation included movies, concerts, amateur dramatics, dances and indoor games in theaters, clubs and hostess houses.[84]

Jefferson Barracks had switched from the 7th Corps Area to the 6th Corps Area in 1922. As such, enrollment for the 1925 CMTC at Jefferson Barracks came from men living in the 6th Corps Area, along with young men from Arkansas and the surrounding 7th Corps Area.

New CMTC young men get issued their military equipment for the 30-day stay at Jefferson Barracks.

Col. Halsey E. Yates assumed command of Jefferson Barracks on 21 March 1922. Yates also assumed command of the 6th Infantry on the same date.

This "baby blimp" was used for instruction at Scott Field, which was the center of the Army's lighter-than-air activities. Officers frequently used the blimp on official business trips to Jefferson Barracks, passing over Belleville and St. Louis.

Aside from the 3,000 men at Camp Custer, the 6th Corps Area sent 500 new candidates to Jefferson Barracks. St. Louis and adjoining counties to the south in Missouri sent men to Jefferson Barracks, while other sections of Missouri sent men either to Fort Des Moines or Fort Leavenworth. The CMTC enrollment in Missouri was especially the concern of Mr. Carl F.G. Meyer of St. Louis who was the State Civilian Aide to the Secretary of War. In his work of enrollment and entertainment at Jefferson Barracks, he was greatly assisted by a Citizen's Committee under the chairmanship of Col. Albert T. Perkins, manager of the United Railways of St. Louis.[85]

On 23 July 1925, the CMTC began at Jefferson Barracks. Young men from Missouri, Illinois and Arkansas arrived at the Jefferson Barracks train station and hiked to the camp area located on the parade ground.

The days of the young men were planned from reveille to taps so that every minute would be occupied. The boys were made "to work hard and play hard." Attractive prizes were offered for both.

The 1st Battalion reported for duty on 23 July, were immediately "processed" and were very soon learning the duties of a soldier and citizen. The training schedule was extremely complete and was rigidly adhered to. The result was a battalion of five hundred boys that any commander could point to with pride.

The men hailed from Arkansas and Missouri: Companies A, B, and C from Arkansas and Company D from Missouri. There was no feeling of hostility within the battalion, but there seemed to be some hard feelings between Illinois of the 2nd Battalion and Arkansas of the 1st Battalion. However, it all passed away harmlessly if one considers harmless such things as throwing buckets of water into bunks and hurling epithets back and forth.

After the companies were served with baseball honors there was very little left, as Company "D" won first, Company "B" second, and Company "A" third place in the baseball league.

The boys from Missouri returned to their respective homes still saying, "You've got to show us," while the boys from Arkansas departed for the sunny southwest still of the opinion that it takes a sharp one to beat a "razorback."

Clarence Weems, of the Jeffersonian staff, noted that so much happened between the beginning of camp on 23 July and the end on 21 August, that it was hard to give even an idea of the 30 days that were spent at Jefferson Barracks. But Weems, with a bit of good luck, hit on a sure way to provide an interesting story of the camp. He happened to pass a friend of his from Winchester, Arkansas, the only and original Aaron "Zero" Zenon and asked him to tell Weems his version of the story at Jefferson Barracks. Zero scratched his head, leaned on one of his bowed legs for a minute with the other making circles in the ground and then agreed. What follows is Zero's story.

"For several years I had been hearing about the Citizen's Military Training Camps held all over the country in the summer, but I had never thought seriously about the question until last fall, when one of my friends back in Winchester, Arkansas, came home from Fort Leavenworth, brim full of tales of the times he had had at camp. He soon got me interested enough so that I wrote to the state CMTC headquarters for information. I found that ever since 1921 the government has been carrying on summer training camps all over the country, as a part of the program of national defense. Any American boy, seventeen or more years of age, who is physically sound may go to one of these encampments. The letter from the CMTC officer told me that the student's transportation to camp is paid by the government, that all food and clothing used during camp are furnished him, and that all he needs to bring with him are a few toilet articles and pieces of linen and a desire to learn."

"My friend kept urging me on, letters kept coming from the CMTC officer and I finally decided to apply for a 1925 camp. I filled out the application blank, secured a certificate of character, took a physical examination, including a smallpox vaccination and inoculation for typhoid and sent in my application. After quite a stream of letters from headquarters, I was notified that I had been definitely accepted for the camp at Jefferson Barracks, beginning 23 July. A little yellow card, bearing instructions to proceed to camp and red-and-yellow stickers for my baggage came several days before I was to leave."

"Wednesday afternoon July 22, I bade farewell to the old corner drug store and the little white cottage under the hill and took the train for Little Rock. There I found the platform crowded with boys, and strange to say, every one of them had a "Citizens' Military Training Camps - National Defense" tag on his suitcase. When they all got packed into three special coaches, there wasn't an empty seat anywhere. Right there I began to see that I was on my way to something big and worthwhile. A stormy night, when spitoons and light bulbs played hide-and-seek from behind carefully turned seatbacks, brought the 'Arkansas Special' to Jefferson Barracks."

"Officers met the seventy or more rookies at the depot and started a line up the hill to the post buildings. The first view of the post - with its rolling parade ground, green with close-cut Bermuda, its long rows of brick barracks and its stars and stripes floating in front of the post hall - presented a pleasing picture from the first. A granite slab bearing the inscription: "Jefferson Barracks, 1827" impressed us with the age and the security of this, one of the early American army posts. It is the home of the 6th Infantry Regiment, which has seen important service in the Revolutionary War, the War with Mexico, the Civil War, the Philippine Campaign, the Cuban Campaign and the World War. I was to learn that its Commander, Colonel David L. Stone, would also be the Commander of the CMTC, and that the officers and men from the 6th Infantry would form the basis for the corps of instructors in camp."

"We got our first taste of Army life in the form of light "chow" at the chaplain's tent. The rookies put down their baggage and went for a handout of sandwiches and lemonade. Most of us had had nothing since supper the night before, and the long ride in the day coach had given us a good appetite."

"Next, the process of classification into companies began. Each man pulled out his little yellow tag and handed it in to an officer seated at a desk. The officer hunted in his card file for the sheet bearing the same serial number as that on the card presented and ordered the man to a company according to the classification previously made. Just across the room was a line of officers, each representing one of the eight companies in the camp. As a man was told to go to any one of the companies, he took his place behind the man from that company."

"The non-commissioned officer leading our group marched us to our company street, where we set our suitcases down and left them for the rest of the day. The first sergeant of our company took over our valuables and we were marched across the field to get our physical examination."

"With blanks for our physical qualifications in our hands, we were started into a long tent. When my turn came, I started in and took a brown sack, which I was soon to know by the dignified term 'barracks bag'. I little dreamed what curious and untried adventures were ahead of me, and I was certain that they would indeed be curious enough when we were commanded, 'Strip, and put your civilian clothes in your barracks bag.' Having fulfilled the command, each rookie filed out and up a flight of stairs to the shower baths. He took his shower, picked up his barracks bag and fell in line along one of the long rooms occupied by doctors and orderlies. The dentist, parked sedately in an open window to insure sufficient light, gazed into the dental recesses of many a gaping mouth and called out to his assistant to 'cross out lower 4 or 'class 2' applying to the victim in hand. From this test, the rookie went on to the scales and under the measuring stick, where his weight and his height were duly found and recorded. The long line moved slowly on and gradually each subject in turn posed for the oculist, the ear, nose and throat specialist, the skin specialist and the lung and throat expert. With blanks fully made out, the line passed on to the clothing room, thoroughly dressed in raincoats and smiles. Measures were taken for shoes, suits and hats, and the line passed on by a long counter, where shoes, breeches, socks, shirts, hats, ties, belts and fatigue clothes were handed out in rapid succession."

"Well thumped and measured, the newcomer swung his two barracks bags on his back and started for the dressing tents. Here he began the real job of turning from a civilian to a soldier. All those unnecessary strings on the bottoms of his breeches, those long rolls of brown leggins that would never hug the legs smoothly and worst of all, those wide, bulky shoes gave the boy fits and fidgets. And yet, when he had finally arrayed himself - woolen shirt, breeches, leggins, shoes, and hat - he felt quite satisfied with the world in general, himself included."

"To me, as to others, all this was new and interesting. As soon as six men were fully outfitted, they were led back to the company street. It wasn't far, but to me, with those stiff shoes on and with two bags on my back, it seemed miles. Arrived at the company street, each one of us was assigned to a tent. Next, we marched to one of the post warehouses, where we checked in our civilian clothes. The company supply room was the next stop. Here each man was loaded with a mattress, a pillow, a cot, bed linen, mosquito net, pack, "T" irons and ornaments for the shirt-collar. Needless to say, we all had to make two trips. Then, with the help of a sergeant - for a CMTC every regular, whether he be private, corporal or sergeant, is known as "sergeant" - the cot was placed, holes were bored for the "T" irons to hold the mosquito net, the pack was adjusted properly, and the puzzling strings and tapes of the United States Army mosquito net were adjusted. By this time, 'chow' was ready, and everybody decided to call it a day."

"The second day was mostly taken up with 'processing' late comers and with adjusting and getting things in final shape around the tents. The third day proved quite a different story. At five o'clock, the bugle called not only the Regulars in the post, but the CMTC greenies as well. There was no time for rubbing eyes and stretching now. Fifteen minutes later, the companies lined up for reveille. The cannon shot and a stirring march by the band put the rookie into a military atmosphere from the first. 'Policing the company street,' was the next order on the program. I really didn't know why any police-duty was necessary; there were no marauders or tramps in sight. But when the captain ordered, 'Pick up every match-stick and piece of paper,' I knew very well that he meant 'clean up'. That was familiar enough, and we filed down the street, behind tents, through the line of officers' quarters, picking up orange peelings, cigarette stubs, match-sticks and what-not."

"From policing the street, we had to move quickly to get back to our tents and make up our bunks and sweep before morning 'chow' at 5:30. Lined up in a column of twos, the hundred or more boys in each company marched up the street along the line of barracks buildings and across in front of the fire-station to the handsome concrete mess hall. Oatmeal, fruit, eggs, toast, butter, potatoes and coffee in abundance were already on the long tables and with the command 'take seats,' the hungry crowd showed that they could use their hands and mouths efficiently."

"At 6:45 o'clock each company formed and marched without hats or shirts, to the parade ground for physical drill. When 'close up', 'cover in file', 'extend on number one', 'rear rank one pace to the left, uncover', and a few other commands had been given and after a fashion executed, Lieutenant Palmer jumped to the low platform and commanded: 'Battalion, (Echoes –'Companee!' 'Platoon!') Atten-SHUN.' Over two thousand heels were supposed to click, and over two thousand arms were supposed to fall to the side, but alas, how few could remember that 'SHUN' was the magic word that no muscle should move until that syllable was uttered, and that at it every arm, every head and every foot should snap into position. "The first exercise will be from the position of hands over head. A full bend forward, keeping the knees straight, thus. Thirty counts. Ready: Exercise! One, two, three, four........" and so on and on for twenty minutes. Arms, legs, chest, head, shoulders, toes - each and all had a few minutes of strenuous exercise. Then, at the command 'double time back to company street,' the companies assembled on number one and started at a rapid pace from the parade ground."

"The rest of the morning was taken up with elementary drill. 'Right face,' 'left face,' 'squads right,' 'squads left,' and 'forward march' echoed from company to company all over the broad drill ground. Operations were stopped for chow at 11:45, and the tired, homesick mob retired in rout to its tents. Baseball, basketball, tennis, volleyball and track were the order for the afternoon, and everyone in camp was required to go out for one of these sports. Many a youth, thinking that he would not be found missing in the afternoon formation, stayed in the shade and quiet of the chaplain's tent, only to find his name posted on the bulletin board under the encouraging heading 'Kitchen Police for tomorrow."

"Retreat' at five-fifteen was carried out in the CMTC program as it is in the Regular Army. Each company marched behind its guide to the parade ground and was drawn up in set formation. At the appointed moment, the bugles sounded 'Retreat' and the command was shouted, 'Parade rest!' Then, with the last blast of the bugles and with the roaring shot from the cannon higher up on the green, the clear notes of the 'Star Spangled Banner' were heard and each company commander gave the order, 'Present arms'. When the last note died away, the command, 'order arms' was given and the regular announcements for the following day were made."

"As for me, the day had been full enough and strenuous enough to make me tired and ready for some amusement. Supper over, I wandered up to the post hall and found that 'Riding Thunder' was being shown inside. Of course, I took in the show. When it was over, I passed by the chaplain's tent and stopped there to have a chat with Chaplain Fell. I found magazines, checker boards, mah jong sets and chessmen on the tables. Writing paper could be had for the asking and stamps were on sale. An hour of writing and reading here and I was ready to turn in by 'Tattoo' at 9:15."

"The next day was Sunday. Instead of waking at 5 o'clock the lazy sleepers could stay in bed till 6 o'clock, with fifteen minutes to get ready for 'Reveille' and a half-hour for breakfast as usual. The services of the Episcopal Church and of the Roman Catholic faith were both held in the Post Chapel with Chaplain Fell and Chaplain Higgins officiating. For Protestants, there was another service, for no particular faith, in the Chaplain's tent."

"Fatigue clothes were the official uniform for Monday morning. The company marched to the company supply room and drew rifles and rifle slings. It was easy for me to recognize the rifle handed to me, covered and soaked in cosmoline as it was. But when it came to the long leather strap, with numerous fasteners and leather 'keepers' scattered around, I really didn't have any idea where or what was what. It took us the whole afternoon to clean our rifles with kerosene and to get our slings adjusted, even with the help of an officer."

"The first day of drill with rifles brought a host of new things to remember. The first principles of the 'manual of arms' had difficulty in soaking through the brains of many of us. 'Right shoulder arms' and 'present arms' and 'order arms' seemed simple indeed when it was done by a trained 'reg'lar,' but when it came to doing it myself, it seemed that it just wouldn't come out right."

"Soon a new feature was brought into the morning program. 'Citizenship' talks were given by each company commander. Our captain, in his first talk, went into the beginnings and development of what we call citizenship. Talks on the Constitution, the American Army, and other subjects related to citizenship were given."

"Immediately after or before this talk to the individual companies, the whole student body of nearly 1,100 was gathered in the grandstand for a short lecture. A talk by Major Carol on 'First Aid,' a lecture on America's spirit of helpfulness and friendliness as shown in Russia, and a talk on 'Citizenship,' by a prominent lawyer from East St. Louis, Ill., were among the talks given at this period."

"After about two weeks of regular drill, we were given three days of work in sighting, to prepare us for shooting on the rifle range. Those on the machine gun range were given similar work, but on a larger scale. I was told to lie prone on the ground and sight through the peep-sight of a rifle laid in two notches in a wooden box. The next step was to sight at a blank sheet, over which a black disk, with a hole in the center for marking, was moved at the order of the student behind the rifle. We were told to sight thus three times and to have the three points formed by the markings connected to form a triangle. The smaller the triangle, the better the score. This was repeated until a fairly small triangle was formed. Then the boxes were moved to a more open space and the rifles were sighted on large targets at a range of two hundred yards. Here the same process was used, except with larger discs and larger triangles".

"On Monday morning of the third week, our company marched out through the post grounds, passed the chapel, and on out the highway toward the U.S. Veterans hospital, where hundreds of veterans of the World War and other wars are given careful treatment. At the fork of the hospital road and the highway, the column turned to the right and started into the woods. Down a hill, around the shoulder, and we were almost on the targets themselves. The 'pit' where the frames for the targets were set up was a long trench protected in front by a concrete wall and overhead by board and earth. Two hundred yards up the hill was the 'firing line' The company, puffing and blowing from the climb, finally got lined up behind the stakes some 15 yards from the firing line. Each one of us advanced to the line in his turn, with wild tales of the rifle that 'kicked like a mule,' ringing in his ears and with his heart pounding fast. But the coach on the firing line saw that the sling was drawn right on the left arms and there wasn't really any room for the rifle to 'kick'. After firing ten shots in practice, I was started on my record, in which I failed to make the required score by one point, due to bad luck and inexperience."

"During the last week of camp, the Authorities gave the boys in camp the biggest treat of the whole month. The St. Paul, 'Excursion Queen of the Mississippi,' drew up at the dock just below the barracks, loaded to the guards with pretty girls. The 1100 sheiks and 'jelly-beans,' dolled out as they were in khakies and hobnail shoes, danced and played the whole day long and almost forgot that they were soldiers. The whole trip was very enjoyable, and we all appreciated it."

"The last formation in the camp was made Wednesday afternoon, August 19th. The medals for success in marksmanship and in the different athletic contests were awarded on the parade ground, in the presence of a large number of citizens from St. Louis. These boys who were lucky enough and good enough to get one of these rewards were lined up in front of the companies drawn up on the grass. I wasn't in that bunch myself. As each prize was awarded, the company fellows of the lucky man gave him a hearty handclapping."

"The ceremony was immediately followed by a farewell message from our Commander, Colonel David L. Stone. He extended an invitation to all of us to consider Jefferson Barracks as our home and to come back here whenever we have the opportunity. He complimented us on our progress since we came to camp. Over and above all else, he emphasized the idea of 'Citizenship.' The regimental colors, which had been entrusted to the CMTC at the beginning of camp, were formally returned to the regiment. Retreat was sounded and the one thousand boys stood for the last time with their rifles at 'present arms' in salute to the flag. A regimental parade followed and all eight companies passed in review before the commanding officers and before the winners in the various contests.

"And now, during the last days of camp, when boys were getting their 'civies' from the warehouse and beginning to think of home, I, for one, want to say that my remembrances of the camp will be pleasant and that I will use any influence I can to bring others here. We owe a debt of appreciation to Colonel Stone, Lieutenant Colonel England, the various regulars and reserve officers, and the vast group of civilians outside, who have had to do with making the CMTC at Jefferson Barracks a success."

That was "Zero's" story. When he had finished, the one thousand and thirty-six other CMTC boys could agree to what he had said. The camp at Jefferson Barracks was a first year camp and the boys turned out from here were not intended to be thoroughly trained; instead, they were put through one of four courses which prepare a young man for a commission. Into these thirty days, many useful lessons and experiences were crowded and many things were learned that would not be forgotten.[86]

After the close of CMTC on 21 August, the garrison returned to its normal routine for the remainder of 1925. Only one further event of consequence took place during 1925. At the end of October, the Chemical Warfare Service, 6th Corps Area, published a memorandum regarding chemical warfare training. In the October 31 memorandum, it stated that Training Memorandum No. 2, Headquarters Jefferson Barracks, included training in Chemical Warfare for all Rifle, National Guard, Headquarters and Service Companies. It also stated that SSgt. Samuel A. Denton, Chemical Warfare Service, would conduct a winter training program.

In compliance with the Training Memorandum a demonstration of White Phosphorus Hand and Rifle Grenades took place at Jefferson Barracks on 25 November for the officers and men of the 1st and 2nd Battalions of the 6th Infantry. Training included the use, nomenclature, functioning, methods of firing, destroying of duds and burning effects of White Phosphorus on the body.[87]

1926

The new year, 1926 began with at Jefferson Barracks with continued training in chemical warfare. A school for officers and another for non-commissioned officers took place from 4 January to 15 January. The schools covered subjects such as chemical agents; physiological effects and their first aid treatment; the care, handling and storage of chemical warfare munitions; the care, handling, nomenclature and fitting of gas masks, and (my favorite) the adjustment of the horse mask-[88]

Col. Stone left for Washington, D.C., on 18 March 1926, to accept an appointment as Assistant Secretary of War. Lt. Col. George Washington England assumed command of Jefferson Barracks. The military history of Lt. Col. England is a part of the history of the 6th Infantry. England joined the army as a volunteer in the 1st District of Columbia Regiment on 12 May 1898, and served in the Spanish-American War. He accepted a commission as a second lieutenant of regulars on 22 November 1901, and was assigned to the 6th Infantry. For a quarter of a century England was one of the 6th Infantry's most competent and energetic officers. He retired from active service on 28 February 1934. [89]

Col. Moor N. Falls relieved England as commanding officer of the post on 4 May 1926. At the time of Col. Falls's arrival, there were 1,200 officers and men on duty at Jefferson Barracks.[90]

13 May was set aside as "Hospital Day" at the Post in honor of Florence Nightingale. About 5,000 visitors witnessed a unique program. One of the featured events was the wheel chair race, won by "Sunny Joe" Morrison, who had been permanently disabled in the Battle of Belleau Wood. Paul Edwards, Charles Docktell and John Tezar, all veterans of World War I, also won prizes.[91]

Col. Falls ordered a week-long training program for the Organized Reserve Officers of the 7th Corps Area in Chemical Warfare to take place from 18 June to 25 June. This was part of the Reserve Officers summer camp held at Jefferson Barracks.[92]

It is interesting to note some of the subject matter covered in this summer training course as it provides the names of some of the officers assigned to Jefferson Barracks at the time. The training memo was issued by Capt. R.G. Cousley, 6th Infantry and Post Adjutant, and stated that Capt. Bollenbeck, Post Executive Officer, was in charge of the training. Capt. Rener and a detachment from Company E, 6th Infantry, provided a talk and practical demonstration on the automatic rifle with range firing on the morning of June 18. In the afternoon, Capt. Egan and a detachment of Company H, 6th Infantry, gave a talk and practical demonstration of the machine gun. On Monday 21 June, 1st Lt. Nelson and a detachment of Headquarters Company gave a talk and demonstration on the 37" Gun and Stokes Mortar. Also on Monday, Capt. Parker and a detachment of Company C, 6th Infantry, provided a demonstration of the Rifle Squad and Platoon. Tuesday morning, 22 June, 1st Lt. Whatley gave a talk on the Service Company and Capt. Slate and a detachment of Company A, 6th Infantry, gave an explanation and demonstration of Scouting and Patrolling. Capt. Hartman and a detachment of Companies I, K and L, 6th Infantry, gave an explanation and demonstration on Rifle Company attack on 23 June. Thursday, 24 June belonged to SSgt. Denton and a detachment of Company G, 6th Infantry, who provided information and demonstrations of Hand and Rifle Grenades and the use of Gas Masks. On Friday, 25 June 1st Lt. Wilson and a detachment of Headquarters Company gave a practical demonstration and explanation of Regimental and Battalion Command Posts.[93]

The 1926 CMTC organized on 7 July. About 1,800 youths participated in the camp that followed the same agenda as the 1925 camp. The first boat excursion took place on 14 July with a dance following the excursion. The Red Cross chaperoned the dance which was attended by about 500 beautiful young ladies from St. Louis. The CMTC included participation in the Washington University field meet.

Another feature of the 1926 CMTC had the students engage in a march and establishment of a camp on 3 August. The students, under the supervision of 6th Infantry personnel, assembled at 2:30 p.m. on 3 August, and began their march carrying full packs, less ammunition and rations. There were three battalions of students with one rolling kitchen for each two companies.

On the morning of 4 August, special field exercises began and mock battle operations commenced. The students marched back to Jefferson Barracks at the end of the day.[94]

A detachment from Jefferson Barracks was stationed at the grounds of the Greater St. Louis Exposition held in Forest Park during the summer. The troops provided added security and gave military demonstrations.[95]

Also in 1926, the building that is today used as the Park Visitors Center underwent alterations and repairs in order to convert it into a tank repair station for use by the 1st Platoon, 6th Tank Corps. The building, originally completed in 1878 for use as a stable, was remodeled, inspected and accepted by the Quartermaster Corps, 6th Corps Area by 12 May 1926.

When finished, the building provided a storehouse and repair shop for tanks, plus sleeping quarters for guards. The Superintendent of Construction at Jefferson Barracks supervised all work and purchases of materials for the project. But unlike most construction projects at military posts, the labor was actually done by enlisted men. Materials for the project cost $356.52, and the enlisted labor amounted to $229.60, bringing the total cost of the project to only $586.12. [This is considerably less than the remodeling done in 2003/2004.][96]

1927

The year 1927 continued much as the previous year had passed. Early in the year SSgt. Samuel A. Denton reported to the Chief, Chemical Warfare Service, 6th Corps Area, that Companies K, L and M, 6th Infantry, at Jefferson Barracks had received instructions and a practical demonstration in the use of the gas mask and C.N. Candles. They also received a lecture on Chemical Warfare agents, First Aid and Chemical Warfare Weapons.[97]

Continuing Chemical Warfare training took place again in February given to the various 6th Infantry organizations at Jefferson Barracks. The 1st Battalion and Headquarters Company received training in chemical agents, First Aid treatment, and individual and collective protection. The 2nd and 3rd Battalions received training in W. P. and C.N. Hand and Rifle Grenades.

Two demonstrations took place on the old cavalry drill grounds. Munitions were issued to the companies after they assembled on the field. Preliminary instructions and a demonstration were provided on the firing of these weapons before the men actually fired them. Company commanders then segregated their companies at a safe distance for firing the hand grenades. The rifle grenades were then fired by company as only one barricade had been constructed. After the C.N. hand grenades were set off the men marched through the cloud to get its effect on the eyes. Many tears were shed and the morale of the march was broken upon entering the cloud.[98]

The memo also reported that Staff Sergeant Denton would be transferred to Fort Sheridan, Illinois, and replaced at Jefferson Barracks by Staff Sergeant Charles F. Barnes. Staff Sergeant Brown instructed the 1st Battalion, 6th Infantry, in the use of hand and rifle grenades, W.P. and C.N. during March.[99]

The rifle range at Arcadia received improvement during 1927, which made it acceptable for target practice once again. From this time forward, until a new range was constructed at Moss Hollow near Barnhart, Missouri, the Arcadia Range was used for annual target practice. Companies I, K and L, 6th Infantry departed in June to participate in the National Rifle Matches at Camp Perry, Ohio.[100]

Detachments of the 331st Infantry from Waukegan, Wisconsin, and the 244th Infantry from Princeton, Illinois, arrived at Jefferson Barracks in early July for basic training. ROTC training also continued at Jefferson Barracks during the summer.

The Citizen's Military Training Camp at Jefferson Barracks had become an institution. The largest camp yet held at Jefferson Barracks, in terms of the number of young men attending, took place in 1927. Almost 1800 boys enjoyed the privileges of the beautiful and historic army post as guests of Uncle Sam. The interest in this movement had increased tremendously and in every way had manifested itself through the cooperation which the Military Training Camps Association received from businesses and individuals throughout the city.

All difficulties seemed to have been overcome and the forecast was that, because of the exceptional facilities available to the young men, the number of applicants desiring to join in this outstanding activity would far outnumber the quota allowed. Great credit must be given to the interest evidenced by Col. Moor D. Falls, in command of Jefferson Barracks, and his staff of officers of the post and the reserves.

While the government supplied the clothing, food and sleeping accommodations, other equipment such as athletic equipment, prizes, medals, entertainments, etc., had to be provided elsewhere. Without the slightest difficulty, these requirements were supplied by an enthusiastic and generous group of men and women, and none of the boys possessed of average capabilities left camp without some souvenir or mark of their prowess on the parade ground or in the athletic contests.

The lumber for a permanent dancing pavilion was supplied gratis by some of the area's prominent lumber yards. The National League Baseball Club generously donated admission to ball games, and through Col. Albert T. Perkins, manager of the United Railways, transportation on the street car for the boys as well as for the young ladies for the semi-weekly dances was made available without cost. The Junior Chamber and other civic organizations contributed beautiful loving cups, medals and badges in great variety and number.

The Moving Picture Industries supplied much constructive and amusing entertainment and so, in every way, the young men were generously remembered.

Special mention should be made of the cooperation given by the Local Chapter of the Red Cross headed by Mrs. Frank Hammer, who supplied the young ladies for the dances, properly chaperoned, much to the delight of the citizen soldiers.

Jefferson Barracks contributed a great deal of work to the development of real American Ideals for coming generations.

The Citizens Military Training Camp at Jefferson Barracks began on 7 July 1927. Early morning trains brought loads of young men who found their way with the help of a guide to the chaplain's tent. Later trains carried still more. Street cars brought the boys from St. Louis and its vicinity. Those who could afford it or if one had enough friends he could afford it, for "five can ride as cheap as one," came in taxis. At the Chaplains' tent, the students learned their companies. From the company orderly tent, the young men went to the "processing" quarters. There they were given a thorough physical and mental examination. They were also given a barracks bag in which to put their civilian clothes, and a raincoat in which they could walk over to the supply tents and the warehouse, where clothing was issued.

Between the processing tents and the warehouse there was a small tent where the rookies' sizes were taken. Boys who had been used to wearing shoes size 7 were surprised when they were told to put down size 8 or 8 ½. They were still surprised when after putting on the socks they tried on their shoes, and they fit perfectly. They were then under the impression that Uncle Sam knew his business. By the time they had passed through the warehouse, the empty barracks bag which they carried over from the processing tent was quite full. From the warehouse, they proceeded to a tent with their company number on it and dressed as well as they could. The result was surprising - they looked just like soldiers. If they were hungry, there was a light form of "chow" consisting of sandwiches and coffee in the chaplain's tent. At twelve, dinner was served, and what a meal! All day long the boys poured in. Those that came after three o'clock were processed and issued clothing the following day. They were very few, however, but they certainly felt out of place.

The afternoon was spent in wandering around and in staring at the high-brow regulars. Supper was served after the impressive ceremony of retreat, and how they enjoyed that first supper. Some had to sit still a while before they could move from their chairs, they had eaten so much. Nearly everybody went to the movies that night. Each had a different reason. Some went because they were used to going every night; some went because they seldom had a chance to see a movie; still others went because they were lonesome and homesick and wanted to forget it. The picture was "Frisco Sally Levy." There was quite a bit of humor in it and it was thoroughly enjoyed by everyone. The first day ended with taps at 10:00.

The next three days were spent in ease, and Friday the oath of allegiance was taken by every boy in camp. It was a soul-stirring moment and each boy repeated the oath with as much feeling as he could put into it.

On Saturday, the boys drilled for the first time. The drilling consisted of the position of a soldier; the position of attention and the facings. The boys learned quickly and they picked up everything as fast as it could be given to them. They were given rest at frequent intervals and the first drill was a decided success. The remainder of the day was a holiday. More than a few of the boys went into town to spend the time giving Saint Louis the "once over," or to see some of the theaters for which it was noted. Sunday morning services were held in the chapel and later in the morning Chaplains Jones and Higgins addressed students who crowded the baseball stands. The speeches were amplified and not one word was lost. The week started on Monday with intensive drill. This time the work of Saturday was reviewed and "squads right" and "squads left" was taken up. During the rest period, every boy received a bottle of milk. They were also lectured at this time by a commissioned officer on Citizenship. In the afternoon, the teams were organized and they played their first games.

Tuesday evening, the first CMTC dance of the season was held. Car loads of pretty girls from St. Louis came out to entertain the boys. The initial dance, like each succeeding one, was an immense success. This was evidenced by the fact that at each following dance more and more girls came.

The rifles were issued on Wednesday. It took the boys many painstaking moments to wipe off the grease with which the rifles were covered. The guns were heavy and at first, they were handled clumsily, but after the boys could handle them with ease, their sense of ownership increased and "next to themselves they liked their rifles best." If some of their girlfriends knew how much the boys cared for their rifles, they would certainly sever their relationships. The boys drilled hard for the rest of the week and Saturday morning was ushered in with a parade, under the command of Col. Fox, 341st Infantry Reserves.

The "competence of the men was astounding," Col. Fox exclaimed after the students passed in review before him, I didn't think it possible. And after only six days of drill, too." Col. Falls who, although he had turned the review over to Col. Fox, was more than a casual observer said, "This year's CMTC has broken all records. Today's exhibition exceeded the expectations of myself and every other officer at the post."

During the third week, while some of the students were having the time of their lives, the rest were practicing sighting and firing on the range. The sighting is preliminary to the actual firing and is essential to the art of marksmanship. The range was a good two miles away and the company left early in the morning and stayed all day. The students fired at targets two hundred yards away, each shot counting from five to nothing, when the target is missed altogether. The majority of the students made marksmanship, a fifty-six or more out of a possible seventy-five.

On Tuesday, 25 July, Jefferson Barracks was honored by the presence of Major General William Lassiter, 6th Corps Area Commander, who reviewed the students passing in parade and inspected their whole camp thoroughly. He later addressed them saying, "You learn to be punctual, to be exact in the performance of duties, and you learn to command. The third thing we teach in this investment in citizenship is defense of your country if necessary."

General Lassiter was thoroughly pleased with the Jefferson Barracks CMTC and stated, "I have visited many camps in many years, and I feel sure from what I have seen here, and the officers I know who are training you, that you are getting the best possible training."

Monday, 1 August, was the beginning of the end. It was visitors' day and a parade was given in the morning at nine o'clock. There was another formation at ten o'clock, with the boys marching over to the ball field and filling the bleachers with as much rapidity as they take their seats when the lieutenant orders "seats" at mess. The speeches were punctuated with outbursts of spontaneous applause. Awards were made to the champion teams, whose pictures were taken immediately afterwards.

General C.P. Summerall, the Chief of Staff of the United States Army, arrived at the post early Wednesday morning, just a few minutes prior to the parade of which he was to be the reviewing officer. The general was highly pleased with the whole performance. He watched the squad formation which followed the parade and the rest of the morning program, which resembled an ordinary morning's drill, including the bottle of milk. He also inspected the whole camp. [The general has the highest position in the army and the CMTC's were highly honored by having him among them.]

A final review and parade before Col. Falls and some visiting guests was held at 8:30. How different this parade was from the first one! The arms were handled with careless ease, all movements in unison. The maneuvering was flawless. As the squads drew up in platoons, the men were like veteran soldiers. The platoons, in perfect step, marched nearer and nearer to the reviewing stand where "eyes right" was given; a few steps further, "front". A couple of minutes, and the platoons formed into a column of squads—the last parade was over. The business of de-processing did not take long and soon the CMTC soldiers were civilians again. They wore the same shabby or good-looking clothes that they brought with them, but they all retained the properties that are essentially a soldier's: the sprightly look, the firm step, head and eyes off the ground and lots of self-assurance. By Friday evening the men were all gone, some back to school, some to work and others to loaf; but it is safe to assume that whatever they did, they would always carry with them the memories of the thirty days spent at the Jefferson Barracks CMTC.[101]

As for the organization of the 1927 CMTC, Major Charles A. Ross commanded the 1st Battalion, which consisted of four companies of 250 men each: A, B, C and D. Company "D" had the distinction of being the first CMTC machine gun company formed at Jefferson Barracks.

Capt. Ralph Slate, 6th Infantry, commanded Company "A", with 1st Lt. William A. Harbold, 6th Infantry, 2nd Lt. C.H. Moore, Infantry-Reserve; and 2nd Lt. H.C. Bebb, Infantry-Reserve serving as the other company officers.

The company contained three men in the Blue Course, fourteen in the White Course, twenty-one in the Red Course and the remainder in the Basic Course. The vast majority of the young men came from Arkansas and Illinois.

Capt. Thomas S. Sinkler, 6th Infantry, commanded Company "B", assisted by 2nd Lt. Homer P. Ford, 6th Infantry; and 2nd Lt. A.F. Newkirk, Infantry-Reserve. Company "B" had four men in the Blue Course, twelve men in the White Course, eighteen in the Red Course, with the remainder in the Basic Course. Almost all of the young men in Company "B" came from Illinois, with a few from Arkansas and Missouri.

Capt. Earl Almon, 6th Infantry, commanded Company "C", with 2nd Lt. William E. Lang, 6th Infantry; and 2nd Lt. W.J. Whipple, Infantry-Reserve; serving as the other officers in the company. Company "C" had four men in the Blue Course, eleven in the White Course, thirteen in the Red Course, and the remainder in the Basic Course. The majority of the men came from Illinois.

Capt. Frank E. Brokaw, 6th Infantry, commanded Company "D". He was assisted by 2nd Lt. William G. Stephenson, 6th Infantry; 1st Lt. L.S. Jobe, Infantry-Reserve; and 2nd Lt. A.N. Hickey, Infanry-Reserve. Two men were taking the Blue Course, eight men the White Course, 180 the Red Course, with the remainder in the Basic Course. The majority of the men came from Illinois and Arkansas.

Major Elbert A. Lyman commanded the 2nd Battalion, which consisted of Companies E, F and G. Capt. Dan H. Rener, 6th Infantry, commanded Company "E", assisted by 1st Lt. Rudolph W. Broedlow, 6th Infantry; 2nd Lt. W.Y. McBurney, Infantry-Reserve; and 2nd Lt. W.W. Brown, Infantry-Reserve; Company "E" contained two men in the Blue Course, ten in the White Course, 110 in the Red Course and seventy in the Basic Course.

1st Lt. James C. White commanded Company F and 1st Lt. Walden S. Lewis, 6th Infantry; 2nd Lt. G.B. Strain, Infantry-Reserve; and 2nd Lt. F.A. Benson, Infantry-Reserve; were the other officers in the company. Company F contained two men in the Blue Course, eleven in the White Course, eighteen in the Red Course, with the remaining 120 in the Basic Course. One hundred sixty-seven of the young men came from Illinois, with forty-seven from Arkansas and thirty-nine from Missouri.[102]

Capt. Harry V. Hand, 6th Infantry, commanded Company G, assisted by 1st Lt. Francis X. Oberst, 6th Infantry; and 2nd Lt. L.B. Kiblinger, Infantry-Reserve. The company had two men in the Blue Course, thirteen in the White Course, fourteen in the Red Course, and 126 in the Basic Course. The company contained the most men from St. Louis, but the majority came from Illinois.[103]

The 1927 CMTC appeared to have the best and most recreational activities of any CMTC to that point. Seven dances were held with 1,750 attractive young girls from St. Louis in attendance. The dances took place each Tuesday and Friday night. Sponsored by the St. Louis Chapter of the American Red Cross, these groups of girls represented the Community Center of St. Louis, The Young Women's Hebrew Association, the Western Union Telegraph Company, the Junior League, the Columbus Girls, the Catholic Woman's Club, the Girls Friendly Class, the Missouri State Life Insurance Company, the Missouri Pacific Railway Company and various smaller organizations.[104]

Through a previous arrangement between the Recreation Officer, Lt. Lee Pollock, and the local Red Cross, all girls attending the dances were chaperoned and were furnished with identification badges. The new open air dance pavilion provided ample room for all the students in camp and the splendid music furnished by the 6th Infantry Dance Orchestra, combined with nimble young dancers from St. Louis, made each event a huge success.[105]

All dances were personally supervised by the Recreation Officer who attended each one and with the assistance of the Provost Marshal, the Red Cross Hostesses, and the Chaperones, saw that no uninvited guests attended and the dances were conducted in a manner to insure success from every standpoint.

Free movies were shown in the open-air theater every Tuesday, Friday and Saturday evening. Through an arrangement made with the St. Louis Film Board of Trade, high class picture films and comedies were secured gratis. The motion picture machines and booth equipment were secured gratis from the National Theater Supply Company of St. Louis.[106]

An Amateur Theatrical Group recruited by the Recreation Officer from the ranks of the students brought forth an abundance of vaudeville talent. The show, held in the post theater on the evening of 30 July, provided an evening of mirth and merriment for a capacity audience.

Through the courtesy of the management of the St. Louis Browns and the World Champion Cardinals, the students, accompanied by the Recreation Officer, attended two games played in St. Louis. Cheerleaders provided ample "rooting" for the home teams and the students made a big hit with the fans.

Two river trips on the Mississippi also provided entertainment for the students. The all-day excursion on the steamer *St. Paul* was one of the outstanding events of the camp. With the syncopated tunes of Bernie Washington's colored jazz orchestra and several hundred girls as dancing partners on board, the students did not "miss a step" all day. The post orchestra on the upper deck, refreshments, and a picnic luncheon added to the pleasure of the occasion and the trip was declared a "perfect day" by everyone on board.[107]

Passive recreation, consisting of games of all kinds, was enjoyed by many students at the recreation tent. Another busy place on the post was the Red Cross House, where a Red Cross Hostess was on duty at all times and the students could play billiards, chess, dominoes, indoor quoits and other games, which were provided by the Red Cross Field Director. In addition to the games, writing materials and magazines were supplied free by the Red Cross.[108]

Under the supervision of Lt. Pollock, an intensive swimming program was conducted. Compulsory attendance for non-swimmers, and efficient instructors furnished by the American Red Cross Life Saving Corps made it possible to teach the two hundred non-swimmers who reported at the beginning of camp how to swim, and with practice and application of the instruction furnished them each one can become a good swimmer. A large number of the expert swimmers were instructed in Red Cross Life Saving and qualified as Life Guards. A swimming meet was also held to determine the best swimmers and divers in camp.[109]

Packing every corner of the chaplain's tent, CMTC students were delighted by seven acts of Orpheum Circuit vaudeville presented 21 July. The trip was arranged by Everett Hays, manager of the theater, and I.J. Scully, the publicity representative. The entire company had dinner with the boys in the big mess hall.

Louis London, brother of Jack London, the famous novelist, acted as master of ceremonies. Ben Castle of the Florence Hedges act opened the show with a song. Barnett and Thomas followed with an excellent soft shoe dance. Barnett, a midget, especially pleased the students. Miss Florence Hedges, well known prima donna, sang the opening number from *Rose Marie* next. The boys insisted upon an encore, which was a second number from the same opera.

John Hough, tenor, sang *On the Road to Mandalay*. Numerous other songs followed, then Kelly and Forsythe, musical comedy stars of Broadway, presented a very humorous dialogue which made the students want to miss the afternoon's drill. However, promptly at 1:00 p.m., the artists stopped their program in order that no man might be absent from his duties.[110]

Lt. C.F. Hamilton supervised the calisthenics. Hamilton, when not performing his military duties, was a high school physical education director in Casey, Illinois. He had also been in charge of regimental exercises while in the regular service. Every drill morning the students would fall out about 7:30 for exercise. After much maneuvering, the regiment was called to "batal-yun-n a-ten-shun!" The exercise would be demonstrated and the director shouted, "In cadence, ex-er-cise!" all of which was done by count. There was exercise for breathing, for the legs, for the body and neck muscles. The exercises lasted half an hour. The platoons then did double time back to the company streets and got ready for the morning's drill. After the break-up of the camp, the chest expansion was taken and compared with the chest expansion at the time of arrival. There was not a single boy who did not have a larger chest than he had before the beginning of camp.[111]

Col. Falls explained the purpose of CMTC athletics. He stated that since the beginning of the Citizen's Military Training Camps in 1921, a study was made by officers responsible for the training of the CMTC students to develop a system of instruction which would give the students and the government a maximum benefit.

The World War had taught the necessity of building up the physical condition of the young men of this country, when it was found that approximately one-third of the available man-power of the United States of military age was so deficient physically as to render it unfit for combat service. Something had to be done.

This then became one of the primary goals of the Citizen's Military Training Camps. To this end, athletic exercises and games were made a part of the schedule of instruction. For the young men who did not ordinarily take part in the athletic training offered in their home localities, a special course was offered.[112]

2nd Lt. William H. Arnold, athletic director for the 1927 CMTC explained the athletic program thusly: "Seventeen hundred and sixty-four boys, every one of them a potential athlete, arrived at Jefferson Barracks, July 6th. Their life, as far as athletics was concerned, had already been planned and schedules published designed to give every man a maximum of outdoor exercise. These schedules and plans were drawn up with the idea in view that athletics, properly conducted, are one of the greatest elements for the upbuilding of the character of young America."

"The host of talent was divided among seven CMTC companies, each of which was under the sheltering wing of one of the companies of the 6th United States Regulars. An athletic officer was appointed in each company as assistant to the Camp Athletic Officer and to organize athletics in the respective companies. In addition to the company athletic officers, each sport of each company was under the direct supervision of a regular non-commissioned officer. These company athletic directors were early impressed with the idea that their main function was to whip the material of their companies into shape for the inter-company competitions to come."

"Athletics were divided into two main classifications - competitive and mass. Competitive athletics consisted of baseball, basketball, indoor ball, swimming, boxing, wrestling, tennis and track and field events. The first classification could only include those boys who were athletes in the beginning and to take care of that large body of students not engaged in competitive sports and who were in need of athletic training, mass athletics were made a part of the summer's work. Consequently, every afternoon of the camp students were, for a short period, engaged in wholesome outdoor exercise."

"The first four days of camp were set aside for the use of the company athletic officers in organizing their teams. On the fourth day of camp hostilities began. Clean, hard-fought games were the order of the camp, and the competition resulted in a close race for the coveted medals and "Best Company" awards."

"In wrestling, strong competition was developed. Some very good matches were held and the victors earned their renown."

"Tennis enjoyed a great summer. Every afternoon of the camp saw the three courts in constant demand."

"Perhaps the greatest amount of fun was derived from mass athletics. In some places, belts can be still felt colliding with parts of the student anatomy."

The first CMTC track and field meet took place on 29 July at Francis Field at Washington University in St. Louis. It was a tremendous success, due primarily to the efforts of Lt. C.F. Hamilton, who had worked with the men since the very beginning of camp. Officials were so pleased with the results of this first meet that it became an annual event.

Company B won the meet with Company D second and Company E taking third place. L.L. DeSollar won individual honors by scoring nine points.

In order that the CMTC could be a complete success, it was necessary that competent leaders be placed in charge of every activity. The purpose of these camps was not primarily to make soldiers, but to improve the type of citizenship found in the students attending them. In order that this could be accomplished it was necessary that the higher and better qualities of young manhood be developed; that the right kind of ideals be fostered and nourished; and that the high standards of American manhood be held up constantly before the students. The burden of this responsibility rested to a large degree upon the chaplains. The moral and spiritual guidance of the boys of the CMTC was entrusted to them.

The chaplains assigned to this important work for the entire period of the camp at Jefferson Barracks in 1927 were Chaplain Nathaniel A. Jones, U.S.A., and Chaplain Clarence J. Higgins, Organized Reserve Corps. Chaplains assigned to assist in this work for shorter periods were Chaplains Niles A. Boropp, Ernest Lack and Robert Lee Logan.

Religious services, both Catholic and Protestant, were conducted every Sunday. While the students were not required to attend, the services were well-advertised and they were advised to improve their spiritual life by faithful attendance. The numbers making use of the opportunity were large and gratifying.

The chaplains visited the hospital daily, ministering to the spiritual and temporal wants of the boys who were sick, giving a word of cheer or encouragement, and rendering any other service needed.

Col. David L. Stone relieved Col. Yates in command of Jefferson Barracks on 2 September 1924. Col. Stone left Jefferson Barracks on 18 March 1926, to become Assistant Secretary of War. Lt. Col. George Washington England assumed command of the post.

Col. Moor N. Falls relieved Lt. Col. George Washington England in command of Jefferson Barracks on 4 May 1926. Col. Falls also served as commanding officer for the 1926, 1927, and 1928 CMTC.

Mrs. Elizabeth Wilson, Red Cross , arranged for local girls to attend CMTC dances. Mrs. Wilson and Lt. L. Pollock, CMTC Recreation Officer, chaperoned all the dances held during the 1927 CMTC.

A large tent known as the Chaplain's Tent stood near the Post Hall. At their leisure, the men gathered in this tent where writing tables were provided and where stationery, pens and ink were furnished, and wrote thousands of letters to their loved ones at home.

The Chaplain's Tent also served as a rendezvous for visitors. Those who visited the Chaplain's Tent seeking to locate their relatives and acquaintances in the CMTC were assisted in finding them and were offered the hospitality of the tent in which to visit them.

There was some kind of entertainment going on in the tent all the time. When there were no entertainers from the city, the men played checkers and other indoor games in the tent and ran a horse-shoe tournament just outside the tent. An hour in the late afternoon was spent in boxing, to the delight of hundreds of fistic enthusiasts. There was a piano in the tent, and not a little of the entertainment was furnished by the men themselves, playing and singing popular songs.

The chaplains, like all other clergymen, understand human nature and realize that their function is to advise, counsel, encourage and to render to the men aid and comfort in every possible way. The boys recognized this function of the chaplains, for they came to them with confidence, bringing to them their joys and sorrows.[113]

Inasmuch as an Army travels on its stomach, feeding eighteen hundred hungry young men three times a day is no laughing matter. For a long while before the first meal was served, Lt. Pettibone and his staff worked hard to organize an efficient corps of men who could satisfactorily handle a whole regiment at one sitting. The initial thing to be considered was a chef who would supervise the cooking. A French chef was selected and anyone of the boys would tell you that he surely knew his stuff.

He had innumerable helpers who attended to the details of preparing the food. Regular Army men helped get the dishes and tables ready for the first meal. Last, but not least by any means, were the immortal K.P.s - the corporals, sergeants and Col. Falls - but most of the rank and file had it about four and five times, at least, during their residence in camp. There were various things to be done. Some boys waited on the tables and fixed them up for the next meal. The dishes had to be washed, so others worked in the small room where the dishwashing machine was located. In that room, the temperature was generally around a hundred degrees Fahrenheit. The dishes had to be carried and stacked in another room where they were dried and made so hot that when the table waiters went to get them to set the tables, they nearly burned their hands. There were also various other things to be done, such as peeling spuds, cleaning pots and pans, and carrying food in from the trucks.

Almost everyone would concede that K. P. wasn't so bad. It was the long hours that they didn't like.

The chef baked an enormous cake as a special favor to the editor of the *Jeffersonian* and it was presented to Company B, the company which subscribed for the highest number of *Jeffersonians*.

It should be noted that as the CMTC grew in size, it became a serious problem for the officers at Jefferson Barracks and the other camp sites. The Quartermaster experienced increasing difficulty in securing enough supplies and equipment to make it the success it had been during the first years of its organization. However, 1927 can be deemed a grand success and thus ended another year of CMTC at Jefferson Barracks.

A disastrous tornado passed over Jefferson Barracks and cut a wide swath several miles long through St. Louis leaving wreckage and ruin in its path on September 29. Entire blocks literally were razed and sixty-nine persons were killed or injured. All available troops from Jefferson Barracks were rushed to the city to join police and civilians in rescuing the trapped from the wreckage, to restore order, and to provide supplies and relief for those left homeless. As this work progressed the troops turned their attention to cleaning the debris, and many days passed in feverish work before the work was completed.[114]

1928

Thus, passed another year at Jefferson Barracks and the year 1928 saw few changes in routine. Otherwise only occasional inspection visits and a review by a general relieved the monotony.

Officer Reserve Corps and CMTC training continued as in past years. Young men from Illinois, Arkansas and Missouri arrived at Jefferson Barracks for the 1928 CMTC in early July. Their training lasted for thirty days.

The young men were divided into three battalions. The 1st Battalion consisted of Companies A and B, each with two hundred men. Major Charles A. Ross, 6th Infantry, commanded the 1st Battalion. Capt. R. Slate, 6th Infantry, commanded Company A, assisted by 1st Lt. C. Moore, Infantry-Reserve; 2nd Lt. C. Higgins, 6th Infantry;

and 2nd Lt. G. Smith, Infantry-Reserve. 1st Lt. Byron Halter, 6th Infantry, commanded Company B, assisted by 2nd Lt. H. Mayes, Infantry-Reserve; 2nd Lt. H. Ford, 6th Infantry; and 2nd Lt. Fred Roberts, Infantry-Reserve.

Capt. G.A. Rose, 6th Infantry, commanded the 2nd Battalion, which consisted of Companies C and K, each with two hundred men. Capt. E. Almon, 6th Infantry, commanded Company C, assisted by Capt. Spainhower, Infantry-Reserve; and 2nd Lt. H. Hay, Infantry-Reserve. Capt. G. Ross, 6th Infantry, commanded Company K, assisted by 1st Lt. Crump Garvin, 6th Infantry; Capt. Vrooman, Infantry-Reserve; 2nd Lt. R. Benard, Infantry-Reserve; and 2nd Lt. John W. Copeland, Infantry-Reserve.

Major L.P. Ford, 6th Infantry, commanded the 3rd Battalion which consisted of three companies, I, L and M, each with two hundred men. Capt. M. Cowley, 6th Infantry, commanded Company I, assisted by 1st Lt. C. Ankerm 6th Infantry; 2nd Lt. H. Bennett, Infantry-Reserve; and 2nd Lt. L. Smith, Infantry-Reserve. Company L was commanded by Capt. George Nielson, 6th Infantry and assisted by 2nd Lt. E. Nelson, Infantry-Reserve; 2nd Lt. Willis S. Matthews, 6th Infantry; and 2nd Lt. C. Ulrich, Infantry-Reserve. Capt. A. Croonquist, 6th Infantry, commanded Company M, assisted by 1st Lt. L.S. Jobe, Infantry-Reserve; 1st Lt. R.H. Vesey, 6th Infantry; and 2nd Lt. H. Lindstrum, Infantry-Reserve.

As in past years, the men participated in military training and drill in the mornings with athletic training after lunch. Men from each company took part in White, Blue, Red and Basic training.[115]

Each afternoon the parade ground was filled with students engaged in some type of sport. There were half a dozen or more baseball games taking place at the same time as basketball, tennis and mass athletics. The annual swimming meet took place on 30 July, and the track and field meet on 1 August. All sports held a tournament to determine a camp champion.

Capt. Stanley G. Backman, 6th Infantry, who had only recently been ordered to Jefferson Barracks after spending five years at the University of Georgia as an Army representative, was in charge of all athletics at the 1928 camp. Intercollegiate rules were used for all athletics, modified to suit camp conditions as regarded size and age of the students.

At Georgia, Backman had been assistant coach of football and baseball, head coach of boxing and dean of men. Before the World War, Backman had been associate coach at the University of Cincinnati. For three years beginning in 1923, he was in charge of athletics for the R.O.T.C. at Camp McClellan, Georgia, and in 1926 was camp athletic officer for the same camp, on the general staff. Backman was assisted by Capt. Lee Pollock, 306th Military Police; 1st Lt. R.W. Broedlow, 6th Infantry; 1st Lt. C.F. Hamilton, 52nd Infantry, at St. Joseph, Illinois; and the following company athletic officers: Company A - 1st Lt. Charles H. Moore, 6th Infantry, reserve at Alton, Illinois; Company B - 2nd Lt. Homer P. Ford, 6th Infantry; Company C - 2nd Lt. H.S. Hayward, Chicago; Company I; 2nd Lt. L.L. Smythe, 344th Infantry, Malden, Illinois; Company K - 2nd Lt. Roland Bernard, 407th Infantry, St. Louis; Company L - 2nd Lt. Willis S. Mathews, 6th Infantry; Company M - 1st Lt. L.S. Jobe, 6th Infantry Reserve, Mattoon, Illinois.[116]

Shortly after the end of CMTC, work began on a project to establish a permanent camp site and the erection of necessary buildings and utilities for CMTC and Officers Reserve Corps encampments at Jefferson Barracks. Work actually began on 14 August, with the selection of a sewer line route. The total cost of this project came to $46,203.57. Six buildings were constructed. Buildings No. 246 and 247 served as CMTC lavatories, Building No. 248 as Post Exchange, Building No. 250 as an officers' lavatory and Building No. 251 an officers kitchen and mess. The total cost of these buildings came to $32,594.11. In addition to the six buildings, new sewer and water lines, curbing, two tennis courts and repairs to the dance pavilion were constructed.

Although the project began in August 1928, final acceptance and payment for the project did not take place until 14 December 1929.[117]

Companies A, B and C, 6th Infantry, and the 1st Platoon, 6th Tank Company, received chemical warfare training during June 1928. All the men in these units received training in gas mask drill and in the wearing of the gas mask during extended order drills and combat exercises over difficult terrain. They also received training in the use of hand and rifle grenades.[118]

In November 1928, extensive training in chemical warfare took place at Jefferson Barracks. Companies B, C, D, E, F, G, H, L and K, 6th Infantry received between six and eight-hours of training covering types of chemical weapons such as toxic gasses and smoke, gas defense, chemical agents and first aid, and the use and care of gas masks. The 1st Platoon, 6th Tank Company received three hours of training in gas mask drill, gas defenses, and the use of gas and smoke. Battery F, 3rd Field Artillery, received two hours of training in gas mask drill, duties of gas sentries, the use of gas and smoke, and the care of material.[119]

Headquarters Company, 6th Infantry, enjoyed a fabulous Christmas dinner of roast turkey, roast loin of pork, oyster dressing, mashed potatoes, candied sweet potatoes, creamed peas, and Parker House rolls, with pumpkin pie, mince pie, coconut and chocolate cake for desert. The festive repast was prepared under the supervision of Mess Sergeant Thomas J. Hilburn. Capt. George C. Nielson, Company Commander and 1st Lt. Rudolph W. Broedlow served as hosts for the one hundred and seven men of Headquarters Company.[120]

1929

An announcement reached Jefferson Barracks on 22 January 1929, that the post was to be raised to the rating of a brigade post and that Brigadier General George H. Estes of the 9th Corps Area of the Pacific Coast had been ordered to assume command of Jefferson Barracks. General Estes assumed command from Col. Moor N. Falls on 16 March 1929. Col. Falls transferred to an executive position with the National Guard in Chicago. In addition, Col. Pegram C. Whitworth assumed command of the 6th Infantry at Jefferson Barracks. Col. Whitworth had been stationed as an Army representative at the University of Arkansas.

While the announcement of the change in status for Jefferson Barracks was recognized as a special honor for the post, the transfer of Col. Falls caused some sad feelings, not due to any lack of honor for General Estes, but because the departing commander had been a capable and considerate individual. As the St. Louis *Globe-Democrat* put it, "a real friend of St. Louis;" a friendship based upon nearly two years of pleasant association.[121]

Brig. General Estes did not assume immediate command of the post upon the departure of Col. Falls on 15 March. Major Louis P. Ford, a Tennessee cadet in 1905, acted as commander until 2 June, when Lt. Col. John Randolph relieved him. Randolph had begun his army career as a private in the 6th Infantry on 31 August 1898.

Gen. Estes finally assumed command of Jefferson Barracks on 11 June 1929. A few weeks later he presided over 1,617 young men attending CMTC at Jefferson Barracks. It had been thirty-four years since Estes had left West Point with his commission as a second lieutenant, but he was not immune to the exuberance of youth, and applied himself with passion to the task of training the young men to shoot.

The 1929 CMTC was officially named Camp Skinker in honor of Capt. Alexander Rives Skinker, a St. Louis native who was killed in action in the Battle of the Argonne, France, on 16 September 1918, while commanding Company I, 138th Infantry, of the 35th Division. He was awarded the Congressional Medal of Honor, the highest decoration for heroism beyond the call of duty that the United States can award. The citation accompanying his award reads as follows: "*Unwilling to sacrifice his men when his company was held up in terrific machine gun fire from iron pill boxes in the Hindenburg line, Captain Skinker personally led an automatic rifleman and a carrier in an attack on the machine guns. The carrier was killed instantly, but Captain Skinker seized the ammunition and continued through an opening in the barbed wire, feeding the automatic rifle until he, too, was killed.*"

The streets in the camp were named for the following World War I heroes all of whom received the Distinguished Service Cross for their actions:

Sergeant Abe Short, Aurora, Arkansas
Capt. Herbert D. Ryman, Mount Pulaski, Illinois
Private Willard D. Petty, Joliet, Illinois
First Lieutenant Joseph W. Emery, Jr., Quincy, Illinois
Private Charles Disalve, St. Louis, Missouri
First Lieutenant Clement P. Dickinson, Clinton, Missouri
Corporal Joseph G. Armisted, San Antonio, Texas.

Col. Charles W. Weeks, 52nd Infantry, and Col. R.L. Floyd, 344th Infantry, commanded the CMTC regiment. First Battalion officers included Major C.A. Ross, 6th Infantry; Major R.A.P. Holderly, 6th Infantry Reserve; and Major Robert G. Evans, 344th Infantry. Second Battalion officers were Lt. Col. Charles T. Smart, 6th Infantry; Lt. Col. Oscar Kaufman, 344th Infantry; and Major Oldham Paisley, 344th Infantry. The 3rd Battalion officers included Capt. F.E. Brokaw, 6th Infantry; and Lt. Col. James A. Walrath, 344th Infantry.

The 1st Battalion consisted of Companies B and C. Company B consisted of 278 young men with three in the Blue course, sixteen in the White, twenty-five in the Red, and the remainder taking the Basic course. Capt. A.G. Hutchinson, 6th Infantry, commanded the company with Capt. Charles E. Guetig, 344th Infantry; 1st Lt. J.H. Carlin, 52nd Infantry; 1st Lt. R.H. Vesey, 6th Infantry; 1st Lt. Max M. Adelman, 344th Infantry; 1st Lt.William E. Reminger, 344th Infantry; and 2nd Lt. Grant Bechtel, 344th Infantry; rounding out the officer corps for the company.[122]

1st Lt. P.E. Hunt, 6th Infantry, commanded Company C with Capt. Charles W. Conrad, 344th Infantry; 1st Lt. E. Rutishauser, 52nd Infantry; 1st Lt. B. Thorman, 344th Infantry; 2nd Lt. C.F. Howard, 6th Infantry; 2nd Lt. G. Pigg, 52nd Infantry; 2nd Lt. Arnold E. Pendell, 344th Infantry; 2nd Lt. Guy S. Peters, 344th Infantry; and 2nd Lt. Byron E. Hargrove, 344th Infantry, assisting. Company C consisted of 275 young men with five in the Blue course, seventeen in the White, twenty-three in the Red and the remainder in the Basic course.

The 2nd Battalion was made up of Companies E and F. Capt. J.R. DeVall, 6th Infantry, commanded Company E, with Capt. Daniel R. Kenshalo, 344th Infantry; 1st Lt. A.T. Newkirk, 52nd Infantry; 1st Lt. Carl D. Olmstead, 344th Infantry; 2nd Lt. P.E. Schewe, 6th Infantry; 2nd Lt. E.A. Thompson, 52nd Infantry; 2nd Lt. Robert Ashley, 344th Infantry; and 2nd Lt. William Below, 344th Infantry, rounding out the company's officer corps. Company E consisted of 275 young men. Four young men participated in the Blue Course, sixteen in the White Course, twenty-nine the Red Course, and the remainder took the Basic Course.[123]

Company F consisted of 277 young men who were commanded by 1st Lt. F.E. Hein, 6th Infantry, whose assistants included Capt. John R. Funkhouser, 344th Infantry; 1st Lt. R.J.C. Griffith, 52nd Infantry; 1st Lt. G. Porman, 52nd Infantry; 1st Lt. John C. Werchman, 532nd Infantry; 2nd Lt. R.W. Hastings, 6th Infantry; 2nd Lt. Robert H. Elliott, 344th Infantry; and 2nd Lt. Leon J. Smyth, 344th Infantry. Company F had five men in the Blue Course, thirteen in the White, twenty-five in the Red and the remaining 234 in the Basic Course.[124]

The 3rd Battalion consisted of Company D, the Howitzer Company and Headquarters Company. Capt. F.E. Brokaw, 6th Infantry, commanded Company D, which contained 250 young men. Company D had ten men in the Blue Course, thirty-two in the White Course, and seventy-five in the Red Course with the remaining 133 in the Basic Course. Capt. Cyrus A. Geers, 344th Infantry; 1st Lt. R.W. Odor, 6th Infantry; 1st Lt. S.T. Holzman, 52nd Infantry; 1st Lt. S.A. Moore, 52nd Infantry; 1st Lt. Richard D. Chapman, 344th Infantry; 2nd Lt. R.S. Watts, 52nd Infantry; 2nd Lt. Harry L. Leatherman, 344th Infantry; and 2nd Lt. Chesney C. Ewing, 344th Infantry, assisted Capt. Brokaw.

The Howitzer Company, nicknamed the "Broom and Bucket Brigade," consisted of 133 young men commanded by 1st Lt. Crump Garvin, 6th Infantry, [and ably assisted] by 1st Lt. W.H. Moore, 52nd Infantry; 1st Lt. A.J. Hohnansky, 52nd Infantry; 2nd Lt. H. Doud, 6th Infantry; 2nd Lt. Fred S. Rippinger, 344th Infantry; and 2nd Lt. Lewis McD. Teirner, 344th Infantry. The Howitzer Company included five young men taking the Blue Course, sixteen in the White Course, seventy-one in the Red Course, and the remaining forty-one in the Basic Course.[125]

Headquarters Company, commanded by 1st Lt. R.W. Broedlow, 6th Infantry, consisted of 129 young men, of which four participated in the Blue Course, eleven in the White Course, seventy-five in the Red Course, and the remaining thirty-nine in the Basic Course. Assisting Lt. Broedlow were 1st Lt. C.C. Higgins, 6th Infantry; 1st Lt. W.P. Delahaunty, 52nd Infantry; 1st Lt. Grover Schubkegal, 344th Infantry; 2nd Lt. E.M. Madson, 52nd Infantry; 2nd Lt. Russell F. Edwards, 344th Infantry; and 2nd Lt. John W. Copeland, 344th Infantry.[1]

All the young men who participated in the 1929 CMTC came from Illinois, Arkansas and Missouri. The vast majority came from Illinois.

Athletics, Recreation, and Publicity for the 1929 camp were grouped in one office with the duties of the three departments interlocking. All were under one officer in charge, and the duties of the assistants were distributed among these three activities.

Athletics and Recreation consisted of the supervision of the following: Baseball, Basketball League, Playground Ball League, Speed Ball League, Boxing Tournament, Wrestling Tournament, Track and Field Meet, Tennis Tournament, Swimming Meet, Swimming Instruction for Non-Swimmers, Physical Proficiency Tests, Volleyball, Amateur Theatricals, C.M.T.C. Dances, Passive Recreation, and free trips to Major League Baseball games in St. Louis. Practically every student in camp engaged in some form of organized athletics. Prizes in the form of medals and cups were awarded in all athletic contests. Over 350 such awards were distributed among the CMTC personnel.

The Publicity Department furnished spot news and weekly letters to approximately 900 newspapers in Missouri, Illinois and Arkansas, and also daily items to all St. Louis publications. This department also published a four-page daily newspaper. *The Camp Skinker News*, printed with linotype composition on regular newspaper stock.

Two thousand copies were printed each day except Sundays and holidays. All composition was donated by the St. Louis *Post-Dispatch* and the printing was done on the Jefferson Barracks press. This newspaper contained cuts and news of activities concerning the CMTC and was undoubtedly one of the most popular features of the camp.

The Red Cross house on the post was open at all times to the CMTC students. This house contained facilities for various games, along with reading and writing materials. The students spent many pleasant hours at the house when not engaged in drill or athletics. Mrs. Gertrude Force of St. Louis was in charge as hostess.[127]

The chaplains assigned to work with the CMTC students during the 1929 camp were Nathaniel A. Jones, Regular Army Post Chaplain; Clarence J. Higgins, Reserves; and Arthur O. Ramsey, Reserves.

Religious services were conducted every Sunday. In their chronological order, these services took place at 8:00 a.m. for a general meeting featuring a moral and patriotic talk; at 8:45 a.m. for Catholic Mass; a 9:30 a.m. mens' bible class; and at 6:30 p.m. a vesper service was held.

The large auditorium in the Post Chapel was fitted up as a recreation center. Writing desks and writing material could be obtained in abundance. Hundreds of letters were written in the auditorium each day. Games such as checkers and dominoes were also furnished. Entertainment was provided by the students themselves or by outside talent. At almost any hour, the young men would be gathered about the piano, playing and singing.

A banking system was established in a room adjacent to the auditorium. Here the boys could deposit their money for safekeeping or draw it out as they needed it. About $7,000 of the students' money was handled by the chaplains during the camp.

The students felt that the chaplains cared about them. They came to the chaplains for advice, information and guidance.[128]

All 1617 young men received three good meals each and every day. The personnel of the CMTC mess prepared each of these meals. That comes to 4,851 individual meals each day for thirty days or approximately 145,530 individual meals. The instructors and officers of the camp must be fed, and all the permanent party of the post also. 1st Lt. Arthur E. Dewey served as CMTC Mess Officer and Staff Sergeant Charles Pinnick as mess supervisor. They supervised the work of sixty-one mess personnel.[129]

Certainly, not of the least importance was the post medical staff whose job it was to maintain the health and welfare of each and every trainee. Major William F. Hall, Medical Corps, served as Post Surgeon. His staff consisted of five other medical doctors, one dentist, Major Thomas L. Smith; and one veterinarian, Capt. Raymond L. Lovell.[130]

Just over a month after the 1929 CMTC concluded, on 11 September, General Estes relinquished command of Jefferson Barracks to Col. Pegram C. Whitworth. After graduating from West Point on 12 June 1894, Whitworth became a second lieutenant in the 18th Infantry. He proved his worth as an army officer in the Philippines, winning three citations for bravery. When the United States entered World War I, Whitworth was made a brigadier general commanding the 72nd Infantry Brigade. Marshal Petain, commander-in-chief of the French armies in the East, decorated Whitworth with the following citation: "A general officer who showed a great courage and remarkable energy at the head of his brigade during the operation of 8 October 1918, near St. Etienne; was able to lead and encourage, with much ability, his men who fought for the first time. Though several times under very violent bombardments, he continued to give orders with great coolness."[131]

The 6th Infantry was reorganized into two battalions on 31 October 1929. The 3rd Battalion was placed on the inactive list. The Jefferson Barracks garrison, at this time, consisted of the entire 6th Infantry, a Quartermaster detachment, a medical detachment, the 1st Platoon of the 6th Tank Company, an ordnance and engineer detachment, and the recruit detachment.[132]

The 1927 CMTC athletic staff. These men oversaw all the various sports activities for the young men attending the camp.

The Chaplain staff for 1927 CMTC.
The chaplains often provided often much needed support for the young men, many of whom were away from home for the first time. Left to right: Capt. Clarence J. Higgins, Capt. N.A. Jones, and 1st Lt. A.C. Ramsey.

Brigadier General George H. Estes relieved Colonel Falls in command of Jefferson Barracks on 16 March 1929, but did not actually assume command until 11 June 1929.

Birdseye view of Jefferson Barracks ca. 1920s.

Capt. Alexander Rives Skinker
The 1929 CMTC was officially named Camp Skinker in honor of Capt. Skinker, a St. Louis native who was killed in action in the Battle of the Argonne on 16 September 1918, while commanding Company I, 138th Infantry, 35th Division. He was awarded the Congressional Medal of Honor.

6th Infantry Regimental Day, 4 November 1926.

The year 1929 went out with a bang at Jefferson Barracks. The Red Cross hut was the scene of the gayest dance of the season on New Year's Eve. A large Christmas tree adorned the center of the ballroom and the colorful costumes of a masked crowd enhanced the atmosphere. (Note: the list of those attending provides the names of all the officers and their significant others stationed at Jefferson Barracks at the time.} Those attending were: Col. and Mrs. Pegram Whitworth; Lt. Col. John Randolph, Miss Margaret Randolph; Major and Mrs. Thomas L. Smith; Major and Mrs. Arthur R. Underwood; Major and Mrs. Louis P. Ford; Major and Mrs. Arthur C. Tipton; Major and Mrs. Henry S. Cole; Major and Mrs. Frank W. Romaine; Capt. Edwin W. Grimmer, Miss Marguerite Grimmer; Capt. Glenn A. Ross; Capt. and Mrs. Arthur G. Hutchinson; Capt. and Mrs. Joseph L. Connelly; Capt. and Mrs. Stanley G. Backman; Capt. and Mrs. Richard M. Sandusky; Capt. and Mrs. Sherman P. Walker; Capt. and Mrs. Nathaniel A. Jones; Capt. Raymond L. Lovell; Capt. and Mrs. Paolo H. Sperati; Capt. and Mrs. John T. Sunstone; Capt. and Mrs. Aubrey J. Bassett, Lt. and Mrs. Ray H. Larkins; Lt. and Mrs. Clifford D. Overflet; Lt. and Mrs. Rudolph W. Broedlaw; Lt. and Mrs. John H. Judd; Lt. and Mrs. John D. Eason; Lt. and Mrs. Clinton J. Anker; Lt. and Mrs. James B. Howatt; Lt. and Mrs. Robert H. Vasey; Lt. and Mrs. Raymond W. Oder; Lt. and Mrs. Nathan A. Smith; Lt. and Mrs. Edwin M. Sutherland; Lt. and Mrs. Arthur L. Moore; Lt. and Mrs. Bryan S. Halter; Lt. and Mrs. Crump Garvin; Lt. and Mrs. Leonard L. Hilliard; Lt. and Mrs. Charles H. Higgins; Lt. and Mrs. August E. Schanze; Lt. and Mrs. Welborn B. Griffith; Lt. and Mrs. Willis S. Matthews; Lt. and Mrs. Howard H. Hastings; Lt. A.E. Dewey, Miss Jane Pelton of St. Louis; Miss Margaret Ellen Thompson; Mr. And Mrs. Carlyle Odor of Columbia, Missouri; and Miss Elizabeth Underwood of Washington, Missouri.[133]

Chapter 9- Decade of the 1930s

For the enlisted men, the army in the decade of the 1930s was a school, an athletic club, an orphan's home, and a boy's camp all rolled into one. That wasn't a bad thing considering that a man got room and board, his clothes, and twenty-one dollars a month.

Twenty-one dollars a month for a private doesn't sound like much, but there was opportunity for advancement if a man stayed in the army long enough. He might make private first class on his first enlistment and possibly corporal in eight to ten years. The army was not a place for an in-and-outer. A popular barracks story illustrates this point: The men of an Infantry company gathered around the bulletin board to read the order promoting a private to private first class. "What is this man's Army coming to?" one soldier complained in disgust. "Hogan is promoted to first class and he only has six years' service. I'm going to transfer to a good outfit." It was not entirely a joke, for a survey of the 2nd Infantry Division at Fort Sam Houston, Texas, in the mid-1930s showed the average length of service for privates to be three years; that of private first class, five years; corporals, twelve years; and sergeants, eighteen years. Sergeants of the first three grades, the elite of the non-commissioned corps, averaged twenty-four years of service.[1]

The officer corps, during the same time period, enjoyed a busy and varied social life. The *St. Louis Post-Dispatch* even ran a weekly column entitled "Jefferson Barracks: Items of Social Interest from the Army Post." It can be seen from reading this column that officers and their wives entertained at frequent dinner parties and dances. There was a bi-monthly bridge club, theater outings, and much more. It also appears that newly arrived or soon-to-be departing officers often made the social column. The February 2, 1930, *Post-Dispatch* printed that Capt. Edward L. Trett, the newly assigned chaplain at Jefferson Barracks, "will hold religious services at the Post Chapel at 11:45 a.m., and vesper services Sunday evening at 6 o'clock." It should be noted that the post had a Sunday School that started at 9:45 a.m.

Another interesting item in the same newspaper told of the arrival the previous week from Washington, D.C., of Stephen Caufin, photophone engineer from the Adjutant General's office. Mr. Caufin had come to Jefferson Barracks to supervise the installation of talking picture apparatus in the Post Theater.[2]

Valentine's Day 1930 provided the opportunity for another gala dance at the Officer's Club. Major Arthur R. Underwood, Major Arthur C. Tipton, Capt. Raymond Lovell, and Lt. Claude D. Collins supervised the arrangements for the dance. It appears that most if not all of the officers of Jefferson Barracks and their ladies attended the dance as the list of attendees is long. When a dance or dinner party was given, it was practically mandatory that all invited would attend.[3]

Desertion had always been a major problem in the army, but during peace time it seemed to present an even bigger headache. During peaceful times the army could be an extremely dull and boring job. Thus, stories like the following concerning deserters could often be found in the newspapers. It seems that two soldiers overpowered their guard at Jefferson Barracks on 10 March and made a daring break for liberty. Robert L. Jolley, 22, of Pittsburgh, Missouri, and Albert F. Laughlin, 22, of Philadelphia, who had escaped from confinement at the post while at work, dashed through the woods to a highway where they stopped a motorist, robbed him of $15, and took his car. Three hours later the two were apprehended by police and faced charges of highway robbery in addition to a military court martial.[4]

Chemical Warfare training maintained its importance during 1930. All organizations at Jefferson Barracks took part in gas mask training from 25 March to 27 March. On 28 March battalion commanders conducted Chemical Warfare training inspection on the parade ground. Each man had to be prepared to answer any of nineteen questions regarding chemical warfare. Examples of the questions are: "What is the odor of chlorine, phosgene or mustard gas?" and "Give four precautions necessary to properly care for a gas mask and give some favorable weather conditions for a gas attack."

In April, the 1st and 2nd Battalions, 6th Infantry, received training in tactical exercises involving the offensive use of tear gas and smoke designed to show the effect of chemical agents in maintaining superiority of fire. Each company trained in the use of hand and rifle smoke and tear gas grenades. 1st Lt. Charles C. Higgins, 6th Infantry, supervised this training in his capacity as the Post Chemical Officer.[5]

In March, the officers and ladies of the post gave a barn dance at Atkinson Hall. Then in April, they gave a dance at the Officer's Club.[6]

In April, Jefferson Barracks hosted a 6th Corps meeting of officers from the Corps Area. Officers who attended the meeting came from all posts in the 6th Corps Area. Col. John A. Paegeloro, Capt. James F. Powell, Capt. George P. Johnson, Lt. William O. Eackerson, and Lt. Milton T. Hankens came from Scott Field. Other officers attending came from Chanute Field in Rantoul, Illinois; the 6th Corps Area Headquarters in Chicago; Fort Sheridan, Illinois; Selfridge Field in Mount Clemons, Michigan; and Fort Wayne in Detroit.[7]

Also in April, Jefferson Barracks collaborated with the local Boy Scout Council to host a Boy Scout Pow-Wow. Members of the St. Louis Boy Scout Campers' Club were invited to the Pow-Wow. All members of the Campers' Club displaying a Campers' Club button were admitted.

Five main divisions were scheduled for the program, including a demonstration of army tanks stationed at the post, a display of military maneuvers, a parade of scouts and soldiers, a camp dinner, and camp games in the barracks' woods. The Army maneuvers took place in the morning; the afternoon was devoted to the games and other scout activities.

The scouts assembled at the south end of the Broadway car line at 9 a.m., carrying a drinking cup, a spoon and a bowl for hunters' stew. Special cars carried them to the barracks; the same specials made the return trip at 4 p.m.

The St. Louis Boy Scout Campers' Club was an organization of scouts who signed up for attendance at one of the camps to be conducted during the summer by the local scout council. These camps included the regular camp at Irondale, Missouri; the Ranger camp on the same grounds, but separate; an all-summer teepee camp; several roving camps; and several special camps such as the ranger ride through the Ozarks.[8]

Major General Frank B. Parker, 6th Corps Area commanding officer, arrived at Jefferson Barracks on May 8 to inspect the post and review the troops. Arriving with General Parker were Col. E.R. Tompkins, Major A.G. Campbell, Major E.J. Carr and Capt. J.R. Francis. Col. Pegram Whitworth, commanding officer of the post, and Capt. Stanley G. Backman met the general and his party at Union Station. Motorcycle police escorted them through traffic to Jefferson Barracks where the troops were in formation on the parade grounds. When the party entered the east gate, a salute was fired, followed by flourishes from the 6th Infantry Band. The general and his party immediately mounted their horses and reviewed the troops. A reception and military ball was given that evening by the officers and ladies of the post in honor of General Parker and his staff.[9] The next afternoon General Parker was the guest of honor at a luncheon given by the Army, Navy and Marine Corps Council of St. Louis at the Statler Hotel.

The summer exodus of troops to attend special training camps began on May 1. Company E left to spend the summer at Camp Custer, Michigan. The company was transported as far as Collinsville, Illinois, by motor truck, then marched 117 miles to Mattoon, Illinois, where a train carried them for the remainder of their trip. Marches of one hundred miles or more were the rule at Jefferson Barracks, and each of the companies leaving during the summer of 1930 "enjoyed" this experience. The 6th Infantry soldiers had reason to enjoy these hikes as on June 15 an incident took place which put to shame any disposition to complain about these 'short' walks. First Sergeant John Gerechter of the Argentine Army walked into the Barracks on that day. He had just reached the last leg of a 11,430 mile hike from Buenos Aires, Argentina to New York, with Chicago and Washington on his itinerary. He had already walked for two years, seven months and ten days when he reached Jefferson Barracks. He had carried a sixty-three-pound pack all the way and had to get his seventh pair of shoes before leaving. He had traversed almost impenetrable jungles and great wastelands, fought off all sorts of wild beasts and reptiles and still looked happy and hearty and fit for the remainder of his journey. His hike was part of a test of time and endurance between the Infantry and the Cavalry; three years before, a Cavalryman had ridden the same route in two years and four months.[10]

Less than a week after the visit by General Parker, Major General Stephen O. Fuqua, Chief of Infantry for the United States Army, arrived from Washington on an inspection tour of Infantry posts of the central states. Col. Whitworth and Capt. Backman met General Fuqua at the Statler Hotel. They then proceeded by official car to Jefferson Barracks where a 13-gun salute was fired, followed by ruffles and flourishes by the 6th Infantry Band. General Fuqua then reviewed the troops, who were in formation on the parade ground. At 1 o'clock a stag luncheon was held in the Officers' Club in honor of the General. After the luncheon, attended by most of the Jefferson Barracks Officer Corps, General Fuqua addressed the officers on the subject: "The Present and Future Developments of the Infantry."[11]

Capt. Paolo H. Sperati and Lt. Edwin M. Sutherland left with Companies A, B, C, D and H of the 6th

Infantry on May 18 to spend a month at the post rifle range at Arcadia. Improvements at the rifle range had been made intermittently during the past three years and comfortable quarters had been built to accommodate all of these troops. They returned around 22 June.

On Memorial Day, 30 May 1930, services were held at the Jefferson Barracks National Cemetery. It had been sixty-five years since Lee's surrender and only eleven of his former followers still survived in St. Louis and fifty-eight Union veterans remained alive. Many were too feeble to take part in the Memorial Day services. The youngest in the area was P.H. Callahan, 81, a Union veteran.

Once flourishing organizations, by Memorial Day 1930 the Grand Army of the Republic and the United Confederate Veterans were represented by a few white-haired men and rapidly diminishing membership lists. It was estimated that there were once 3,000 Confederate veterans in the St. Louis area and 3,000 to 5,000 Union veterans.

In its peak year, the Confederate group numbered 20,000 to 25,000 in Missouri. The Union veterans had shrunk likewise from 25,000 to 500.

The G.A.R. posts represented were the Ranson Post, the Neumann Post, the Hassendeubel Post, the Harry P. Harding Post, and the Frank P. Blair Post. The Confederate veterans belonged to the St. Louis Camp No. 731 of the United Confederate Veterans.[12]

Most of St. Louis stopped work on May 30 and in some form or another observed the sixty-second Memorial Day since Commander-in-Chief John A. Logan of the Grand Army of the Republic set aside May 30 as a day "for strewing with flowers or otherwise decorating the graves of comrades who died in the defense of their country during the late 'rebellion.' "

In compliance with General Logan's "hope that it will be kept up from year to year," patriotic civic and military organizations had planned the customary services in public places and cemeteries for the purpose of honoring war dead in and around St. Louis. A downtown parade, followed by grave decoration and a memorial service, was the feature of the day in St. Louis. Assembling on Twelfth Boulevard north of Market Street shortly after noon, veterans of the several wars and subsidiary patriotic organizations marched to Washington Avenue and east to Fourth Street, then boarded cars for Jefferson Barracks.

Probate Judge Charles W. Holtcamp, past department commander of the United Spanish War Veterans and A.G. Abreau, Cuban Consul in St. Louis, were speakers at the Barracks services. Following re-formation at the National Cemetery, the various organizations proceeded to their sections to decorate the graves of their comrades.

The largest observance in the St. Louis area took place in Webster Groves, where 7500 members of civic, patriotic and military organizations and school children marched in a parade. The procession, which assembled at 9:30 a.m., was preceded on its route by an army airship and a squadron of army airplanes under command of Col. John A. Pagelow, commandant of Scott Field. As the airship hovered over the monument at Big Bend and Lockwood, three volleys of flowers were let loose.

Civil War veterans, both North and South, those who took part in the Spanish-American War and World War I, the Red Cross, American Legion auxiliaries, Gold Star Mothers, Boy Scouts and Girl Scouts, schools, churches, religious organizations and luncheon clubs participated in the parade.[13]

A special service took place at the Jefferson Barracks National Cemetery on 5 June, when the body of Louis E. Roedner, private in Company L, 38th Regiment, 3rd Division, who had been killed in action on October 24, 1918, was laid to rest. Pvt. Roedner had been killed by high explosives while acting as a runner in the Meuse-Argonne offensive. He had been buried in France for nearly twelve years.[14]

Another special summer activity took place at Soldier Field in Chicago from 21 June to 29 June. A detachment of twenty-four enlisted men and twenty-six members of the 6th Infantry Band attended the 6th Corps Area Military Tournament and Exposition.[15]

Troops also came from Fort Sheridan, Fort Wayne, Selfridge Field, Chanute Field, and Scott Field. They represented all the arms of the service: infantry, artillery, cavalry, engineers, medical, and signal corps. Defense plans of the Sixth Corps Area against attack by land, water, and air were demonstrated. The infantry repulse of an imaginery attack was presented as the defense that the army had been working. This was followed by support from the artillery, cavalry, and tanks and the protection provided by the air service, particularly by means of smoke curtains which was laid by the Chemical Warfare service. The climax of the show was the reproduction of "The Battle of Chateau-Thierry," in which practically every combat arm of the service was used.[16]

By the middle of 1930, radio station WFFT began operations at Jefferson Barracks. It had been built, licensed and operated by Sergeants Snooks, Cooley, and Ross.[17]

In April 1928, the War Department set aside $85,000 for an addition and improvements to the central hospital building. This work had just begun when Sgt. Paul W. Holmes wrote on 4 July 1930 regarding the "old hospital" moved from the original river site as follows: "About the only relics of the original construction of this hospital are the two great open fire places in the Surgeon's and Registrar's offices. We can visualize this building back in the roaring "nineties" when it was heated by iron stoves and open grates and lighted by coal oil lamps of the mid-Victorian period. Two of these shining brass lamps still do duty when the electricity fails as it does occasionally."[18]

The seventh Citizen's Military Training Camp opened on 7 July 1930 and lasted until 5 August. It was the largest camp held to date with over 1600 young men from Missouri, Illinois and Arkansas attending. The name of the 1930 camp was "Camp Joseph Britton" in honor of a St. Louisan, Sergeant Joseph Britton, formerly of Company I, 138th Infantry, who was killed at Varennes, France, on 26 September 1918. For gallantry in action and bravery beyond the call of duty, he was posthumously awarded the Distinguished Service Cross.

The morning program of instruction included calisthenics, training in citizenship, personal hygiene, and military drill. The afternoons were devoted to athletics and recreation.

Col. Pegram Whitworth served as commanding officer of the camp, with Lt. Col. John Randolph serving as executive officer. Capt. R.M. Sandusky served as adjutant; Capt. Glenn A. Ross as plans and training officer; Capt. Stanley G. Backman as athletic, recreation and publicity officer; Capt. A.J. Bassett as supply officer; and Lt. C.C. Higgins as personnel adjutant.[19]

Battalion commanders for the CMTC included Major Louis P. Ford, 6th Infantry, 1st Battalion; Major Arthur R. Underwood, 6th Infantry, 2nd Battalion; and Lt. Col. R.A.P. Holderly, 6th Infantry Reserve, 3rd Battalion. The 1st Battalion included Companies A, B, C and D. The 2nd Battalion consisted of Companies E, F, G and H; and the 3rd Battalion included Companies I, K, L and the Band.

Capt. J.T. Sunstone, 6th Infantry, commanded Company A with 2nd Lt. L. Clarke, 6th Infantry his second in command. Company A consisted of 162 young men. Capt. A.G. Hutchinson, 6th Infantry, commanded Company B with 2nd Lt. B.M. Greeley, 6th Infantry, next in line. Company B consisted of 170 young men. Capt. P.H. Sperati, 6th Infantry, commanded Company C assisted by 2nd Lt. C.F. Howard, 6th Infantry, and 2nd Lt. Gerard A. Byrne, 6th Infantry Reserve. This company consisted of 160 young men. 1st Lt. Crump Garvin, 6th Infantry, commanded Company D with 1st Lt. Cyrus C. Covalt, 6th Infantry Reserve and 2nd Lt. Fred Bender, 6th Infantry Reserve, assisting. Company D consisted of 158 young men. 1st Lt. E.M. Sutherland, 6th Infantry, commanded Company E with 2nd Lt. R.G. Crandall, 6th Infantry serving as his assistant. Company E was made up of 162 young men. 1st Lt. R.W. Broedlow, 6th Infantry, commanded Company F and 2nd Lt. J.W. Hammond, 6th Infantry, served as his second in command. Company F consisted of 162 young men. Capt. S.P. Walker, 6th Infantry, commanded Company G with 2nd Lt. J.C. Stephenson, 6th Infantry, as the second officer. Company G consisted of 160 young men. 1st Lt. J.C. Catte, 6th Infantry, commanded Company H with 2nd Lt. W.B. Griffith, 6th Infantry, assisting. Company H consisted of 160 young men. 1st Lt. R.W. Oder, 6th Infantry, commanded Company I with 1st Lt. Erwin Larson, 6th Infantry Reserve, and 1st Lt. Fred H. Roberts his assistants. Company I consisted of 164 young men. Capt. D.C. Overfelt, 6th Infantry, commanded Company K with Capt. Kenneth H. Knowlton, 6th Infantry Reserve, serving as his second in command. Company K consisted of 160 young men. Capt. J.L. Connolly, 6th Infantry, commanded Company L with the other officers, Capt. John H. Rapp, 6th Infantry Reserve, Capt. Joseph H. Catlin, 52nd Infantry Reserve, and 2nd Lt. Fred A. Benson, 6th Infantry Reserve. Company L consisted of 164 young men. There was also a CMTC Band composed of fifty-three young bandsmen. This made the total number of attendees at the 1930 Jefferson Barracks CMTC stand at 1835.

Each company had young men from Illinois in the 6th Corps Area who represented the majority in each company and young men from Missouri and Arkansas in the 7th Corps Area. Forty-two young men from St. Louis and the immediate area attended.[20]

A provisional battalion of 221 officers and men of the 6th Infantry at Jefferson Barracks reported at Camp Perry, Ohio, on 13 August for special duty at the National Rifle Matches. They were to prepare the camp for other troops and rifle teams which reported August 17. Almost 2,000 troops took part in the four-week encampment.[21]

On 8 September, it was reported that military and civilian authorities were investigating the fatal shooting of William M. Fitzpatrick, First Sergeant, Sixth Tank Company at Jefferson Barracks. He was killed near the military reservation the previous night.[22]

Officers were looking for Cpl. James M. Hill, 6th Tank Company, in connection with the fatal shooting. Orders for the arrest of Cpl. Hill came after Sgt. Albert Francis testified that Hill shot Fitzpatrick in Francis' quarters. Both Fitzpatrick and Hill had been drinking. According to Hill' wife.[23]

In a totally different vein, hunting and trapping was forbidden on the Jefferson Barracks Reservation as of 3 October 1930. This was an effort to conserve the vanishing wildlife on parts of the reservation.[24]

1931

"Hold Soldier As Robber of Ober's," a headline of the sort that all too often seemed to find its place in the newspaper. Low pay may have contributed to this dilemma, but whatever the cause soldiers did not seem to be exempt from criminal behavior. Anyway, this headline appeared in the *Lawrence Daily Journal-World* on 7 January 1931. It seems that a young soldier by the name of Harry E. Barnes, 16, of Peoria, Illinois, had been arrested by Lawrence, Kansas authorities at Jefferson Barracks. Barnes and an unknown companion broke into Ober's Clothing Store in Lawrence and stole $500 worth of merchandise.

It seems that Barnes made only one mistake. He tore an identification card from an old wallet which he left behind, but on the remaining portion of the card Chief of Police W.J. Cummings found part of a name and part of the name of a town. With this clue, Cummings traced Barnes, a regular army private, back through several transfers to find that he enlisted at Peoria, then went to Des Moines, Iowa, then to Detroit, and later to Illinois again. Chief Cummings found Barnes was arrested at Columbia, Missouri, three days after the robbery, and had been turned over to the military at Jefferson Barracks on an A.W.O.L. charge. At Christmas, 1930, Barnes was restored to good standing and assigned to a troop at the Barracks.

Chief Cummings finally talked to the Commandant at Jefferson Barracks after being told by military authorities that he could have custody of Barnes without the proper red tape comparable to "an act of congress." Cummings got his man and returned with him to Lawrence. The loot taken from Ober's Clothing Store included five pile overcoats, four pairs of officer's boots, three sheepskin lined coats, several pairs of riding pants, two sweaters, two cigarette lighters, and shoes, belts, ties, and caps. Barnes had sold most of these items in Kansas City two days after the burglary. Barnes told Cummings that he did not know the name of his accomplice.

There was little change in the routine at Jefferson Barracks during 1931. During April and May, training in chemical warfare took place. Each of the two battalions of the 6th Infantry at Jefferson Barracks conducted two tactical exercises in which gas and smoke was used. All units had an average of fourteen hours of instruction as required by the Headquarters, 6th Corps Area Training Directive.[25]

Although by 1931 the CMTC had become a routine yearly event, it still presented the most significant break of the year from the long boring routine of garrison. The Jefferson Barracks CMTC opened on July 7 with 1949 youths attending. The largest number to date.

The first order of business was the discarding of civilian clothes and manners at the first inspection tent. The young citizen soldiers proceeded through a systematic health examination by officers who functioned as they would when inspecting a new draftee during war times.

Then, clad only in raincoats and shoes, a ragged line of youths hurried through the army's processing system which transformed a civilian into a man in uniform, eager to be assigned to tents of the CMTC.

By noon on the first morning, more than 500 youths had received their khaki uniforms and by sundown most of the 1949 recruits had been scheduled to be outfitted. All but three of the student soldiers were from Missouri and Illinois. One youth came from Iowa, one from Kansas and one from South Dakota. There were fifty-two boys from St. Louis.

Only a portion of the time was devoted to military drill. Citizenship and first aid classes were held during a part of each morning, while supervised athletics took up the afternoons. Each youth was required to pass a swimming test before camp ended.

Many of the young men arrived in camp in groups traveling in dilapidated cars bearing chalked or painted legends. They anticipated tenting together, but friends were intentionally separated and given new tent mates. One of the objectives of the camp was to afford residents of different communities a chance to get acquainted and exchange ideas.[26]

Refreshed by bottles of milk and a cool breeze the young citizen soldiers went through their first drill during the morning of July 9. Divided into squads, the summer soldiers were told how to stand properly, salute smartly and execute simple squad movements. Lessons were also given in military courtesy.

Squads dotted the parade ground under the watchful eyes of 6th Infantry officers as noncoms barked their orders, interjecting an occasional "please" in deference to the youth and inexperience of the student soldiers. Each recruit received a bottle of milk during one or two 15-minute rest periods during the morning drill.[27]

As James Munday, a 1931 attendee, put it; "We drilled four hours a day in the shade of the ancient oak trees, within the perimeter of the old military cemetery. At our first morning break, they would serve us bottles of chocolate milk. I thought I'd died and gone to heaven!"[28]

The CMTC troops were assigned to companies, A through H, Headquarters and Band. The regulars in each company aided in instructing the youths. Each company, including CMTC troops and regulars, contained around 250 men, full war times strength.

By 90 July, enrollment at Camp Howze stood at 1600, all but five from Missouri and Illinois. About one hundred youths were rejected for physical disabilities and some of those who received orders failed to report. (P-D, 7/9/1931)

The 1931 CMTC was officially named for Sergeant James Adrian Howze, Jr., "whose loyalty to his country, exceptional courage and gallantry in action above and beyond the call of duty should be an inspiration to the young men of this camp."

Sergeant Howze, prior to enlisting in the Regular Army at the outbreak of World War I, was a resident of Webster Groves, Missouri. While serving as a sergeant in Battery C, 10th Field Artillery, 3rd Division, American Expeditionary Force, he was mortally wounded in action. He died on 17 June 1918 at Base Hospital No. 4 at Nampes, France. Sgt. Howze was awarded the Croix de Guerre and English and French citations. The streets in the camp were also named for the following World War I heroes: Thomas P. Mannion, Laurence J. Stephens, Lee T. Goff, Robert R. Shaw, Joseph A. Moll, Andrew P. Dunker and Walter F. Runge.[29]

Facilities for housing and training the student soldiers were better than ever before. In 1930, a permanent camp site was laid out and several improvements were added. Electrically-lighted tents which had wood floors were called home for country and city boy alike, until the close of camp on August 5.

The government allowed seventy cents a day to feed each student soldier. This is twice the allowance for the Regular Army, and assured a varied and healthful diet, arranged and prepared by Army mess personnel. Despite hot weather and a strenuous program, most boys gained weight.

For the first time, no young men from Arkansas attended the Jefferson Barracks camp as that state had its own encampment, Camp Pike.

The government appropriated $66,835 for the expenses of the Jefferson Barracks camp. A portion of this sum had been spent for a sports stadium seating 3500, where the boxing and wrestling bouts were held. The public was invited to attend these matches, held in the evening, at no charge.

The entertainment program, in addition to athletics, included weekly dances under the auspices of the Red Cross and St. Louis civic organizations, and two visits to Sportsman's Park to view major league baseball games. Medals and trophies for winners in the various athletic and military competitions were donated by the St. Louis Chamber of Commerce.[30]

After a week in camp, the new student soldiers had learned thirty-seven bugle calls. From sunrise to sunset the bugles blew, each call signaling a different activity in the crowded days' schedule. Beginning with reveille at 5:45 a.m. and ending with taps at 10:45 p.m. Of course, the bugle call for mess was the first call learned by the youths.[31]

Major General Frank B. Parker, commander of the 6th Corps Area, arrived on 16 July and informally inspected the CMTC. General Parker commended Col. Whitworth and his officers and men "for the generally high conditions existing at Jefferson Barracks; for the teamwork and high morale present in your command."[32]

Following two weeks of close order drill and instruction in the use of a rifle, half of the citizen soldiers in camp began firing on the rifle range on the morning of 20 July. The entire week was devoted to range practice, including machine gun firing.[33]

Running, jumping and vaulting under a blazing sun, about 250 youths at the Jefferson Barracks camp competed for track and field honors on July 29. Clad in track suits and marching behind their company guidons the

250 athletes, representing all ten companies, paraded in review before Col. Whitworth. Company C won the closely contested track meet.

Medals were awarded the next Saturday, 1 August, after a review and inspection by General Parker.

Competition for the rifle team of seven men which represented Camp Howze at the area match at Camp Custer on 10 August had been narrowed to ten marksmen by 30 July. The thirteen winners of this match went on to compete at the national match at Camp Perry, held on 22 August.[34]

Heads erect, shoulders back and with rifles at the proper angle, the youths of the Jefferson Barracks CMTC passed in review before General Parker during their final exercises on 1 August. The effect of the professional training at the hands of the 6th Infantry Regiment was apparent in the straight platoon fronts and the perfect marching step. The small-town youth had lost his shuffle and the city boy his peculiarities in walking during the month at Jefferson Barracks.

General Parker, who made a minute inspection of each company preceding the review, said the training in which the government had expended $66,000, had resulted "very satisfactorily. The general appearance and bearing of these boys is excellent," the General asserted.

Following the review, Col. Whitworth presented the various awards for military and athletic achievement. Arthur L. Worsec, 3287 Oregon Avenue, a student at Cleveland High School, won the rifle marksmanship award with a perfect score of 100 shots at 200 yards. Vincent J. Tiefenbrunn, 3633 Lierman Avenue, won second place. Both were members of Company B. The two best pistol shots were Rupert F. Bunham of Jerseyville, Illinois, and Graham Jackson, 8551 Enright Avenue, St. Louis County. Leading machine gunners were Edgar B. Biffle of Bloomfield, Missouri, and Fred Williams of Eldorado, Illinois.

"Best Student" awards were as follows: Basic Course: B.T. Gangle, Dupo, Illinois; Red Course: J.E. Kopta, Robinson, Illinois, and Fred L. Henly, Caruthersville, Missouri; White Course: Fred J. Biggs, Neelyville, Missouri and William Grimes, Jr., Orient, Illinois; Blue Course: Fielding H. Cooster, Webster Groves and S.F. Janeke, Dupo, Illinois.

The month-old young soldiers spent 3 and 4 August turning in their uniforms and equipment, and reclaiming their civilian attire. They departed on Wednesday morning, 5 August.[35]

At the close of camp, Army doctors examined the youths selected at random to learn the physical effects of the training. The examinations disclosed an average weight gain of seven pounds and a gain of one inch in chest expansion.[36]

Camp Perry served as host for the National Rifle Matches again in 1931. The 6th Infantry from Jefferson Barracks again provided soldiers to prepare and support this four-week encampment and the contests that took place. However, things did not go as smoothly as in the past. First, Pvt. James Cartern, 19, received fatal injuries when a car knocked him from his bicycle.[37] In yet another incident Pvt. Dan Bacchatta passed away from pneumonia in September while serving with the 6th Infantry at Camp Perry.[38]

Remember the "Dinky" street car that began serving Jefferson Barracks way back in 1896? Well, on 17 September 1931, the St. Louis Public Service Company asked for authority to abandon its street car line to Jefferson Barracks and substitute motor bus service.[39]

A good example of Christmas Dinner for all personnel at Jefferson Barracks can be gleaned from the menu for the Service Company, 6th Infantry. The Service Company, commanded by 1st Lt. William W. Brier, partook of roast turkey and pork with giblet gravy, oyster dressing, candied sweet potatoes, creamed peas, bread, butter, and cranberry sauce. For dessert, they had minced pie and fruit cake with apples, oranges, bananas and grapes topped off with hot coffee, candy and nuts. A better time and a better meal would have been hard to find anywhere.

Menus of this sort are always a good source for the names of the men in a unit. As mentioned, 1st Lt. Brier commanded the Service Company, whose First Sergeant was Howard L. Mounday; Ira G. Elliott and Philip S. Murphy were Master Sergeants with the names of all the unit's personnel listed under their rank.[40]

1932

The year 1932 started, passed and ended much as most of the 1920s and 1930s. With few exceptions, normal garrison duty was the order of the day. The 6th Infantry Regiment garrisoned Jefferson Barracks, with Col. Whitworth commanding the regiment and the post.

Perhaps this is a good time to explain a bit about recruits and garrison duty. When a recruit joined the army in the 1920s and 1930s, he enlisted for the regiment of his choice and received basic training as a member of the company, troop or battery to which he was permanently assigned. Until he completed his training under the supervision of a non-commissioned officer, usually a corporal, the new soldier performed no other duty.[41]

A man enlisted for three years, and this meant three years' "good time." Any time lost that was not in the line of duty was tacked onto the end of the term of enlistment. If a man was absent without leave, he had to make good the number of days he was gone, plus the time he spent in the guardhouse as punishment. Bad time in the hospital as the result of venereal disease had to be made up, as was time in the hospital as a result of an accident not in the line of duty. If a soldier was hurt in a brawl and went to the hospital, it was not in the line of duty and he had to make up the time lost. There was no pay for such bad time, but the soldier still received three square meals and a bunk wherever he was.[42]

A unique feature of the pre-World War II Army was the purchased discharge, a right that passed into military history with the horse. After twelve months' good time, a soldier could purchase his discharge for the cash price of $120, no questions asked. After two years, the price went down to $100, then it dropped in increments of $10 a year to a minimum of $30.[43] A purchased discharge was an honorable discharge.

A dishonorable discharge was the result of a conviction by a general court-martial for a serious offense, such as murder, robbery, larceny or desertion. The most common of these was desertion, but the culprits were seldom apprehended and the army made no attempt to find them. If a man was absent without leave for more than ninety days, he was dropped from the rolls and forgotten.[44]

Minor violations were handled within the company by "company punishment," which meant restriction to the post or barracks or extra duty on Sundays or holidays. Being late for formation, wearing improper uniform, or having a dirty duty rifle fell into this category. In repeated or more severe cases, the penalty was reduction in rank or loss of specialist's rating.[45]

A soldier's day began at six in the morning, everyday, except Sunday and holidays, with reveille. Garrison duty for the infantry in the 1930s followed a routine training schedule that covered close order drill, extended order or tactical formations, marksmanship and physical conditioning. Sometimes there would be classroom work or lectures, but these were held to a minimum.[46]

The basic formation was the squad, and all drill, marching and tactics were centered on the movement of the squad. Theoretically, there were eight men in a squad, although squads were seldom at full strength because men were absent on furlough, in the hospital, or on special duty. The squad leader was a corporal, or an acting corporal in many cases, usually a man with several enlistments.[47]

A routine morning would be spent in close-order drill, tactical drill, use of weapons and physical training. Special units, such as communications platoons, mounted sections, and supply and headquarters clerks worked on those jobs. Sometimes there would be classes on gas warfare, map reading, mob control and message writing.[48]

Normally, three men, privates or privates first class, would be assigned to work Kitchen Police (KP). Two men would assist the cook by making coffee, peeling potatoes and performing tasks that did not involve the actual preparation of meals. They also did such distasteful jobs as washing pots, scrubbing floors and cleaning garbage cans. The third man was the dining room orderly who set the tables and cleared the dining area when the meal was finished. All three men served tables during the meal, seeing that empty service bowls were refilled and pitchers were kept full of coffee, water, tea or whatever drink was served. Some soldiers disliked the job, but it wasn't hard work and in bad weather it beat drilling or guard duty. Also, there was plenty of coffee at all times, and leftover pie was a fringe benefit. No one liked to pull Kitchen Police on Sundays and holidays, but a man could find a buddy to take his place for five dollars, the going rate. Since five dollars equaled twenty-five percent of a private's monthly pay, it indicates the value placed on a day in the kitchen.[49]

A company would have two cooks, a first and second, both privates first class with specialists' rating, and they seldom performed any other duty except to fire their weapons when the unit was on the firing range. The mess sergeant, a three-striper, was in charge of the entire mess.[50]

Weekday afternoons were devoted to cleaning up grounds or equipment or other housekeeping chores. Team sports were popular, and there was usually an athletic contest in the afternoons. If a man did not have any other duty, he could be found on the athletic field.[51]

At 10 o'clock in the evening, the bugler of the guard stepped out into the quadrangle and blew tattoo. This signal notified the NCO in charge of quarters for each company that it was time to turn out the lights in squad rooms and the dayroom and for everyone in the outfit to quiet down. At a quarter past 10:00 the bugler blew taps, which meant that everything was finished for the day.[52]

When the infantryman went to the field he carried his weapon, a full pack and a cheese sandwich. Those packs were the subject of much discussion, and the consensus was that they each weighed at least seventy-five pounds. Nobody ever got around to putting one on a scale, and their top weight was more like forty pounds. At the first rest period, the cheese sandwiches were devoured, and by supper time everyone was ready to eat their rifle sling.[53]

The rate of march was two and a half miles per hour, fifteen miles per day of steady hiking was the norm.[54]

For the Infantry private, unburdened by responsibility, being in the field was a picnic. He didn't have to shine his shoes, pull K.P. or stand guard duty.[55]

Officers at Jefferson Barracks learned in mid-February that Jefferson Barracks had been designated to conduct the Sixth Corps indoor athletic meet for the year 1932. The meet consisted of contests in boxing and basketball between teams from Fort Sheridan, Illinois; Fort Brady, Fort Wayne, and Selfridge Field in Michigan; Chanute Field and Scott Field in Illinois; and Jefferson Barracks. The meet was scheduled to take place between 21 – 26 March.[56]

From 2 March through 11 March company NCOs received eight hours of chemical warfare instruction by battalion and regimental gas officers. Then from 11 March to 17 March battalion and company NCOs instructed the remainder of their companies. On 18 March, four hours of training was given in smoke and tear gas problems. Sixth Corps Area Chemical Warfare officers gave ten hours of instruction to company officers and NCOs from 21 March to 25 March. Battalion officers received two hours of training in gas defense and tactical use of chemical agents.

The instruction of company NCOs included the characteristics of gases, relative persistency, methods of distribution, removal of agents, tactical uses, physiological action, use of the gas mask and first aid and protection against gas.

During 24 March, battalion training demonstrations for the officers of the post and senior St. Louis Police officials were given in the methods of handling and distributing gas. Terrain was chosen to represent the vicinity of the Ford Motor Plant in Dearborn, Michigan, and a riot was re-enacted to show proper defense, making use of tear gas and smoke. One section was used as "defenders" and three companies were used as the "mob." Gas was laid, through which the mob had to advance to reach its objective. Behind the gas screen was a reserve consisting of a mobile squad of riflemen and a machine gun. Few members of the 'mob' penetrated the gas screen.

In another problem on 24 March, elements of the 2nd Battalion were confronted with the situation where a mob was attempting to destroy certain stores in stone buildings. Companies E and F represented the mob. Company G, with elements of Headquarters Company attached were defending the stone buildings. Machine guns were placed in commanding positions. Headquarters Company, divided into two parts, was in reserve. Upon the approach of the mob Company G laid a gas and smoke screen, but due to an unfavorable wind and conditions of the terrain the gas was not dense enough to stop the mob and other measures were required.[57]

In May, the Officer Reserve Corps received chemical warfare training at Arcadia. Jefferson Barracks officers supervised this training in which smoke, HC and MI and MII candles were used.[58]

During the period, 6 – 19 July, chemical warfare instruction was conducted at the U.S. Rifle Range in Arcadia, Missouri. General instruction in the tactical use of lacrimatory and smoke candles was given to the 312th Heavy Tank Regiment, and a demonstration involving the use of smoke candles was conducted by the 2nd Platoon, 5th Tank Company.[59]

The final Chemical Warfare training of 1932 took place on 2 October. Lieutenants Roger S. Daley, Louis W. Turner and Roscoe C. Higgins, all 1932 graduates of the U.S. Military Academy, were enrolled in Army Extension Courses that included "Defense Against Chemical Warfare," "Protection Against Chemical Warfare," and "The Employment of Chemical Agents in Troop Training and Suppression of Disorders."[60]

In June, the 6th Infantry, less Company D, moved to Soldier Field in Chicago to attend the Washington Bi-Centennial Military Tournament. The 6th won the distinction of being the crack infantry regiment participating in the event.[61]

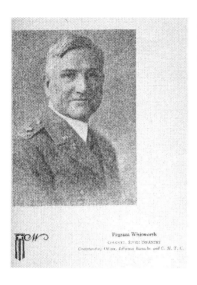

Col. Pegram C. Whitworth assumed command of the 6th Infantry at Jefferson Barracks in January 1929, then relieved General Estes in command of the post on 11 September 1929.

Young men of the CMTC in formation.

Lt. Gen. Walter Krueger
As a Lt. Col. Krueger relieved Col. Pegram Whitworth in command of Jefferson Barracks on 7 July 1932. General Krueger commanded the U.S. 6th Army in the Pacific during World War II.

Lt. Col. Walter Krueger relieved Col. Whitworth as commander of Jefferson Barracks on 7 July 1932. Col. Whitworth left for Fort Sam Houston at San Antonio, Texas, to serve on the general staff. Lt. Col. Krueger, a native of Germany, had enlisted as a volunteer private during the Spanish-American War, and had compiled an enviable record as a soldier during his thirty-four years in the army. In mid-1899, he joined the Regular Army as a private and spent the next four years on Luzon, taking part in many engagements during the Philippine Insurrection and rising through the ranks to second lieutenant.

Krueger served in the United States except for another tour in the Philippines, 1908-1909, until World War I. During this time, he served as an infantry commander, a National Guard inspector-instructor, and an assistant in the Office of the Chief of the Militia Bureau. He also graduated from the Infantry-Cavalry School and the General Staff College. By 1916 when he was promoted to captain, he had become an authority on German infantry, cavalry and artillery tactics.

In early 1918, he joined the American Expeditionary Force in France. After attending the General Staff College at Langers, Krueger served at the front as assistant chief of staff for operations with the 26th Division and later the 84th Division. In October 1918, he took command of the AEF Tank Corps during the Meuse-Argonne Offensive. His wartime record earned him the Distinguished Service Cross and the Distinguished Service Medal. After the armistice, he became assistant chief of staff for operations of the VI Corps in France and later the IV Corps in Germany.

Between the wars, when promotions came at a snail's pace, Krueger rose steadily, becoming a colonel in 1932, a brigadier general in 1936, a major general in 1939 and a lieutenant general in May 1941. He served on the faculty of the Infantry School, the Army War College and the Naval War College. He also gained vast experience in troop command at the regimental level until 1934, then commanded the 16th Brigade, 2nd Division, and VIII Corps from 1938 to 1940. He was appointed commanding general of the 3rd Army and the Southern Defense Command in 1941.

Upon the request of General Douglas MacArthur, Krueger was transferred to Australia in February 1943 to command the newly created American 6th Army. Eventually consisting of eleven divisions, the 6th Army secured the Lae-Salamaua area and the Huon Peninsula of Northeast New Guinea and the western end of New Britain and the Admiralty Islands. Bypassing Japanese strongholds in a 600-mile leap northward along the New Guinea coast in April 1944, Kruger's Army seized the Hollandia-Walde regions of Netherlands New Guinea.

Moving north in September 1944, Krueger's 6th Army captured Morotai and invaded Leyte in the central Philippines. With the invasion of Luzon in January 1945, Krueger's Army, possessing over 280,000 troops, engaged General Tomoyeshi Yamashita's Japanese Army of nearly the same strength in the largest campaign of the Pacific war.

Krueger's leadership in over twenty major operations in the Southwest Pacific earned him a promotion to general in March 1945, and numerous American and Allied decorations. He was preparing his army to spearhead Operation Olympic, the invasion of Kyushu scheduled for autumn, when Japan surrendered in August. Subsequently, he and his army moved to Japan and assumed occupation duties. The 6th Army was deactivated in early 1946, and Krueger returned to the United States. He retired during the summer of 1946.[62]

Krueger's work at Jefferson Barracks began with the convening of the CMTC, the Officers' Reserve Corps and regular recruiting service.[63] The CMTC once again began in early July and ran until early August with young men from Missouri and Illinois attending.

In 1932, almost 37,500 young men completed CMTC in fifty-one camps throughout the country. Almost 100,000 applicants applied, a new all-time high. As much as the War Department and the MTCA might have wished the increase to be attributed to continued improvement in recruiting, the surge in applicants were more likely due to the nation's worsening economy.[64]

Despite the country's economic woes new construction continued at Jefferson Barracks. In a completion report dated 27 September 1932, construction and completion of kitchens and mess additions to Barracks No. 25 and 26 are described.

The 6th Infantry celebrated its 120th anniversary on 4 November 1932. A feature of the celebration was a parade in which all brides and grooms since the last anniversary celebration rode in wagons while bachelor officers trekked along astride mules.[65]

Perhaps the most colorful individual that had ever been stationed at the Barracks was Major Tarriagaki of the Japanese Army, who spent six months there during 1932-1933. He was not only colorful in personality, but in regalia, as his uniforms were dazzling in color, extravagant in texture and replete in decoration. Tarriagaki was here as an observer through an arrangement by which the United States entertained a certain number of officers of the army of the "Rising Sun" in return for a like courtesy on the part of Japan. Tarriagaki was accorded the dignity of an honorary member of the Jefferson Barracks staff, lived in officer's quarters and two lieutenants were assigned to look after his personal comfort and entertainment. He participated in post activities and was not self-conscious about demonstrating his prowess, particularly horsemanship. Prior to leaving, he gave an elaborate banquet to the officers and their ladies at the Chase Hotel in St. Louis. One of the oddest incidents of his story was recalled by Major Paul A. Petty, who was in charge of the commissary at the time. Tarriagaki purchased several dolls which he had sent to the post and packed for shipment to his family in Tokyo. During packing it was discovered that the dolls were made in Japan.[66]

A person might be led to wonder where Major Tarriagaki was in World War II when General Krueger, his host at Jefferson Barracks, was advancing on Japanese bases in the Pacific, but this information cannot be found.

Major Robert C. Cotton, executive officer at Jefferson Barracks, was elevated to the rank of lieutenant colonel and served temporarily as commander of the post during the absence of Col. Krueger. Col. Cotton retired from the Army on 31 October 1940.[67]

1933

As 1932 ended and 1933 began, plans for new construction at Jefferson Barracks were taking shape. A new theater building, four double sets of non-commissioned officer's quarters, and the conversion of the boiler room in the pump house into a set of non-commissioned officer's quarters were all almost set to begin construction.

The project for construction of a Post Theater building started first. Major Frederick Schoenfeld, Post Quartermaster, was designated as the officer in charge of construction and 1st Lt. William H. Arnold, 6th Infantry, was assigned to assist Major Schoenfeld. In addition, Warrant Officer Luther Davis, Quartermaster Corps, was detailed to assist Lt. Arnold. (Note: today this building is St. Bernadette's Church.)

An existing wooden structure occupied the site chosen for the theater building, B-82, originally constructed as a CMTC lavatory and at the time used as the post salvage warehouse. Demolition of this structure began on 25 August 1932. Prisoner labor was used entirely for this project with tools and equipment already available on the post.

Excavation for the fan room began immediately after demolition of B-82 had been completed. Excavation progressed slowly due to a lack of proper equipment. Then, after the top soil had been removed, hard clay was found making it necessary to plow before scrapers could be used. Mule teams pulled the plows and scrapers until the depth of the excavation made their use impracticable. An old artillery tractor was then used. In addition, at fourteen feet four inches an eight-inch terra cotta sewer main was encountered, which prevented the necessary depth from being achieved. In the end, the location of the fan room had to be changed to the southeast corner of the building.

These difficulties were probably standard operating procedure in the Jefferson Barracks area, but they certainly slowed construction and raised costs. The total cost of the completed project came to $20,028.64. The officers in charge including Post Commander Col. Walter Krueger signed off on the completion and acceptance of the building on 4 May 1933.

It should also be mentioned that the U.S. Army Motion Picture Service furnished the draperies for the stage, doors and windows and 574 opera chairs.[68]

Excavation for the construction of four double sets of non-commissioned officer's quarters began on 6 December 1932. Progress was slow due to continuous rain, snow and cold weather and the breaking down of the shovel. Footings were started on 28 December and brick laying on 3 January 1933. January provided unseasonably good weather, February was typical winter weather, then March and April turned good again. Plastering started on 26 April and the entire project was completed on 17 July 1933.

Unlike the Theater project, in which a good deal of prisoner and soldier labor was used, this project had a general contractor who sub-contracted the different aspects of the project. There were approximately forty-two skilled and forty-six unskilled laborers employed at various times during the progress of the work.

The total cost of this project came to $54,884.44. Final payment was made to the contractor on 26 July 1933.[69]

The last construction project for 1933 was the alteration of Building No. 33, converting the old boiler room into one set of non-commissioned officer's quarters. The south half of B-33 was to be modified by putting in a new opening in the exterior brick work for doors and windows, bricking up old openings, the installation of plumbing, bathroom fixtures, floors, partitions, plastering, woodwork and interior decorating and a new slate roof.

The object of the project was to provide quarters for the attendant in charge of the pumping station occupying the other half of the building.

Approval for this project came on 19 January 1933 at an estimated cost of $2100.00. All work was accomplished by purchase and hire and progressed smoothly. Materials cost $9348.40, and hired labor $1151.60, bringing the total cost to the estimated total of $2100. Final payment was made 27 May 1933, and Major Frederick Schoenfeld signed off on the project.[70]

"Spit and Polish," those were the words of the day. They were even more the words of the day from 1932 to 1934, when Col. Walter Krueger was commanding officer. Born in Prussia, Krueger, at the time the youngest colonel in the Army, was the only private to attain four-star general rank. Men who served under him at Jefferson Barracks remember his mania for keeping everything trim and neat. He would sneak around, they say, on surprise inspections to every corner of the barracks, into the kitchens and the latrines. The prisoners worked regularly extracting every blade of grass from the blocks of limestone in the gutters along the parade ground, and the men waxed and polished the floors of their barracks. The plain wooden floors were cleaned with sand rock and lye water and then waxed. Johnson's Wax was applied with a Johnson bar consisting of a piece of rug wrapped around a weight on a long handle. At a later date, the floors were covered with "battleship linoleum," which was a quarter inch thick and would not chip or scratch. "Shine the brass!" Col. Krueger ordered, and every bit of visible brass everywhere would sparkle. Brass cuspidors were placed in the corners of almost every barracks room. Filled with fresh water, they shone, ready for use, but they were never used. They were for show; cigarettes and cigar butts were thrown in a butt can that was removed and hidden during regular inspections.[71]

There were white-glove inspections not just of the barracks, but of the enlisted men's quarters as well. In the D.C. Building, there was always great anxiety on Saturday morning. As the officers made their rounds, there would be knocks of warning on the beaverboard walls separating the quarters to notify the neighbors that the officers were approaching and to give them time to put away their home brew or other unwelcome or unsightly objects.

The brass shone in the enlisted men's quarters as well. The flower vases, fashioned from sawed-off shells, glowed on delicate white doilies that women had crocheted. The prisoners did the hard work, such as cutting the grass, cleaning the walks, hauling coal and washing the windows, for enlisted men as well as for officers. Such was the attention to cleanliness that the clothes of the lowest enlisted man's children were usually spotless. Even the prostitutes who turned up regularly at noon on payday at the trolley station seemed to have dressed in keeping with the polished look of the post. With frizzled hair showing the recent effect of the hot curling iron and faces heavily made up, they often wore evening dresses of bright red or green satin, but because their assignations were usually somewhere in the woods, they also wore tennis shoes so that they might more readily cope with the difficult terrain.[72]

In addition to the regular inspections of the barracks, there were frequent eight or ten-mile hikes with full packs, and in the summer visits to the rifle range at Arcadia, Missouri, where each man had to qualify. It was to Arcadia that the mules were retired when they became too old for service. The mules were treated like soldiers, each had his serial number (the mules were branded on the left hip) and like the soldier each one had to be accounted for and provided with a decent retirement. One summer the regiment hiked to Battle Creek, Michigan, for maneuvers, taking twenty-one days and nights. Along with the other constant inspections there were, of course, the routine "short-arm" inspections (for venereal disease). At one such inspection, a Bandsman was found to have gonorrhea, but rather than having to pay the usual penalty of being busted and having his pay docked, he was able to beat the system. By asking that she be examined, he was able to prove that he had contracted the disease from his wife, who had picked it up from another man while her husband was away on the rifle range. The man lost his wife, but kept his rating.[73]

"Shine the brass!" the Colonel ordered, for a Bandsman like William Jay Smith's father there was plenty of brass to shine. A photograph of the 3rd Cavalry Band in 1894 shows the men in tunics with three rows of buttons and helmets with large metal plaques in front that make them look as if they have just walked off the stage from some comic opera. Smith's father's uniform was not that fancy, but it took just as much care. To begin with, every button had to be polished, and as they were heavily embossed, the task took attention and elbow grease. A button board, purchased from the Post Exchange, was used to polish the buttons. It was V-shaped, made of heavy cardboard and made to hook around each button. A combination of salt, vinegar and scrubbing powder was used first, followed by jeweler's rouge and a final polishing with a Blitz Cloth. (In 1843, a school for infantry brigade drill had been established at Jefferson Barracks, and, it was here that the 3rd Infantry, because of its glittering look on parade, won the nickname of "Buffsticks," from the constant use of just such a slotted button board."

The brass was quite enough in itself, but the leggings were a real nightmare. The ordinary canvas leggings or puttees worn in World War I, had been replaced by wool wrap-around leggings, and winding these properly was an art in itself. You had to start from the top of the shoe in just the proper way so that if it rained the water would run off each succeeding layer. In addition, for parades the Band wore white canvas leggings, the strings of which had to be bleached and the brass tips of the strings polished. The leggings themselves had to be scrubbed with brushes. The Band also had to wear white web belts, which the men had to scrub or "blanco" with a Paris-green powder. And every brass eyelet on the belt had to be polished. For this job Smith's father had what was called a "whirlgig," in which a polishing surface would descend in whirling yoyo-fashion on each eyelet. This tool did its work so effectively that it was much in demand and was frequently rented out to his fellow Bandsmen.[74]

Special care had to be taken with rifles. The gunstocks were made to shine like brass. One of the sergeants in Company B was known as "Gunrack" Miller because he was so particular about his rifle that he never wanted to take it from the rack. He would put linseed oil on the gunstock and rub it for hours over and over with the palm of his hand.[75]

Col. Krueger decided at one point that he did not like the color of the men's shoes or garrison belts, and soon the order went out for them to be dyed a darker brown. This was not easily accomplished, and it took constant surveillance to keep the results from looking messy.[76]

Ordinarily the men wore a woolen serge uniform in winter, one that had to be cleaned and pressed and kept pressed, with a straight black cotton necktie, and in summer a khaki uniform and a thin khaki necktie. The khakis - or "sun tans" - were, of course, washable, but since they had to be starched, they were not always so easy to handle. Some of the officers, not content with the way the Post Laundry did their khaki trousers, took them to the wives of enlisted men so that they could get special attention. Capt. James Tiston, a bachelor living at the Officers' Club, sought out Mrs. Velma Gholson, the wife of Sgt. Gholson of Company B. Capt. Tiston explained to her that he wanted his trousers starched so stiff they would stand up. Mrs. Gholson obliged, but the next week Capt. Tiston sent a note, saying, "A little more starch. The third time she decided to prepare them as she did the nurses' caps, by washing and drying them first and then putting them through hot starch. Capt. Piston was delighted and strutted out like a knight who had donned new armor for the weekly review. Unfortunately, it rained, and he found himself encased in what amounted to plaster. The following week he sent a final request, "Not quite so much starch, please."[7]

The sun tans, starched or not, were at least fairly cool. But Col. Krueger decided that khaki for summer was messy and that wool was the thing. Although it was warm, it had the advantage of absorbing perspiration, which did not show through until the men were ready to keel over in the one-hundred-degree heat. The men would return from the Friday afternoon reviews soaked to the skin, and then the woolen uniform would have to be readied for the next day. Col. Krueger also enjoyed making speeches, and from time to time he would assemble the men of the regiment in the Post Theater and address them on the subject of discipline, "You must learn to be led before you can learn to lead," he would tell them.[78]

While much of a soldier's time was ordinarily spent in carrying out orders, a good amount also was spent in finding ways to not carry them out or in beating the system in one way or another, which under Col. Krueger became increasingly difficult. The routine of the day went something like this: 5:30 a.m. reveille; 6:00 a.m. breakfast; at 7:30 a.m. the entire regiment would line up on the parade ground in undershirts and trousers for half an hour of calisthenics and butts manual; 8:00 a.m. drill call [for the line companies squad drill; for the Band, rehearsal]; 11:30 a.m. guard mount [the changing of the guard], which was always held in front of the old Company H on the corner of the parade ground next to the Headquarters Building; 12:00 noon chow; from 1:00 p.m. to 3:00 p.m. fatigue. [Some men had special assignments and others rested. During this period, the old soldiers would stretch out on their bunks, and the young recruits, fearing their wrath, were careful not to disturb them, would tiptoe in stocking feet up glossy stairs still smelling from their heavy application of floor wax.] The regiment would fall out about 4:00 p.m. for review for about an hour [or on Friday for the regular weekly review]. At 5:00 p.m. retreat sounded. Before Col. Krueger's time, the band had not been required to turn out for retreat; a single bugler (buglers were not connected with the band) had sufficed. But Col. Krueger decided that the full band should be present for retreat seven days a week. At 6:00 p.m. chow was served, followed at 9:00 p.m. by tattoo and 10:00 p.m. taps played, at which time lights went out except in the latrines and entrances. If poker or crap games were in progress, they moved to the latrines or somewhere like the tailor's shop in the basement that was tucked away from general view, and there they frequently continued all night long.[79]

"Happy Days Are Here Again!" This was the title of an article in the 12 April 1933 issue of the St. Louis *Post-Dispatch*. Beer is on sale at Jefferson Barracks for the first time in thirty-one years. For seventeen years prior to prohibition, since 1902, army regulations, prohibiting intoxicants on government reservations, forbade its sale. But the ban on beer, now legally declared to be non-intoxicating, was lifted at Jefferson Barracks on Sunday when a radiogram was received from the Secretary of War authorizing its distribution.

The beverage may be sold, however, only in the restaurant at the Post Exchange and in the Officers' Club. It may be sold only at army posts in states which permit its distribution.

Officers and enlisted men may buy and drink their beer at the barracks but civilians, including the recruits in the forestry conservation camp, are not permitted to purchase it there. Nor are the soldiers permitted to obtain beer in the city and take it to the barracks.

This regulation was issued, it was said, to avert the possibility of any beer containing more than the prescribed 3.2 percent of alcoholic content being imported to the post.

Companies A and G, 6th Infantry, and the band left for Fort Sheridan, Illinois, on 3 May 1933, for a short period of training. After the training, they proceeded to Chicago to participate in "A Century of Progress" exposition. They did not return to Jefferson Barracks until 15 November.

Oftentimes Col. Krueger had to be absent from the post. During these absences in 1933, Lt. Col. Irving M. Madison acted as commander. Madison was a veteran of the 6th Infantry who had been assigned to the 6th Infantry after graduation from West Point. He served with the 6th Infantry overseas and came to Jefferson Barracks with the regiment. Madison was promoted to the rank of colonel 1 October 1934.[80]

Without a doubt the biggest event, possibly for the nation, and certainly impacting Jefferson Barracks in 1933, was the creation of the Civilian Conservation Corps [CCC]. President Franklin D. Roosevelt introduced the idea for the CCC in his first inaugural address on 21 March 1933. The same day legislation to create the program, Senate Bill 5.598 [the Robinson-Wagner Bill] "... for the relief of unemployment through performance of useful public works and other purposes" or Emergency Conservation Work [ECW], as it was known, was presented by Roosevelt to the 73rd U.S. Congress. It passed both houses of Congress and Roosevelt signed it into law on 31 March. On 5 April 1933, Roosevelt issued Executive Order No. 61601, which established the CCC and appointed a director, Robert Fechner. The order directed that the program was to be supervised jointly by four Cabinet departments: War, Labor, Agriculture, and Interior by means of a CCC Advisory Council composed of representatives from each of the supervising departments.

Also on 5 April, War Department corps area commanders were tasked to commence enrollment. The first CCC enrollee was selected April 7 and subsequently lists of unemployed men were supplied by state and local welfare and relief agencies for immediate enrollment. Less than a month after the bill was introduced, on 17 April 1933, the first camp, NF-1, Camp Roosevelt, was established at George Washington National Forest near Luray, Virginia. By 1 July 1933, there were 1,463 working camps with 250,000 junior enrollees [18 to 25 years of age], 28,000 veterans, 14,000 Native Americans and 25,000 locally enrolled {or experienced) men. The typical enrollee was a U.S. citizen, unmarried, unemployed male, 18 to 20 years of age. Each enrollee volunteered, and upon passing a physical and after a period of conditioning, was required to serve a six-month period with the option to serve as much as two years. Enrollees worked forty hours a week over five days, sometimes including Saturdays if poor weather dictated. In return, he received $30 a month {with a compulsory allotment of $25 sent to a family dependent} as well as food, clothing and medical care.

Each CCC camp was located in the general area of particular conservation work to be performed, and organized around a complement of up to 200 civilian enrollees in a designated numbered "company" unit. Each camp was structured to generally have barracks for fifty enrollees each, official technical staff quarters, medical dispensary, mess hall, recreation hall, education building, lavatory and showers, technical/administrative offices, tool room, blacksmith shop and motor pool garages. The enrollees were organized into work details called "sections" of twenty-five men each, according to the barracks in which they resided. Each section had an enrollee "leader" and "assistant leader" who were accountable for the men at work and in the barracks. Over this company organization each camp had a dual-authority supervisory staff: Department of War personnel, generally reserve officers, who were responsible for overall camp operation, logistics, education and training; and technical service civilians, a camp "superintendent" and "foreman," employed by the Department of the Interior and the Department of Agriculture, responsible for the type of field work.[81]

The CCC performed 300 possible types of work projects within ten approved general classifications: 1) Structural Improvement: bridges, fire lookout towers, service buildings; 2) Transportation: truck trails, minor roads, foot trails, and airport landing fields; 3) Erosion Control: check dams, terracing, and vegetable covering; 4) Flood Control: irrigation, drainage, dams, ditching, channel work, riprapping; 5) Forest Culture: planting trees and shrubs, timber stand improvement, seed collection, nursery work; 6) Forest Protection: fire prevention, fire-pre-suppression, firefighting, insect and disease control; 7) Landscape and recreation: public camp and picnic ground development, lake and pond site clearing and development; 8) Range: stock driveways, elimination of predatory animals; 9) Wildlife: stream improvement, fish stocking, food and cover planting; 10) Miscellaneous: emergency work, surveys, mosquito control.[82]

The responses to the six-month experimental conservation program were enthusiastic, and on 1 October 1933, Director Fechner was instructed to arrange for a second period of enrollment. The Civilian Conservation Corps was probably the most popular of all the New Deal "alphabet" relief agencies.

Jefferson Barracks served as a CCC district headquarters for CCC camps in southern Illinois [1935-1939] and Missouri [1939-1942]. It was also the site of one of the largest reconditioning camps, readying enrollees for their work in America's forests and parks system.

With pounding of hammers and rasp of saws, the Civilian Conservation Corps Camp took final shape, the strangest encampment ever to be erected at Jefferson Barracks. What follows is a description of the CCC camp at Jefferson Barracks and how it came about. "Without military duties or discipline, some 900 men recruited from destitute families to work in national reforestation projects were conditioning themselves for the labor ahead, gaining practical experience by putting the camp in shape to withstand rains which left it ankle deep in mud."

"A pick and shovel gang, composed partly of Negroes, dug ditches, the Negroes singing as they swung their picks. A few yards away about forty men were sawing up boards and nailing them together to form tent floors."

"Another detachment was busied walling the sides of the recreation pavilion, breaking the wall with a long narrow window with a hinged shutter running the length of the building. Unperturbed by the noise, men within the hall wrote letters and worked jig-saw puzzles. Officers of the barracks have requested donations of writing paper, puzzles and magazines to put there."

"Hard by the tents men were making rock paths. Others were stringing wires, so that each tent might have electric light. More of 200 of the recruits sat idle, nursing temporarily sore arms occasioned by the effects of typhoid serum."

"Cooks selected from the recruits have already taken over the field kitchens, but appetites had not diminished at dinner today as the men devoured "hot dogs," sauerkraut, stewed corn, boiled potatoes, slaw, rice pudding and bread and butter."

"While no definite orders have been received officers at the Barracks said today the camp will last probably two weeks after reaching its full complement, rather than from the time the first recruits arrived last week...."

"Some of the campers were stripped to the waist as they worked. Others wore odd combinations of work clothes."

"Part of the Army of the unemployed until rescued by President Roosevelt's reforestation program, which gives each worker $30 a month, $25 of which he must agree to send home, the campers range from college graduates to those who never finished grammar school."

"While all the recruits have passed a physical examination to determine whether they are fit for work, the requirements are much lower than those of an Army draft. A bad eye or flat feet, for example, are not sufficient to disqualify a man to work in the wood...."[83]

In June 1933, the *Neighborhood Link News* had this to say about the Jefferson Barracks CCC camp. "The khaki tents of six separate camps dotted the hillsides at Jefferson Barracks as 10,000 recruits of the Civilian Conservation Corps engaged in varied activities designed to condition them for work in far western forests."

Built in 1932, Theater No. 1 provided entertainment for thousands of soldiers. It was one of the first new construction projects under Col. Krueger.

When the 138th came back to St. Louis, May 9, 1919.

William Jay Smith
Smith in front of his father's tent at the Century of Progress Exposition in Chicago in 1933.

"Not since World War days has such activity been observed at the government reservation. The conservation contingent encamped there is the largest in the country and entails an expenditure of $2500 a day, spent in St. Louis, for rations alone."

"Mayor Dickman and his cabinet visited the camp recently at the invitation of Col. Krueger, commandant at the Barracks, and stood in the chow line with four hundred St. Louis members of the Corps for the noon day meal."

"Eating out of mess kits, the Mayor's party lunched on fish, potatoes, peas, cucumber salad, bread and butter, pudding and coffee, the same fare served the men. All of the food was prepared by recruits, who have shown an aptitude for camp cookery."

"After lunch, the visitors were escorted through the company "streets," viewed with admiration efficient sanitation arrangements, and were surprised to learn an underground sewage system for 6,000 men had been installed at a total cost of $90. The $90 went for pipe, draining into a limestone fault leading to the Mississippi River. Labor was furnished by the recruits...."

"By July 1, all but about 500 of the campers are scheduled to report for reforestation duty, virtually all of them going to projects on the Pacific coast. The fifty-three companies in camp, most of them from Southern Illinois, will be equipped to meet conditions they will encounter in various localities. Men assigned to Oregon camps, for instance, will be issued overcoats."

"Work details have built new roads leading to the six camps, have cleared the woods of underbrush, obtaining fuel for the 106 field ranges which go into action three times a day."

"Working day and night, the Regular Army personnel at the Barracks has so systematized the camps that new arrivals, even those reporting late at night, are assured of hot meals and prompt assignment to tents. Even the officers' golf course, near the Veteran's Hospital, has been converted into a camp. Each camp accommodates from 200 to 800 men."

"About 850 of the campers are Negroes...."

"Morale of the recruits, officers said, has been excellent, and visitors remarked upon the alacrity and the geniality with which the men went about their work."[84]

Col. Robert C. Cotton, 6th Infantry at Jefferson Barracks, served as the principal speaker for the Memorial Day observance at Edwardsville, Illinois. Col. Cotton majored in history at Georgetown University while stationed in Washington, D.C., and was considered an authority on military and U.S. history. Unlike past Memorial Day observances, the 1933 program took only a little more than one and a half hours instead of the all afternoon affairs of previous years.[85]

CMTC had escaped Congress's scalpel through 1932, but the War Department saw what was coming. The Democratic-controlled Houses' subcommittee on War Department appropriations was set to perform radical surgery with its draft of the 1933 fiscal year appropriations bill, which was to fund CMTC.

The lame-duck Hoover administration's proposed budget for the 1934 fiscal year cut CMTC's funding in half, down to a lean $1 million dollars. This would reduce the number of trainees from 37,500 to 13,000. With its former quota of 35,000 cut in half, the War Department made the decision to accept no first-year candidates.[86]

The Army's inability to accept new applicants, or even some of those with past CMTC training, had no immediate dampening effect on applications. A new record for the number of applications, 106,834, was received in 1933. The army conducted forty-nine camps in 1933; Jefferson Barracks hosted one of these camps, but the number of attendees came to only about half of those attending in 1932.[87]

After the conclusion of the 1933 CMTC in early August, the Post resumed its normal garrison activities for the remainder of the year. If one peruses the *St. Louis Post-Dispatch,* "Jefferson Barracks Social Items From the Army Post", the reader can see that the Jefferson Barracks officers and their wives continued a variety of dinners and teas, many of them centering around Col. and Mrs. Walter Krueger. There certainly was no shortage of such events for the officers and their families. The enlisted men, however, were left to their own devices to overcome the boredom of routine garrison life.

A fight of a different kind took center stage for army doctors at Jefferson Barracks during September. On September 5, the United States Army joined the Federal Public Health Service and other local agencies in a study of a mysterious "Sleeping sickness" epidemic which had been responsible for 74 deaths in the greater St. Louis area since its outbreak here on 30 July. Major James S. Simmons, bacteriologist, arrived in St. Louis with aides, equipment, and experimental animals and prepared to set up his own laboratory at Jefferson Barracks to determine if insects transmitted the disease from person to person. Local health officials were informed his studies would include a study of the possibility that encephalitis was spread by insects. More than 500 cases had been reported in St. Louis.[88]

The Army surgeons set up their equipment in a hospital building built during World War I at Jefferson Barracks. The Army surgeons brought 10,000 adult mosquitoes and 5,000 eggs as well as 35 rabbits and 12 monkeys. These were used to transfer the sleeping sickness germs from human patients to the animals.[89]

Fatalities from "sleeping sickness" rose sharply during the first week of September. During this week 45 deaths had been reported, with ten deaths reported 7 September 7, bringing the total death count to 92. Dr. Margaret Smith, assistant pathologist at Washington University, had discovered the presence of virus in the kidney, proving that the disease was one of the virus type, but no other information had as yet been uncovered.[90]

Armistice Day activities brought on a new event to the celebration in 1933. The Jefferson Barracks football team coached by F. Saunders played the B & E Independent team at Alton, Illinois at 3:30 p.m. The Barracks team was considered one of the best teams in the area, averaging 182 pounds per man (this certainly has changed). The two teams also appeared in the Armistice Day parade in Alton.[91]

On 24 November, the Civil Works Administration announced projects it said would employ 9,076 men in Missouri. The work outlined was to cost approximately $100,000. The War Department would spend $52,000 of the total at Jefferson Barracks, the St. Louis Medical Depot, and in non-military projects at Jefferson Barracks National Cemetery and at cemeteries at Jefferson City and Springfield.

The coast and geodetic survey was to employ 375 men; and national forests 8,500 men. The Bureau of Chemistry and Soils employed 11 men for ten weeks at Bethany, Missouri.[92]

1934

One of the times when the monotony of garrison life could be broken was once a year when the men went to the target range to train and qualify. For the 6th Infantry at Jefferson Barracks that rifle range was located at Arcadia, Missouri. The men usually went to the range by battalion. It took five days to march to Arcadia and another five days to return. Two weeks was normally spent at the range.

The 1903 Springfield .30-.06 bolt-action clip-fed rifle was the standard infantry small arms weapon of the time. It was the finest infantry weapon known to man and the biggest source of military training, hard work, and sport the Regular Army knew. It was also the means by which a soldier could earn extra pay because qualification on the firing range as an expert rifleman paid $5 a month, and as a sharpshooter $3 a month, when the money was available. During the hard times of the 1930s, only experts received the extra pay. This made competition at the range keener as an extra $5 a month could be 25 percent of a privates' pay and bought a lot of beer and Bull Durham tobacco.[93]

While at the firing range, the infantrymen practiced firing from several different positions. The positions were standing, (or offhand as it was called,) sitting, kneeling and prone. The rifle sling, used for carrying the rifle, was used when firing from all the different positions as an aid for accurate firing. Standing, sitting and kneeling positions were used at distances of 200 and 300 yards, both for slow and rapid fire. The prone position was used at 500 yards. Hitting a bullseye twenty inches in diameter at 500 yards -over a quarter of a mile- required a keen eye and a steady hand. Within the bullseye was another circle, the V-ring, half the diameter of the bullseye, and an expert rifleman was expected to put at least half his shots in the smaller area.[94]

The best sporting test came at 200 yards, firing offhand at an 8-inch bullseye. A record course was ten shots, with no time limit, although five minutes was ample and experienced shooters fired faster, using a rhythmic cadence that grouped the hits within a small area.[95]

Scoring was five points for a bullseye, then four and three in the next outer rings, with any hit on the scoring surface outside the three rings being worth two points. There was no score of one. Forty was a good offhand score, and few shooters could top forty-five. A perfect score of fifty was rare.[96]

The Regular Army did not keep a list of casualties inflicted on shooters by their own weapons, but these occurred in large numbers. Hardly a man left the firing line without a black eye, a bloody nose, a bruised cheek, a fractured jaw or broken teeth. The Springfield packed tremendous power, propelling a bullet with a muzzle velocity of more than 2,800 feet per second, and the recoil would punch a man unmercifully.[97]

The daily routine under Col. Krueger was bad enough, recalled William Jay Smith's father, but it was followed, when General Preston D. Brown took command of the 6th Corps Area, by what the men called "General Brown's reign of terror." General Brown instituted a nightly bed check at 11:00 p.m. Only married men were exempt and those who tried to avoid it, as one bandsman did by filling his bed with two hefty barracks bags, were readily apprehended. Two men, speeding back from St. Louis for bed check after a night on the town, wheeled into a sink hole and both were killed. Bed check was stopped shortly afterward.[98]

The life of an enlisted man at Jefferson Barracks, in addition to being monotonous at times, could be tough, full of written and unwritten regulations. In one of Bill Mauldin's famous cartoons two generals are shown contemplating a spectacular sunset. "It's a beautiful view," one says to the other. "Is there one for the enlisted men?" If an enlisted man dared to walk out in the company of an officer to look at the sun setting behind the parade ground at Jefferson Barracks at the time that I knew it, he would have had to keep a pace or two to his left and rear. And he would, of course, always have to show the utmost respect in addressing him. An enlisted man was required to give his rating, name and serial number and to refer to the officer in the third person. One of the men who served with Smith's father was private William F. Alden, later, in World War II, he became a Master Sergeant, who became historian of the 6th Infantry. Like many of the recruits of the day, he came from a small town in southern Illinois. When he first arrived at the post, the men in his squad room found on his bunk his hometown newspaper with an article about him bearing the headline: LOCAL BOY JOINS ARMY. From that day on, he was known by all the men as "Local Boy."

Alden recalled going in to see Capt. Henderson, the commanding officer of service company, to request permission to get married.

'Local Boy,' standing at attention, said, "Sir, Private William F. Alden, Serial Number 6829056, desires the permission of the company commander to be married on the 28th day of September 1934, if it so pleases the commanding officer."

"Sit down, Alden," Capt. Henderson replied. "You know you're a damn fool. Any man who asks a woman to share the military is a damn fool."

Then, after a long tirade outlining all that Alden would be putting his bride through, he concluded: "I'll send a letter along, and we'll see what we get back." And that meant that there would be no problem.[99]

William Jay Smith described his father's bootleg business. "How it was that we entered the "Bootleg Business" I am not quite sure. But it began with our moving in the spring of 1930 from the Barracks to what was known as the Boston house. A sergeant named Boston, who had retired to St. Augustine, Florida, to manage a national cemetery, owned the sizeable two-story square frame structure which looked out on the North gate entrance to Jefferson Barracks. The address, 9988 South Broadway, indicated that it was indeed the last house."

"The North Gate, the main gate to the Barracks, consisted of two large gate posts made of white limestone blocks topped with black-painted cannon balls. Next to the gate posts was the sentry box, where the guard on duty stopped each car as it approached the gate to inquire about the purpose of its visit, its destination, and then, usually without further ado, to wave it past. Although cars were rarely turned away, the guard made clear to each driver that he was entering a special domain. Even the Dinky or Toonerville Trolley, whose tracks into the Barracks curved past the North Gate opposite the Boston house, had to stop long enough for the guard to make sure that all was right on board before it could proceed."[100]

The Smith family had shared the Boston house with close friends, the O'Hara family. Sgt. O'Hara, his wife and three children occupied the three ground-floor rooms and the Smith's the three upstairs rooms, all sharing the one bathroom on the second floor. In the fall of 1931, the O'Hara's departed for Long Beach, California, as Sgt. O'Hara had retired from the Army. The Smith's were once again faced with the difficult problem of having to move. To solve this problem, Private Smith came up with the proposal of going into the "Bootleg Business" and took over the entire house. "His idea was to make home brew and invite his fellow bandsmen from the Barracks to share with him and thus make a small profit which would take care of our increased rent and give us an easy and comfortable place to live in. My mother was not exactly enchanted by the plan, especially since she did not drink herself, but she did not oppose it on moral grounds. She was quite aware that there were bootleg joints all over St. Louis County and that most of them were frequented by my father. If the police cared that the law was being broken, they never gave any indication of it. As long as the establishments were quiet, they didn't object, and the army itself would be the last to object. The bootlegger was after all only offering a needed service. There were so many bootleggers in Lemay that it was said that you could fall off one porch and onto another and never miss a round of drinks. A man named

Singer ran a bootleg joint down the street from us in a large white frame house. He had been in business for years and raked in the money from his military customers. His place was their first stop off the base."[101]

"Liquor had always been available in one way or another on the post. When the regular ration of early days was discontinued, whiskey was provided by the sutler who ran the garrison's general store. When the sutler was forbidden to sell spirits, the men would exchange provisions purchased from him for spirits obtained from civilians. My father was not the first enlisted man to engage in the production of home brew. Sgt. Daley, who produced home brew and wine, made the mistake of selling it at the rifle range at Arcadia and was caught. Sgt. Ailsworth, whose wife "Madam Queen" became celebrated throughout the garrison for her bright curly hennaed hair, had taken his own supply of home brew in a hay wagon and had hidden it at one point in the ammunition dump of a sinkhole to avoid detection."[102]

"The procedure for making it was simple. Two large cans of malt were needed for the ten-gallon crock. The cans of malt with their yellow labels, resembling yellow cans of Mexican tamales but bigger and fatter, covered with reproductions of medals won at various fairs and expositions had an appropriate plump German appearance. Water was heated on the gas range in the kitchen in a large kettle and the two cans of malt were stirred in. When the mixture cooled and yeast had been added, it was taken to the cellar and poured into the crock, which was then covered over with cheese cloth and tied with a string to keep out gnats and bugs. The mixture was left overnight, and the next day a large Irish potato was cut into three pieces and tossed into the crock. The starch in the potato pieces would cause the yeast to settle to the bottom."

"Although it was advisable to wait longer, our brew was ready for bottling in two or three days. A short piece of hose was dropped into the crock and the brew siphoned out into bottles that contained a small amount of sugar. You had to be careful not to drop the hose down too close to the bottom, so as not to get the yeast all stirred up. Then you would draw in on the hose to get the brew started. Since Richie and I were designated to help with the bottling, we also had to siphon off the stuff to get it started. While I now think that there is nothing more refreshing than a good cold beer, I then found the taste or even the smell of my father's abhorrent. I recall it as having the smell of old wet Army shoes and the taste of a soggy blanket."

"When the bottles were filled, each one was set under the simple capper that brought down the cap on the bottle, sealing it airtight, and that was that. The bottles were put in cases, the cases stacked up, and the brew was ready for drinking."

"The home brew was deposited in the Kelvinator in the kitchen, and it did not stay long. The men on the post were ready to drink anything they could find. Soon there were any number of thirsty bandsmen gathered around our dining table. The beer was priced at ten cents a pint. It was sometimes bottled in quart bottles and sold by the glass, at five cents a glass. Before long, men from all the other companies were arriving every evening, and considering the amount of brew consumed, there should have been a profit. But from the beginning my father made the mistake of giving credit. He was forced to do so because most of the men had no cash whatever during the month; it all came on payday and disappeared at once...."[103]

"Some of the men came regularly and paid up. There was Beerbaum, a thin blond horn player, a graduate of the University of Illinois. We were, of course, at the height of the Great Depression, and many of the men had turned to the military when there was no place else to turn. There was another college graduate, a full-blooded Indian, six feet four inches tall, "Big Ike," a Sioux, the star of the band's basketball team. The men called him "Chief." He was a gentle, kind man, who from time to time brought his tall blonde wife, just as blonde as he was dark. She had a job in North St. Louis, and they came together usually only on weekends. Another Indian member of the band and also a steady customer was "Little Ike," a Comanche. A Polish-American clarinet player named Trask sometimes brought his very Polish girlfriend. Another young clarinet player from southern Illinois, Clyde Maynard, brought his pretty young wife Louise. She did not like the army life at all, and soon managed to persuade her husband to give it up. She and Clyde, who both were favorites of my mother became life-long friends, and mine as well."

"Although there were in general few women customers, there was one regular one, Adele Grimble, the wife of Sgt. Grimble. The Grimbles had been our next-door neighbors in the Knights of Columbus building on the post, and now lived around the corner on Teddy Avenue. Dell Grimble, had served for years as secretary to the supply officer of the post, and her husband was a barber. Together they knew all the gossip. Dell Grimble, a plumpish little woman with delicate, doll-like features and a quick laugh, was a descendant of the original settlers of Carondelet who had deeded the land of the Barracks to the army in 1826. She naturally took a proprietary interest in the reservation, and was a mine of information about it. Her mother, the wife of Pvt. "Pop" Stewart, who operated the hog ranch on the post, still spoke the French that her family had always spoken. I began to take weekly lessons with her when I was only eight or nine, and by the time I came to study French in high school, I already had a certain proficiency in the language....".

"Most of our bootlegging customers were loners, men like Holbrook, the snare drummer, a small man with a shriveled-up face. Or Sgt. "Cat" Collins of Service Company, a solid red-faced, square-shouldered man in his fifties who had served in Panama and elsewhere overseas, an old-timer who had no end of stories to tell. "Cat" Collins took the part of Santa Claus every Christmas Eve in the Post Chapel. Then there was Upchurch, perhaps the steadiest customer. He was an emaciated, gray-haired wisp of a man with black horn-rimmed glasses and a roll-your-own, Bull Durham cigarette constantly dangling from his mouth. As prim and precise as a country school teacher, he took down the orders at the Commissary on regular printed forms."

"Upchurch became a permanent fixture and his consumption of home brew did nothing to fatten him up, but he went on consuming it all the same. He would run up a bill of $100 or more and still be there every evening soon after retreat. He was deeply in debt to us when we closed down our bootlegging operation years later."

"During the week, no session in the evening lasted very late; most of the men had to be back on the post and in their bunks in time for reveille at 5:30 the next morning. That usually meant that, not having money for carfare, they would have to walk back the mile through the woods. My father had to be up and off at seven in the morning. The big gatherings took place on weekends, especially after payday. Because the men just came and stayed, my mother was persuaded to provide them with food. She cooked huge meals, baked ham, fried chicken and turkey, with cornbread and her own hot rolls. A delicious dinner with all the fixings was priced at only fifty cents...."

"It became clear as time went by that home brew and food were not bringing in much money. So, my father decided to begin dealing in hard liquor...His leather case, which he then opened, fitted neatly around a 5-gallon can of pure alcohol. The oak barrel was soon installed on its side in a frame on the shelf of the closet in the middle room upstairs, which was the bedroom that Richie and I shared. My father would cut the alcohol in half, adding five gallons of water to the oak barrel, whose charcoal-lined interior would color the alcohol in due time. To speed up the process my father tried putting prunes into the barrel, but the prunes gave the liquor a bitter taste. He again consulted the experts, and the gentleman caller brought along with his next leather-encased delivery, an electric needle about six inches long. It was a steel rod like a soldering iron. The needle would be plugged in, and, when red, would be inserted in the hole in the barrel and remain there for two or three days. The alcohol would then absorb the flavor and the coloring from the barrel, and the whiskey, selling for forty cents a half-pint and seventy-five cent a pint, was as fine as any that could be acquired in the country. At least it was cut in a clean and decent way, and in those days that was just about all anyone could ask."

"In the process of the 'cutting' the alcoholic vapors that emerged from my closet made me feel when I went to bed that I was about to be hauled off to an operating room. The room had been intended as a kitchen, and the large gunmetal gray sink that greeted me when I awoke gave me the sensation of being locked up in some evil and foul-smelling laboratory...."[104]

During the first half of 1934, Col. Krueger, preparing the 6th Infantry for war games, intensified the activity at the Barracks. The society columns of the *St. Louis Post-Dispatch* on Sunday, 20 April, carried an announcement of the schedule of summer parades: "A battalion parade every Monday and Tuesday afternoon at 4:30 p.m., and a full regimental parade, with machine gun troops and supply wagons in the line, every Friday at the same time." The 6th Infantry Band would give a concert each Wednesday afternoon and on Thursday mornings there would be special drills on the parade grounds. While Col. Krueger was intent on keeping his regiment abreast of change, he also revived some of the oldest army customs. One Wednesday afternoon the band played a concert on the lawn in front of the quarters of Lt. and Mrs. Daniel Hundley, who was the youngest bride on the post. On a Wednesday in May, the band gave another concert in front of the Commanding Officer's quarters to honor Mrs. Krueger, who celebrated her birthday that day. But for the wedding of his daughter Dorothy to Lt. Aubry de Witt Smith on June 6, 1934, Col. Krueger pulled out all the stops. The wedding was prepared with all the care of the most intricate military maneuver.

The engagement picture that was featured in the central position of the society section of the *St. Louis Post-Dispatch* showed Dorothy Jane Krueger in an almost military stance. The article stated that Miss Krueger was an excellent horse-woman who played tennis and swam. Beside her commanding presence, the faces of the other prospective brides paled in comparison. Lt Smith, the son of Mrs. Kathryn Smith of Boonville, Missouri, and a graduate of the U.S. Military Academy, was on duty as a student at the Infantry School at Fort Benning, Georgia. The couple were to be married in June, when Lt. Smith graduated.[105]

Monday and Tuesday of the week of the Smith-Krueger marriage had the highest temperatures ever recorded for so early in the season, and a few scattered showers in the area were not enough to make any appreciable difference to the men lined up in their stiff serge uniforms to honor the daughter of their commanding officer. The first military wedding at Jefferson Barracks in many years, it was announced, would take place with the proper pomp and ceremony "on the terraced slope overlooking the Mississippi River, and more than one thousand guests, including all the officers and enlisted men of the Barracks and their wives, had been invited."

The bride came out in her heavy satin dress with a high neckline in front. The dress buttoned to the waist in back with small satin buttons. She was on her father's arm and carried white gardenias. Col. Krueger wore highly polished leather riding boots and his Sam Browne belt.

After the ceremony, the bride and groom walked back from the altar under an arch of crossed sabers held by the ushers and all the officers of the 6th Infantry. After passing below the sparkling shark teeth of the drawn sabers, the couple mounted upon the spring seat of a Service Company covered wagon beside Private "Pop" Higby, who, because of his great white moustache, was known as "Handlebar Hank." Pop Higby, who never wore the regular campaign hat but rather an old Spanish-American War hat, always drove the service wagon. He chewed tobacco, and it was his custom to spit in his hands as he took up his reins and urged the mules forward. For the wedding, he wore white gloves, but those who watched him closely saw that he spat as usual into them before setting out. Around the parade ground time after time the wagon went to the cheers of the thousands of spectators, and each time it passed in front of the guardhouse the cannon was fired. "Sparkplug," Sgt. Harry Becker's mongrel dog, darted out each time the cannon went off and lifted his leg against it, as he usually did at reveille and at retreat.

At a reception held afterward at the Officer's Club, the bride cut the heart-shaped wedding cake with the bridegroom's saber. While the officers enjoyed their wedding cake and champagne, the enlisted men and their families gathered around picnic tables the mess sergeants had set up on the edges of the parade ground. It was a day none of us would forget; the handsome smiling couple striding under the drawn sabers and then perched on top of the mule-drawn wagon represented the best that the Army could provide.[106]

The popularity of the CCC continued unabated in 1934. By January, the second year of the program, 300,000 men were enrolled. In July 1934, this was increased by 50,000. An article in the *Neighborhood Link News* on August 9 stated that there were 3,500 CCC boys at Jefferson Barracks taking preliminary training in the fine art of wielding axes, rakes and scythes before being assigned to the various forest preserves.

These CCC boys came from all over the Midwest. Many stayed in one of the camps at Jefferson Barracks but others came for examinations and conditioning. An example of this occurred during April when Lt. Col. O.A. Clark, of Jefferson Barracks, and several other officers traveled to Edwardsville Township, Illinois, to conduct examinations on 147 Madison County, Illinois, boys to be enrolled in the CCC. The first 50 young men left the next morning by train from St. Louis. It was reported that at Jefferson Barracks the men would be put through additional examinations and conditioning for work in the field. These young men were from all sections of Madison County, Illinois.[107]

Only a short time before the 1934 CMTC was to begin, on 24 June, Col. Walter C. Short succeeded Col. Krueger as commander of Jefferson Barracks.

Walter Short, born in Fillmore, Illinois, on 30 March 1880, graduated from the University of Illinois in 1901 and received a commission as second lieutenant in March 1902. Short had a successful, although unremarkable, military career. He was stationed at the Presidio of San Francisco in April 1903 and then transferred to the 25th Infantry at Fort Reno, Oklahoma. [1903-1907]. Following a brief tour of duty in the Philippines [1907-1908], he joined the 6th Infantry in Nebraska. Other assignments took Short to Alaska, California and Fort Sill, Oklahoma, where he became the secretary of the School of Musketry and commander of the 12th Infantry. Short then served with General Pershing's expeditionary force in Mexico with the 16th Infantry. During World War I, Short served as a small-arms training officer in Georgia. In June 1917, he went to France with the 1st Division. Holding the temporary rank of lieutenant colonel, Short was attached to the training section of the General Staff from April to November 1918. His professionalism won him the Distinguished Service Medal for "conspicuous service in the inspecting and reporting upon the front-line conditions" and for his efficiency in training machine gun crews. He was given the nickname of "Machine Gun" because of his keen interest in the development and utility of that weapon. He wrote a book on the subject.

Short saw combat during the battles of Aisne-Marne, St. Mihiel and the Meuse-Argonne. He held numerous staff positions after his return to the United States. While serving in these positions he served at Fort Leavenworth, with the 6th Division in Illinois, and Washington, D.C. Short came to Jefferson Barracks after serving as assistant chief of Insular Affairs. From Jefferson Barracks, Short became assistant commandant at the Infantry School at Fort Benning, Georgia. In December 1936, he became a brigadier general and in February 1938, the commander of the 2nd Brigade at Fort Ontario, New York. He then commanded [June 1938] the 1st Infantry Brigade at Fort Wadsworth, New York, the 1st Division at Fort Hamilton, New York, and upon promotion to major general in 1940, he transferred to Columbia, South Carolina.

On 8 February 1941, Short took command of the Hawaiian Department with the temporary rank of lieutenant general. Following the Japanese attack on Pearl Harbor, Short was demoted to major general and relieved of command on 17 December 1941. Under pressure, Short applied for retirement, which became effective 28 February 1942.

During retirement, Short worked for Ford Motor Company in Dallas, Texas, until 1946. He died in 1949 of a chronic heart ailment complicated by emphysema. He is buried in Arlington National Cemetery.[108]

CMTC opened at Jefferson Barracks in early July 1934, with about half as many participants as in 1932. Jefferson Barracks was one of forty-eight camps throughout the country.[109]

Paul R. Hughes, St. James, Missouri, provided the biggest problem faced during the CMTC training period at Jefferson Barracks. Hughes, 18, weighed 297 pounds and stood 5 feet 11 inches tall. He took a size 50 pants, a size 20 shirt and then could not button the collar, and size 12 ½ shoes. The Quartermaster had a real problem.[110]

An interesting sidelight to activities at Jefferson Barracks in 1934 took place on Saturday and Sunday, 22 and 23 April, when the 1st Cavalry passed through on its way from Fort Knox, Kentucky, to Fort Riley, Kansas. The 1st Cavalry had organized at Jefferson Barracks in 1833 as the 1st Dragoons. When it had organized at Jefferson Barracks the 6th Infantry had been stationed at the post, so the officers of the two organizations took the opportunity to celebrate the event. The old cavalrymen were not impressed with the new modernized unit, which was propelled by motors instead of the noble horse. A cavalry on wheels just was not a cavalry to them.[111]

The 6th Infantry made a "leap-frog" march to Camp Custer, Michigan, for the 1934 summer maneuvers. The regiment divided into three sections and camps were placed about forty miles apart. One-third of the regiment was moved by motor trucks to within thirteen or fourteen miles of the first camp and left to hike the remaining distance. The trucks then returned to meet the second section, which had also marched approximately thirteen or fourteen miles, and transported it to the camp. The third section, which had been left behind to break camp, was then met by the trucks and carried to camp. This procedure was repeated between camps until the entire regiment had reached its destination. A detachment moved ahead with kitchen, headquarters and staff officers' equipment to prepare a new camp each day.[112]

Approximately 700 officers and men of the 6th Infantry and the Second Platoon of the 6th Tank Company made its first camp at the American Legion Park in Edwardsville, Illinois. Capt. Edward C. Phillips, Executive Officer at Jefferson Barracks, spent the day of 2 August in Edwardsville making arrangements for the camp that was to last from Saturday afternoon until Monday morning. The stopover on Sunday resulted from army regulations prohibiting marching on Sundays.

A model camp was to be established at Legion Park on the level portion of the golf course. The public was invited to visit the camp after 9 a.m. Sunday. The 30-piece band that accompanied the 6th Infantry gave a concert at 4 p.m. on Sunday.

A detachment of 50 soldiers, with all the animals and horse-drawn vehicles of a U.S. Army regiment, passed through Edwardsville and made camp at Granite City on 2 August. Animals in the detachment consisted of 20 riding horses, 40 draft horses with rolling kitchens, and 24 one-horse machine gun carts. The detachment with the unit's horses departed Jefferson Barracks ahead of the main column as it can travel only around 25 miles per day, thus allowing the main column to catch up during the march to Camp Custer.[113]

The outfit left Monday morning for Litchfield, Illinois. It planned to travel 35 to 45 miles a day. The men walked about 10 miles each day and rode in trucks the remainder of the distance to each camp.[114]

On 6 November 1934, the 6th Infantry held its Regimental Day exercises. Activities began at 7:00 a.m. with the 6th Infantry Band conducting a Reveille March, followed at 9:00 a.m. by a Regimental Parade. Major W.B. Zimmerman, Chaplain, gave the Invocation. This was followed by a history of the 6th Infantry by Capt. R.A. Byars. Col. Short then addressed the regiment and the 6th Infantry Band and played the 6th Infantry March. Dinner, by companies, began at 12:15 p.m. The afternoon was spent in many different military competitions. At 6:00 p.m., there was a complimentary picture show in the new post theater, followed by a Regimental Dance at 8:45 p.m. in Atkinson Hall. Taps ended the day at 11:00 p.m.

The day's activities were presided over by the 6th Infantry staff officers: Col. Walter C. Short, commander; Capt. William H. Irvine, Adjutant; 2nd Lt. Louis W. Truman, Assistant Adjutant; Capt. Walter C. Phillips, Plans and Training Officer; and Capt. James C. Reed, Supply Officer.[115]

1935

The year 1935 was in most respects a mirror image of the previous year. Again, the monotony of routine garrison life was broken only occasionally by special outings, the overseeing of the CCC, and the one month CMTC in July.

In February, Capt. John D. Eason received orders to report for duty at Honolulu. Eason would return to Jefferson Barracks five years later to take command of Reception Center No. 1772, and the Induction Station.[116]

William Jay Smith described life at Jefferson Barracks in the 1930s in his book *Army Brat*. From Smith's book the reader can glean a sense of what the enlisted men did to overcome the boredom of army life at a post in the Midwest. In reality, especially at the time, some of their recreational activities bordered on the sad and ridiculous, but they also show what real life could be like.

One such incident concerns Sgt. Walter Payne of the 6th Infantry. Early one Sunday morning, a policeman found Sgt. Payne of Jefferson Barracks sprawled in a gutter near the intersection of Broadway and Rutger, halfway to downtown St. Louis. His trousers were lowered and he was bleeding profusely. His penis had been cut off and stuffed into the pocket of his uniform. The policeman called an ambulance, got the sergeant to a hospital and saved his life.

Sgt. Payne had apparently been discovered *in flagrante delicto* by an irate husband, who had taken immediate and explicit revenge.

The news soon made the rounds of the garrison.

"He was cut off at the front," someone said.

"They removed his bayonet," said another.

"They silenced his reveille," said a third.[117]

On another occasion, Sgt. "Tex" Schanley, one of the crack soldiers of the 6th Infantry, went on board the steamer *St. Paul* after having led the Memorial Day Parade. Midway on the trip, a drunken Schanley jumped overboard into the paddle wheel of the steamer.

Word went around that he had contracted syphilis; others said that he had been rejected by his girlfriend; still others reported that "Tex" had taken his life because he was more blessed than most men "built like a mule," and too much for any woman. Several of his buddies accompanied his body back to Texas.[118]

Sex and liquor were the primary concerns of the enlisted man, and both could be had in places not far off the post. St. Louis in the 1920s and 1930s was one of the most notorious centers of prostitution in the country, if not the world. Brothels ringed the waterfront and downtown areas of the city, and immediately across the river in East St. Louis was "The Valley," covering several acres. Here hundreds of largely black women attended their customers in rickety wooden cribs. But the men from Jefferson Barracks seldom had to go so far; the prostitutes came to them. On payday, they would appear at the streetcar station in their bright green and red satin dresses, wearing tennis shoes, and often carrying blankets under their arms. In 1927, the venereal disease rate at Jefferson Barracks was one of the highest in the army.

Smith goes on to say that when he was a teenager and on the way to his favorite swimming hole, he would sometimes come on a couple making love in the underbrush. It didn't take him long to learn the facts of life.[119]

Sgt. And Mrs. Layton had moved to a house midway between the North Gate and the parade ground, and Sgt. Layton was among the first enlisted men to acquire a car. In his Model A sedan, he took William Smith and his friends around the countryside, and it seemed the height of pleasure to have all the familiar places, houses, trees, fields, horses flying past as they turned on those high wheels. Before long, the cars began to multiply and young people who borrowed their parents' cars were off exploring what night life there was adjacent to the post.[120]

With the automobiles, roadhouses sprang up near the Barracks, and they also held their secrets. Smith and his friends went to one on Telegraph Road where the black singer offered up her song with a special flourish.[121]

During Smith's high school years, a new Post Theater had been built beside the Hospital, and on summer evenings Smith and his brother would put on their white duck trousers and walk off through the woods to the picture show. Usually they had canteen checks, which their father had won or collected in exchange for drinks, to cover the entrance fee, but there were times when they did not. They discovered that the window to the toilet on the side of the building was always left open, and since it was at ground level they could hoist their legs over the window ledge and climb in. They would wait until the picture started, and in the dark, find a seat with their friends, a good proportion of the audience was young people.[122]

The reader of William Jay Smith's book can catch a glimpse of the area around Jefferson Barracks when Smith describes his and his family's life. After high school, William Jay Smith attended Washington University in St. Louis. During his freshman year at Washington University, with their bootlegging days behind them, Smith's mother took a job at the Post Laundry to help pay the rent. Smith shared a ride to Wash. U. every day with his friend Jack Glascock, a major's son, who had enrolled to take courses until he could get into West Point. Jack would pick Smith up every morning, but usually in the afternoon William would have to take a long streetcar ride with several transfers home, as their schedules did not match up.

Toward the end of his freshman year, the Smith's heard that the Boston family, the owner of their house at the North Gate, was returning to St. Louis and wanted their home back. William's father frequented Regnier's tavern just beyond the West Gate of the Barracks. He learned that a small brick bungalow, owned by Joe Regnier's son, Jo-Jo, was for rent just down the road, on the corner of Sigsbee and Telegraph. This is where the Smith family moved and where they found themselves on 7 December 1941. It was a brick bungalow like so many built in the 1930s in the area, a sturdy, solid, incredibly ugly, four rooms with a cellar, an attic, a fenced-in yard behind, and a front porch high off the ground, where no one ever sat.[123]

The shift between high school and college can be very abrupt, but William said that it was a miraculous crossing of a deep chasm; at times, he wanted to destroy the bridge by which he had crossed and to blot out any reminders of his life with the army. Smith's R.O.T.C. uniform was one such reminder, and he wore it as little as possible. In his sophomore year, he hung it up and only occasionally attended class. He had taken ROTC in the first place only to avoid taking gym. Most of his friends at the Barracks had moved away or were soon to leave. Dean Short, his best friend and the son of Col. Walter Short, the commandant, had gone with his parents to Fort Benning, and afterward to West Point. Tommy Reagan had also gone to West Point, and Smith never saw either of them again. But Smith still lived on the edge of the Barracks and there were constant reminders that his connection with the military was not over. During his freshman year, he still lived in the Boston house, where he slept and studied, perched almost literally above the North Gate. He drove through the post almost every day, past the scenes of his childhood, to pick up his mother at the Post Laundry. On Telegraph Road, after they moved, his father would still come home daily with the large commissaries, and when Smith returned at night he would sometimes find him at the kitchen table drinking with his fellow bandsmen. But more and more his off-duty hours were spent at taverns, at Regnier's at the West Gate or at the Blue Goose, farther out in the country. Regnier's, a few hundred feet from the gate, was a two-story brick structure with a dark high-ceilinged barroom on the ground floor and a large apartment upstairs occupied by Joe Regnier and his family. In the spring and summer there were tables out under the trees behind the building. Presided over by stout and matter-of-fact Joe Regnier (always willing to listen to the soldier's complaints about the happenings on the post) and his handsome muscular bartender son, Regnier's was a favorite gathering place for men of the 6th Infantry. It resembled a good many of the German beer houses and beer gardens in South St. Louis. The Regniers, like many of the other inhabitants of the area, could probably trace their ancestry back to the original French settlers of Carondelet's Vide Poche, but by then they seemed to have adopted the atmosphere of their German neighbors.

All that was needed to give the place a complete feeling of *Gemutlichkeit* was a uniformed brass band pumping away on summer evenings. Even if there was no band, there were numerous bandsmen without instruments, but with plenty of talk. Smith's father became a legendary figure in the establishment. When sometimes in the late afternoon Smith stopped by to pick up his father for dinner, he would introduce William proudly as his son, the college boy. Smith noticed that his father's stories took precedence over those of the other men at the bar. This was a matter of protocol; deference was shown to old-timers, whatever their rating, even after duty hours. His father became a real hero when one evening he accidentally got locked inside. He went to the bathroom late in the evening, and, heavy with beer, fell asleep and did not come out. So much time went by that Joe Regnier thought that he had gone home, and when closing time came he locked up without checking the bathroom. When Smith's father came to an hour or so later, he tried to find his way through the dark to the door. His stumbling between the tables brought Joe down the stairs with his pistol at the ready. Only Smith's father's familiar snarl kept Joe from firing into the dark at the supposed intruder. The scene, reenacted on both sides of the bar, became a perennial favorite with the customers.[124]

Responding to the favorable public opinion to alleviate unemployment, Congress approved the Emergency Relief Appropriation Act of 1935 on 8 April of that year. This Act included continued funding for the CCC program through 31 March 1937. The age limit was expanded to 28, to include more young men. Enrollment had peaked at 505,782 in 2,900 camps by 31 August 1935, followed by a reduction to 350,000 in about 2,019 camps by 30 June 1936. During this period, the public response to the CCC program was overwhelmingly positive. A Gallup poll of 18 April 1936, asked, "Are you in favor of the CCC camps?" Eighty-two percent of the respondents said yes.

The territory of the Jefferson Barracks District of the CCC increased in 1935 to include fifty-two work camps. Each camp was equipped with suitable furniture, recreation and reading rooms, a library that included current newspapers and magazines, radios, victrolas and in some cases pianos. Pool tables, ping-pong tables, bowling alleys and gym equipment were installed in many camps. Each camp had baseball, football and basketball teams that competed with other camps and at the end of each particular season tournaments were held to determine district champions. Facilities in nearby towns were available for CCC members to attend church and community events, and local theaters usually cut prices of admission to enrollees. Arrangements and supervision for all of these events were handled by the executive staff, and the planning and supervision of project work was managed by the technical staff.[125]

Major General Stuart Heintzelman, commanding the Seventh Corps Area, announced on 4 April that 4,000 young men were to be trained in the Citizen's Military Training Camps in the Seventh Corps Area with camps located at Jefferson Barracks; Fort Snelling, Minnesota; Fort Lincoln, North Dakota; Fort Riley, Kansas; Fort Des Moines, Iowa, Camp Pike, Arkansas; Fort Crook, Nebraska; and Fort Leavenworth, Kansas. Jefferson Barracks trained young men in the basic course as well as Infantry.

General Heintzelman stated that the purpose of the camps was to "develop the manhood of this nation by bringing together young men of high type from all walks of life, in the same uniform, on a common basis of equality and under the most favorable conditions of outdoor life; to teach them the privileges, duties, and responsibilities of American citizenship; to inculcate self-discipline and obedience; and to develop these young men physically, mentally, and morally."[126]

CMTC began at Jefferson Barracks on 2 July with Col. Short in overall command and the 6th Infantry officers and enlisted men plus reserve officers in charge of the daily activities of attendees. Approximately 1,700 youths from Missouri, Illinois, and Arkansas began the month-long camp. This figure amounted to nearly three times the number trained in 1934.[127]

Maybe it was the result of powerful lobbying, some improvements in the economy, a new feeling of hope generated by Roosevelt's New Deal, or the frightening developments in Europe and Asia, or a combination of these things, but Congressional appropriations for defense increased for Fiscal Year 1936. Congress's generosity resulted in CMTC receiving an appropriation of $2 million for the 1935 camps. A quota of nearly 34,000 was established, and 30,084 young men trained at forty-nine camps, with almost 54,000 applying.[128]

At the same time as CMTC was going on at Jefferson Barracks, a two-week Reserve Officers training camp was held. Col. Marshall A. Goff, commanding officer of the 404th Infantry, announced that 404th officers came from a territory in Wisconsin within the Superior-La Crosse-Madison area.[129]

During the summer of 1935, the 6th Infantry participated in the Bi-Centennial celebration of the settlement of Ste. Genevieve, Missouri. A pageant portraying historical highlights of its two hundred-year existence was an eight-day event during which the 6th Infantry soldiers appeared in many scenes, in addition to many parades and drills. The event drew thousands of visitors from all over the Midwest. The Jefferson Barracks troops marched the sixty miles from the Post to Ste. Genevieve and set up camp on the outskirts of the town.[130]

Captain Harry Kirsner
Kirsner enlisted in the Army in 1908, moved through the ranks, and was finally appointed a Second Lieutenant during World War I. During the 1930s he served as quartermaster for CMTC, CCC, and the post. Capt. Kirsner developed the U.S. Army blanket, that scratchy wool thing, which was issued to every soldier. Capt. Kirsner's son, Sheldon grew up at Jefferson Barracks and piloted B-17s in the 8th Air Force during World War II, before serving at the post after the war and settling down in St. Louis after his military career.

6th Infantry Headquarters Company in 1933

Lt. Gen. Walter C. Short
Col. Short relieved Lt. Col. Krueger in command of Jefferson Barracks on 24 June 1934. Short commanded the Hawaiian Department on 7 December 1941 when the Japanese attack took place.

A warrant charging assault to kill was issued on 22 June against Pvt. Thomas L. Owens, a soldier stationed at Jefferson Barracks, in connection with the shooting of Clifford Johnson, a carpenter. Johnson, whose right arm was fractured, said he was walking down a road with a woman companion when the soldier came up, drew a pistol, and fired four times at him and twice at the woman. Owens, who was unable to raise bond, was held in jail. No explanation or motive had been uncovered.[131]

Like his predecessors, Col. Short's duties often took him away from the post, leaving the post under the temporary command of several capable officers. They included Capt. Paul H. Weiland, Major William A. Smith, Lt. Col. Frederick A. Barker, Capt. John H. Cochran and Major James A. Summersett. All of these officers, with the exception of Lt. Col. Barker, who retired April 30, 1935, and Major Summersett, who served in the Air Corps, were veterans of foreign wars. Capt. Brown retired due to a disability received in the line of duty on 31 October 1936.

One of Col. Short's absences came about when he was appointed commanding officer of the annual National Rifle and Pistol Matches at Camp Perry, Ohio. This event was held from 1 September to 18 September. As commanding officer Short shouldered many duties. Over 6,000 competitors had to be comfortably sheltered and fed; safety precautions and sanitary measures enforced; and in fact, the colonel had to be "mayor" of this huge tent city.

The National Rifle and Pistol Matches had been held for many years under the auspices of a special act of Congress. The program of shooting was divided into two parts. The first was devoted to the great national matches such as the national team match and the individual match which were promoted directly by the War Department. The second part listed the many matches sponsored by the National Rifle Association. This part also featured the Junior matches for teenage boys and girls.[132]

On 24 September, the 6th Infantry from Jefferson Barracks took part in the annual American Legion parade in downtown St. Louis. In colorful peacetime demonstration, 70,000 veterans of World War I marched to the cheers of thousands of spectators along the two-mile route of march. More than 125 musical organizations, including 100 drum and bugle corps, and many crack drill teams excited the crowd.[133]

The 6th Infantry at Jefferson Barracks held its Regimental Day on 4 November 1935. This was always an important, as well as a festive day to celebrate the present and past of a regiment, in this case the proud 6th Infantry. The 6th Infantry band played reveille at 7:00 a.m. At 9:00 a.m. came a regimental parade where each company paraded in review. The band then gave a concert, followed by the invocation by Major W.B. Zimmerman, Chaplain. Col. Short addressed the assembled troops and visitors and the band played the 6th Infantry March. Dinner was served at 12:10 by company. At 2:00 p.m., the Jefferson Barracks and Scott Field football teams played. Complimentary picture shows were at 6:00 and 8:00 p.m., and at 8:45 was a regimental dance in Atkinson Hall. The day ended with taps at 11:00 p.m.

The 6th Infantry roster of officers at Jefferson Barracks included Col. Walter C. Short, commander; Lt. Col. William A. Smith, Executive Officer; Major John H. Cochran, Adjutant; Major Walter C. Phillips, Plans and Training Officer; Major George Read, Jr., Regimental Supply Officer; and 1st Lt. Louis W. Trieman, Assistant Adjutant. Battalion commanders included Major Nels L. Soderholm, 1st Battalion; Major James A. Summersett, 2nd Battalion; and Major James R. Urquhart, 4th Battalion. There were also four unassigned officers: Major Alexander M. Stark, Jr., Major William L. Brown, Major Lester H. Harnhill, and Capt. Emmet M. Connor. Major Cochran commanded the band and Warrant Officer George H. Buckholz served as Band Leader. Capt. A.J. Regnier commanded Headquarters Company; 1st Lt. Walden B. Coffey commanded Company A; 2nd Lt. Herman H. Kaesser, Jr., commanded Company B; 2nd Lt. R.W. Jenna, Company C; Capt. J.D. Frederick, Company D, 2nd Lt. L.K. White, Company E; Capt. W.G. Muller, Company F, Capt. LeRoy E. McGraw, Company G; Capt. Wayne C. Smith, Company H; and Capt. R.S. Henderson, Service Company.[134]

1936

The year 1936 began, passed and ended pretty much as the previous year. The Headquarters 7th Civilian Conservation Corps Area remained at Jefferson Barracks and during the month of July, the CMTC held its annual encampment.

In February, Representative Thomas C. Hennings, D-Missouri, announced that he had been advised of the approval for three WPA, {Works Progress Administration} projects totaling $17,200 for improvements at Jefferson Barracks. The projects provided $2,408 for repairs of the stables, $7,172 for improvement of the grounds, and $7,620 for work at the National Cemetery.[135]

The number of applications for CMTC went up eight percent from the number of applicants in 1935, to 58,327. The number of camps increased by two, as 31,480 young men attended CMTC in 1936.[136]

The 6th Infantry continued to garrison Jefferson Barracks. Col. Walter C. Short remained in command of Jefferson Barracks and the 6th Infantry, until he was recalled to service with the Bureau of Insular Affairs on July 1. Col. Joseph A. Atkins relieved Col. Short in command of Jefferson Barracks, the 6th Infantry, and the CCC District.

Col. Atkins was born in Georgia on 13 November 1876. He graduated from Emory College with a Bachelor of Science degree in 1898 and received an appointment to the U.S. Military Academy June 19, 1900. He graduated and received a commission as a Second Lieutenant of Infantry 15 June 1904. Later military education included graduation from the Army War College in 1930 and the Chemical Warfare School, Field Officers' Course, in 1930.

Col. Atkins was promoted to first lieutenant in 1911 and to Captain in 1916. On 5 August 1917, he was promoted to Major (temporary) and on 31 August 1918 he was promoted to lieutenant colonel, U.S.A. He was stationed at Washington, D.C. as Infantry Representative with the Technical Staff of the Ordnance Department, and in the office of the Chief of Infantry from 13 December 1919 to 1 February 1921. Col. Atkins served as Assistant Chief of Staff, 1st Division, from 1 February 1921, to 30 June 1921; with the War Department General Staff, Washington from 1 July 1921 to 31 July 1923; as post and 3rd Battalion Commander, 12th Infantry, at Fort Washington from 1 August 1923 to 31 July 1925; with the War Department General Staff as Assistant to the Secretary of the General Staff, Washington from 1 August 1925 to 30 June 1928; and as Secretary, General Staff, from 1 July 1928, to 31 August 1929. He was promoted to lieutenant colonel on 13 August 1928. From 15 August 1929 to 30 June 1930, Col. Atkins was student officer at the Army War College. From 16 September 1930 to 16 June 1934 he served as Assistant Executive Officer, the Infantry School, Fort Benning, Georgia; and from 20 June 1934 to 26 June 1936 as Commanding Officer, 3rd Battalion of the 29th Infantry, Field Artillery School, Fort Sill, Oklahoma. Col. Atkins reached the grade of colonel 1 August 1935.

As of the time that Col. Atkins reached Jefferson Barracks, he was on the Initial General Staff Eligible List. He had won the Victory Service Medal with four battle clasps. He was awarded the Distinguished Service Medal with the following citation:

"For exceptionally meritorious and distinguished services. He served with the Third Division as assistant chief of staff, G-3, from December 1917, until March 1918; acting chief of staff and G-3, from March 1918, to 27 May 1918; G-3, from 28 May to 11 June, and from 1 September to 19 September 1918; and as G-3, 36th Division from September 1918, to March 1919. By his tireless energy, devotion to duty and high military attainments, he contributed in a large measure to the successes by the commands with which he served."[137]

On a sad note, no trace could be found of the body of James H. Bailey, 25, infantry band drum major at Jefferson Barracks, who leaped into the Mississippi River from an excursion steamer the night of June 1. Bailey, in civilian clothes, had accompanied three companions from the barracks on a boat trip. Edward Abbot, one of the men, said Bailey remarked, "I'm going to jump in the water." He broke free from Abbot's restraining grasp and leaped. Bailey was from Weatherford, Texas, and was said to be a good swimmer.[138]

On a lighter note, fifty 6th Infantry soldiers from Jefferson Barracks participated in the marching and battlefront scenes of "Sons of Guns," presented for seven performances at St. Louis' outdoor municipal theater beginning 29 June.[139]

During the summer of 1936, the 6th Infantry took part in the 2nd Army maneuvers in Michigan. This was the most extensive military tournament held in the United States up to that time. Approximately 60,000 regulars and militia participated in these maneuvers.[140]

The regiment that a soldier served in could certainly produce a sense of pride in an individual. The 6th Infantry had a long and distinguished history, having been constituted 11 January 1812 in the Regular Army as the 11th Infantry Regiment. It organized during March to May 1812 in Vermont, New Hampshire, and Connecticut. It then consolidated with the 25th, 27th, 29th and 37th Infantry Regiments during May to October 1815 to form the 6th Infantry Regiment.

During the War of 1812, the regiment served on the Canadian border. Then in 1832, the regiment saw action in a series of engagements known as the Black Hawk War against the Sac and Fox Indians. On 2 August 1832, the 6th Infantry caught the Indians at the junction of the Bad Axe River with the Mississippi River, in present day Wisconsin, and soundly defeated the Indians, earning the Campaign Streamer for the Black Hawk War. In 1837, units of the regiment left Jefferson Barracks for Florida via Louisiana. As part of a force commanded by Zachary

Taylor, the regiment entered the Second Seminole War in eastern Florida in 1837. It was the first "guerrilla-style" war fought by U.S. troops.

At the onset of the Civil War, the regiment received orders to move east from Fort Humboldt in northwest California and join Federal forces. According to one biographer of the time, "Several of the Regiment's best and bravest officers, honest in the mistaken construction of the Constitution and true to their convictions as to their duty, tendered their resignations and gave themselves to the Confederate cause." During the Civil War, the 6th U.S. Infantry Regiment lost two officers and twenty-nine enlisted men killed or mortally wounded, and one officer and forty-three enlisted men by disease. A total loss of seventy-five.

For six years after the Civil War, the regiment served at various stations in Georgia and South Carolina. It moved to Fort Hays, Kansas, in October 1871. For the next several years, the regiment saw duty on the frontier in Kansas, Colorado, the Dakotas, Iowa, Wyoming, Idaho and Utah. In 1872, the regiment was in the Dakota Territory fighting many engagements against hostile Indians. In 1872 and 1873, the regiment earned two Campaign Streamers: North Dakota 1872 and North Dakota 1873. The next several years saw the regiment in action during the Indian Wars, and they were awarded four Campaign Streamers: Montana 1879, Little Big Horn, Cheyenne and Utes.

In 1880, the regiment moved to Fort Thomas, Kentucky, where it remained until called to action in June 1898 in the Spanish-American War. On 1 July 1898, the 6th Infantry took the brunt of the fighting during the charge up San Juan Hill. It carried its standard high and bravely, always forward, and won the battle.

In late July 1898, the regiment sailed for the Philippines to help quell the insurgents in the Philippine-American War. The Moro tribe was one of the toughest enemies the 6th ever faced, every one of them fought to the death, and preferred to do it in hand-to-hand combat. The regiment fought more than fifty engagements, and left with Campaign Streamers for Jolo, Negros in 1899, and Panay in 1900. In March 1905, the regiment returned to the Philippines to do battle with the Moros again. For three days in 1906, elements of the regiment fought in the First Battle of Bud Dajo, one of the fiercest conflicts of the entire island campaign. The successful ending to the battle broke the Moro strength and ended the fighting in that part of the island. One of the 6th Infantry soldiers, Capt. Bernard A. Byrne, received the Medal of Honor for service in the Philippines.

Following service in the Philippines, the 6th Infantry returned to the Presidio of San Francisco, California. In May 1914, it entered into service on the Mexican border. In March 1916, it proceeded to San Antonio, Chihuahua, as part of the Punitive Expedition under Brigadier General John J. Pershing. In February 1917, Pershing's force withdrew from Mexico and the regiment moved to Fort Bliss. The regiment earned another Campaign Streamer, Mexico 1916-1917.

On 18 November 1917, the 6th Infantry was assigned to the 5th Division. In December 1917, the regiment was assigned to the 10th Brigade, 5th Division and began training stateside. In the latter part of May 1917, the 6th Infantry Regiment was declared ready for introduction to combat and placed at the disposal of the French, for service at the front. In July 1918, a strategic offensive plan was agreed upon by the Allied commanders, the immediate purpose of which was to reduce the salients which interfered with further offensive operations. One of these was the St. Mihiel salient. The 1st U.S. Army was organized on 10 August and directed to launch an offensive on 12 September to reduce this salient. The 6th was destined to play an important role in this operation. On 1 December 1918, the 6th Infantry conducted a march from Luxembourg to the city of Trier, Germany. They were the first American troops to enter that ancient city.

The 6th was relieved from assignment to the 5th Division in August 1921. On 24 March 1923, it was assigned to the 6th Division. It served with the 6th Division until relieved on 16 October 1939.

Between World War I and World War II, the regiment returned to the United States, where they continued to train to become one of the best regiments in the Army. In 1936, they were designated a mechanized unit. The regiment left Jefferson Barracks for Fort Knox, Kentucky in February 1941[141]

The enlisted man of the army gained an affinity to his "Outfit." The infantry company, cavalry troop or artillery battery was the smallest unit with both tactical and administrative capabilities and duties. It was able to fight on its own resources for a limited time and could handle the necessary business of supply and personnel management. To the enlisted soldier, it was "the outfit," and he seldom called it anything else. The outfit provided everything a man needed- food, clothing, shelter and security from the outside world, where no one was in charge. On the last day of each month, the outfit paid a soldier enough to keep him in Bull Durham tobacco, buy a few beers and make a trip to town if that was what he wanted. In return, the soldier was required to be present most of the time, carry out orders given him in a reasonably efficient manner without too much complaining and do nothing to disgrace the uniform or the outfit. The last requirement was the most important.[142]

The boss of the outfit was the "Old Man," officially the commanding officer, usually a captain or first lieutenant with considerable service behind him. Sometimes he was a new second lieutenant just out of the military academy at West Point on his first assignment. In that case, the pink-cheeked, beardless youth was still the Old Man, but primarily he was an observer learning the ways of the regulars, while the first sergeant kept the outfit running. Occasionally, the Old Man was a captain in his forties, maybe even fifties, sweating out enough service for retirement, at the end of the line, militarily speaking. This was the result of a lenient policy that rewarded past service, usually in World War I, and allowed an officer to leave the Army with honor and retirement pay. Because of the limited number of officers, there was only one commissioned rank in the outfit. If there were two, the second one was probably one of the new second looies just out of West Point. An officer might be in command of two outfits at the same time, when the commander of one was absent, since an officer was always required to be on hand.[143]

Next in the chain of command was the first sergeant, also called the "first soldier," the "topkick," or merely the "top." He was the ramrod of the outfit, the man who kept it running. Most likely he was a veteran of World War I or the Mexican border campaign, but sometimes he went back as far as the Philippine Insurrection. When the commanding officer was absent, the topkick had full responsibility until the Old Man returned.[144]

The platoon sergeants were on the next rung of the ladder, responsible for the performance of the squads assigned to their platoons. They saw that the training progressed according to the schedule and that discipline was maintained. Most had five or six enlistments, or more, in the Army.[145]

The outfit also had a mess sergeant, a supply sergeant and a clerk who were responsible for their special departments and reported directly to the first sergeant. The corporals, lowest of the noncommissioned ranks, were squad leaders, in charge of the smallest tactical units of the military machine. A corporal was the leader in direct contact with the privates of his squad and responsible for their conduct and performance of duty. He might have two or three enlistments behind him, or he could be nearing retirement with thirty years of service on his record.[146]

Privates were a diverse lot. There were recruits on their first enlistment learning the basics of soldiering. Although some had enough after one enlistment and left to look for a job on the outside, many re-upped and made it a career. There were old-timers who had knocked around the Army, the Navy and the Marine Corps, enlisting in one branch, then another, as the mood suited them. Unable to take the responsibility that went with higher rank, or not wanting it, those men served out their time because it was the only life they knew or wanted. Privates also fell into the category of the smart soldier who liked the service and made it his career and who could be relied on to do his duty well and was prepared for advancement. When a vacancy in the noncommissioned ranks occurred, he was considered for promotion. Some of these men had enlisted for West Point Preparatory School, failed to make the grades necessary for entry into the academy, but chose to remain in the army. Others had been to private military schools, tried the army and found it little different so they stayed.[147]

Outfits were small, seldom more than ninety men at full strength, and the men were close because of the barracks life. They knew each other's qualifications, temperaments and sense of humor or lack of it. There were no secrets, and if a man tried to hide something he was suspect.[148]

The brigade commander was a brigadier general, with a staff consisting of an executive officer, a major, an S-1, administration and personnel; S-2, military intelligence; S-3, operations and training, and an S-4, logistics. The S-2 and S-3 were combined, due to the shortage of officers available for this duty. The brigade commander also had an aide-de-camp, a lieutenant.[149]

The enlisted section of brigade headquarters included the sergeant major, a topographical draftsman and two clerks.[150]

The two regiments of the brigade were identical in organization, each consisting of three battalions, a headquarters company and a service company. Each battalion was made up of three rifle companies and a machine gun company. The companies were lettered from A to M, with the J being omitted. Each regimental commander, a colonel, was served by a staff, which was organized in the same way as the brigade staff. The regimental commander did not rate an aide-de-camp. There were no medical personnel assigned to the brigade. Regimental aid stations were manned by medical detachments from division. Regimental headquarters company furnished personnel for the administrative staff of the regiment, communications, and a weapons platoon armed with mortars and anti-tank guns. Service Company furnished transportation for the regiment, which prior to the adoption of motor vehicles in 1935 was mule drawn.[151]

A battalion was often commanded by a major, although the Table of Organization authorized a lieutenant colonel for the position. The battalion was also entitled to a staff the same as the regiment, but in most cases, it would likely be a patchwork of personnel drawn from the companies for a specific training exercise.[152]

Total strength of the brigade, including the two regiments, was approximately 2,500 officers and men.[153]

Major holidays were always special for the soldiers at Jefferson Barracks, or at any post for that matter. Only those soldiers with special duty were required to report on holidays such as Thanksgiving and Christmas, and they would be relieved so that they could partake in the festive and delicious meals served on those special days.

A good example of one of these meals can be taken from the Thanksgiving Day menu served to the Headquarters Company, 6th Infantry, on 26 November 1936. The meal started with oyster soup and crackers, with stuffed olives, celery and shrimp salad served next. Then came the roast turkey with chestnut dressing, cranberry sauce, roast pork, mashed potatoes, creamed peas, creamed asparagus, and candied sweet potatoes for the main course. For dessert, the men had pumpkin pie, coconut cake, fruit cake, and minced pie. After dinner, the men could enjoy assorted candy and mixed nuts. The meal was topped off with cigars or cigarettes, sweet cider and coffee.

1937

The year 1937 opened as no other year in recent memory. A soldier is trained to answer the call of duty whether it be in time of war or at home during peaceful times. On the home front, soldiers can be called to fight the ravages of flood, fire or any other disaster that imperils the country.

The soldiers at Jefferson Barracks have answered this call to duty many times, but possibly never to a greater degree than during the unprecedented floods of the Ohio River and its tributaries in January and February 1937. As the headquarters of the Civilian Conservation Corps for this district, a major share of the responsibility for the protection of southern Illinois and southeastern Missouri centered on Jefferson Barracks and its commanding officer, Col. Joseph Atkins. Cities, villages and farms were inundated as far as twenty miles from the channel of the Ohio River; many lives were imperiled and thousands were driven from their homes. Practically the entire strength of the 6th Infantry from Jefferson Barracks and the CCC District, including trucks, tents and all other facilities necessary to meet the emergency were rushed to the flood stricken area. Contact was established with other posts, civilian groups and the Red Cross in order to maintain an efficient organization. Communities were evacuated and thousands of refugees were fed, sheltered, clothed and given medical attention, while thousands of soldiers and CCC boys worked day and night building and repairing levees to hold the flood waters back and to bring the raging rivers and streams under control. The city of Cairo, Illinois, was saved from destruction by a three-foot bulkhead built on top of the levee, and great areas of southeastern Missouri were spared devastation by the heroic and tireless energy of these troops. Many deeds of heroism marked this mid-winter battle with the turbulent elements. Drenched in the icy waters, men labored to the limits of exhaustion unmindful of time, discomfort, or danger. Charles G. Fowler of CCC Company No. 695 risked his life to save a buddy from drowning, and was rewarded with a Certificate of Valor by CCC Director Robert Fechner, .

Company 695 was located at Dixon Springs, Illinois. It had originated 18 July 1934 at Jefferson Barracks. During the flooding in February 1937, the entire company was used to augment the work of relieving the suffering. Things operated on a war-time 24-hour basis, with a shift of four crews preparing meals throughout the day and night.[154]

During this time of intense activity for both the 6th Infantry at Jefferson Barracks and the Jefferson Barracks CCC District, Col. Joseph A. Atkins, commanded the 6th Infantry, Jefferson Barracks and the Jefferson Barracks CCC District. Lt. Col. George R. Hicks served as executive officer.

Lt. Col. George R. Hicks, District Executive Officer, was born in Sioux City, Iowa, 24 August 1885. He attended Lake Forest University, Iowa State College and the U.S. Military Academy, graduating in 1911. He served with the 26th Infantry from 1911 to 1914; the 15th Infantry, U.S. Expeditionary Force in China from 1915 to 1917; the 8th Infantry in 1918; the 1st Hawaiian Infantry in 1919; the 44th Infantry in 1920; the 20th Infantry in 1921; on the Infantry School staff from 1922 to 1925; the Command and General Staff School in 1926; with R.O.T.C. at Creighton University from 1927 to 1930; and with O.R.C., 102nd Division from 1930 to 1936, after which he arrived at Jefferson Barracks.[155] Probably one of the busiest officers during the flood activities in 1937 was District Quartermaster, Capt. Harry Kirsner. Capt. Kirsner was born in Poland on 21 February 1890. He enlisted as a private in the U.S. Army on 24 April 1908. He moved up through the grades of Elect. Sgt. 2nd Class, Master Elect., Q.M. Sgt. Sr. Grade, 59th Company and Non-commissioned Staff Coast Artillery Corps and Quartermaster, Q.M. Corps until 19 August 1918, when he was commissioned second lieutenant, Q.M. Corps. He was promoted to first lieutenant 13 November 1918, and honorably discharged 25 October 1919. He was re-appointed Quartermaster Sgt., Sr. Grade, Q.M. Corps, 8 December 1919, and served in that capacity until 13 September 1920, when he was commissioned first lieutenant, Q.M. Corps, and promoted to captain 1 September 1934.

Capt. Kirsner was assigned as Base Supply Officer CCC at Jefferson Barracks from 28 May 1933 to 31 March 1935. When the CCC re-organized and separated from the Regular Army accountability on 1 April 1935, he was assigned duties as CCC District Quartermaster at Jefferson Barracks. He performed additional service as Flood Relief Quartermaster in January and February 1937.[156]

The Jefferson Barracks Civilian Conservation Corps District comprised about two-thirds of the state of Illinois, extending throughout the southern and central portions from Cairo to a northern boundary formed by a line east and west of Peoria. Before this administrative district was formed, the 6th Corps Area was organized into twenty-three forestry districts and several supply bases. Instructions were issued by Headquarters, 6th Corps, in March 1935, changing this set-up to that of five district organizations. The Jefferson Barracks District became one of these five districts.

The former 21st, 22nd and 23rd Forestry Districts, with the supply base at Jefferson Barracks, were combined under this new reorganization plan. Jefferson Barracks became the district headquarters and the post commander became the District Commander of CCC activities. At this time the district was comprised of forty work camps, divided into three sub-districts with a Commanding Officer over each and the Headquarters Company located at Jefferson Barracks.

Shortly after organization as a district in the summer of 1935, the CCC activities gained their greatest expansion. A peak of fifty-two work camps was reached in the district. To provide greater administrative efficiency, five sub-districts were established instead of three. In November 1935, four companies were moved from the district to Wisconsin. The following January, the district personnel was further reduced by the departure of five companies to the 9th Corps Area and the discontinuance of one company, thus dropping the number to forty-two work camps.

The next change of importance was a reorganization within the district. This was accomplished by the discontinuance of the sub-districts as administrative divisions and the establishment of four Inspection Areas, with one inspector assigned to each instead of Sub-District Commanders as formerly. This change was accomplished in June 1936.

The Headquarters Company at Jefferson Barracks was disbanded on 27 May 1937; all work formerly done by members of this company was assigned to civilian employees. With further general reductions in the CCC due to improved employment conditions throughout the country, the number of companies was further reduced to thirty-three as of 1 August 1937. Of these companies, six were employed in forestry work, five in state parks, one on state conservation projects, seventeen on soil conservation and four on drainage. Five of the camps were comprised of veterans of the Great War and the other twenty-eight were junior companies comprised of young men, two companies were comprised of young colored men. The strength of the district at that time was 128 reserve officers; including ninety-one line officers, twenty-one medical officers, six chaplains, three dental officers and one veterinarian. There were ninety-seven civilian employees, thirty-three educational advisers, nine contract surgeons, and 5,047 enrollees. Four contract clergymen of the Roman Catholic faith were employed from local churches to serve personnel of this faith.[157]

An extensive program of general improvement had been inaugurated at Jefferson Barracks during the fall of 1935, under supervision of the Federal Works Projects Administration, to utilize idle and penniless workers during the Great Depression. This was increased in 1936 to include $77,052.63 for paving, $96,715.17 for remodeling buildings and $5,000 for building roads through the National Cemetery. This program was extended in 1937 to include construction of a stone wall around the National Cemetery, for roads essential to fire prevention through the wooded areas of the reservation, for repairs to barracks, construction of pipe lines, a side-track to the ordnance storehouses, additions to the commissary buildings, for clearing timber and underbrush and making further extensions to the paving system. The total amount appropriated for these improvements was in the neighborhood of $2,500,000, and the number of WPA workers given employment ranged from a few hundred to 3,500.[158]

Easter Sunday, 28 March 1937, saw a huge celebration at Jefferson Barracks for the garrison and the surrounding community. The Third Annual Easter Sunrise Services were held at Jefferson Barracks at 6:00 a.m. More than 6,000 attended this service, sponsored by the Carondelet Ministries Alliance. A chorus-choir of 100 voices under the direction of Mrs. Helen Sneeds Parson presented special numbers and led the congregational singing.[159]

Extremely sad news hit Jefferson Barracks on 10 May when it was learned that three non-commissioned officers of the 6th Infantry had been killed early that day in an automobile accident three miles east of the post. Cpl. Paul D. Outhouse, 25, Co. B, Patoka, Illinois, was killed instantly. Cpl. Hugh P. Snell, North Platte, Nebraska, died a few minutes later, and Sgt. Fred H. Everett, Co. C, died in a Cape Girardeau hospital. The veteran Everett had served in the Army for 31 years. The three had been on their way to the Arcadia, Missouri, Rifle Range.[160]

Infantry tanks, assigned to the 6th Infantry at J.B., made their first public appearance at Scott Field on Sunday, 27 June, in connection with the Sons of the American Legion celebration held that day. In addition to the tanks, Jefferson Barracks sent its crack 6th Infantry Military Band. Two National Guard Flying Units as well as one Naval Air Unit participated in the event. More than 40,000 visitors watched the military demonstrations. Sons of Veterans squadrons from all over southern Illinois and greater St. Louis entered in a track and field meet and rifle competition the morning of the 27th. Twenty-three drum and bugle corps competed for cash prizes in the afternoon.[161]

6 July marked the beginning of the thirteenth annual CMTC at Jefferson Barracks. It took 158 tents to house the approximately 1400 young men between the ages of 17 and 24 who attended the 4-week course in military drill and citizenship. The camp lasted until 4 August.[162]

In the 30-day course, students spent the first two weeks at drilling, the third week at target practice, and the final week at "polishing off," a process that included hikes and extended order drill, as well as considerable close order drill.[163] More than 2,000 CMTC trainees and 6th Infantry regulars participated in a brigade review at 4:00 p.m. at Jefferson Barracks on 16 July. Col. H.C. Bonesteel, Fort Sheridan, Illinois, commanded the 6th Infantry and Col. Robert L. Floyd, Chicago, commanded the CMTC Regiment. Reserve officers from the 342nd and 343rd Infantry commanded all of the companies. A contingent of 72 reserve officers from the 343rd Infantry arrived on 15 July to take over the training of the enrollees. Lt. Col. Ray Mahon commanded the First Battalion and Lt. Col. Arthur L. Simpson commanded the Second Battalion.[164]

At the request of the officers in charge of the CMTC encampment at Jefferson Barracks, the St. Louis Red Cross sponsored a series of dances on Friday evenings at the Barracks.[165]

The 6th Infantry left Jefferson Barracks on 2 September 1937, to take part in army maneuvers in Texas. The convoy included 850 officers and men plus 118 motor vehicles. Their first night was spent at Lebanon, Missouri, then moved on with Missouri Highway Patrol escort. The 6th did not return until 21 November. The regiment was at full peace-time strength at this time, with thirty-nine officers and 1,115 enlisted men, and special troops at Jefferson Barracks that included twelve officers and 117 enlisted men of the medical, ordnance, quartermaster and signal corps.[166] These maneuvers included almost 11,000 officers and enlisted men from throughout the country in a test of a new motorized infantry division. The division assembled at Fort Sam Houston and Camp Bullis, Texas, in September, then conducted a series of combat tests. Early in October broader tests of the powers of the division took place at Camp Bullis, then a week's extended march and field maneuvers started during the first week of November. Attack and pursuit tests were conducted for one day in the Mineral Wells area and the final day of the test saw the entire division march from Mineral Wells to San Antonio, a distance of 279 miles.[167]

In his book, *Army Brat*, William Jay Smith gave us some insight into the everyday life of the soldier at Jefferson Barracks and what he could do for rest and relaxation. Smith goes on to point out that "there was always violence just below the surface of military life, a violence that led many men to blow their tops, get busted and sent to the guardhouse. But it was only in boxing that physical combat was given official sanction. Competition among the companies was so intense that men were promoted solely on their ability in the ring and were prepared like leashed animals for the regular inter-company "smokers" during the year or for the summer bouts. The competition, especially during the terrible August heat which, even under the best of circumstances, put us all on edge, was so keen that it affected everyone on the garrison, including the wives who shared every detail of their husbands' lives, and, of course, their children. Officers' wives were not exempt, indeed, some seemed to find as much release in the boxing as the men themselves."

"The wife of Major Ford, a supply officer, was out every evening. With her red hair in its mannish cut, a cigarette dangling from her mouth, she cursed like a trooper in a rich husky voice, urging her troops on. Her troops were not the men in the ring (although she found time to shout at them also), but her squad of young boys selling popcorn. The profits from the sale of popcorn went to the recreation fund for the benefit of the entire garrison, and Mrs. Ford was determined to raise as much money as possible."[168]

One place in the Barracks remote from riotous activity was the main Barber Shop, located in the basement under the old Post Theater and chapel at one corner of the parade ground. Although the shop was below ground, it gave the impression of being at the surface, with windows opening out into bays of limestone. Next to the Barber Shop was the Post Library, an odd and uneven collection of mostly popular novels and detective stories.[169]

Another place of great quiet was the Post Hospital, situated on the far west of the parade ground and set back from the other buildings. The dark wide screen porches that surrounded it, hiding the red brick, and the shade trees before it made it seem a smudge or a great oblong shadow on the landscape. The corridors inside the hospital were as dark as the porches, the brown linoleum floors were kept polished to a keen gloss. The wards were all white and gleaming, but in the somber hallways the ceiling fans turned like dark tongues, and the white-uniformed nurses making their rounds stood out like white teeth in the shadowy throat of a monster.[170]

1938

Jefferson Barracks was typical of all army posts in the 1930s. Typically, the army was for single men, with a system designed for maximum performance of military duty with a minimum of outside problems. If a man was married, he could not enlist. No regulation existed that prohibited marriage, but an enlisted man had to obtain permission to marry from his company commander or he could not re-enlist at the completion of his current term of service.[171]

Non-commissioned officers of the first three grades, the staff, technical, or first and master sergeants, were governed by different regulations and, if married, were furnished quarters on the post. They made up a small fraction of the enlisted ranks, however. Those senior non-commissioned officers who were bachelors lived in private rooms in barracks and when off duty pursued their own interests, generally keeping aloof from the lower ranks.[172]

The majority of soldiers who made up the line companies, batteries, and troops, were single, and they took their fun where they found it in bars, dance halls, or in games of chance, with nice women or women not so nice, as long as their pay lasted. When a man was broke, he stayed on the post, went to the movies on credit, played pool in the dayroom, or fired small-caliber weapons on the company's indoor range. Some even read books.[173]

All the old tricks, shortsheeting, the hotfoot, shoes tied together, knotted socks, were repeated at every opportunity. Each new recruit who joined the outfit was sent to the supply room for such non-existent equipment as left-handed ramrods and bunk stretchers, only to draw the wrath of an annoyed supply sergeant.[174]

Starting with the base pay for a private at $21 per month, pay rose to $30 for a private first class. A corporal drew a base of $42, and a sergeant, sometimes a veteran of twenty or twenty-five years-service with a war or two behind him, drew a base salary of $54 per month. The upper non-commissioned grades fared better - a staff sergeant drew $72, first and technical sergeants $84, and a master sergeant the sum of $126 as their base pay. Because most men, especially the non-coms, had more than four years' service, they drew longevity pay on top of the base. This additional pay, or "fogy," increased base by five percent for each four year's good time. Privates and Privates First Class could also draw extra pay as specialists in a variety of fields, for example, as bugler, teamster, cook, radio operator, etc. Pay for specialist first class was $30 per month; second class, $25; third class, $20; fourth class, $15, fifth class, $6, and sixth class, $3. Specialists pay was not increased by a fogy.[175]

Officers could not expect to become wealthy in the military. The pay of the chief of staff, the top man in the army, was $666.67 per month, plus $117.30 for quarters and rations. Major generals received the same pay and allowances as the chief of staff, which seems hardly fair for the chief. Brigadier generals were paid $500 per month, with the same allowances as the other general ranks. Colonels with twenty-six years of service drew $466.67, but were paid $500 after thirty years. Lieutenant colonels with twenty years were paid $379.17 per month, and it went to $479 after thirty years. Majors with fourteen years behind them drew $250, and their top salary was $437.50 at thirty years. Captains with less than seventeen years were paid $220 per month, but it could go as high as $375 if they lasted thirty years in that rank. A first lieutenant was worth $166.67 to start, but his pay could go as high as $300 in thirty years, if he hadn't quit before that time. A second lieutenant started at $125 per month, one dollar less than a master sergeant. The ration allowance was $15.30 per month for all ranks, without dependents.[176]

Sports was an important part of military life during the 1930s. Physical contests gave men a chance to work off steam, helped build esprit de corps in regiments and provided free entertainment for the garrison. This was a fringe benefit enjoyed by all ranks because there was never an admission charge for any sporting event. The quality of athletics was high, for competition was keen and there were plenty of candidates for both team and individual contests. Athletes who made the regimental teams may not have been professionals in the strict meaning of the word, but they came close. They were allowed all the time necessary to practice. They were well coached, and were relieved of duty that would interfere with the sport. There was some recruiting of good athletes, but many volunteered solely to be able to take part in organized athletics. In the Depression years, opportunities in professional sports were limited and the pay was low. The security provided by military service was an added benefit.[177]

More soldiers played the game of baseball than any other team sport, for each company put a team on the field and men were encouraged to play. During the summer when troops were in garrison, there would be games each afternoon, and off-duty personnel would turn out to cheer their buddies. There were battalion and regimental leagues, as well as inter-post leagues, which were the "major leagues" of service baseball. These were made up of outstanding players selected from the company teams for their ability. It was, in effect, a farm system. Managers were officers who had played the game at West Point or other colleges or were senior non-commissioned officers, some with professional experience. Although a member of a regimental team was a soldier first, he was excused from such unpleasant work details as kitchen police, stable call, or pulling targets during the playing season or when in training. This was an incentive to be on the team, and a man who made the regimental squad could depend on promotion in rank as well. Also, a good baseball player could stay in training and play the game while awaiting a tryout with a minor league team, and more than one man got his chance that way. The best example was Dizzy Dean, who began his baseball career at Fort Sam Houston in 1928 pitching for the post laundry team. In 1929, Dizzy bought his discharge to play for the San Antonio Public Service Club and the following year he began his professional career with a St. Louis Cardinals minor league team. In 1934, he was voted the outstanding athlete of the year by the Associated Press while playing for the Cardinals. For years, fans at Fort Sam Houston talked about the way Dean could throw a baseball and how Sgt. Jimmy Brought, the coach of the 12th Field Artillery team, saw his potential and helped him get a start.[178]

A large number of visitors attended the Army Day exercises at Jefferson Barracks that were held on April 6, 1938. Visitors witnessed - probably for the first-time, an elaborate exhibition of the latest inventions of warfare, including the new .50 caliber machine guns, anti-aircraft guns, tanks, artillery pieces and small arms. The St. Louis Chapter of the Military Order of World War Veterans gave a banquet in the evening at the Coronado Hotel in St. Louis, which was attended by the post officers and their ladies.[179]

The Missouri State rifle and pistol matches took place in Jefferson City on 14 and 15 May. The 6th Infantry team from the post won the high-powered rifle team competition with a team from Washington University taking second and the 138th Infantry National Guard finishing third. Frank Rossio, 6th Infantry finished second in the individual high-powered rifle competition. Rossio also won the service rifle match with Thomas Bennett, 6th Infantry, in third place.[180]

Major General Hugh A. Drum visited the Post on 27 May 1938 for an inspection and review of the post and troops. Major General Karl Truedell accompanied General Drum. A mock battle provided entertainment for the Jefferson Barracks guests. Major Audrey J. Bassett commanded 450 officers and men in a bloodless clash with an equal number of men under the command of Major Virgil N. Cordero. Despite the fact that Major Cordero had the advantage of a tank unit, Major Bassett's forces held its assigned sector, the north half of the reservation or "Gettysburg Ridge," against the furious attacks of the enemy for four long hours, from 2:00 until 6:00 p.m. The engagement was officially declared a draw, and all differences settled at the mess hall. Both commanding officers had survived a real baptism of fire on the fields of battle in France, during World War I.[181]

On 7 July, the CMTC once again took center stage at Jefferson Barracks. Despite the fact that President Roosevelt's proposed budget had cut CMTC funding to one million dollars from the previous year's 2.3 million, the popularity of CMTC with Congress paid off, and the full amount was restored to the Army appropriation bill. Perhaps reflecting the recession, almost 8,000 more men applied for camp in 1938 than had applied in 1937. A total of fifty camps were conducted, and almost 4,500 more men completed the four-week course than did the previous year.[182]

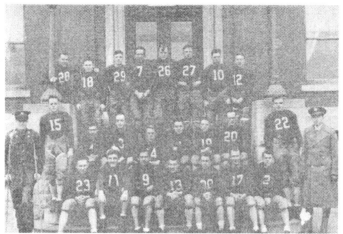

Jefferson Barracks football team ca. 1930s.
This picture was taken in front of the post gymnasium (now the Missouri Civil War Museum)

Jefferson Barracks basketball team ca. 1930s.
This picture was taken behind the post mess hall, "White Elephant".

Jefferson Barracks soccer team ca. 1930s.

At Jefferson Barracks, inexperienced Reserve Officers, under the supervision of Regular Army officers, "mustered in' 1,500 Missouri and Illinois youths. Starting at 7:30 a.m., the rookie civilian-soldiers processed in at a rate of 200 per hour. Advanced medical students of the ROTC aided medical corps physicians with the physicals, then the rookies received military clothing piece by piece, following measurement of each individual.

Once all the processing had been completed, mornings, except Sundays, were devoted to military drill. Swimming, basketball, baseball, and other games took care of the trainees' afternoons. Prizes were awarded for excellence in athletics and marksmanship and to generally outstanding students. The students could attend dances, boxing and wrestling matches in the evening.

The 1,500 enrollees in the CMTC at Jefferson Barracks and 1,200 members of the 6th Infantry staged a joint parade the afternoon of 22 July. Congressman C. Arthur Anderson and a number of newspaper editors from Missouri and Illinois attended as special guests of Col. Atkins. Under the command of Lt. Col. E.H. Bertram, second in command at the Barracks, the 6th Infantry put on a demonstration of Butt's Manual of Special Drills before the regular parade began. Col. Phillip Fox, commander of the 343rd Infantry, U.S. Reserve Corps, commanded the CMTC units.

Also in the reviewing line was Lt. Col. Oldham Paisley of Marion, Illinois, in charge of the 344th Infantry, Egyptian Fusiliers. These troops were encamped at the Barracks for unit training.[183]

The entire population of Jefferson Barracks was interested in the parade of the 7th Cavalry Corps through St. Louis on its way to Fort Knox, Kentucky, on 3 November. Brigadier General Adna R. Chaffee, who had been decorated for gallantry and had risen to the rank of major general during World War I, commanded the 84 officers and 1,951 men who were mounted on 637 armored cars and trucks. The route of march had been chosen to test the ability with which armored divisions could be moved through a large city. The results were more than satisfactory. The division left Columbia, Missouri, at 6:30 a.m.; entered St. Louis via route 40 at 11:00 a.m.; and passed over the Municipal Bridge to East St. Louis in just one hour.[184]

The very next day, 4 November, the 6th Infantry celebrated the regiment's 149th anniversary. The 6th Infantry Band played reveille at 7:30 a.m., then after breakfast the regiment marched to the North Gate at 9:00 a.m. Once at the North Gate, the band played a selection of march music. Chaplain Walter B. Zimmerman gave the invocation, and Major Ray H. Green, Post Quartermaster, presented the North Gate Sentry House to the Post Commander, Col. Joseph A. Atkins. Col. Atkins then addressed the gathering and deposited historical material in the Sentry House archives. The regiment then had dinner, by company, followed by an afternoon of military games and competition. The day's festivities came to an end with a complimentary picture show in the Post Theater at 6:00 and 8:00 p.m.[185]

From the Organizational Day program, we can learn the names of the officers and men who made up the Jefferson Barracks garrison. In addition to Col Atkins, the Jefferson Barracks staff consisted of Col. Shepperd B. Philphot, Regimental Executive for Supply; Lt. Col. George R. Hicks, Provost Marshal and Post Exchange Officer; Major Virgil N. Cordero, Adjutant; Major Edward P. Earle, Plans and Training Officer; and Capt. Roy M. Thoroughman, Assistant Adjutant and Recruiting Officer.

1939

News that Col. Atkins' tenure as commander of Jefferson Barracks was to end on 10 February 1939 was received with regret at the post and in St. Louis, early in the year. Col Atkins had not only met successfully all the difficult situations that had confronted his administration of the post during a period of transition - the many problems involved in directing the CCC, the CMTC and the ROTC- but also had given a measure of cooperation to the city and public that had won the highest praise. Much of his success can be attributed to exceptional education and experience.

Lt. Col. George R. Hicks, who had served as a major in the American Expeditionary Force; Lt. Col. Shepperd B. Philpot, also an overseas veteran; and Major Cordero were temporary commanders of the post, during absences of Col. Atkins. Both Hicks and Philpot retired on 31 December 1940.

Col. Harry B. Crea arrived from St. Petersburg, Florida, to relieve Col. Atkins as commander of the Post on 10 February 1939. Col. Crea had served overseas and had remained after the close of World War I as Executive Officer of the 50th Infantry at Mayen and Coblenz, Germany, until the recall of the troops of occupation in 1922. He had been in charge of National Guard instruction in the Florida area prior to coming to Jefferson Barracks.[186]

During an inspection of Jefferson Barracks on 7 April, Major General Henry Gibbons was stricken with a heart attack and remained at the post hospital until he recovered. Gibbons was then serving his fortieth year in the army, having entered the military at the outbreak of the Spanish-American War on May 19, 1898. General Gibbons retired shortly after leaving Jefferson Barracks.[187]

Remember, that during all of the 1930s the CCC maintained a presence at Jefferson Barracks. On 31 May, the St. Louis office of the Federal Bureau of Investigation announced the arrest of Robert A. Smith, 20, a CCC enrollee, assigned to Jefferson Barracks. Donald B. Norris, in charge of the FBI's St. Louis office stated that the arrest came after an exhaustive examination of thousands of signatures of CCC men at the post. Norris went on to say that Smith had admitted killing C.K. Wickiser, a salesman, in a Butte, Montana, hotel on 20 October 1938.

A tip that Smith had come to St. Louis in Wickizer's automobile to join a CCC camp led authorities to St. Louis, where it was found that Smith had enrolled in a CCC camp in Carrollton, Illinois, then been transferred to a camp in Leroy, Illinois, then on to Jefferson Barracks. After his arrest, Smith told Norris that Wickizer had picked him (Smith) up while he had been hitchhiking near Helena, Montana. When they got to Butte Smith went to Wikizer's hotel room and beat him to death with a hobnailed shoe, robbed him of $6, and took his car.[188]

Smith was returned to Butte the second week in June. There he faced murder charges.[189]

The fourteenth annual CMTC opened on 12 July with approximately 1,400 enrollees. 6th Infantry personnel had pitched 264 tents just south of the main parade grounds to house the enrollees. 6th Infantry officers and 73 reserve officers were in charge of the camp.[190]

Perhaps the highlight of the 1939 CMTC came on August 4 when the young men received their first taste of battle. They moved up to front at "Argonne Heights," a mock battlefield in the vicinity of the Barracks. For the mock battle, the regiment was divided, one battalion scheduled to "dig in" and protect the "Heights," and the other, constituting the enemy, attacked in an attempt to drive the former back.

After the battle the battalions united to participate in the first hike of the 30-day camp, and that night spent their first night sleeping in pup tents on the ground. The hike covered 6 miles and was made with full pack, weighing about 10 pounds. The regiment returned to camp the next day.

After the final review the day before the camp demobilized on 9 August, Col. H.B. Crea, commanding officer of Jefferson Barracks, said that he had witnessed the training of youthful citizens in four CMTC camps, and that those in this camp had been more responsive to army routine than those of the others. After the review, scheduled for 8:00 a.m., all assembled in the CMTC bowl where awards for scholarship and athletic achievements were made. The next day the young soldiers de-processed by turning in their military equipment and uniforms and donning their civilian clothes once again. They then mustered out and received their mileage allowance to return home.

When large numbers of men were at Jefferson Barracks for training, it was customary to bring to the post officers of reserve units whose training consisted of working with the CMTC men. In 1939, Lt. Col. Oldham Paisley was commanding officer of the 344th Illinois Infantry, better known as the Egyptian Fusiliers. The officers of this unit arrived for training with the CMTC. Staff officers for the whole training were appointed by the Commanding Officer of Jefferson Barracks. These included Plans and Training, Camp Surgeon, Camp Supply and Assistant Camp Supply Officer, Camp Mess Officers, Camp Chaplain, Camp Publicity Officers and Camp Athletic Officers. These posts all came from permanent party officers at Jefferson Barracks.

General Ford, who visited the 1939 camps, and for whom a parade was given on 1 August, expressed himself as "very pleased" with the accomplishments of CMTC. Certainly, the personnel of Jefferson Barracks had done everything possible in their power to make the camps, CMTC, ROTC and ORC, successful.

Another youth program, the National Youth Administration [NYA], began in December 1939 at Jefferson Barracks and continued for seven months. Consultations between officials of the National Youth Administration of St. Louis and post executives led to the conclusion that a large number of NYA boys could be employed and give benefits to both the youths and the War Department. The result was that an application for a total of $50,630 was approved by the Federal Security Agency for the NYA and the War Department to cover the cost of labor, material and equipment. 69 boys between the ages of 18 and 24 were assigned to work at the post on 7 December 1939. This number represented approximately a third of the project quota. By rotation of shifts, a total of 200 boys were utilized for a period of seven months. When this project expired, a new one was sponsored and approved, providing a quota of 400 boys for work at the post. The wide field of work especially provided by this plan gave the youths a chance to try several trades or occupations, such as auto mechanics, landscaping, plumbing, etc. Boys were assigned to work in the offices, laundry, pressing room, repair shops, high pressure oil-burning heating plants, in maintenance duties, as assistant plumbers, pipe fitters, pipe layers, meter readers, in electric lighting repair and installations, steam fitting, carpentry, packing, crating, operating woodworking machinery, warehousing and in miscellaneous functions in the warehouse, grocery and commissary. They also assisted in surveying parties as rodmen and linemen. The importance and success of the program can be attested to by the fact that it was used as a model for similar projects at other posts throughout the United States.[191]

The year 1939 brought a fresh outbreak of war among the great powers of Europe and plunged American public opinion into uncertainty. As far as Jefferson Barracks was concerned, there was no uncertainty as to its duties. Whatever the future might be for America, the Barracks had to be prepared for the possibility of war. Coincident with the outbreak of the European struggle, Col. Crea, Lt. L.C. Macon and Capt. Huelett commenced tours of St. Louis manufacturing districts and munitions plants to determine St. Louis' manufacturing capability, both for the immediate needs of the Barracks and for the larger needs of the nation, and to build good relations between the Army and its supporting civil functions.

November brought the Army, Navy and Marine Council to Jefferson Barracks for a meeting, and on 11 December the Military Affairs Committee of both the House and Senate of the U.S. Congress made a survey of the Post, doubtless in connection with the nation's facilities for military expansion.[192]

During September 1939, the army inaugurated an intensive recruiting campaign with Capt. R.A. Thoroughman and Capt. Hamer P. Ford as recruiting officers. Officials expected that 2,000 men could be recruited from the St. Louis area. Recruiting stations opened in St. Louis, Poplar Bluff and Sikeston, Missouri.

Jefferson Barracks became the reception post for these recruits. They arrived at first in groups of twenty to thirty each day, and were kept for approximately one week. They were quartered in Atkinson Hall, and distributed for mess among nine organizational messes on the post. Each man was issued one complete uniform, with toilet articles, and given two dollars for incidentals. As the weeks went by, the number of recruits arriving at and passing through the Barracks grew and placed a considerable strain on the post facilities. By 10 October there were about 400 enlistees waiting to be processed. Many of the recruits sought entrance to the Artillery. Such men had to be shipped to the West Coast for training. Indicative of the number of men is an entry in the post diary for 1939 stating that Capt. Gilbreth left for the Pacific Coast on November 3 with 277 enlisted men.[193]

Such numbers of men must have taxed not only residential facilities but also existing arrangements for transportation. This formed the first evidence for the need of a separate Induction Station and Reception Center, as well as a new type of shipping and receiving service at Jefferson Barracks.

Along with the expansion of its military activities, a reconstruction and rehabilitation program was approved for the Barracks with money allotted from State WPA funds. A total of $2,670,178 came from this source and $340,450 from Federal WPA funds. About 1,600 of the 3,000 WPA workers assigned to the post were regularly employed, including 200 of 400 skilled workers. Whereas the program for 1938 had been primarily confined to ground improvements, the program for 1939 included the completion of projects undertaken the previous year, along with renovation and construction of buildings. A part of this program was the development of Little Big Horn Run, now known as Sylvan Springs, to make a picnic and recreation area, for the commanding officer of the post had always been conscious of the necessity for facilities which would assist in maintaining morale. Work on this project was commenced in February 1939, and in later years the work was to be enlarged.[194]

Buildings on the post were in a bad state of repair. Termites had eaten into the foundation stays of several buildings to the extent that it was doubtful if they were habitable. The six barracks buildings and two converted stables were inadequate for the housing of the garrison, and rehabilitation of officer's quarters had also become necessary. Major General Stanley H. Ford and his aide Major Basse spent 28 January at the Barracks in consultation concerning construction and improvements. Major General Henry Gibbons, Quartermaster General, also made an inspection on 6 April.[195]

The approach of war in Europe resulted in an acceleration of the 6th Infantry training program, in keeping with the nation-wide expansion of the army's size and activities. The usual spring rifle program at the Arcadia Range was cancelled, and the 1st Battalion was ordered to join the 2nd Battalion in intensive field work and conditioning in preparation for maneuvers. A mobilization test was completed on 6 May. Overnight training was instituted on 16 May, with the regiment leaving the post at 2:00 p.m. and returning at 10:00 a.m. the following morning. These tests included both defense and attack exercises and critique conferences for the officers. By 25 May, the 6th Infantry was ready to depart for summer maneuvers at Camp Williams, Wisconsin.[196]

Earlier in the year, in February, a series of training films were shown at the post theater. There is no previous record of the use of this type of visual education and it is probable that they represent the post's first use of a training aid.[197]

Upon its return from summer maneuvers, the 6th Infantry resumed its rifle training at Arcadia. Marching and bivouacking were incidental to the Arcadia expeditions. Arcadia is approximately 90 miles from Jefferson Barracks - the journey there and back entailed long daily marches for the infantrymen.

It must be understood that the regiment seldom functioned as one unit. The trips to Arcadia were undertaken one battalion at a time. Meanwhile men, sometimes consisting of a few men and sometimes a whole company, undertook special duty in other states. During December 1939, Capt. Pierce is reported as having taken fifty men for special duty at Fort Snelling, Minnesota, and during the reserve training period in the summer of 1940, Company K was at Des Moines, Iowa, on duty with the CMTC, remaining there until shortly before the final departure of the 6th Infantry from Jefferson Barracks. Even the band had special duties to perform outside its regular military duty with the infantry. During the recruiting campaign of September 1939, the 6th Infantry Band initiated the work of canvassing by a series of tours in a number of Missouri towns.[198]

During the remaining months of 1939 the 6th Infantry was almost constantly on maneuvers. The entire regiment went to Camp Joseph Robinson at Little Rock, Arkansas, for winter maneuvers. The first contingent left the Barracks on 2 November and the remainder followed two days later. Even the tank company attended these maneuvers. Returning to the Barracks on 6 February 1940, the regiment left on 1 March with forty-nine officers and 1,029 enlisted men for Fort Knox, Kentucky. [This time it was to take part in the spring maneuvers extending into four states with Louisiana as the central point.][199]

The fires that broke into a world conflagration had been kindled in Europe, and there was a rising lump in the throat of the United States. What the future held in store for this nation was uncertain, but that it must prepare for whatever that might be was certain. World War I had left only unpleasant memories, and the isolationists were strong, but careful observers foresaw the necessity for a strong, well-equipped army, and the processes of creating, training and maintaining that army were undergoing reorganization.

Congress had made liberal army appropriations, and the campaign for recruiting was being pressed with renewed vigor. Lt. Col. Ford, who had been designated recruiting officer for Missouri, opened stations at various points throughout the state, and recruits were being received at Jefferson Barracks in ever increasing numbers. This called for general expansion of the post. Many new buildings were needed, facilities had to be added, and all departments enlarged.

Two battalions each of the 1st and 20th Infantry, with twenty-four officers and 1,175 men under the command of Col. John B. Hester, arrived at the Barracks on 8 November and departed 10 November.

The 6th Infantry Band returned from Camp Robinson to participate in the Armistice Day Parade, and on 14 November the first detachment of the tank company left for Camp Robinson.

The congressional military committee, headed by U.S. Senator Thoas, visited the post on 11 December. Officers from Scott Field, Fort Leavenworth, Fort Chanute and the Belleville, Illinois Chamber of Commerce were at the post to meet the committee. One of the questions to be determined was the changes and expansion necessary to prepare this post as a replacement center for Air Corps ground units. Members of the committee expressed themselves as highly pleased with conditions at the Barracks.

Col. Joseph A. Atkins
Col. Atkins commanded Jefferson Barracks and the 6th Infantry Regiment.

Col Joseph A. Atkins with the 6th Infantry in review formation with Col. Joseph A. Atkins front and center. Col. Atkins relieved Col. Short in command of Jefferson Barracks on 1 July 1936.

Chapter 10 - Jefferson Barracks Begins to Expand and the Army Air Corps Takes Over

The 61st Coast Artillery with fifty officers and 1,300 men came rolling into the Barracks in 290 motor cars and trucks on 28 May 1940. While at Jefferson Barracks, it gave an anti-aircraft and searchlight demonstration which attracted a large crowd of visitors.

The 6th Infantry returned from Army maneuvers on June 1, and after ten days rest, the 2nd Battalion marched to the Arcadia Rifle Range.

On 5 July 1940, the 6th Infantry received orders to prepare for the permanent evacuation of Jefferson Barracks. On 6 August, Col. Crea left with the 1st and 3rd Battalions for Fort Knox, which became the regimental headquarters. The 2nd Battalion, under the command of Major Cyril B. Spicer, entrained for Fort Benning, Georgia, on 12 August. On the same day, Capt. Francis H. Boos arrived with Company E, 3rd Infantry, from Fort Snelling, Minnesota.

Lt. Col. Frank H. Pritchard arrived with the 11th Air Corps School Squadron, activated at Scott Field, on 3 September 1940, to take charge of the Barracks and convert it into an Air Corps Replacement and Training Base, the first post in the country to be selected for that purpose. A week later, 125 reserve officers arrived for ten days duty. On 12 September, an order was received to induct all reserve officers qualifying in this group into the service for one-year active duty.[1]

Perhaps the best description of the first days of Jefferson Barracks as a Air Corps Replacement and Training Center can be found in a memoir written by Col. Leslie I. Neher, USAF (retired) in December 1987. According to Neher the Air Corps occupation of Jefferson Barracks started with the mobilization of the 13th Air Corps School Squadron at Scott Field, Illinois. The first formation of the squadron occurred at sunrise on Saturday, 14 September 1940 when more than 400 enlisted men formed in double line in the southern portion of the building area at Scott Field.

Capt. Leslie I. Neher, Field Artillery Reserve, had arrived the day before and was assigned to the 13th School Squadron. Headquarters did not know where the squadron was located and suggested a search mission. Capt. Neher located an area where unassigned enlisted men were quartered and found several sergeants searching for information regarding the assignment of several hundred enlisted men. He ordered a roll call at sunrise the following morning.

The formation at sunrise on Saturday morning disclosed that the 13th Squadron was the only squadron to have an officer present. The enlisted men that had not been assigned or posted to the roll of the 13th Squadron were dismissed and returned to their barracks. The 13th was quickly formed into squads and marched (herded is a better word) to the mess hall for breakfast.

The squadron consisted of approximately fifty enlisted men that were in their second or third enlistments and included a master sergeant and a first sergeant. More than a hundred men were in civilian clothes, and had not received a single day of military education or training. The first hours after breakfast were spent in organizing the squadron and making assignments into squads and platoons (later termed as flights) with assignments to barracks. Headquarters had made no assignment of barracks and other unorganized squadrons were "outranked" for barracks space.

It was shortly before noon that a "runner" from Headquarters arrived with compliments to the Captain and a request to meet the adjutant immediately at headquarters.

Capt. Fay O. Dice, Adjutant, stated that the 13th School Squadron would proceed on Monday morning to Jefferson Barracks, Missouri, by motor transportation and man the post, until Washington (War Department, Chief of the Air Corps) ordered the squadron back to Scott Field.

Many changes were made in the assignments of enlisted men in order to make the squadron self-sufficient when detached from an established base. It took the direct order of the Field Commander, Lt. Col. Wolcott P. Hayes, Air Corps, to open the "shop" of the quartermaster in order that uniforms might be issued to the recruits of the 13th Squadron. The uniforms were drawn in bulk and issued at an unoccupied barracks on Sunday morning. It was a very busy Sunday for Capt. Neher who wished to relieve the 6th Infantry, then a mere skeleton force at Jefferson Barracks. Neher had recently served on a special mission (training exercise) at Fort Knox that included select troops of the 6th Infantry, and he had been impressed with the combat effectiveness of the 6th.

The big question was, could Air Corps troops man an Army post? There were approximately fifty enlisted men that had served in the Infantry, Artillery and Cavalry. They were highly experienced and were later found to be well adapted to post missions.

The truck convoy departed from the main gate of Scott Air Field at eight o'clock and it was later learned that the last truck was halted by Lt. Col. Leo F. Post and two cooks were removed. The Monday morning movement of the 13th Squadron crossed the Mississippi River on the south bridge and turned downstream. It was admitted to Jefferson Barracks by the 6th Infantry gate guards.

A company of the 6th Infantry was waiting for the arrival of the Air Corps troops and a "change-of-command" exercise was quickly arranged. The courtesy formations were held on the parade grounds while the trucks for the squadron and for the infantry company were parked on the road near the river side of the parade grounds.

The First Sergeant approached the squadron commander and asked, "What the hell do we do now?"

Any enlisted man that had served at Jefferson Barracks was directed to "front and center" and a plan was quickly formulated to house the squadron and to relieve the guards of the 6th Infantry.

The 13th School Squadron had relieved the famous 6th Infantry of a long tenure of service in the west. In fact, Jefferson Barracks was at this stage an Air Corps post.

The fact that the 13th Squadron contained some fifty experienced enlisted men enabled the squadron to quickly assume those duties that the 6th Infantry had performed for the past one hundred or so years. Those former members of the 6th Infantry that had re-enlisted in the Air Corps were most valuable in assisting in locating other services of the post, such as the quartermaster, medical services and chaplain.

The first service that was performed by the Air Corps was that of relieving the infantry guard of general prisoners. An unexpected incident occurred when a newly enlisted soldier was given two general prisoners to guard on a work detail of cutting wood in a remote portion of the post. The two prisoners gained possession of the shotgun carried by the guard and broke out the handle of the gun when they hit the guard over the head. They abandoned the gun and left the guard in a coma lying on the ground. The area was quickly surrounded and the two prisoners solicited a ride, on the adjoining highway, from a plain-clothed state policeman patrolling in an unmarked car. The prisoners were placed on bread and water for three days in solitary confinement, were given extended sentences, and were transferred to an Army disciplinary barracks.

One night, just a few days after the 13th Squadron had garrisoned Jefferson Barracks, the St. Louis police telephoned from Union Station and stated that young civilians from Kentucky and Tennessee were hungry and would like to have transportation to the Barracks. A truck brought them to Jefferson Barracks where a hot meal awaited. Thus, Jefferson Barracks was an Air Corps Basic Training Station and the mission of the post was evident.

Immediately there were problems arising as the mission of the squadron became known. One of the first was the refusal of the quartermaster to outfit more than six or eight recruits per day. After a few days in which there was a constant arrival of recruits, the 13th Squadron devised battering rams and forcefully removed padlocks from quartermaster warehouses that contained both Army and Civilian Conservation Corps equipment, including clothing. There was at that time a "summer house" near the parade ground and all uniforms, cots, blankets, etc. were carried from the warehouses to the "summer house." The following day saw all uniformed men "fitted" by CCC type service.

Many of the tents that were drawn from the quartermaster were unfit for service. Only the best were placed on wooden platforms that had housed the ROTC and CMTC personnel during past summer months. A local tentmaker provided repairs to the tents and the Air Corps troops settled in for the winter.

The 13th Squadron became a tentative or provisional group organization. A single officer had commanded the 13th when it arrived at Jefferson Barracks and it was several days before additional officers were assigned. Several of these were junior officers that had seen CCC service and had recently received commissions from approved colleges and universities. The officers were quartered in the Officers Club building. Meals were served in the club dining room and cots were placed in several of the rooms.

Unfortunately, there was a feeling of distrust between the regular officers and the reserve officer. Even when a judgment must be made of the two classes of officers, that by 1940 the regular officers had completed some twenty years of professional service, a period for the Army that contained extreme scarcity of federal funding and a retrospective system that dated to the early twenties. The morale and consequently the efficiency of the Army was very low. The officers of the Reserve Corps had seen promotions consistent with proper training periods, and "time-in-grade" programs. Predicable, perhaps, was the attitude of the regular officer toward the reserve officers that had penetrated the ranks of the Army, including the Air Corps. This unfortunate attitude existed toward the CCC-trained officer that had seen one, two, three, four, or even more years in uniform under mobilization conditions.

The Civilian Conservation Corps did assist the Army in 1940 with rather large quantities of trucks, cots, blankets, kitchen equipment, automobiles, etc. that went into Army quartermaster warehouses, when the CCC saw its ranks depleted and the draft became effective in August 1940. It was the surplus CCC equipment in storage at Jefferson Barracks that provided the first uniforms of the recruits of the early fall of 1940. The draft was effective 28 August 1940, and the flow of recruits soon followed.

The 13th School Squadron, when it arrived at Jefferson Barracks, contained perhaps 150 enlisted men that had never fired an Army weapon. A sinkhole contained a supply of ammunition, stored in a warehouse, that was used to qualify the recruits for duty that required the use of weapons. All men of the squadron qualified according to Army regulation. A colonel from Corps Area arrived and requested to view the Corps Area reserve of small arms ammunition. There was only a small lot that remained, and the colonel returned to headquarters with a negative report that none at Jefferson Barracks knew that the sinkhole containing the reserve ammunition was for the Corps.

The 13th School Squadron had completed the mission of organizing the post of Jefferson Barracks for an Air Corps Basic Training Station and Reception Center. All recruits and excess officers and enlisted men were transferred to other school squadrons and on 26 October the squadron returned to Scott Field. The squadron provided service for administration and service for the radio school of that station.

The squadron had spent one month and eleven days at Jefferson Barracks, Missouri.

This was certainly an extremely busy time at Jefferson Barracks, but while all the changeover from Regular Army to Army Air Corps was happening the annual CMTC had to be carried out. To get an intimate look at CMTC in 1940 from enrollee Paul S. Kuhns, Jr., who kindly answered my request for information regarding his experiences at the 1940 CMTC. As we look at the information that he provided, I believe that we can get a glimpse into what all enrollees experienced.

What follows is Mr. Kuhns' recollections. "I became aware of the C.M.T.C. program during the winter of 1939-40 while attending Harris Junior College in St. Louis. There was no particular advertising, possibly a notice on a bulletin board. A Clarence Hulett may have talked about it amongst the students. Clarence attended Harris, but lived on the post at J.B. as an 'Army Brat'. In any case I decided to apply for the 'thirty days of rest and recreation' as we laughingly referred to it. There was some paper work and the usual physical exam required. On the appointed day, probably July 1, 1940, I reported to J.B. and was put through the processing to become a 'Basic' recruit in the infantry program. Seems to me one could go for four years to complete the entire sequence. The 'Basic' year was followed by Red, White, and Blue veterans, these latter ones were given NCO roles to fill. There weren't nearly so many of those - for what reason I'm not sure, possibly ratings to qualify, natural attrition. Trainees came from a fairly wide area, including other states. We were a mixed 'bag' of young men to say the least, but since we were all volunteers, we were all eager to learn and to please.":

"We were arranged into rifle companies, I being in Company A under the command of William P. Havens, First Lieutenant, Engineer Reserve. I remember Lt. Havens as a middle-aged man, well into his forties. Our housing consisted of standard G.I. Tents set on wooden floors. However, while six beds are shown, my records indicate there were only four of us in Tent No. 19, Warren H. Weisz, a 'White' trainee, Harold S. Bourgoin, Raymond Ashby, and I, all 'Basics'. A W.H,. Ogden, Lt. Col. is listed as the First Bn. Admin. Officer...."

"The tents were arranged along a company street which lay north-south, the south end being not far from what is now an elementary school. The camp lay for the most part on what is now the school play yard. There were several permanent small buildings lying south of the tent area, in an east-west line. The first was the PX, then an orderly room and several latrine-showers. Meals were served at the post mess hall, referred to in the manual as Atkinson Hall, the large white, stucco building, still standing. As trainees we marched to the mess hall by units, but since we didn't all eat at the same speed, groups were assembled as people emerged from the mess hall, and then marched back as platoon-sized groups formed."

"The tents were comfortable to the degree possible in St. Louis July weather, but these were pre-air-conditioning days, so what we didn't know we didn't miss."

"A curious custom prevailed during the night. Since the company streets were located at considerable distance from the latrines, metal wash tubs were set out at intervals, partially filled with water. The idea of course was to use these 'chamber pots' instead of urinating on the ground around the tents. Enough light was provided by overhead lamps to make this possible. The funny part was to watch, or be part of, the crews assigned to empty these containers in the morning. These old wash tubs had two handles, one on each side, so two people had to carry them. They were awkward at best, but filled with liquid they were fairly heavy, and even by keeping step the carriers couldn't avoid sloshing. This resulted in laughter by the carriers, heightened by the jeers and calls of the on-lookers, so that many were the times when the tubs were dropped or one carrier let go resulting in the contents cascading over the legs of his partner. These 'urinals' were the source of much merriment."

"The training program included most of the fundamental rifle company subjects, drilling, facings, etc. We were issued World War I rifles to carry, never fired. One day of actual firing was provided using .22 cal. weapons kept at the firing range on the post. Pre-firing instruction was rudimentary, showing the 'sight picture' by means of tin cut-outs fastened to a stick, that sort of thing. Unfortunately, I missed all that by virtue of being on K.P. duty at the mess hall. During the day the K.Ps were marched out to the range, handed a rifle, and told to shoot at the target. It was required that all trainees have this experience. Needless to say, my score did not win any prizes, but I knew enough from my BB gun days to get off my rounds and not hit any bystanders. That was a disappointing day for me, as I recall even now. Since there was a lot of competition for 'points', it didn't seem fair that the K.P.s should be dealt with in such a cavalier fashion."

"Aside from close-order and extended-order drill, and inspections, there was one day at least devoted to platoon and squad combat tactics - creeping through the woods toward the 'enemy'", following hand signals - all great fun. Another time we were 'interviewed' by the officers as if being inducted for real service. There were many questions devoted to determining skills or aptitudes we might have. Little did we realize that within two or three years most of us would be going through all that again - in earnest."

"First-aid was yet another subject given some time, primarily in the area of heat exhaustion and sun stroke because of the hot weather. Our uniforms actually contributed to the problem. While the fabric was cotton khaki, we wore long-sleeved shirts, long pants, neckties, all fully buttoned. The concession to heat was the hat issued, a sort of ersatz pith helmet made of pressed paper-board. They were fairly durable, and they did shade one's head and face, but they were also hot and sweaty to wear. Air was supposed to circulate through them, and, to some extent it did, but not enough to alleviate the problem. There were many cases of heat exhaustion. Sun stroke was rare, if at all. One time, during a formal review held on a hot afternoon, the entire regiment was drawn up on the parade ground in front of the brick barracks, the line stretching from one end of the field to the other. There we stood, at 'attention', while some dignitary addressed the group. Soon the bodies began to topple. Looking down the line I could see man after man lying prostrate, having fainted from the heat and from standing stiffly. No one seemed to know what to do. The attitude seemed to be that as a soldier one was supposed to withstand such things. Only weaklings fainted. Eventually medics did begin to pick up these poor souls and drag them back to some shade to recover. I felt so superior knowing enough to stand slightly relaxed, and to shift my weight slightly if I felt the least bit 'whoozy'.

"Guard duty was another memorable experience. As a seventeen-year-old youth, and an 'only child' to boot, I had firmly-established habits of sleep, influenced from early childhood by my mother. This guard-duty business was REALLY 'off the chart' for me. I was familiar with the stories about such things being a part of military life, and the consequences of failing in one's duty, etc., but to be confronted with reality was quite another thing, indeed. We were 'on duty' for twenty-four hours, four on and four off, etc. There was no difficulty until the night/early morning hours. I was posted to guard a gate in the rail fence along the north side of the camp. There was an overhead light shining there which kept the area in a state of quasi darkness. All went well enough until the wee hours of the morning. Not getting my usual eight hours of uninterrupted slumber came down heavily upon me. There I stood 'in a military manner', with my trusty empty rifle, slightly chilly, struggling with heavy eyelids and fading resolve. I was nagged by the knowledge of the humiliation connected with failure to perform my duty, and somewhere in my mind were thoughts of being shot for falling asleep. At one point, I gave up and sat briefly on the bottom rail of the gate and let Morph us take control. Five or ten minutes of that revived me slightly so that reason prevailed and when I let my eyes shut again, at least I was leaning against the gate 'in a military manner'. Since no enemy stormed my post, and the sergeant-of-the-guard was probably having his own problems, my digression was never discovered and I lived on to be on guard duty again under more serious circumstances, but that night under the street light will live forever in my memory."

"Earlier I alluded to Kitchen Police (K.P.) duty. All the 'Basic' trainees were given the opportunity to appreciate all that went into supplying food to large numbers of hungry men. Actually, I always rather enjoyed K.P., then and later. I was not unfamiliar with food preparation, and neatness and cleanliness have always been habitual.

The large containers and vats and boilers and stoves were impressive, and the regular cooks were friendly and kind. My later army experience substantiated this feeling. As Will Rogers might have said, 'I never met an Army cook I didn't like'. At J.B. maybe the feeling was mutual for I spent little time mopping floors and washing dishes, but was put to work in actual food preparation. I'll never forget stirring gravy in one of those vast kettles, standing on a bench to reach the top and using what seemed like a canoe paddle. Now THAT'S a pot of gravy. Not only that, I thought the food was good. There wasn't enough fruit for my taste, but what the heck, this WAS the Army after all. The thing about SOME mess halls that did bother me was the pervasive odor of 'institutional' soap. This always conjured up visions of prisons or insane asylums. At J.B. I didn't feel that, yet to me there was always an aura of World War. Everything had an 'old' look about it, the equipment we were issued was not new of course, and while it probably was devoted to the C.M.T.C. program, I often wondered what happened to the 'doughboy' who had it before me. Then, too, there were the 1903 rifles we carried, and the Whippet tank on display at post headquarters to add to this atmosphere."

"A lot of time was devoted to athletics and physical training. We were permitted to use the post swimming pool on occasion, then located east of the mess hall. I recall that too because I nearly drowned, although seventeen years old I still didn't know how to swim, and bouncing up and down in the pool I bounced down into the deep end over my head. After a brief period of panic I managed to thrash my way to safety...."[2]

What follows is a typical day in the life of a CMTC trainee:

4:00 a.m. - a lonely cock crows...snores are heard from the tents.

5:00 a.m. - Continued snores with a few creaking cots.

5:15 a.m. - Basics start to get up. Blues and Whites still snore.

5:30 a.m. - First Call - Blues and Whites turn over; Basics begin to make their bunks; Activity in camp increases.

5:45 a.m. - Reveille - All companies rush to fall in; Blues and Whites tuck in shirt tails, tie ties, and with a frawsy look fall in.

6:00 to 6:15 a.m. - Pick up those loose match sticks and cigarette butts...Clean the area.

6:20 a.m. - Chow (food to uouse civies)...nothing needed here.

7:30 a.m. - March to that **/:#@?77 drill field.

10:00 a.m. - Much activity on the drill field...How about letting me drink out of your canteen?...Boys it's too hot for drill...FALL IN!!!

12:15 p.m. - Chow (none to soon) hotter than...blazes (Ha fooled you) That was a snooze...What? FALL IN AGAIN!!!!!

1:00 p.m. - Formation for athletics...Hey let's see that ol' Pill c'mon putter' here...Aw you couldn't hit a bull with a bass fiddle.

1:30 p.m. - Sick Call...Sgt. Can I go get some medicine for my mosquito bite?

4:00 p.m. - Parade...I'd like to catch the fellow who invented these things...I've sweat thru my shirt again.

5:30 p.m. - CHOW

7:00 p.m. - Amusement...gals...fisticuffs...pop and ice cream...

9:00 p.m. - Lights out sweetheart (beg your pardon)

11:00 p.m. - Snore snore snore...Another day gone to the dogs...or wherever they go.

(Signed) Your Exhausted Reporter "As viewed by Co. I"[3]

The 1940 camp was named Camp Britton in honor of Sgt. Joseph Britton, 138th Infantry, who died from gas in France. Sgt. Britton received the Distinguished Service Cross posthumously for taking his platoon into Varennes under heavy machine gun fire and returning with 24 prisoners. Company streets were named for other men from Missouri, Illinois, and Arkansas who received similar posthumous awards.[4]

The 1940 CMTC graduation exercises took place for the approximately 1,400 young men in attendance at Jefferson Barracks on 30 July. The program included a Track and Field Meet on Monday afternoon and a parade Tuesday morning. The regiment assembled in final review on the parade grounds at 8 o'clock Tuesday morning. Presentation of scholarships and awards took place at the Bowl area at 9 o'clock. Col. Harry B. Crea, Commander of the 6th Infantry, and Col. Paul S. Bliss, Commander of the CMTC regiment, made the presentations of scholarships to go to Wentworth, Missouri, and Kemper Military Academies and also a Scabbard and Blades scholarship of $100.

Equipment returns and mileage payments were completed on Wednesday morning. Then the new young soldiers returned to their homes.[5]

Lt. Col. Raymond R. Brown

Appointed to command Jefferson Barracks on 18 September 1940, Brown commanded during the vast enlargement of facilities at the post in order to meet the impending emergency of World War II. It was at the time of Brown's appointment that Jefferson Barracks became the first Army Air Corps Basic Training Center (BTC No. 1).

6th Infantry Holdovers

Anyone with questions about earlier days at Jefferson Barracks might be referred to the men pictured here, all veterans who served with the 6th Infantry, which was quartered at Jefferson Barracks for many years before the Army Air Forces took over in the fall of 1940. Still stationed at the post with the AAFTTC were, left to right, kneeling, W.O. (J.G.) Harmon W. Barbee, MSgt. James Parmentier, TSgt. Jake W. Martindale, and W.O. (J.G.) Ralph W. Rausch. Standing, MSgt. Leon Price, SSgt. Valentine M. Treslley, TSgt. Neil J. Woods, and SSgt. Wilburn C. McGeher.

Capt. Daniel R. Baugh

A native of Pineville, Kentucky, Baugh attended the University of Kentucky, graduating in 1923. He enrolled in the Reserve Officers Training Corps and was commissioned a 2nd Lt. of Infantry upon graduation. In 1924 he attended the Infantry School at Fort Benning, then assumed duties as commandant of cadets at the Locust grove Academy in Georgia and at Gordon Military College in Barnesville, Georgia. With the establishment of the CCC in 1935, Baugh was called to serve at Boise, Idaho, as company commander and district inspector. He came to J.B. on 20 November 1940.

After Lt. Col. Pritchard returned to Scott Field on 18 September 1940, Major Raymond R. Brown was appointed Commanding Officer. Brown was the first Commanding Officer of the Post who had spent his entire Army career in the Air Corps or in its predecessor, the Aviation Section of the Signal Corps. During the first World War, Brown served as a private first-class in the Aviation Section until his appointment as second lieutenant on 28 September 1918. He rose to the rank of first lieutenant on 1 July 1920. After receiving his degree of LLS from the Jefferson School of Law at Kentucky in 1924, he became a captain on 1 October 1933. This promotion was followed by another on 12 October 1937, when he was appointed temporarily as a major, a rank he held until June 7, 1941, when he received a temporary appointment as lieutenant colonel. In 1935, Major Brown graduated from the Air Corps Technical School after previous service at Mitchell Field, New York and Park Field, Tennessee. When he was assigned to Jefferson Barracks, he was serving as Provost Marshal of the Air Corps Technical School, at Lowry Field at Denver, Colorado.

Under Major Brown's command, the enlargement of facilities at Jefferson Barracks was further sped up to meet the impending emergency. On 6 September, there were 3,500 enlisted men in training at the Post, under the supervision of 400 regulars. On 6 February 1941, there were 102 officers and 5,676 enlisted men at the Post.

Jefferson Barracks officially became the first and most important Air Corps Replacement Center in the United States. On 21 February 1941, five million dollars was appropriated for improvements and 275 frame buildings were added as rapidly as possible to increase the Post accommodations to 17,000. The new buildings were to occupy the golf course south of the permanent brick buildings and west of the National Cemetery and Argonne Hill northwest of the hospital group and parade grounds. In addition to barracks, mess and recreation halls, two chapels, two theaters and units for basic school work, extensions were to be made to the hospital group.

Hundreds of cottage-style 16-foot square hutments were replacing tents among the rolling wooded hills. Each hutment was furnished comfortably with a heating stove and fire extinguisher. A guest's hall where visiting relatives of the enlisted men could get overnight accommodations, a $150,000 post auditorium, and a $100,000 cold storage plant were later additions.

The post print shop was established in early April 1941. A staff of newspaper men was gathered and given pens that were mightier than the sword for the moment, and the first edition of the Barracks newspaper appeared. It initially had no name. A prize was offered to the soldier who supplied the most appropriate name. Pvt. Donald S. Permar, Flight 2, 31st School Squadron, suggested *The Hub*. A board of officers selected it from the hundreds of names submitted, because the Barracks was then the only Air Corps basic training center, and recruits were sent here from to all parts of the United States.

At the beginning of its designation as an Air Corps facility, Jefferson Barracks presented something of a nightmare as far as administration was concerned. On 23 August 1940, when it was announced that the post would be used for housing Air Corps recruits, the post was to be under the control of the Commanding Officer of the Air Corps Technical School at Scott Field, Illinois. A letter addressed to the Commandant of the Air Corps Technical School at Chanute Field in Rantoul, Illinois, ordered the Commandant to direct that the Commanding Officer of Scott Field was to take over Jefferson Barracks from the Commanding General of the 7th Corps Area.

At this time, however, a mixture of administrations became evident, as Jefferson barracks was not an exempt station and was therefore also under the 7th Corps Area Headquarters. Moves were begun during November 1940 to sever the connections with Scott Field and to make Jefferson Barracks an independent station. Despite the fact that the Chief of the Air Corps had requested that the War Department designate Jefferson Barracks as a separate station, no official action was forthcoming. As late as 28 January 1941, Jefferson Barracks was still dependent on Scott Field for authority to make promotions. However, as far as instruction was concerned, the program at Jefferson Barracks was handled directly by the Commanding Officer and Washington.

Let's backtrack for a moment so that we can more fully understand the significance of Jefferson Barracks becoming the first Basic Training Center (BTC No. 1) for the Army Air Corps. Jefferson Barracks, one of the oldest fortresses of what was once the American frontier, was suddenly attached to the youngest instrument of modern warfare, the United States Army Air Corps. The historical post was destined not to lose its connection with the frontiers of change. In the transition it became the first, and remained for some time the only, basic training center for ground forces of the Army Air Corps.

But the year 1940 was not the Post's first experience of aerial activities. You may recall that as early as 1923 a detachment of the 6th Infantry went to Lambert Field near St. Louis to act as a guard during the Pulitzer National Air Races. This was a humble beginning but doubtless played a part in the smooth operation of an event which, along with similar competitions, contributed to the technical development of aviation. It may be recalled that only nine months later, American Army fliers paid the first aerial visit to Tokyo. Soon the development of the aeroplane as a weapon of war began to influence procedure at the Barracks. In April 1938, anti-aircraft guns made their appearance on the Post in connection with the celebration of Army Day. Later that same year, a sham battle took place, both sides using scout planes integrated with the work of the Infantry. Still later, vast crowds attended a huge display in which the latest in anti-aircraft guns and searchlights were demonstrated. Jefferson Barracks was becoming fully conscious of the sort of warrior which it might have to train.

Jefferson Barracks' transition to the Air Corps intensified the Post's importance as a molding place for soldiers, but in 1940 there arose a whole series of new problems. In addition to the problems of adequate supplies and facilities, an issue common to all democracies on the eve of war was the urgent and fundamental question; precisely what constituted a sound basic training for a member of the ground forces of a rapidly expanding fighting air arm? Was it sufficient to give a man a hasty orientation and pack him off to one of the technical schools which train the innumerable experts required to maintain a modern air fleet? Should he be a soldier, physically fit, alert, and disciplined as well as a technician? It must be remembered that in modern war there was no such thing as a static front line. At any time, the men of a ground crew could be called upon to defend themselves and to assist in destroying the enemy.

Strictly speaking, this was a problem for the War Department. But unlike its older sister, the Royal Air Force, the Air Corps had no written history to turn to for records of past procedures, mistakes and achievements.

In such a situation, the great importance of Jefferson Barracks was immediately apparent. Jefferson Barracks had to become the laboratory, in which all plans would be tested, from which all the data of trial and error or deliberate experiment had to be accumulated, analyzed and revised.

Attendant upon the development of training procedures many administrative changes had to be made. New offices had to be created and old ones grown in size and scope. Distinguished men, such as Major Howard Rusk of the Medical Corps, had to work out solutions to problems incidental to the training of men, prove their value and moved on to higher posts of national service. And what may be loosely called the cultural activities of the Barracks, which cater to the physical, moral and spiritual needs of the enlisted men, had to be expanded in a way which would astonish the infantryman of prewar days. All of these developments became integral to the central problem of making soldiers.[6]

The original organizations that relieved the 6th Infantry at Jefferson Barracks did return to Scott Field. However, their men formed the cadres for the 26th, 27th and 28th School Squadrons which transferred back to Jefferson Barracks. These three squadrons are the parent organizations of all training groups on the Post.[7]

With but a few changes, a 1938 map of Jefferson Barracks provides a picture of Jefferson Barracks as it was before the Air Corps took over the Post in the fall of 1940 and affords a suitable landmark to guide us in discussing the physical growth of the Post from January 1939 to 7 December 1941. The Post covered approximately 1700 acres extending along the west bank of the Mississippi River for one and one third miles. As one examines the 1938 map, several landmarks catch the eye, the South Target Range, the Veterans Hospital in the southeast area overlooking the river, the National Cemetery north of the Veterans Hospital and Sherman Avenue cutting across the middle of the reservation from east to west. The south side of Sherman Avenue was lined with permanent buildings facing the area which was the Parade Grounds during World War II. The character of the terrain is indicated by the large number of sink holes and ridges marked on the map. The names of the various areas are reminiscent of America's history from the days of Indian fighting pioneers to the World War, i.e., Gettysburg Ridge, Argonne Ridge, Seminole Run, Third Infantry Woods and Black Hawk Run. Most of the ground covered with hutments, hospitals, theaters, drill fields, PXs and paved roads had in 1939 been covered with oak trees and underbrush and was dotted with innumerable sink holes.

The number of paved roads in 1938 was limited to a few main avenues, supplemented by unpaved trails. In addition to Sherman Avenue and a number of short paved streets in the central section, there were three main paved roads: Leavenworth Road running to the Veterans Hospital, Grant Avenue extending from the east end of the Parade Ground to the North Gate, and Sheridan Avenue connecting the center of the Post with the West Gate. In the rest of the Post area, there were a few unpaved trails, most of which were not named.

Most of the permanent buildings on Sherman Avenue had been in existence since the 1890s. These extended from Building No. 1 (Headquarters), at the intersection of Grant and Sherman, to Building No. 68, opposite Randolph Place. The permanent buildings on the south side of Kearny Street were also in existence in

1938, as well as Mess Hall No. 1. With the warehouses, Post Office, Gymnasium, Officers' Quarters north of the Parade Ground, and a few other scattered buildings, this list accounts for most of the permanent buildings on the Post in 1938. The existing warehouses were located inconveniently in sink holes in the northeast sector and made necessary a large motor pool for transportation of supplies. (These buildings now comprise the museums in the historic park area.) As early as March 1940, before the Air Corps took over the Post, barracks accommodations were inadequate for the garrison.[8]

The facilities taken over officially by the Air Corps consisted of permanent barracks housing approximately 1550 men and a training camp housing 1500 men, Atkinson Mess Hall where 1500 men could be served, and a post cafeteria. The decision was made in September 1940 to provide tent camps for the temporary accommodation of Air Corps recruits. When the 1st School Squadron arrived 3282 tents were available, each tent equipped with bunk beds, clothes racks, Sibley stoves, electric lights and wooden floors.[9]

As to the matter of training facilities, there was but one parade ground on the Post, one small gymnasium and limited facilities for target practice. There was a 24-target 165-yard range, a pistol range and a 1,000-inch range, according to the report of an inspection done in March 1940.[10]

During 1937, 1938 and 1939, a good deal of road repair and building renovation was carried on with the assistance of the WPA. In 1939, for example, approximately $2,500,000 of WPA funds was allotted for work on the Post. This work consisted primarily of road improvements, building repairs, the erection of new quarters for officers and nurses, and a new medical barracks. One should not be left with the impression that Jefferson Barracks was an insignificant Army camp in a state of disrepair in 1939. It is only by comparison with the state of the Post in 1943 that it appears small and undeveloped. The report made by an inspection in 1938, for example, contained this statement: "Was impressed with the amount of work done under the direction of the Construction Quartermaster and am sure Jefferson Barracks will, after the project is completed, be one of the 'show' posts of the Army."[11]

From 1939 to 1941, Jefferson Barracks increased its population from approximately 1300 to over 11,000 and was transformed from the headquarters of the 6th Infantry, into a large Air Corps basic training center. The long list of buildings constructed during this period includes that 145 barracks, six 2,000-man mess halls, numerous hospital and administrative buildings, post exchanges, chapels and store houses. Large areas were cleared and graded, miles of roads and sidewalks were laid, and sewers, pipe lines and other service facilities were completed. These facts indicate the size and nature of the building program during 1940-41.[12]

Tentative long-range plans for the construction of new facilities at Jefferson Barracks were drawn up by the Commanding Officer, Major Raymond R. Brown, along with the Office of Post G-4 and the Construction Quartermaster. The plans were sent to Washington for approval on 28 October 1940. Jefferson Barracks was the only Army Air Corps Reception and Replacement Center of its kind then contemplated under the National Defense program. Plans called for the erection of 275 buildings to provide proper facilities for housing 17,000 men. In January 1941, the total cost of this new construction, plus additions to existing facilities, was estimated to be approximately $5,000,000. Other plans called for the construction of three cantonment areas, a reception center, a 376-bed hospital installation and numerous service buildings and utilities.[13]

Extensive expansion occurred during 1941 in the region known as Area No. 1, which was located south of the central part of Jefferson Barracks and west of the National Cemetery. The temporary construction date was submitted on 21 January 1941, although actual construction did not begin for four months. Preparation of the ground for this 6,000-man cantonment was begun almost immediately after submitting the preliminary plans. Topographic and layout surveys were completed in March; in April, almost the entire surface had been cleared by the WPA. The company of Cameron Joyce had been awarded the contract to grade the area, and began work on March 18, completing the grading in June.[14]

Of the four bids submitted for construction of 146 buildings in this area, the low bid of $1,112,600, was submitted by Joseph A. Bass Company of Minneapolis. The contractor moved his machinery into the area on May 13, eight days after the contract had been awarded.[15]

In May 1941, the plan for a single 6,000-man mess hall in the area was changed to three 2,000-man mess halls. Less steel and a cost of less than half of that for a 6,000-man hall determined that the three buildings be constructed. Work was started on these mess facilities on 17 June 1941, by O'Driscoll and Grove, Inc.[16]

The contract for the work begun on 13 May required that construction be completed in 105 days. Accordingly, 26 buildings were accepted by the commanding officer on September 16, and ninety-six more on 3 October. The commanding officer accepted Building 803, Theater No. 3, which had been built for $60,400 on

October 3. By the middle of November 1941, all buildings in Area No. 1 had been completed. This included a total of 154 buildings: 96 barracks, 3 mess halls, 2 schools, 24 day rooms, 12 company supply buildings, 6 group administrative buildings, 3 recreation buildings, 2 post exchanges and 1 each company administration, theater, infirmary, fire house, chapel and technical training building.[17]

Area No. 2 was planned as a 2,000-man cantonment area to be located in the section north of the hospital known as Argonne Ridge. Plans were made in January 1941 for clearing and grading thirty acres on which barracks, supply buildings, a water tank, theater, post exchange and other types of buildings were to be constructed. The estimated cost at that time was $692,010, and construction was planned to begin early in the spring. Most of the buildings were to be temporary frame structures.

Evans Construction, of Springfield, Illinois, was awarded the contract for this work. Clearing and grading was completed in early May 1941, and on 14 May the contractor moved equipment into the area and began excavating for footings. By 28 August, sixteen buildings had been completed and accepted at a cost of $136,633. By 7 December 1941, 55 buildings in Area No. 2 had been completed and accepted. These buildings included 32 barracks buildings, four company supply buildings, eight day rooms, two group administration buildings, and one each recreation building, school, administration, 2000-man mess hall, guard house, infirmary, fire house, theater and post exchange.[18]

Also in January 1941, plans for Area No. 3 were announced. This area was to be much the same as Area No. 2, a 2000-man cantonment located north of Sheridan Avenue and east of Black Hawk Run. Evans Construction was also awarded the contract for Area No. 3. After clearing and grading, actual construction began on 14 May. By 7 December 1941, (Pearl Harbor), thirty-seven buildings had been completed and accepted. The buildings included sixteen barracks buildings, eight day rooms, four company supply buildings, two group administration buildings, and one each, chapel, school, administration, recreation building, 2000-man mess hall, trade testing building and processing building.[19]

One of the main projects included in the 1941 building program was the construction of additional hospital facilities. At the beginning of 1940, the Station Hospital consisted of only three buildings. By Pearl Harbor, the hospital complex consisted of fifty-one buildings. In January 1941, the number of beds available was 151 with emergency space in the Post Gymnasium and barracks. By the end of 1941, the estimated maximum bed capacity had been raised to 750 by the addition of eighteen ward buildings.[20]

The hospital area, designated as Area No. 4, was located on level ground to the west of the Parade Ground. A total of thirty-seven buildings had been completed and accepted by 14 November 1941. These buildings included sixteen wards, a Dental Clinic, Laboratory, Infirmary, Mess Hall, Hospital Quarters and three Store Houses.[21]

As a result of the passage of the Selective Service Act of 1940, Headquarters of the 7th Corps Area announced on 28 October 1940, that plans had been made for the establishment of eleven induction stations in the area for the reception of Selective Service men. Jefferson Barracks was to be the site of one of the reception centers. Construction of Reception Center No. 1772 at Jefferson Barracks had actually been authorized on October 9, 1940. It was to be one 1000-man type center. With the exception of later additions, the project was completed in about four months, allowing the processing of Selective Service men to begin on 1 March 1941.

The site selected for the Reception Center was in the extreme northeast corner of the reservation, three-fourths of a mile from the nearest post buildings. These facilities were a separate unit under the jurisdiction of 7th Corps Area Headquarters and not a part of the Air Corps establishment. The stated objective of the Reception Center was "to receive men coming to it from Selective Service Boards and to induct them into the Armed Services of the United States, process them and get them supplied and equipped, and to transfer them to the various Replacement Training Centers and units of Field Forces throughout the country to receive their basic training."[22]

The plan for the Reception Center at Jefferson Barracks included twenty 63-man barracks to be used for the trainees and permanent personnel, plus four similar barracks for the Headquarters Company. A building for a Military Police detachment of fifteen was to be located near the entrance to the Reception Center. A large Mess Hall was to be built near the barracks, as well as buildings for processing, supply, recreation etc. Owing to the large amount of paper work in a Reception Center, and the need for centralized administration, a large Headquarters building, thirty feet by 120 feet, was planned. Test rooms, processing buildings, records offices and clothing warehouses had to be constructed. By the end of 1941, thirty-one buildings had been completed in the Reception Center.[23]

In addition to the areas already mentioned, an estimated $1,339,410 for other construction during 1941 was planned. These included improvements in the utility services, recreation facilities, warehouses, communications and mess structures.[24]

As the size of the camp increased, it was natural that there should be problems in providing adequate water. The Medical Corps estimated that 100 gallons of water per day per soldier would be needed. To supply this minimum supply of water, a 500,000-gallon storage tank in Area No. 1 and a 300,000-gallon tank in Area No. 2 were completed by 15 November 1941, by the Pittsburgh-Des Moines Steel Company. A booster pump for the water system was also constructed during the period on leased land at South Broadway, about one mile north of the Post limits.[25]

Seven new warehouses were also constructed south of the main area of the Post. The WPA began construction on 16 April 1941, completing two by 30 June, and the remainder by 15 November. At the east end of this area, a cold storage building for quartermaster and commissary storage was built by Dickie Construction Company.[26]

Railroad connections between the main line of the Missouri Pacific and the warehouse area was completed by mid-November. The WPA did the excavation work for the spur track and sidings. The actual laying of 6750 feet of siding track was done by Longwill Scott, Inc.[27]

The recreational and social facilities at Jefferson Barracks were greatly increased by construction in the areas known as the Civic Center, near Areas No. 1 and No. 2. Here, Service Club No. 1 was built, and adjacent to it a Guest House. The contract for both of these buildings went to Darr-Williams Company. In August and September, the Beverage House, dance floor, and Amphitheater in Sylvan Springs opened for use. Post Exchange and WPA funds had been used for construction of these projects.[28]

A new main Post Office was built during 1941 on the corner of Kearny Street and Sheridan Road to replace the old one which was converted to the Non-Commissioned Officers' Club. Improvements and additions to the laundry, General Mess, and Headquarters were also made.[29]

The construction programs at Jefferson Barracks in 1941 encountered difficulties similar to those encountered throughout the country. Jefferson Barracks felt the pressure of labor groups and had to face the difficulties of shortages of certain critical materials. When these problems had been solved, an extremely wet fall hampered construction.

On 21 June 1941, the A.F. of L. union members doing construction work in the four camp areas objected to WPA workers painting buildings which private contractors had erected. The crisis came on 1 July when approximately 1500 A.F. of L. craftsmen went on strike over this issue. There was a delay of a week while these skilled workers refused to work as long as WPA workers were permitted to do rough painting. Work was resumed on July 8 after the WPA men had been transferred to other jobs. The strike made it necessary to postpone the date for completion of many of the projects.[30]

The huge demand for steel and other important metals could not be immediately met in a nation that had suddenly turned to producing vast quantities of armaments. It was partially due to a lack of steel that the 6000-man mess building in Area No. 1 had been changed to three 2000-man buildings. In addition, aluminum and steel kitchen equipment could not be obtained when needed, delaying the use of mess facilities.[31]

The cost of the work completed by 15 November 1941, was $5,033,296. For most of this new development, the standard mobilization type of temporary construction was used, although a few permanent brick buildings were erected. The building program was carried on under the direction of the Construction Quartermaster until February 28, 1941, when it was transferred to the Engineer Corps.[32]

Perspective on the construction program carried out at Jefferson Barracks from 1939 to 1941 can be gained by looking at it as a small but vital part of the vast picture of a nation girding itself for war. The creation of a giant Air Force made up a large part of the National Defense Program, and the installations at Jefferson Barracks were designed to advance this program. By the time of the attack at Pearl Harbor, Jefferson Barracks was relatively well equipped with the military installations required for the role it was to play during the years of World War II.

Plans and Training

Since its origin, the Air Corps Training Program at Jefferson Barracks went through a process of continuous and simultaneous growth and change. It gradually took form to meet the varying circumstances of wartime conditions. From the beginning, certain principles, later to be set out precisely, in a directive from higher headquarters had been fairly clear and had been Post policy. It was understood that the essential mission of the Post was "to receive, equip, classify and provide basic instructions for recruits in preparation for entrance into Air Corps Technical Schools."

The training objectives were:

1) To provide thorough basic military training of the individual soldier, including the early development of his physical and mental coordination;

2) To provide group instruction planned to school the recruit in subordination of the individual to the accomplishment of the group mission;

3) To provide a minimum four-week training schedule for recruits at the replacement training center; and

4) To provide provisions for advanced training of the recruits who remain at the replacement training center longer than the four-week period.[1]

By 5 October 1940, a definite three-week training schedule was in existence at Jefferson Barracks. The essentials covered included: Military Courtesies, six hours; Articles of War, four hours; Personal hygiene and First Aid, twelve hours; Wearing of the Uniform, eight hours; Alpha and Math Tests, two hours; School of the Soldier, including physical training, position of soldier, facings, squad drill, platoon and company drill, marching, firing riot gun and pistol, gas mask and gas drill, for a total of 127 hours; Interior Guard Duty, six hours; Government Insurance, three hours; and Miscellaneous, twenty-four hours.[33]

However clear in principle, this training program had to be put into actual operation and it inevitably suffered for some time from "normal" lack of coordination, misunderstandings, errors and weaknesses found among the several training organizations, all of which can be charged to inexperience. In addition to inexperience, many problems such as difficulties in setting up the organization, inadequacy of personnel, peace-time inertia, and inadequate living conditions and recreational activities were to be expected and did exist. This, to be sure, did not mean that the training program was encountering anything more than normal difficulties.

As an illustration of early difficulties, it can be recalled that the 11th and 13th School Squadrons, on their arrival at Jefferson Barracks from Scott Field, had to borrow beds from the District CCC. The whole problem of clothing, housing and equipment was a difficult one.

With the creation of the 26th, 27th and 28th School Squadrons and their assignment to Jefferson Barracks in November 1940, the training program gained momentum. The 27th Squadron received, processed and clothed the men, after which they were transferred to the 28th for training. The 28th was responsible for all training, there being at that time no Post S-3 as such. After training, the men transferred to the 26th, which handled the shipping.[35]

With the increasing activity of the Post, the facilities of the 28th were taxed, and training problems began to arise. Those difficulties brought on recommendations which led eventually to segregation of trainees, depending upon the extent of their prior training and the establishment of several casual companies. These companies were later demobilized and attached to their respective squadrons.[36]

In the spring of 1941, the 31st and 39th School Squadrons were organized. The 39th operated as a mess squadron.

By 1 March 1941, the Post had issued a Training Directive entitled "Disciplinary and Basic Training," providing for a four-week course. This course was to be followed by a twelve-week training period, called "Disciplinary and Basic Training Advanced." As the majority of the trainees were shipped out to Technical Schools or were by-passed by the end of the four-week period, not many received the twelve-week advanced training.

The four-week "Disciplinary and Basic Training Course" in substance consisted of the following schedule:

First Week

1) Four hours drill in School of the Soldier each day except Wednesday and Friday, on which days two hours drill was given.

2) Lectures by squadron officers on subjects such as School of the Soldier, military courtesy and customs of the service, military discipline, uniform regulations, military sanitation, care of clothing and equipment, and tent pitching.

Second Week

1) Schedule for drill same first week.

2) Lectures by squadron officers on the care and cleaning and operating of .30 caliber rifle, manual of arms, squadron and platoon drill, Government Insurance, care and use of the gas mask, chemical warfare, defense against air attack.

Third Week

1) Four hours of company drill with rifle on Monday and Tuesday. Two hours company drill with rifle on Wednesday and four hours of company drill with rifle on Friday.

2) Lectures by squadron officers on subject of interior guard duty, first aid, riot duty, company drill and ceremonies, organization of Air Corps, duties of Charge of Quarters, care and operation of the automatic pistol.

Fourth Week

1) Four hours of company drill with rifle each day except Wednesday and Friday, on which days two hours drill was given.

2) Lectures by squadron officers given to men who had previously missed lectures due to inoculations and fatigue details.

The twelve-week advanced course covered somewhat the same training as the basic course, but in more detail and was more intensive.[37]

In April 1941, Major M.I. Carter arrived from Chanute Field, Illinois, and was assigned to be in charge of training at Jefferson Barracks. Carter became the first Post S-3, Plans and Training. He organized the three existing School Squadrons into Training Squadrons. Each squadron was a complete unit, responsible for the processing, training and shipping of its men.[38]

As outlined in "Procedure of Operation, Air Corps Replacement Training Center, Jefferson Barracks, Missouri, October 1941," the Squadrons remained the basic training organizations. They continued to carry the responsibilities for the actual training. The training schedules furnished them were "furnished as a training guide. Each Squadron was to prepare a training schedule covering the subjects indicated and broken down to give the time, place and instructor for each subject covered in the training guide."

A Plans and Training Officer was to be appointed by each Squadron Commander "to properly coordinate the training program to Post S-3 and each Squadron and to insure a vigorous training program in all its phases." It was the responsibility of this officer "to prepare a schedule, make substitution of instructors and subjects, where necessary conduct meetings between all training personnel, and to prepare necessary reports in connection therewith."[39]

Due to the rapid expansion of the Post, one of the important S-3 functions was the coordinating of fatigue details required throughout the Post. The aim, so far as possible, was to use men who had completed their training and were waiting shipment. There were times when outgoing shipments were so heavy that it taxed the Post facilities to keep all men in training and also to do the work involved in carrying out the expansion program and in maintaining high morale.

Time was also found to fill in a number of gaps and develop a more fully rounded program. As examples, five outstanding items can be noted.

1) In November 1940, the first NCO school was organized. Its purpose was to train the men to handle their squadron jobs more efficiently. The school was conducted five days a week from 1:00 p.m. to 5:00 p.m. The total number of hours was 150. The non-commissioned officers were thoroughly instructed in their various specialized duties in company administration as a whole. These men were destined soon to form cadres for other organizations both at Jefferson Barracks and at other basic training centers, in the Technical Training Command.[40]

2) In August 1941, the first drill instructor school was organized. The Squadrons were short of personnel and the average ratio was one drill instructor to one hundred men. The students in this course were chosen for qualities of leadership and initiative. The greater part of the training was close order drill. From all reports this school was highly successful.[41]

3) In September 1941, the school for permanent party of the training squadrons was opened. This course ran for five weeks, and classes were held on Tuesday and Thursday nights. Subjects taught were organization, administration, supply, military courtesy, military discipline and related subjects. The purpose of this course was to give the men a working knowledge of the duties within the squadron, in addition to their regular jobs.

4) In cooperation with the Trade Test Center, an evening school was maintained for those who wished to brush up on their mathematics and related subjects before attending technical schools. Attendance was wholly voluntary.

5) An officers' school was organized in the summer of 1941, meeting at night twice a week. This course lasted five weeks, and covered administration, military law, courts martial, duties of the Squadron Commanding Officer, duties of the squadron Adjutant and Military Training.[42]

At the same time, during the summer and fall of 1941, many drill areas were built to supplement the main parade ground, which, to start with, was the only place available for drill. In addition, S-3 prepared a plan for a new lay-out for the parade ground. The Review Stand was moved from the South to the North side; the gravel marching area was constructed so that in case of rain prior to a parade, the parade could still be held. In September 1941, S-3 built the first obstacle course. During the fall of 1941, each Squadron built its own course.[43]

By July 1941, Post growth necessitated the activation of new Squadrons. The old organizations were becoming too large and unwieldy. The 354th, 355th, 356th, 357th, 358th, 359th and 360th School Squadrons were formed. This soon necessitated a decentralization of the S-3 function, and, by 20 August 1941, four provisional groups were organized on orders from higher headquarters. The first group was composed of the 26th and 27th School Squadrons; the second, the 38th and 31st; the third, the 354th, 355th and the 356th; and the fourth was composed of the 357th, 358th and 359th. In November 1941, the fifth provisional group was formed composed of the 39th and 360th Squadrons. This last group functioned as a mess group.[44]

The Squadron Commanding Officer and his Plans and Training Officer were still responsible for the training program in each squadron. The provisional group officer was detailed as an Assistant Post Executive and was primarily a staff officer and not a commander. As a staff officer, his duties were to assist the Post Commander in the exercise of his command function; specifically, he performed the duties of coordination and supervision with respect to the administration, training and messing of several school squadrons of his group; all orders issued by him were by virtue of the authority delegated to him by the Post Commander.

The Group Supervising Officer was not authorized to maintain an Office of Record, nor any staff of officers or enlisted men, and had no group headquarters.

The status of the Group Supervising Officer was considered somewhat analogous to that of S-3, except that, instead of being "charged with those functions of the staff which relate to organization training and combat operations," he was charged with those functions of the staff which related to all the four sub-divisions of Command Duties. In carrying out his duties, it was intended that he deal directly with each of the S- sections of Post Headquarters.

It was believed that the group supervisor plan had limited success in actual operation, due primarily to lack of command function in the group supervisor's authority. This was, however, the background and beginning of the Wing System to be instituted later.[45]

Another problem reared its head near the end of this period. New squadrons were being activated for the new Air Corps Training Centers at Sheppard Field, Texas, and Keesler Field, Mississippi. The Jefferson Barracks personnel contributed to the formation of the cadres that organized these Training Centers. While the drain of officers and enlisted men created a problem of replacement, which at first was of limited scope, this was a matter destined to recur often and to leave its mark many times on Jefferson Barracks.[46]

Health

A wide range of factors must be considered in any discussion of health conditions on a military post. One factor which must be mentioned in any discussion of the health conditions at Jefferson Barracks is the climate of the region. The climatic conditions in the region in which Jefferson Barracks is located caused numerous problems for the medical officers at the post. Jefferson Barracks is located on the west bank of the Mississippi River at the southern limit of the St. Louis metropolitan area. The humidity is high, and the temperature varies from occasional near-zero weather in the winter to sultry summer days when the temperature can hit 100 degrees. Sudden changes in temperature result in numerous respiratory infections among unacclimated troops, as in 1940 when a common cold epidemic swept the Post. The hot summer weather, and the presence of numerous sink-holes in the area, increased the difficulty of controlling disease carrying flies and mosquitoes. Adding to this problem was the fact that a large percentage of the personnel at the Post were unseasoned recruits.

The Station Hospital at Jefferson Barracks operated, in 1939, under the administrative control of the Air Corps Technical Training Command, whose headquarters were at Tulsa, Oklahoma. The Hospital and Dental Clinic provided medical care not only for military personnel stationed at Jefferson Barracks, but also for men at Scott

Field, Parks Air College and at other points in the vicinity of St. Louis. This service was provided in some cases for civilian employees and civilian dependents of military personnel.

During 1939 when the United States was at peace, the average strength of the command at Jefferson Barracks was 1188 men, ranging from the high point of 1439 in October to 336 in December, when troops were away on maneuvers. From 1939 to 1941, Jefferson Barracks increased its population from approximately 1100 men to over 11,000. Such rapid expansion is another factor in creating health problems.[47]

The Station Hospital which served the Post in 1939 was headed by Lt. Col. P.J. Carroll, who was serving as Surgeon and Commanding Officer of the medical staff. Lt. Col. Carroll was assisted by a staff of six medical officers, two dental officers and one contract physician.

On 3 August 1939, Lt. Col. Carroll wrote a detailed description of the problems of the medical staff at Jefferson Barracks to Col. Kent Nelson, at 7th Corps Area Headquarters. Carroll stated that a staff of eight medical officers was required to perform the normal functions satisfactorily. Even before the rapid expansion of 1940-41, medical personnel problems existed. Carroll's letter stated that "since a staff of five was assigned here, the work has grown steadily so that we have three times the work that was formerly here. Physical examinations alone take up the entire time of one officer and often times we are obliged to give him help. There are many outside physical examinations to do and it leaves us without the services of one officer. Scott Field is sending more and more work, including women and children. This work will increase shortly. Parks Air College will start in on us soon. With the present work alone, we just can't stand the strain without additional help." Absences of medical officers due to illness, accompanying troops to the rifle range at Arcadia, and attendance at Army Medical Schools placed an added burden on the medical staff.[48]

During 1940, the medical staff was expanded to cope with the sudden rise in personnel on the Post. By December 1940, just after the Air Corps took over, there were fifteen medical officers on duty, and the population of the Post had risen to 4405. When compared with the figures for 1939, this census reveals a much greater proportional increase in Post population than in medical staff. This situation occurred frequently during the period of expansion.[49]

During 1941, the strength of Jefferson Barracks increased still more rapidly due to the enactment of the Selective Service Act of 1940 and the expansion of the Air Corps. The monthly average for the year was 7457, and ranged from 4936 in January to 11,512 in December. By December, the medical staff had been increased to twenty-nine officers. The Dental Corps increased to sixteen officers at the same time. Despite these increases, the medical staff was about forty percent under authorized strength during the third quarter of 1941 and twenty percent under during the fourth quarter.[50]

On 1 January 1939, Lt. Col. Lawrence K. Anderson commanded the Dental Service at Jefferson Barracks. Only two officers made up the entire Dental Service at the Post, and for a part of the year Lt. Col. Anderson was confined to Walter Reed General Hospital. Anderson died on December 27, 1939. During the latter part of that year, 1st Lt. Martin P. Sullivan carried on the work alone as Post Dental Surgeon. 1st Lt. Ernest R. Rumpeltes, Dental Corps Reserve, reported for extended active duty on 21 December 1939. More Dental Corps Reserve officers reported for either short terms of active duty or, in the case of four officers, for extended terms of duty during 1940. Lt. Col. Clement J. Gaynor, Dental Corps, reported for duty at Jefferson Barracks on 5 September 1940, to replace Anderson.[51]

Under the command of Lt. Col. Gaynor, the Dental Service grew rapidly during 1941, to meet the mounting demands for dental work on the Post. Beginning on 1 January 1941, with seven dental officers on duty, the staff was increased to sixteen officers by the end of the year. This number was still inadequate for the increased work load placed on the Dental Service by the expansion of the AAFTTC and the enormous number of men needing dental treatment. During the year, the permanent staff was assisted by forty-eight Dental Corps Reserve officers who were on short periods of duty for a total of 534 days. The number of enlisted men in the dental service increased from seven at the beginning of 1941 to fourteen at the end of the year. In spite of this increase, at the end of 1941 Col. James R. McDowell, Medical Corps and the new Station Hospital commanding officer, estimated that twenty additional officers for all services were needed.[52]

There was no evidence of a shortage of trained nurses, although the number of regular nurses was at no time large. On 1 January 1939, there were six regular Army nurses and six CCC nurses stationed permanently at the Post. A year later, there was one Chief Nurse, nine regular Army nurses, five CCC nurses and one civilian dietician assigned. At the beginning of 1941, there were thirteen regular Army nurses, one CCC nurse and one civilian dietician. The nursing staff was assisted by several reserve nurses, who numbered forty at the time of Pearl Harbor.[53]

In 1940, before the Air Corps took over the Post, the hospital plant consisted of three buildings. Building 30 was utilized as the Detachment Barracks. Building 69 was the Main Hospital building and Building 40 was used as an additional ward. With the great influx of men late in 1940 and during 1941, hospital facilities were expanded at a rapid rate, so that by the end of 1941, fifty-one buildings were in use. Of this number, three were permanent structures used for the hospital proper, two were permanent barracks converted into wards and forty-one were temporary frame structures. Five temporary barracks built for housing troops of the Air Corps were assigned to the medical staff for use as quarters for medical personnel.[54]

The bed capacity of the Station Hospital on 1 January 1941, was estimated to be 425. Of this number, 151 beds were in hospital buildings and 274 beds were in barracks and in the Post Gymnasium. In February 1941, one thirty-three bed ward was occupied, and by the end of the year the estimated maximum bed capacity was 750, based on seventy-two square feet of floor space per bed. Plans were being made at that time to add fifteen more wards in order to raise the total number of beds to 1250.[55]

There were 260 patients remaining in the hospital on 1 January 1941, and 375 at the end of the year. A total of 8,054 dispositions were made during the year.[56]

Morale

Before the arrival of the Air Corps, the administration of morale activities appears to have been left to Company Commanders, under the general supervision of an officer responsible for such facilities as were then at the Barracks. The earliest record of such officers' duties is a Special Order dated December 18, 1939, detailing 2nd Lt. Donald P. Hull to the care of the theater, library, athletics and recreation. The A & R (Athletics and Recreation) Officer, which was the Post agency for morale activities as outlined by the Morale Division of the Adjutant General's Department in Washington, D.C., was not attached to any other staff organization at the Barracks.

The Commanding Officers of Companies and, later, of Training Groups, arranged their own programs and submitted them to this office for approval. Once approved, these programs went into operation in the individual Training Groups through Plans and Training Clerks, who were usually non-commissioned officers.

Such was the situation when the Air Corps arrived at Jefferson Barracks in September 1940. Before the end of the year, the personnel of the A & R Office had to be almost doubled, and by late 1940, consisted of "approximately seven officers and fifteen enlisted men."[57]

In March 1941, the War Department separated the Morale Division from the Adjutant General's Department, creating an independent organization under the Chief of the Morale Branch. As a result of this change, Morale Officers were appointed on military posts throughout the United States. Capt. Daniel R. Baugh became the first such officer at Jefferson Barracks. The appointment was made on 12 May 1941, and created an anomalous situation. S-3 had been established in April 1941, to direct Plans and Training; the A & R Office was concerned in part with training, and remained in existence. Now a new office had been created that impinged upon the functions of both.[58]

The confusion cleared up when the A & R Office was discontinued. With the continuance of athletics as part of the regular training program, the athletic functions of the A & R Office were merged into S-3. The recreational programs devolved upon the Morale Officer, whose department was to become the Special Service Office, in 1942.[59]

The Chaplain's Department was concerned with less tangible problems of morale. Before the arrival of the Air Corps, Lt. Col. Edward L. Branham, Chaplain for the 7th Corps Area, made Jefferson Barracks his headquarters. There was no chapel on the Post and much of the Chaplain's administrative work consisted of raising funds from churches and outside organizations. Relieved of this burden after Congress authorized appropriations for the work of Chaplain's Departments, chaplains were able to spend some of their time assisting the Plans and Training Officers in matters such as sex lectures, contributing to physical and mental health.

As the strength of the Post expanded rapidly, from 657 in September 1940 to 11,512 in December 1941, the organization of the Chaplain's Department enlarged to handle the increased work. In November 1940, Capt. Noel T. Adams was appointed Post Chaplain and by October 1941, his staff had been augmented by the appointment of eight chaplains. The personnel seemed adequate to staff the Chaplain's Office and the offices attached to four new chapels, decentralized throughout the Barracks.[60]

Chaplain Adams, while acting as Chairman of the Post Morale Board from 5 February 1941, to 12 April 1941, created a voluntary band. There had been no martial music on the Post since the departure of the 6th Infantry. The voluntary musicians, on Special Off-Duty and Special Duty Passes issued by squadron commanders, practiced in the basement of the Guest House, under the leadership of Sgt. [later CWO] Bennie Maniscalco. The band was used for Retreat Parades and for the opening and closing of shows and boxing matches. This was the nucleus from which the ACRTC Band was activated at Jefferson Barracks on 1 May 1941.[61]

The only office concerned with morale at Jefferson Barracks which was not a function of the Army was the Red Cross. There was no Field Office at Jefferson Barracks when the Air Corps moved in. The Red Cross work on the Post had proved so light in 1939 that the office had been moved to Scott Field, leaving only a secretary at the Veterans Administration Building. Both offices were merely part of the Midwestern Area, with headquarters in St. Louis. An office opened at Jefferson Barracks on 17 December 1940, with Mr. VonThurn in charge. He maintained his office at the Veterans' Hospital, but by March 1941, work had increased sufficiently to warrant the appointment of another secretary and a case worker, Mr. Ralph Digby. By October 1941, the Red Cross case load at Jefferson Barracks had increased to about 300 cases per month. Mr. George Skillstead became Field Director and was in charge at the time of Pearl Harbor.[62]

A morale program is only as good as the facilities available for its operation. When the Air Corps arrived at Jefferson Barracks, there were few facilities for catering to the needs of the growing body of men being trained for war. There was one Post Exchange, [with a capital value of approximately $3000,] and one theater; no Service Club or Chapel existed, and the only Guest House was the two-roomed Hostess House established at the Station Hospital. The only halls available for dancing or stage shows were the Post Gym, which was also the Library; and Atkinson Hall, which was the General Mess. The Boxing Arena, commonly known as the "Sink Hole," was unusable in winter. To make matters worse, these facilities were all centrally located, and therefore inaccessible to enlisted men in remote parts of the Post, such as the Reception Center.

When the rapid expansion of Jefferson Barracks began, the most urgent need was for a Service Club and a Guest House. The Hostess House already mentioned was not available to the wives and relatives of healthy trainees. Accordingly, plans went forward on 21 January 1941, for the construction of both a Service Club and a Guest House, situated on that area of the Post known as 1300. These buildings were completed in July and August 1941. The Guest House was furnished, and the Service Club Cafeteria was operated by the Post Exchange.[63]

The construction of the Post's best developed recreational area was extremely complicated: commenced in 1939, built by civilian labor and Army personnel, and at various times under the jurisdiction of the Quartermaster, the WPA and the Post Exchange. This is Sylvan Springs, which combined a dance floor, a club room, a sunken garden and an amphitheater all in one area. In accepting this project for the Post, Col. Crea, Post Commander, made a brief speech which was prophetic of the popularity of Sylvan Springs.[64]

The Main Post Exchange, one of the oldest in the U.S., was completely remodeled by the Quartermaster during this period. From a small one-room store it became a modern shop containing a meat and grocery market, a tailor shop, a barber shop, a soda fountain, a bowling alley, a lunch room and a photograph studio. At the same time, capital had to be accumulated for the growth of decentralized Post Exchange stores. By 7 December 1941, the net worth of the Jefferson Barracks Exchange was approximately $65,000.

Jefferson Barracks was expanded by a series of area developments, plans for all of which were prepared in January 1941. Each of these areas contained buildings devoted to recreation and the non-military needs of enlisted men. Area No. 1 contained twenty-four Day Rooms, three Recreation Buildings, a Theater, two Post Exchanges and a Chapel. Area No. 2 contained eight Day Rooms, a Recreation Building, a Post Exchange and a Theater. Area No. 3 contained eight Day Rooms, a Recreation Building and a Chapel. In addition to these areas designated for the use of enlisted men, the Hospital expanded by adding a Chapel. A Chapel was also built in the 1300 Area, close to the Service Club and Guest House. Another Post Exchange was constructed in the tent area and another Post Exchange and Recreation Building erected for the Reception Center and Induction Station.[65]

By 7 December 1941, the Post contained forty Day Rooms, six Recreation Buildings, three Theaters and four Chapels. Five Post Exchanges had been constructed, and with this decentralization, barber shops, tailor shops and soda fountains became available to officers and men that resided in the new more remote areas.[66]

In the days when the 6th Infantry occupied Jefferson Barracks, the Post Swimming Pool was available to enlisted men, but rapid expansion made this impossible. Therefore, Post authorities made arrangements with local YMCA, YWCA and the Knights of Columbus for enlisted men to use their facilities for free or at reduced prices.

Library facilities also proved inadequate. An Air Corps BTC (Basic Training Center) ships men to many technical schools, and the more thoughtful of the enlisted men frequently desire to spend spare time studying in advance for their future occupations. Early in 1940, the Library was so small and so little used that it operated in Building No. 66 without an attendant. In September 1940, the Library moved into the Gymnasium, which was no longer used for training, and about a year later 5000 new volumes covering a wide range of scientific and military subjects became available.[67]

By the time that the United States was thrust into war, the vigorous building program at Jefferson Barracks had provided the Post with adequate facilities for a diverse program to benefit the morale of its ever-increasing body of enlisted men.

The A & R Office, responsible for morale in 1940, emphasized athletics and indoor games. A program of tournaments was conducted, and the Post developed teams which began to be known beyond Post boundaries. In addition, a Post newspaper, the *Hub* began on 15 April 1941, and appeared weekly. By covering the activities of the Post, items of interest to the personnel, and by its own comic strip cartoons and photos, the *Hub* became a strong morale builder. The first several issues came out without a name for the newspaper. A contest to name the newspaper presented a $5.00 prize to Pvt. Donald S. Parmar, who suggested the title of *Hub*. The reason behind this name was that Jefferson Barracks was the only Air Corps Replacement Training Center in the United States and therefore it was the center from which all ground troops were distributed throughout the Air Corps.[68]

Motion pictures provided the most popular spare-time activity for enlisted men. Prior to Pearl Harbor, the Post offered a varied program in its three theaters, but the films shown had already been released to the civilian population for several months. After Pearl Harbor, the Army Motion Picture Service and film producers reached an agreement whereby military theaters could obtain first releases. Stage shows supplemented the films. These were amateur productions drawing on Post talent in their initial stages, but they later became a regular feature of entertainment at Sylvan Springs.

The establishment of Sylvan Springs made dancing possible almost every night when the weather cooperated. Partners for the soldiers at first were provided by the Red Cross or other local organizations on a somewhat haphazard basis. It later became possible to arrange convoys of partners to visit the Post for Saturday evening dances. The Post's own recreation orchestra, which had been organized in November 1940, provided the music.[69]

As part of the morale program, there were the usual visits of celebrities, particularly after the organization of the USO. Some of these were film stars. Others came to give demonstration boxing matches, or to inaugurate spare-time recreation clubs. In June 1941, Thomas E. Dewey, later Governor of New York, visited the Post in connection with the organization of the USO.[70]

In May 1941, Jefferson Barracks went on the air. Radio station KMOX installed a complete recording unit on the Post, preparatory to inauguration of a series of broadcasts based on interviews with interesting members of the Command.[71]

Mess

With the conversion of Jefferson Barracks to Air Corps purposes and the rapid expansion of personnel, it readily became apparent that any system whereby each squadron operated its own mess would not be in the interests of efficiency. Accordingly, the 39th School Squadron, originally activated as a Training Squadron and made up of men from various other training squadrons, was designated as mess squadron. Shortly afterwards, Post growth necessitated further expansion of mess personnel and the 360th School Squadron was formed with the 39th furnishing the initial cadre. These two squadrons later became the basic squadrons for a provisional group, under the provisional group set-up. These two are the parent organizations of all mess squadrons on the Post.[72]

During the early months, the general mess operated with only a few experienced cooks, butchers and bakers available. However, the ability of a few old-timers to make use of whatever recruits came along soon relieved the situation.

At this time, the highly systematic selection and training program for cooks and bakers was only in its infancy. A good example of this can be found in the May 1941addition to the 39th School Squadron, of the first group of Selective Service trainees classified as mess personnel. They were clerks, truck divers, mechanics, photographers and everything else imaginable. There wasn't a cook, baker or butcher in the lot. After receiving their basic training, they were sent to learn the general mess system.[73]

The biggest problem, of course, was overcrowding. For a considerable time, all the mess operations were conducted in one building, Atkinson Hall. Even the cooks' quarters were located in an alcove on the second floor. Congestion reached a peak when about 7700 men were being fed in this building each day. That meant that more than 23,000 meals had to be prepared and served in a mess hall which had a seating capacity of only 1,250. Congestion was so great that at "chow time" the lines waiting to pass the serving tables would stretch literally hundreds of feet. It took an average of two and a half hours to feed all the men. Five temporary mess halls, each with a capacity of 2,000 men, were constructed to help resolve the overcrowding problem. Outside each of these temporary mess halls were large hot water baths used exclusively for cleaning the mess kits which were used to relieve the shortage of metal trays and dishes. These hot water baths were converted metal truck bodies whose openings had been welded together.[74]

In August 1941, the first wooden-type mess hall opened. Within several months, four more opened. Three of these were placed next to each other and were intended to service an area containing 6,000 men. However, before too long having three such facilities in the same area caused too much congestion.

Also, the Post personnel continued to increase, and soon these mess halls were all operating at capacity. By the time of Pearl Harbor, the mess system was feeding approximately 13,000 men in these limited facilities.[75]

Shipping & Receiving

One of the notable accomplishments of the Post was the creation and performance of the Shipping and Receiving Office. In the beginning, these important functions were performed by a number of different agencies on the Post. one department handled shipping, another receiving and other correlating functions were handled by the squadrons concerned.

In March 1941, Capt. I.G. Siemens, Post Executive Officer, concluded that these functions could be best handled if combined into one agency whose sole responsibility would be the shipment of men leaving the Post and the receiving of those entering it. Although there was no known precedent or provision in Army Regulations for the establishment of such an agency, the step was taken.[76]

Many problems had to be overcome in order to create a well functioning organization of this type. Difficulties included obtaining sufficient railway equipment, having squadrons properly prepare for shipping, and getting sufficient advance notice from stations shipping men to Jefferson Barracks. Finding a suitable place for the assembly and instruction of a large body of men created no small problem in itself.

The baggage also created a difficult problem. When the men arrived and physical examinations and roll calls had been conducted, their baggage became a serious handicap and tended to slow down procedure, since the department did not have an assembly place within a short distance of the office. To overcome this, each shift appointed a baggage orderly. His duty was to pick up baggage at the depot and transport it to the organization in which the men were attached. To complicate matters, the limited housing facilities on the Post necessitated distributing men on one order to several different organizations. After the baggage orderlies became familiar with their work, this proved to be a satisfactory system.

The book of instructions provided by the Shipping and Receiving Department served as a model for Army Posts in all parts of the country. In fact, the system of having a separate agency to handle shipping and receiving came into widespread use throughout the country.[77]

In the pre-Air Corps period and for some time after, the Quartermaster organization performed the following activities: Quartermaster Office, Quartermaster Detachment, Utilities, Railway Transportation, Motor Transportation, Quartermaster Property and Procurement, Commissary Sales, Bakery, Laundry, Salvage and Reclamation and Fiscal. Superimposed on this organization was the supervision of a very large construction program as well as a large WPA project. For the performance of these duties, the Quartermaster Office was designated as Construction Quartermaster.[78]

Not until the summer of 1941 did the mounting pressure of expanding Air Corps duties bring on a decentralization of the Quartermaster function. In May 1941, an Air Corps Supply Station was established at Jefferson Barracks, when it became apparent that the Air Service Command at Wright Field could render valuable service. Within a short time, a large volume of steel office furniture and machines, as well as, technical equipment began to arrive. In July 1941, the War Department decentralized the utilities. This branch operated under guidance of the parent Quartermaster organization until such time as it could be fully organized and staffed. The Utilities did not actually separate and become independent until late December 1941, at which time jurisdiction passed to the Corps of Engineers. From that time, there was a Post Engineer's Office, an independent activity.[79]

The problems of the Quartermaster Office were many, particularly from a personnel standpoint. Despite the steady increase in workload, a commensurate increase in personnel was not reflected. Some of the key personnel had to devote 12 to 16 hours a day in order to accomplish their numerous responsibilities. Despite the volume of work and the limited personnel available to handle it, and notwithstanding frequent changes in administration, morale was exceedingly good. Long and tedious hours were devoted "gladly to the accomplishment of assignments."[80]

Headquarters Organization and Administration

As there are few records of the 6th Infantry's last days at Jefferson Barracks, what will be discussed here will begin at the Air Corps takeover in September 1940. The overall picture is one of a growing departmentalization and a gradual sharpening of the lines dividing the functions of the administrative offices. It is a picture of expanding staff, beginning with a limited organization in September 1940, and developing into a complex administrative structure by the time of Pearl Harbor, in December 1941.

Lt. Col. Fred Pritchard only commanded from 3 to 18 September 1940, so it was left to Major Raymond Brown to develop the administrative processes necessary for the smooth and efficient administration of a large military post like Jefferson Barracks. Major Brown faced a daunting task, as the duties of Post Commander included the safety and defense of the Post, the welfare of all military personnel, discipline, conduct, bearing and appearance of military personnel under his command and proper condition of quarters. In order to perform these duties, a Post Commander must have a staff of officers who are qualified to assume specific responsibilities under his direction. Major Brown selected staff officers to fill gaps in the existing administrative machinery. In order to iron out any problems that arose, daily staff meetings became a regular occurrence.[81]

The creation of the office of Post S-4, Logistics, is typical of the manner in which other offices were created. It was set up to meet a situation for which the existing organization was inadequate. Charged with a number of diverse responsibilities in the beginning, it was later split up into several separate units, as the burden of work became too great for efficient operation.

During September and October 1940, there was no Post S-1, S-2, S-3, or S-4 and no Executive Officer, but soon difficulties arose concerning clothing issue which made necessary the establishment of an S-4 office. When the problem of clothing issue became acute, Lt. Byron C. Swanson was assigned the office of Post S-4, mainly because of his previous CCC experience with this type of work. As S-4 Officer, Lt. Swanson's primary responsibility centered on the urgent problem of clothing issue, but he also became responsible for all Air Corps property on the Post. After about three months, further departmentalization took place when Lt. Swanson became Clothing Issue Officer, and Lt. Marion G. Ferguson succeeded him as Post S-4. Assistant S-4, Capt. Gilbert C. Moore, later became S-4 officer and continued in this capacity until he transferred to Camp Wallace, Texas. Capt. Ernest H. Knight acted as head of S-4 for a short time and was succeeded by Major Rudolph W. Eldien. On September 3, 1941, Capt. Walter W. Woodruff became the S-4 Officer.[82]

During September and October 1940, it was felt that an Adjutant and S-4 Officer were the officers most urgently needed for handling the problems at hand. The duties of an Adjutant can be best described as issuing the orders that carry out post policies as formulated by the Commanding Officer's staff, and seeing that those orders are carried out with dispatch and precision. Under Major Brown, Capt. C.M. Anderson performed the work of Adjutant. On 13 November 1940, Capt. Lonnie M. Johnson became Adjutant with Lt. L.A. Peterson and Lt. B.W. Alden as assistant Adjutants. In September 1941, Capt. Lee W. Fulton replaced Johnson.[83]

Major Brown's staff was augmented in November 1940, when Capt. Isaac G. Siemens became Executive Officer. He continued in this capacity during 1941. As Executive Officer, Capt. Siemens acted as the principal assistant to Major Brown. The duty of the Executive Officer is to transmit the orders of the Commanding Officer to those individuals who exercise control and to coordinate the work of subordinate officers in order to insure the efficient functioning of the staff. As the strength of the Post increased during 1941, these duties could not be properly performed by only one officer and on 13 May 1941, Capt. Daniel R. Baugh was relieved as Commanding Officer of the 27th School Squadron and assumed the duties of Assistant Executive Officer.[84]

The Executive Officer's staff further expanded in August 1941, when five provisional groups organized in order to assist the Commanding Officer in his duties with regard to training. An experienced officer supervised each group as an Assistant Executive Officer and Group Supervisor.[85]

Due to the many problems which arose incidental to the establishment of Jefferson Barracks as an Air Corps Center, and due to the large numbers of men who arrived during the latter part of 1940, little military training could be carried on. As Major Swanson said in describing the early weeks of the new administration, "All the time was used in solving problems of clothing, housing and equipment." Before an S-3 Office, Plans and Training, was created, training had to be handled by one squadron.[86]

In April 1941, Major M.I. Carter arrived at Jefferson Barracks from Chanute Field to be in charge of training. Carter became the first Post S-3 Officer, and as such, he organized the three existing School Squadrons into training squadrons. Under this set-up, each squadron became responsible for receiving, training and shipping its own men.

In general, the S-3 function coordinated all departments, executed the training program, prepared training directives, and supervised and inspected all processing and training of recruits in order to achieve efficient administration of the training program.[87]

During the early weeks of the Air Corps period, the Adjutant handled personnel work in addition to his other duties. In December 1940, 1st Lt. Leonard S. Carroll became S-1, Personnel and Organization Officer; 2nd Lt. Ronald E. Tomlin served as Assistant S-1 Officer. The responsibility of an S-1 Officer was primarily personnel management, record keeping and advising the commanding officer in regard to personnel policies. The close relationship between the S-1 Office and morale problems is shown by the fact that Capt. Lonnie M. Johnson, formerly Post Adjutant, served as both S-1 Officer and Morale Officer during the spring of 1941.[88] Due to the large numbers of men on the Post during 1941, classification and trade testing, normally S-1 functions, were performed by separate offices.

The general expansion of Jefferson Barracks during the spring of 1941 created the need for a Headquarters and Headquarters Squadron. Therefore, on 16 April 1941, the Headquarters and Headquarters Squadron was activated. At the time of its activation, the organization had one officer and one enlisted man. Capt. Lonnie M. Johnson became Squadron Commanding Officer and Porter L. Prince became Squadron First Sergeant. 1st Lt. Lee W. Fulton became Squadron Adjutant and 2nd Lt. Albert W. Hand became Squadron Supply Officer on 18 April.[89]

Five days after activation, 145 special duty enlisted men transferred from the 26th, 27th, 31st and 39th School Squadrons to work as administrative personnel in the new squadron. Therefore, the Squadron's enlisted men staffed practically all the administrative offices on the Post.[90]

The first quarters for the new unit was in Building No. 29, adjacent to Post Headquarters. Then, in June 1941, the Squadron moved from its first home in Building No. 29, next door into Building No. 28 on Sherman Street facing the Parade Grounds.[91]

Capt. Johnson remained as Squadron Commanding Officer until relieved 16 June 1941, by Capt. Loren T. Sorenson, who had been relieved from his duty with the 354th School Squadron. Capt. Sorenson remained in charge until May 1942.[92]

By 30 June 1941, the Squadron consisted of 27 assigned officers, 33 attached officers, 193 assigned enlisted men and 21 attached enlisted men.[93]

The turnover in personnel effected the Headquarters Squadron, like all Post personnel. On 23 July 1941, Capt. Ross L. Freeman became Supply Officer and 1st Lt. Vincent J. Van Meter became Squadron A & R (Athletics & Recreation) Officer, relieving Lt. Hand. On 25 July, the Squadron lost seven enlisted men who transferred to the newly activated Wichita Falls, Texas, and Biloxi, Mississippi, facilities. However, by the end of July, the enlisted strength of the Squadron reached 214. At the same time, the Squadron consisted of 81 assigned officers and 50 attached officers. 1st Lt. Henry E. Wood relieved Capt. Fulton as Adjutant on 9 October 1941, and Staff Sgt. Anthony C. Raffa took over as 1st Sergeant on 24 October.[94]

By 14 August 1941, the enlisted strength of the Squadron had dropped to 191. Enlisted strength held at around this number for the remainder of 1941[95]

The Commanding Officer's staff further increased on 13 November 1940, when an S-2, Intelligence and Security Office was established with Major Ralph W. Pierce at its head. The primary duty of a Post Intelligence Officer is to keep the Commanding Officer informed as to conditions on the Post. The functions of Post S-2 comprise the collection, evaluation and dissemination of information concerning espionage, sabotage, subversive activities, treason, sedition, and dissatisfaction among the personnel of the command. By February 1941, Capt. William E. Keefe and 2nd Lt. Charles W. Owens became part of the S-2 staff, as assistants to Major Pierce. Lt. Martin J. Mallette became Assistant Post S-2 in July 1941.[96]

During the Air Corps period, and for some time thereafter, the Quartermaster Officer had a wide range of responsibilities, with one of the most important being supervision of the construction program. Many of these duties were of the same nature as those normally performed by an S-4 office and by the Corps of Engineers. The building program placed a heavy burden on the Quartermaster staff until 28 February 1941, when construction work transferred to the Corps of Engineers.[97]

As for officers, the Quartermaster report provides the following information: "Officers in the Quartermaster Corps who held the office of Construction Quartermaster until such time as the Post S-4 was established were Lt. Col. Edwin S. Brewster and Lt. Col. Floyd D. Jones. In addition, the regular duties of the Post Quartermaster functions were their responsibility. Lt. Col. Roland T. Fenton also acted as Construction Quartermaster for a short period of time.[98]

On 1 July 1941, the Utilities Office separated from the Quartermaster Department. Prior to this date, the repairs and utilities work at Jefferson Barracks had been done by a member of the staff of the Quartermaster Department.[99]

During the first half of 1941, the Post Quartermaster was charged with the procurement, installation, operation and maintenance of all fire protection and fire fighting equipment. On 1 October 1941, the Post Utilities Officer became fire marshal, relieving the Post Quartermaster of this responsibility.[100]

These details are presented in order to demonstrate the process by which various offices of the headquarters were created.

Major Brown created the Post Administrative Inspector's Office, on 6 March 1941. Major William R. Butler became Administrative Inspector at that time with Capt. Carl J. Stumpf as his assistant. Stumpf later became the Administrative Inspector. The duties of an Administrative Inspector can be summarized briefly as the responsibility of seeing that all Post activities are carried on in accordance with Army regulations and in accordance with the wishes of the Commanding Officer. The newly created office made regular organization inspections and submitted reports. As the strength of Jefferson Barracks increased rapidly in 1941, the staff increased. On July 5, Capt. Levi J. Baker and 1st Lt. Robert H. Gregory became Assistant Administrative Inspectors. On 4 August 1941, 1st Lt. Milan Vydareny became part of the staff and on 22 October 1941, Capt. Victor H. Wohlford joined the staff. In spite of these additions, the Administrative Inspector was handicapped in the performance of his duties by the lack of an adequate staff, and by the fact that the Inspector had several additional duties which required a great deal of his time. The report of an inspection made by a representative of the Inspector General's Department in December, 1941, stated that, for the reasons just mentioned, "This section is not obtaining the results that can be expected of it."[101]

The Classification Division and the Trade Test Center was established late in 1940, and experienced difficulties similar to those encountered by other offices on the Post at that time. Facilities were taxed to capacity by the great influx of recruits, and expansion of facilities and staff was soon urgently needed. Lt. Morris Hearst took charge of the Trade Test Center, during the early months of 1941.[102]

The Classification Division was established as an administrative unit at Jefferson Barracks in November 1940. One officer and twelve enlisted men staffed the Center, and in the early spring of 1941, two officers and twenty-one enlisted men joined the organization. 2nd Lt. Albert W. Hand, assigned on December 18, 1940, became the first officer in charge of the Classification Division.[103]

Established before World War I, the Post Exchange had been in continuous operation. The administration of this organization was well established before the beginning of the Air Corps period. On 25 September 1940, Capt. Isaac G. Siemens was assigned to act as Exchange Officer, in addition to his other duties. Capt. Guinter served as Post Exchange Officer from 6 May 1941, until 20 August 1941, when Major James B. Patton relieved him. The main problem facing the Post Exchange Officer during this time came about due to the rapid expansion. Facilities had to be provided for the increasing the capacity of the Post Exchange and provide welfare equipment and other facilities for the thousands of men stationed at Jefferson Barracks.[104]

At the beginning of the Air Corps period the Athletics and Recreation Officer served as the principal officer responsible for the manifold activities related to morale. This office expanded rapidly during the latter part of 1940 and in the early months of 1941, and an independent Morale Office was established. Capt. Daniel R. Baugh, a former CCC officer, became the first Morale Officer for the Post on 12 May 1941. Capt. E.K. Hampel, former Assistant Morale Officer, became Morale Officer on 1 July 1941. The Athletics and Recreation Office remained in existence for some time, but later in 1941 it merged with S-3, pursuant to a training directive issued from Chanute Field, 15 August 1941.[105]

Chaplain Noel T. Adams, appointed in November 1940, directed the Chaplains' Department. The staff gradually enlarged as the strength of the command increased during 1941, and by October eight additional chaplains had been appointed.[106]

Mess operations on the Post began 3 September 1940, under the control of Capt. Carl J. Stumpf, Mess Officer, assisted by a staff of one mess sergeant and six cooks.[107]

In the latter part of March 1941, a Shipping and Receiving Office was created as a separate unit in the administrative structure. The office was established in order to centralize control of all shipping and receiving. Lt. Rudolph W. Eldien headed this office.[108]

On 5 July 1941, Major Brown established the Provost Marshal's Office. Prior to that time, the Police and Prison Office had been charged with the responsibility for all prisoners confined in the Guard House, the protection of buildings and property on the Post and the proper organization and functioning of the guard. On 25 September 1940, 1st Lt. Byron C. Swanson was detailed as Police and Prison Officer and Provost Marshal.[109]

Capt. Arthur J. Stanley Jr. became Provost Marshal on 5 July 1941, replacing Major Petrus F. Meert. The two offices were separated due to the fact that the combined duties placed too much responsibility upon one officer. The Provost Marshal was appointed special staff officer of the Commanding Officer, being responsible to the Commanding Officer for the proper functioning of the interior guard, the Police and Prison Office, and the Military Police. Capt. Stanley served as Provost Marshal until the assignment of Capt. Frank E. Bartlett on 21 July 1941. On 2 October 1941, Capt. Walter R. Lindersmith succeeded Capt. Bartlett.[110]

The Finance Office during 1939, 1940 and the early months of 1941, held the position of a Class B office under the supervision of the Finance Officer in St. Louis. An agent officer handled financial matters during the latter part of 1940 and early 1941. 1st Lt. Albert J. LeBreton served as the agent in charge. A disbursing officer established agent offices on posts where the volume of work did not warrant an independent disbursing office. The inspector's report in March 1941, concluded that with a strength of over 5,000 men at that time and with substantial increases expected in the future, "it is not believed that prompt and efficient payment can then be made by an agent officer. These activities warrant the stationing of a finance officer at this Post." The recommendation of the inspector caused the Finance Office to be discontinued as a Class B office and activated as an independent disbursing office on 1 May 1941. Major Robert R. Eakins, who had arrived at Jefferson Barracks in April 1941, became the first Finance Officer, relieving Lt. LeBreton, and remained at that post continuously during the period until Pearl Harbor. Seven enlisted men assisted Eakins as of May 1941. The Finance Officer's duties included handling payroll, as well as, making payments for the Quartermaster, Ordnance and Utilities Department. By 7 December 1941, the staff had grown to twenty-eight enlisted men.[111]

As noted earlier, the chief administrative task facing Major Brown during 1940-41 was the creation and supervision of an adequate staff to assist the Commanding Officer in fulfilling his responsibilities. Starting from scratch in September 1940, Major Brown built up the administrative machinery necessary for the efficient administration of Jefferson Barracks in just over one calendar year.

Perhaps a short biography of some of the department heads that assisted Major Brown in the administration of Jefferson Barracks from the beginning of the Air Corps period in September 1940 until 7 December 1941, would be appropriate here.

Capt. Isaac G. Siemens, served as Post Executive Officer from October 1940, to December 1941, was a veteran of eighteen months overseas duty in the Field Artillery during World War I, Capt. Siemens had fought in four major battles, for which he received the Silver Star with citation. He received a reserved commission as a second lieutenant of Field Artillery in 1925, became a first lieutenant in 1928, and a captain in 1932. He became a major on 8 November 1941, shortly before his transfer from Jefferson Barracks, to duty in the office of the Chief of Air Corps, in Washington, D.C.

When Jefferson Barracks became an Air Corps Replacement Training Center in September 1940, Capt. Siemens had been serving as staff officer with the CCC headquarters, which had been moved from Jefferson Barracks to Illinois in 1939. In his first month at Jefferson Barracks, he served as Post Inspector and Post Exchange Officer.[112]

Lt. Albert W. Hand headed the Classification Section during 1940-41. This section fell under the direct supervision of the Executive Officer. Commissioned in the Coast Artillery in 1938, Lt. Hand had received his military education at Wentworth Military Academy in Lexington, Missouri; at the University of Kansas; and during three summers with the National Guard. His first tour of duty after receiving his commission was with the CCC at Centaur, Missouri. He came to Jefferson Barracks with the first small group of new officers assigned there following the Post's establishment as an Air Corps Training Center.[113]

Capt. Daniel R. Baugh served as a key member of the small group of officers who assisted Major Brown. Baugh came to Jefferson Barracks on 20 November 1940. Initially placed in charge of the 27th Technical School Squadron, Baugh served successively as Assistant Executive Officer, Morale Officer and S-3 and Post Plans and Training Officer.

Capt. Baugh's military career began at the University of Kentucky, where he graduated in 1923. A member of the ROTC, he immediately received a commission as a second lieutenant of Infantry. The following year he attended the Infantry School at Fort Benning, Georgia, and shortly thereafter became commandant of cadets at the Locust Grove Academy, Georgia, and Gordon Military College in Barnesville, Georgia, a position he held until 1935. Baugh then served with the CCC at Boise, Idaho, as company commander and district inspector. He remained on duty there until his assignment to Jefferson Barracks.[114]

Lt. Byron C. Swanson served as one of the original seventeen officers responsible for the administration and operation of the Post as an Air Corps Training Center. Serving first as S-4 Officer, and then transferring to S-3 of the provisional group which directed plans and training for all training squadrons, Swanson remained in a position of high authority throughout the Post's early history.

Graduating from Coe College in 1935, and spending the following year at West Point, Lt. Swanson then entered the CCC service, serving at Spalding, Nebraska, and as camp commander at Custer, South Dakota.

Called to Jefferson Barracks in September 1940, he served first as S-4 Officer under the Post's new administrative organization. He organized the Clothing Issue Department and took responsibility for all Air Corps property used on the Post. When the duties of Clothing Issue grew to such magnitude that it required his full-time attention, he was relieved of his additional duties, and devoted all his efforts to the latter department until June 1941. For the remainder of the year, he served as S-3 of the provisional group.[115]

As the CCC District Quartermaster stationed at Jefferson Barracks from September 1940, until his transfer to the Air Corps in March 1941, Lt. Rudolph W. Eldien brought with him many years of experience as a military administrator. CCC administration, as was the case with many other officers of the new base, formed most of the background of Lt. Eldien's experience. On 14 March 1934, he was assigned to duty in the Black Duck Camp in Minnesota, and had continued on active duty since that date. During the following years he served with ten different CCC units in four states. At the Troy, Missouri, camp where he served for four years, his unit was judged "Outstanding Camp" of fifty such organizations in nine of twenty-one competitions.

Lt. Eldien's first assignment after his transfer to Jefferson Barracks was as S-3 Officer, where his first task included the compilation of the manual, "Procedure of Operations," which outlined functions of the Post. Four months later, he was appointed to the important position of Shipping and Receiving Officer, which he retained during 1941.[116]

Assigned to Jefferson Barracks on 27 March 1941, Major Merlin I. Carter began serving almost immediately as the first Post Plans and Training Officer, a key position which he held at the close of the year. A graduate of the University of Iowa in 1928, Major Carter studied flying at March Field and Kelly Field, and received a commission in the Air Corps in 1929. Service at Marshall Field, Fort Riley, Kansas; Chanute Field, Rantoul, Illinois; and Barksdale Field, Shreveport, Louisiana, followed, and on 1 April 1935, he received a promotion to first lieutenant.

In 1937, he was stationed at Wheeler Field, Hawaii, and in March 1939, he returned to Chanute Field. He was promoted to captain on September 4, 1939, and the rank of major on 15 March 1941, shortly before his transfer to Jefferson Barracks.[118]

When Lt. Col. Floyd D. Jones came to Jefferson Barracks as Post Quartermaster in November 1941, he had completed nearly twenty-four years of Army service. Since Jefferson Barracks was then in the process of rapid expansion of both personnel and facilities, Lt. Col. Jones seemed extremely well fitted for the jobs at hand, having spent most of his career in the construction division of the Quartermaster Corps.

The colonel held a degree in engineering from Iowa State College, and had been commissioned a first lieutenant with the Engineers upon entering the Army 23 June 1917. On 4 April 1918, he rose to the rank of captain, serving in the General Engineering Depot in Washington.

After a short interval as a civilian engineer following the Armistice, Capt. Jones rejoined the Army on 1 July 1920, with the Quartermaster Department, and at various times he acted as chief of construction operations at Fort Mason, California, as supervisor of utilities on Corregidor Island, and as assistant to the post quartermaster at Fort Monroe and Cargley Field, Virginia. In 1928, he attended the Quartermaster School, graduating in June 1929.

Supervising construction jobs with Seventh Corps Area Headquarters in Omaha and in the Philippines marked the years 1929 to 1938. On 1 August 1935, he rose to the rank of major. While helping to establish training schools in the 9th Corps Area, he attained the rank of lieutenant colonel.[1]

Preceding Lt. Col. Jones as Post Quartermaster, Lt. Col. Roland T. Fenton was responsible for the duties of providing supplies and quarters for the personnel of the Post upon its establishment as an Air Corps unit. From March 1940, until November 1941, Lt. Col. Fenton supervised much of the expansion of the Post, and assumed a large share in the direction and planning of the many new facilities required for its efficient operation.

Lt. Col. Fenton had served as a second lieutenant of Cavalry during World War I, from 15 August 1917, until 7 October 1918, when he became a first lieutenant of Infantry. He held this rank until 22 September 1920, when he joined the Quartermaster Corps. He held the rank of captain until his promotion to major on 1 August 1935, and was made lieutenant colonel 18 August 1940.[118]

Lt. William W. Quinn, a member of a family of soldiers with a long military background, assisted the Quartermaster and served as Quartermaster Property Officer during the critical early period. He was commissioned at West Point on 13 June 1933, and advanced to first lieutenant 13 June 1936. Lt. Quinn had served at Jefferson Barracks with the CCC District Headquarters. Other CCC assignments in Illinois and Missouri followed, and on 1 September 1940, he took up the duties here with the CCC as Property Officer in charge of ordnance, salvage, signal and motor transport.

Called to active duty at this station on 15 May 1941, he became property officer of the Post, and was promoted to captain on 9 June 1941.[120]

Another important member of the special staff assisting Major Brown included Major Robert R. Eakins, Post Finance Officer, who arrived at Jefferson Barracks on 10 April 1941, and opened the Finance Office two weeks later. Major Eakins entered the Army as an enlisted man, through a vocational candidate's course at the University of Kansas, which he completed after the armistice ending World War I. He remained an enlisted man until July 1919, during which time he served at Leavenworth, Kansas, and Camp Funston as a Master Sergeant and chief clerk in the Finance Office. He continued in the same capacity as a civilian at Fort Riley, Kansas, following his discharge. He received a reserve commission in 1922.[121]

Lt. Col. James R. McDowell, an Army Medical Corps doctor since World War I, served as Post Surgeon during the early Air Corps period when hospital facilities were strained to the utmost and the staff overworked.

McDowell received a commission as a 1st Lieutenant on 19 July 1918, as an emergency officer. After the war, he successfully passed the examination for the Regular Army Medical Corps and became a 1st lieutenant on 1 July 1920. He advanced to the rank of captain on 8 February 1923; to major on 8 February 1932; and to Lt. Col. on 8 February 1940. In 1920, McDowell graduated from the Army Medical School and Field Service School. In 1931, he successfully completed the advanced course. Before coming to Jefferson Barracks, McDowell had been stationed in Iceland and for two years in Hawaii.[122]

The tremendous problem of feeding the thousands of trainees assigned to Jefferson Barracks as the main basic training center of the Air Corps' Technical Training Command belonged to Capt. Charles A. Rose in March 1941. Under his supervision, mess operations were successfully decentralized from the General Mess Hall to many smaller buildings erected during 1941.

Capt. Rose's military career began with ROTC training during his undergraduate days at the University of Missouri. After six years in the banking business, Capt. Rose was recalled to active duty in 1933. He worked with the CCC, where one of his units at Roaring River State Park won the Army and Navy Journal Award as the outstanding camp in the 7th Corps Area.

Promoted to captain in March 1941, he transferred to the Air Corps and was assigned to Jefferson Barracks. He attended the Mess School at Fort Riley, before assuming his position as General Mess Officer. In addition to these duties, he served as supervisor of the 4th Divisional Group, which included the 39th and 360th Squadrons and the Bakers' and Cooks' School.[123]

One of the most important assignments at Jefferson Barracks was the Office of Post Engineer. After December 1941, it was headed by Major Harold S. Martin. Martin supervised all construction projects and maintenance work at the Post as well as 330 Civil Service workers at the Post.

A former electrical, mechanical and civil engineer for the City of Los Angeles, Martin attended the California Institute of Technology for three years, leaving in 1920. He returned to college twenty years later and received his degree in June 1940 from the University of South Carolina.

He became an Army reserve officer in 1927, and was recalled to active duty as a captain in December 1940. During his time as a reserve officer, he had been recalled to active duty at various times with the Quartermaster Corps, the Coast Artillery and the Engineers.

His first assignment in 1941 was in Washington, D.C., in the Quartermaster Corps. He transferred to Jefferson Barracks in January 1941; and transferred as a major to the Corps of Engineers in December 1941.

In addition to his duties as Post Engineer, Major Martin was in charge of Engineers at 2nd District Headquarters, the Forest Park Reservation Camp, Spring and Chouteau Recreation Camp (for colored troops), and the leased facilities of the St. Louis Ordnance District and Babler Park MP Training Camp.[124]

Capt. Kenneth M. Banie proved to be one of the most successful training supervisors on the Post during its early days as an Air Corps Training Center. He served as commandant of the 26th School Squadron during this time.

Commissioned as a reserve officer of Infantry upon graduation in 1933 with a B.A. degree from the University of Wichita, Capt. Banie was called to active duty in April 1935 at the CCC Kansas District Headquarters at Fort Riley. Transferring to Fort Leavenworth in November 1935, Banie resigned to take a business position. He became a captain on the reserve list in 1940, and on 5 July 1941, was called to active duty at Jefferson Barracks.

After a month of service on the Post Inventory Board, Capt. Banie became adjutant of the 26th School Squadron, and on 1 October became the squadron commander.[125]

One of the busiest sections at Jefferson Barracks throughout the early period of its history as an Air Corps unit was the Reception Center, which was commanded from the date of its activation, 31 January 1941, by Lt. Col. John D. Eason. Born in South Carolina and educated at The Citadel, Eason enlisted as an Infantry private shortly after his 21st birthday in the midst of World War I. Five months later, Eason received a commission as a 2nd lieutenant, a rank he retained until 1 July 1920.

Between the wars Eason served eleven tours of duty, all with Infantry commands. At various times he was stationed in the Philippines, Tientsin, China, and Hawaii. From September 1929 until April 1935, he was stationed at Jefferson Barracks with the 6th Infantry. He received a promotion to captain 1 October 1934, and was placed in charge of Co. G. On 1 July 1939, he became a major, and was assigned to head the Reception Center at Jefferson Barracks upon its activation. He received advancement to Lt. Colonel in September 1941.[126]

In order to carry out the provisions of the Selective Service and Training Act of 1940, Reception Centers as contemplated in the War Department Mobilization Plan were organized. Reception Center No. 1772 was allocated to Jefferson Barracks and activated on 10 February 1941, pursuant to General Order No. 3, Headquarters 7th Corps Area, dated 31 January 1941. The Reception Center, consisting of a Headquarters and Headquarters Company, a Receiving Battalion and four Receiving Companies, was first established in Building 67-E, just east of Theater No. 1, on the Main Post. When construction of temporary buildings was completed in the northeast corner of the military reservation, the Reception Center moved on 1 March 1941.

The Commanding Officer at the date of activation was Major John D. Eason and Capt. Harry C. Heald served as Adjutant. Two days later Capt. Walter D. Holliday relieved Capt. Heald.

On the activation date, the strength of the organization stood at 14 officers and 193 enlisted men. Officers had come from a special training class at Headquarters 7th Corps Area; the Reception Center at Fort Snelling, Minnesota; and Fort Leavenworth, Kansas. Three reserve officers, formerly non-commissioned officers of the

Regular Army, had been ordered directly to this station for Reception Center duty. The original cadre of enlisted men came from Fort Des Moines, Iowa, and had been on detached duty at Jefferson Barracks since November 1940. Just prior to activation another cadre transferred in from Fort Snelling and Fort Crook, Nebraska. These men came from the 3rd Infantry, 6th Medical Battalion and Headquarters and Military Police Company, 6th Division.

The Reception Center served, roughly, the area consisting of the eastern half of Missouri a part of the 7th Service Command under the direction of Major General F.E. Uhl. The objectives of Reception Center No. 1772 were to receive men coming to it from the Selective Service Boards and to induct them into the Armed Services of the United States; to process them and get them supplied and equipped; and to transfer them to the various Replacement Training Centers and units of Field Forces throughout the country to receive their basic training.

The problem confronting the new Reception Center was seeing to it that the newly inducted soldiers were properly fed, quartered, given physical examinations, classified, immunized, adequately supplied with clothing and equipment, and transferred to their proper Training Centers. Initially the greatest handicap was the lack of a suitable building for classification. It became necessary to use a barracks building until a processing building was constructed.

On 1 March 1941, when the Reception Center moved to its new area, it received men for processing that night. Due to experience gained by the cadre that had visited the Reception Center at Fort Leavenworth, processing went along smoothly and the assigned mission was accomplished. The following figures are indicative of the success of the mission: during the period from 1 March 1941, through 30 July 1943, a total of 125,735 men processed and transferred to Replacement Training Centers and units of the Field Forces.

Originally constructed as a 1,000-man Reception Center, facilities began to be over-loaded after December 7, 1941. During January 1942, it became necessary to supplement housing by the use of tents. By the end of the year, 7,175 tents were in use. Their use in this climate for men just entering the service was unsatisfactory and early in 1943, nineteen Theater of Operations Type buildings were added. This provided adequate housing for the maximum number of men that could normally be processed. It became necessary during the formative part of the Reception Center's career to construct a storehouse for stocks of clothing and equipment required to be carried by Reception Centers.[127]

At time of activation, 14 officers and 193 enlisted men made up the personnel of the Reception Center. By mid-1943, 45 officers and 311 enlisted men made up its personnel.[128]

At the date of activation, 22 buildings made up the Reception Center. By mid-1943 the Reception Center consisted of 49 buildings. The buildings included an Induction Station, Mess Hall, Information Building, Office Quarters, Warehouse, Temporary Barracks, Latrines and Bachelor Officer Quarters.[129]

At the time of activation, the Reception Center consisted of dirt/mud roads, board walks, no grading, no parking lots and dirt, excavated for buildings, that had not been hauled away. The beautification of the Reception Center involved careful planning and plenty of labor over a two-year period. Starmar Park, built during the summer of 1941, was named for Lt. Starmar, former 1st Sergeant of Co. A, who moved on to the European Theater.[130]

During 1943, a plan submitted to the Commanding Officer suggested that the streets in the Reception Center be given names of military significance such as Bataan Avenue, Tunisia Drive, Guadalcanal Avenue and Malta Road. This plan received the Commander's approval and the roads were so named.[131]

Turnover of permanent party personnel proved to be very high. Of the personnel present at activation, only one officer and thirteen enlisted men remained by mid-1943. These men included Major Walter D. Holliday, Master Sergeant Dale D. Cornell, Master Sergeant Lewis W. Rose, 1st Sgt. Lawrence Bernard, 1st Sgt. Orlin D. Oxenreider, 1st Sgt. George Goodwin, Technical Sgt. Herald O. Winchester, Staff Sgt. James P. Barrett, Sgt. Eugene F. Beck, Sgt. Edward Durham, Sgt. Clement Weiss, Sgt. Marvin H. Gayhart, Sgt. Gerald A. McConnell and Cpl. Edgar R. Wells.[132]

In spite of the frequent turnover, morale remained high and the organization functioned smoothly and efficiently. This can be at least in part attributable to the excellent recreational opportunities offered to all who cared to participate. During 1942, the Reception Center Missions baseball team captured the Post championship with a record of 23 and 4. Playing on the Missions team were Jim Babcock, a former All-American basketball player from Denver University; Johnny Sturm of the New York Yankees; George Archie of the St. Louis Browns and many other prominent players in the sports world.[Remember where a recruit goes first is the Reception Center, and from there it is not that difficult to become permanent party in the Reception Center.][133]

The following officers served as Commanding Officer of Reception Center No. 1772: Major John D. Eason served from February 10 until relieved by Major Lee A. Pollack on March 10, 1942. Pollack in turn was relieved by Lt. Col. Fred L. Jones on August 31, 1942 and on March 8, 1943, Major Clinton E. John relieved Jones. Major, later colonel, Eason served in the Southwestern Pacific after leaving Jefferson Barracks, and Capt. Elmer C. Witz, another Reception Center officer, was killed in action on Bataan.[134]

Another colorful personality who served at the Reception Center a few days was Pvt. Oscar Johnson, the millionaire President of the St. Louis Symphonic Society and the principal stockholder of the International Shoe Company of St. Louis. Pvt. Johnson said, as he was being fitted for a pair of shoes manufactured by his own company, "I will be glad to do whatever is expected of me."[135]

When the Japanese struck Pearl Harbor, 7 December 1941, all visitors were excluded from the Reception Center and special guards were posted day and night. This remained in effect for almost six weeks. The Reception Center also maintained a guard at the Medical Depot on Arsenal Street. for two weeks.

In bringing to a close this history of Reception Center No. 1772, the following extract from General Order No. 1, dated 2 March 1942, shows to some extent, what had happened since activation: "During the past twelve months, this station has been transformed from the drab picture of muddy walks, unpaved roads, unpainted barracks and a grassless, treeless and shrubless area to the pleasing appearance of freshly painted barracks, yards upon yards of newly laid sod, transplanted trees and shrubbery, with a background of vine covered trellises."[1]

Operating and occupying the same location as the Reception Center was an Induction station. Major Brown received notice of the establishment of an induction station from 7th Corps Area commander, Major General Bishop on 23 October 1940. In the same letter, Major Brown received orders to have the induction station in operation by 12 November 1940.[137]

During the latter part of October and the early part of November 1940, the Missouri Recruiting District recruited personnel for the new induction station. The first group of personnel, consisting of about fourteen men, were assigned to the Induction Station in early November 1940. For the first two weeks, the enlisted men of the organization took part in intensive training in administrative procedures. They were ready to begin induction in the latter part of November.

The Induction Station originally came under the supervision of Col. Ford Richardson, Recruiting Officer for the Missouri Recruiting District. Col. Richardson had his headquarters in the Federal Building in St. Louis.[138]

Capt. John R. Andie became the first commanding officer of the Induction Station in the latter part of November 1940, and arrived at the Station soon afterwards. Lt. Ernest Kretschmar served as Executive Officer. Promoted to captain shortly after his arrival, Capt. Kretschmar, who arrived shortly before Andie, took an active part in the preliminary arrangements prior to the opening of the Induction Station.[139]

Capt. Kretschmar relieved Capt. Andie on 27 November 1941. He served as commanding officer until the middle of March 1942.[140]

Lt. Robert L. Kasha served as the first medical officer of the Induction Station, beginning in November 1940. He remained as Chief Medical Officer until relieved by Major John R. Daly in February 1942.[141]

Visiting medial officers from the Post Hospital assisted at the Induction Station during its early months. During April 1941 the Station began getting its own staff. Major Charles H. Coughlan, Col. Luther H. Wilmoth, Capt. Levin H. Peek, Capt. Wilbur P. McDonald, Capt. Dwight A. Mater, Major Richard D. Nierling and Capt. Frederick J. Vollmar were all assigned duty at the Induction Station between 15 April and 30 April 1941. Capt. Lee E. Juhl reported 15 May 1941; Capt. John J. Prusmack reported on 22 May 1941; Capt. Bennett R. Wood on 28 May 1941; Capt. Joseph C. Epstein and Capt. Jacob B. Cier on 15 October 1941; and Capt. Marion B. Allen reported on 1 December 1941.[142]

Sgt. Oscar G. Hopson served as acting first sergeant of the Induction Station during the early period and Master Sergeant Charles F. Krementz served as chief clerk. Both of these enlisted men remained at the Station on 7 December 1941.[143]

In the beginning, selectees arrived at the Induction Station by train and were met by members of the Induction Station personnel, who marched them to the Induction building. Under the original plan the Post Gymnasium, Building No. 17, served for medical examinations; the old Post Exchange, Building No. 224, served as the administrative offices; and the west half of Barracks Building No. 67 served as sleeping quarters. This arrangement lasted only a short time when the entire Building No. 67 was turned over to the Induction Station. Under the new arrangement, the physical examinations took place in the basement, the administrative offices took up the first floor, and sleeping quarters were located on the second floor.[144]

On 23 September 1941, the Induction Station moved to its new location in the Reception Center. These quarters consisted of two barracks buildings, Nos. 328 and 329, and one single story unit No. 330. Building No. 328 provided sleeping quarters for the personnel, No. 329 served as administrative offices, and No. 330 served as the medical building. At the time, these quarters provided ample space, but with the huge increase of inductees to come, more room had to be provided.[145]

The Induction Station received its first selectees on 27 November 1940. The selectees, all from St. Louis, left Union Station about 8:30 a.m. after having a breakfast of hot coffee and rolls served by Salvation Army workers. Several hundred people, including draft officials and relatives, bid them farewell and a black school's drum and bugle corps gave them a departing concert.[146]

According to the 28 November 1940, issue of the St. Louis *Globe Democrat*: "A raw December wind which blew a few flakes of snow greeted the rookies as their train arrived at the Barracks about 9:15 a.m. After single file formation from the train, their baggage was trucked to the Induction Station and the men formed by waiting officers in the new three-abreast formation to the parade grounds."

"There a reception committee of 3,700 Aviation Corps recruits, including 843 recruits in campaign hats who would shortly be moving to California for Hawaii awaited them. Major Raymond R. Brown expressed the hope the men would profit by their training. and Col. Ford Richardson, Army Recruiting Officer for Missouri, pointed out the draft law was enacted for the common defense. In the parlance of the aviation base, the men were welcomed with 'happy landings'. Then the long, colorful history of the Barracks was recited by Mayor Bernard Dickmann."

Of the 95 men who reported for induction this first day, 76 were sworn into the Army, 11 were rejected and eight were held over for further examination.[147]

After the accepted men had been sworn in, they were loaded on a special train at 7:30 p.m. and sent directly to the Reception Center at Fort Leavenworth. Lt. Col. Griswold of 7th Corps Area Headquarters at Omaha, and Major Brown and his staff were on hand to bid the draftees good-bye. Lt. Col. Griswold accompanied the contingent to Fort Leavenworth.

From the opening of the Induction Station to 8 December 1941, no leave of any type was granted to newly inducted men. They generally shipped to a reception center on the same day that they got their physical examinations. For a short period, these men shipped to the Reception Center at Fort Leavenworth and, subsequently, they shipped to the Reception Center at Little Rock, Arkansas, until the opening of the Reception Center at Jefferson Barracks.

From 27 November 1940, to 23 September 1941, while the Induction Station was located on the Main Post, the number of Selective Service men reporting each day for induction rarely exceeded 100. Generally, fifty to seventy-five men received examinations. When the Station moved to the northeast corner of the Post the number of selectees reporting increased to around 150 per day and remained steady at that figure, until 7 December 1941.[148]

It is interesting to note that during the early period under consideration, selectees were drafted for one year of training in the Army. The country was not at war. Most of the men expected to return home after a year. All this changed on 7 December 1941, and with that change came a change in attitude and philosophy in the work of the Induction Station. From that date, a grim, determined purpose replaced the playful half-joking attitude that previously characterized the work of induction.

It has been attempted through the proceeding pages to provide a history of the early period of Jefferson Barracks as an Air Corps Technical Training facility. A great deal of construction and the establishment of basic infrastructure departments had to be accomplished during this period. However, the training of volunteers and Selective Service men had to be accomplished at the same time. An inspection tour conducted by Major Charles T. Arnett, Inspector General Department from 6 December until 11 December 1941, detailed areas of concern.

In his report, Major Arnett stated that the administration, supervision and control at Jefferson Barracks rated unsatisfactory. Arnett reported that "although the purpose of this school is to give basic military training to Air Corps recruits and selectees before sending them to one of the technical schools, it is believed this is not being accomplished. There appear to be two reasons for this: the first is that it becomes necessary in many cases, in order to fill quotas to the technical schools on schedule, to send men out before completion of the four weeks course they are supposed to receive. The second is that the training is not satisfactory even for those who are present for the full period. This is due to a laxity in carrying out the scheduled curriculum. With only four weeks available in which to accomplish so much in the case of each individual soldier entering, it is necessary that advantage be taken of every moment in training. Such is not the case."

Arnett cited an example of the 358th School Squadron Area that he inspected at 10:45 a.m. He stated that none of the over 500 trainees attached to the squadron were receiving instruction and apparently had not received any training during the entire morning. The explanation was that the regular instructors were on other duty relating to guarding defense areas in St. Louis. This was right after Pearl Harbor and Jefferson Barracks troops had been called upon to guard many areas such as the bridges leading into and out of St. Louis, power plants, and military related manufacturing plants. But Arnett pointed out that several squadron officers and non-commissioned officers were present and should have seen that instruction went on even though the regular instructors were absent.[149]

Arnett went on to report that the administrative section did not seem to be obtaining the results that should be expected of it. He stated that the cause seemed to be a lack of an adequate number of enlisted men to provide assistance and that the Administrative Inspector had several additional duties requiring a great amount of his time.

Arnett did report that adequate housing and general police of the Post seemed excellent. He reported that as of his inspection there existed housing for approximately 25,000 men in temporary barracks suitable for 10,000 men and tentage for another 10,000 men in addition to the permanent housing on the post.[150]

Major Brown refuted Major Arnett's report stating that he believed that Arnett failed to understand or take Into consideration certain conditions and problems with which the Post had been and was still confronted. Brown went on to state that in September 1940, when the Air Corps Replacement Training Center was established at Jefferson Barracks, two under strength School Squadrons had been loaned from Scott Field. These Squadrons had been largely composed of inexperienced enlisted men. From this original small group of enlisted personnel one Headquarters Squadron and twelve School Squadrons had been formed. In addition, one Headquarters Squadron and ten School Squadrons had been formed for Sheppard Field at Wichita Falls, Texas, and one Headquarters Squadron and eight School Squadrons for Keesler Field in Biloxi, Mississippi. Major Brown stated that Jefferson Barracks had to continually give up experienced personnel in order to do everything possible to assist the Air Corps Technical Training Command and the Air Corps. Brown also stated that in September 1940, there were approximately 15 officers made available. Of these only two were Regular Army and the remainder were reserve officers with no training for the type of duty required of them. The number of Reserve Officers gradually increased until by 5 July, 1941, some 130 officers had been received. This number of officers provided barely enough officer personnel for the proper operation of the Replacement Training Center. During November 1941, 92 of these officers transferred to Sheppard Field and Keesler Field. This again created a condition where the officer personnel was entirely inadequate at Jefferson Barracks.

Requests for additional officers and enlisted men had been frequently made. Again, on 7 November 1941, a request for 1,000 additional enlisted men and 103 officers was made in order to provide proper training of 10,000 men.

The Inspector General arrived on 6 December 1941, and on 7 December 1941, the Japanese attacked Pearl Harbor. Higher headquarters directed Brown to place the Emergency War Plan in operation. This directive necessitated utilization of the Jefferson Barracks Combat Force, composed of some 400 officers and assigned men whose normal duty was the supervision and instruction of trainees. These men remained on this extra-ordinary duty during the time that the Inspector General conducted his inspection.[151]

Endnotes

Chapter 1 – October 1894 Through 1897

[1] *St. Louis Post-Dispatch*, September 18, 1894.

[2] *Report of the Secretary of War: Being Part of the Message and Documents communicated to the Two Houses of Congress at the Beginning of the 2nd Session of the 54th Congress. Volume I, p. 527.*

[3] *Omaha World Herald*, February 13, 1895.

[4] Alexander Scammel Brooks Keyes served as a private and sergeant, then sergeant major of the 59th Massachusetts Infantry from October 31, 1863, to June 30, 1864, when he became a 2nd lieutenant in the 1st Battalion Massachusetts Artillery, on July 5, 1864. He was honorably mustered out October 20, 1865. On February 23, 1866, Keyes became a 2nd lieutenant in the 12th Infantry. He transferred to the 30th Infantry on September 21, 1866, where he was promoted to 1st lieutenant on February 9, 1867. He served as regimental adjutant from November 10, 1868, to March 23, 1869. Assigned to the 10th Cavalry on April 2, 1870, Keyes became a captain on December 6, 1873, and a major in the 3rd Cavalry on October 20, 1892. Keyes retired on August 27, 1896.

[5] *Kansas City Times*, July 1, 1895.

[6] Samuel Marmaduke Whitside had served at Jefferson Barracks previously, on duty with the Mounted Recruit Service. He arrived at Jefferson Barracks April 27, 1883, serving on Detached Service as Recruiting Officer at Rochester, New York, and Chicago, Illinois, until; he transferred back to his regiment on November 26, 1883. He joined the Army as a private in the General Recruiting Service and then as a sergeant major, 6th Cavalry, from November 10, 1858, to November 4, 1861, when he became a 2nd lieutenant in the 6th Cavalry. He was promoted to 1st lieutenant on January 25, 1864, and to captain on October 20, 1866. He became a major in the 7th Cavalry on March 20, 18885 and then a lieutenant colonel, 3rd Cavalry on July 17, 1895, transferring to the 5th Cavalry on October 15, 1895. He became colonel of the 10th Cavalry on October 16, 1898. On January 3, 1901, he was promoted to brigadier general of volunteers and on May 29, 1902, to brigadier general, U.S.A. Whitside retired on June 9, 1902.

[7] National Archives (N.A.), Jefferson Barracks Post Returns, December, 1895, M617, Roll 549.

[8] N.A., Jefferson Barracks Post Returns, December 1895, M617, Roll 549. Officers at Jefferson Barracks included: Lt. Col. Guy V. Henry, commanding the Post and 3rd Cavalry; Capt. John S. Seibold, Chaplain and in charge of the Post School; Major Robert H. White, Surgeon; Capt. Samuel R. Jones, Post Quartermaster; Capt. John B. Johnson, commanding Troop B; Major Henry W. Wessells, Jr., commanding the 2nd Squadron and in charge of the Post Garden; Major Alexander S.B. Keyes, commanding the 3rd Squadron and Range Officer; 1st Lt. and Adjutant Parker W. West, commanding Troop M, Recruit Detachment and Recruit Office for General Service; 1st Lt. Tyree R. Rivers, 3rd Cavalry Quartermaster and Commissary of Subsistence and in charge of the Post Exchange; Capt. George F. Chase, commanding Troop D; 1st Lt. David H. Boughton, duty with Troop H; 1st Lt. Franklin O. Johnson, duty with Troop I; 1st Lt. Arthur Thayer, commanding Troop A; 1st Lt. Charles A. Hedekin, duty with Troop B, 2nd Lt. Kirby Walker, duty with Troop D, 2nd Lt. Henry H. Pattison, duty with Troop B, Post Treasurer and Ordnance Officer (relieved January 1, 1896); and 2nd Lt. Clyde E. Hawkins, duty with Troop A, 1st Lt. George H. Morgan was awarded the Medal of Honor on July 15, 1892, for distinguished conduct in action against hostile Indians at the Big Dry Wash, Arizona, on July 17, 1882, by gallantly holding his ground at a critical moment and firing upon the advancing enemy until he was disabled by a shot, while serving as a 2nd Lt., 3rd Cavalry, and serving as a volunteer with Lt. West's command of Indian scouts and Troop I, 6th Cavalry.

[9] *Kansas City Times,* February 15, 1895.

[10] *Kansas City Times*, January 8, 1896.

[11] *Kansas City Times*, January 15, 1896.

[12] *Kansas City Times*, January 19, 1896.

[13] *St. Louis Republic*, February 15, 1896.

[14] *St. Louis Republic*, March 4, 1896.

[15] *St. Louis Republic*, March 21, 1896.

[16] Letter from Captain and Assistant Quartermaster Samuel R. Jones to Quartermaster-General, U.S. Army, Washington, D.C., dated April 22, 1896.

[17] *Annual Reports of the War department for the Fiscal Year Ended June 30, 1897. Report of the Secretary of War, Miscellaneous Reports*, p. 323. Hereafter cited as *Annual Report 1897*.

[18] *Morning Olympian*, May 29, 1896.

[19] Four hundred seventy-five recruits transferred from Jefferson Barracks to their permanent regiments during the year.

[20] N.A., Jefferson Barracks Post Returns, June, July, August 1896, M617, Roll 549.

[21] *Annual Report 1897*, p. 494-495, 584-592.

[22] *Annual Reports 1897, Miscellaneous Report*, p. 333.

[23] *Annual Report 1897, Miscellaneous Report*, p. 283.

[24] *St. Louis Republic*, May 31, 1896.

[25] *Charlotte Observer*, May 22, 1896.

[26] *Chicago Inter Ocean*, September 20, 1896.

[27] *St. Louis Republic*, October 13, 1896.

[28] *St. Louis Republic*, October 6, 1896.

[29] *Omaha World Herald*, November 20, 1896.

[30] *Chicago Inter Ocean*, November 20, 1896.

[31] N.A., Jefferson Barracks Post Returns, January 1896, M617, Roll 549.

[32] *St. Louis Republic*, December 22, 1896.

[33] N.A., Jefferson Barracks Post Returns, January 1897, M617, Roll 549. Officers at Jefferson Barracks included the following: [all are 3rd Cavalry officers unless noted] Lt. Col. Guy V. Henry, commanding Post and Regiment; Major Henry W. Wessells, Jr., commanding 2nd Squadron; Major J.B. Girard, Surgeon; 1st Lt. Parker W. West, Adjutant and commanding Troop M and Recruit Detachment; 1st Lt. Tyree R. Rivers, Quartermaster and Commissary Officer; Capt. George F. Chase, Troop D, sick in quarters since January 29; Capt. George K. Hunter, commanding Troop K; Capt. George H. Morgan, commanding Troop H; Capt. Daniel H. Boughton, commanding Troop B; 1st Lt. Thomas B. Dugan, commanding Troop I; 1st Lt. Arthur Thayer, commanding Troop A; 1st Lt. J.T. Mason Blunt, Troop K; 1st Lt. Charles A. Hedekin, Troop B; 1st Lt. Edwin M. Suplee, Troop D; 2nd Lt. Kirby Walker, Troop D; 2nd Lt. J.T. Conrad, Troop K and in charge of General Mess, Post Exchange and Post Garden; and Lt. Harry H. Pattison, Troop B and Range Officer; 2nd Lt. Clyde E. Hawkins, Troop A; 2nd Lt. John Morrison, Jr., Troop L; 2nd Lt. Ola W. Bell, Troop L; 1st Lt. Michael M. McNamee, 9th Cavalry, Troop H, duty with 3rd Cavalry, Troop I and Post Treasurer; 1st Lt. Alfred C. Merillat, Troop M.

[34] *St. Louis Republic*, February 20, 1897.

[35] Pamphlet, *Construction Costs at Jefferson Barracks, Missouri*, reproduced by the National Archives.

[36] *St. Louis Republic*, January 15, 1897.

[37] *St. Louis Republic*, January 24, 1897.

[38] *St. Louis Republic*, April 26, 1897.

[39] *St. Louis Republic*, June 4, 1897.

[40] *Dallas Morning News*, March 24, 1897.

[41] *St. Louis Republic*, April 7, 1897.

[42] *St. Louis Republic*, April 24, 1897.

[43] N.A., Jefferson Barracks Post Returns, June 1897, M617m, Roll 549.

[44] Arlington National Cemetery Website. Francis B. Heitman, *Historical Register and Dictionary of the United States Army, From Its Organization, September 29, 1789, to March 2, 1903*, Volume I, p. 523. Hereafter cited as Heitman, *Historical Register*.

[45] *St. Louis Republic*, June 22, 1897.

[46] *St. Louis Republic*, June 25, 1897.

[47] *St. Louis Republic*, May 23, 1897.

[48] *St. Louis Republic*, May 27, 1897.

[49] *St. Louis Republic*, June 4, 1897.

[50] *St. Louis Republic*, June 15/16, 1897.

[51] *Aberdeen Daily News*, June 15, 1897.

[52] *Idaho Falls Times*, August 19, 1897.

[53] N.A., Jefferson Barracks Post Returns, July 1897, M617, Roll 549.

[54] N.A., Jefferson Barracks Post Returns, September 1897, M617, Roll 549.

[55] *St. Louis Republic*, August 15, 1897.

[56] N.A., Jefferson Barracks Post Returns, October 1897, M617, Roll 549. Capt. George K. Hunter commanded, 1st Lt. J.Y. Mason Blunt and 2nd Lt. Julius T. Conrad.

[57] *St. Louis Republic*, October 16, 1897, and *Omaha World Herald*, October 17, 1897.

[58] *St. Louis Republic*, November 11, 1897.

[59] *New Haven Register*, December 23, 1897.

Chapter 2- Jefferson Barracks and the War with Spain

[1] Troop M, 3rd Cavalry, consisted of two officers and only three enlisted men.

[2] Major John P. Baker was a Civil War veteran who had achieved the rank of brevet lieutenant colonel of volunteers during the war. He retired 24 July 1902.

[3] David F. Trask, *The War with Spain in 1898*, p.1. Hereafter cited as Trask, *War with Spain*.

[4] Trask, *War with Spain*, p. xii.

[5] Trask, *War with Spain*, p. xiii.

[6] Trask, *War with Spain*, p. 35.

[7] Trask, *War with Spain*, p. 56.

[8] Trask, *War with Spain*, p. 57.

[9] *St. Louis Globe-Democrat*, 16 May 1898.

[10] *Report of the Adjutant General of Missouri, 1897-1898*, p.

[11] *St. Louis Globe-Democrat*, 20 August 1898.

[12] Porter, *A History of Battery A*, p. 34-36, Missouri History Museum Collection.

[13] Nambour, *Yarns of Battery A*.

[14] *Report of the Adjutant General of Missouri, 1897-1898*, p. 454. Porter, *A History of Battery A*, p. 46. Capt. Rambouillet and 20 others re-enlisted in the U.S. Volunteer Infantry and went to the Philippines, where Rambouillet gained distinction for gallantry and efficient service.

[15] *St. Louis Globe-Democrat*, 5 May 1898.

[16] *St. Louis Globe-Democrat*, 6 May 1898.

[17] *St. Louis Republic*, 11 May 1898.

[18] Ruby Beatrice Waldeck, *Missouri in the Spanish-American War*, p. 47, 48. Hereafter cited as Waldeck, *Spanish-American War*.

[19] *St. Louis Globe-Democrat*, 22 May 1898.

[20] Waldeck, *Spanish-American War*. p. 49.

[21] *St. Louis Globe-Democrat*, 4 June 1898.

[22] *St. Louis Globe-Democrat*, 24 May 1898.

[23] Waldeck, *Spanish-American War*. p. 50.

[24] *St. Louis Globe-Democrat*, 21 July 1898.

[25] *St. Louis Globe-Democrat*, 28 June 1898.

[26] *St. Louis Globe-Democrat*, 27 July 1898.

[27] *St. Louis Globe-Democrat*, 7 August 1898.

[28] *Report of the Adjutant General of Missouri, 1897-1898*, p. 144. Batsdorf, Cavender, and Webster were then at the mercy of Governor Stephens. Early in 1899 the regiment was declared inefficient and disbanded. It was then reorganized with different officers.

[29] *St. Louis Globe-Democrat*, 6 May 1898.

[30] *Report of the Adjutant General of Missouri, 1897-1898*. p. 207.

[31] *Sedalia Daily Capital*, 12 June 1898.

[32] *St. Louis Globe-Democrat*, 19 July 1898.

[33] *Correspondence Relating to the War With Spain*, p. 601. Hereafter cited as *Correspondence*.

[34] *Correspondence*, p. 601.

[35] *Sedalia Daily Capital*, 4 March 1899.

[36] *Kansas City Times,* 1 May 1898.

[37] *Report of the Adjutant General of Missouri, 1897-1898,* p.246.

[38] *Correspondence,* p. 601.

[39] *St. Louis Globe-Democrat,* 9 June 1898.

[40] *Correspondence,* p. 601.

[41] *St. Louis Globe-Democrat,* 10 October 1898.

[42] *Correspondence,* p. 601.

[43] *Report of the Adjutant General of Missouri, 1897-1898,* p. 309. Co. A came from Carrollton; Co. B from Mound City; Co. D from Bethany; Co. E from Maryville; Co. F from Hannibal; Co. H from Chillicothe; Co. I from Warrensburg; Co. M from Fulton; and Companies C, K, and G from St. Joseph.

[44] *Report of the Adjutant General of Missouri, 1897-1898,* p. 350/351.

[45] *St. Louis Globe-Democrat,* 2 June 1898.

[46] This information came from 1st Lt. George L. Rollins, Regimental Adjutant.

[47] *St. Louis Globe-Democrat,* 27 May 1898.

[48] *St. Louis Republic,* 28 April 1898.

[49] *Kansas City Times,* 28 April 1898.

[50] *St. Louis Globe-Democrat,* 27 May 1898.

[51] *Kansas City Times,* 29 April 1898.

[52] *Kansas City Times,* 1 May 1898.

[53] *St. Louis Globe-Democrat,* 26 April 1898.

[54] *Columbia Herald,* 20 May 1898.

[55] *Report of the Adjutant General of Missouri, 18978-1898,* p. 350.

[56] *Report of the Adjutant General of Missouri, 1897-1898,* p. 350.

[57] *St. Louis Globe-Democrat,* 8 September 1898.

[58] *St. Louis Globe-Democrat,* 8 September 1898.

[59] *Kansas City Times,* 2 August 1898.

[60] *Correspondence,* p. 602.

[61] *St. Louis Globe-Democrat,* 29 May 1898.

[62] *St. Louis Globe-Democrat,* 18 June 1898.

[63] *St. Louis Republic,* 22 June 1898.

[64] *St. Louis Republic,* 11 June 1898.

[65] *St. Louis Globe-Democrat,* 30 June 1898. The Webster Groves company was recruited in Pacific, Eureka, Clayton, Kirkwood, Ferguson, and other towns in St. Louis County.

[66] *St. Louis Republic,* 25 June 1898.

[67] *St. Louis Republic,* 14 July 1898.

[68] *Report of the Adjutant General of Missouri, 1897-1898,* p. 138.

[69] *Report of the Adjutant General of Missouri, 1897-1898,* p. 138.

[70] *Correspondence,* p. 602.

[71] Information taken from www.spanamwar.com. History of the 6th Missouri Volunteer Infantry.

[72] *St. Louis Republic,* 27 February 1898. Before war was declared, Missouri had one Rear-admiral, Edward C. Mathews; two Lt. Commanders, 13 Lieutenants, one Junior Lieutenant, four Ensigns, three men in the Paymaster Department, and five assistant surgeons.

[73] *Sedalia Daily Capital,* June 25, 1898.

[74] *St. Louis Globe-Democrat,* June 26, 1898.

[75] *St. Louis Republic,* June 10, 1898.

[76] *St. Louis Republic,* May 22, 1898.

[77] *St. Louis Republic,* June 13, 1898.

[78] *St. Louis Republic,* June 14, 1898.

[79] *St. Louis Republic,* July 20, 1898. Fulton was an assumed name. His real name was Walter Pannill.

[80] *Major General Report, 1898,* p. 369.

[81] *Misc. Reports, 1898,* p. 75/76.

[82] *St. Louis Republic,* May 8, 1898.

[83] *St. Louis Republic*, May 10, 1898.

[84] N.A., Jefferson Barracks Post Returns, August 1898, M617, Roll 550.

[85] N.A., Jefferson Barracks Post Returns, September 1898, M617, Roll 550.

[86] Roger D. Cunningham, *Kansas City's African-American "Immunes" in the Spanish-American War, Missouri Historical Review*, Missouri State Historical Society, Volume 100, April 2006.

[87] *St. Louis Republic*, September 27, 1898.

[88] N.A., Jefferson Barracks Post Returns, November 1898, M617, Roll 550.

[89] N.A., Jefferson Barracks Post Returns, November 1898, M617, Roll 550.

[90] *St. Louis Republic*, November 9, 1898.

[91] N.A., Jefferson Barracks Post Returns, December 1898, M617, Roll 550.

[92] Total casualties, in killed and wounded during the war with Spain: in Cuba, 23 officers and 237 men killed, 99 officers and 1,332 men wounded; in Puerto Rico, 3 men killed and 4 officers and 36 men wounded; in the Philippines, 17 men killed and 10 officers and 96 men wounded.

[93] *St. Louis Republic*, December 11, 1898.

Chapter 3 - Philippine Insurrection - 1899

[1] Brian McAllister Linn, *The U.S. Army and Counterinsurgency in the Philippine War, 1899-1902*, p.2/3. Hereafter cited as Linn, *The U.S. Army and Counterinsurgency.*

[2] Linn, *The U.S. Army and Counterinsurgency*, p. 8.

[3] Linn, *The U.S. Army and Counterinsurgency*, p. 8.

[4] Linn, *The U.S. Army and Counterinsurgency*, p. 8/9.

[5] Linn, *The U.S. Army and Counterinsurgency*, 9.

[6] Heitman, *Historical Register*, p. 762.

[7] Linn, *The U.S. Army and Counterinsurgency*, p. 10/11.

[8] Linn, *The U.S. Army and Counterinsurgency*, p. 12.

[9] Linn, *The U.S. Army and Counterinsurgency*, p. 12.

[10] *Annual Reports of the War Department for the Fiscal Year Ended June 30, 1899, Report of the Secretary of War, Miscellaneous Reports*, p. 3-12. Hereafter cited as *Annual Reports, 1899, Misc.*

[11] N.A., Jefferson Barracks Post Returns, January 1899, M617, Roll 550.

[12] N.A., Jefferson Barracks Post Returns, February 1899, M617, Roll 550.

[13] N.A., Jefferson Barracks Post Returns, March 1899, M617, Roll 550.

[14] N.A., Jefferson Barracks Post Returns, March 1899, M617, Roll 550.

[15] N.A., Jefferson Barracks Post Returns, April 1899, M617, Roll 550.

[16] N.A., Jefferson Barracks Post Returns, April 1899, M617, Roll 550.

[17] N.A., Jefferson Barracks Post Returns, April 1899, M617, Roll 550.

[18] Major Henry W. Webb, *The Story of Jefferson Barracks*, p. 113. Hereafter cited as Webb, *Jefferson Barracks.*

[19] N.A., Jefferson Barracks Post Returns, June 1899, M617, Roll 550.

[20] N.A., Jefferson Barracks Post Returns, May 1899, M617, Roll 550.

[21] N.A., Jefferson Barracks Post Returns, June 1899, M617, Roll 550.

[22] N.A., Jefferson Barracks Post Returns, June 1899, M617, Roll 550.

[23] N.A., Jefferson Barracks Post Returns, July 1899, M617, Roll 550.

[24] N.A., Jefferson Barracks Post Returns, August 1899, M617, Roll 550 & *Annual Reports of the War Department for the Fiscal Year Ended June 30, 1899, Report of the Major-General Commanding the Army*, Part 1, p. 3-7. The following officers transferred during August: Capt. Francis H. Hardie, Troop G, 3rd Cavalry; Capt. George K. Hunter, Troop K, 3rd Cavalry; 1st Lt. Julius T. Conrad, Adjutant, 3rd Cavalry; 2nd Lt. John Morrison, Jr., Troop K, 3rd Cavalry; 2nd Lt. Godwin Ordway, Troop G, 3rd Cavalry; and acting assistant Surgeon A. von Clossman, who accompanied Troop K, 3rd Cavalry, to Seattle.

[25] N.A., Jefferson Barracks Post Returns September 1899 & *War Department Report, 1899*, Part 1. Other 38th U.S. Volunteer Infantry officers who joined in September included 1st Lt. William G. Donne, 1st Lt. Fred A. Thompson, Capt. William H. Collier, Capt. Ross A. Nichols, Capt. John S. Powell, Capt. John L, Jordan, Capt. Claude E.

Sawyer, Capt. Beverly A. Read, Capt. Robert M. Nolan, Capt. John W. Moore, Capt. William J. Warden, Capt. John E. Weber, Capt. Clarence L. Grinstead, 1st Lt. Joseph L. Kraemer, 1st Lt. Reuben D. Blanchard, 1st Lt. Douglas H. Jacobs, 1st Lt. John E. Morris, 1st Lt. Thaddeus P. Seigle, 2nd Lt. John R. Maxwell, 2nd Lt. Elisha G. Abbott, 2nd Lt. Walter C. Hudson, 2nd Lt. Samuel G. Shortle, 2nd Lt. William O. Thornton, 2nd Lt. Charles J. Weinheimer, and 2nd Lt. Fred Burg.

[26] *Annual Report of the War department for the Fiscal Year Ended June 30, 1899, Reprot of the Secretary of War, Miscellaneous Reports*, p. 3-12.

[27] N.A., Jefferson Barracks Post Returns, September 1899, M617, Roll 550.

[28] N.A., Jefferson Barracks Post Returns, M617, Roll 550. Other 49th U.S. Volunteer Infantry officers who joined in September included 1st Lt. Isaac W. Mahoney, 1st Lt. William D. Pritchard, Capt. Charles W. Jefferson, Capt. William R. Staff, Capt. Thomas Campbell, Capt. Floyd Crumbly, Capt. Emmanuel D. Bass, Capt. John C. Proctor, 1st Lt. Charles Sperlock, 1st Lt. Elbert W. Maiden, 1st Lt. William H. Butler, 1st Lt. James W. Thomas, 2nd Lt. Henry F. Falls, 2nd Lt. Robert Gough, 2nd Lt. Beverly Perea, and 2nd Lt. George E. Payne.

[29] *Fort Worth Morning Register*, September 29, 1899.

[30] *Annual Reports of the War Department for the Fiscal Year Ended June 30, 1899, Part 1*, p. 380-381.

[31] *Annual Reports of the War Department for the Fiscal Year Ended June 30, 1899, Part 3*, p. XV.

[32] *Annual Reports of the War Department for the Fiscal Year Ended June 30, 1899, Reports of Chiefs of Bureaus*, p. 9.

[33] *Annual Reports of the War Department for the Fiscal Year Ended June 30, 1899, Part 1*, p. 369-375.

[34] N.A., Jefferson Barracks Post Returns, October 1899, M617, Roll 550. Other officers in the 49th U.S. Volunteer Infantry that joined during October included Major Carter P. Johnson, former captain in the 10th Cavalry; Major Ernest Hinds, former 1st Lt. in the 2nd Artillery; Major George W. Kirkman, former captain in the 12th Infantry; Capt. and Regimental Adjutant Robert Gage; Capt. and Regimental Quartermaster Gilbert Smith; 1st Lt. and Commissary Officer Fred Dibler; 1st Lt. William D. Prichard; Capt. Edward L. Baker; Capt. William D. Edward; Capt. William M. Hawkins; Capt. Louis W. McNabb; Capt. Frank R. Steward; Capt. Robert G. Woods; 1st Lt. Robert Blakeman; 1st Lt. William H. Butler; 1st Lt. L.H. Jordan; 1st Lt. Lafayette Tillman; 2nd Lt. G.E. Campbell; 2nd Lt. Alfred M. Ray; 2nd Lt. H.F. Wheaton; and acting Assistant Surgeon Joseph H. Carroll.

[35] N.A., Jefferson Barracks Post Returns, October 1899, M617, Roll 550.

[36] *Annual Reports of the War Department for the Fiscal Year Ended June 30, 1899, Part 1, p. 375.*

[37] N.A., Jefferson Barracks Post Returns, November 1899, M617, Roll 550.

[38] *Idaho Statesman*, November 9, 1899.

[39] *Helena Independent*, November 9, 1899.

[40] Webb, *Jefferson Barracks*, p. 114 & *Annual Reports of the War Department for the Fiscal Year Ended June 30, 1899*, Part 3, p. 1931.

[41] N.A., Jefferson Barracks Post Returns, November 1899, M617, Roll 550. The civilians included one clerk at $100 per month; one Clerk at $75 per month; one clerk at $60 per month; one plumber at $75 per month; one blacksmith at $60 per month; one engineer at $75 per month; one Pack Master at $100 per month; one assistant engineer at $60 per month; one laborer at $40 per month; four laborers at $30 per month; seven teamsters at $30 per month; one wagon master at $50 per month; one clerk at the Recruit Rendezvous at $100 per month.

[42] *Fort Worth Morning Register*, November 3, 1899.

[43] N.A., Jefferson Barracks Post Returns, December 1899, M617, Roll 550.

[44] *Annual Reports of the War Department for the Fiscal Year Ended June 30, 1900, Report of the Lieutenant-General Commanding the Army, Part 1*, p. 44-70. Hereafter cited as *Annual Reports of the War Department, 1900.* Units of the 6th Infantry that had previously served at Jefferson Barracks took part in twenty-five combat actions in the Philippines between July 19, 1899, and December 19, 1899. Units of the 3rd Cavalry took part in twelve combat actions in the Philippines between November 11, 1899, and December 12, 1899. The 6th Infantry suffered nine enlisted men killed and twenty-one wounded. In addition to Lt. Grubbs, 1st Lt. Augustus C. Ledyard of the 6th Infantry was killed in action. Lt. Ledyard was killed December 8, 1899, in action in South Negros. The 3rd Cavalry suffered two men killed and thirteen wounded (some of those wounded could have belonged to the 34th U.S. Volunteer Infantry as this unit participated in the action on December 4 with the 3rd Cavalry, when twelve men were wounded.

[45] *Annual Reports of the War Department for the Fiscal Year Ended June 30, 1900, Report of the Lieutenant-*

General Commanding the Army, Part 2, p. 321.

[46] *Annual Reports of the War Department, 1900,* Part 5, p. 171-172.

[47] N.A., Jefferson Barracks Post Returns, January 1900, M617, Roll 550.

[48] N.A., Jefferson Barracks Post Returns, January 1900, M617, Roll 550.

[49] *Annual Reports of the War Department, 1900,* Part 4, p. 625-628.

[50] *Annual Reports of the War Department, 1900,* Part 4, p. 640-649.

[51] *Annual Reports of the War Department, 1900,* Part 4, p. 10-24.

[52] N.A., Jefferson Barracks Post Returns, March 1900, M617, Roll 550.

[53] Heitman, *Historical Register,* p. 325.

[54] N.A., 5th Cavalry Regimental Returns, April 1900, M744, Roll 57. N.A., 6th Cavalry Regimental Returns, April 1900, M744, Roll 67.

[55] N.A., 5th Cavalry Regimental Returns, April/May 1900, M744, Roll 57.

[56] N.A., Jefferson Barracks Powder Depot Returns, April 1900,

[57] N.A., 6th Cavalry Regimental Returns, May 1900, M744, Roll 67.

[58] *Annual Reports of the War Department, 1900,* Part 6, p. 520.

[59] *Annual Reports of the War Department, 1900,* Part 3, p. 28/29.

[60] *Annual Reports of the War Department, 1900,* Part 3, p. 30.

[61] N.A., Jefferson Barracks Powder Depot Post Returns, May 1900,

[62] *St. Louis Republic,* May 30, 1900.

[63] *Annual Reports of the War Department, 1900,* Part 3, p. 208-216.

[64] N.A., Jefferson Barracks Post Returns, June 1900, M617, Roll 550.

[65] N.A., Jefferson Barracks Post Returns, June 1900, M617, Roll 550. N.A., 5th Cavalry Regimental Returns, June 1900, M744, Roll 57.

[66] N.A., Jefferson Barracks Post Returns, June 1900, M617, Roll 550.

[67] N.A., Jefferson Barracks Powder Depot Returns, June 1900,

[68] *Annual Reports of the War Department, 1900,* Part 3, p. 36.

[69] *Annual Reports of the War Department, 1900,* Part 3, p. 40.

[70] N.A., Jefferson Barracks Post Returns, July 1900, M617, Roll 550. The following 5th Cavalry officers transferred during July: 1st Lt. John M. Jenkins; Capt. Charles H. Watts; 1st Lt. Lawrence J. Fleming; 1st Lt. James J. Hornbrook; 2nd Lt. William D. Forsyth; Capt. Augustus C. Macomb; 1st Lt. Nathaniel F. McClure; 2nd Lt. William S. Balentine; Capt. Eben Swift; Capt. William E. Almy; and 1st Lt. James McCarlin.

[71] N.A., Jefferson Barracks Post Returns, August 1900, M617, Roll 550.

[72] N.A., Jefferson Barracks Post Returns, August 1900, M617, Roll 550.

[73] N.A., Jefferson Barracks Post Returns, August 1900, M617, Roll 550. The general prisoners were Pvt. John H. Kane, Troop D, 5th Cavalry; Pvt. Chris Crawford, Battery H, 4th Artillery; and Pvt. Henry Waller, Company M, 16th Infantry.

[74] N.A., Jefferson Barracks Powder Depot Returns, August 1900,

[75] N.A., Jefferson Barracks Post Returns, September 1900, M617, Roll 550.

[76] N.A., Jefferson Barracks Post Returns, September 1900, M617, Roll 550.

[77] N.A., Jefferson Barracks Post Returns, October 1900, M617, Roll 550.

[78] N.A., Jefferson Barracks Post Returns, November 1900, M617, Roll 550.

[79] N.A., Jefferson Barracks Post Returns, November 1900, M617, Roll 550.

[80] N.A., Jefferson Barracks Post Returns, December 1900, M617, Roll 550.

[81]. *Annual Reports of the War Department, 1900,* Part 7, p. 382.

[82] *Annual Reports of the War Department, 1900,* Part 7, p. 418.

[83] Leon Wolff, *Little Brown Brother: How the United States Purchased and Pacified the Philippine Islands at the Century's Turn,* p. 317/318. Hereafter cited as Wolff, *Brown Brother*

[84] *Annual Reports of the War Department, 1900, Misc. Reports,* p. 3-5.

[85] *Annual Reports of the War Department, 1900,* Part 5, p. 363/364. Part 3, p. 38, 40, 42, 45, 47, 48, 219, 220, 231-233. *Annual Reports of the War Department for the Fiscal Year Ended June 30, 1901, Report of the Lieutenant-General Commanding the Army in Five Parts,* Part 3, p. 9, 101-105, 239, 240, 250. Hereafter cited as *Annual Reports of the War Department, 1901. Annual Reports of the War Department, 1901,* Part 4, p. 6-10. *Annual*

Reports of the War Department, 1901, Part 5, p. 7, 12, 14-19, 23-28, 30, 32, 34-39, 275-297, 395-413.

[86] *Annual Reports of the War Department, 1901,* Part 4, p. 6-10.

[87] N.A., Jefferson Barracks Post Returns, January 1901, M617, Roll 550.

[88] N.A., Jefferson Barracks Post Returns, January 1901, M617, Roll 550.

[89] N.A., Jefferson Barracks Post Returns, January 1901, M617, Roll 550.

[90] N.A., Jefferson Barracks Post Returns, February 1901, M617, Roll 550.

[91] N.A., Jefferson Barracks Post Returns, February 1901, M617, Roll 550.

[92] N.A., Jefferson Barracks Post Returns, March 1901, M617, Roll 550.

[93] N.A., Jefferson Barracks Post Returns, March 1901, M617, Roll 550.

[94] N.A., Jefferson Barracks Post Returns, March 1901, M617, Roll 550.

[95] Webb, *Jefferson Barracks,* p. 116.

[96] N.A., Jefferson Barracks Post Returns, April 1901, M617, Roll 550.

[97] N.A., Jefferson Barracks Post Returns, May 1901, M617, Roll 550.

[98] *Idaho Statesman,* May 31, 1901.

[99] N.A., Jefferson Barracks Post Returns, May 1901, M617, Roll 550.

[100] N.A., Jefferson Barracks Post Returns, June 1901, M617, Roll 550.

[101] N.A., Jefferson Barracks Post Returns, July 1901, M617, Roll 550.

[102] N.A., Jefferson Barracks Post Returns, August 1901, M617, Roll 550.

[103] N.A., Jefferson Barracks Post Returns, August 1901, M617, Roll 550.

[104] N.A., Jefferson Barracks Post Returns, August 1901, M617, Roll 550. Officers at Jefferson Barracks and their duties included: Major James B. Hickey, commanding Post & 1st Battalion, 11th Cavalry; Capt. Francis A. Winter, Post Surgeon; 1st Lt. & Squadron Adjutant Theodore B. Taylor; Capt. John T. Haines, commanding Troop A, 11th Cavalry; Capt. Allstine W. Rowell, commanding Troop D, 11th Cavalry; Capt. Edward M. Leary, commanding Troop B, 11th Cavalry; 1st Lt. Guy Cushman, Troop B, 11th Cavalry; 1st Lt. Frank P. Amos, commanding Troop C, 11th Cavalry; 2nd Lt. John Symington, Troop A, 11th Cavalry; 2nd Lt. George H. Baird, Troop C, 11th Cavalry; 2nd Lt. Daniel D. Tompkins, Troop C, 11th Cavalry & Post Quartermaster & Commissary Officer; 2nd Lt. William G. Meade, Troop D, 11th Cavalry and commanding Recruit Detachment; 1st Lt. Henry Watterson, Jr., 29th Infantry; 2nd Lt. Fred H. Turner, 23rd Infantry; and Contract Surgeon Parker G. Dillon, in charge of the hospital at the Arcadia Rifle Range.

[105] N.A., Jefferson Barracks Post Returns, September 1901, M617, Roll 550. The following officers joined with the 4th Cavalry: Major Frank A. Edwards, commanding the 3rd Squadron; Capt. Henry C. Bernson, commanding Troop K; 1st Lt. Charles S. Haight, Troop L; 1st Lt. B.H. Dorcy, Troop M; 1st Lt. Charles T. Boyd, Troop I; 2nd Lt. Charles J. Naylor, Troop M; Capt. Robert A. Brown, Troop M; 1st Lt. Guy V. Henry, Troop K; and 2nd Lt. Albert J. Mohr, Troop I.

[106] N.A., Jefferson Barracks Post Returns, September 1901, M617, Roll 550.

[107] N.A., Jefferson Barracks Post Returns, September 1901, M617, Roll 550.

[108] N.A., Jefferson Barracks Post Returns, October 1901, M617, Roll 550.

[109] N.A., Jefferson Barracks Post Returns, October 1901, M617, Roll 550.

[110] N.A., Jefferson Barracks Post Returns, October 1901, M617, Roll 550.

[111] N.A., Jefferson Barracks Post Returns, October 1901, M617, Roll 550.

[112] N.A., Jefferson Barracks Post Returns, November 1901, M617, Roll 550.

[113] N.A., Jefferson Barracks Post Returns, January to December 1901, M617, Roll 550.

[114] N.A., Jefferson Barracks Post Returns, November 1901, M617, Roll 550.

[115] N.A., Jefferson Barracks Post Returns, November 1901, M617, Roll 550.

[116] N.A., Jefferson Barracks Post Returns, December 1901, M617, Roll 550.

[117] N.A., Jefferson Barracks Post Returns, December 1901, M617, Roll 550.

[118] Heitman, *Historical Register,* p. 398.

[119] N.A., Jefferson Barracks Post Returns, December 1901, M617, Roll 550.

[120] *Trenton Evening News,* December 20, 1901.

[121] *Annual Reports of the War Department for the Fiscal Year Ended June 30, 1901, Report of the Secretary of War, Miscellaneous Reports,* p. 7-9.

[122] *Annual Reports of the War Department for the Fiscal Year Ended June 30, 1901, Report of the Lt.-General*

Commanding the Army, in five parts, Part 1, p. 28/29. Hereafter cited as *Annual Report 1901*, Part 1.

[123] *Annual Report 1901*, Part 1, p. 28/29.

[124] *Annual Report 1901*, Part 1, p. 29/30.

[125] *Annual Report 1901*, Part 1, p. 29/30.

[126] Wolff, *Brown Brothers*, p. 342-345 and Linn, *The U.S. Army and Counterinsurgency*, p. 75.

[127] Wolff, *Brown Brothers*, p. 345/346.

[128] Wolff, *Brown Brothers*, p. 346 and Heitman, *Historical Register*, p. 441.

[129] Wolff, *Brown Brothers,* p. 358/359.

[130] Wolff, *Brown Brothers*, p. 360.

[131] N.A., Jefferson Barracks Post Returns, January 1902, M617, Roll 550.

[132] *Idaho Statesman*, January 27, 1902.

[133] N.A., Jefferson Barracks Post Returns, January 1902, M617, Roll 550.

[134] N.A., Jefferson Barracks Post Returns, January 1902, M617, Roll 550.

[135] N.A., Jefferson Barracks Post Returns, February 1902 and March 1902, M617, Roll 550.

[136] N.A., Jefferson Barracks Post Returns, February 1902 and March 1902, M617, Roll 550.

[137] N.A., Jefferson Barracks Post Returns, March 1902, M617, Roll 550.

[138] N.A., Jefferson Barracks Post Returns, March 1902, M617, Roll 550.

[139] Heitman, *Historical Register*, p. 850.

[140] N.A., Jefferson Barracks Post Returns, April 1902, M617, Roll 550.

[141] N.A., Jefferson Barracks Post Returns, April 1902, M617, Roll 550.

[142] N.A., Jefferson Barracks Post Returns, April 1902, M617, Roll 550.

[143] *Annual Reports of the War Department for the Fiscal Year Ended June 30, 1902, Volume IX, Report of the Lt.-General Commanding the Army and Department Commanders*, p. 92. Hereafter cited as *Annual Reports, 1902, Volume IX*

[144] N.A., Jeffersobn Barracks Post Returns, May 1902, M617, Roll 550. Officers arriving in May included: Major Henry W. Sprole; 2nd Lt. Frank Keller, Squadron Quartermaster and Commissary officer; Capt. Joseph A. Gaston, Troop F; 1st Lt. Osmun Latrolee, Jr., Troop H; 2nd Lt. Thomas H. Cunningham, Troop F; 2nd Lt. Sebring C. Megill, Troop E; 2nd Lt. Joseph C. Righter, Troop H; 2nd Lt. Albert E. Phillips, Troop G; Contract Surgeon William H. Moncrief; and Contract Surgeon Robert P. Coke.

[145] N.A., Jefferson Barracks Post Returns, May 1902, M617, Roll 550.

[146] *Salt Lake Telegram*, May 30, 1902.

[147] N.A., Jefferson Barracks Post Returns, June 1902, M617, Roll 550.

[148] N.A., Jefferson Barracks Post Returns, January through June 1902, M617, Roll 550.

[149] N.A., Jefferson Barracks Post Returns, June 1902, M617, Roll 550.

[150] N.A., Jefferson Barracks Post Returns, July 1902, M617, Roll 550.

[151] N.A., Jefferson Barracks Post Returns, July 1902, M617, Roll 550.

[152] N.A., Jefferson Barracks Post Returns, July 1902, M617, Roll 550.

[153] N.A., Jefferson Barracks Post Returns, August 1902, M617, Roll 550.

[154] N.A., Jefferson Barracks Post Returns, August 1902, M617, Roll 550.

[155] *Annual Reports, 1902*, Volume IX, p. 54-62.

[156] *Annual Reports*, 1902, Volume IX, p. 54-62.

[157] *Annual Reports of the War Department for the Fiscal Year Ended June 30, 1902, Report of the Secretary of War and Reports of Bureau Chiefs*, Volume I, p. 400.

[158] *Annual Reports of the War Department for the Fiscal Year Ended June 30, 1902, Report of the Secretary of War and Reports of Bureau Chiefs*, Volume I, p. 52. Hereafter cited as *Annual Reports, 1902, Volume I*.

[159] *Annual Reports*, 1902, Volume I, p. 28.

[160] N.A., Jefferson Barracks Post Returns, August 1902, M617, Roll 550.

[161] *Salt Lake Telegram*, August 28, 1902.

[162] N.A., Jefferson Barracks Post Returns, September 1902, M617, Roll 550.

[163] N.A., Jefferson Barracks Post Returns, November 1902, M617, Roll 550.

[164] N.A., Jefferson Barracks Post Returns, October 1902, M617, Roll 550.

[165] *Annual Reports of the War Department for the Fiscal Year Ended June 30, 1903, Volume II, Armament,*

Transportation, and Supply, p. 119/120.

[167] N.A., Jefferson Barracks Post Returns, November 1902, M617, Roll 550, and N.A., Regimental Returns, 8th Cavalry, November 1902, M744, Roll 83.

[167] N.A., Jefferson Barracks Post Returns, December 1902, M617, Roll 550.

Chapter 4: Jefferson Barracks and the Army Reorganize

[1] N.A., Jefferson Barracks Post Returns, January 1903, M617, Roll 550.

[2] Richard B. Crossland and James T. Currie, *Twice the Citizen*, p. 13/14. (Hereafter cited as Crossland and Currie, *Twice the Citizen).

[3] Crossland and Currie, *Twice the Citizen*, p. 14.

[4] *Annual Reports of the War Department for the Fiscal Year Ended June 30, 1903, Reports of the Secretary of War, Chief of Staff, Adjutant-General, Inspector-General, and Judge-Advocate-General*, Volume I, p. 3-5. (Hereafter cited as *Annual Report 1903*, Volume I),

[5] *Annual Report 1903*, Volume I, p. 9.

[6] N.A., Jefferson Barracks Post Returns, February and March 1903, M617, Roll 550.

[7] N.A., Jefferson Barracks Post Returns, April 1903, M617, Roll 550.

[8] *Annual Reports 1903*, Volume I, p. 437.

[9] N.A., Jefferson Barracks Post Returns, May 1903, M617, Roll 550.

[10] *Times Picayune*, May 6, 1903.

[11] N.A., Jefferson Barracks Post Returns, June and July 1903, M617, Roll 550.

[12] *Annual Reports 1903*, Volume III, p. 78-95.

[13] Webb, *Jefferson Barracks*, p. 117.

[14] *Annual Reports 1903*, Volume III, p. 78-95.

[15] *Annual Reports 1903*, Volume III, p. 94/95.

[16] N.A., Jefferson Barracks Post Returns, August 1903, M617, Roll 550.

[17] N.A., Jefferson Barracks Post Returns, August 1903, M617, Roll 550.

[18] N.A., Jefferson Barracks Post Returns, August 1903, M617, Roll 550.

[19] N.A., Jefferson Barracks Post Returns, September 1903, M617, Roll 550.

[20] N.A., Jefferson Barracks Post Returns, September 1903, M617, Roll 550.

[21] N.A., Jefferson Barracks Post Returns, October 1903, M617, Roll 550.

[22] N.A., Jefferson Barracks Post Returns, October 1903, M617, Roll 550.

[23] N.A., Jefferson Barracks Post Returns, November 1903, M617, Roll 550.

[24] N.A., Jefferson Barracks Post Returns, November 1903, M617, Roll 550.

[25] N.A., Jefferson Barracks Post Returns, December 1903, M617, Roll 550.

[26] N.A., Jefferson Barracks Post Returns, December 1903, M617, Roll 550.

[27] N.A., St. Louis Powder Depot Returns, December 1903, M617, Roll 550.

[28] Webb, *Jefferson Barracks*, p. 118.

[29] *Annual Reports of the War Department for the Fiscal Year Ended June 30, 1904, Reports of the Secretary of War, Chief of Staff, The Military Secretary, Inspector-General, and Judge-Advocate-General*, Volume I, p. 5. (Hereafter cited as *Annual Report 1904*, Volume I)

[30] *Annual Reports 1904*, Volume III, p. 63-80.

[31] Webb, *Jefferson Barracks*, p. 118.

[32] N.A., St. Louis Powder Depot Returns, January 1904, M617, Roll 550.

[33] N.A., Jefferson Barracks Post Returns, January 1904, M617, Roll 550.

[34] *The Idaho Daily Statesman*, January 23, 1904.

[35] N.A., Jefferson Barracks Post Returns, January and February 1904, M617, Roll 550.

[36] Edward M. Coffman, *The Regulars: The American Army 1898-1941*, p. 103/104. (Hereafter cited as Coffman, *Regulars).

[37] Coffman, *Regulars*, p. 104, 105-107.

[38] Coffman, *Regulars,* p. 109/110.

[39] N.A., Jefferson Barracks Post Returns, February 190-4, M617, Roll 550.

[40] *Annual Reports 1904*, Volume III, p.63 and Heitman, *Historical Register*, p. 285.

[41] N.A., Jefferson Barracks Post Returns, March 1904, M617, Roll 550.

[42] Heitman, *Historical Register*, p. 432.

[43] Webb, *Jefferson Barracks*, p. 118.

[44] N.A., Jefferson Barracks Post Returns, April 1904, M617, Roll 550.

[45] Coffman, *Regulars,* p. 108/109.

[46] N.A., Jefferson Barracks Post Returns, April 1904, M617, Roll 550.

[47] N.A., Jefferson Barracks Post Returns, May 1904, M617, Roll 550.

[48] Webb, *Jefferson Barracks,* p. 119.

[49] N.A., Jefferson Barracks Post Returns, May 1904, M617, Roll 550.

[50] N.A., Jefferson Barracks Post Returns, June 1904, M617, Roll 550.

[51] *Annual Reports 1904,* Volume III, p. 63-80.

[52] *Annual Reports of the War Department for the Fiscal Year ended June 30, 1904, Armament, Transportation, and Supply,* Volume II, p. 169-170. Hereafter cited as *Annual Report 1904,* Volume II.

[53] N.A., Jefferson Barracks Post Returns, June 1904, M617, Roll 550.

[54] N.A., Jefferson Barracks Post Returns, July 1904, M617, Roll 550.

[55] N.A., Jefferson Barracks Post Returns, July 1904, M617, Roll 550.

[56] N.A., Jefferson Barracks Post Returns, August 1904, M617, Roll 550.

[57] N.A., Jefferson Barracks Post Returns, August 1904, M617, Roll 550.

[58] N.A., Jefferson Barracks Post Returns, August 1904, M617, Roll 550.

[59] N.A., Jefferson Barracks Post Returns, September 1904, M617, Roll 550.

[60] N.A., Jefferson Barracks Post Returns, October 1904., 617, Roll 550. The following officers joined the post: 9th Cavalry officers were Capt. Charles Young, Capt. John Nance, Capt. John B. Christian, 1st Lt. Holand E. Rubottom, 1st Lt. James E. Fechet, 1st Lt. Winston Pilcher, 1st Lt. John T. Sayles, 2nd Lt. Edwin L. Cox, 2nd Lt. John H. Howard, 2nd Lt. Branford R. Camp, and 2nd Lt. Thomas B. Esty. The following officers left Jefferson Barracks: 4th Cavalry included Lt. Col. Samuel W. Fountain, 1st Lt. Ben H. Dorcy, 2nd Lt. Charles J. Naylor, Capt. Harry C. Benson, Capt. James B. Hughes, Capt. John O'Shea, 1st Lt. Charles S. Haight, 1st Lt. Alvan C. Gillem, 1st Lt. Jens E. Stedge, 1st Lt. William B. Renziehausen, 2nd Lt. William S. Martin, 2nd Lt. Anton Jurich, Jr., 2nd Lt. Albert J. Mohn, and 2nd Lt. Alexander M. Milton; 11th Cavalry included Capt. James G. Harbord, Capt. Powell Clayton, Jr., 1st Lt. Edmond R. Tompkins, 1st Lt. Eben Swift, Jr., and 2nd Lt. Stephen C. Reynolds.

[61] N.A., Jefferson Barracks Post Returns, October 1904, M617, Roll 550.

[62] N.A., Jefferson Barracks Post Returns, November 1904, M617, Roll 550.

[63] N.A., Jefferson Barracks Post Returns, December 1904, M617, Roll 550.

[64] N.A., Jefferson Barracks Post Returns, December 1904, M617, Roll 550.

Chapter 5 - The Quiet Before the Storm

[1] *Annual Reports of the War Department for the Fiscal Year Ended June 30, 1905, Reports of the Secretary of War, Chief of Staff, The Military Secretary, Inspector-General, and Judge-Advocate-General,* Volume I, p. 1-13. Hereafter cited as *Annual Reports, 1905,* Volume I.

[2] N.A., Jefferson Barracks Post Returns, January 1905, M617, Roll 550.

[3] *Annual Reports, 1905,* Volume I, p. 1-13.

[4] It was Capt. Poore's wife Benny Poore who in 1917 wrote a poignant description of life and travel after a lifetime in the Regular Army.

[5] N.A., Jefferson Barracks Post Returns, February 1905, M617, Roll 550.

[6] N.A., Jefferson Barracks Post Returns, 1905, M617, Roll 550.

[7] Coffman, *Regulars.* P. 100/101.

[8] *Annual Reports, 1905,* Volume I, p. 359 and *Annual Reports of the War Department for the Fiscal Year Ended June 30, 1905, Division and Department Commanders,* Volume III, p. 80. Hereafter cited as *Annual Reports, 1905,* Volume III.

[9] *Annual Reports, 1905,* Volume III, p. 75-95.

[10] *Tuscan Daily Citizen,* February 21, 1905.

[11] N.A., Jefferson Barracks Post Returns, March and April 1905, M617, Roll 550.

[12] N.A., Jefferson Barracks Post Returns, March 1905, M617, Roll 550.

[13] N.A., Jefferson Barracks Post Returns, March and April 1905, M617, Roll 550.

[14] *Annual Reports, 1905,* Volume I, p. 285/286.

[15] *Annual Reports, 1905,* Volume I, p. 287.

[16] N.A., Jefferson Barracks Post Returns, April 1905, M617, Roll 550.

[17] N.A., Jefferson Barracks Post Returns, May 1905, M617, Roll 550.

[18] N.A., Jefferson Barracks Post Returns, June 1905, M617, Roll 550, and Webb, *Jefferson Barracks,* p. 120.

[19] Webb, *Jefferson Barracks,* p. 120.

[20] N.A., Jefferson Barracks Post Returns, June 1905, M617, Roll 550.

[21] *Annual Reports, 1905,* Volume III, p. 94/95.

[22] N.A., Jefferson Barracks Post Returns, June 1905, M617, Roll 550.

[23] N.A., Jefferson Barracks Post Returns, July, August, and September 1905, M617, Roll 550.

[24] *Aberdeen Daily News,* August 25, 1905.

[25] N.A., Jefferson Barracks Post Returns, October 1905, M617, Roll 550.

[26] Untitled History of Jefferson Barracks, p. 108.

[27] N.A., Jefferson Barracks Post Returns, November 1905, M617, Roll 550.

[28] N.A., Jefferson Barracks Post Returns, December 1905, M617, Roll 550.

[29] Webb, *Jefferson Barracks,* p. 120.

[30] N.A., Jefferson Barracks Post Returns, January 1906, Roll 551.

[31] N.A., Jefferson Barracks Post Returns, January through June 1906, M617, Roll 551.

[32] N.A., Jefferson Barracks Post Returns, January through June 1906, M617, Roll 551.

[33] *St. Louis Post-Dispatch,* January 3, 1906.

[34] *St. Louis Post-Dispatch,* January 7, 1906.

[35] Coffman, *Regulars,* p. 91.

[36] N.A., Jefferson Barracks Post Returns, March 1906, M617, Roll 551.

[37] N.A., Jefferson Barracks Post Returns, March 1906, M617, Roll 551 and *Kansas City Star,* March 22, 1906.

[38] N.A., Jefferson Barracks Post Returns, April 1906, M617, Roll 551.

[39] N.A., Jefferson Barracks Post Returns, June 1906, M617, Roll 551.

[40] *Annual Reports of the War Department for the Fiscal Year Ended June 30, 1906, Reports of the Secretary of War, Chief of Staff, The Military Secretary, Inspector-General, and Judge-Advocate-General,* Volume I, p. 545. Hereafter cited as *Annual Reports, 1906,* Vol. I.

[41] *Annual Reports of the War Department for the Fiscal Year Ended June 30, 1906, Armament, Transportation, and Supply,* Volume II, p.88. Hereafter cited as *Annual Reports, 1906,* Vol. III.

[42] *Annual Reports, 1906,* Vol. II, p. 88.

[43] *Annual Reports, 1906,* Vol. II, p. 88.

[44] *Annual Reports, 1906,* Vol. II, p. 101.

[45] *Annual Reports of the War Department for the Fiscal Year Ended June 30, 1906, Reports of Division and Department Commanders,* Volume II, p. 117. Hereafter cited as *Annual Reports, 1906,* Vol. III.

[46] *Annual Reports, 1906,* Vol. II, p. 591/592.

[47] *Annual Reports, 1906,* Vol. I, p. 592.

[48] *Annual Reports, 1906,* Vol. I, p. 597.

[49] *Annual Reports, 1906,* Vol. II, p. 598.

[50] *Annual Reports, 1906,* Vol. II, p. 153.

[51] *Annual Reports, 1906,* Vol. II, p. 154.

[52] N.A., Jefferson Barracks Post Returns, August 1906, M617, Roll 551.

[53] Webb, *Jefferson Barracks,* p. 121 and Untitled History, p. 109/110.

[54] N.A., Jefferson Barracks Post Returns, August 1906, M617, Roll 551.

[55] N.A., Jefferson Barracks Post Returns, September 1906, M617, Roll 551.

[56] N.A., Jefferson Barracks Post Returns, October 1906, M617, Roll 551.

[57] N.A., Jefferson Barracks Post Returns, October 1906, M617, Roll 551.

[58] N.A., Jefferson Barracks Post Returns, November & December 1906, M617, Roll 551.

[59] *Annual Reports of the War Department for the Fiscal Year Ended June 30, 1907*, Volume III, p. 101. Hereafter cited as *Annual Reports, 1907*, Vol. III.

[60] *Annual Reports, 1907*, Vol. III, p. 57-86.

[61] *Oregonian*, November 1, 1906.

[62] *Annual Reports of the War Department for the Fiscal Year Ended June 30, 1907*, Volume I, p. 250. Hereafter cited as *Annual Reports, 1907*, Vol. I.

[63] N.A., Jefferson Barracks Post Returns, January 1907, M617, Roll 551. The following is a list of officers present and their duties: Major William B. Bannister, Post Surgeon; 1st Lt. Will L. Pyles, Assistant Surgeon and Recruiting Officer; 1st Lt. William A. Powell, Assistant Surgeon and Recruiting Officer; 1st Lt. John R. Bosley, Assistant Surgeon and Recruiting Officer; 1st Lt. James D. Fife, Medical Department on temporary duty; Capt. Lester W. Cornish, 9th Cavalry, commanding 15th Recruit Company; Capt. John T. Geary, Artillery Corps, commanding 17th Recruit Company; Capt. William T. Littlebrandt, 12th Cavalry, commanding 16th Recruit Company; Capt. Howard L. Laubach, 23rd Infantry, commanding 19th Recruit Company and Summary Court Officer; Capt. Gaston S. Turner, 7th Infantry, reported February 20 and commanding 15th Recruit Company; 1st Lt. Francis McConnell, 17th Infantry, Commissary and Mess Officer; 1st Lt. William L. Luhn, 5th Cavalry, Depot Adjutant and Signal Officer; 1st Lt. Allen Parker, 26th Infantry, commanding 18th Recruit Company; 1st Lt. Wilson G. Heaton, 13th Cavalry, duty with 18th Recruit Company; 1st Lt. John P. Hasson, 6th Cavalry, commanding 16th Recruit Company; 1st Lt. Daniel D. Gregory, 5th Cavalry, duty with 15th Recruit Company; Capt. William C. Cannon, QM Department, Post Quartermaster; 1st Lt. John R. Musgrove, Artillery Corps, duty with 16 Recruit Company and Ordnance Officer; 2nd Lt. Nelson A. Goodspeed, 3rd Cavalry, duty with 19th Recruit Company; 1st Lt. Eugene J. Ely, 5th Cavalry duty with 17th Recruit Company; James S. Ruby, Ordnance Sergeant since October 9, 1906; James R. Gillespie, QM Sgt. since February 4, 1906; Sergeant First Class August Nickel, Engineer Corps, Post Engineer Sgt. since October 17, 1905; Sgt. George S. Lewis, Hospital Corps and Post Hospital Steward since July 2, 1905; Paul L. Spaney, Post Commissary Sgt. since February 2, 1906; Sgt. Henry Dunn, Signal Corps, Post Signal Sgt.; Sgt. Charles E. Rafter, Post Hospital Steward since July 6, 1905; and Sgt. Lewis F. King, Post Hospital Steward since December 19, 1905.

[64] N.A., Jefferson Barracks Post Returns, January 1907, M617, Roll 551.

[65] *Fort Worth Star-Telegram*, January 22, 1907.

[66] N.A., Jefferson Barracks Post Returns, February through June 1907, M617, Roll 551.

[67] *Evening News* (California), April 10, 1907.

[68] N.A., Jefferson Barracks Post Returns, May, June and July 19007, M617, Roll 551.

[69] *Oregonian*, May 26, 1907.

[70] *Anaconda* (Montana) *Standard*, August 11, 1907.

[71] N.A., Jefferson Barracks Post Returns, March 1907, M617, Roll 551.

[72] N.A., Jefferson Barracks Post Returns, May 1907, M617, Roll 551.

[73] *The Columbus Enquirer-Sun* (Georgia), February 2, 1907.

[74] *Annual Reports of the War Department for the Fiscal Year Ended June 30, 1907, Reports of Quartermaster-General, Commissary-General, Surgeon-General, Paymaster-General, Chief Signal Officer, Chief of Artillery, Board of Ordnance and Fortification*, Volume II, p. 129. Hereafter cited as *Annual Reports, 1907*, Vol. II.

[75] *Annual Reports, 1907*, Vol. II, p. 16.

[76] *Annual Reports, 1907*, Vol. I, p. 235.

[77] *Annual Reports, 1907*, Vol. I, p. 236.

[78] *Annual Reports, 1907*, Vol. II, p. 232.

[79] *Annual Reports, 1907*, Vol. II, p. 7-27.

[80] *Annual Reports, 1907*, Vol. II, p. 7-27.

[81] *Annual Reports, 1907*, Vol. II, p. 220.

[82] *Annual Reports, 1907*, Vol. III, p. 57-86.

[83] *Annual Reports, 1907*, Vol. III, p. 57-86.

[84] *Annual Reports, 1907*, Vol. III, p. 241/242.

[85] *Annual Reports, 1907*, Vol. II, p. 233.

[86] *Annual Reports, 1907*, Vol. II, p. 186.

[87] N.A., Jefferson Barracks Post Returns, July 1907, M617, Roll 551.

[88] N.A., Jefferson Barracks Post Returns, August 1907, M617, Roll 551.

[89] N.A., Jefferson Barracks Post Returns, September 1907, M617, Roll 551.

[90] N.A., Jefferson Barracks Post Returns, October 1907, M617, Roll 551.

[91] Webb, *Jefferson Barracks,* p. 121 and Untitled History, p. 119.

[92] Webb, *Jefferson Barracks,* p. 121.

[93] *Philadelphia Inquirer,* October 21, 1907.

[94] *Charlotte Observer,* November 26, 1907.

[95] N.A., Jefferson Barracks Post Returns, November 1907, M617, Roll 551.

[96] N.A., Jefferson Barracks Post Returns, November 1907, M617, Roll 551.

[97] N.A., Jefferson Barracks Post Returns, December 1907, M617, Roll 551.

[98] N.A., Jefferson Barracks Post Returns, December 1907, M617, Roll 551.

[99] N.A., Jefferson Barracks Post Returns, January 1908, M617, Roll 551.

[100] N.A., Jefferson Barracks Post Returns, February 1908, M617, Roll 551.

[101] N.A., Jefferson Barracks Post Returns, March 1908, M617, Roll 551.

[102] N.A., Jefferson Barracks Post Returns, April 1908u, M617, Roll 551.

[103] Crossland and Currie, *Twice the Citizen,* p. 17/18.

[104] N.A., Jefferson Barracks Post Returns, May 1908, M617, Roll 551.

[105] N.A., Jefferson Barracks Post Returns, June 1908, M617, Roll 551.

[106] *Annual Reports of the War Department for the Fiscal Year Ended June 30, 1908, Reports of the Secretary of War, Chief of Staff, The Adjutant-General, Inspector-General, Judge-Advocate-General,* Volume I, p. 402-406. Hereafter cited as *Annual Reports, 1908,* Vol. I.

[107] *Annual Reports, 1908,* Vol. I, p. 20/21.

[108] N.A., Jefferson Barracks Post Returns, July 1908, M617, Roll 551.

[109] N.A., Jefferson Barracks Post Returns, August 1908, M617, Roll 551.

[110] N.A., Jefferson Barracks Post Returns, September 1908, M617, Roll 551.

[111] N.A., Jefferson Barracks Post Returns, October, November, and December 1908, M617, Roll 551.

[112] N.A., Jefferson Barracks Post Returns, January 1909, M617, Roll 551.

[113] Coffman, *Regulars,* p. 150.

[114] N.A., Jefferson Barracks Post Returns, January 1909, M617, Roll 551.

[115] *Philadelphia Inquirer,* January 10, 1909.

[116] N.A., Jefferson Barracks Post Returns, May, June, and July 1909, M617, Roll 551.

[117] N.A., Jefferson Barracks Post Returns, May and July 1909, M617, Roll 551.

[118] *Fort Worth Star-Telegram* (Texas), July 5, 1909.

[119] N.A., Jefferson Barracks Posts Returns, August 1909, M617, Roll 551.

[120] N.A., Jefferson Barracks Post Returns, September 1909, M617, Roll 551.

[121] N.A., Jefferson Barracks Post Returns, October 1909, M617, Roll 551.

[122] N.A., Jefferson Barracks Post Returns, October 1909, M617, Roll 551.

[123] N.A., Jefferson Barracks Post Returns, November 1909, M617, Roll 551.

[124] N.A., Jefferson Barracks Post Returns, November 1909, M617, Roll 551.

[125] N.A., Jefferson Barracks Post Returns, December 1909i, M617, Roll 551.

[126] N.A., Jefferson Barracks Post Returns, December 1909, M617, Roll 551.

[127] Webb, *Jefferson Barracks,* p. 122.

[128] N.A., Jefferson Barracks Post Returns, January 1910, M617, Roll 551.

[129] N.A., Jefferson Barracks Post Returns, January 1910, M617, Roll 551.

[130] N.A., Jefferson Barracks Post Returns, January 1910, M617, Roll 551.

[131] N.A., Jefferson Barracks Post Returns, February 1910, M617, Roll 551.

[132] N.A., Jefferson Barracks Post Returns, March 1910, M617, Roll 551.

[133] N.A., Jefferson Barracks Post Returns, March 1910, M617, Roll 551.

[134] N.A., Jefferson Barracks Post Returns, April 1910, M617, Roll 551.

[135] N.A., Jefferson Barracks Post Returns, May 1910, M617, Roll 551.

[136] N.A., Jefferson Barracks Post Returns, May 1910, M617, Roll 551.

[137] N.A., Jefferson Barracks Post Returns, June through December 1910, M617, Roll 551.

[138] N.A., Jefferson Barracks Post Returns, January through December 1910, M617, Roll 551.

[139] Webb, *Jefferson Barracks,* p. 122.

[140] Webb, *Jefferson Barracks,* p. 122.

[141] N.A., Jefferson Barracks Post Returns, January 1911, M617, Roll 551.

[142,] N.A., Jefferson Barracks Post Returns, January 1911, M617, Roll 551.

[143] N.A., Jefferson Barracks Post Returns, January 1911, M617, Roll 551.

[144] N.A., Jefferson Barracks Post Returns, February 1911, M617, Roll 551.

[145] N.A., Jefferson Barracks Post Returns, March 1911, M617, Roll 551.

[146] N.A., Jefferson Barracks Post Returns, March 1911, M617, Roll 551.

[147] Unknown Author, Untitled History of Jefferson Barracks, p. 111.

[148] N.A., Jefferson Barracks Post Returns, April 1911, M617, Roll 551.

[149] Dwight D. Eisenhower, *At Ease: Stories I Tell To Friends,* p. 106/107. Hereafter cited as Eisenhower, *At Ease.*

[150] N.A., Jefferson Barracks Post Returns, May 1911, M617, Roll 551.

[151] N.A., Jefferson Barracks Post Returns, June 1911, M617, Roll 551.

[152] N.A., Jefferson Barracks Post Returns, July 1911, M617, Roll 551.

[153] N.A., Jefferson Barracks Post Returns, July 1911, M617, Roll 551.

[154] N.A., Jefferson Barracks Post Returns, August 1911, M617, Roll 551.

[155] N.A., Jefferson Barracks Post Returns, August 1911, M617, Roll 5651.

[156] N.A., Jefferson Barracks Post Returns, September 1911, M617, Roll 551.

[157] Webb, *Jefferson Barracks,* p. 122, Unknown Author, Untitled History of Jefferson Barracks, p. 111/112.

[158] N.A., Jefferson Barracks Post Returns, October, November, and December 1911, M617, Roll 551.

[159] Coffman, *Regulars,* p. 98.

[160] Coffman, *Regulars,* p. 98/99.

[161] Coffman, *Regulars,* p. 119.

[162] N.A., Jefferson Barracks Post Returns, January 1912, M617, Roll 551. The remainder of the officers at Jefferson Barracks included the following: Lt. Col. Oscar I. Straub, Coast Artillery Corps; Capt. Jennings B. Wilson, 8th Infantry; Adjutant; Capt. Stanley H. Ford, Quartermaster Department, Quartermaster and Constructing Quartermaster; Capt. Charles H. Errington, 11th Infantry, Commissary and Mess Officer, and Post Treasurer; 1st Lt. Fred C. Miller, 30th Infantry, Post Exchange and Laundry Officer and in charge of Receiving Barracks; 1st Lt. Jesse M. Holmes, 27th Infantry, Assistant Adjutant and Prison, Signal, Engineer, and Ordnance Officer; Capt. William H. Peck, Coast Artillery Corps, commanding 18th Recruit Company; Capt. George E. Houle, 26th Infantry, commanding 16th Recruit Company, Summary Court Officer; 1st Lt. Thomas M./ Knox, Cavalry, commanding 27th Recruit Company; Capt. Dennis P. Quinlan, 5th Cavalry, commanding 15th Recruit Company; 1st Lt. Otis R. Cole, Infantry, commanding 23rd Recruit Company; 1st Lt. John R. Starkey, 2nd Field Artillery, duty with 27th and 15th Recruit Company; 1st Lt. Olney Place, 13th Cavalry, duty with 16th Recruit Company; 1st Lt. Reuben C. Taylor, duty with 18th Recruit Company; and 1st Lt. Arthur T. Dalton, 20th Infantry, absent sick at the Army and Navy Hospital at Hot Springs, Arkansas.

[163] N.A., Jefferson Barracks Post Returns, January, February and March 1912, M617, Roll 551.

[164] N.A., Jefferson Barracks Post Returns, March 1912, M6t17, Roll 551.

[165] *Aero Magazine,* February 19, 1912.

[166] N.A., Jefferson Barracks Post Returns, April 1912, M617, Roll 551.

[167] N.A., Jefferson Barracks Post Returns, May 1912, M617, Roll 551.

[168] N.A., Jefferson Barracks Post Returns, July through December 1912, M617, Roll 551.

[169] Webb, *Jefferson Barracks,* p. 123.

[170] *Daily Herald* {Mississippi), August 24, 1912.

[171] *New Orleans Times Picayune,* August 27, 1912.

[172] Crossland and Currie, *Twice the Citizen,* p. 22/23.

[173] Crossland and Currie, *Twice the Citizen,* p. 23/24.

[174] N.A., Jefferson Barracks Post Returns, January 1913, M617, Roll 551.

[175] N.A., Jefferson Barracks Post Returns, February 1913, M617, Roll 551.

[176] N.A., Jefferson Barracks Post Returns, March 1913, M617, Roll 551`.

[177] *Pueblo Gazette-Telegraph* {Colorad0), March 9, 1913.

[178] N.A., Jefferson Barracks Post Returns, April 1913, M617, Roll 551.

[179] N.A., Jefferson Barracks Post Returns, April 1913, M617, Roll 551.

[180] N.A., Jefferson Barracks Post Returns, May 1913, M617, Roll 551.

[181] N.A., Jefferson Barracks Post Returns, May 1913, M617, Roll 551.

[182] N.A., Jefferson Barracks Post Returns, June 1913, M617, Roll 551.

[183] N.A., Jefferson Barracks Post Returns, July 1913, M617, Roll 551.

[184] N.A., Jefferson Barracks Post Returns, July 1913, M617, Roll 551.

[185] N.A., Jefferson Barracks Post Returns, Augusts and September 1913, M617, Roll 551.

[186] Oberlin College Archives and Heitman, *Historical Register,* p. 202.

[187] N.A., Jefferson Barracks Post Returns, October 1913, M617, Roll 551.

[188] N.A., Jefferson Barracks Post Returns, November 1913, M617, Roll 551.

[189] N.A., Jefferson Barracks Post Returns, December 1913, M617, Roll 551.

[190] Coffman, *Regulars,* p. 125.

Chapter 6 - 1914: World War I Begins in Europe

[1] N.A., Jefferson Barracks Post Returns, January 1914, M617, Roll 551. Officers at Jefferson Barracks in January 1914 in addition to Col. Beacom were Major James M. Kennedy, Medical Corps, Surgeon and Recruiting Officer; Capt. Charles L. Foster, Medical Corps, Assistant Surgeon & Recruiting Officer; Capt. Harry G. Humphreys, Medical Corps, Assistant Surgeon and Recruiting Officer; Capt. Guy V. Rukke, Medical Corps, Assistant Surgeon and Recruiting Officer; Capt. Henry C. Pillsbury, Medical Corps, Assistant Surgeon and Recruiting Officer; 1st Lt. John A. McAlister, Dental Surgeon; Capt. Frederick Lawton, Quartermaster Corps, Post Quartermaster and Laundry Officer; Capt. Francis H. Lomax, Coast Artillery, Adjutant, Summary Court Officer and commanding 14th Recruit Company; Capt. George W. England, Police Officer, Assistant Quartermaster and Mess Officer; 1st Lt. John R. Starkeu, 6th Field Artillery, Assistant Adjutant and Signal, Ordnance, Prison, and Engineering Officer; 1st Lt. Francis H. Burr, Infantry, Post Exchange, Athletic Officer, and Librarian, in charge of Receiving Barracks; Capt. Andrew E. Williams, Cavalry, commanding 18th Recruit Company; Capt. Fredrick M. Jones, Cavalry, commanding 15th Recruit Company; Capt. Alexander M. Wetherill, Infantry, commanding 27th Recruit Company and Summary Court Officer; Capt. Charles C. Farmer, Cavalry, commanding 23rd Recruit Company; 1st Lt. John M. Craig, 20th Infantry, commanding 16th Recruit Company during absence of Capt. Houle; 1st Lt. Jesse M. Holmes, 27th Infantry, on duty with 15th Recruit Company; 1st Lt. Walter W. Merrill, Field Artillery, on duty with 18th Recruit Company; Capt. George E. Houle, Infantry, commanding 16th Recruit Company; 1st Lt. Julius C. Peterson, Coast Artillery, on detached service at Fort Monroe to determine his fitness for promotion; 1st Lt. Talbot Smith, 6th Cavalry, on detached service conducting recruits to Panama Canal Zone; and Lt. Col. Thomas W. Griffiths, 19th Infantry, relived from duty at Jefferson Barracks on January 2 and left on January 13, 1914.

[2] N.A., Jefferson Barracks Post Returns, January 1914, M617, Roll 551.

[3] N.A., Jefferson Barracks Post Returns, February 1914, M617, Roll 551.

[4] N.A., Jefferson Barracks Post Returns, March 1914, M617, Roll 551.

[5] N.A., Jefferson Barracks Post Returns, April 1914, M617, Roll 551.

[6] N.A., Jefferson Barracks Post Returns, May 1914, M617, Roll 551.

[7] N.A., Jefferson Barracks Post Returns, June 1914, M617, Roll 551.

[8] N.A., Jefferson Barracks Post Returns, July 1914, M617, Roll 551.

[9] N.A., Jefferson Barracks Post Returns, July 1914, M617, Roll 551.

[10] Souvenir Program of the Good Time Party in the Jefferson Barracks Collection.

[11] N.A., Jefferson Barracks Post Returns, August 1914, M617, Roll 551.

[12] Martin Gilbert, *The First World War: A Complete History,* p. 31. Hereafter cited as Gilbert, *First World War.*

[13] Gilbert, *First World War,* p. 32.

[14] Gilbert, *First World War,* p. 16/17.

[15] Gilbert, *First World War,* p. 34.

[16] Gilbert, *First World War,* p. 54.

[17] Coffman, *Regulars,* p. 203.

[18] N.A., Jefferson Barracks Post Returns, September 1914, M617, Roll 551.

[19] Gilbert, *First World War,* p. 67.

[20] Gilbert, *First World War,* p. 67.

[21] Gilbert, *First World War,* p. 72.

[22] Gilbert, *First World War,* p. 84.

[23] N.A., Jefferson Barracks Post Returns, October, November, and December 1914, M617, Roll 551.

[24] N.A., Jefferson Barracks Post Returns, October 1914, M617, Roll 551.

[25] N.A., Jefferson Barracks Post Returns, November 1914, M617, Roll 551.

[26] N.A., Jefferson Barracks Post Returns, December 1914, M617, Roll 551.

[27] Webb, *Jefferson Barracks,* p. 123.

[28] N.A., Jefferson Barracks Post Returns, January 1915, M617, Roll 551. In addition to Col. Beacom the following officers served at Jefferson Barracks: Major James M. Kennedy, Medical Corps, Surgeon and Recruiting Officer; Capt. William A. Wickline, Medical Corps, Assistant Surgeon and Recruiting Officer; Capt. Charles L. Foster, Medical Corps, Assistant Surgeon and Recruiting Officer; Capt. Harry G. Humphreys, Medical Corps, Assistant Surgeon and Recruiting Officer; Capt. Guy V. Rukke, Medical Corps, Assistant Surgeon and Recruiting Officer; 1st Lt. John A. McAlister, Dental Surgeon; Capt. Frederick G. Lawton, Quartermaster Corps, Post Quartermaster and Laundry Officer; Capt. Francis H. Lomax, Coast Artillery Corps, Adjutant and Summary Court Officer and commander of 14th Recruit Company; Capt. George W. England, Infantry, Police and Mess Officer and assistant Quartermaster; Capt. John M. Craig, 27tyh Infantry, Assistant adjutant, Signal, Ordnance, Prison and Engineering Officer and commanding casuals; 1st Lt. Francis H. Burr, Infantry, Post Exchange and athletic Officer and Librarian; Capt. Andrew E. Williams, Cavalry, commanding 18th Recruit Company; Capt. Alexander M. Wetherill, Infantry, commanding 27th Recruit Company and Summary Court Officer; Capt. Albert R. Dillingham, Infantry, commanding 16th Recruit Company; Capt. Fredrick M. Jones, Cavalry, commanding 15th Recruit Company; 1st Lt. John G. Donovan, Coast Artillery Corps, duty with 27th Recruit Company; 1st Lt. Talbot Smith, Cavalry, duty with 15th Recruit Company; 1st Lt. John G. Tyndall, 6th Field Artillery, duty with 23rd Recruit Company; 1st Lt. George C. Kelcher, 26th Infantry, duty with 16th Recruit Company; 1st Lt. John R. Starkey, 6th Field Artillery, relieved January 6; and 1st Lt. Walter W. Merrill, 6th Field Artillery.

[29] N.A., Jefferson Barracks Post Returns, January 1915, M617, Roll 551.

[30] N.A., Jefferson Barracks Post Returns, January 1915, M617, Roll 551.

[31] Gilbert, *First World War,* p. 125.

[32] Gilbert, *First World War,* p. 127.

[33] Gilbert, *First World War,* p. 127/128.

[34] Gilbert, *First World War,* 128.

[35] N.A., Jefferson Barracks Post Returns, February 1915, M617, Roll 551.

[36] Gilbert, *First World War,* p. 132.

[37] N.A., Jefferson Barracks Post Returns, March 1915, M617, Roll 551.

[38] N.A., Jefferson Barracks Post Returns, April 1915, M617, Roll 551.

[39] Gilbert, *First World War,* p. 144.

[40] N.A., Jefferson Barracks Post Returns, May 1915, M617, Roll 551.

[41] N.A., Jefferson Barracks Post Returns, May 1915, M617, Roll 551.

[42] Gilbert, *First World War,* p. 157.

[43] Crossland and Currie, *Twice the Citizen,* p. 26/27.

[44] N.A., Jefferson Barracks Post Returns, June 1915, M617, Roll 551.

[45] N.A., Jefferson Barracks Post Returns, July 1915, M617, Roll 551.

[46] N.A., Jefferson Barracks Post Returns, July 1915, M617, Roll 551.

[47] N.A., Jefferson Barracks Post Returns, August 1915, M617, Roll 551.

[48] *Macon Weekly Telegraph,* August 8, 1915.

[49] N.A., Jefferson Barracks Post Returns, September 1915, M617, Roll 551.

[50] N.A., Jefferson Barracks Post Returns, September 1915, M617, Roll 551.

[51] N.A., Jefferson Barracks Post Returns, October 1915, M617, Roll 551.

[52] *New Orleans Times Picayune,* October 8, 1915.

[53] N.A., Jefferson Barracks Post Returns, November 1915, M617, Roll 551.

[54] N.A., Jefferson Barracks Post Returns, November 1915, M617, Roll 551.

[55] Gilbert, *First World War,* p. 210.

[56] Heitman, *Historical Register,* p. 592.

[57] N.A., Jefferson Barracks Post Returns, December 1915, M617, Roll 551.

[58] N.A., Jefferson Barracks Post Returns, December 1915, M617, Roll 551.

[59] *Grand Forks Herald,* December 24, 1915.

[60] Gilbert, *First World War,* p. 217.

[61] Gilbert, *First World War,* p. 219.

[62] N.A., Jefferson Barracks Post Returns, January 1916, M617, Roll 551.

[63] N.A., Jefferson Barracks Post Returns, January 1916, M617, Roll 551.

[64] N.A., Jefferson Barracks Post Returns, January 1916, M617, Roll 551.

[65] N.A., Jefferson Barracks Post Returns, February 1916, M617, Roll 551.

[66] N.A., Jefferson Barracks Post Returns, March 1916, M617, Roll 551.

[67] Coffman, *Regulars,* p. 195.

[68] Coffman, *Regulars,* p. 197, Crossland and Currie, *Twice the Citizen,* p. 27/28.

[69] Coffman, *Regulars,* p. 199.

[70] Gilbert, *First World War,* p. 236/237.

[71] N.A., Jefferson Barracks Post Returns, April 1916, M617, Roll 551.

[72] N.A., Jefferson Barracks Post Returns, April 1916, M617, Roll 551.

[73] N.A., Jefferson Barracks Post Returns, May 1916, M617, Roll 551.

[74] N.A., Jefferson Barracks Post Returns, June 1916, M617, Roll 551.

[75] Crossland and Currie, *Twice the Citizen,* p. 27/28.

[76] Coffman, *Regulars,* p. 199 and Crossland and Currie, *Twice the Citizen,* p. 28.

[77] N.A., Jefferson Barracks Post Returns, July 1916, M617, Roll 551.

[78] Heitman, *Historical Register,* p. 928.

[79] N.A., Jefferson Barracks Post Returns, July 1916, M617, Roll 551.

[80] N.A., Jefferson Barracks Post Returns, August 1916, M617, Roll 551.

[81] N.A., Jefferson Barracks Post Returns, September and October 1916, M617, Roll 551.

[82] N.A., Jefferson Barracks Post Returns, September and October 1916, M617, Roll 551.

[83] N.A., Jefferson Barracks Post Returns, November 1916, M617, Roll 551.

[84] *Dictionary of American Military Biography,* Volume II.

[85] N.A., Jefferson Barracks Post Returns, November 1916, M617, Roll 551.

[86] N.A., Jefferson Barracks Post Returns, November 1916, M617, Roll 551.

[87] N.A., Jefferson Barracks Post Returns, November 1916, M617, Roll 551.

[88] 1916 Thanksgiving Day Menu, Jefferson Barracks Collection.

[89] N.A., Jefferson Barracks Post Returns, December 1916, M617, Roll 551.

[90] N.A., Jefferson Barracks Post Returns, December 1916, M617, Roll 551.

[91] Program/Menu, General Mess at Jefferson Barracks for Christmas 1916, Jefferson Barracks Collection.

[92] Gilbert, *First World War,* p. 299/300.

[93] Gilbert, *First World War,* p. 303.

Chapter 7 – War Comes to the United States – 1917

[1] *Kansas City Star,* February 10, 1917.

[2] Gilbert, *First World War,* p. 306.

[3] Gilbert, *First World War,* p. 308.

[4] Gilbert, *First World War,* p. 312.

[5] Gilbert, *First World War,* p. 318.

[6] *Idaho Statesman,* March 16, 1917.

278

This building was located just west of the road leading to the cemetery. When the dairy was discontinued in 1936 the building became a paint shop.

[8] *Aberdeen Daily News,* April 6, 1917.

[9] *Aberdeen Daily News,* April 10, 1917.

[10] *Aberdeen Daily News,* April 16, 1917.

[11] *Pueblo Chieftain,* April 27, 1917.

[12] Sunday Magazine, *St. Louis Post-Dispatch,* April 8, 1917.

[13] Crossland and Currie, *Twice the Citizen,* p. 29/30.

[14] *Colorado Gazette-Telegraph,* May 10, 1917.

[15] *Aberdeen Daily News,* May 19, 1917.

[16] *Aberdeen Daily News,* May 26, 1917.

[17] *St. Louis Post-Dispatch,* May 19, 1917.

[18] *St. Louis Post-Dispatch,* May 6, 1917.

[19] *St. Louis Post-Dispatch,* May 6, 1917.

[20] Crossland and Currie, *Twice the Citizen,* p. 31.

[21] *Kansas City Star,* June 12, 1917.

[22] *Fort Worth Star-Telegram,* June 16, 1917.

[23] *Kansas City Star,* June 16, 1917.

[24] Webb, *Jefferson Barracks,* p. 124.

[25] Heitman, *Historical Register,* p. 738 and Ancestry.com.

[26] *Aberdeen American,* July 1, 1917.

[27] *Kansas City Star,* July 11, 1917.

[28] *Belleville News Democrat,* September 29, 1917.

[29] *Belleville News Democrat,* October 1, 1917. The Jefferson Barracks players included Mabry, Gromann, Sass, Brown, Rucker, Westhouse, White, Vogtmann and Moran.

[30] *Belleville News Democrat,* September 4, 1917.

[31] *St. Louis Post-Dispatch,* August 22 & December 28, 1917.

[32] *Duluth News-Tribune,* November 17, 1917.

[33] *Kansas City Star,* December 13, 1917.

[34] *Kansas City Star,* December 13, 1917.

[35] *Duluth News-Tribune,* December 11, 1917.

[36] *Dallas Morning News,* December 11, 1917.

[37] *Grand Forks Herald,* December 12, 1917.

[38] *Kansas City Star,* December 15, 1917.

[39] *Kansas City Star,* December 15, 1917.

[40] *Kansas City Star,* December 15, 1917.

[41] *United Press,* December 15, 1917.

[42] Webb, *Jefferson Barracks,* p. 294.

[43] Gilbert, *First World War,* p. 359.

[44] Gilbert, *First World War,* p. 372.

[45] Gilbert, *First World War,* p. 393.

[46] Gilbert, *First World War,* p. 397.

[47] *St. Louis Post-Dispatch,* January 1, 1918.

[48] *St. Louis Post-Dispatch,* January 4, 1918.

[49] *St. Louis Post-Dispatch,* January 4, 1918.

[50] *St. Louis Post-Dispatch,* January 4, 1918.

[51] *St. Louis Post-Dispatch,* January 5, 1918.

[52] *St. Louis Post-Dispatch,* January 6, 1918.

[53] *St. Louis Post-Dispatch,* January 6, 1918.

[54] *St. Louis Post-Dispatch,* January 9, 1918.

[55] *St. Louis Post-Dispatch,* January 31, 1918.

[56] *St. Louis Post-Dispatch,* January 13, 1918.

[57] *St. Louis Post-Dispatch,* January 13, 1918.

[58] *St. Louis Post-Dispatch,* January 16, 1918.

[59] *St. Louis Post-Dispatch,* January 16, 1918.

[60] *St. Louis Post-Dispatch,* January 16, 1918.

[61] *St. Louis Post-Dispatch,* January 16, 1918.

[62] *St. Louis Post-Dispatch,* January 18, 1918.

[63] *St. Louis Post-Dispatch,* January 24, 1918. Privates from St. Louis included Homer W. Atrchison, Howard L. Badoliet, Everett S. Ballew, Paul B. Barnnett, Fred E. Beincke, Malcolm A. Black, William Y. Brown, John Bloss, John R. Campbell, C.C. Conrad, John S. Cooks, Sam R. Corbet, Wyman M. Cromer, John C. Davis, Arthur C. Detriet, William E. Esser, Oliver Dincan, Raymond L. Fitzgerald, Louis R. Flori, William H. Frohoff, Paul E. Gundelfinger, Paul James, Jake Kessler, Stephen H. Kleekamp, Daniel H. Dreutzer, Edwin C. Lemme, E.T. McIvers, J.C. McCabe, J.H. McCaleb, David M. McDonald, Mortimer W. Mears, Herbert A. Milbank, Louis Miller, Paul W. Moffit, John V. Moran, F.S. Morris, Arthur F. Neimeir, Charles R. Odell, William G. Ogen, Bernard G. Otten, F.C. Passek, F.L. Pickering, Arthur F. Poepping, James Price, Edward G. Queveroux, C.H. Russell, Frank A. Sexto, Joe K. Shields, Joseph A. Sicking, Charles V. Smith, Joseph H. Smith, J.J. Slattery, George A. Steeg, Harvey O. Stevens, F.G. Stubblefield, Henry C. Taylor, August Uhl, Edwin J. Uhl, George B. Shessell, Frank Winens, Robert B. Wilson, William H. Wilson, Carl F. Zerr.

[64] *St. Louis Post-Dispatch,* January 28, 1918.

[65] *St. Louis Post-Dispatch,* February 12, 1918.

[66] *St. Louis Post-Dispatch,* February 3, 1918.

[67] *St. Louis Post-Dispatch,* February 5, 1918.

[68] *St. Louis Post-Dispatch,* February 11, 1918.

[69] *St. Louis Post-Dispatch,* February 15, 1918.

[70] *St. Louis Post-Dispatch,* February 18, 1918.

[71] *St. Louis Post-Dispatch,* February 26, 1918.

[72] *St. Louis Post-Dispatch,* February 27, 1918.

[73] *St. Louis Post-Dispatch,* February 28, 1918.

[74] Gilbert, *First World War,* p. 399.

[75] *St. Louis Post-Dispatch,* March 1, 1918.

[76] *St. Louis Post-Dispatch,* February 20, 1918.

[77] *St. Louis Post-Dispatch,* March 5, 1918.

[78] *St. Louis Post-Dispatch,* March 5, 1918.

[79] *St. Louis Post-Dispatch,* March 5, 1918.

[80] *Daily Herald* [Mississippi], March 15, 1918.

[81] *St. Louis Post-Dispatch,* March 24, 1918.

[82] *Grand Forks Herald,* March 30, 1918.

[83] *Kansas City Star,* June 16, 1918.

[84] Gilbert, *First World War,* p. 401.

[85] Gilbert, *First World War,* p. 404.

[86] Gilbert, *First World War,* p. 404.

[87] Gilbert, *First World War,* p. 406.

[88] Gilbert, *First World War,* p. 409/410.

[89] *St. Louis Post-Dispatch,* April 1 and April 2, 1918.

[90] *St. Louis Post-Dispatch,* April 2, 1918.

[91] *St. Louis Post-Dispatch,* April 3, 1918.

[92] *St. Louis Post-Dispatch,* April 16, 1918.

[93] Webb, *Jefferson Barracks,* p. 125.

[94] *St. Louis Post-Dispatch,* April 28, 1918.

[95] Gilbert, *First World War,* p. 416.

[96] Completion Report of Construction Work at Jefferson Barracks, Missouri.

[97] *St. Louis Post-Dispatch,* May 1, 1918.

[98] *St. Louis Post-Dispatch,* May 3, 1918.

[99] *St. Louis Post-Dispatch,* May 4, 1918.

[100] *St. Louis Post-Dispatch,* May 4, 1918.

[101] *St. Louis Post-Dispatch,* May 5 and May 12, 1918.

[102] *St. Louis Post-Dispatch,* May 7, 1918.

[103] *St. Louis Post-Dispatch,* May 12, 1918.

[104] *Kansas City Star,* May 29, 1918.

[105] *St. Louis Post-Dispatch,* June 15, 1918.

[106] *Kansas City Star,* June 15, 1918.

[107] *St. Louis Post-Dispatch,* June 16, 1918.

[108] *St. Louis Post-Dispatch,* June 21, 1918.

[109] *St. Louis Post-Dispatch,* June 22, 1918.

[110] *St. Louis Post-Dispatch,* June 24, 1918.

[111] *St. Louis Post-Dispatch,* June 25, 1918.

[112] *St. Louis Post-Dispatch,* June 26, 1918.

[113] *St. Louis Post-Dispatch,* June 27, 1918.

[114] Gilbert, *First World War,* p. 430.

[115] *St. Louis Post-Dispatch,* June 30, 1918.

[116] *Kansas City Star,* July 8, 1918.

[117] *St. Louis Post-Dispatch,* July 3, 1918.

[118] *St. Louis Post-Dispatch,* July 15, 1918.

[119] *St. Louis Post-Dispatch,* July 22, 1918.'

[120] Gilbert, *First World War,* p. 437.

[121] Gilbert, *First World War,* p. 442.

[122] *St. Louis Post-Dispatch,* July 18, July 19, and July 20, 1918.

[123] *St. Louis Post-Dispatch,* August 3, 1918.

[124] *Oregonian* September 8, 1918 and *Duluth News-Tribune,* August 11, 1918.

[125] *St. Louis Post-Dispatch,* August 22, 1918.

[126] *Kansas City Star,* August 30, 1918.

[127] *St. Louis Post-Dispatch,* September 18, 1918.

[128] *St. Louis Post-Dispatch,* August 26, 1918.

[129] *St. Louis Post-Dispatch,* August 22, 1918.

[130] *St. Louis Post-Dispatch,* August 3, 1918.

[131] *St. Louis Post-Dispatch,* August 6 and August 7, 1918.

[132] *St. Louis Post-Dispatch,* August 11, 1918.

[133] *St. Louis Post-Dispatch,* August 12, 1918.

[134] *St. Louis Post-Dispatch,* August 19, 1918.

[135] *Idaho Statesman,* September 20, 1918, and *Kansas City Star,* September 21, 1918.

[136] *St. Louis Post-Dispatch,* September 5, 1918.

[137] *St. Louis Post-Dispatch,* September 7, 1918.

[138] *St. Louis Post-Dispatch,* September 25, 1918.

[139] Gilbert, *First World War,* p. 460.

[140] Gilbert, *First World War,* p. 465.

[141] Gilbert, *First World War,* p. 465-467.

[142] *St. Louis Post-Dispatch,* October 3, 1918.

[143] *Belleville News Democrat,* October 4, 1918.

[144] *St. Louis Post-Dispatch,* October 11, 1918.

[145] *St. Louis Post-Dispatch,* October 4, 1918.

[146] *St. Louis Post-Dispatch,* October 9, 1918.

[147] Gilbert, *First World War,* p. 477.

[148] Webb, *Jefferson Barracks,* p. 126.

[149] Untitled History of Jefferson Barracks, p. 296.

[150] *St. Louis Post-Dispatch,* November 1, 1918.

[151] *St. Louis Post-Dispatch,* November 2, 1918.

[152] *St. Louis Post-Dispatch,* November 7, November 9, and November 11, 1918.

[153] *St. Louis Post-Dispatch,* November 20, 1918.

[154] N.A., Jefferson Barracks Post Returns, October and December 1918, M617, Roll 551.

Chapter 8 – Years of Peace: 1919 and the 1920s

[1] Crossland and Currie, *Twice the Citizen,* p. 33.

[2] Crossland and Currie, *Twice the Citizen,* p. 33.

[3] Crossland and Currie, *Twice the Citizen,* p. 34.

[4] Webb, *Jefferson Barracks,* p. 126.

[5] Webb, *Jefferson Barracks,* p. 126.

[6] *St. Louis Post-Dispatch,* January 14, 1919.

[7] Webb, *Jefferson Barracks,* p. 126.

[8] N.A., Jefferson Barracks Post Returns, March 1919, M617, Roll 551.

[9] N.A., Jefferson Barracks Post Returns, April 1919, M617, Roll 551.

[10] N.A., Jefferson Barracks Post Returns, May 1919, M617, Roll 551.

[11] N.A., Jefferson Barracks Post Returns, June 1919, M617, Roll 5651.

[12] N.A., Jefferson Barracks Post Returns, July through December 1919, M617, Roll 551.

[13] *St. Louis Post-Dispatch,* October 19, 1919.

[14] *St. Louis Post-Dispatch,* December 22, 1919.

[15] *St. Louis Post-Dispatch,* December 22, 1919.

[16] *St. Louis Post-Dispatch.* December 22, 1919.

[17] *St. Louis Post-Dispatch,* December 22, 1919.

[18] Jefferson Barracks 1919 Christmas Menu, Jefferson Barracks Collection.

[19] *St. Louis Post-Dispatch,* December 19, 1919.

[20] *St. Louis Post-Dispatch,* December 30, 1919.

[21] Gilbert, *First World War,* p. 515/516.

[22] Gilbert, *First World War,* p. 508.

[23] Gilbert, *First World War,* p. 517/518.

[24] Edward M. Coffman, *The Old Army: A Portrait of the American Army in Peacetime, 1784-1898,* Preface IX-X. Hereafter cited as Coffman, *Old Army.*

[25] N.A., Jefferson Barracks Post Returns, January 1920, M617, Roll 551.

[26] N.A., Jefferson Barracks Post Returns, February and March 1920, M617, Roll 551.

[27] Webb, *Jefferson Barracks,* p. 127. A few months later General Wood was defeated for the nomination for president at the Republican National Convention in Chicago. Warren G. Harding, a "Dark Horse," received the nomination.

[28] N.A., Jefferson Barracks Post Returns, June and July 1920, M617, Roll 551.

[29] N.A., Jefferson Barracks Post Returns, August 1920, M617, Roll 551.

[30] N.A., Jefferson Barracks Post Returns, November 1920, M617, Roll 551.

[31] N.A, Jefferson Barracks Post Returns, December 1920, M617, Roll 551.

[32] *St. Louis Post-Dispatch,* January 2, 1921.

[33] *St. Louis Post-Dispatch,* January 2, 1921.

[34] Untitled Manuscript on Jefferson Barracks by unknown author, p. 115.

[35] Untitled Manuscript on Jefferson Barracks by unknown author. P. 115.

[36] *St. Louis Post-Dispatch,* April 10, 1921.

[37] *St. Louis Post-Dispatch,* July 14, 1921.

[38] *St. Louis Post-Dispatch,* September 11, 1921.

[39] *Oregonian,* March 7, 1921.

[40] Donald M. Kington, *Forgotten Summers: The story of the Citizen's Military Training Camps 1921-1940,* p. 12. Hereafter cited as Kington, *Forgotten Summers.*

282

[41] Kington, *Forgotten Summers,* p. 14.

[42] Kington, *Forgotten Summers,* p. 14.

[43] *St. Louis Post-Dispatch,* July 12, 1921.

[44] *St. Louis Post-Dispatch,* July 15, 1921.

[45] *St. Louis Post-Dispatch,* July 24, 1921.

[46] *St. Louis Post-Dispatch,* July 28, 1921.

[47] *St. Louis Post-Dispatch,* July 27, 1921.

[48] William Jay Smith, *Army Brat: A Memoir,* p. 14. Hereafter cited as Smith, *Army Brat.*

[49] Smith, *Army Brat,* p. 18-20.

[50] Smith, *Army Brat,* p. 7/8.

[51] Smith, *Army Brat,* p. 8-11.

[52] Smith, *Army Brat,* p. 12/13.

[53] Smith, *Army Brat,* p. 20.

[54] Smith, *Army Brat,* p. 20. *St. Louis Post-Dispatch,* November 4, 1921.

[55] Smith, *Army Brat,* p. 21/22. *St. Louis Post-Dispatch,* November 2, 1921.

[56] *St. Louis Globe-Democrat,* November 4, 1921.

[57] *St. Louis Globe-Democrat,* November 4, 1921.

[58] *St. Louis Post-Dispatch,* November 5, 1921.

[59] Smith, *Army Brat,* p. 26/27.

[60] Smith, *Army Brat,* p. 27/28.

[61] *St. Louis Post-Dispatch,* January 7, 1922.

[62] *St. Louis Post-Dispatch,* January 20, 1922.

[63] Webb, *Jefferson Barracks,* p. 128.

[64] *St. Louis Post-Dispatch,* February 12, 1922.

[65] Memo dated April 24, 1922, also listed local recruiting officers.

[66] *St. Louis Post-Dispatch,* May 2, May 28, and May 29, 1922.

[67] *St. Louis Post-Dispatch,* July 21, 1922.

[68] *Olympia Record* [Washington], July 24, 1922.

[69] *Fort Worth Star-Telegram,* October 31, 1922.

[70] *Jeffersonian 1922,* Annual of the CMTC.

[71] *Kansas City Star,* August 29, 1922.

[72] *St. Louis Post-Dispatch,* March 9, 1922.

[73] Webb, *Jefferson Barracks,* p. 130.

[74] *St. Louis Post-Dispatch,* July 5, 1922.

[75] Webb, *Jefferson Barracks,* p. 130.

[76] *St. Louis Post-Dispatch,* October 12, 1923.

[77] *St. Louis Post-Dispatch,* November 17, 1923.

[78] Smith, *Army Brat,* p. 28-34.

[79] *Dallas Morning News,* July 26, 1924.

[80] Webb, *Army Brat,* p. 311.

[81] *St. Louis Post-Dispatch,* December 14, 1924.

[82] Smith, *Army Brat,* p. 45/46.

[83] *Jeffersonian 1925,* p. 11.

[84] *Jeffersonian 1925,* p. 11.

[85] *Jeffersonian 1925,* p. 23.

[86] *Jeffersonian 1925,* p. 31-39.

[87] Memo dated December 1, 1925, from Headquarters 6th C.A. [Coast artillery] to The Chief, C.W.S. [Chemical Warfare Service], Washington, D.C.

[88] Memo dated December 31, 1925, to Headquarters 6th Corps Area to The Chief C.W.S., Washington, D.C. and Annex No. I, Training Memo No. 3, Hq., Jefferson Barracks, Mo., dated December 8, 1925.

[89] Cullom, Volume VII, p. 386.

[90] Post Order No. 80. Jefferson Barracks Collection.

[91] *St. Louis Post-Dispatch,* May 13, 1926.

[92] Annex No. 1, Training Memo No. 6, dated May 10, 1926. Jefferson Barracks Collection.

[93] Training Memo No. 10, dated June 17, 1926, Jefferson Barracks Collection.

[94] Training Memo No. 3, dated October 3, 1926, issued by Col. Falls in Jefferson Barracks Collection.

[95] Webb, *Jefferson Barracks,* p. 316/317.

[96] Completion Report Covering Alterations and Repairs on Building No. 8-P, dated May 12, 1926, in Jefferson Barracks Collection.

[97] Memo: Report of activities, 6th Corps Area, to Chief C.W.S., Washington, D.C., dated January 3, `1927, in Jefferson Barracks Collection.

[98] Memo: Report of Activities, 6th Corps Area, for the month of February 1027, dated March 1, 1927, in Jefferson Barracks Collection.

[99] Memo: Report of activities, 6th Corps Area, for the month of March 1927, dated April 1, 1927, in Jefferson Barracks Collection.

[100] Webb, *Jefferson Barracks,* p. 317.

[101] *Jeffersonian 1927,* p. 93-96.

[102] *Jeffersonian 1927,* p. 73.

[103] *Jeffersonian 1927,* p. 76.

[104] *Jeffersonian 1927,* p. 81.

[105] *Jeffersonian 1927,* p. 81.

[106] *Jeffersonian 1927,* p. 81.

[107] *Jeffersonian 1927,* p. 83.

[108] *Jeffersonian 1927,* p. 83.

[109] *Jeffersonian 1927,* p. 83.

[110] *Jeffersonian 1927,* p. 84.

[111] *Jeffersonian 1927,* p. 84.

[112] *Jeffersonian 1927,* p. 85.

[113] *Jeffersonian 1927,* p. 97.

[114] *St. Louis Post-Dispatch,* November 4, 1927.

[115] *Jeffersonian 1928,* p. 31-37.

[116] *Jeffersonian 1928,* p. 38-40.

[117] These are the cement block buildings still standing just off Sheridan to the south of St. Bernadette Church. Completion Report covering Establishment of Citizen's Military Training Camp (C.M./T.C. and O.R.C.,) Jefferson Barracks, Missouri, in Jefferson Barracks Collection.

[118] Memo: Report of Chemical Warfare Activities for the month of June 1928, dated 3 July 1928, in Jefferson Barracks Collection.

[119] Memo: Report of Chemical Warfare Activities for the month of June 1928, dated 3 July 1928, in Jefferson Barracks Collection.

[120] Menu: Christmas Dinner, 1928, Headquarters Company, 6th Infantry, Jefferson Barracks, Missouri, in Jefferson Barracks Collection.

[121] *St. Louis Globe-Democrat,* January 22, 1929.

[122] *Jeffersonian, 1929,* p. 13.

[123] *Jeffersonian, 1929,* p. 23.

[124] *Jeffersonian, 1929,* p. 24.

[125] *Jeffersonian, 1929,* p. 38.

[126] *Jeffersonian, 1929,* p. 41.

[127] *Jeffersonian, 1929,* p. 44.

[128] *Jeffersonian, 1929,* p. 43.

[129] *Jeffersonian, 1929,* p. 46.

[130] *Jeffersonian, 1929,* p. 44.

[131] Cullum, Volume VII, p. 361

[132] Webb, *Jefferson Barracks,* p. 321,

[133] *St. Louis Post-Dispatch,* January 5, 1930.

Chapter 9 – Decade of the 1930s

[1] Coffman, *Old Army,* p. 3.

[2] *St. Louis Post-Dispatch,* February 2, 1930.

[3] *St. Louis Post-Dispatch,* February 16, 1930.

[4] *The Daily Independent* [Murphysboro, Illinois], March 11, 1930.

[5] Memo: Chemical Warfare Training, dated March 6, 1930, in the Jefferson Barracks Collection.

[6] *St. Louis Post-Dispatch,* March 16, 1930, and April 13, 1930.

[7] *St. Louis Post-Dispatch,* April 6, 1930.

[8] *St. Louis Post-Dispatch,* April 9, 1930.

[9] *St. Louis Post-Dispatch,* May 11, 1930.

[10] Webb, *Jefferson Barracks,* p. 321/322.

[11] *St. Louis Post-Dispatch,* May 18, 1930.

[12] *St. Louis Post-Dispatch,* May 30, 1930.

[13] *St. Louis Post-Dispatch,* May 30, 1930.

[14] *St. Louis Post-Dispatch,* June 6, 1930.

[15] Webb, *Jefferson Barracks,* p. 322.

[16] *Southtown Economist* [Illinois], May 27, 1930.

[17] Webb, *Jefferson Barracks,* p. 323.

[18] Webb, *Jefferson Barracks,* p. 323 and *Jefferson Barracks News* [Jefferson Barracks, Missouri], July 4, 1930.

[19] *St. Louis Post-Dispatch,* June 18, 1930.

[20] *Jeffersonian,* p.

[30] *St. Louis Post-Dispatch,* July 5, 1931.

[31] *St. Louis Post-Dispatch,* July 15, 1931.

[32] *St. Louis Post-Dispatch,* July 16, 1931.

[33] *St. Louis Post-Dispatch,* July 20, 1931.

[34] *St. Louis Post-Dispatch,* July 30, 1931.

[35] *St. Louis Post-Dispatch,* August 2, 1931.

[36] *St. Louis Post-Dispatch,* August 5, 1931.

[37] *Newark Advocate* and *American Tribune,* September 5, 1931.

[38] *The Lima News* [Ohio], September 4, 1931.

[39] *Neighborhood Link News,* September 17, 1931.

[40] Menu, Christmas Day, 1931, Service Company, 6th U.S. Infantry, Jefferson Barracks, Missouri, in the Jefferson Barracks Collection.

[41] Coffman, *Old Army,* p. 516.

[42] Coffman, *Old Army,* p. 6.

[43] Coffman, *Old Army.* p. 7.

[44] Coffman, *Old Army.* p. 718.

[45] Coffman, *Old Army.* p. 8.

[46] Coffman, *Old Army.* p. 10/11.

[47] Coffman, *Old Army.* p. 11.

[48] Coffman, *Old Army.* p. 12/13.

[49] Coffman, *Old Army.* p. 15.

[50] Coffman, *Old Army.* p. 15.

[51] Coffman, *Old Army.* p. 16.

[52] Coffman, *Old Army.* p. 16/17.

[53] Coffman, *Old Army.* p. 19.

[54] Coffman, *Old Army.* p. 19.

[55] Coffman, *Old Army.* p. 21.

[56] *Joplin News Herald,* February 17, 1932.

[57] Memo: Headquarters, Jefferson Barracks, Missouri, Col. Whitworth, 6th Infantry, Commanding, in the Jefferson Barracks Collection.

[58] Memo: *Report of Chemical Warfare Activities for the Month of May 1932,* dated June 17, 1932, in the Jefferson Barracks Collection.

[59] Memo: *Report of Chemical Warfare Activities for the Month of July 1932,* from Headquarters 6th Corps Area, Chicago, Illinois, dated August 13, 1932, in the Jefferson Barracks Collection.

[60] Memo: *Report of Chemical Warfare Activities for the Month of October 1932,* from Headquarters 6th Corps Area, dated November 17, 19332, in Jefferson Barracks Collection.

[61] Webb, *Jefferson Barracks,* p. 324.

[62] *Dictionary of American Military Biography,* Volume II, p. 579-581.

[63] *St. Louis Post-Dispatch, June 17, 1932.*

[64] Kington, *Forgotten Summers,* p. 128.

[65] *St. Louis Globe Democrat,* November 5, 1932.

[66] Webb, *Jefferson Barracks,* p. 352/353.

[67] Webb, *Jefferson Barracks,* p. 326.

[68] Completion Report covering "Erection of a Theater Building at Jefferson Barracks, Missouri, in the Jefferson Barracks Collection.

[69] Completion Report for Four Double Sets of N.C.O. Quarters at Jefferson Barracks, Missouri, in the Jefferson Barracks Collection.

[70] Completion Report covering conversion of Boiler Room at Pump House, Building No. 33, into One Set of N.C.O. Quarters, at Jefferson Barracks, Missouri, in the Jefferson Barracks Collection.

[71] Smith, *Army Brat,* p. 46/47.

[72] Smith, *Army Brat, p. 47/48.*

[73] Smith, *Army Brat, p. 48.*

[74] Smith, *Army Brat, p. 48/49.*

[75] Smith, *Army Brat, p. 49.*

[76] Smith, *Army Brat, p. 49/50.*

[77] Smith, *Army Brat, p. 50.*

[78] Smith, *Army Brat, p. 50/51.*

[79] Smith, *Army Brat, p. 51/52.*

[80] *Official Army Register, 1941,* p. 531.

[81] *Your CCC, A Handbook for Enrollees,* p. 8-13.

[82] Perry H. Merrill, *Roosevelt's Forest Army: A History of the CCC,* p. 9.

[83] *Neighborhood Link News,* April 27, 1933.

[84] *Neighborhood Link News,* June 8, 1933.

[85] *Edwardsville Intelligencer,* May 25, 1933.

[86] Kington, *Forgotten Summers,* p. 129/130.

[87] Kington, *Forgotten Summers,* p. 130.

[88] *Fayetteville* [Arkansas] *Daily Democrat,* September 5, 19i33.

[89] *Waterloo* [Iowa] *Daily Courier,* September 8, 1933.

[90] *The Sheboygan* [Wisconsin] *Press,* September 8, 1933.

[91] *Alton Evening Telegraph,* November 10, 1933.

[92] *Joplin Glove,* November 25, 1933.

[93] Coffman, *Old Army,* p. 28.

[94] Coffman, *Old Army,* p. 28/29.

[95] Coffman, *Old Army, p. 29.*

[96] Coffman, *Old Army, p. 30.*

[97] Coffman, *Old Army, p. 32.*

[98] Coffman, *Old Army, p. 52.*

[99] Smith, *Army Brat,* p. 52/53.

[100] Smith, *Army Brat,* p. 68/69.

[101] Smith, *Army Brat,* p. 71/72.

[102] Smith, *Army Brat,* p. 72/73.

[103] Smith, *Army Brat,* p. 75/76.

[104] Smith, *Army Brat,* p. 74-79.

[105] Smith, *Army Brat,* p. 145/146.

[106] Smith, *Army Brat,* p. 146-148.

[107] *Edwardsville Intelligencer,* April 12, 1934.

[108] *Dictionary of American Military Biography,* Volume II, p. 1000-1002.

[109] Kington, *Forgotten Summers,* p. 130.

[110] *Jefferson City Post-Tribune,* July 30, 1934.

[111] *St. Louis Globe Democrat,* April 24, 1934.

[112] Webb, *Jefferson Barracks,* p. 329.

[113] *Edwardsville Intelligencer,* August 3, 1934.

[114] *Edwardsville Intelligencer,* August 2, 1934.

[115] Program for 6th Infantry's 1934 Regimental Day Exercises, in the Jefferson Barracks Collection.

[116] *Neighborhood Link News,* February 28, 1935.

[117] Smith, *Army Brat,* p. 152.

[118] Smith, *Army Brat,* p. 152/153.

[119] Smith, *Army Brat,* p. 153.

[120] Smith, *Army Brat,* p. 154.

[121] Smith, *Army Brat,* p. 155/156.

[122] Smith, *Army Brat,* p. 157.

[123] Smith, *Army Brat,* p. 182/183.

[124] Smith, *Army Brat,* p. 182/183.

[125] Webb, *Jefferson Barracks,* p. 329/330.

[126] *Joplin Globe,* April 4, 1935.

[127] *Joplin Globe,* July 3, 1935.

[128] Kington, *Forgotten Summers,* p. 134/135.

[129] *La Crosse* [Wisconsin] *Tribune and Leader Press,* July 19, 1935.

[130] Webb, *Jefferson Barracks,* p. 330.

[131] *The Sunday News and Tribune* [Jefferson City, Missouri] June 23, 1935.

[132] *The Tyrone* [Pennsylvania] *Daily Herald,* September 2, 1935.

[133] *Ironwood* [Michigan] *Daily Globe,* September 24, 1935.

[134] Program for 6th Infantry Regimental Day at Jefferson Barracks, Missouri, November 4, 1935, in the Jefferson Barracks Collection.

[135] *Jefferson City Pot-Tribune,* February 17, 1936.

[136] Kington, *Forgotten Summers,* p. 171/172.

[137] Official Annual CCC, Jefferson Barracks, CCC District, 6th Corps Area, 1937, p. 9 and p. 135.

[138] *The Morning Avalanche* [Lubbock, Texas], June 2, 1936.

[139] *Joplin Globe,* June 28, 1936.

[140] Webb, *Jefferson Barracks,* p. 331.

[141] *History of the 6th Infantry.*

[142] Coffman, *Old Army,* p. 37.

[143] Coffman, *Old Army,* p. 37/38.

[144] Coffman, *Old Army,* p. 38.

[145] Coffman, *Old Army,* p.38.

[146] Coffman, *Old Army,* p. 38.

[147] Coffman, *Old Army,* p. 38/39.

[148] Coffman, *Old Army,* p. 39.

[149] Coffman, *Old Army,* p. 41.

[150] Coffman, *Old Army,* p. 41.

[151] Coffman, *Old Army,* p. 41.

[152] Coffman, *Old Army,* p. 41.

[153] Coffman, *Old Army,* p. 42.

[154] Official Annual, 1937, CCC, Jefferson Barracks, CCC District, 6th Corps Area, p. 45 and p. 131.

[155] Official Annual, 1937, CCC, Jefferson Barracks, CCC District, 6th Corps Area, p. 10.

[156] Official Annual, 1937, CCC, Jefferson Barracks, CCC District, 6th Corps Area, p. 10.

[157] Official Annual, 1937, CCC, Jefferson Barracks, CCC District, 6th Corps Area, p. 19/20; Headquarters staff from Jefferson Barracks were as follows: Col. Joseph A. Atkins, 6th Infantry Commanding Officer; Lt. Col. George R. Hicks, 6th Infantry, Executive Officer; Capt. Harry Kirsner, Q./M.C., Quartermaster; Capt. C.E. Grey, Finance Dept., Finance Officer; Major Walter B. Zimmerman, Chaplain; 1st Lt. Charles C. Trendley, Infantry Reserve, Adjutant; 1st Lt. George B. Can Zee, Infantry Reserve, Assistant Adjutant; Capt. I.A. Chesbro, Field Artillery Reserve, Property Officer; 1st Lt. Walter J. Williams, Field Artillery Reserve, Executive Officer, District Quartermaster Office; 1st Lt. Thomas D. Patterson, Cavalry Reserve, Purchasing and Contracting Officer; 1st Lt. William G. Johnson, Quartermaster Reserve, Subsistence Officer; 1st Lt. Clarence H. Lewis, Signal Corps Reserve, Warehouse Officer; Dr. J.L. Conover, Surgeon; Mr. E.M. Jasper, District Adviser.

[158] Webb, *Jefferson Barracks,* p. 333/334.

[159] *Neighborhood Link News.*

[160] *Jefferson City Post-Tribune,* May 15, 1937.

[161] *Edwardsville, Intelligencer,* June 22, 1937.

[162] *St. Louis Post-Dispatch,* July 6, 1937.

[163] *St. Louis Post-Dispatch,* August 4, 1937.

[164] *St. Louis Post-Dispatch,* July 16, 1937.

[165] *Neighborhood Link News.*

[166] Webb, *Jefferson Barracks,* p. 334.

[167] *The Light* [San Antonio, Texas], July 19, 1937.

[168] Smith, *Army Brat,* p. 117/118.

[169] Smith, *Army Brat,* p. 119/120.

[170] Smith, *Army Brat,* p. 120/121.

[171] Coffman, *Old Army,* p. 64.

[172] Coffman, *Old Army,* p. 64.

[173] Coffman, *Old Army,* p. 64/65.

[174] Coffman, *Old Army,* p. 71.

[175] Coffman, *Old Army,* p. 82/83.

[176] Coffman, *Old Army,* p. 85.

[177] Coffman, *Old Army,* p. 86.

[178] Coffman, *Old Army,* p. 86/87.

[179] Webb, *Jefferson Barracks,* p. 334/335.

[180] *Jefferson City Post-Tribune,* May 16, 1938.

[181] *St. Loui Star-Times,* May 28, 1838,

[182] Kington, *Forgotten Summers,* p. 175.

[183] *St. Louis Post-Dispatch,* July 23, 1938.

[184] *St. Louis Post-Dispatch,* November 3, 1938.

[185] Program for Organizational Day, 6th U.S. Infantry, Jefferson Barracks, Missouri, November 4, 1938, in the Jefferson Barracks Collection.

[186] *St. Louis Globe Democrat,* February 16, 1939.

[187] *Official Army Register, 1941,* p. 1057.

[188] *Reno Evening Gazette,* May 31, 1939.

[189] *The Billings Gazette,* June 2, 1939.

[190] *Jefferson City Daily Capital News,* July 12, 1939.

[191] U.S. Air Force History Center, Maxwell Air Force Base, Alabama, Microfilm Reel A2378, p. 242/2453. Hereafter cited as USAF History Center.

[192] USAF History Center, Reel A2378, p. 244/245.

[193] USAF History Center, Reel A2378, p. 245.

288

[194] USAF History Center, Reel A2378, p. 246/247.
[195] USAF History Center, Reel A2378, p. 247.
[196] USAF History Center, Reel A2378, p. 248/249.
[197] USAF History Center, Reel A2378, p. 249.
[198] USAF History Center, Reel A2378, p. 249/250.
[199] USAF History Center, Reel A2378, p. 250.

Chapter 10 – Jefferson Barracks Begins to Expand and the Army Air Corps Tales Over

[1] Untitled and Unpublished history of Jefferson Barracks, p. 342. Jefferson Barracks Collection
[2] Letter from Paul Kuhns, Jr. to the Curator of Jefferson Barracks Museum, dated December 5, 1990, in the Jefferson Barracks Collection.
[3] Newsletter, *Campus Chatter,* Volume 1, No. 2, July 30, 1940.
[4] *Ye Olde Lemay Times.*
[5] Newsletter, *Campus Chatter,* Volume 1, No. 3, July 30, 1940.
[6] USAF History Center, Reel A2378, p. 224-228.
[7] USAF History Center, Reel A2378, p. 253.
[8] USAF History Center, Reel A2378, p. 254-256.
[9] USAF History Center, Reel A2378, p. 256.
[10] USAF History Center, Reel A2378, p. 256.
[11] USAF History Center, Reel A2378, p. 257.
[12] USAF History Center, Reel A2378, p. 257/258.
[13] USAF History Center, Reel A2378, p. 258.
[14] USAF History Center, Reel A2378, p. 259/260.
[15] USAF History Center, Reel A2378, p. 260.
[16] USAF History Center, Reel A2378, p. 260.
[17] USAF History Center, Reel A2378, p. 260/261.
[18] USAF History Center, Reel A2378, p. 261/262.
[19] USAF History Center, Reel A2378, p. 262/263.
[20] USAF History Center, Reel A2378, p. 263.
[21] USAF History Center, Reel A2378, p. 264.
[22] USAF History Center, Reel A2378, p. 265/266.
[23] USAF History Center, Reel A2378, p. 265/266.
[24] USAF History Center, Reel A2378, p. 267.
[25] USAF History Center, Reel A2378, p. 267.
[26] USAF History Center, Reel A2378, p. 268.
[27] USAF History Center, Reel A2378, p. 268.
[28] USAF History Center, Reel A2378, p. 269.
[29] USAF History Center, Reel A2378, p. 269.
[30] USAF History Center, Reel A2378, p. 268-270.
[31] USAF History Center, Reel A2378, p. 270.
[32] USAF History Center, Reel A2378, p. 271.
[33] USAF History Center, Reel A2378, p. 273.
[34] USAF History Center, Reel A2378, p. 274/275.
[35] USAF History Center, Reel A2378, p. 276.
[36] USAF History Center, Reel A2378, p. 276/277.
[37] USAF History Center, Reel A2378, p. 277/278.
[38] USAF History Center, Reel A2378, p. 278.
[39] USAF History Center, Reel A2378, p. 279.
[40] USAF History Center, Reel A2378, p. 280.
[41] USAF History Center, Reel A2378, p. 281.

[42] USAF History Center, Reel A2378, p. 281.
[43] USAF History Center, Reel A2378, p. 282.
[44] USAF History Center, Reel A2378, p. 282.
[45] USAF History Center, Reel A2378, p. 282-284.
[46] USAF History Center, Reel A2378, p. 284.
[47] USAF History Center, Reel A2378, p. 295.
[48] USAF History Center, Reel A2378, p. 296/297.
[49] USAF History Center, Reel A2378, p. 296/298.
[50] USAF History Center, Reel A2378, p. 298.
[51] USAF History Center, Reel A2378, p. 299.
[52] USAF History Center, Reel A2378, p. 300.
[53] USAF History Center, Reel A2378, p. 301.
[54] USAF History Center, Reel A2378, p. 302.
[55] USAF History Center, Reel A2378, p. 302/303.
[56] USAF History Center, Reel A2378, p. 305.
[57] USAF History Center, Reel A2378, p. 312/313.
[58] USAF History Center, Reel A2378, p. 314.
[59] USAF History Center, Reel A2378, p. 314.
[60] USAF History Center, Reel A2378, p. 315.
[61] USAF History Center, Reel A2378, p. 316.
[62] USAF History Center, Reel A2378, p. 316/317.
[63] USAF History Center, Reel A2378, p. 317/318.
[64] USAF History Center, Reel A2378, p. 319.
[65] USAF History Center, Reel A2378, p. 320.
[66] USAF History Center, Reel A2378, p. 320.
[67] USAF History Center, Reel A2378, p. 321/322.
[68] USAF History Center, Reel A2378, p. 322/323.
[69] USAF History Center, Reel A2378, p. 323/324.
[70] USAF History Center, Reel A2378, p. 324.
[71] USAF History Center, Reel A2378, p. 324.
[72] USAF History Center, Reel A2378, p. 325.
[73] USAF History Center, Reel A2378, p. 335/336.
[74] USAF History Center, Reel A2378, p. 338.
[75] USAF History Center, Reel A2378, p. 339.
[76] USAF History Center, Reel A2378, p. 339/340.
[77] USAF History Center, Reel A2378, p. 340/341.
[78] USAF History Center, Reel A2378, p. 342.
[79] USAF History Center, Reel A2378, p. 342/343.
[80] USAF History Center, Reel A2378, p. 343.
[81] USAF History Center, Reel A2378, p. 345/346.
[82] USAF History Center, Reel A2378, p. 346/347.
[83] USAF History Center, Reel A2378, p. 348.
[84] USAF History Center, Reel A2378, p. 348.
[85] USAF History Center, Reel A2378, p. 349.
[86] USAF History Center, Reel A2378, p. 349.
[87] USAF History Center, Reel A2378, p. 350.
[88] USAF History Center, Reel A2378, p. 350.
[89] USAF History Center, Reel A2378, p. 785.
[90] USAF History Center, Reel A2378, p. 786.
[91] USAF History Center, Reel A2378, p. 787.
[92] USAF History Center, Reel A2378, p. 788.
[93] USAF History Center, Reel A2378, p. 788.

[94] USAF History Center, Reel A2378, p. 789.
[95] USAF History Center, Reel A2378, p. 789.
[96] USAF History Center, Reel A2378, p. 351.
[97] USAF History Center, Reel A2378, p. 352.
[98] USAF History Center, Reel A2378, p. 352.
[99] USAF History Center, Reel A2378, p. 352.
[100] USAF History Center, Reel A2378, p. 353.
[101] USAF History Center, Reel A2378, p. 353/354.
[102] USAF History Center, Reel A2378, p. 354/355.
[103] USAF History Center, Reel A2378, p. 355.
[104] USAF History Center, Reel A2378, p. 355/356.
[105] USAF History Center, Reel A2378, p. 356/357.
[106] USAF History Center, Reel A2378, p. 357.
[107] USAF History Center, Reel A2378, p. 357.
[108] USAF History Center, Reel A2378, p. 358.
[109] USAF History Center, Reel A2378, p. 358/359.
[110] USAF History Center, Reel A2378, p. 359.
[111] USAF History Center, Reel A2378, p. 359-361.
[112] USAF History Center, Reel A2378, p. 365/366.
[113] USAF History Center, Reel A2378, p. 366/367.
[114] USAF History Center, Reel A2378, p. 367/368.
[115] USAF History Center, Reel A2378, p. 368/369.
[116] USAF History Center, Reel A2378, p. 369.
[117] USAF History Center, Reel A2378, p. 370.
[118] USAF History Center, Reel A2378, p. 370/371.
[119] USAF History Center, Reel A2378, p. 372.
[120] USAF History Center, Reel A2378, p. 372/373.
[121] USAF History Center, Reel A2378, p. 373.
[122] USAF History Center, Reel A2378, p. 373/374.
[123] USAF History Center, Reel A2378, p. 375/376.
[124] USAF History Center, Reel A2378, p. 376/377.
[125] USAF History Center, Reel A2378, p. 378.
[126] USAF History Center, Reel A2378, p. 378/379.
[127] USAF History Center, Reel A2378, p. 736/737.
[128] USAF History Center, Reel A2378, p. 738.
[129] USAF History Center, Reel A2378, p. 738.
[130] USAF History Center, Reel A2378, p. 739.
[131] USAF History Center, Reel A2378, p. 739.
[132] USAF History Center, Reel A2378, p. 739.
[133] USAF History Center, Reel A2378, p. 739.
[134] USAF History Center, Reel A2378, p. 740.
[135] USAF History Center, Reel A2378, p. 740.
[136] USAF History Center, Reel A2378, p. 741.
[137] USAF History Center, Reel A2378, p. 493/494.
[138] USAF History Center, Reel A2378, p. 774.
[139] USAF History Center, Reel A2378, p. 774.
[140] USAF History Center, Reel A2378, p. 775.
[141] USAF History Center, Reel A2378, p. 775.
[142] USAF History Center, Reel A2378, p. 775/776.
[143] USAF History Center, Reel A2378, p. 780.
[144] USAF History Center, Reel A2378, p. 776/777.
[145] USAF History Center, Reel A2378, p. 777.

[146] USAF History Center, Reel A2378, p. 778.
[147] USAF History Center, Reel A2378, p. 778.
[148] USAF History Center, Reel A2378, p. 779.
[149] USAF History Center, Reel A2378, p. 631/632.
[150] USAF History Center, Reel A2378, p. 632.
[151] USAF History Center, Reel A2389, p. 634/635.

292

Bibliography

Archives

Government Documents

Report of the Secretary of War: Being Part of the Messages and Documents communicated to the Two Houses of Congress at the Beginning of the First Session of the 54th Congress, Volume I, Washington, Government Printing Office, 1895.

Report of the Secretary of War: Being Part of the Messages and Documents communicated to the Two Houses of Congress at the Beginning of the 2nd Session of the 54th Congress, in 3 volumes, Volume I, Washington, Government Printing Office, 1896.

Annual Reports of the War Department for the Fiscal Year Ended June 30, 1897, Report of the Secretary of War, Miscellaneous Reports, Washington, Government Printing Office, 1898.

Annual Reports of the War Department for the Fiscal Year Ended June 30, 1898, Report of the Major-General Commanding the Army, Washington, Government Printing Office, 1898.

Annual Reports of the War Department for the Fiscal Year Ended June 30, 1899, Report of the Major-General Commanding the Army, Washington, Government Printing Office, 1899.

Annual Reports of the War Department for the Fiscal Year Ended June 30, 1899, Reports of Chiefs of Bureaus, Washington, Government Printing Office, 1899.

Annual Reports of the War Department for the Fiscal Year Ended June 30, 1899, Report of the Secretary of War, Miscellaneous Reports, Washington, Government Printing Office, 1899.

Annual Reports of the War Department for the Fiscal Year Ended June 30, 1900, Report of the Lieutenant-General Commanding the Army, in Seven Parts, Washington, Government Printing Office, 1900.

Annual Reports of the War Department for the Fiscal Year Ended June 30, 1900, Report of the Secretary of War, Miscellaneous Reports, Washington, Government Printing Office, 1900.

Annual Reports of the War Department for the Fiscal Year Ended June 30, 1901, Report of the Lieutenant-General Commanding the Army, in Five Parts, Washington, Government Printing Office, 1901.

Annual Reports of the War Department for the Fiscal Year Ended June 30, 1901, Report of Chiefs of Bureaus, Washington, Government Printing Office, 1901.

Annual Reports of the War Department for the Fiscal Year Ended June 30, 1901, Report of the Secretary of War, Miscellaneous Reports, Washington, Government Printing Office, 1901.

Annual Reports of the War Department for the Fiscal Year Ended June 30, 1902, Volume I, Report of the Secretary of War and Reports of the Bureau Chiefs, Washington, Government Printing Office, 1902.

Annual Reports of the War Department for the Fiscal Year Ended June 30, 1902, Volume IX, Report of the Lieutenant-General Commanding the Army & Department Commanders, Washington, Government Printing Office, 1902.

Annual Reports of the War Department for the Fiscal Year Ended June 30, 103, Volume I, II, II, Washington, Government Printing Office, 1903.

Annual Reports of the War Department for the Fiscal Year Ended June 30, 1904, Volume I, Reports of the Secretary of War, Chief of Staff, The Military Secretary, Inspector-General, & Judge-Advocate-General, Washington, Government Printing Office, 1904.

Annual Reports of the War Department for the Fiscal Year Ended June 30, 1904, Volume II, Armament, \ Transportation, & Supply, Washington, Government Printing Office, 1904.

Annual Reports of the War Department for the Fiscal Year Ended June 30, 1904, Volume III, Reports of Division and Department Commanders, Washington, Government Printing Office, 1904.

Annual Reports of the War Department for the Fiscal Year Ended June 30, 1905, Volume I, Reports of the Secretary of War, Chief of Staff, The Military Secretary, Inspector-General, & Judge-Advocate-General, Washington, Government Printing Office, 1905.

Annual Reports of the War Department for the Fiscal Year Ended June 30, 1905, Volume III, Division & Department Commanders, Washington, Government Printing Office, 1905.

Annual Reports of the War Department for the Fiscal Year Ended June 30, 1906, Volume I, Reports of the Secretary of War, Chief of Staff, The Military Secretary, Inspector-General, & Judge-Advocate-General, Washington, Government Printing Office, 1906.

Annual Reports of the War Department for the Fiscal Year Ended June 30, 1906, Volume II, Armament, Transportation, and Supply, Washington, Government Printing Office, 1906.

Annual Reports of the War Department for the Fiscal Year Ended June 30, 1906, Volume III, Reports of Division and Department Commanders, Washington, Government Printing Office, 1906.

War Department, U.S.A., Annual Report, 1907, Volume II, Reports of Quartermaster-General, Commissary-General, Surgeon-General, Paymaster-General, Chief Signal Officer, Chief of Artillery, Board of Ordnance And Fortification, Washington, Government Printing Office, 1907.

War Department, U.S.A., Annual Report, 1907, Volume III, Washington, Government Printing Office, 1907.

War Department Annual Reports, 1908, Volume I, Reports of the Secretary of War, Chief of Staff, the Adjutant General, Inspector-General, Judge-Advocate-General, Washington, Government Printing Office, 1908.

War Department Annual Reports, 1914, Volume I, Reports of Secretary of War, Chief of Staff, Adjutant-General, Inspector-General, Chief of Coast Artillery, Military Academy, Military Parks, Chickamauga, Gettysburg, Shiloh, Vicksburg, Washington, Government Printing Office, 1914.

National Archives and Records Administration, Washington, D.C.

Returns from United States Military Posts, 1800-1916, M617, Rolls 549, 550, and 551.

Returns from Regular Army Infantry Units, June 1821-December 1916, M665: Rolls 10, 11, 85, 139, 169, 178.

Returns from Regular Army Cavalry Units, 1833-1916, M744: Rolls 33, 34, 47, 48, 57, 58, 67, 92, 93, 100, 101, 103, 104.

Returns from Regular Army Engineer Battalions, September 1846-June 1916, M690: Roll 4.

Returns from Regular Army Artillery Regiments, June 1821-January 1901, M727: Roll 8.

United States Air Force History Center, Maxwell Air Force Base, Microfilm Reels: A2378, A2379, !2380, A2381, A2384, and A2440.

Newspapers and Periodicals

St. Louis Post-Dispatch
St. Louis Republic
St. Louis Globe-Democrat
St. Louis Star-Times
Jefferson Barracks Hub
Neighborhood Link News (Lemay, Missouri)
Jefferson City Post-Tribune (Jefferson City, Missouri)
Daily Capital News (Jefferson City, Missouri)
Belleville News Democrat (Belleville, Illinois)
Edwardsville Intelligencer (Edwardsville, Illinois)
Alton Evening Telegraph (Alton, Illinois)
Omaha World Herald (Omaha, Nebraska)
Kansas City Times (Kansas City, Missouri)
Kansas City Star (Kansas City, Missouri)
Morning Olympian (Olympia, Washington)
Charlotte Observer (Charlotte, North Carolina)
Chicago Inter Ocean (Chicago, Illinois)
Southtown Economist (Chicago, Illinois)
Aberdeen Daily News (Aberdeen, South Dakota)
New Haven Register (New Haven, Connecticut)
Sedalia Daily Capital Sedalia, Missouri)

294

Idaho Statesman (Boise, Idaho)
Dallas Morning News (Dallas, Texas)
Fort Worth Morning Register (Fort Worth, Texas)
Fort Worth Star-Telegram (Fort Worth, Texas)
Trenton Evening News (Trenton, New Jersey)
Salt Lake Telegram (Salt Lake City, Utah)
Daily Citizen (Tucson, Arizona)
The Oregonian (Portland, Oregon)
The Anaconda Standard (Montana)
The Columbus Enquirer-Sun (Columbus, Georgia)
Aero Magazine
New Orleans Times Picayune (New Orleans, Louisiana)
Daily Herald (Chicago, Illinois)
Pueblo Gazette-Telegraph (Pueblo, Colorado)
Pueblo Chieftain (Pueblo, Colorado)
Colorado Gazette-Telegraph Colorado Springs, Colorado)
Macon Weekly Telegraph (Macon, Georgia)
Grand Forks Herald Grand Forks, North Dakota)
Duluth News-Tribune (Duluth, Minnesota)
United Press
Olympia Record (Olympia, Washington)
The Daily Independent (Murphysboro, Illinois)
*The Times Recorder (*Zanesville, Ohio)
The Lima News (Lima, Ohio)
Joplin News Herald (Joplin, Missouri)
Joplin Globe (Joplin, Missouri)
Fayetteville Daily Democrat Fayetteville, Arkansas)
Waterloo Daily Courier Waterloo, Iowa)
The Sheboygan Press (Sheboygan, Wisconsin)
The Tyrone Daily Herald (Tyrone, Pennsylvania)
Ironwood Daily Globe (Ironwood, Michigan)
The Light (San Antonio, Texas)
The Billings Gazette (Billings, Montana)
Reno Evening Gazette (Reno Nevada)

Published Primary Sources

Jeffersonian, Jefferson Barracks CMTC Annual, 1921, 1933, 1935, 1926, 1927, 1928, 1929, 1930, 1931.

Books and Articles

Coffman, Edward M. *The Regulars: The American Army 1898-1941.* Cambridge, Massachusetts: The Belknap Press of Harvard University Press, 2004.
Crossland, Richard B. and Carrie, James T. *Twice the Citizen: A History of the United States Army Reserve, 1908-1983.* Fredonia Books, 2002.
Cunningham, Roger. *Kansas City's African-American "Immunes" in the Spanish-American War.* State History Society, Volume 100, No. 3, April 2006.
Gilbert, Martin. *The First World War: A Complete History.* New York: Henry Holt and Company, 1994.
Heitman, Francis B., *Historical Register and Dictionary for the United States Army: From Its Organization, September 29, 1789, to March 2, 1903.* Washington: Government Printing Office, 1903.

Kington, Donald M., *Forgotten Summers: The Story of the Citizen's Military Training Camps 1921-1940.* Two Decades Publishing, 1995.

Linn, Brian McAllister, *The U.S. Army and Counterinsurgency in the Philippine War, 1899-1902.* Chapel Hill, University of North Carolina Press, 1989.

Merrill, Perry H., *Roosevelt's Forest Army: A History of the Civilian Conservation Corps, 1933-1942.* Perry H. Merrill Dr., 1`984.

Smith, William Jay. *Army Brat: A Memoir By William Jay Smith.* New York: Persea Books, 1980.

Spiller Roger J., Editor. *Dictionary of American Military Biography.* Volumes I, II, and III. Westport, Connecticut: Greenwood Press, 1984.

Trask, David F. *The War With Spain in 1898.* Lincoln, Nebraska: University of Nebraska Press, 1981.

Wolff, Leon. *Little Brown Brothers: How the United States Purchased and Pacified the Philippine Islands at the Century's Turn.* New York: History Book Club, 2006.

Unpublished Manuscripts

Webb, Henry W., Major, U.S. Air Corps, *The Story of Jefferson Barracks,* 1944.

Author Unknown, *The History of Jefferson Barracks.*

Index

302